THE
THE SUNDA

Good University Guide

2015

John O'Leary

With

Dr Nicki Horsemar

IN ASSOCIATION WITH

milkround SCHOOL LEAVERS

D0263697

Published in 2014 by Times Books

HarperCollins Publishers
Westerhill Road
Bishopbriggs
Glasgow G64 2QT
www.harpercollins.co.uk

First published in 1993 by Times Books. Twenty-first edition 2014

ISBN 978-0-00-759188-6

Dr Nicki Horseman was the lead consultant for UoE Consulting Ltd, which has compiled the main university
league table and the individual subject tables for this guide on behalf of *The Times, The Sunday Times* and
HarperCollins.

Please see chapters 4 and 5 for a full explanation of the sources of data used in the ranking tables. The data
providers do not necessarily agree with the data aggregations or manipulations appearing in this book and are
also not responsible for any inference or conclusions thereby derived.

Project editor: Christopher Riches
Design, editorial and additional research: Edenside Computing Services Ltd

Printed and bound in Great Britain by Clays Ltd, St Ives plc.

MIX
Paper from
responsible sources
FSC C007454

Find out more about HarperCollins and the environment at:
www.harpercollins.co.uk/green

Contents

About the Author

John O'Leary is a freelance journalist and education consultant. He was the Editor of *The Times Higher Education Supplement* from 2002 to 2007 and was previously Education Editor of *The Times*, having joined the paper in 1990 as Higher Education Correspondent. He has been writing on higher education for more than 30 years and is a member of the executive board of the QS World University Rankings. He is the author of *Higher Education in England*, published in 2009 by the Higher Education Funding Council for England. He has a degree in politics from the University of Sheffield.

Acknowledgements

We would like to thank the many individuals who have helped with this edition of *The Times and Sunday Times and Sunday Times Good University Guide*, particularly Greg Hurst, Education Editor of *The Times*, Alastair McCall, Editor of *The Sunday Times* University Guide, and Dr Nicki Horseman, the lead consultant for UoE Consulting Ltd, which has compiled the main university league table and the individual subject tables for this guide on behalf of *The Times*, *The Sunday Times* and HarperCollins Publishers; to the members of *The Times and Sunday Times Good University Guide* Advisory Group for their time and expertise: Patrick Kennedy, Consultant, Collective Intelligence Ltd; Christine Couper, Head of Planning and Statistics, University of Greenwich; Jim Galbraith, Senior Strategic Planner, University of Edinburgh; Alison Hartrey, Head of Planning, SOAS London; Mark Langer-Crame, Senior Planning Officer, Cardiff University; Aaron Morrison, Principal Planning Officer, De Montfort University; Komal Patel, Strategic Planning Officer, Imperial College, London; Dr Sarah Taylor, Head of Strategy Development, Aberystwyth University; Tom Wale, Senior Planning Officer, Loughborough University; Tom Wright, Senior Planning Manager, Northumbria University; James McLaren and Denise Jones of HESA for their technical advice; Martin Ince, Alice Hancock, Greta Keenan and Sue O'Leary for their contributions to the book.

We also wish to thank the publishers of the QS World University Rankings, the Academic Ranking of World Universities and *Times Higher Education* for permission to reproduce some of their main league tables, and all the university staff who assisted in providing information for this edition.

How to Use This Book

The Times and Sunday Times Good University Guide 2015 will help you to select the subject and university of your choice and to guide you through the whole process of getting to university. The answers to the questions below will help you to get the most out of the information we offer.

How do I choose a course?
» The first half of chapter 1 provides advice on what you should consider when choosing a subject area and relevant courses within that subject.
» The tables near the beginning of chapter 2 give details of the employment prospects for all major subjects.
» Chapter 5 provides details for 66 different subject areas (as listed on page 68).
» For each subject there is a league table that provides our assessment of the ranking of universities offering courses in the particular subject area.
» For each subject we also provide some background information and details of employment prospects.
» Specific advice for international students is given in chapter 12.

How do I choose a university?
» The second half of chapter 1 provides advice on choosing a university.
» If you are considering studying abroad, chapter 3 provides guidance and practical information.
» Central is the main *Times and Sunday Times* league table on pages 60–64. This ranks the universities by assessing their quality not just according to student satisfaction (drawn from the National Student Survey) but also through seven other factors, including research quality, the spending on services and facilities, and graduate employment prospects. This table gives an indication of the overall performance of each university.
» The second half of the book contains two pages on each university, giving a general overview of the institution as well as data on student numbers, how to contact the university, the accommodation provided by the university, and the fees and financial support for 2015–16, wherever possible. Note that details for support for 2015–16 had not been released for some institutions when this book was prepared in August 2014.
» In addition, chapter 10 provides information on sport and sporting facilities across all the universities.
» For those considering Oxford or Cambridge, details of admission processes and of all the colleges can be found in chapter 13.
» Specific advice for international students is given in chapter 12.

How do I apply?
» Chapter 6 outlines the application procedure for university entry.
» It starts by advising you on how to complete the UCAS application, and then takes you through the process that we hope will lead to your university place for autumn 2015.
» Specific information about applying to Oxford and Cambridge is given in chapter 13.

Can I afford it?

» Chapters 7 and 8 outline the costs of studying at university (including the payment of fees) as well as sources of funds (including student loans, grants and bursaries).

» Chapter 9 provides advice on where to live while you are there.

» Accommodation charges for 2014 15 for each university are given in the university profiles in chapter 14. Figures for 2015–16 were not available when this book was printed.

How will university enhance my career?

» The employment prospects and average starting salaries for the main subject groups are given in chapter 2.

» Universities are now doing more to increase the employability of their graduates. Some examples are given in chapter 2 – and check whether your chosen universities provide similar services.

How do I find out more?

» In each university profile (chapter 14) contact details are given (including email addresses and websites), so you can obtain more information on any university you are interested in.

» At the end of each chapter, a selection of useful websites is given.

» A further listing at the back of the book provides contact details for higher education institutions that are not covered elsewhere within the book.

» *The Times and Sunday Times Good University Guide* website at **www.thetimes.co.uk/tto/ education/gooduniversityguide** or **www.thesundaytimes.co.uk/gooduniversityguide** will keep you up to date with developments throughout the year and contains further information and online tables

Introduction

For those with the right qualifications, 2015 might be the best year in living memory in which to apply for a degree. There will be fewer 18-year-olds in the population and universities in England will finally be freed of any restrictions on the number of places they can fill. They are gearing up for unprecedented levels of competition, with the private sector preparing to undercut their £9,000 fees in popular subjects. While the top institutions will still be highly selective, applicants could find themselves in a buyer's market elsewhere.

Plenty of good judges question whether the new, unregulated market in higher education will be affordable. Some think funding will have to be cut or new restrictions introduced before long – and there is the additional complication of a general election, with the possibility of lower fees if Labour wins. But the ground rules have been set for 2015–16 and candidates hoping to start courses then should have more choice than ever. Universities were already able to admit as many students as they like, provided they had grades of at least ABB at A level, or the equivalent, but this covered only 30 per cent of those taking A level and a smaller proportion of other qualifications. Now every place is up for grabs.

With some prestigious universities looking to expand, admissions officers will find it difficult to know where to pitch their offers to recruit enough students to ensure that their courses are viable. Even some in the Russell Group of research universities got that wrong when the restrictions were first relaxed for high-grade candidates, and this is a much more wide-ranging change. In short, uncertainty will reign and this may be the year to be more ambitious with at least some applications. It is clear that some universities dropped their entry requirements in 2013 and 2014 in order to keep up recruitment, and it will be no surprise if more follow suit in the coming year.

The level of demand for places in 2015 and beyond cannot be taken for granted, however, in spite of this year's recovery. The 18-year-olds who have applied for places since the fees went up were already on track for higher education before the Government imposed higher charges. Sixth-formers and college students who are weighing up their options in the coming months embarked on A levels or other qualifications in the full knowledge of what a degree would cost. With some of the leading employers expanding their recruitment at 18, the Government funding many more apprenticeships and economic recovery promising higher levels of employment, some may try to avoid the undoubtedly high costs of higher education.

An era of change

Although £9,000 fees have hardly been popular and may well be at issue in next year's election, they have not led to the protracted slump in the demand for higher education that many critics predicted. After a year's decline as higher fees were introduced, the numbers applying for – and starting – degrees are now growing once more. More surprisingly, so are the numbers coming from low-income families and areas of low participation in higher education. It seems that only a post-election commitment to reduce the fees in the near future would be likely to depress demand for places dramatically in 2015, as applicants waited for a cheaper option.

What has changed with higher fees, however, is the pattern of applications and enrolments. Students are plainly opting in larger numbers for subjects that they think will lead to well-paid jobs. While there has been a recovery in some arts and social science subjects in 2014, the trend towards the sciences and some vocational degrees is unmistakeable. Languages have suffered particularly – perhaps partly because they tend to be four-year degrees – and so have courses associated with parts of the economy that were hardest hit in the recession. Building is one example, where numbers are down even though the subject is only just outside the top ten for employment prospects, with three-quarters of graduates going straight into a professional job.

The vast majority of students take a degree primarily to improve their career prospects, so some second-guessing of the employment market is inevitable. But most graduate jobs are not subject-specific and the best brains in the country are hard-pressed to predict employment hotspots four or five years ahead, when today's applicants will be looking for jobs. Computer science is a good example of the pitfalls. Demand for the subject plummeted when the "dotcom bubble" burst and courses closed. Now parts of the IT industry are booming again and there is a skills shortage. Applications for the subject have shot up, but no one can be certain of market conditions in such a fast-moving industry so far ahead.

Just as it may be unwise to second-guess employment prospects, the same goes for the competition for places in different subjects. Universities may close or reduce the intake to courses that have low numbers of applicants while some of the more selective institutions may make more places available, especially to candidates who achieve good grades at A level. Bristol, Birmingham, Exeter and University College London have all taken hundreds more students than usual since the restrictions were relaxed for high-grade candidates. Now universities such as Essex have announced that they intend to grow substantially, while the University of St Mark and St John plans to double in size to achieve economies of scale and become more secure.

Even without an increase in £9,000 fees to allow for inflation, it seems that universities of all types see the expansion of undergraduate provision as a sensible strategy. But even those that are expanding may do so only in areas of strength. In the absence of clear announcements, applicants are still best advised to go for the courses and universities that meet their requirements, rather than trying to play the system.

Certainly, fee levels are unlikely to play a significant part in applicants' choices of university – other than in Scotland and Northern Ireland, where there are big financial incentives to study at a home university. The continuing absence of fees north of the border has been particularly influential in dissuading Scottish students from studying elsewhere. But there has been little evidence that candidates have been swayed by differences of a few hundred pounds in the fees charged by universities in England. Even those differences have almost disappeared: the 20 universities that are charging less than £9,000 for any of their degrees will dwindle to a handful in 2015–16. In any case, applicants know that they have up to 30 years to repay their loans and graduates will all pay the same proportion of their salary (9 per cent) once they pass the threshold of £21,000 a year. Some will repay for a lot longer than others, but that will depend on salary levels, rather than any marginal differences in the size of loans.

Using this *Guide*

Last year's merger of *The Times* and *Sunday Times* university guides began a new chapter in the ranking of higher education institutions in the UK. The two guides had 35 editions between them and, in their new form, provide the most comprehensive and authoritative assessments of undergraduate education at UK universities. The publication of this book follows nearly a week of coverage in the two newspapers and online.

Two more universities are included in the main table this year: St Mary's University, Twickenham, which has been awarded university status since the last edition of the *Guide*, and the University of South Wales, which was formed last year from the merger of Glamorgan and Newport universities. The additions mean that only four public universities are absent this year, at least one of which will be included next year. The current absentees, which instructed the Higher Education Statistics Agency not to release data on their performance, are University College Birmingham, Liverpool Hope, Trinity Saint David and Wolverhampton.

With seven new universities joining the table last year when the Government reduced the minimum number of students required for university status, our ranking is substantially bigger than it was at the beginning of the decade. However, two of the universities created in 2013 – the Norwich University of the Arts and the Royal Agricultural University – were considered too specialised to be compared usefully with more mainstream universities. In addition, new private universities such as the University of Law, Regent's University and UPP University, do not currently have the necessary data to be included.

Some famous names in UK higher education have never been ranked because they do not fit the parameters of a system that is intended mainly to guide full-time undergraduates. The Open University, for example, operates entirely through distance learning, while the London and Manchester Business Schools have no undergraduates. Specialist institutions, like some university colleges, appear in relevant subject tables.

There are also two new subject tables, bringing the total to 66. Last year, physiotherapy and radiography were extracted from the group of subjects entitled "Allied to Medicine" because of the large numbers applying in those specialisms. The new edition contains the first tables for Animal Sciences and Creative Writing, both of which have been popular in recent years. Sadly, both appear at the foot of the comparison of graduate prospects. Other subject tables will be added in due course because there is growing demand for information at this level. A survey of international students by Hobsons, the education software and services company, found that international students were more influenced by subject rankings than those for whole institutions, and there is no reason to believe that domestic applicants think differently.

There has been no change in the basic methodology behind the tables, however. Unlike most of the rankings that have sprung up in recent years, this *Guide* has remained as consistent as possible in the methods used to compare universities. A change of name has not altered that philosophy. The only minor change has been the return to using two years' employment figures in the subject tables, rather than the single year used in the last *Guide*.

There was no alternative to last year's system because the recategorisation of graduate jobs by the Higher Education Statistics Agency meant that only one year's data was available. Using two years' figures reduces the risk of exaggerated swings where student cohorts are small and has increased the number of universities in some subject tables.

As in previous years, the methodology has been scrutinised by a review group comprising academic planning officers from a variety of different types of university.

This year's tables

This year's results show considerable movement, especially in the subject tables, where Warwick tops five rankings – more than any non-Oxbridge university has ever managed and enough to secure the award of University of the Year. Warwick's successes include economics and accounting and finance, as well as the new table for creative writing. It is only two behind Oxford for the number of rankings it leads, but once again Cambridge dominates, topping 33 of the 66 tables.

Our main table also shows change, starting right at the top. Last year, there was only one point separating Cambridge from Oxford; in this edition, there is not even that. For the first time since the inaugural edition of the *Guide*, more than 20 years ago, there is a dead heat between the two universities at the top. The result underlines the fact, evident throughout all the years of the table, that there is little to choose between Oxford and Cambridge, especially in terms of the undergraduate education they offer.

The gap continues to widen between the two ancient rivals and their nearest challengers. St Andrews has replaced the London School of Economics in third place, but Scotland's leading university is almost 130 points behind the leaders. Other movements in the upper reaches of the table have seen big rises by Loughborough and Leeds into the top 20. Cardiff remains clearly the leading university in Wales and Queen's, Belfast is the long-established leader in Northern Ireland.

Further down the table, impressive gains have been made by Falmouth, De Montfort and the University for the Creative Arts, all of which have jumped more than 20 places this year. But perhaps the most significant trend is the continued appearance of a number of post-1992 universities above – in some cases, well above – some older foundations. The first edition of *The Times Good University Guide* predicted the development of a new pecking order in an era of growing competition between universities, many of which had just acquired that title. It has taken longer than many expected and the top third of the table is still monopolised by old universities, but the previous binary division is breaking down.

The standard bearer for the modern universities is Coventry, a classic city-centre former polytechnic, which is now higher in the table, at 42nd, than any of its peer group has ever been. Coventry has higher rates of student satisfaction than any university, old or new, and has taken the award for Top Modern University for the second year in a row. It is joined in the top 50 by Oxford Brookes, with Falmouth, Nottingham Trent

2015 *Guide* Award Winners

University of the Year	**Warwick**
Runner-up	**Leeds**
Shortlisted	**St Andrews**
	Loughborough
	Coventry
Top for Student Experience	**Coventry**
Top for Graduate Prospects	**London School of Economics**
Top in Scotland	**St Andrews**
Top in Wales	**Cardiff**
Top Modern University	**Coventry**

and De Montfort not far behind. At the same time, Salford has slipped out of the top 100 and Aberystwyth is only seven places from following suit. Five other pre-1992 universities are outside the top 50, with more in danger of joining them.

Another surprising feature of this year's table is the poor performance of many Scottish universities. Despite the advantages in student recruitment conferred by the absence of fees for Scottish students and a generous conversion rate for Scottish qualifications in the UCAS points tariff, 11 of the 15 universities north of the border have fallen in this year's ranking. Only St Andrews appears in the top 20 and there are just four Scottish universities in the top 40. The decline may be no more than a blip, but it may call into question some institutional strategies. Ten of the universities had seen declines in student satisfaction, suggesting that free tuition is not enough on its own.

Making the right choices

Anyone hoping to embark on a degree in 2015 will be well advised to tread carefully and muster as much comparative information as possible before making their choices. This *Guide* is intended as a starting point, a tool to help navigate the statistical minefield that will face applicants, as universities present their performance in the best possible light. There is a chapter on the impact of the fee changes, as well as one focusing on all-important employment issues along with the usual ranking of universities and 66 subject tables.

Whatever their appetite for expansion, most of the leading universities will remain highly selective, particularly in popular subjects. Even when the demand for places dropped in 2012, there were between five and six applications (not applicants) to the place across the whole higher education system. The figure was almost double that at the most popular universities. The demand for places is far from uniform, however; even within the same university the level of competition will vary between subjects. The entry scores quoted in the subject tables in Chapter 5 offer a reliable guide to the relative levels of selectivity, but the figures are for entrants' actual qualifications. The standard offers made by departments will invariably be lower.

Making the right choice in 2015 will require a mixture of realism and ambition. Most sixth-formers and college students have a fair idea of the grades they are capable of attaining, within a certain margin for error. Even with five choices of course to make, there is no point in applying to a course where the standard offer is so far from your predicted grades that rejection is virtually certain. But, in this year of uncertainty for admissions officers, there is no harm in using at least one of your choices to apply to a university at the upper end of your possible grades.

One change that has already taken place and which will no doubt continue in 2015 may also affect your choices. With the relaxation of recruitment restrictions, universities that once took pride in their absence from Clearing are now continuing to recruit after A-level results day. As a result, the use of insurance choices – the inclusion of at least one university with lower entrance standards than your main targets – is likely to decline further. It is still a dangerous strategy, but there is now more chance of picking up a course at a leading university if you aimed too high with all your first-round choices. Oxford and Cambridge will not be appearing in the Clearing lists and you are most unlikely to find courses in medicine there, but there will be a wider range of universities to choose from than ever before.

Candidates with better grades than they expected may also find more options available in the Adjustment Period that runs for five days after results have been published. Although only 1,220 students found places this way in 2013, the numbers may rise as the system becomes better known, especially in the new de-regulated era. Universities at the very top of the table may still be full, but there should be more opportunities to "trade up" if your grades are better than your highest offer.

The long view

School-leavers who enter higher education in 2015 were not born when our first league table was published and most will never have heard of polytechnics, even if they attend a university that once carried that title. But it was the award of university status to the 34 polytechnics, 22 years ago, that was the inspiration for the first edition of *The Times Good University Guide*. The original poly, the Polytechnic of Central London, had become the University of Westminster, Bristol Polytechnic was now the University of the West of England and – most mysteriously of all – Leicester Polytechnic had morphed into De Montfort University. The new *Guide* charted the lineage of the new universities and offered the first-ever comparison of institutional performance in UK higher education.

The university establishment did not welcome the initiative. The vice-chancellors described the table as "wrong in principle, flawed in execution and constructed upon data which are not uniform, are ill-defined and in places demonstrably false." The league table has changed considerably since then, although Oxford and Cambridge still reign supreme. While consistency has been a priority for the *Guide* throughout its 21 years, only six of the original 14 measures have survived. Some of the current components – notably the National Student Survey – did not exist in 1992, while others have been modified or dropped at the behest of the expert group of planning officers from different types of universities that meets annually to review the methodology and make recommendations for the future.

While ranking is hardly popular with academics, the relationship with universities has changed radically, and this *Guide* is quoted on numerous university websites. As Sir David Eastwood, now vice-chancellor of the University of Birmingham, said in launching an official report on university league tables that he commissioned as Chief Executive of the Higher Education Funding Council for England: "We deplore league tables one day and deploy them the next."

Most universities have had their ups and downs over the years, although Oxford and Cambridge have tended to pull away from the rest. Both benefited from the introduction of student satisfaction ratings and from the extra credit given to the top research grades – the two measures that carry an extra weighting in our table. They also have famously high entry standards, much the largest proportions of first and upper-second class degrees and consistently good scores on every other measure. Several other famous names have been among the chasing pack throughout. The London School of Economics, Imperial College and University College London have seldom been out of the top five, while Warwick and, in recent years, Durham and St Andrews have all been fixtures in the top ten.

There have been spectacular rises, however. Exeter, for example, was 36th in the inaugural table and only one place better off in the 2003 *Guide*, but is now enjoying its fourth year in the top ten. Lancaster has slipped out of the top ten, but is still 25 places better off than it was in 1993. Even more impressively, Lincoln was only five places off the bottom of the table eight years ago. Since then, it has moved 50 places up the table and into the top half, cementing a position among the highest-placed universities to be established in the last 20 years.

Higher education has changed enormously since this book was first published. The number of universities has increased by another third and the full-time student population has rocketed. Individual institutions are almost unrecognisable from their 1993 forms. Greenwich, for example, had less than 8,500 students then, compared with more than 18,500 now. Manchester Metropolitan, the largest of the former polys, had little more than 10,000 full-time students in 1993, compared with almost 28,000 last year. The diversity of UK higher education is celebrated as one of its greatest strengths, and the modern universities are neither encouraged nor anxious to compete with the older foundations on some of the measures in our table.

The next 20 years may see another transformation in the higher education landscape, with the private sector competing strongly with established universities in some fields and distance learning becoming more popular as there is greater investment in Massive Open Online Courses (MOOCs) and the cost of full-time degrees rises. There may, indeed, be university closures and mergers, although they have been predicted before and seldom come about. Universities are among the most enduring of the UK's institutions, and will take some shifting.

Why university?

Particularly if the UK economy continues its modest recovery, more young people will be tempted to write off higher education, once the cost of living has been added to the growing fees burden and the attractions of university life balanced against loss of potential earnings. There are plenty of self-made millionaires who still swear by the University of Life as the only training ground for success. Yet even by narrow financial criteria it would be rash to dismiss higher education. With so many more competing for jobs, a degree will never again be an automatic passport to a fast-track career. But graduates' financial prospects remain much brighter than school leavers', as are their prospects in other important areas, such as health.

Even for those who cannot or do not wish to afford three or more years of full-time education after leaving school, university remains a possibility. The modular courses adopted by most universities enable students to work through a degree at their own pace, dropping out for a time if necessary, or switching to part-time attendance. Distance learning is another option, and advances in information technology now mean that some nominally full-time courses are delivered mainly online.

For many – perhaps most – students, the university experience is not what it was in their parents' day. There is more assessment, more crowding, more pressure to get the best possible degree while also finding gainful employment for at least part of the year. The proportion of students achieving first-class degrees has risen significantly, while an upper second (rather than the previously ubiquitous 2:2) has become the norm. Research shows that the classification has a real impact in the labour market.

Most graduates do not regret their decision to go to university, however. Students from all over the world flock to British universities, and they offer a valuable resource for those on their doorstep. No league table can determine which is the right university for any candidate, but this *Guide* should provide some of the information necessary to draw up a shortlist for further investigation.

1 What and Where to Study

Choosing a university and degree course is a potentially life-changing decision. Many graduates end up living and working near their university; they often make their closest friends in their student days and may even meet their future partner there. For a growing number of applicants, however, the process appears to be almost exclusively about future career prospects. Applications and enrolments since the introduction of £9,000 fees are beginning to show clear patterns that favour particular subjects and universities, and may make life increasingly difficult for others.

The primary motivation for most students in going to university has always been long-term betterment, but the stakes have never been as high. It is not surprising that growing numbers should decide to play it safe, as they see it, in choosing what and where to study. Although most graduate jobs continue to be open to students of any discipline, some arts subjects may now seem more of a gamble and there may be pressure at home to go for a science or business subject, if you have the right qualifications.

Of course, it would be perverse not to take employment prospects into account when you may be leaving university with debts of £50,000, however enlightened the repayment regime. If higher fees are encouraging students to think more carefully about what (and whether) to study, that should be considered a redeeming feature. But there must more to the decision than money: not least, the chances of your chosen course being within your capabilities and maintaining your interest for three years – indeed, possibly much longer than that if it is then going to determine your field of employment.

Ideally, higher education should broaden your options in later life, not narrow them. Most of today's graduates will work in several different fields during their careers. In any case, no one can be sure which skills will be required in four or more years' time, when today's applicants enter the graduate labour market. Some subjects and universities will be more marketable than others, but which ones? This *Guide* may give some pointers – medicine is unlikely to go into decline, for example – but times do change. Computer science, for instance, went through years of falling numbers after the dotcom bubble burst, before recovering strongly in the last two years. Applications for the architecture and building group of subjects remain 20 per cent behind the totals reached before the recession.

Why applicants have reached some of the conclusions they have remains a mystery. Languages, for example, have been hardest hit in terms of applications and enrolments.

Yet French, German and Spanish are all in the top 30 (out of 66) in our employment table, and classics, Russian, Italian and Asian languages are not far behind. Business leaders are constantly stressing the need for linguists, but sixth-formers appear not to believe them. In this case, decisions made on entry to the sixth-form may be the biggest factor behind falling applications – the numbers taking languages at A level have been dropping for a number of years, perhaps because they are seen as more difficult than other arts subjects.

There will be a number of different factors influencing your choice of university and course, ranging from the limitations imposed by your qualifications to favoured geographical locations. You may want to stay within reach of home – or to get as far away as possible. You may have heard good things about a particular course from friends, or a teacher. This *Guide* – and the tables it contains – offers a reality check to supplement such opinions, and the opportunity to narrow down your options.

Key reasons for going to university

To improve job opportunities	**76%**
To improve knowledge in an area of interest	**63%**
To improve salary prospects	**61%**
To specialise in a certain subject/area	**59%**
Obtain an additional qualification	**58%**
To become more independent	**48%**
Essential for my chosen profession	**48%**
Meet new people	**44%**
It's the obvious next step – just what you do	**40%**
To experience a different way of life	**38%**
My parents expected me to	**27%**
To have a good social life	**26%**
I didn't want to get a job straight away	**24%**
I didn't know what else I wanted to do	**20%**
Can live at home and still go to university	**13%**
All my friends were going	**12%**

Sodexo University Lifestyle Survey 2014

Is higher education for you?

Before you start, there is one important question to ask yourself: what do you want out of higher education? The answer will make it easier to choose where (and if) to be a student. With three in ten school-leavers going on to university, it is easy to drift that way without much thought, opting for the subject in which you expect the best A-level grades, and looking for a university with a reasonable reputation and a good social life. Your career will look after itself – you hope.

With graduate debt soaring, however, and job prospects varying widely between subjects, now is the time to look at your own motivation. Some – though not as many as predicted – opted out of higher education in the first year of higher fees, while others appear to be rethinking their course choice. The choices of these first cohorts were limited by the subjects they were taking, or had already taken, in the sixth-form. More may be steered towards apparently lucrative courses in future.

Love of a subject is an excellent reason for taking a degree, and one that allows you to focus almost exclusively on the search for a course that corresponds with your passions. If, however, higher education is a means to an end, you need to think about career ambitions and look carefully at employment rates for any courses you might consider. These are examined in more detail in chapter 2.

Many graduates look back on their student days as the best years of their lives, and there is nothing wrong with wanting to have a good time. Remember, though, that you will be paying for it later (literally) and there will be more studying than partying. If you have not enjoyed sixth-form or college courses, you may be better off in a job and possibly becoming one of the hundreds of thousands each year who return to education later in life.

Setting your priorities

Even in the world of £9,000 fees, there are good reasons to believe that the right degree will still be a good investment. Research by London Economics for the million+ group of universities suggested that, on average, a degree would add £115,000 to lifetime earnings. The most recent Labour Force Survey showed working-age graduates earning 50 per cent more on average than non-graduates.

The majority of graduate jobs are not subject-specific; employers value the transferable skills that higher education confers. Rightly or wrongly, however, most employers are influenced by which university a graduate attended, so the choice of institution remains as important as ever.

Those who want to add value to their degree in the jobs market will find that growing numbers of universities are offering employment-related schemes that are considered in more detail in chapter 2. In many cases, this will involve work experience or extra activities organised by the careers service. Some universities, such as Leicester, now run certificated employability programmes, while others, such as Liverpool John Moores, have built such skills into degree programmes. Such programmes are also highlighted in chapter 2 and in the institutional profiles in chapter 14.

Narrowing down the field

Once you have decided that higher education is for you, the good news is that, as long as you start early enough, finding the right university can be relatively straightforward. Media attention focuses on the scramble for places on a relatively small proportion of courses where competition is intense, but there are plenty of places at good universities for candidates with the basic qualifications – it's just a matter of finding the one that suits you best. For older applicants, relevant work experience and demonstrable interest in a subject may be enough to win a place.

If anything, the problem is that of too much choice, although universities have reduced the number of degree combinations in anticipation of tougher financial conditions. Students prepared to move away from home will still have more than 100 universities and numerous specialist colleges to consider, most with hundreds – even thousands – of course combinations on offer. Institutions come in all shapes and sizes, so there is work to do at the outset narrowing down your options.

Deciding what you want to study may reduce the field considerably – there are only eight institutions offering veterinary medicine for example, although the total is around 100 in subjects such as law and English. By the time you have factored in personal preferences about the type or location of your ideal university, the list of possibilities may already be reduced to manageable proportions.

After that, you can take a closer look at what the courses contain and what life is really like for students. Prospectuses and university websites will give you an accurate account of course combinations, and important facts like the accommodation available to new students, but it is their job to sell the university. To get a true picture, you need more – preferably a visit not just to the university, but to the department where you would be studying. If that is not possible, there are plenty of other sources of objective information, such as the National Student Survey (which is available online, with a range of additional data about the main courses at each institution, at **www.unistats.com**).

Some students' unions publish alternative prospectuses, giving a "warts and all" view of the university, and those that do not provide this service may be able to arrange a brief

The UCAS tariff

Tariffs for selected qualifications are given below. The full range of acceptable qualifications and their tariff values are given at **www.ucas.com/how-it-all-works/explore-your-options/entry-requirements/tariff-tables**.

GCE AS/AS VCE	GCE AS Double Award	GCE A level/A VCE	A level with additional AS (9 units)	GCE/AVCE Double Award	Points	Advanced Higher	Higher
				A*A*	280		
				A*A	260		
				AA	240		
				AB	220		
			A*A	BB	200		
			AA	BC	180		
			AB		170		
				CC	160		
			BB		150		
		A*	BC	CD	140		
					130	A	
	AA	A	CC	DD	120		
	AB		CD		110	B	
	BB	B		DE	100		
	BC		DD		90	C	
	CC	C	DE	EE	80		A
					72	D	
	CD				70		
					65		B
A	DD	D	EE		60		
B	DE				50		C
C	EE	E			40		
					36		D
D					30		
E					20		

UCAS tariff for the International Baccalaureate

Points for the International Baccalaureate (IB) are awarded to candidates who achieve the IB Diploma.

IB Dip.	Points	IB Dip.	Points	IB Dip.	Points	IB Dip.	Points	IB Dip.	Points
45	720	40	611	35	501	30	392	25	282
44	698	39	589	34	479	29	370	24	260
43	676	38	567	33	457	28	348		
42	654	37	545	32	435	27	326		
41	632	36	523	31	413	26	304		

discussion with a current student, either by phone or email. Some alternative prospectuses and other apparently random students' views can be found at **www.realuni.com**. Your school or college may put you in contact with someone who went to a university that you are considering. Guides and collections of statistics may give you valuable information about a course or a university, but there is no substitute for personal experience.

What to study?

Most people seeking a place in higher education start by choosing a subject and a course, rather than a university. If you take a degree, you are going to spend at least three years immersed in your subject. It has to be one you will enjoy and can master – not to mention one that you are qualified to study. Many economics degrees require maths A level, for example, while most medical schools demand chemistry or biology. The UCAS website (**www.ucas.com**) contains course profiles, including entrance requirements, which is a good starting point, while universities' own sites contain more detailed information. In chapter 5, we describe 66 subject areas and provide league tables for each of them.

Your school subjects and the UCAS tariff

The official yardstick by which your results will be judged is the UCAS tariff, which gives a score for each grade of most UK qualifications considered relevant for university entrance, as well as for the International Baccalaureate (IB). This tariff has become controversial as more subjects and types of qualifications have been included in it. Top scores in the IB, for example, earn considerably more points than the maximum for four, let alone three, A levels.

While the majority of universities use the tariff to make offers of places, many of the leading institutions prefer to stipulate the grades that they require. This allows them to specify the subjects in which particular grades must be achieved, as well as to determine which vocational qualifications are relevant to different degrees. In certain universities, some departments, but not others, will use the tariff to set offers. There has been debate within UCAS about scrapping the tariff altogether, but it will still be in place for applications for courses beginning in 2015. Course profiles on the UCAS website and/or universities' own sites should show whether offers are framed in terms of grades or tariff points. It is important

---

"Soft" subjects

The London School of Economics would prefer to see only one subject from this list in your mix of A-level subjects.

» Accounting
» Art and design
» Business studies (especially when combined with Economics)
» Communication studies
» Design and technology
» Drama/theatre studies (some departments)
» Home economics
» Information and communication technology
» Law
» Media studies
» Music technology (music is acceptable)
» Sports studies
» Travel and tourism

Those studying either accounting or law at A level "should not be put off applying to the LSE, as, depending on their overall academic profile, they may be made an offer". General studies and critical thinking A levels will only be considered as fourth A-level subjects and will not therefore be accepted as part of a conditional offer.

to find out which, especially if you are relying on points from qualifications other than A level or Scottish Highers.

"Soft" subjects

There is a related issue for many of the most selective universities about the subjects studied in the sixth-form or at college. Not only are growing numbers of students applying with vocational (usually BTEC) qualifications, but the variety of A-level courses now available includes many subjects that top universities usually will not consider on a par with traditional academic subjects. For many years a minority of universities have refused to accept General Studies as a full A level for entrance purposes (although even some leading universities do). The growth of supposedly "soft" subjects, such as media studies and photography, has prompted a few universities to produce lists of subjects that will only be accepted alongside at least two traditional academic subjects.

The Russell Group of 24 leading universities published an extremely useful report (updated in 2013), called *Informed Choices*, on the post-16 qualifications preferred by its members for a wide range of degrees. Although it names media studies, art and design, photography and business studies among the vocational subjects that would normally be

---

Admissions tests

Some of the most competitive courses now have additional entrance tests. The most significant tests are listed below. Note that registration for many of the tests is before 15 October and you will need to register for them as early as possible. All the tests have their own websites.

Some universities also administer their own tests; details are given at: **www.ucas.com/how-it-all-works/explore-your-options/entry-requirements/ providers-own-tests**

Law

Law National Admissions Test (LNAT): for entry to law courses at Birmingham, Bristol, Durham, Glasgow, King's College London, Nottingham, Oxford, SOAS, University College London.

Mathematics

Mathematics Admissions Test (MAT): for entry to mathematics at Imperial College, London and mathematics and computer science at Oxford.

Sixth Term Examination Papers (STEP): for entry to mathematics at Cambridge and Warwick (also encouraged by Bath, Bristol, Imperial College London, King's College London, Loughborough, Oxford and University College London).

Medical subjects

BioMedical Admissions Test (BMAT): for entry to medicine, veterinary medicine and biomedical sciences at Brighton and Sussex Medical School (graduate entry), Cambridge, Imperial College London, Leeds, Oxford, Royal Veterinary College, University College London.

Graduate Medical School Admissions Test (GAMSAT): for graduate entry to medicine and dentistry at Cardiff, Exeter, Liverpool, Nottingham, Plymouth, St. George's, University of London, Swansea.

Health Professions Admissions Test (HPAT-Ulster): for certain health profession courses at Ulster.

UK Clinical Aptitude Test (UKCAT): for entry to medical and dental schools at Aberdeen, Cardiff, Central Lancashire, Dundee, Durham, East Anglia, Edinburgh, Exeter, Glasgow, Hull York Medical School, Keele, King's College London, Leicester, Manchester, Newcastle, Nottingham, Plymouth, Queen Mary, University of London, Queen's University, Belfast, Sheffield, Southampton, St Andrews, St George's, University of London, Warwick (graduate entry).

given this label, it does not subscribe to the notion of a single list of "soft" subjects. The report suggests you choose at most a single vocational course and primarily select from a list of "facilitating subjects", which are required for many degrees and welcomed generally at Russell Group universities. The list comprises: maths and further maths, English, physics, biology, chemistry, geography, languages (classical and modern) and history. In addition their guide indicates the "essential" and "useful" A-level subjects for 60 different subject areas studied at Russell Group universities.

For most courses at most universities, there are no such restrictions, as long as your main subjects or qualifications are relevant to the degree you hope to take. Nevertheless, when choosing A levels it would be wise to bear the Russell Group lists in mind if you are likely to apply to one or more of the leading universities. At the very least, it is an indication of the subjects that admissions tutors may take less seriously than the rest. Although only the London School of Economics identifies "non-preferred" subjects publicly (see page 19), others may adopt less formal weightings.

Vocational qualifications

The Education Department has announced that many vocational qualifications will be downgraded in school league tables from 2014. This can only add to the confusion surrounding the value placed on diplomas and other qualifications by universities. The engineering diploma has won near-universal approval from universities (for admission to

---

Cambridge University
Cambridge Law Test: for entry to law, taken at Cambridge during interview process.
Modern and Medieval Languages Test (MML): for entry to modern and medieval languages at Cambridge, taken at Cambridge during interview process.
Thinking Skills Assessment (TSA) Cambridge: mainly for computer science, economics, engineering, human, social and political sciences, land economy, natural sciences, psychological and behavioural sciences at most Cambridge colleges, taken at Cambridge during interview process. See also STEP and BMAT above.

Oxford University
Specific registration is required for the following subject tests. Tests taken on 5 November 2014, usually at candidate's educational institution.
Classics Admissions Test: classics.
Thinking Skills Assessment (TSA) Oxford: economics and management, experimental psychology, geography, philosophy, politics and economics (PPE), psychology.
Physics Aptitude Test: engineering, materials science, physics.
English Literature Admissions Test: English.
History Aptitude Test: history.
Modern Languages Admissions Tests: modern languages, courses including linguistics.
Oriental Languages Aptitude Test: oriental studies.
See also LNAT, MAT and BMAT above.
For fine art, music and philosophy, there will be a test at interview in December 2014.
Full details at **www.ox.ac.uk/admissions/undergraduate_courses/applying_to_oxford/tests**

University College London
Thinking Skills Assessment (TSA) UCL: for entry to European social and political studies; the test is arranged in the interview process.

engineering courses and possibly some science degrees), but some of the other diplomas are in fields that are not on the curriculum of the most selective universities. Regardless of the points awarded under the tariff, it is essential to contact universities direct to ensure that a diploma or another vocational qualification will be an acceptable qualification for your chosen degree.

Admission tests

The growing numbers of applicants with high grades at A level have encouraged the introduction of separate admission tests for some of the most oversubscribed courses. There are national tests in medicine and law that are used by some of the leading universities, while Oxford and Cambridge have their own tests in a number of subjects. The details are listed on pages 20–21. In all cases, the tests are used as an extra selection tool, not as a replacement for A level or other general qualifications.

Making a choice

Your A levels or Scottish Highers may have chosen themselves, but the range of subjects across the whole university system is vast. Even subjects that you have studied at school may be quite different at degree level – some academic economists actually prefer their undergraduates not to have taken A-level economics because they approach the subject so differently. Other students are disappointed because they appear to be going over old ground when they continue with a subject that they enjoyed at school. Universities now publish quite detailed syllabuses, and it is a matter of going through the fine print.

The greater difficulty comes in judging your suitability for the many subjects that are not on the school or college curriculum. Philosophy and psychology sound fascinating (and are), but you may have no idea what degrees in either subject entail – for example, the level of statistics that may be required. Forensic science may look exciting on television – more glamorous than plain chemistry – but it opens fewer doors, as the type of work portrayed in *Silent Witness* or *Raising the Dead* is very hard to find.

Academic or vocational?

There is frequent and often misleading debate about the differences between academic and vocational higher education. It is usually about the relative value of taking a degree, as

The ten most popular subject areas for applications, 2014	
1 Subjects allied to medicine	327,620
2 Business and administrative studies	310,690
3 Creative arts and design	287,040
4 Social studies	237,100
5 Biological sciences	216,480
6 Engineering	134,810
7 Law	117,240
8 Sciences combined with social sciences or arts	110,210
9 Medicine and dentistry	93,390
10 Physical sciences	91,940
UCAS, applications by 30 June 2014	

The ten most popular subject areas for acceptances, 2013	
1 Business and administrative studies	60,990
2 Creative arts and design	51,645
3 Subjects allied to medicine	49,475
4 Biological sciences	44,415
5 Social studies	40,930
6 Engineering	27,155
7 Law	23,740
8 Computer sciences	21,710
9 Physical sciences	19,325
10 Education	17,860
UCAS 2013	

opposed to a directly work-related qualification. But it also extends to higher education itself, with jibes about so-called "Mickey Mouse" degrees in areas that were not part of the higher education curriculum when most of the critics were students.

Such attitudes ignore the fact that medicine and law are both vocational subjects, as are architecture, engineering and education. They are not seen as any less academic than geography or sociology, but for some reason social work or nursing, let alone media studies and sports science, are often looked down upon. The test of a degree should be whether it is challenging and a good preparation for working life. Both general academic and vocational degrees can do this.

Nevertheless, it is clear that the prospect of much higher graduate debt is encouraging more students into job-related subjects. This is understandable and, if you are sure of your future career path, possibly also sensible. But much depends on what that career is – and whether you are ready to make such a long-term commitment. Some of the programmes that have attracted public ridicule, such as surf science or golf course management, may narrow graduates' options to a worrying extent, but often boast strong employment records.

As you would expect, many vocational courses are tailored to particular professions. If you choose one of these, make sure that the degree is recognised by the relevant professional body (such as the Engineering Council or one of the institutes) or you may not be able to use the skills that you acquire. Most universities are only too keen to make such recognition clear in their prospectus; if no such guarantee is published, contact the university department running the course and seek assurances.

Total number of full-time undergraduates by subject area, 2012–13

Business and administrative studies	188,965
Subjects allied to medicine	147,620
Creative arts and design	143,210
Biological sciences	139,130
Social studies	131,890
Engineering and technology	96,365
Languages	81,900
Physical sciences	63,940
Computer sciences	59,600
Law	57,865
Education	55,975
Historical and philosophical studies	54,780
Medicine and dentistry	46,235
Mass communications and documentation	38,595
Mathematical sciences	29,600
Architecture, building and planning	29,230
Agriculture and related subjects	11,685
Veterinary sciences	4,800
Total: All subjects	**1,385,675**
HESA 2014	

Even where a course has professional recognition, bear in mind that a further qualification may be required to practise. Both law and medicine, for example, demand additional training to become a fully qualified solicitor, barrister or doctor. Nor is either degree an automatic passport to a job: only about half of all law graduates go into the profession. Both law and medicine also provide a route into the profession for graduates who have taken other subjects. Law conversion courses, though not cheap, are increasingly popular, and there are a growing number of graduate-entry medical degrees.

One way to ensure that a degree is job-related is to take a "sandwich" course, which involves up to a year in business or industry. Students often end up working for the organisation which provided the placement, while others gain valuable insights into a field of employment – even if only to discount it. The drawback with such courses is that, like the year abroad that is part of most language degrees, the period away from university inevitably disrupts living arrangements and friendship groups. But most of those who take this route find that the career benefits make this a worthwhile sacrifice.

Employers' organisations calculate that more than half of all graduate jobs are open to applicants from any subject, and recruiters for the most competitive graduate training schemes often prefer traditional academic subjects to apparently relevant vocational degrees. Newspapers, for example, often prefer a history graduate to one with a media studies degree; computing firms are said to take a disproportionate number of classicists. A good degree classification and the right work experience are more important than the subject for most non-technical jobs. But it is hard to achieve a good result on a course that you do not enjoy, so scour prospectuses, and email or phone university departments to ensure that you know what you are letting yourself in for. Their reaction to your approach will also give you an idea of how responsive they are to their students.

Studying more than one subject

You may find that more than one subject appeals, in which case you could consider Joint Honours – degrees that combine two subjects – or even Combined Honours, which will cover several related subjects. Such courses obviously allow you to extend the scope of your studies, but they should be approached with caution. Even if the number of credits suggests a similar workload to Single Honours, covering more than one subject inevitably involves extra reading and often more essays or project work.

However, there are advantages. Many students choose a "dual" to add a vocational element to make themselves more employable – business studies with languages or engineering, for example, or media studies with English. Others want to take their studies in a particular direction, perhaps by combining history with politics, or statistics with maths. Some simply want to add a completely unrelated interest to their main subject, such as environmental science and music, or archaeology and event management – both combinations that are available at UK universities.

At most universities, however, it is not necessary to take a degree in more than one subject in order to broaden your studies. The spread of modular programmes ensures that you can take courses in related subjects without changing the basic structure of your degree. You may not be able to take an event management module in a single-honours archaeology degree, but it should be possible to study some history or a language. The number and scope of the combinations offered at many of the larger universities is extraordinary. Indeed, it has been criticised by academics who believe that "mix-and-match" degrees can leave a graduate without a rounded view of a subject. But for those who seek breadth and variety, close scrutiny of university prospectuses is a vital part of the selection process.

What type of course?

Once you have a subject, you must decide on the level and type of course. Most readers of this *Guide* will be looking for full-time degree courses, but higher education is much broader than that. You may not be able to afford the time or the money needed for a full-time commitment of three or four years at this point in your life.

Part-time courses

Tens of thousands of people each year opt for a part-time course – usually while holding down a job – to continue learning and to improve their career prospects. The numbers studying this way have dropped recently, but that may change as the new funding arrangements, which give most part-time students access to loans for the first time, become better known and accepted.

Under these arrangements, loans are available for students whose courses occupy between a quarter and three-quarters of the time expected on a full-time course. Repayments are on the same conditions as those for full-time courses, except that repayments will begin after three years of study even if the course has not been completed by then. The downside is that many universities have increased their fees in the knowledge that part-time students will be able to take out student loans to cover fees and employers are now less inclined to fund their employees on such courses. Nevertheless, the change should still be beneficial overall. At Birkbeck, University of London, for example, full-time fees are £9,000 a year, with part-timers paying in proportion to the number of credits they take. For the first time, students need pay nothing up front if they take out income-contingent loans.

Part-time study can be exhausting unless your employer gives you time off, but if you have the stamina for a course that will usually take twice as long as the full-time equivalent, this route should still make a degree more affordable. Part-time students tend to be highly committed to their subject, and many claim that the quality of the social life associated with their course makes up for the quantity of leisure time enjoyed by full-timers.

Distance learning

If you are confident that you can manage without regular face-to-face contact with teachers and fellow students, distance learning is an option. Courses are delivered mainly or entirely online or through correspondence, although some programmes offer a certain amount of local tuition. The process might sound daunting and impersonal, but students of the Open University (OU), all of whom are educated in this way, are among the most satisfied in the country, according to the results of the annual National Student Survey. Attending lectures or oversized seminars at a conventional university can be less personal than regular contact with your tutor at a distance.

Of course, not all universities are as good at communicating with their distance-learning students as the OU, or offer such high-quality course materials, but this mode of study does give students ultimate flexibility to determine when and where they study. Distance learning is becoming increasingly popular for the delivery of professional courses, which are often needed to supplement degrees. The OU now takes students of all ages, including a growing number of school-leavers, not just mature students.

In addition, there is now the option of Massive Open Online Courses (MOOCs) provided by some of the leading UK and American universities, usually free of charge. As yet, such courses are the equivalent of a module in a degree course, rather than the entire qualification. Some are assessed formally but none is likely to be seen by employers as the equal of a conventional degree, no matter how prestigious the university offering the course. That may change – some commentators see in MOOCs the beginning of the end of the traditional, residential university – but their main value at the moment is as a means of dipping a toe in the water of higher education. For those who are uncertain about committing to a degree, or who simply want to learn more about a subject without needing a high-status qualification, they are ideal.

Several leading UK universities are beginning to offer MOOCs through the Futurelearn platform, run by the Open University (**http://futurelearn.com**). But the beauty of MOOCs is that they can come from all over the world. Perhaps the best-known providers are Coursera (**www.coursera.org**), which originated at Stanford University, in California, and now involves a large number of American and international universities including Edinburgh, and edX (**www.edx.org**), which numbers Harvard among its members.

Foundation degrees

Even if you are set on a full-time course, you might not want to commit yourself for three or more years. Two-year vocational Foundation degrees have become a popular route into higher education in recent years. Many other students take longer-established two-year courses, such as Higher National Diplomas or other diplomas tailored to the needs of industry or parts of the health service. Those who do well on such courses usually have the option of converting their qualification into a full degree with further study, although many are satisfied without immediately staying on for the further two or more years that completing a BA or BSc will require.

Other short courses

A number of universities are experimenting with two-year degrees, squeezing more work into an extended academic year. The so-called "third semester" makes use of the summer vacation for extra teaching, so that mature students, in particular, can reduce the length of their career break. Several universities are offering accelerated degrees as part of a pilot project initiated under the last government. But only at the University of Buckingham, the UK's longest-established private university, is this the dominant pattern for degree courses. Other private institutions – notably BPP University – are following suit.

Other short courses, usually lasting a year, are designed for students who do not have the necessary qualifications to start a degree in their chosen subject. Foundation courses in art and design have been common for many years, and are the chosen preparation for a degree at leading departments, even for many students whose A levels would win them a degree place elsewhere. Access courses perform the same function in a wider range of subjects for students without A levels, or for those whose grades are either too low or in the wrong subjects to gain admission to a particular course. Entry requirements are modest, but students have to reach the same standard as regular entrants to progress to a degree.

Yet more choice

No single guide can allow for personal preferences in choosing a course. You may want one

---

Subjects with highest ratio of applications to acceptances, 2013

1	Medicine	11.2
2	Dentistry	9.7
3	Nursing	9.2
4	Veterinary medicine	9.2
5	Medical technology	8.8
6	Anatomy, physiology and pathology	8.2
7	Training teachers	7.3
8	Pharmacology, toxicology and pharmacy	6.8
9	Economics	6.6
10	Mechanical engineering	6.2

UCAS 2013 (for subjects with over 1,000 acceptances)

Universities with the highest application to place ratio, 2013

1	London School of Economics	12.1
2	Buckingham	11.9
3	Aberdeen	11.8
4	Edinburgh	9.2
5	Keele	8.9
6	Liverpool	8.3
=7	Bristol	8.2
=7	Dundee	8.2
9	King's College London	8.1
10	St Andrews	7.9

UCAS 2013

of the many degrees that incorporate a year at a partner university abroad, or to try a six-month exchange on the Continent through the European Union's Erasmus Programme. Either might prove a valuable experience and add to your employability. Or you might prefer a January or February start to the traditional autumn start – there are plenty of opportunities for this, mainly at post-1992 universities.

In some subjects – particularly engineering and the sciences – the leading degrees may be Masters courses, taking four years rather than three (in England). In Scotland, most degree courses take four years and some at the older universities will confer a Masters qualification. Those who come with A levels may apply to go straight into the second year. Relatively few students take this option, but it is easy to imagine more doing so in future at universities that charge students from other parts of the UK the full £9,000 for all years of the course.

Where to study

Once you have decided what to study, there are still several factors that might influence your choice of university or college. Obviously, you need to have a reasonable chance of getting in, you may want reassurance about the university's reputation, and its location will probably also be important to you. On top of that, most applicants have views about the type of institution they are looking for – big or small, old or new, urban or rural, specialist or comprehensive. Campus universities tend to produce the highest levels of student satisfaction, but big city universities continue to attract sixth-formers in the largest numbers. You may surprise yourself by choosing somewhere that does not conform to your initial criteria, but working through your preferences is another way of narrowing down your options.

Non-academic factors considered when choosing a university

Location-related

Close to transport links	35%
Able to live away from parental home but close enough for support	33%
Quality of accommodation	24%
Cost of accommodation	22%
Low cost of living	19%
Able to live at parental home	18%
Opportunities for part-time jobs	10%

University-related

Good impression from open days	50%
Campus university	38%
Attractive environment	38%
City centre university	23%
Active social life / good social facilities	23%
IT / Resource / study facilities	22%
Financial support available (bursaries; sponsorship, etc)	19%
Clubs and societies	14%
Good sporting facilities	8%
Good catering and retail facilities	3%

Sodexo University Lifestyle Survey 2014

Entry standards

Unless you are a mature student or have taken a gap year, your passport to your chosen university will be a conditional offer based on your predicted grades, previous exam performance, personal statement, and school or college reference. A lucky few may get an offer that is so low that success is a foregone conclusion – because the university considers them outstanding and needs no further evidence of their potential. But at most universities, only those who already have their grades receive unconditional offers.

Supply and demand dictate whether you will receive an offer. Beyond the national picture, your chances will be affected both by the university and the subject you choose. A few universities (but not many) at the top of the league tables are heavily oversubscribed in every subject; others will have areas in which they excel, but may make relatively modest demands for entry to other courses. Even in many of the leading universities, the number of applicants for each place in languages or engineering is still not high. Conversely, three As at A level will not guarantee a place on one of the top English or law degrees, but there are enough universities running courses to ensure that three Cs will put you in with a chance somewhere.

University prospectuses and the UCAS website will give you the "standard offer" for each course, but in some cases this is pitched deliberately low in order to leave admissions staff extra flexibility. The standard A-level offer for medicine, for example, may not demand A*s, but nearly all successful applicants will have one or more.

The average entry scores in our subject tables give the actual points obtained by successful applicants – many of which are far above the offer made by the university, but which give an indication of the pecking order at entry. The subject tables (in chapter 5) are, naturally, a better guide than the main table (in chapter 4), where average entry scores are influenced by the range of subjects available at each university.

Location

The most obvious starting point is the country you study in. Most degrees in Scotland take four years, rather than the UK norm of three. It goes without saying that four years cost more than three, especially given the loss of the year's salary you might have been earning after graduation. A later chapter will go into the details of the system, but suffice to say that students from Scotland pay no fees, while those from the rest of the UK do. Nevertheless, Edinburgh and St Andrews remain particularly popular with English students, despite charging them £9,000 a year for the full four years of a degree. The number of English students going to Scottish universities actually increased by almost a quarter in 2012 and increased again in 2013, despite the fact that there would be no savings on fees, perhaps because the institutions tried harder to attract them. More than 4,000 students went north, while the numbers coming in the opposite direction dropped to 1,600.

Close to home

Far from crossing national boundaries, however, growing numbers of students choose to study near home, whether or not they continue to live with their family. This is

Most popular universities by applications, 2013		Most satisfied with student union	
1 Manchester	55,845	1 Sheffield	94%
2 Manchester Metropolitan	51,920	2 Leeds	91%
3 Nottingham	51,140	3 Loughborough	89%
4 Edinburgh	50,755	4 Dundee	86%
5 Leeds	48,445	=5 Cardiff	85%
6 Birmingham	39,955	=5 Reading	85%
7 Bristol	39,660	7 Bath	84%
8 Sheffield Hallam	39,520	8 Keele	83%
9 Kingston	38,590	=9 Newcastle	82%
10 Southampton	36,690	=9 Plymouth	82%
		=9 Teesside	82%
UCAS 2013		National Student Survey 2014	

understandable for Scots, who will save themselves tens of thousands of pounds by studying at their own fees-free universities. But there is also a gradual increase in the numbers choosing to study close to home either to cut living costs or for personal reasons, such as family circumstances, a girlfriend or boyfriend, continuing employment or religion. Some simply want to stick with what they know.

The trend for full-time students who do go away to study, is to choose a university within about two hours' travelling time. The assumption is that this is far enough to discourage parents from making unannounced visits, but close enough to allow for occasional trips home to get the washing done, have a decent meal and see friends. The leading universities recruit from all over the world, but most still have a regional core.

University or college?

This *Guide* is primarily concerned with universities, the destination of choice for the vast majority of higher education students. But there are other options – and not just for those searching for lower fees. A number of specialist higher education colleges offer a similar, or sometimes superior, quality of course in their particular fields. The subject tables in chapter 5 chart the successes of various colleges in art, agriculture, music and teacher training in particular. Some colleges of higher education are not so different from the newer universities and may acquire that status themselves in future years, as ten did in 2012–13 and one more in the following year.

Further education colleges

The second group of colleges offering degrees are further education (FE) colleges. These are often large institutions with a wide range of courses, from A levels to vocational subjects at different levels, up to degrees in some cases. Although their numbers of higher education students have been falling in recent years, the new fee structure presents them with a fresh opportunity because they tend not to bear all the costs of a university campus. For that reason, too, they may not offer a broad student experience of the type that universities pride themselves on, but the best colleges respond well to the local labour market and offer small teaching groups and effective personal support.

FE colleges are a local resource and tend to attract mature students who cannot or do not want to travel to university. Many of their higher education students apply nowhere else. But, as competition for university places has increased, they have become more of an option for school-leavers, as well as for their own students, to continue their studies, as they always have done in Scotland. Ministers hope that they will now also become more attractive by virtue of price.

Their predominantly local, mature student populations do FE colleges no favours in comparisons with universities. But it should be noted that 16 per cent of their graduates were unemployed six months after graduation in 2011, compared with 10 per cent at universities. The average salary of 2011 FE graduates at that time was £15,000, compared with a university equivalent of £19,000. This may be why not all of the 10,000 extra places reserved for FE colleges were filled in 2012, although the total number of entrants showed a modest rise.

Both further and higher education colleges are audited by the Quality Assurance Agency and appear in the National Student Survey, where their results usually show wide variation. Some demonstrate higher levels of satisfaction among their students than most universities, while others are at the bottom of the scale

Private universities and colleges

The final group of colleges that present an alternative to university has been insignificant in terms of size until recently, but may also prosper under the new fee regime. This is the private sector, seen mainly in business and law, but also in some other specialist fields. The best-known currently is BPP University, which became a full university in 2013 and offers degrees, as well as shorter courses, in both law and business subjects. Like Buckingham, BPP offers two-year degrees with short vacations to maximise teaching time – a model that other private providers are likely to follow. Fees were £7,000 a year for a two-year degree in 2014.

At the other end of the cost spectrum, the New College of the Humanities took its first students in 2012. Offering economics, English, history, law and philosophy, the college is charging £17,814 a year in 2014–15 for guaranteed small-group teaching and some big-name visiting lecturers. Up to 30 per cent of students will be offered bursaries for degree courses validated by the University of London.

Two other private institutions have been awarded university status in the last two years. Regent's University, attractively positioned in London's Regent's Park, caters particularly for the international market with courses in business, arts and social science subjects priced at £15,054 a year for courses starting in Spring 2015. However, about half of the students at the not-for-profit university, which offers British and American degrees, are from the UK or other parts of Europe. The University of Law, as its name suggests, is more specialised. It has been operating as a college for more than 100 years and claims to be the world's leading professional law school. Law degrees, as well as professional courses, are available in London and Manchester, with fees totalling £18,000 for a two-year course.

There are also growing numbers of specialist colleges offering degrees, especially in the business sector. Greenwich School of Management, with more than 3,500 students on two London campuses, is probably the largest in terms of full-time students, but there are others that have forged partnerships with universities or are going it alone. The ifs School of Finance, for example, also dates back more than 100 years and now has university college status (as ifs University College) for its courses in finance and banking. Some others that rely on international students have been hit by tougher visa regulations, but the Government is keen to encourage the development of a private sector to compete with the established universities.

The top universities for student satisfaction in the 2015 *Times and Sunday Times* table		The top universities for services and facilities spend per student in the 2014 *Times and Sunday Times* table	
1	Coventry	88.4%	1	Oxford	£3,506
=2	Bath	87.1%	2	Cambridge	£3,246
=2	Keele	87.1%	3	Imperial College	£2,833
4	Surrey	86.9%	4	Middlesex	£2,595
5	East Anglia	86.5%	5	Durham	£2,544
6	Exeter	86.4%	6	University College London	£2,453
7	St Andrews	86.3%	7	Northampton	£2,439
=8	Loughborough	85.7%	8	Essex	£2,401
=8	Essex	85.7%	9	Leicester	£2,384
10	Cambridge	85.6%	10	London School of Economics	£2,381

City universities

The most popular universities, in terms of total applications, are nearly all in big cities – generally with other major centres of population within that two-hour travelling window. For those looking for the best nightclubs, top sporting events, high-quality shopping or a varied cultural life – in other words, most young people, and especially those who live in cities already – city universities are a magnet. The big universities also, by definition, offer the widest range of subjects, although that does not mean that they necessarily have the particular course that is right for you. Nor does it mean that you will actually use the array of nightlife and shopping that looks so alluring in the prospectus, either because you cannot afford to, because student life is focused on the university, or even because you are too busy working.

Campus universities

City universities are the right choice for many young people, but it is worth bearing in mind that the National Student Survey shows that the highest satisfaction levels tend to be at smaller universities, often those with their own self-contained campuses. It seems that students identify more closely with institutions where there is a close-knit community and the social life is based around the students' union rather than the local nightclubs. Few UK universities are in genuinely rural locations, but some – particularly among the more recently promoted – are in relatively small towns. Several longer-established institutions in Wales and Scotland also share this type of setting, where the university dominates the town.

Importance of Open Days

The only way to be certain if this, or any other type of university, is for you is to visit. Schools often restrict the number of open days that sixth-formers can attend in term-time, but some universities offer a weekend alternative. The full calendar of events is available at **www. opendays.com** and on universities' own websites. Bear in mind, if you only attend one or two, that the event has to be badly mismanaged for a university not to seem an exciting place to someone who spends his or her days at school, or even college. Try to get a flavour of several institutions before you make your choice.

How many universities to pick?

When that time comes, of course, you will not be making one choice but five; four if you are applying for medicine, dentistry or veterinary science. (Full details of the application process are given in chapter 6.) Tens of thousands of students each year eventually go to a university that did not start out as their first choice, either because they did not get the right offer or because they changed their mind along the way. UCAS rules are such that applicants do not list universities in order of preference anyway – indeed, universities are not allowed to know where else you have applied. So do not pin all your hopes on one course; take just as much care choosing the other universities on your list.

The value of an "insurance" choice

Until recently, nearly all applicants included at least one "insurance" choice on that list – a university or college where entry grades were significantly lower than at their preferred institutions. This practice has been in decline, presumably because candidates expecting high grades think they can pick up a lower offer either in Clearing or through UCAS Extra, the service that allows applicants rejected by their original choices to apply to courses that still have vacancies after the first round of offers. However, it is easy to miscalculate and leave yourself without a place that you want. You may not like the look of the options in Clearing, leaving yourself with an unwelcome and potentially expensive year off at a time when jobs are thin on the ground.

The lifting of recruitment restrictions in 2015 will increase competition between universities and almost certainly see more of the leading institutions taking part in Clearing; a number joined the process for the first time in recent years in 2014. For those with good grades, this will make it less of a risk to apply only to highly selective universities. However, if you are at all uncertain about your grades, including an insurance choice remains a sensible course of action – especially since entry requirements have risen in response to increased demand for places. Even if you are sure that you will match the standard offers of your chosen universities, there is no guarantee that they will make you an offer. Particularly for degrees demanding three As at A level, there may simply be too many highly qualified applicants to offer places to all of them. The main proviso for insurance choices, as with all others, is that you must be prepared to take up that place. If not, you might as well go for broke with courses with higher standard offers and take your chances in Clearing, or even retake exams if you drop grades. Thousands of applicants each year end up rejecting their only offer when they could have had a second, insurance, choice.

Reputation

The reputation of a university is something intangible, usually built up over a long period and sometimes outlasting reality. Before universities were subject to external assessment and the publication of copious statistics, reputation was rooted in the past. League tables are partly responsible for changing that, although employers are often still influenced by what they remember as the university pecking order when they were students.

The fragmentation of the British university system into groups of institutions is another factor: the Russell Group represents 24 research-intensive universities, nearly all with medical schools; the Million+ group contains many of the former polytechnics and newer universities; the University Alliance provides a home for 20 universities, both old and new, that did not fit into the other categories; while GuildHE represents specialist colleges and the newest universities. The Cathedrals Group is an affiliation of 16 church-based universities and colleges, some of which are also members of other groups. The university profiles in

---

Checklist

Choosing a subject and a place to study is a major decision. Make sure you can answer these questions:

Choosing a course

» What do I want out of higher education?
» Which subjects do I enjoy studying at school?
» Which subject or subjects do I want to study?
» Do I have the right qualifications?
» What are my career plans and does the subject and course fit these?
» Do I want to study full-time or part-time?
» Do I want to study at a university or a college?

Choosing a university

» What type of university do I wish to go to: campus, city or smaller town?
» How far is the university from home?
» Is it large or small?
» Is it specialist or general?
» Does it offer the right course?
» How much will it cost?
» Have I arranged to visit the university?

chapter 14 give the affiliation of each university.

Many of today's applicants will barely have heard of a polytechnic, let alone be able to identify which of today's universities had that heritage, but most will know which of two universities in the same city has the higher status. While that should matter far less than the quality of a course, it would be naïve to ignore institutional reputation entirely if that is going to carry weight with a future employer. Some big firms restrict their recruitment efforts to a small group of universities (see chapter 2), and, however short sighted that might be, it is something to bear in mind if a career in the City or a big law firm is your ambition.

Cost

Quite apart from the level of fees, the cost of studying in different parts of the UK inevitably varies. Some cities – notably London – are notoriously expensive for students and non-students alike. But even these comparisons can be complicated by the availability of part-time employment – an important factor for a growing number of students today. The 2010 NatWest survey rated London as the cheapest place in the UK to study once earning opportunities are taken into account, although no other surveys have reached this conclusion since. If you intend to take part-time employment while studying, check that your chosen university has a "job shop", or some other organisation to help students find reasonably paid work.

Accommodation costs listed alongside the university profiles in this *Guide* are probably the nearest proxy for a cost-of-living indicator. The *Guide* also includes a summary of the bursaries available at each university. The size of bursaries varies enormously, as do the rules governing eligibility. Scholarships are awarded for other achievements, regardless of family income.

Facilities

Universities compete for the best students not only through their courses but, increasingly, also through non-academic facilities. Accommodation is the main selling point for those living away from home, but sports facilities, libraries and computing equipment also play an important part. Even campus nightclubs have become part of the facilities race that has coincided with the introduction of top-up fees.

Many universities guarantee first-year students accommodation in halls of residence or university-owned flats. But it is as well to know what happens after that. Are there enough places for second- or third-year students who want them, and if not, what is the private market like? Rents for student houses vary quite widely across the country and there have been tensions with local residents in some cities. All universities offer specialist accommodation for disabled students – and are better at providing other facilities than most public institutions. Their websites give basic information on what is provided, as well as contact points for more detailed inquiries.

Special-interest clubs and recreational facilities, as well as political activity, tend to be based in the students' union – sometimes knows as the guild of students. In some universities, the union is the focal point of social activity, while in others the attractions of the city seem to overshadow the union to the point where facilities are underused. Students' union websites are included with the information found in the university profiles (chapter 14).

Sources of information

With more than 120 universities to choose from, the Unistats and UCAS websites, as well as guides such as this one, are the obvious places to start your search for the right course. Unistats now includes figures for average salaries at course level, as well as student satisfaction ratings and some information on contact hours, although this does not distinguish between lectures and seminars. The site does not make multiple comparisons easy to carry out but it does contain a wealth of information for those who persevere. Once you have narrowed down the list of candidates, you will want to go through undergraduate prospectuses. Most are available online, where you can select the relevant sections rather than waiting for an account of every course to arrive in the post. Beware of generalised claims about the standing of the university, the quality of courses, friendly atmosphere and legendary social life. Stick, if you can, to the factual information.

If the material that the universities publish about their own qualities is less than objective, much of what you will find on the internet is equally unreliable, for different reasons. A simple search on the name of a university will turn up spurious comparisons of everything from the standard of lecturing to the attractiveness of the students. These can be seriously misleading and are usually based on anecdotal evidence, at best. Make sure that any information you may take into account comes from a reputable source and, if it conflicts with your impression, try to cross-check it with this *Guide* and the institution's own material.

Useful websites

The following websites will help you find out more about the topics discussed in this chapter. The best starting point is the UCAS website (**www.ucas.com**). On the site there's lots of information on courses, universities and the whole process of applying to university. In addition UCAS has an official presence on Facebook (**www.facebook.com/ucasonline**) and Twitter (**@UCAS_online**) and now also has a series of video guides (**www.ucas.tv**) on the process of applying, UCAS resources and comments from other students.

For statistical information which allows limited comparison between universities (and for full details of the National Student Survey), visit: **www.unistats.com**
For an alternative view of universities: **www.realuni.com**

On appropriate A-level subject choice, visit: **www.russellgroup.ac.uk/informed-choices**
UK Course Finder: **www.ukcoursefinder.com**
For a full calendar of university and college open days: **www.opendays.com**

Students with disabilities: Disability Alliance: **www.disabilityalliance.org/personal-care-university**

University groupings

GuildHE: colleges, specialist institutions and new universities: **www.guildhe.ac.uk**
Million+ : a group of newer universities: **www.millionplus.ac.uk**
Russell Group: large research-intensive universities: **www.russellgroup.ac.uk**
The University Alliance: old and new universities: **www.unialliance.ac.uk**
The Cathedrals Group: church-based universities: **www.cathedralsgroup.org.uk**

2 Graduate Employment Prospects

The graduate labour market has emerged from a five-year trough, according to Government figures published early in 2014. Not since the second quarter of 2008, when the banking crisis was turning into a worldwide recession, has the employment rate been as high. And the "young graduate high-skilled employment rate", which more closely resembles the measure used in *The Times and Sunday Times* league tables, is higher than it has been since 2009.

Of course, competition for graduate jobs remains stiff – there are now 12 million graduates in the UK, and in London they represent 60 per cent of the working-age population. But every survey shows that throughout their careers, graduates fare better in the labour market than those without a degree, both in salary terms and in avoiding unemployment. Unfortunately, the rates for individual universities are collected just six months after graduation, but statisticians insist that they are representative of later career patterns. In the absence of a better alternative, these are the figures used to measure employment in this *Guide*.

At the end of 2013, the unemployment rate for those who had graduated six months earlier was 11 per cent, two percentage points better than in the previous year. Average starting salaries had also risen, although by little more than 1 per cent. The tables later in this chapter give a more detailed picture of the differences between subjects, while the rankings in chapters 4 and 5 include figures for each university and subject area.

Government reports take a longer-term view of the whole labour market, which continue to support the case for taking a degree if you have the opportunity. Up to the age of 30, the employment rate for graduates was 87 per cent in March 2014, compared with 62 per cent for others. The median salary for all working-age graduates was £31,500, compared with £20,750 for non-graduates, a premium that remains one of the largest in the western world.

The downside in recent years – which must be a major consideration in an era of £9,000 fees – has been the sizeable proportion of graduates in jobs that are not classified as requiring a degree. Although the percentage has fallen for the first time in five years, it still stands at more than 47 per cent for recent graduates, compared with 37 per cent in 2001. This particular shift reflects changes in the labour market, as well as the very considerable growth in the number of people graduating. Employers look for graduates in roles that would not have been seen as their natural territory in years gone by, not only because graduates are more readily available, but also because they may bring an extra dimension to the tasks they perform.

Inevitably, national surveys average out the experiences of millions of people. This chapter will begin to tease out the often contrasting prospects of graduates in different subjects and different types of institution. The Office for National Statistics (ONS), for example, in its 2013 Graduates in the Labour Market survey, found that 67 per cent of graduates from Russell Group universities were in high-skilled jobs, earning £18.60 an hour, compared with 53 per cent of those from other universities, who earned £14.97 an hour. As the ONS acknowledged, part of the discrepancy was due to the larger proportion of Russell Group graduates who had taken subjects such as medicine, which lead naturally to high-earning jobs. The report did not try to gauge whether there was still a gap in other subjects.

Similarly, a 2014 report for the Million Jobs Campaign, which promotes apprenticeships, found that 46 per cent of graduates from post-1992 universities were earning less than the average young person with a higher apprenticeship. This rose to more than 60 per cent in the humanities and business subjects. But, as with the ONS report, only a close examination of individual universities' employment rates in your subject – possibly supplemented by the salary figures on the Unistats website (**www.unistats.com**) – will tell you whether national trends apply to your chosen course.

It should be noted that the definition of a graduate job is a controversial one. The statistics include internships and temporary jobs, for example, which may or may not lead to permanent employment. New universities in particular often claim that the whole concept of a graduate job immediately after graduation fails to reflect the employment reality for their alumni, especially in subjects such as media studies or art. In any case, a degree is about enhancing your whole career and your view of the world, not just your first job out of college.

Average annual pay for graduates with undergraduate degrees by the subject of their degree

	Annual pay
Medicine	£45,604
Engineering	£42,016
Physical/environmental subjects	£35,984
Architecture	£34,996
Maths or computer science	£34,008
Languages	£30,420
Social sciences and law	£30,004
Business and finance	£30,004
Education	£30,004
Agricultural sciences	£28,600
Biological sciences	£27,976
Humanities	£27,976
Medical related subjects	£27,508
Technology	£27,508
Linguistics, English and classics	£26,416
Arts	£21,944
Media and information studies	£21,008

Survey covered male graduates aged between 21 and 64, and female graduates aged between 21 and 59.
Labour Force Survey, as quoted in Graduates in the UK Labour Market 2013, Office for National Statistics

No one can predict the changes that may take place in the four or more years before those starting a degree in 2015 begin their careers. But anyone choosing a course now will want to know what they can do to insulate themselves against the possibility of joining the growing band of unemployed or underemployed graduates after they leave university.

The good news is that it is not just Government reports that suggest the worst may be over. *The Times* Top 100 employers, surveyed by High Fliers for the 2014 *Graduate Market* report, expected to have 8.7 per cent more vacancies than in 2013. This represented the largest pool of vacancies since 2007 and followed a 2.5 per cent increase in 2013.

The biggest growth in vacancies is expected at public sector employers, accounting and professional services firms, city investment banks, retailers, and engineering and industrial companies. Teach First was planning the biggest single recruitment, looking for more than 1,500 graduates.

However, the High Fliers survey covers only the upper end of the market. For the boom years of graduate employment to return, there will have to be stronger recruitment by small- and medium-sized companies. Increasingly, there will also be a greater proportion of self-employed graduates – and not simply because they cannot find the jobs they want. Many universities report growing demand for the services they provide to help to those who want to set up their own companies.

Subject choice and career opportunities

The tables on pages 38–41 will help you assess whether your course will pay off in career terms, at least to start with. They show both the amount you might expect to earn with a degree in a specific subject, and the odds of being in work. They reflect the experiences of those who graduated in 2013, and the picture may be less gloomy by the time you leave university. But there is no reason to believe that the pattern of success rates for specific subjects and institutions will have changed radically.

The Higher Education Statistics Agency (HESA) collects data on what graduates do straight after graduation (sometimes called graduate destinations) and on their average salaries. Positive destinations in our tables include those who go on to postgraduate study, but they make no allowances for the variety of entry routes into different areas of employment. Degrees in social work, for example, can sometimes involve a placement after final exams, so people taking these courses can seem to be unemployed when they might in fact have reasonable job prospects.

The table of employment statistics does reveal some unexpected results. For example, only 68 per cent of computer science graduates are working in graduate jobs or doing further study. More traditional engineering subjects fare a little better. The table also shows that some subjects, especially sciences such as physics, chemistry and geology, have a higher expectation than others, such as art and design or hospitality, that their graduates will undertake further study. In both physics and Celtic studies, more than 40 per cent of graduates continued to study. Those going into art and design appreciate that it, too, has its own career peculiarities. Periods of freelance or casual work may be an occupational hazard at the start of their career, and perhaps later on as well. One less surprising result: doctors and dentists are virtually guaranteed a job if they complete a degree successfully, as are nurses. HESA found that only one medic in 100 was unemployed six months after graduating.

This is the second year of a new classification developed by the Higher Education Statistics Agency to distinguish between "graduate-level" work and jobs that do not normally require a degree. In the table, subjects are ranked on "positive destinations", which include professional jobs and further study, whether or not combined with a job. Some similar tables do not make a distinction between different types of job. These tend to give the misleading impression that all universities and subjects offer uniformly rosy employment prospects.

The second table, on pages 40–41, gives average earnings of those who graduated in 2013, six months after leaving college. It contains interesting – and in some cases surprising – information about early career pay levels. Few would have placed social work or librarianship and information management in the top 20 fields for graduate pay, while business studies and accounting appear in 22nd and 24th place respectively. Those positions

What graduates are doing six months after graduation by subject studied

Subject, ranked by the total of the first four columns on right	Professional job	Professional job and studying	Studying	Non-professional job and studying	Non-professional job	Unemployed
1 Medicine	93%	1%	5%	0%	0%	1%
2 Dentistry	91%	7%	0%	0%	1%	2%
3 Nursing	91%	3%	2%	0%	2%	3%
4 Radiography	89%	2%	2%	0%	3%	5%
5 Pharmacology and pharmacy	77%	6%	8%	1%	5%	4%
6 Veterinary medicine	87%	1%	2%	0%	5%	5%
7 Physiotherapy	86%	2%	1%	0%	6%	4%
8 Civil engineering	66%	2%	12%	1%	9%	10%
9 Chemical engineering	62%	1%	17%	1%	7%	12%
10 Mechanical engineering	66%	2%	11%	1%	10%	10%
11 Building	72%	3%	3%	0%	11%	10%
12 General engineering	63%	3%	12%	1%	8%	13%
13 Physics and astronomy	36%	5%	36%	1%	9%	13%
14 Architecture	62%	4%	9%	2%	11%	12%
15 Chemistry	37%	3%	34%	1%	13%	12%
16 Other subjects allied to medicine	57%	4%	11%	2%	16%	10%
17 Electrical and electronic engineering	58%	2%	12%	1%	14%	13%
18 Mathematics	41%	7%	23%	2%	15%	12%
19 Town and country planning and landscape	55%	5%	11%	2%	15%	12%
20 Economics	50%	7%	13%	1%	15%	13%
21 Education	56%	2%	12%	2%	22%	6%
22 Aeronautical and manufacturing engineering	56%	2%	13%	1%	15%	13%
23 Land and property management	65%	0%	5%	1%	14%	15%
24 Anatomy and physiology	35%	3%	28%	3%	21%	10%
25 Russian	43%	3%	20%	3%	17%	14%
26 Iberian languages	45%	4%	19%	2%	20%	11%
27 Computer science	59%	1%	8%	1%	16%	15%
28 German	43%	4%	19%	2%	20%	12%
29 French	44%	3%	18%	2%	20%	12%
30 Social work	56%	3%	6%	1%	22%	11%
31 Geology	38%	2%	26%	1%	17%	15%
32 Theology and religious studies	34%	4%	25%	3%	23%	10%
33 Law	28%	5%	29%	6%	22%	11%
34 Materials technology	44%	2%	19%	2%	22%	12%
35 Librarianship and information management	56%	0%	8%	1%	22%	12%
36 Food science	50%	3%	10%	2%	24%	11%

Subject, ranked by the total of the first four columns on right	 Professional job	Professional job and studying	Studying	Non-professional job and studying	Non-professional job	Unemployed
37 Celtic studies	24%	1%	37%	2%	21%	15%
38 Classics and ancient history	31%	3%	25%	4%	22%	14%
39 Politics	38%	3%	20%	3%	22%	14%
40 Italian	44%	3%	14%	2%	21%	15%
41 Middle Eastern and African studies	35%	7%	18%	3%	20%	17%
42 Music	39%	4%	16%	3%	27%	11%
43 East and South Asian studies	45%	2%	15%	1%	21%	16%
44 History of art, architecture and design	35%	3%	20%	3%	27%	12%
45 Biological sciences	28%	2%	28%	3%	25%	14%
46 Geography and environmental sciences	35%	3%	20%	3%	27%	13%
47 Philosophy	32%	3%	22%	4%	24%	16%
48 Sport science	38%	4%	14%	3%	31%	9%
49 Business studies	49%	3%	6%	1%	28%	13%
50 History	29%	3%	22%	4%	29%	13%
51 Accounting and finance	39%	9%	8%	3%	27%	14%
52 English	30%	3%	21%	4%	30%	12%
53 Linguistics	34%	4%	16%	3%	31%	13%
54 Agriculture and forestry	40%	5%	8%	3%	30%	15%
55 Social policy	34%	3%	14%	4%	32%	13%
56 Anthropology	34%	2%	15%	3%	32%	14%
57 American studies	35%	2%	14%	4%	31%	14%
58 Art and design	47%	1%	5%	2%	32%	13%
59 Psychology	27%	4%	16%	5%	36%	12%
60 Archaeology	30%	2%	15%	4%	35%	14%
61 Drama, dance and cinematics	39%	2%	7%	2%	38%	13%
62 Communication and media studies	41%	1%	5%	2%	36%	15%
63 Hospitality, leisure, recreation and tourism	40%	1%	4%	2%	40%	13%
64 Sociology	28%	2%	13%	4%	41%	13%
65 Creative writing	27%	2%	12%	3%	38%	18%
66 Animal science	19%	2%	13%	3%	54%	10%
Total	**47%**	**3%**	**13%**	**2%**	**24%**	**11%**

HESA 2012/13 DLHE return

What graduates earn six months after graduation by subject studied

	Subject	Professional employment	Non-professional employment
1	Dentistry	£30,395	/.
2	Chemical engineering	£29,582	£20,577
3	Medicine	£28,548	..
4	General engineering	£26,362	£16,906
5	Economics	£26,283	£16,604
6	Mechanical engineering	£26,076	£17,671
7	Aeronautical and manufacturing engineering	£25,343	£15,715
8	Veterinary medicine	£24,934	£14,500
9	Electrical and electronic engineering	£24,639	£15,801
10	Civil engineering	£24,524	£18,265
11	Physics and astronomy	£24,523	£14,308
12	Materials technology	£24,289	£16,625
13	Mathematics	£24,075	£16,260
14	Computer science	£23,699	£15,890
15	Social work	£23,643	£14,747
16	Librarianship and information management	£22,899	£15,536
17	Land and property management	£22,722	£15,430
18	Nursing	£22,580	£15,207
19	Building	£22,479	£15,948
20	Geology	£22,319	£14,698
21	Radiography	£22,286	£19,150
22	Business studies	£22,144	£16,565
23	Physiotherapy	£22,013	£14,047
24	Accounting and finance	£21,952	£16,903
25	Philosophy	£21,869	£14,838
26	Chemistry	£21,821	£15,180
27	Classics and ancient history	£21,723	£14,790
28	Politics	£21,628	£15,866
29	Town and country planning and landscape	£21,451	£15,865
30	Other subjects allied to medicine	£21,328	£13,935
31	Geography and environmental sciences	£21,252	£14,803
32	Education	£21,176	£14,333
33	Russian	£21,031	£14,126
34	Anatomy and physiology	£20,992	£15,095
35	Food science	£20,965	£15,434
36	Agriculture and forestry	£20,721	£16,113
37	Theology and religious studies	£20,606	£15,421
38	Iberian languages	£20,603	£16,051
39	Italian	£20,374	£16,128
40	History	£20,045	£14,818
41	Biological sciences	£20,008	£14,399
42	Social policy	£19,918	£15,089

Subject	Professional employment	Non-professional employment
43 Pharmacology and pharmacy	£19,763	£16,821
44 French	£19,664	£15,912
45 Sociology	£19,652	£15,246
46 Anthropology	£19,637	£14,780
47 Law	£19,598	£15,739
48 German	£19,442	£15,159
49 Middle Eastern and African studies	£19,302	£17,390
50 Hospitality, leisure, recreation and tourism	£19,265	£15,861
51 East and South Asian studies	£19,258	£16,220
52 Linguistics	£18,919	£15,120
53 Archaeology	£18,838	£14,646
54 Psychology	£18,773	£14,622
55 Sport science	£18,554	£14,139
56 Architecture	£18,528	£15,587
57 History of art, architecture and design	£18,491	£15,083
58 English	£18,483	£14,554
59 Celtic studies	£18,326	£13,324
60 Communication and media studies	£18,270	£14,725
61 American studies	£18,046	£14,854
62 Art and design	£17,964	£14,366
63 Animal science	£17,854	£15,180
64 Drama, dance and cinematics	£17,308	£14,177
65 Music	£17,118	£14,299
66 Creative Writing	£16,903	£14,276
Average	**£21,982**	**£15,156**

NOTE: .. indicates a suppressed mean salary based on 7 or fewer graduates
HESA 2012/13 DLHE return

underline the differences between starting salaries and long-term prospects in different jobs. Over time the accountants may well end up with big rewards. Incidentally, the top non-City pay for a graduate is thought to be with the European Commission and the supermarket group Aldi. Despite its budget image, Aldi pays graduates training to be area managers £41,000 in their first year and adds an Audi A4, whereas the Commission is offering £41,500.

HESA also reported good news in September 2013 on the longer-term outlook for students, based on questioning those who had graduated in 2009. Of the UK graduates surveyed, 87.1 per cent were in employment, 6.7 per cent were studying full-time and only 3.2 per cent were unemployed, compared with 7.2 per cent when the same cohort was surveyed six months after graduation. The median salary of the 2009 graduates had risen from £21,000 to £27,500 over the same three and a half year period. A lucky few had seen their incomes rise by over £20,000 and 87.1 per cent had had some increase despite tricky times for the UK economy.

Enhancing your employability

Universities are well aware of the difficulties in the graduate employment market and have been introducing all manner of schemes to try to give their graduates an advantage in the labour market. Many have incorporated specially designed employability modules into degree courses; some are certificating extra-curricular activities to improve their graduates' CVs; others are stepping up their efforts to provide work experience to complement degrees.

Opinion is divided on the value of such schemes. Some of the biggest employers restrict their recruitment activities to a small number of universities, believing that these institutions attract the brightest minds and that trawling more widely is not cost-effective. These companies, often big payers from the City of London and including some of the top law firms, are not likely to change their ways at a time when they are more anxious than ever to control costs. Widening the pool of universities from which they set out to recruit is costly, and unnecessary in a buyers' market like the one we see today. As before, they will expect outstanding candidates who went to other universities to come to them, either on graduation or later in their careers.

The best advice for those looking to maximise their employment opportunities (and who isn't?) must be to go for the best university you can. But most graduates do not work in the City and most students do not go to universities at the top of the league tables.

Universities targeted by the largest number of top employers in 2013–14

1	(2)	Nottingham
2	(3)	Manchester
3	(4)	Cambridge
4	(7)	Oxford
5	(4)	Bristol
6	(9)	Bath
7	(1)	Warwick
8	(10)	Leeds
9	(12)	Imperial College
10	(16)	University College London
11	(8)	Birmingham
12	(6)	Durham
13	(11)	Sheffield
14	(13)	Loughborough
15	(14)	Edinburgh
16	(15)	London School of Economics
17	(18)	Newcastle
18	(20)	Exeter
19	(17)	Southampton
20	(19)	Strathclyde

Last year's position in brackets
Source: Graduate Employment Market in 2014, High Fliers

University schemes

If a university offers extra help towards employment, it is worth considering whether its scheme is likely to work for you. Some are too new to show results in the labour market, but they may have been endorsed by big employers or introduced at an institution whose graduates already have a record of success in the jobs market. In time, these extras may turn into mandatory parts of degree study, complete with course credit.

At Liverpool John Moores University, for example, the World of Work (WoW) programme was devised with the help of the CBI, Shell, Sony, and Marks and Spencer. Taken by students in all subjects, including postgraduates, it offers classes in CV writing, interview skills, finance, entrepreneurship and negotiation skills, among many other topics. There are guest lectures and demonstrations related to the eight employment-related skills that WoW is intended to develop, and employers carry out mock interviews to assess students' strengths and weaknesses. It began as an option and is now part of all courses.

Hertfordshire is another institution which has demonstrated a sustained focus on its students' job prospects. It was arguably the first of many universities to describe itself as "business-facing". Employer groups are consulted on the curriculum and often supply guest lecturers on degree courses. Like some other universities, such as Derby, it offers career development support to graduates throughout their working life.

Other universities, such as Exeter, have taken a different tack and are helping students make the most of their voluntary and extra-curricular activities by certificating them. The Exeter Award gives credit for attendance at skills sessions and training courses, active participation in sporting and musical activities, engagement in work experience and voluntary work. The university already claimed to have more students than any other involved in voluntary activities. It believes that the award will encourage employers to take more notice of them.

The York Award is another well-established example of this type of scheme that has the involvement of organisations from the public, private and voluntary sectors. The university has found that employers value a combination of academic study, work experience and leisure interests. The scheme offers York students a framework to gain recognition for activities that are not formally recognised through the degree programme. Among the subjects on an extensive list of courses are networking, time management, counselling and understanding different cultures.

The value of work experience

As the table earlier in this chapter showed, there are big differences in the average employment prospects for different subjects. The majority of graduate jobs are open to applicants from any discipline. For these general positions, employers tend to be more impressed by a good degree from what they consider a prestigious university than by an apparently relevant qualification. Here numeracy, literacy and communications – the arts needed to function effectively in any organisation – are of vital importance.

Specialist jobs – for example in engineering or design – are a different matter. Employers may be much more knowledgeable about the quality of individual courses, and less influenced by a university's overall position in league tables, when the job relies directly on knowledge and skills acquired as a student. That goes for the likes of medicine and architecture as well as the new vocational areas such as computer games design or environmental management.

In either case, however, work experience has become increasingly important. The High Fliers survey showed that employers in *The Times* 100 expected to fill a record 37 per cent of their vacancies with graduates who had already worked for them, whether in holiday jobs, internships or placements. Sandwich degrees, extended programmes that include up to a year at work, have always boosted employment prospects. Graduates often end up working where they undertook their placement. And while a sandwich year will make your course longer, it will not be subject to a full year's fees.

Many conventional degrees now include shorter work placements that should offer some advantages in the labour market. Not all are arranged by the university so, unless you have an opening that you would like to pursue, that is something to establish and weigh in the balance when choosing a course. The majority of big graduate employers offer some provision of this nature, although access to it can be competitive.

If your chosen course does not include a work placement, you may want to consider arranging your own part-time or temporary employment. The majority of supposedly full-time students now take jobs during term time, as well as in vacations, to make ends meet. But such jobs can boost your CV as well as your wallet. Even working in a bar or a shop shows some experience of dealing with the public and coping with the disciplines of the workplace. Inevitably, the more prosperous cities are likely to offer more employment opportunities than rural areas or conurbations that have been hard hit in the recession.

The ultimate work-related degree is one sponsored by an employer or even taken in the workplace, something that ministers have encouraged recently. Middlesex University provides tailored programmes for Dell and Marks and Spencer, among other organisations, and has more than 1,000 students taking courses run by its Institute of Work Based Learning. Most such courses are provided for people already employed by the companies concerned, rather than as a route into the company. But they may come to be considered as an alternative to entering full-time higher education straight from school or college.

Consider part-time degrees

Another option, also favoured by ministers, is part-time study. Although enrolments have fallen sharply both leading up to and since the 2012 increases in fees, there are now loans available for most part-time courses. Employers may be willing to share the cost of taking a degree or another relevant qualification, and the chance to earn a wage while studying has obvious attractions.

Part-time study requires a high degree of commitment – knuckling down to an essay or an assignment after a hard day at work is not easy – but it does reduce the cost of higher education for those in work. Bear in mind, however, that most part-time courses take twice as long to complete as the full-time equivalent. If your earning power is linked to the qualification, it will take that much longer for you to enjoy the benefits.

Plan early for your career

Whatever type of course you choose, it is sensible to start thinking about your future career early in your time at university. There has been a growing tendency in recent years for students to convince themselves that there would be plenty of time to apply for jobs after graduation, and that they were better off focusing entirely on their degree while at university. In the current employment market, all but the most obviously brilliant graduates need to offer more than just a degree, whether it be work experience, leadership qualities demonstrated through clubs and societies, or commitment to voluntary activities. Many students finish a degree without knowing what they want to do, but a blank CV will not impress a prospective employer.

The leading employers told High Fliers that they are not interested in graduates with no previous work experience and that any such applicants would have "little or no chance" or a place on their graduate programmes. He may be overstating the case, but Martin Burchall, High Fliers' Managing Director, claimed that work placements and internships were now "just as important as getting a 2:1 or first-class degree".

Useful websites

Prospects, the UK's official graduate careers website:
www.prospects.ac.uk
For information on internships, graduate schemes and career advice:
www.milkround.com
HESA Longitudinal survey on graduate employment: **www.hesa.ac.uk/pr195**
High Fliers: **www.highfliers.co.uk**

3 Going Abroad to University

Successive surveys in 2014 found that about four sixth-formers in ten were considering going abroad to take a degree. Most will not do so in the end but, with fees of £9,000 at home, it is no surprise that an overseas university has become an option. The numbers considering it had almost doubled in a year, according to the British Council. Almost nine out of ten thought a degree from an overseas university would help them to stand out in the employment market, but more than half were also motivated by increased fees. American and Dutch universities, in particular, are mounting regular recruitment campaigns – mainly, but not exclusively at Independent schools.

Even Government ministers are now encouraging more students to go abroad, and have set up a taskforce to encourage more mobility both in and out of the UK. David Willetts, until recently the Universities Minister, saw overseas study – especially in economically powerful countries like China and the United States – as beneficial both for individuals' career prospects and future trading performance.

Continental universities are now much cheaper than those in England and even those in the United States are not out of reach: state universities can be cheaper per year than their UK counterparts, while Ivy League institutions offer generous scholarships and bursaries. So far, however, the exodus predicted by many commentators has not really got started. There may well be an increase in 2014, but the traditional reluctance of UK students to study abroad, even in exchange schemes, appears to be winning out. There was an impressive 77 per cent rise in the number of Britons at Dutch universities in 2012, but they still totalled less than 1,000 of the 2.5 million UK student population. There were more than 9,000 UK students in the USA in 2013 but, despite reports of many more inquiries to US universities, this represented only a small increase on the previous year.

Nevertheless, it would be surprising if high fees at home and an increasingly international graduate labour market did not encourage at least gradual growth in overseas study. There is good reason for applicants to spread the university net more widely. Research by QS, publishers of the World University Rankings, found that 60 per cent of employers worldwide – and 42 per cent of those in the UK – gave extra weight to an international student experience when recruiting graduates. Of course, everything will depend on what and where that experience was. Harvard is going to carry more weight than the University of Lapland, which has tried to attract British students. But leaving the UK to study certainly need not hold back your career or provide an inferior education.

Indeed, most students who go abroad are motivated by a desire to study at a "world-class" institution, according to a study for the Department of Business, Innovation and Skills. Often the trigger is failure to win a place at a leading UK university and being unwilling to settle for second best. Other motivations included a desire for adventure and a belief that overseas study might lead to an international career.

The question is how to judge a university that may be thousands of miles from home against more familiar names in the UK. This chapter will make some suggestions, including the use of the growing number of global rankings that are available online or in print.

It is possible to have your academic cake and eat it by going on an international exchange or work placement organised by a UK university, or even to attend a British university in another country. Nottingham University has campuses in China and Malaysia; Middlesex can offer Dubai or Mauritius, where students registered in the UK can take part or all of their degree. Other universities, such as Liverpool, also have joint ventures with overseas institutions which offer an international experience (in China, in Liverpool's case) and degrees from both universities.

In most cases, however, an overseas study experience means a foreign university. Until recently, this was usually for a postgraduate degree – and there are still strong arguments for spending your undergraduate years in the UK before going abroad for more advanced study. Older students taking more specialised programmes may get more out of an extended period overseas than those who go at 18 and, since first degrees in the UK are shorter than elsewhere, it may also be the more cost-effective option.

If cost is the main consideration, however, even the generally longer courses at Continental universities can work out cheaper than a degree in the UK. The main obstacle, apart from British students' traditional reluctance to take degrees anywhere else, concerns the language barrier. Although there are now thousands of postgraduate courses taught in English at Continental universities, first-degree programmes are still much thinner on the ground. A few universities, like Maastricht in the Netherlands, have made a serious pitch for business from the UK and are offering a wide range of subjects in English. Maastricht doubled its UK intake in 2012 and now has almost 300 UK students. But most European universities teach undergraduates in the host language – and, up to now, that has always deterred UK students.

The obvious alternative lies in American, Australian and Canadian universities, all of which are keen to attract more international students. Here, cost and distance are the main obstacles. Four-year courses add considerably to the cost of affordable-looking fees, while the state of the pound has been another serious disadvantage. Add in the natural reluctance of most 18-year-olds to commit to life on the other side of the world (or even just the Atlantic), and the prospect of a dramatic increase in student emigration lessens considerably.

Where do students go to?

There is remarkably little official monitoring of how many students leave the UK, let alone where they go. But it seems that for all the economic advantages of studying in Continental Europe, the USA remains by far the most popular student destination. Most surveys put Canada, France and Germany (in that order) as the biggest attractions outside the USA.

A few British students find their way to unexpected locations, like South Korea or Slovakia, but usually for family reasons or to study the language. The figures suggest that British students are more attracted to countries that are familiar or close at hand, and where they can speak English. Many are doubtless planning to stay in their adopted country after they graduate, although visa regulations may make this difficult.

Studying in Europe

More than 10,000 UK students now attend Continental European universities and colleges, according to UNESCO. But international statistics pick up those whose parents emigrated or are working abroad, as well as those who actually leave the UK to take a degree. A minority are undergraduates, if only because the availability of courses taught in English is so much greater at postgraduate level.

The increased interest in Continental universities arises both from the generally low fees they charge and from the growth in the number of courses offered in English. Lund University in Sweden, for example, which is ranked in the top 100 in the world by QS and *Times Higher Education*, had more than 600 applications from the UK in 2012 – 15 per cent up on the previous year – and has added science and business degrees to its five BA programmes taught in English. Even then, however, the undergraduate portfolio will be dwarfed by the 90 MAs taught in English.

Fees will remain low, or even non-existent, for UK students attending public universities in other EU countries because they are entitled to study there for the same fees as local residents. In the EU, you will also be able get a job while studying. Farther afield, your student visa might not allow you to take on paid work.

Undergraduates can study at a French university for £150 a year but, not surprisingly, nearly all first degrees are taught in French. Only 58 of the 870 programmes taught in English and listed on the Campus France website (**www.campusfrance.org/en**) are at the Licence (Bachelors equivalent) level – and 19 of them have some teaching in French. Germany is much the same, despite attracting large numbers of international students. The DAAD website (**www.daad.de/en**) lists 149 undergraduate programmes taught wholly or mainly in English – 24 more than last year – but many are at private universities like Jacobs University in Bremen, which charges €12,455 a semester. There are cheaper alternatives in the public sector – tuition fees are "optional" for the BSc in applied chemistry at the University of Applied Sciences in Aachen – but they remain relatively scarce.

Any potential saving has to be considered with care. Despite the Bologna process – an intergovernmental agreement which means that degrees across Europe are becoming

Top ten European countries, as destinations for UK students, 2012		Top ten student cities in the world	
1 France	3,186	1 Paris	France
2 Ireland	2,062	2 London	United Kingdom
3 Germany	1,411	3 Singapore	Singapore
4 Netherlands	888	4 Sydney	Australia
5 Spain	505	=5 Zurich	Switzerland
6 Czech Republic	435	=5 Melbourne	Australia
7 Switzerland	395	7 Hong Kong	Hong Kong
8 Norway	346	8 Boston	Unites States of America
9 Italy	259	9 Montreal	Canada
10 Sweden	255	10 Munich	Germany
UNESCO Institute for Statistics, 2014		QS Best Student Cities in the World, 2013	

more similar in content and duration – most Continental courses are longer than their UK equivalents, adding to the cost and to your lost earnings from attending university. And, of course, you will have higher travel costs. It is harder to generalise about the cost of living. It can be lower than the UK in southern Europe, but frighteningly high in Scandinavia. You can cut down the cost of an international experience and hedge your bets about committing yourself to a full course overseas by opting instead for an exchange scheme. UK universities have exchange partners all over the world, providing opportunities for everything from a summer school of less than a month to a full year abroad.

The most common offering is the EU's Erasmus scheme, which funds exchanges of between three months and a year, the work counting towards your degree. More than 2 million students throughout Europe have used the scheme, and there are 2,000 universities to choose from in 30 countries. Applications, which are made through universities' international offices, must be approved by the UK university as well as by the Erasmus administrators. Erasmus students do not pay any extra fees and they are eligible for grants to cover the extra expense of travelling and living in another country.

Studying in America

American universities remain the first choice of British students going abroad to take a degree, just as the UK is the first choice for Americans. Regardless of any special relationship, this is not surprising since international rankings consistently show US and UK universities to be the best in the world (as well as teaching in English).

Around half of the British students taking courses in the USA are undergraduates. Already by far the most popular student destination, the attractions of an American degree have multiplied since fees trebled in England. The Fulbright Commission, which promotes American higher education, has seen a 30 per cent increase in the number of Britons taking US university entrance exams. Even before the latest rise in UK fees, the top American universities had seen demand rise sharply: Harvard received 41 per cent more applications from the UK in 2010–11, Yale 23 per cent and Pennsylvania 50 per cent more.

The sheer depth of the US university system means that if you are thinking of studying abroad, the USA is almost bound to be on the list of possibilities. Tuition fees at Ivy League institutions are notoriously high – Harvard's were $44,000 in 2014–15 and the university put the full cost of attendance at up to $68,000 a year – but generous student aid programmes ensure that most pay far less than the "sticker price". Outside the Ivy League, the fee gap for UK students is narrower, although fees at many state universities have shot up in the last three years as politicians have tried to balance the books. At Texas A&M University, for example, ranked in the top 200 in the world, international students still only paid $12,500 a year for tuition, about £7,500 at the time of writing, although the university put undergraduates' total costs at $36,000. Fees are lower than that at the State University of New York, although the university puts the total cost for those living on campus at $33,000.

The individual systems of state universities and private universities mean that there is a great variation in the financial support given to international students. Fulbright advises students considering a US degree to assess and negotiate a funding package at the same time as pursuing their application. Otherwise, they may end up with a place they cannot afford, losing valuable time in the quest for a more suitable one.

Which countries are best?

Anyone going abroad to study will be in search of a memorable and valuable all-round experience, not just a good course. Most international students are motivated by location – both the country and the city in which a university is based – as well as by the reputation of the institution. QS publishes an annual ranking of student cities, based on quality of life indicators as well as the number of places at world-ranked universities. Paris topped the ranking in 2013, with London second, Singapore third and Sydney fourth.

Many Asian countries are looking to recruit more foreign students, both as part of a broader internationalisation agenda and to compensate for falling numbers of potential students at home. Japan is a case in point. The high cost of living may put off many potential students, as may the unfamiliarity of its language, but more support is being offered to attract foreign students and more courses are being taught in English. However, as with any non-English speaking country, the language of instruction is only part of the story. You will need to know enough of the local language to manage the shops and the transport system, and, of course, to make friends and get the most out of being there.

Another option of growing interest is China. While you may not believe the whole of the story that China is about to take over the world, it has already grown massively in importance. Its university system is growing in quality, especially at the C9 group of international institutions, which have become known as the Chinese Ivy League. Familiarity with China is unlikely to be a career disadvantage for anyone in the 21st century. Some see Hong Kong, which has several world-ranked universities and a familiar feel for Britons, as the perfect alternative to mainland Chinese universities.

Will my degree be recognised?

Even in the era of globalisation, you need to bear in mind that not all degrees are equal. At one extreme is the MBA, which has an international system for accrediting courses, and a global admissions standard. But with many professional courses, study abroad is a potential hazard. To work as a doctor, engineer or lawyer in the UK, you need a qualification which the relevant professional body will recognise. It is understandable that to practise law in England, you need to have studied the English legal system. For other subjects, the issues are more to do with the quality and content of courses outside UK control.

There are ways of researching this issue in advance. One is to contact NARIC, the National Recognition Centre for the UK (**www.ecctis.co.uk/naric**). NARIC exists to examine the compatibility and acceptability of qualifications from around the world. The other approach is to ask the UK professional body in question – maybe an engineering institution, the Law Society or the General Teaching, Medical or Dental Councils – about the qualification you propose to study for.

Which are the best universities?

Going abroad to study is a big and expensive decision, and you want to get it right. Whether your ultimate aim is to become an internationally mobile high-flyer, or simply to broaden your experience, you will want to know that the university you are going to is taken seriously around the world.

At the moment there are three main systems for ranking universities on a world scale. One is run by QS (Quacquarelli Symonds), an educational research company based in London (**www.topuniversities.com**). Another is by Shanghai Ranking Consultancy, a company set up by Shanghai Jiao Tong University, in China, and is called the Academic Ranking of World Universities (ARWU) (**www.arwu.org**). These two have been joined by *Times Higher Education* (**www.timeshighereducation.co.uk**), a weekly magazine with no connection to *The Times*, which produced its own ranking for the first time in 2010, having previously published the QS version.

There are several more international ranking systems that an online search might throw up, but most are either specialist – like the Webometrics ranking of universities' web activity – or limited in their readership and influence. Some are still developing: the European Commission's U-Multirank, for example, has produced only one edition, limited to physics, engineering and business studies, but may become a more widely used source of information in time.

The QS system uses a number of measures including academic opinion, employer opinion, international orientation, research impact and staff/student ratio to create its listing, while the ARWU uses measures such as Nobel Prizes and highly cited papers, which are more related to excellence in scientific research. *The Times Higher* has added a number of measures to the QS model, including research income and a controversial global survey of teaching quality. Despite these different approaches, many universities appear in all three rankings. If you go to a university that features strongly in any of the tables, you will be at a place that is well-regarded around the world. After all, even the 200th university on any of these rankings is an elite institution in a world with more than 4,000 universities. The top 50 universities in all three rankings are listed on the following pages.

These systems tend to favour universities which are good at science and medicine. Places that specialise in the humanities and the social sciences, such as the London School of Economics, can appear in deceptively modest positions. In addition, the rankings tend to look at universities in the round, and contain only limited information on specific subjects. QS published the first 26 global subject rankings in 2011 and has since increased this to 30. One advantage of the QS ranking system is that 10 per cent of a university's possible score comes from a global survey of recruiters. So you can look at this column of the table for an idea about where the major employers like to hire. Note that the author of this *Guide* has a role in developing the QS Rankings.

Other options for overseas studies

If you decide that studying abroad for a complete degree is too much, a number of options remain open. A language degree will typically involve a year abroad, and a look at the UCAS website will show many options for studying another subject alongside your language of choice. UK universities offer degrees in information technology, science, business and even journalism with a major language such as Chinese.

Many universities offer a year abroad, either studying or in a work placement, even to those who are not taking a language. At Aston University, for example, 70 per cent of students do a year's work placement and a growing number do so abroad. China and Chile have been among recent destinations. Other universities offer the opportunity to take credit-bearing courses with partner institutions overseas. American universities are again the most popular choice. The best approach is to decide what you want to study and then see if there is a UK university that offers it as a joint degree or with a placement abroad. Be aware that employers and academics alike sometimes look askance at joint degrees. Make sure that all the universities involved are well-regarded, for example by looking at their rankings on one or other of the websites mentioned at the end of the table.

Useful websites

Prospects: studying abroad: **www.prospects.ac.uk/studying_abroad.htm**
Association of Commonwealth Universities: **www.acu.ac.uk**
Campus France: **www.campusfrance.org/en**
College Board (USA): **www.collegeboard.org**
DAAD (for Germany): **www.daad.de/en**
Education Ireland: **www.educationinireland.com/en**
Erasmus Programme (EU): **www.britishcouncil.org/erasmus**
Finaid (USA): **www.finaid.org**
Fulbright Commission: **www.fulbright.co.uk**
Study in Australia: **www.studyinaustralia.gov.au**
Study in Canada: **www.studyincanada.com**
Study Overseas: **www.studyoverseas.com**

The top 50 universities in the world in 2014 according to QS World University Ranking (QS), the Academic Ranking of World Universities (ARWU) and *Times Higher Education* (THE)

QS Rank	Institution	Country	ARWU Rank	Institution	Country	THE Rank	Institution	Country
1	Massachusetts Institute of Technology	USA	1	Harvard University	USA	1	California Institute of Technology	USA
=2	University of Cambridge	UK	2	Stanford University	USA	=2	Harvard University	USA
=2	Imperial College London	UK	3	Massachusetts Institute of Technology	USA	=2	University of Oxford	UK
4	Harvard University	USA	4	University of California, Berkeley	USA	4	Stanford University	USA
=5	University College London	UK	5	University of Cambridge	UK	5	Massachusetts Institute of Technology	USA
=5	University of Oxford	UK	6	Princeton University	USA	6	Princeton University	USA
7	Stanford University	USA	7	California Institute of Technology	USA	7	University of Cambridge	UK
8	California Institute of Technology	USA	8	Columbia University	USA	8	University of California, Berkeley	USA
9	Princeton University	USA	=9	University of Chicago	USA	9	University of Chicago	USA
10	Yale University	USA	=9	University of Oxford	UK	10	Imperial College London	UK
11	University of Chicago	USA	11	Yale University	USA	11	Yale University	USA
12	ETH Zurich (Swiss Federal Institute of Technology)	Switz.	12	University of California, Los Angeles	Switz.	12	University of California, Los Angeles	USA
13	University of Pennsylvania	USA	13	Cornell University	USA	13	Columbia University	USA
=14	Columbia University	USA	14	University of California, San Diego	USA	14	ETH Zurich (Swiss Federal Institute of Technology)	Switz.
=14	Johns Hopkins University	USA	15	University of Washington	USA	15	Johns Hopkins University	USA
16	King's College London	UK	16	University of Pennsylvania	USA	16	University of Pennsylvania	USA
=17	École Polytechnique Fédérale de Lausanne	Switz.	17	Johns Hopkins University	USA	17	Duke University	USA
=17	University of Edinburgh	UK	18	University of California, San Francisco	USA	18	University of Michigan	USA

Rank	University	Country
19	Cornell University	USA
20	University of Toronto	Canada
21	McGill University	Canada
22	National University of Singapore	S'pore
23	University of Michigan	USA
24	École Normale Supérieure, Paris	France
=25	Australian National University	Australia
=25	Duke University	USA
27	University of California, Berkeley	USA
28	University of Hong Kong	Hong Kong
29	University of Bristol	UK
30	University of Manchester	UK
=31	Seoul National University	S. Korea
=31	University of Tokyo	Japan
33	University of Melbourne	Australia
34	Northwestern University	USA
35	École Polytechnique Paris Tech	France
36	Kyoto University	Japan
=37	University of California, Los Angeles	USA
=37	University of Sydney	Australia
39	Nanyang Technological University	S'pore

Rank	University	Country
19	ETH Zurich (Swiss Federal Institute of Technology)	Switz.
20	University College London	UK
21	University of Tokyo	Japan
=22	Imperial College London	UK
=22	University of Michigan	USA
=24	University of Toronto	Canada
=24	University of Wisconsin, Madison	USA
26	Kyoto University	Japan
27	New York University	USA
=28	Northwestern University	USA
=28	University of Illinois, Urbana-Champaign	USA
30	University of Minnesota, Twin Cities	USA
31	Duke University	USA
32	Washington University in St Louis	USA
33	Rockefeller University	USA
34	University of Colorado at Boulder	USA
35	Pierre and Marie Curie University, Paris 6	France
36	University of North Carolina at Chapel Hill	USA
37	University of British Columbia	Canada
38	University of Manchester	UK
=39	University of Texas at Austin	USA

Rank	University	Country
19	Cornell University	USA
20	University of Toronto	Canada
21	University College London	UK
22	Northwestern University	USA
23	University of Tokyo	Japan
24	Carnegie Mellon University	USA
25	University of Washington	USA
26	National University of Singapore	S'pore
27	University of Texas at Austin	USA
28	Georgia Institute of Technology	USA
29	University of Illinois, Urbana-Champaign	USA
30	University of Wisconsin, Madison	USA
31	University of British Columbia	Canada
32	London School of Economics	UK
33	University of California, Santa Barbara	USA
34	University of Melbourne	Australia
35	McGill University	Canada
36	Karolinska Institute	Sweden
37	École Polytechnique Fédérale de Lausanne	Switz
38	King's College London	UK
39	University of Edinburgh	UK

The top 50 universities in the world in 2014 according to QS World University Ranking (QS), the Academic Ranking of World Universities (ARWU) and *Times Higher Education* (THE)

QS Rank	Institution	Country	ARWU Rank	Institution	Country	THE Rank	Institution	Country
40	Hong Kong University of Science and Technology	HK	=39	University of Copenhagen	Denmark	=40	New York University	USA
=41	New York University	USA	41	University of California, Santa Barbara	USA	=40	University of California, San Diego	USA
=41	University of Wisconsin, Madison	USA	42	University of Paris Sud, Paris 11	France	42	Washington University in St Louis	USA
=43	University of British Columbia	Canada	43	University of Maryland, College Park	USA	43	University of Hong Kong	HK
=43	University of Queensland	Australia	44	University of Melbourne	Australia	44	Seoul National University	S. Korea
45	University of Copenhagen	Denmark	=45	University of Edinburgh	UK	45	Peking University	China
46	Chinese University of Hong Kong	HK	=45	University of Texas Southwestern Medical Center at Dallas	USA	46	University of Minnesota	USA
47	Tsinghua University	China	47	Karolinska Institute	Sweden	47	University of North Carolina at Chapel Hill	USA
48	University of New South Wales	Australia	47	University of California, Irvine	USA	48	Australian National University	Australia
49	Heidelberg University	Germany	=49	Heidelberg University	Germany	49	Pennsylvania State University	USA
50	University of Amsterdam	Neth.	=49	University of Munich	Germany	=50	Boston University	USA
						=50	Tsinghua University	China

We gratefully acknowledge permission to reproduce these three rankings. The full QS World University Rankings 2014–15 can be consulted at **www.topuniversities.com**, the full Academic Ranking of World Universities 2014 at **www.arwu.org** and the full *Times Higher Education* 2013–14 rankings at **www.timeshighereducation.co.uk**.

For information on the recognition in the UK of international degrees, visit the National Recognition Centre for the UK (NARIC): **www.naric.org.uk**

4 The Top Universities

Universities publish reams of statistics about themselves – more than ever now that the Government insists on greater transparency. But even some of the official attempts to provide prospective students with better information can leave the reader more confused, rather than less. Our main table has been developed over 20 years to focus on the fundamentals of undergraduate education and make meaningful comparisons in an accessible way.

What distinguishes a top university? And who is to say that one course is better than another – especially when the university system is so reluctant to make any such comparison? Critics of league tables insist that this is because every university has different priorities, and every course has a different ways of approaching a subject. Students must choose the one that suits them best. So they must. Not everyone would find the top universities to their taste, even if they were able to secure a place. But that does not mean that there are not important differences in the quality of universities and the courses they offer. These, in turn, can have a crucial bearing on future employment prospects.

The table in this chapter offers applicants and others with an interest in higher education a means to assess the standing of UK universities with undergraduate education in mind. The institutions will have their own ideas about what should go into comparisons of this type, but ours has stood the test of time because it uses the statistics that universities themselves employ to measure their own performance and combines them in a way that generations of students have found revealing.

Every element of the table in this chapter has been chosen for the light it shines on the undergraduate experience and a student's future prospects. The selection of these eight measures and the way in which they are combined give a particular view of universities' overall strengths, and it is one that has stood the test of time. Unlike some others, *The Times and Sunday Times Good University Guide* has placed a premium on consistency, confident that the measures are the best available for the task. Some changes have been forced upon us. Universities stopped assessing teaching quality by subject, when this was the most heavily weighted measure in the table, for example. However, the arrival of the National Student Survey ten years ago has enabled the student experience to be reflected in the table.

The basic information that applicants need, however, in order to judge universities and their courses does not change. A university's entry standards, staffing levels, completion rates, degree classifications and graduate employment rates are all vital pieces of intelligence for anyone deciding where to study. Research grades, while not directly involving undergraduates, bring with them considerable funds and enable a university to attract top academics.

Any of these measures can be discounted by an individual, but the package has struck a chord with readers. The ranking is the most-quoted of its type both in Britain and overseas, and has built a reputation as the most authoritative arbiter of changing fortunes in higher education. The measures used are kept under review by a group of university administrators and statisticians, which meets annually. The raw data that go into the table in this chapter and the 66 subject tables in chapter 5 are all in the public domain and are sent to universities for checking before any scores are calculated.

Indeed, while the various official bodies concerned with higher education do not publish league tables, several produce system-wide statistics in a format that invites comparisons. The Higher Education Funding Councils' Research Assessment Exercise was one early example of this. The Higher Education Statistics Agency (HESA), which supplies most of the figures used in our tables, also publishes annual "performance indicators" on everything from completion rates to research output at each university.

Any scrutiny of league table positions is best carried out in conjunction with an examination of the relevant subject table – it is the course, after all, that will dominate your undergraduate years and influence your subsequent career.

How *The Times and Sunday Times* league table works

The table is presented in a format that displays the raw data, wherever possible. In building the table, scores for student satisfaction and research quality were weighted by 1.5; all other measures were weighted by 1. The indicators were combined using a common statistical technique known as Z-scores, to ensure that no indicator has a disproportionate effect on the overall total for each university, and the totals were transformed to a scale with 1000 for the top score.

For entry standards, student–staff ratio, good honours and graduate prospects, the score was adjusted for subject mix. For example, it is accepted that engineering, law and medicine graduates will tend to have better graduate prospects than their peers from English, psychology and sociology courses. Comparing results in the main subject groupings helps to iron out differences attributable simply to the range of degrees on offer. This subject-mix adjustment means that it is not possible to replicate the scores in the table from the published indicators because the calculation requires access to the entire dataset.

The Z-score technique makes it impossible to compare universities' total scores from one year to the next, although their relative positions in the table are comparable. Individual scores are dependent on the top performer: a university might drop from 60 per cent of the top score to 58 per cent but still have improved, depending on the relative performance of other universities.

Only where data are not available from HESA are figures sourced directly from universities. Where this is not possible scores are generated according to a university's average performance on other indicators.

The organisations providing the raw data for the tables are not involved in the process of aggregation, so are not responsible for any inferences or conclusions we have made. Every care has been taken to ensure the accuracy of the tables and accompanying information, but no responsibility can be taken for errors or omissions.

The Times and Sunday Times league table uses eight important measures of university activity, based on the most recent data available at the time of compilation:

» Student satisfaction
» Research quality
» Entry standards
» Student–staff ratio

» Services and facilities spend
» Completion
» Good honours
» Graduate prospects

Student satisfaction

This is a measure of students' views of the quality of their courses. The National Student Survey (NSS) was the source of this data. The NSS is an initiative undertaken by the Funding Councils for England, Northern Ireland and Wales. It is designed, as an element of the quality assurance for higher education, to inform prospective students and their advisers in choosing what and where to study. The survey encompasses the views of final-year students on the quality of their courses. Data from the survey published in 2014 were used.

» The National Student Survey covers six aspects of a course: teaching, assessment and feedback, academic support, organisation and management, learning resources and personal development, with an additional question gauging overall satisfaction. Students answer on a scale from 1 (bottom) to 5 (top) and the measure is the percentage of positive responses (4 and 5) in each section, averaged to produce the final score.

» The survey is based on the opinion of final-year students rather than directly assessing teaching quality. Most undergraduates have no experience of other universities, or different courses, to inform their judgements. Although all the questions relate to courses, rather than the broader student experience, some types of university – notably medium-sized campus universities – tend to do better than others.

» Scottish universities were not automatically included in the survey, although all 15 opted to take part in the 2014 survey.

Research quality

This is a measure of the quality of the research undertaken in each university. The information was sourced from the 2008 Research Assessment Exercise (RAE), a peer-review exercise used to evaluate the quality of research in UK higher education institutions undertaken by the UK Higher Education funding bodies. Additionally, academic staffing data for 2007–08 from the Higher Education Statistics Agency have been used.

» A research quality profile was given to every university department that took part. This profile used the following categories: 4* world-leading; 3* internationally excellent; 2* internationally recognised; 1* nationally recognised; and unclassified. The Funding Bodies decided to direct more funds to the very best research by applying weightings. The English, Scottish and Welsh funding councils have slightly different weightings. Those adopted by HEFCE (the funding council for England) for funding in 2013–14 are used in the tables: 4* is weighted by a factor of 3 and 3* is weighted by a factor of 1. Outputs of 2* and 1* carry zero weight. This results in a maximum score of 3.

» The scores in the table are presented as a percentage of the maximum score. To achieve the maximum score all staff would need to be at 4* world-leading level.

» Universities could choose which staff to include in the RAE, so, to factor in the depth of the research quality, each quality profile score has been multiplied by the number of staff returned in the RAE as a proportion of all eligible staff.

» Estimations of the eligible staff for each university were made drawing from publicly available data that have been quality assured by universities themselves. The eligible staff data include all staff directly responsible for teaching and research (excluding those on part-time contracts of less than 20 per cent of a full-time position as they were not eligible), with an adjustment made to remove more junior staff on research-only contracts. An adjustment has also been made to reflect patterns of staffing in those institutions which carry out further education as well as higher education. The calculations were checked against the figures published by a number of universities that declared the proportion of eligible staff entered for assessment.

Estimation was necessary because, as you will see from the note on page 56, HESA decided not to publish data on numbers of staff in university departments who were eligible to be submitted in the RAE. The proportion of staff entered by each university had been considered sufficiently important to be included in the grades used in every previous RAE to give an indication of the ethos and overall quality of departments. The methodology used in *The Times and Sunday Times* league table attempts to replicate that process as accurately as possible, given the restrictions imposed by HESA.

Entry standards

This is the average score, using the UCAS tariff (see page 18), of new students under the age of 21 who took A and AS Levels, Scottish Highers and Advanced Highers and other equivalent qualifications (eg, International Baccalaureate). It measures what new students actually achieved rather than the entry requirements suggested by the universities. The data comes from HESA for 2012–13. The original sources of data for this measure are data returns made by the universities themselves to HESA.

» Using the UCAS tariff, each student's examination results were converted to a numerical score. HESA then calculated an average for all students at the university. The results have then been adjusted to take account of the subject mix at the university.
» A score of 360 represents three As at A level. Although all but six of the top 50 universities in the table have entry standards of at least 360, it does not mean that everyone achieved such results – let alone that this was the standard offer. Courses will not demand more than three subjects at A level and offers are pitched accordingly. You will need to reach the entry requirements set by the university, rather than these scores.

Student–staff ratio

This is a measure of the average number of students to each member of the academic staff, apart from those purely engaged in research. In this measure a low value is better than a high value. The data comes from HESA for 2012–13. The original sources of data for this measure are data returns made by the universities themselves to HESA.

» The figures, as calculated by HESA, allow for variation in employment patterns at different universities. A low value means that there are a small number of students for each academic member of staff, but this does not, of course, ensure good teaching quality or contact time with academics.
» Student–staff ratios vary by subject, for example the ratio is usually low for medicine. In building the table, the score is adjusted for the subject mix taught by each university.

Services and facilities spend

The expenditure per student on staff and student facilities, including library and computing facilities. The data comes from HESA for 2011–12 and 2012–13. The original data sources for this measure are data returns made by the universities to HESA.

» This is a measure calculated by taking the expenditure on student facilities (sports, grants to student societies, careers services, health services, counselling, etc.) and library and computing facilities (books, journals, staff, central computers and computer networks, but not buildings) and dividing this by the number of full-time-equivalent students. Expenditure is averaged over two years to even out the figures (for example, a computer upgrade undertaken in a single year).

Completion

This measure gives the percentage of students expected to complete their studies (or transfer to another institution) for each university. The data comes from the HESA performance indicators, based on data for 2012–13 and earlier years.

» This measure is a projection, liable to statistical fluctuations.

Good honours

This measure is the percentage of graduates achieving a first or upper second class degree. The results have been adjusted to take account of the subject mix at the university. The data comes from HESA for 2012–13. The original sources of data for this measure are data returns made by the universities themselves to HESA.

» Four-year first degrees, such as an MChem, are treated as equivalent to a first or upper second.
» Scottish Ordinary degrees (awarded after three years of study) are excluded.
» Universities control degree classification, with some oversight from external examiners. There have been suggestions that since universities have increased the numbers of good honours degrees they award, this measure may not be as objective as it should be. However, it remains the key measure of a student's success and employability.

Graduate prospects

This measure is the percentage of the total number of graduates who take up graduate-level employment or further study. The results have been adjusted for subject mix. The data come from HESA for 2013 graduates.

» HESA surveys graduates six months after graduation to find out what they are doing and the data are based on this survey.

2015 Rank	2014 Rank	Institution	Student satisfaction (%)	Research quality (%)	Entry standards	Student–staff ratio	Services and facilities spend per student (£)	Completion (%)	Good honours (%)	Graduate prospects (%)	Total
=1	1	Cambridge	85.6	45.0	616	11.6	3246	98.9	88.6	88.7	1000
=1	2	Oxford	85.4	44.3	580	11.0	3506	98.9	91.5	82.5	1000
3	4	St Andrews	86.3	28.0	523	11.8	2346	96.9	88.3	79.1	873
4	5	Imperial College	83.5	33.0	576	11.7	2833	97.1	85.9	89.9	855
5	3	London School of Economics	78.3	38.7	537	11.8	2381	96.3	79.3	83.4	848
6	6	Durham	85.3	29.7	525	15.6	2544	95.8	84.8	79.5	847
7	8	Exeter	86.4	28.0	459	16.6	2356	96.5	84.6	79.6	820
8	10	Warwick	84.0	29.0	510	13.9	2314	95.7	81.0	78.1	811
9	9	University College London	79.0	33.0	521	10.2	2453	93.6	86.7	81.8	801
10	7	Bath	87.1	23.3	489	16.6	1784	95.2	80.2	85.4	795
11	=12	Surrey	86.9	20.3	422	15.4	2167	91.0	79.0	81.8	781
12	=12	Lancaster	84.2	28.3	448	14.9	1752	93.9	77.6	78.0	771
13	21	Loughborough	85.7	24.7	406	15.6	1956	93.5	78.0	80.0	761
14	17	East Anglia	86.5	21.0	431	13.0	2229	92.2	74.3	70.3	757
15	16	Birmingham	82.8	24.0	439	14.5	2375	94.2	81.1	84.3	751
16	11	York	82.6	29.0	446	15.0	1995	93.2	80.0	73.8	742
17	=29	Leeds	84.3	22.7	434	14.7	2068	94.4	81.0	74.8	737
18	20	Southampton	82.2	23.0	431	12.8	2058	92.5	78.4	77.9	735
19	15	Bristol	80.4	29.7	483	14.1	2030	95.5	83.1	80.2	730
20	14	Leicester	83.2	20.0	401	12.9	2384	93.1	79.0	73.9	729
21	=18	Sheffield	83.0	27.3	439	14.9	1801	93.9	78.5	76.9	717
=22	22	Edinburgh	77.4	32.7	489	13.8	2188	90.4	83.7	73.1	716
=22	=18	Newcastle	85.3	21.7	438	15.2	1762	94.2	76.9	78.8	716

=22	23	Nottingham	82.2	24.0	442	14.1	1961	94.0	78.0	79.2	716
25	32	Sussex	82.1	25.7	411	16.5	2114	90.5	76.3	76.1	712
26	25	Glasgow	83.9	24.3	487	15.2	2131	87.4	74.5	79.9	710
27	=33	Cardiff	83.0	21.0	423	13.0	1442	95.6	78.0	81.7	700
28	26	Manchester	81.9	28.7	443	13.9	1734	93.2	73.8	75.7	695
29	27	King's College London	78.7	23.3	470	11.4	2090	92.5	81.1	80.1	694
30	=33	Kent	84.1	17.0	372	13.6	1376	91.4	74.7	75.2	693
31	24	SOAS London	79.8	21.7	422	11.6	2027	85.6	84.0	64.2	688
32	39	Essex	85.7	22.7	343	16.1	2401	86.6	64.7	65.2	684
33	35	Reading	83.7	22.7	376	14.7	1594	91.4	72.5	71.8	682
=34	=29	Aston	84.0	13.3	381	16.2	1735	91.6	75.2	77.1	675
=34	28	Royal Holloway	82.4	27.7	405	15.4	1462	92.3	74.0	62.8	675
36	36	Liverpool	79.8	20.0	414	12.7	2134	92.5	76.8	72.7	656
37	37	Queen Mary, London	80.0	23.0	424	12.0	2233	90.8	70.3	70.3	654
38	=29	Queen's, Belfast	83.3	18.7	391	15.5	1739	92.2	72.6	75.1	651
39	42	Strathclyde	82.3	16.7	470	19.3	1753	85.7	74.4	77.9	644
40	44	Keele	87.1	12.7	384	15.2	1131	89.2	67.5	72.3	631
41	38	Heriot-Watt	82.9	18.0	424	16.4	1736	82.4	70.5	73.2	630
42	45	Coventry	88.4	2.3	313	15.3	1355	87.6	66.1	71.2	623
43	47	Swansea	81.5	16.0	341	15.5	1680	90.1	70.7	78.6	619
44	40	Aberdeen	80.4	20.7	444	15.5	1859	82.5	71.0	74.3	616
45	49	Dundee	84.6	15.7	409	14.9	1422	84.2	71.7	70.7	615
46	43	City	80.0	14.3	394	17.5	2023	87.4	69.6	74.2	605
47	46	Brunel	84.4	17.0	352	16.9	1741	86.0	63.4	60.0	597
48	41	Buckingham	85.1	..	330	11.3	1894	80.2	43.5	75.3	595
49	50	Oxford Brookes	83.3	5.7	369	16.9	1416	89.1	69.6	67.9	586
50	56	Bangor	85.4	16.0	305	17.8	1169	85.1	61.2	66.6	573
51	=77	Falmouth	81.1	2.0	316	23.0	1877	88.6	70.4	70.9	565

2015 Rank	2014 Rank	Institution	Student satisfaction (%)	Research quality (%)	Entry standards	Student–staff ratio	Services and facilities spend per student (£)	Completion (%)	Good honours (%)	Graduate prospects (%)	Total
52	61	Nottingham Trent	83.1	4.3	320	17.2	1568	86.9	66.6	63.5	564
53	51	Stirling	80.3	13.7	380	15.7	1517	83.3	62.8	70.5	562
54	86	De Montfort	82.4	6.0	313	18.1	1571	87.4	66.5	69.1	560
55	48	Goldsmiths, London	79.2	24.7	346	16.9	1052	82.6	76.7	55.7	558
56	59	Northampton	85.3	1.3	280	19.8	2439	84.1	61.1	60.2	556
57	55	Portsmouth	83.0	5.3	314	18.6	1431	88.1	71.2	66.3	555
58	63	Hull	83.0	11.0	333	17.8	1472	85.4	66.7	63.5	552
59	=52	Arts University, Bournemouth	82.3	0.3	331	14.9	640	90.4	62.6	66.2	551
60	=57	Lincoln	82.9	5.0	338	18.6	1450	87.6	57.9	67.6	549
61	=57	Winchester	83.5	4.0	322	17.3	1139	89.2	70.0	51.7	542
62	=77	Sheffield Hallam	83.0	4.0	321	18.4	1705	86.1	65.6	59.7	540
63	=64	Harper Adams	85.3	2.0	342	19.8	1183	88.3	52.8	67.0	539
64	=52	Robert Gordon	81.3	5.3	384	19.3	1246	81.3	63.2	80.5	538
65	68	Chichester	84.5	1.7	306	18.7	1125	89.8	63.7	58.1	532
66	62	Northumbria	81.3	2.7	365	17.8	1486	87.8	63.8	61.8	528
67	=52	Chester	83.8	1.0	302	16.9	1509	82.2	61.8	65.8	527
68	60	West of England	79.7	4.7	339	20.0	1750	84.7	70.0	68.3	526
69	=73	Ulster	83.3	11.0	310	17.7	1524	80.6	65.3	58.2	523
70	70	Bath Spa	83.0	3.0	332	20.0	1046	87.3	71.0	56.4	522
71	83	Liverpool John Moores	82.8	3.7	336	19.7	1308	84.4	70.6	61.5	518
72	69	Edge Hill	83.9	0.7	308	16.8	1614	85.2	59.3	58.3	517

73	80	Roehampton	82.6	7.7	287	20.2	2153	81.8	62.1	56.9	515
74	99	University for the Creative Arts	77.7	5.0	324	12.5	1901	84.7	56.1	49.5	511
75	94	Middlesex	81.7	5.0	287	20.5	2595	76.5	59.3	56.8	506
76	=84	Bradford	79.3	10.0	320	18.6	1426	83.6	65.8	72.4	505
=77	88	Central Lancashire	82.1	3.7	337	16.8	1836	79.8	57.5	59.3	504
=77	66	Huddersfield	82.3	2.0	334	18.3	1288	81.6	60.0	69.5	504
79	=96	Hertfordshire	78.3	3.3	344	18.3	1736	83.3	66.8	68.5	499
80	=73	Plymouth	81.8	6.7	316	16.2	1285	84.6	63.0	57.9	496
81	=84	Derby	83.5	1.0	305	16.8	1370	83.1	60.2	54.4	495
82	76	Brighton	79.4	9.7	319	18.3	1118	84.2	67.3	65.8	494
83	=91	Gloucestershire	80.6	2.0	295	23.6	1499	87.6	69.9	58.0	492
84	81	Glasgow Caledonian	79.2	3.0	370	20.9	1588	80.9	68.5	67.9	490
85	=77	University of the Arts London	73.4	20.3	343	18.7	1562	87.1	64.3	55.0	488
86	=71	Queen Margaret, Edinburgh	80.2	3.3	339	20.5	1321	79.7	73.1	63.3	487
87	=64	York St John	80.2	1.0	302	21.1	1207	91.3	63.5	64.5	485
88	67	Bournemouth	78.1	4.3	336	21.6	1372	87.3	64.5	63.6	484
89	89	Manchester Metropolitan	79.3	4.3	343	18.2	1206	83.0	65.8	60.2	483
90	87	Cardiff Metropolitan	82.5	3.3	304	20.3	1392	85.3	52.9	58.7	482
=91	=91	Birmingham City	81.0	2.3	317	21.2	1563	82.8	63.3	63.0	479
=91	104	Leeds Trinity	83.4	1.7	280	23.6	1236	84.8	56.0	65.8	479
93	82	Aberystwyth	77.9	20.3	325	20.0	1167	86.1	63.2	52.8	476
94	93	Teesside	82.8	1.7	324	18.8	1329	81.0	58.6	58.0	467
95	95	Cumbria	82.3	0.3	288	20.8	816	84.9	66.9	62.1	465
96	90	Canterbury Christ Church	80.9	1.7	277	18.9	1166	82.1	66.7	59.9	460
97	100	Edinburgh Napier	81.6	3.0	348	21.6	1019	75.1	67.3	61.2	457
98	101	Greenwich	82.3	3.0	312	21.5	1403	82.0	63.3	49.0	453
99	=96	Sunderland	81.4	4.7	302	17.9	1359	80.3	54.3	50.9	451
100		St Mary's, Twickenham	80.6	2.7	294	22.4	1005	81.5	60.7	63.8	449

2015 Rank	2014 Rank	Institution	Student satisfaction (%)	Research quality (%)	Entry standards	Student–staff ratio	Services and facilities spend per student (£)	Completion (%)	Good honours (%)	Graduate prospects (%)	Total
101	108	Staffordshire	81.2	1.0	273	17.7	1416	80.8	58.5	55.9	448
=102	=106	Bishop Grosseteste	83.9	0.3	279	30.2	446	92.0	57.0	67.0	447
=102	=71	St Mark and St John	82.9	0.3	276	19.2	803	82.9	51.1	64.0	447
104	=73	Newman	83.1	0.3	302	18.1	1370	77.2	52.7	57.2	445
105	98	Salford	76.4	9.3	341	17.0	1481	77.6	64.3	56.8	440
106	105	Abertay	78.8	3.0	330	21.3	1436	73.2	64.3	61.1	435
107	102	Worcester	79.3	0.3	300	21.1	984	85.4	58.5	60.7	426
108	115	Bedfordshire	81.9	1.7	225	20.9	1440	82.3	50.7	59.3	425
109	112	West London	78.5	2.0	256	18.3	1637	77.6	52.0	67.6	424
110	110	Anglia Ruskin	83.4	1.7	252	23.0	1279	82.5	51.6	58.5	422
111	103	Leeds Metropolitan	78.9	2.0	280	19.9	1188	79.5	61.2	55.6	420
112	=106	Westminster	77.7	5.0	317	20.3	1359	79.1	64.1	50.6	418
113	109	Glyndŵr	76.9	1.3	289	20.1	1815	78.0	53.5	63.7	407
114		South Wales	77.0	3.7	322	21.6	1313	80.8	59.9	55.4	404
115	114	Southampton Solent	77.2	0.7	299	18.8	1335	76.4	61.1	50.5	398
116	113	Buckinghamshire New	76.4	0.7	250	22.2	2051	82.9	53.3	53.7	390
117	111	Kingston	75.7	3.3	298	19.4	1378	79.6	59.0	54.4	376
118	117	West of Scotland	78.9	4.7	299	22.0	1279	67.8	58.5	58.4	370
119	120	East London	81.1	4.0	278	26.3	1451	67.4	54.2	50.5	360
120	119	Bolton	79.1	2.0	276	19.9	927	71.9	50.6	57.4	355
121	116	Highlands and Islands	78.9	2.0	298	..	545	67.4	70.6	49.1	324
122	118	London South Bank	77.7	2.7	233	24.2	1250	72.4	59.7	45.0	320
123	121	London Metropolitan	74.1	3.3	239	21.5	619	70.5	51.3	45.1	253

Notes on the Table

University College Birmingham, Liverpool Hope, Trinity Saint David, University of Wales, and Wolverhampton have refused the release of data, so do not appear in this year's league table.

The following universities provided specific data as follows: Bedfordshire, Central Lancashire, De Montfort, Exeter, Northumbria, University College London and Ulster provided replacement services and facilities spend per student data; Bedfordshire, Glyndŵr and Sheffield Hallam provided replacement good honours data; and Bangor, Cardiff, Central Lancashire, Exeter, Hull, Northumbria, Queen Mary, London and Ulster provided replacement student–staff ratio data.

Statement from the Higher Education Statistics Agency (HESA) regarding the use of staffing data in looking at Research Assessment Exercise performance:

This analysis of the results of the Research Assessment Exercise 2008 makes use of contextual data supplied under contract by the Higher Education Statistics Agency (HESA). It is a contractual condition that this statement should be published in conjunction with the analysis. HESA holds no data specifying which or how many staff have been regarded by each institution as eligible for inclusion in RAE 2008, and no data on the assignment to Units of Assessment of those eligible staff not included. Further, the data that HESA does hold is not an adequate alternative basis on which to estimate eligible staff numbers, whether for an institution as a whole, or disaggregated by Units of Assessment, or by some broader subject-based grouping.

5 The Top Universities by Subject

Knowing where a university stands in the pecking order of higher education is a vital piece of information for any prospective student, but the quality of the course is what matters most – particularly in the short term. Your chosen course, rather than the character of the whole university, will determine what you get out of taking a degree and may have a big bearing on your employment prospects. As the latest Research Assessment Exercise (RAE) in 2008 confirmed, the most modest institution may have a centre of specialist excellence, and even famous universities have mediocre departments. This section offers some pointers to the leading universities in a wide range of subjects. With a number of universities reviewing the courses they will offer in the future, it is possible that not all institutions listed in a particular subject area will be running courses in 2015.

The subject tables in this *Guide* also include scores from the National Student Survey (NSS). These distil the views of final-year undergraduates on several aspects of their course, including teaching quality, assessment and feedback, and the quality of learning resources. The three other measures used are research quality, students' entry qualifications and graduate employment prospects. None of the measures are weighted.

The tables include the research grades drawn from the deliberations of expert assessors in the 2008 RAE. No data have been released on the proportion of academics entered for assessment, for example, so it has not been possible to mirror the approach adopted in the main institutional ranking (see pages 60–64). Data supplied by the Higher Education Statistics Agency (HESA) are used to calculate average entry qualifications and the employment prospects of graduates. The graduate prospects information draws a distinction between different types of employment: professional employment and non-professional employment. The tables give the percentage of "positive destinations" by adding those undertaking further study to the total in professional employment.

Many subjects, such as dentistry or sociology, have their own table, but others are grouped together in broader categories, such as "other subjects allied to medicine". For the first time the specialisms of animal science and creative writing are now in separate subject tables. Scores are not published where the number of students is too small for the outcome to be statistically reliable. In the NSS, a 50 per cent response rate is required from a minimum of 30 students. If there is no student satisfaction score, then to qualify for inclusion in the table a university has to have data for at least two of the other measures.

Cambridge is again the most successful university. It tops 33 of the 66 tables. Oxford has the next highest number of top places with 7, followed by Warwick with 5, while 16 other universities also gain top spots. The subject rankings demonstrate that there are "horses for courses" in higher education. This year, one specialist institution, the Courtauld Institute, was top (for history of art). In our new tables, Nottingham topped animal science and Warwick, creative writing. For a summary of top universities by subject, see pages 196–8,

Research quality

This is a measure of the quality of the research undertaken in the subject area. The information was sourced from the 2008 Research Assessment Exercise (RAE), a peer-review exercise used to evaluate the quality of research in UK higher education institutions, undertaken by the UK Higher Education Funding Bodies.

For each subject, a research quality profile was given to those university departments that took part, showing how much of their research was in various quality categories. These categories were: 4* world-leading; 3* internationally excellent; 2* internationally recognised; 1* nationally recognised; and unclassified. The funding bodies decided to direct more funds to the very best research by applying weightings. The English, Scottish and Welsh funding councils have slightly different weightings. Those adopted by HEFCE (the funding council for England) for funding in 2012–13 are used in the tables: 4* is weighted by a factor of 3 and 3* is weighted by a factor of 1. Outputs of 2* and 1* carry zero weight. This results in a maximum score of 3.

The scores in the table are presented as a percentage of the maximum score. To achieve the maximum score all staff would need to be at 4* world-leading level.

Staffing data to show how many of a department's academics were submitted in the RAE are not currently available. Some research ratings shown could relate to a relatively low proportion of the academic staff in the department.

Entry standards

This is the average UCAS tariff score for new students under the age of 21, based on A and AS Levels and Scottish Highers and Advanced Highers and other equivalent qualifications (including the International Baccalaureate), taken from HESA data for 2012–13. Each student's examination grades were converted to a numerical score using the UCAS tariff (see page 18 for details) and added up to give a total score. HESA then calculated an average score for each university.

Student satisfaction

This measure is taken from the National Student Survey results published in 2013 and 2014. A single year's figures are used when that is all that is available, but an average of the two years' results is used in all other cases. The score for each university represents the percentage of final-year undergraduates declaring themselves satisfied or very satisfied with their course, averaged over the seven sections of the survey (teaching, assessment and feedback, academic support, organisation and management, learning resources, personal development and overall satisfaction).

Graduate prospects

This is the percentage of graduates undertaking further study or in a professional job, in the annual survey by HESA six months after graduation. Two years of data (2012 and 2013 graduates) are aggregated to make the data more reliable. A low score on this measure does not necessarily indicate unemployment – some graduates may have taken jobs that are not categorised as professional work. The averages for each subject are given close by the relevant subject table in this chapter and in a table in chapter 2 (see pages 38–41).

The Education table uses a fifth measure: teaching quality, as measured by the outcomes of Ofsted inspections of teacher training courses.

The subjects listed below are covered in the tables in this chapter:

Accounting and Finance
Aeronautical and Manufacturing
  Engineering
Agriculture and Forestry
American Studies
Anatomy and Physiology
Animal Science
Anthropology
Archaeology
Architecture
Art and Design
Biological Sciences
Building
Business Studies
Celtic Studies
Chemical Engineering
Chemistry
Civil Engineering
Classics and Ancient History
Communication and Media Studies
Computer Science
Creative Writing
Dentistry
Drama, Dance and Cinematics
East and South Asian Studies
Economics
Education
Electrical and Electronic Engineering
English
Food Science
French
General Engineering
Geography and Environmental Sciences
Geology
German

History
History of Art, Architecture and Design
Hospitality, Leisure, Recreation and
  Tourism
Iberian Languages
Italian
Land and Property Management
Law
Librarianship and Information Management
Linguistics
Materials Technology
Mathematics
Mechanical Engineering
Medicine
Middle Eastern and African Studies
Music
Nursing
Other Subjects Allied to Medicine
  (see page 165 for included subjects)
Pharmacology and Pharmacy
Philosophy
Physics and Astronomy
Physiotherapy
Politics
Psychology
Radiography
Russian and East European Languages
Social Policy
Social Work
Sociology
Sports Science
Theology and Religious Studies
Town and Country Planning and Landscape
Veterinary Medicine

Accounting and Finance

Accounting and finance come a surprisingly long way down the employment table – outside the top 50 subjects – but those who do find graduate jobs are relatively well paid. At an average of almost £22,000 in 2013, they were close to the top 20, but the 14 per cent unemployment rate was well above the norm for all subjects. It seems that students are yet to be convinced that the graduate labour market has recovered from the effects of the recession. Applications and enrolments in accounting – much the bigger of the two subjects – continued to decline in 2013 after a 10 per cent drop when the fees went up. Demand for finance degrees rose for the second year in a row.

Employment rates have improved in the new table, although only Robert Gordon registered positive destinations (graduate-level jobs or further study) for more than 90 per cent of graduates. Only four universities, compared with nine last year, slipped below 40 per cent on this measure. Many universities are now offering work placements to try to improve the employment rate. One student in five takes a further qualification, but relatively few (8 per cent) do so full-time.

Warwick makes the leap from equal fifth place to top the latest table, thanks mainly to a big increase in student satisfaction. It is actually not in the top three for any single indicator, but holds off Strathclyde with a strong performance across the board. Bath has dropped from first to fourth place, while Strathclyde benefits from the generous points awarded to Scottish qualifications in the UCAS tariff, which gives the university a higher average entry score than the London School of Economics. High satisfaction rates are spread throughout the table, the best being at Salford, in 30th place. Even East London, only 12 places off the bottom of the table, recorded 93 per cent satisfaction. But high research grades at some traditional universities ensured that Robert Gordon, at 14th, was the only post-1992 institution to reach the top 30.

Some of the leading universities will demand maths A level and all will welcome it. But, with 91 universities qualifying for the table, there is considerable variation in entry standards. Four universities, compared with two last year, average more than 500 points at entry, two had averages of less than 200 points. Some 140 institutions expect to offer accounting, either alone or in combination, in 2015.

Employed in professional job:	39%	Employed in non-professional job and studying:	3%
Employed in professional job and studying:	9%	Employed in non-professional job:	27%
Studying:	8%	Unemployed:	14%
Average starting professional salary:	£21,952	Average starting non-professional salary:	£16,903

Accounting and Finance	Research quality %	Entry standards	Student satisfaction %	Graduate prospects %	Overall rating
1 Warwick	41.7	507	88.1	82.7	100.0
2 Strathclyde	38.3	525	87.2	81.0	98.9
3 Lancaster	41.7	455	87.3	85.7	98.3
4 Bath	43.3	497	84.9	80.8	97.7
5 Aston	30.0	405	90.6	82.6	94.9
6 Glasgow	21.7	509	87.7	82.5	94.5
=7 Loughborough	30.0	429	87.3	84.9	94.1

Accounting and Finance cont

	Research quality %	Entry standards	Student satisfaction %	Graduate prospects %	Overall rating
=7 Queen's, Belfast	28.3	418	87.5	88.2	94.1
=7 Surrey	23.3	420	93.3	75.7	94.1
10 Leeds	36.7	440	86.0	75.6	93.7
11 London School of Economics	43.3	521	75.7	77.6	92.1
12 Exeter	25.0	459	84.9	82.9	92.0
13 Cardiff	46.7	402	85.6	60.5	91.9
14 Robert Gordon	10.0	429	88.9	93.0	91.4
15 Newcastle	23.3	437	85.7	82.5	91.2
16 Reading	23.3	416	87.0	81.3	91.0
17 Nottingham	36.7	414	84.0	71.6	90.8
18 Durham	28.3	420	86.3	72.7	90.5
19 Manchester	38.3	436	82.9	67.0	90.4
20 Bristol	25.0	441	84.0	77.3	89.7
21 Queen Mary, London	28.3	393	84.6	77.4	89.3
22 Edinburgh	23.3	444	82.1	82.1	89.1
23 Heriot-Watt	21.7	434	85.8	73.2	88.9
24 Birmingham	31.7	411	83.2	70.3	88.6
25 City	28.3	450	81.1	71.5	88.0
26 Southampton	28.3	420	79.0	80.4	87.3
27 Sheffield	30.0	371	82.4	75.1	87.2
28 Kent	27.4	397	80.5	77.5	86.6
29 East Anglia	21.7	399	85.3	68.3	86.5
30 Salford	13.3	328	95.4	55.1	85.7
31 Dundee	16.7	404	84.3	66.4	84.3
32 Portsmouth	15.0	316	85.0	79.5	83.7
33 Swansea	20.0	333	82.7	75.0	83.4
34 Liverpool	23.3	397	80.9	63.6	83.2
35 Aberdeen	20.0	401	76.8	78.4	82.7
36 Coventry		294	94.5	66.9	82.6
37 De Montfort	18.3	298	87.9	61.2	82.4
38 Stirling	15.0	378	81.7	71.6	82.3
=39 Bangor	31.7	275	85.1	55.3	82.2
=39 Keele	21.7	356	84.1	57.8	82.2
41 Birmingham City	11.7	277	93.2	53.3	81.7
42 Essex	25.0	339	85.0	49.4	81.5
=43 Huddersfield	10.0	347	82.9	74.4	81.2
=43 Kingston	21.7	309	88.2	47.2	81.2
45 Manchester Metropolitan	15.0	317	89.0	52.0	81.1
46 Aberystwyth	13.3	314	87.4	58.9	80.8
47 Hull	18.3	304	85.3	57.1	80.2
=48 Glasgow Caledonian	5.0	367	86.8	59.0	80.1
=48 Ulster	15.0	324	84.6	60.3	80.1
50 Lincoln		312	88.8	67.1	79.7

51	Brunel	21.7	327	85.6	43.7	79.5
52	Northumbria	6.7	370	84.6	60.0	79.4
53	Chester		283	84.4	85.1	79.3
54	Bradford	25.0	343	78.7	56.8	79.1
=55	Edinburgh Napier	5.0	337	88.5	51.5	78.7
=55	Liverpool John Moores	1.7	318	88.8	58.5	78.7
57	West of England	20.0	328	79.5	61.2	78.6
=58	Middlesex		293	92.4	49.3	77.9
=58	Sussex		386	80.9	70.3	77.9
60	South Wales	8.3	323	85.5	52.3	77.4
=61	Sheffield Hallam	11.7	310	83.7	53.8	77.0
=61	Westminster	13.3	325	81.9	55.0	77.0
63	Greenwich	10.0	302	88.7	40.8	76.9
64	Hertfordshire	15.0	338	81.5	50.6	76.8
65	Central Lancashire	13.3	345	82.7	45.7	76.5
=66	Derby		259	92.1	46.5	76.1
=66	Gloucestershire		259	83.7	75.3	76.1
68	Winchester		299	87.3	55.0	76.0
69	Nottingham Trent	13.3	297	78.4	65.2	75.8
70	Plymouth	13.3	265	86.4	43.2	75.6
71	Bournemouth	13.3	327	78.3	57.4	75.3
72	York St John		242	80.7	83.3	75.2
=73	London South Bank	10.0	194	91.9	39.7	75.0
=73	Worcester		337	83.4	55.7	75.0
75	Northampton		243	88.6	52.1	74.3
76	Brighton	28.3	279	74.6	48.3	73.5
77	West of Scotland	13.3	322	78.3	47.5	73.2
78	Oxford Brookes		306	82.7	53.9	73.1
79	Canterbury Christ Church		260	85.0	53.0	72.8
80	East London		246	93.3	26.2	72.5
=81	Leeds Metropolitan		247	85.7	42.3	70.8
=81	Staffordshire		223	85.0	49.1	70.8
83	Bedfordshire		203	85.6	44.9	69.7
=84	Buckinghamshire New	6.7	176	83.7	42.9	68.9
=84	Southampton Solent		241	81.0	49.4	68.9
86	West London		218	81.5	47.3	68.0
87	Cardiff Metropolitan		273	79.2	43.7	67.8
88	Anglia Ruskin		215	79.0	49.1	66.7
89	Edge Hill		262	77.1	37.5	64.9
90	London Metropolitan		204	81.0	33.0	64.6
91	Bolton	3.3	241	71.0	47.8	63.2

Aeronautical and Manufacturing Engineering

In common with other branches of the discipline, aeronautical engineering bounced back in 2013 following a small decline at the introduction of higher fees. More so than in many subjects, apprenticeships at leading firms like Rolls-Royce provide an attractive alternative to a degree, but both applications and enrolments were up by over 5 per cent and another rise is on the way for 2014. The much smaller area of manufacturing engineering held its own, with modest increases. Prospective applicants will be encouraged by further improvement in the salary table, which sees the subjects placed seventh out of the 66 groups. However, they do less well for the proportion of engineers going straight into graduate-level jobs or further study. Although the unemployment rate has improved, it is still above average and the subjects remain outside the top 20 overall.

Most of the courses in this ranking focus on aeronautical or manufacturing engineering, but it includes some with a mechanical title. To add to the confusion, manufacturing degrees often go under the rubric of production engineering (*see* General Engineering and Mechanical Engineering). Cambridge has maintained a comfortable lead, registering by far the best scores for research, entry standards and graduate prospects. With 97 per cent positive destinations, it is more than 6 percentage points ahead of its nearest challengers in the jobs market. Last year, the University of the West of England (UWE) achieved full employment in this table, but it could only manage 84 per cent this time.

Many universities demand maths and physics at A Level, and give extra credit for further maths, computing and/or design technology. Entry grades are high at the leading universities, with Cambridge averaging almost 650 points and Bristol, Imperial College and Bath more than 500. Only one university averages less than 250 points, and where three Bs at A level was enough to secure a place at about a quarter of the universities in last year's table, the number is now down to five.

Below Cambridge, there is considerable movement this year. Imperial College takes second place, with Southampton dropping eight places, reversing its gains of last year. Leeds and Bristol, in third and fourth, have each moved up six places. Leeds benefits from the top satisfaction rate. Liverpool John Moores is the leading post-1992 university and is joined in the top 20 by UWE. Almost 60 per cent of the 2013 graduates went straight into high-level work, and there was less variation between institutions than in 2012. Only two universities were below 50 per cent for the proportion of leavers in graduate jobs or further study.

Aeronautical and Manufacturing Engineering	Research quality %	Entry standards	Student satisfaction %	Graduate prospects %	Overall rating
1 Cambridge	60.0	647	91.0	97.0	100.0
2 Imperial College	46.7	565	83.8	79.3	86.9
3 Leeds	39.2	437	94.0	70.7	84.2
4 Bristol	43.3	532	76.7	90.7	84.0
5 Bath	25.0	544	85.2	86.7	83.1
6 Newcastle	31.7		84.5	90.3	82.6
7 Sheffield	45.0	446	79.1	86.6	82.0
8 Surrey	35.0	453	81.9	88.1	81.4
9 Nottingham	41.7	410	80.5	85.7	80.6

10 Southampton	30.0	487	79.0	89.2	80.0
11 Loughborough	36.7	429	77.4	86.7	78.6
12 Liverpool	35.4	409	84.0	75.6	78.5
13 Queen's, Belfast	31.7	387	88.9	70.7	78.2
14 Strathclyde	26.2	470	80.3	71.8	75.5
15 Manchester	36.7	444	79.4	64.9	75.4
16 Glasgow	21.7	477	77.1	79.4	74.7
17 Liverpool John Moores	33.3		85.2	51.6	72.6
18 Swansea	21.7	344	79.6	81.8	72.3
19 West of England	25.0	316	75.4	84.0	70.7
20 Brunel	23.3	375	79.5	67.7	70.6
=21 Hertfordshire	26.7	333	76.9	72.3	69.8
=21 West of Scotland		350	84.3	84.0	69.8
23 Queen Mary, London	21.7	389	81.7	58.1	69.7
24 Ulster		310	90.8	73.1	69.4
25 Coventry	7.4	303	87.1	73.2	69.3
26 Aston	18.3	374	78.3	66.0	68.4
27 Plymouth	8.3	256	87.8	66.7	67.0
28 Portsmouth	18.3	287	79.5	67.7	66.6
29 City	21.7	353	74.6	62.1	65.9
30 Staffordshire	20.0	238	74.5	78.9	65.5
31 Salford	23.3	318	68.7	68.9	63.9
32 Sussex		367	73.7	73.7	63.0
=33 Sheffield Hallam	15.0	277	79.1	54.0	62.4
=33 South Wales	23.3	328	67.6	63.4	62.4
35 Brighton	26.7	339	76.0	35.3	61.7
36 Manchester Metropolitan	11.7	289	75.7	54.1	60.3
37 Kingston	11.7	307	72.3	47.7	57.8

Employed in professional job:	56%	Employed in non-professional job and studying:		1%
Employed in professional job and studying:	2%	Employed in non-professional job:		15%
Studying:	13%	Unemployed:		13%
Average starting professional salary:	£25,343	Average starting non-professional salary:		£15,715

Agriculture and Forestry

The separation of animal sciences from agriculture and forestry has produced some big changes in this year's agriculture table. Nottingham has fallen from first position to seventh, and Newcastle has taken over at the top with by far the best employment record. Reading, which shared top place four years ago, moves back up to second after a drop last year, while Queen's, Belfast has edged ahead of Glasgow.

Applications and enrolments edged up in 2013, both for agriculture and the small cohort taking forestry. But the two subjects have among the lowest ratios of applicants to acceptances, with fewer than two applicants to each place in forestry. This is reflected in the entry grades: of the 15 universities with enough entrants for scores to be compiled, only Oxford Brookes and Kent averaged more than 400 points. Nevertheless, only three

Agriculture and Forestry cont

universities average less than 300 points and none less than 250.

Satisfaction rates have improved this year, with only one institution dropping below 70 per cent. Plymouth had the most satisfied students, but was still restricted to the bottom half of the table because only a third of graduates went on to high-level employment or further study. The rate was even lower at Cumbria and only Newcastle managed positive destinations for more than three-quarters of its graduates. Overall, the subjects are not in the top 50 for employment, but the new table sees a big increase in average earnings, placing agriculture and forestry 36th out of 66 subject groupings. The unemployment rate of 15 per cent was one of the highest, but those who found graduate jobs were paid an average of £20,721.

Two of the 19 institutions in the table, Harper Adams and the Royal Agricultural University, are specialist universities. Harper Adams, which held on to fifth position, is the highest-placed of ten post-1992 universities in the ranking. Glasgow and Highlands and Islands are Scotland's only representatives, but Scotland's Rural College, one of several institutions with too little data to qualify for this table, is now the only place to take a full degree in agriculture north of the border. Aberdeen offers forestry and plant and soil science, while Highlands and Islands provides a number of forestry courses, including sustainable forest management. At least a quarter of those enrolling for degrees in agriculture and more

Agriculture and Forestry	Research quality %	Entry standards	Student satisfaction %	Graduate prospects %	Overall rating
1 Newcastle	18.3	358	82.3	81.6	100.0
2 Reading	21.7	372	85.6	64.6	99.8
3 Queen's, Belfast	13.3	368	83.5	67.1	95.9
4 Glasgow	21.7	353			95.8
5 Harper Adams	8.3	339	85.6	72.7	94.6
6 Oxford Brookes		438		54.5	93.4
7 Nottingham	30.0	371	78.1	43.8	93.3
8 Kent		414	82.0	53.8	89.8
9 West of England	18.3			48.1	89.6
10 Greenwich	13.3	365		41.9	86.3
11 Aberystwyth	21.7	321	74.9	46.2	85.5
12 Bangor	18.3	277	79.9	50.7	85.2
13 Plymouth	3.3		86.9	33.3	82.5
14 Central Lancashire		366		43.7	81.8
15 Lincoln	6.7		67.2	64.5	79.5
16 Royal Agricultural University	5.0	313	71.6	56.9	79.4
17 Nottingham Trent		284	76.2	58.7	78.6
18 Highlands and Islands	1.7			50.0	78.0
19 Cumbria	0.0	264	79.7	30.4	72.1

Employed in professional job:	40%	Employed in non-professional job and studying:		3%
Employed in professional job and studying:	5%	Employed in non-professional job:		30%
Studying:	8%	Unemployed:		15%
Average starting professional salary:	£20,721	Average starting non-professional salary:		£16,113

than a third in forestry do so without A levels, often coming with relevant work experience. About one in seven arrives through the Clearing system.

American Studies

Warwick has been deposed at the top of the American studies table for the first time in almost a decade, partly because it did not have enough entrants in 2013 to compile a score on that measure. More significantly, however, it suffered a big drop in student satisfaction while the new leader, Manchester, increased its score in the National Student Survey by 10 percentage points. The two universities already tied for the best research performance and Manchester now has by far the highest entry scores. Such swings are commonplace in subjects with small intakes: fewer than 500 students begin full-time degrees in American studies each year.

Applications fell by about 10 per cent in 2013, possibly influenced by poor graduate prospects. American Studies is among the bottom ten subjects for both employment and earnings. Average starting salaries for those in professional jobs have dropped for the second year in a row and more than a third of graduates started their careers in "non-professional" jobs. Only one university – Birmingham, in joint third place – recorded positive destinations for more than three-quarters of its graduates. Indeed, just five of the 17 universities in the table topped 60 per cent on this measure.

Entry standards have declined in the new table, although only one university averages less than 250 points on the UCAS tariff. Scores in the National Student Survey remain high, however, only one university dropping below 80 per cent satisfaction. Hull has the most satisfied students, with 93 per cent of final-year undergraduates giving their approval. Some courses offer the opportunity of a year at an American or Canadian university as part of a four-year degree. The leading universities are likely to expect English or history at A level or the equivalent.

More than 30 universities and colleges expect to offer American studies in some form in 2015. Some focus on Latin America, whereas most concentrate on the culture and politics of the United States and Canada. Of the Scottish universities, only Aberdeen and Stirling feature in the UCAS lists, and both have a Latin American focus. Nine out of ten students taking American studies have A levels or equivalent qualifications and there is an impressive level of firsts and 2:1s.

American Studies	Research quality %	Entry standards	Student satisfaction %	Graduate prospects %	Overall rating
1 Manchester	45.0	434	89.3	50.7	100.0
2 Warwick	45.0		83.8	58.1	95.8
=3 Birmingham	28.3	404	81.1	83.0	95.5
=3 Sussex	40.0	402	84.2	58.2	95.5
5 East Anglia	30.0	415	89.8	52.2	94.9
6 Leicester	30.0	398	89.0	54.0	94.0
7 Hull	25.0	329	93.0	58.5	92.3
8 Kent	41.7	345	81.4	61.5	92.2

	Research quality %	Entry standards	Student satisfaction %	Graduate prospects %	Overall rating
9 Nottingham	31.7	390	80.9	56.1	89.8
10 Essex	25.0	334	84.7	60.9	88.2
11 Keele	23.3	383	84.6	51.2	87.9
12 Portsmouth	25.0	284	88.6	54.1	86.5
13 Swansea	16.7	316	83.3	70.6	86.0
14 Liverpool	21.7		72.3	69.2	80.0
15 Winchester		293	88.4	32.4	74.1
16 Derby		289	87.3	28.6	72.4
17 Canterbury Christ Church		247	82.0	44.8	70.8

Employed in professional job:	35%	Employed in non-professional job and studying:		4%
Employed in professional job and studying:	2%	Employed in non-professional job:		31%
Studying:	14%	Unemployed:		14%
Average starting professional salary:	£18,046	Average starting non-professional salary:		£14,854

Anatomy and Physiology

This table covers a broad range of courses, including the biomedical science degrees that have been growing in popularity over recent years. Very few actually have the title of anatomy or physiology, but they include degrees in cell biology, neurosciences and pathology. The subjects are a popular choice, with eight applications for every place. The 33,000 applications in 2013 represented the sixth successive increase and there was a 9 per cent increase in the number of new enrolments. In some cases, the courses are used as a fall-back for candidates whose real target was medical school, so average entry qualifications at some of the leading universities are extremely high – 665 points in Cambridge's case. There is a considerable range, however, with four universities averaging less than 300 points.

Cambridge remains top of the table, but Oxford, which has the best research score, has narrowed the lead slightly. Dundee, which split the two ancient universities last year, has slipped to tenth. The most satisfied students are at Coventry, only seven places off the bottom of the table, followed by Keele, which also fails to make the top 20. The best employment record is at fifth-placed Glasgow Caledonian, which also the highest-placed post-1992 university and the new leader in Scotland. Student satisfaction is generally high, but there is wide variation in graduate prospects: from more than 90 per cent positive destinations at three post-1992 universities to less than 40 per cent at another.

Anatomy and physiology are just outside the top 20 subjects for the proportion of graduates going straight into professional jobs or further study. More than a third go on to postgraduate courses. The subjects are rather lower in the earnings table, at just below £21,000, although there has been an increase of almost £1,000 since last year for those starting in professional jobs. Universities often demand at least two science subjects – usually biology and chemistry – although some new universities will accept just one science.

Employed in professional job:	35%	Employed in non-professional job and studying:	3%
Employed in professional job and studying:	3%	Employed in non-professional job:	21%
Studying:	28%	Unemployed:	10%
Average starting professional salary:	£20,992	Average starting non-professional salary:	£15,095

Anatomy and Physiology

		Research quality %	Entry standards	Student satisfaction %	Graduate prospects %	Overall rating
1	Cambridge	33.3	665	87.4	86.6	100.0
2	Oxford	46.7	588	81.1	82.3	96.4
3	University College London	35.1	539	82.0	77.4	91.1
4	Queen's, Belfast	30.0	412	89.6	80.0	90.3
5	Glasgow Caledonian	13.3	398	90.0	95.0	89.3
6	Manchester	35.0	455	84.0	72.0	88.1
7	Leeds	30.0	441	88.2	66.6	87.3
=8	Aberdeen	16.7	472	91.0	68.0	86.7
=8	Newcastle	30.0	446	88.0	63.5	86.7
10	Dundee	38.3		84.3	65.4	86.6
11	Loughborough	33.0	396	87.0	67.6	86.2
12	King's College London	31.7	449	82.1	72.5	86.1
13	Glasgow	28.3	488	79.9	74.9	85.9
14	Salford	15.0	376	87.8	85.4	85.5
15	Huddersfield		384	88.3	94.5	84.2
16	Brighton	15.0	303	89.2	86.4	84.0
17	Nottingham	16.7	464	86.9	63.4	83.0
18	Liverpool	25.0	431	86.5	56.5	82.3
19	Leicester		423	91.3	70.8	81.5
20	Bristol	28.3	445	79.5	61.8	81.1
21	Portsmouth	28.3	339	84.0	65.5	80.9
22	Sussex	31.7	437	76.6	61.3	79.9
23	Keele		380	91.7	66.5	79.2
24	Manchester Metropolitan	15.0	313	82.6	79.3	79.0
25	Northampton	6.7	259	83.4	92.5	78.7
26	Reading	15.0	368	82.0	71.4	78.6
27	Edinburgh	28.3		77.9	65.5	78.4
28	Sheffield Hallam	8.3	336	89.8	62.9	78.1
29	Queen Margaret, Edinburgh	1.7	330	85.4	78.6	77.4
30	Coventry	6.7	284	92.9	61.5	77.3
31	Central Lancashire	13.3	347	85.2	54.5	75.2
32	East London	16.7	260	85.1	59.7	74.4
33	Oxford Brookes	16.7	363	88.2	37.8	74.3
34	Ulster		340	77.9	80.4	73.6
35	Plymouth	6.7	323	79.8	58.0	70.5
36	St George's, London	16.7	359	71.5		69.5
37	Westminster		290	70.6	64.2	64.1

Animal Science

Animal Science is one of two new tables in *The Times and Sunday Times Good University Guide* this year, a reflection of growing interest in the group of subjects under this heading. Extracted from the agriculture category, degree courses range from animal behaviour to equine science and veterinary nursing. Together they recorded among the biggest increases in both applications and enrolments in 2013. Applications grew by 18 per cent and the 2,500 new enrolments represented an increase of more than 20 per cent.

Nottingham is the first leader of the Animal Science table and, in spite of the growing numbers nationally, one of only seven universities with enough students and graduates to have a full set of indicators including an entry in the 2008 Research Assessment Exercise (RAE). Surrey has the highest entry grades and the best employment score, so would almost certainly have finished higher than fourth in the table if it had entered the RAE in this field. By far the most satisfied students are at Anglia Ruskin, but it too was absent from the RAE.

There is a less happy debut for animal science in the employment table, where it finishes bottom. Although the 10 per cent unemployment rate is better than the average for all subjects, more than half of all new graduates in 2013 started their careers in jobs that were categorised as "non-professional". Inevitably, this translates into some unusually low scores in the this table; Edinburgh Napier's score of less than 5 per cent going on to a graduate

Animal Science	Research quality %	Entry standards	Student satisfaction %	Graduate prospects %	Overall rating
1 Nottingham	30.0	388	85.8	57.5	100.0
2 West of England	18.3			65.4	96.3
3 Royal Veterinary College	25.0	377	85.4	52.4	95.8
4 Surrey		445	81.3	81.8	91.9
5 Liverpool	18.3	420	72.5	67.9	91.2
6 Reading	18.3	379	83.8		91.0
7 Aberystwyth	21.7	311	83.9	23.6	84.0
8 Harper Adams	8.3	380	85.1	20.0	83.2
9 Bristol	13.3	408	72.0		82.1
10 Plymouth	3.3	340	86.9	37.5	81.6
11 Lincoln	6.7	364	72.3	59.0	80.2
12 Central Lancashire		389		21.4	78.1
13 Anglia Ruskin		275	92.1	18.5	75.1
14 Edinburgh Napier		329	87.8	4.8	74.7
15 Nottingham Trent		320	76.7	33.0	72.2
16 Greenwich	13.3	288		14.0	72.1
17 Chester		345	72.6	20.3	69.9
18 Middlesex		296	78.2	13.3	68.2

Employed in professional job:	19%	Employed in non-professional job and studying:	3%
Employed in professional job and studying:	2%	Employed in non-professional job:	54%
Studying:	13%	Unemployed:	10%
Average starting professional salary:	£17,854	Average starting non-professional salary:	£15,180

job or further study may be the lowest ever published in the *Guide*. Even those who do find graduate-level jobs average less than £18,000 nationally, which is in the bottom four for all subjects.

Anthropology

Anthropology has been enjoying an apparently unlikely boom since £9,000 fees were introduced. Instead of prompting a decline, as its own association predicted, higher charges have coincided with a 70 per cent increase in applications over two years in which the number of students starting degrees has topped 1,000 for the first time and carried on growing. Some attribute the subject's rise in popularity to television series, but there has been no firm explanation. Much of the growth has come in joint Honours degrees, pairing the subject with everything from accountancy to linguistics or law. The number of universities in the table has jumped from 20 to 28 this year, and 47 have courses advertised for 2015 on the UCAS website.

There are no subject-specific requirements for most degree courses, although some Russell Group universities favour candidates with biology or another science at AS level. The subject has tended to be the preserve of old universities, but there are nine post-1992 institutions in the latest table. Cambridge maintains its accustomed leadership, with Oxford still in second place. The London School of Economics, which ties with St Andrews for third, had the top research score in the 2008 Research Assessment Exercise, when 40 per cent of its work was judged to be world-leading. Brunel, in ninth place, again boasts much the most satisfied students, with an impressive 96 per cent score on this measure. Roehampton is the only post-1992 university in the top half of the table.

Employment prospects will be the main concern of those considering a degree in anthropology. Success rates fluctuated while smaller numbers were taking the subject, but it has been close to the bottom ten for the proportion of graduates going into "professional" jobs or further study in last two years. This is reflected in the table, with 12 of the 28 universities reporting positive destinations for less than half of their graduates. Cambridge has the best score, but it is still below 80 per cent. Nationally, more than a third of graduates started out in "non-professional" jobs, although the picture was brighter in salary terms. Anthropology remains in the top 50 of the 66 subject groups for those who do secure graduate-level jobs.

Anthropology	Research quality %	Entry standards	Student satisfaction %	Graduate prospects %	Overall rating
1 Cambridge	45.3	536	82.6	78.7	100.0
2 Oxford	35.0	542	84.6	72.7	96.0
=3 London School of Economics	48.3	454	80.5	68.3	94.1
=3 St Andrews	35.0	506	85.0	70.2	94.1
5 University College London	40.0	479	79.7	70.5	92.2
6 SOAS, London	43.3	458	83.7	50.0	89.7
7 Durham	31.7	463	81.3	67.4	88.6
8 Sussex	35.0	412	85.9	59.0	87.9

	Research quality %	Entry standards	Student satisfaction %	Graduate prospects %	Overall rating
9 Brunel	30.0	323	96.1	52.5	86.0
10 Manchester	30.0	389	83.2	62.3	84.6
11 Aberdeen	38.3	384	80.5	46.8	82.4
12 Kent	27.1	364	80.0	63.8	81.2
13 Roehampton	36.7	286	87.8	46.0	81.1
=14 Edinburgh	36.7	484	58.1	66.1	79.2
=14 Leeds		437	85.1	73.8	79.2
16 Goldsmiths, London	35.0	352	80.2	44.0	79.0
17 Liverpool John Moores	21.7	346	85.3	52.7	78.5
18 Queen's, Belfast	41.7	330	79.2	36.8	78.3
19 Chester		307	90.8	64.6	74.3
20 Oxford Brookes	15.0	358	82.5	48.8	74.1
21 Glasgow	20.0		85.9	35.0	73.4
22 Bournemouth	18.3	335	82.4		73.2
23 Stirling		394	79.6	40.5	66.6
24 East London	20.0	242	74.5	41.9	65.4
25 Southampton Solent		315	80.1	31.2	61.4
26 Aberystwyth		314	76.0	32.2	59.5
27 Birmingham City		310	70.8	40.5	58.6
28 Sheffield Hallam		303	74.1	34.0	58.5

Employed in professional job:	34%	Employed in non-professional job and studying:	3%
Employed in professional job and studying:	2%	Employed in non-professional job:	32%
Studying:	15%	Unemployed:	14%
Average starting professional salary:	£19,637	Average starting non-professional salary:	£14,780

Archaeology

Archaeology remains a niche subject with only around 500 students starting degrees each year, but 57 universities and colleges still plan to run degree courses in 2015. Most of them are in the new table, which has five more universities than last year. Applications have stabilised since the decline that followed the introduction of £9,000 fees. Many of those attracted onto courses are mature students – often retired – who are studying the subject out of interest and not for career progression. Archaeology is in the bottom ten for employment prospects, although those who find graduate jobs fared a little better in the latest table.

Durham has taken over from Oxford at the top of the table. It shared the best results in the last Research Assessment Exercise with eighth-placed Reading and performed strongly on the other indicators. Oxford has the highest entry standards, while York, in fifth place, again recorded the best of a high set of scores in the National Student Survey, satisfying almost 95 per cent of final-year undergraduates. In another repeat of last year's table, Robert Gordon (RGU) registered by far the best employment score, a full 10 percentage points ahead of any other institution. Still the only post-1992 university in the top 20, RGU saw almost 90 per cent of its graduates go straight into professional jobs or further study, compared with less than 50 per cent at 14 universities.

Archaeology produces consistently high levels of satisfaction. Only two universities in the ranking failed to satisfy at least 70 per cent of their students in the results published in 2014. The increase in the number of universities offering the subject has had the effect of spreading out entry scores, which now range from less than 200 points to almost 550. There are no specific subject requirements for a degree in archaeology, although geography, history and science subjects are all considered relevant. One student in five stays on for a postgraduate qualification, either full or part-time.

Employed in professional job:	30%	Employed in non-professional job and studying:	4%
Employed in professional job and studying:	2%	Employed in non-professional job:	35%
Studying:	15%	Unemployed:	14%
Average starting professional salary:	£18,838	Average starting non-professional salary:	£14,646

Archaeology	Research quality %	Entry standards	Student satisfaction %	Graduate prospects %	Overall rating
1 Durham	48.3	473	89.6	74.5	100.0
2 Oxford	45.0	546	83.8	72.0	98.6
3 Cambridge	40.0	536	82.6	78.7	97.9
4 University College London	40.0	503	91.8	59.8	96.3
5 York	36.7	387	94.7	75.9	96.0
6 Exeter	31.7	421	85.1	78.0	91.7
7 Glasgow	23.3	426	91.1	69.2	90.4
8 Reading	48.3	346	88.2	60.2	90.0
9 Leicester	38.3	372	87.4	60.2	87.9
10 Queen's, Belfast	35.0	326	89.8	64.1	87.3
11 Liverpool	38.3	381	86.7	52.1	85.8
12 Sheffield	36.7	370		58.5	85.7
13 Newcastle	26.7	352	93.7	53.4	85.3
14 Southampton	36.7	371	85.6	50.0	83.8
15 Birmingham	23.3	410	81.9	62.5	83.2
16 Manchester	30.0	321	92.3	48.7	82.9
17 Edinburgh	33.2	483	69.3	60.0	81.9
18 Robert Gordon		383	79.7	89.4	81.4
19 Aberdeen	23.3	410	82.7	53.7	81.3
20 Nottingham	33.3	365	78.9	56.9	81.0
21 Keele		389	90.4	63.7	80.4
22 Cardiff	28.3	354	80.6	57.6	80.2
23 Dundee		456	85.6	52.2	77.8
24 Coventry		315	87.9	66.8	76.7
=25 Bradford	30.0	282	79.0	56.3	76.3
=25 Bristol	26.7	373	68.4	65.5	76.3
27 Abertay		364	81.8	68.4	76.1
28 West of England		402	80.8	58.2	74.6

	Research quality %	Entry standards	Student satisfaction %	Graduate prospects %	Overall rating
29 Bournemouth	18.3	320	84.4	43.6	74.2
30 Derby		278	92.3	52.6	73.7
31 Kent	6.7	310	79.4	64.4	73.4
32 Nottingham Trent	13.3	332	79.2	53.2	73.1
33 De Montfort		282	88.2	57.3	72.9
34 Central Lancashire	10.0	325	85.7	43.0	72.6
35 Lincoln		327	78.2	64.6	71.7
36 Glasgow Caledonian		348	77.3	62.8	71.6
37 Liverpool John Moores		318	80.5	60.5	71.4
38 Swansea		316	79.9	57.7	70.2
39 Chester		286	82.3	57.4	70.1
40 Canterbury Christ Church		272	88.4	47.4	70.0
41 Winchester	6.7	286	82.8	44.9	68.9
42 Hull		315	84.5	43.4	68.8
=43 Huddersfield		279	77.6	61.4	68.4
=43 West of Scotland		296	80.3	53.3	68.4
45 Staffordshire		299	84.2	44.5	68.3
46 Teesside		339	79.0	39.0	65.9
47 Birmingham City		332	77.7	38.5	64.8
48 Greenwich		325	75.2	42.3	64.1
49 South Wales		343	73.1	39.9	63.2
50 Anglia Ruskin		182	85.2	40.4	62.6
51 West London		212	74.7	51.5	61.4
52 Worcester		278	74.1	37.5	60.3
53 London South Bank		226	70.1	21.7	51.8

Architecture

Architecture seems not to have recovered from the recession in the minds of degree applicants. The demand for places fell in 2013 and appears to have dropped again in 2014, with enrolments moving in the same direction. Yet employment prospects are good: architecture is 14th out of the 66 subject groups for the proportion of graduates finding high-level work or continuing to study. Two-thirds of those completing courses in 2013 went straight into a professional role and the unemployment rate fell from 16 per cent to 12 per cent. Starting salaries are low – just outside the bottom ten, at £18,500 – but later career prospects are much brighter.

The length of courses may be one reason that architecture is yet to share in the recovery taking place in other subjects. Qualification usually takes seven years, in which the first degree is but a step on the way. With fees of £9,000 a year, that is a considerable commitment, especially when course materials can add another £1,000 to the burden. Nevertheless, there were still six applications per place in 2013 and satisfaction rates are higher after graduation than during the course itself. Three years into their careers, architects are among the least likely of all graduates to say that they wished they had taken a different degree or chosen a different profession.

Bath has regained top place in the table, having lost it last year to Cambridge, which has now slipped to fourth. Student satisfaction is the main cause: Bath registered its usual high rate while Cambridge dropped by more than 10 percentage points. For the first time, Bath also has the highest entry standards in the subject. Coventry had the most satisfied students, but still does not make the top 20, partly because it did not enter the 2008 Research Assessment Exercise in architecture. The best employment score is at Edinburgh, in third place, behind Sheffield overall.

Some universities ask for art at A level, while others look for a mix of art and science subjects. Candidates may be asked to produce a portfolio of work if they have not taken an art or design-based A level. Entry standards remain relatively high: five universities average more than 500 points on the UCAS tariff and only one is below 250 points. The table contains one name that may be unfamiliar: Manchester School of Architecture is a joint enterprise between Manchester and Manchester Metropolitan universities.

Employed in professional job:	62%	
Employed in professional job and studying:	4%	
Studying:	9%	
Average starting professional salary:	£18,528	

Employed in non-professional job and studying:	2%	
Employed in non-professional job:	11%	
Unemployed:	12%	
Average starting non-professional salary:	£15,587	

Architecture	Research quality %	Entry standards	Student satisfaction %	Graduate prospects %	Overall rating
1 Bath	40.0	579	90.6	91.1	100.0
2 Sheffield	43.5	510	84.5	87.0	94.3
3 Edinburgh	40.0	527	81.6	92.9	94.1
4 Cambridge	46.7	568	75.3	90.9	93.8
5 Cardiff	35.0	494	82.5	92.1	91.8
6 University College London	48.3	501	77.3	84.1	90.9
7 Newcastle	36.7	436	84.4	86.3	89.4
8 Manchester School of Architecture	24.3	441	90.4	77.3	87.0
9 De Montfort	31.7	314	87.9	87.0	85.3
10 Northumbria	20.0	386	88.3	84.5	84.7
11 Liverpool	45.0	427	73.1	81.8	84.5
=12 Brighton	45.0	352	80.8	71.7	82.8
=12 West of England	18.3	353	87.6	85.3	82.8
14 Nottingham	20.0	487	80.3		82.5
=15 Kent		391	89.6	92.1	82.3
=15 Strathclyde	16.7	435	78.2	90.5	82.3
17 Liverpool John Moores	30.0	350	88.7	67.6	81.7
18 Robert Gordon	16.7	416	80.5	83.3	80.9
19 Dundee	16.7	462	80.7		80.4
20 Edinburgh Napier	15.0	345	91.6	68.4	79.3
21 Plymouth	25.0	376	84.3	66.9	79.1
=22 Coventry		311	92.8	81.0	77.9

Architecture cont

	Research quality %	Entry standards	Student satisfaction %	Graduate prospects %	Overall rating
=22 Oxford Brookes		430	88.0	72.0	77.9
=22 Sheffield Hallam	18.3	359	02.0	74.4	77.9
25 Lincoln	15.0	372	81.2	76.5	77.3
26 Westminster	33.3	362	77.8	63.6	76.7
27 Ulster	31.7	320	86.1	54.2	76.3
28 Queen's, Belfast		394	86.5	73.5	76.2
29 Nottingham Trent	10.0	331	80.7	76.6	74.2
30 Huddersfield		337	84.7	77.6	74.1
31 University for the Creative Arts		327	87.8	72.0	73.8
32 Kingston		360	86.1	69.5	73.6
33 Greenwich	20.0	400	76.9	56.5	72.5
34 Anglia Ruskin		264	89.0	70.8	71.7
35 Cardiff Metropolitan		296	81.6	79.5	71.6
36 Portsmouth	3.3	344	79.9	70.3	71.1
=37 Arts University Bournemouth	3.3	287	82.7	73.3	71.0
=37 Glasgow Caledonian	30.0		80.6	46.2	71.0
39 London Metropolitan	23.3	363	68.3	68.8	70.9
40 University of the Arts London		381	74.2	76.9	70.5
41 Derby		299	86.3	63.8	69.9
42 Leeds Metropolitan		314	80.0	71.9	69.5
43 Central Lancashire	16.7	363	67.8	68.9	68.9
44 Salford	38.3		71.5	47.1	68.2
45 Birmingham City		326	80.1	63.0	67.8
46 Northampton		261		76.0	67.6
47 Bolton	20.0		61.5	80.8	67.0
48 East London		276	86.4	52.6	66.2
49 Middlesex		288	80.6	51.3	63.5
50 Southampton Solent		207	78.1	57.6	60.8
51 London South Bank		267	74.0	53.3	60.0

Art and Design

Demand for places in art and design has yet to return to the boom days before £9,000 fees were introduced, but it is heading in the right direction. Applications and enrolments were both up in 2013, especially in the smaller area of fine art, and the trend appeared to continue in 2014. Only nursing attracts more applications than art and design, despite the fact that the subjects always feature near the bottom of the tables for employment and earnings. This year they are in the bottom ten for the numbers going into graduate-level jobs or further study, and the bottom five for starting salaries. However, artists and designers have always accepted that they are likely to have a period of lowly paid self-employment early in their career while they find a way to pursue their vocation.

Most courses in art and design are at post-1992 institutions – including three more specialist arts universities, created in the last two years – but older foundations monopolise the top ten. Oxford, the oldest of them all, where fine art is taught at the Ruskin School of Drawing, retains top place. Not surprisingly, it has by far the highest entry standards. Only 14 of the 78 universities average more than 400 points, but most artists would argue that entry grades are of less significance than in other subjects. Selection in art and design rests primarily on the quality of candidates' portfolios and many undergraduates enter through a one-year Art Foundation Course.

Glasgow has moved up from fifth place to second, with the best employment prospects. Although not in the top 40, Essex again has the most satisfied students, fractionally ahead of Winchester, which is just outside the top 50. Only four universities satisfied fewer than 70 per cent of students in the 2014 National Student Survey. University College London, where students attend the Slade School of Fine Art, shares the best research score with Kent. Falmouth has overtaken the University of the West of England as the leading post-1992 institution, in 12th place.

Employed in professional job:	47%	Employed in non-professional job and studying:	2%
Employed in professional job and studying:	1%	Employed in non-professional job:	32%
Studying:	5%	Unemployed:	13%
Average starting professional salary:	£17,964	Average starting non-professional salary:	£14,366

Art and Design	Research quality %	Entry standards	Student satisfaction %	Graduate prospects %	Overall rating
1 Oxford	41.7	531	87.8	76.9	100.0
2 Glasgow	35.0		87.5	79.3	94.2
3 Lancaster	43.3	432	85.8	69.2	92.0
=4 Newcastle	45.0	467	89.8	51.4	91.1
=4 University College London	46.7	479	88.1	50.9	91.1
6 Loughborough	43.2	430	84.0	62.9	89.3
7 Leeds	36.2	425	86.2	64.2	89.0
8 Goldsmiths, London	37.7	393	87.1	62.2	87.5
9 Reading	45.6	389	76.5	73.7	87.0
10 Edinburgh	23.8	464	83.6	62.4	86.7
11 Brunel	11.7	409	83.0	77.4	85.3
12 Falmouth	13.3	370	87.5	72.7	84.4
13 West of England	26.7	384	85.7	59.2	83.2
14 Dundee	41.7	400	84.6	45.1	82.6
15 Coventry	18.0	376	85.4	64.7	82.3
16 Westminster	38.3	411	81.7	49.1	82.2
17 Brighton	45.0	360	81.2	52.7	81.7
18 Oxford Brookes	20.0	455	80.6	52.5	81.2
19 Kent	46.7	357	74.4	61.1	81.1
20 Nottingham Trent	15.0	356	84.4	65.9	80.6
21 Northumbria	25.0	403	78.0	57.6	79.7
22 Manchester Metropolitan	21.7	442	74.3	57.7	79.3
23 Bournemouth	33.3	326	76.8	64.8	78.8

		Research quality %	Entry standards	Student satisfaction %	Graduate prospects %	Overall rating
24	Kingston	10.0	402	80.0	61.4	78.6
25	Lincoln	8.3	367	82.7	63.0	78.4
=26	Norwich University of the Arts	15.0	343	87.1	56.0	78.3
=26	Southampton	11.7	381	86.1	53.1	78.3
=28	Birmingham City	40.0	356	78.5	48.2	77.9
=28	De Montfort	18.3	352	83.2	56.7	77.9
30	Heriot-Watt	26.7	405	63.1	73.5	77.6
31	University of the Arts London	33.1	370	74.7	54.8	77.3
=32	Arts University Bournemouth	3.3	331	84.8	65.3	76.9
=32	Cardiff Metropolitan	30.0	318	84.2	49.3	76.9
34	Bangor		282	86.5	73.3	76.7
35	South Wales	30.0	325	78.9	54.8	76.3
36	Hertfordshire	26.7	363	80.5	47.2	76.2
37	Abertay		393	79.5	61.9	75.9
38	Bath Spa	10.0	389	78.8	55.4	75.7
39	Essex		307	93.8	50.4	75.0
40	Sheffield Hallam	30.0	322	79.5	48.8	74.7
41	Robert Gordon	18.3	373	70.1	61.5	74.1
42	Chester	1.7	320	79.6	67.3	74.0
43	Plymouth	25.0	337	80.8	44.9	73.9
=44	Cumbria	3.3	319	93.1	42.0	73.6
=44	Derby	11.7	324	85.2	48.4	73.6
46	Middlesex	11.7	320	83.2	52.0	73.5
=47	Staffordshire	3.3	311	88.2	51.0	73.4
=47	University for the Creative Arts	13.3	338	81.7	49.8	73.4
49	Northampton	1.7	318	83.8	57.5	73.2
50	Greenwich		298	84.9	60.0	73.0
=51	Gloucestershire	6.7	349	80.9	51.4	72.7
=51	Winchester		253	93.7	52.6	72.7
53	Huddersfield		359	76.5	61.2	72.6
54	Ulster	28.3	326	79.8	40.8	72.5
55	Central Lancashire	5.0	331	77.8	55.5	71.1
56	Anglia Ruskin	13.3	306	82.5	45.6	71.0
57	Salford	10.0	335	78.2	47.5	70.3
58	Liverpool John Moores	11.7	392	74.2	41.3	70.0
59	Sunderland	16.7	319	83.8	34.7	69.9
60	Teesside		344	77.6	52.5	69.8
61	Chichester		330	86.8	39.3	69.7
62	West London	6.7	256	83.1	52.6	69.2
63	Edinburgh Napier	8.3	391	63.3	58.9	69.0
64	Worcester		302	80.9	50.8	68.7
65	Portsmouth	3.3	326	83.1	40.0	68.6
66	Bolton	0.0	305	77.3	55.0	68.3

67 Canterbury Christ Church		297	81.0	49.6	68.2
=68 Leeds Metropolitan	8.3	296	79.0	44.1	67.3
=68 Southampton Solent	10.0	328	76.5	40.9	67.3
70 Aberystwyth		370	78.6	36.5	67.1
71 Buckinghamshire New	13.3	284	75.5	47.4	67.0
72 East London	20.0	301	73.1	40.3	66.1
73 Glyndŵr	1.7	284	75.1	51.1	65.4
74 London Metropolitan	3.3	306	74.7	42.4	64.3
75 Glasgow Caledonian		388	64.1	45.5	63.7
76 Bedfordshire		237	84.3	38.8	63.5
77 London South Bank		238	81.0	37.8	61.8
78 York St John		318	66.5	46.5	61.5

Biological Sciences

Biology and the various more specialist degrees in the same area have been among the biggest winners in the drift towards the sciences since £9,000 fees were introduced. Applications in 2014 were 16 per cent up on 2010, the last year unaffected either by the prospect or the reality of higher fees, as universities prepared for a third successive increase in enrolments. Admissions officers have had plenty of warning of this trend since the numbers taking biology A level have been rising for several years. The subjects remain well ahead of chemistry and physics in terms of applications, with microbiology offering the stiffest competition, at more than six applications to the place in 2013. Many of the leading universities will demand two sciences at A level, or the equivalent – usually biology and chemistry – for any of the biological sciences.

Cambridge and Oxford (in that order) make it ten years in a row at the head of the table. Indeed, the top four are unchanged for the second successive year. Cambridge's Natural Sciences degree boasts some of the highest entry grades in any subject, averaging 665 points. However, neither of the ancient universities registered the best score in the 2008 Research Assessment Exercise. That distinction was shared by Manchester and Dundee. Gloucestershire again had the most satisfied biologists, but dropped further down the table, to 66th. Like last year, Nottingham Trent is the highest-placed modern university, but it has dropped out of the top 30.

Entry standards are up slightly, but employment scores and graduate salaries are surprisingly modest. Apart from Cambridge, the only university to see 80 per cent of those finishing courses go straight into graduate-level employment or go on to postgraduate study was Robert Gordon, in 58th place. The biological sciences are only just in the top 50 in the employment table and not a great deal higher for graduates' starting salaries, which barely averaged £20,000 in 2013. A third of students stay on for a postgraduate qualification, either full or part-time, but the 14 per cent unemployment rate is well above average for all subjects.

Employed in professional job:	28%	Employed in non-professional job and studying:	3%
Employed in professional job and studying:	2%	Employed in non-professional job:	25%
Studying:	28%	Unemployed:	14%
Average starting professional salary:	£20,008	Average starting non-professional salary:	£14,399

Biological Sciences

	Research quality %	Entry standards	Student satisfaction %	Graduate prospects %	Overall rating
1 Cambridge	33.3	665	87.4	86.7	100.0
2 Oxford	37.4	574	87.0	79.2	96.0
3 York	36.7	457	91.3	72.3	92.6
4 Sheffield	36.7	471	86.8	73.5	90.9
5 Manchester	38.3	456	87.6	69.1	90.2
6 Glasgow	28.3	487	86.7	75.0	89.6
7 Surrey	33.3	438	86.2	76.3	89.4
8 Bath	23.3	463	88.1	75.8	88.4
9 University College London	35.1	512	80.4	73.0	88.2
10 Bristol	29.0	470	85.8	71.5	87.8
11 St Andrews	23.3	511	86.4	70.2	87.7
12 Exeter	23.3	431	90.1	72.0	87.6
13 Lancaster	33.3	427	86.5	68.0	87.1
14 King's College London	35.0	430	85.6	67.0	86.9
15 Imperial College	35.0	541	72.9	79.1	86.6
16 Edinburgh	30.0	492	83.1	67.3	86.2
17 Durham	23.3	524	79.9	75.8	86.0
18 Nottingham	28.3	418	84.8	69.6	85.0
19 Dundee	38.3	476	80.6	60.3	84.8
20 Warwick	23.3	457	83.8	71.0	84.7
21 East Anglia	23.3	436	88.0	63.6	84.5
22 Kent	15.0	392	91.8	67.1	83.8
23 Leicester	21.7	419	86.4	67.5	83.6
24 Birmingham	23.3	431	78.9	79.4	83.3
25 Newcastle	30.0	402	84.0	64.2	83.1
26 Cardiff	28.3	425	83.1	64.7	83.0
27 Leeds	30.0	408	82.4	65.2	82.7
28 Royal Holloway	33.3	389	81.0	66.1	82.4
29 Southampton	23.3	416	81.8	69.4	81.9
30 Sussex	24.4	422	82.0	65.6	81.5
31 Aberdeen	28.3	416	84.1	54.5	80.7
32 Strathclyde	28.3	448	76.9	65.1	80.5
33 Queen's, Belfast	13.3	379	82.8	73.7	79.7
34 Nottingham Trent	30.0	308	82.3	65.7	79.5
35 Aston	26.7	374	83.1	58.4	79.3
36 Keele	5.0	387	87.3	66.6	78.4
37 Heriot-Watt	16.7	415	81.5	62.7	78.2
38 Coventry		274	89.9	78.7	78.0
39 Swansea	6.7	356	85.4	70.2	77.8
40 Essex	16.7	336	85.4	62.1	77.7
41 Reading	15.0	377	84.9	59.2	77.6
42 Huddersfield	8.3	340	83.9	71.8	77.2
43 Abertay	21.7	374	79.7	61.8	77.0

44 Liverpool	20.0	410	79.8	58.6	76.9
45 Oxford Brookes	10.0	357	84.2	64.9	76.6
46 Bath Spa	0.0	284	89.5	72.2	76.4
47 Portsmouth	25.6	319	81.2	57.5	76.0
48 Bradford	16.7	312	81.7	65.3	75.7
49 Brunel	15.0	359	83.1	57.5	75.5
50 Glasgow Caledonian	13.3	392	79.9	60.7	75.2
51 Edinburgh Napier	6.7	364	84.5	60.8	75.1
=52 Queen Mary, London	16.7	406	75.5	63.1	74.8
=52 West of England	27.5	346	79.7	50.7	74.8
54 Edge Hill		263	86.7	73.6	74.6
55 St George's, London	16.7	398	76.1	61.4	74.4
56 Brighton	18.3	305	82.0	57.1	73.9
57 West of Scotland	23.3	298	82.0	52.1	73.8
58 Robert Gordon		353	75.4	80.6	73.1
59 Kingston	11.7	280	84.0	59.0	73.0
60 Bangor	11.7	318	82.7	56.7	72.9
=61 Hertfordshire	15.0	318	77.1	64.6	72.8
=61 Plymouth	14.7	343	85.0	45.1	72.8
63 Sheffield Hallam	8.3	340	81.7	57.2	72.4
64 Manchester Metropolitan	15.0	333	80.4	53.4	72.2
65 Cardiff Metropolitan	8.3	225	85.5	62.2	72.0
=66 Gloucestershire		284	96.2	40.0	71.9
=66 Hull	8.3	344	83.6	50.9	71.9
68 Stirling	18.7	402	72.1	56.0	71.5
69 Ulster		292	82.5	63.2	70.5
70 East London		282	81.7	64.9	70.2
71 Northampton		247	91.0	49.1	70.1
72 Northumbria	13.3	350	72.4	61.1	69.9
73 Canterbury Christ Church		247	81.8	66.4	69.6
74 Bedfordshire	8.3	234	83.9		69.2
75 Liverpool John Moores	13.6	328	80.6	40.5	68.5
76 Central Lancashire		341	81.2	51.5	68.4
=77 Bolton		257	76.2	71.6	68.1
=77 Staffordshire		255	81.1	61.3	68.1
79 Roehampton	1.7	276	79.5	59.0	67.8
80 Middlesex		264	82.1	56.3	67.7
=81 Derby	5.0	307	81.9	45.9	67.6
=81 St Mary's, Twickenham	3.3	301	81.1	50.0	67.6
83 Anglia Ruskin		250	86.1	48.3	67.3
84 South Wales	3.3	358	75.2	51.7	66.6
85 Teesside		347	74.2	55.0	65.7
=86 Greenwich		370	76.5	45.4	65.3
=86 Leeds Metropolitan		244	78.7	56.8	65.3
=88 Chester	5.0	289	78.6	45.9	65.2
=88 Salford	15.0	307	74.0	42.8	65.2
90 Westminster		286	79.2	45.0	63.9

Biological Sciences cont	Research quality %	Entry standards	Student satisfaction %	Graduate prospects %	Overall rating
91 Aberystwyth		333	73.1	49.3	63.2
92 Bournemouth		312	70.7	38.9	62.9
93 Sunderland		247	76.4	48.3	62.0
94 Worcester		286	69.2	57.7	61.8
95 London South Bank	11.7	206	68.6	54.8	61.1
96 London Metropolitan	1.7	262	74.8	27.6	56.8

Building

Building is just outside the top ten subjects for employment prospects and in the top 20 for starting salaries in graduate-level jobs, averaging nearly £22,500 in 2013. Only nine of the 66 subject groupings had a lower unemployment rate and three-quarters of those finishing degrees went straight into graduate-level jobs. This encouraging message is yet to filter through to sixth-forms and colleges, however. The numbers of applications and enrolments for building have almost halved since the recession began in 2008, with another drop on the way in 2014. Applicants and careers advisers can be forgiven for not realising the scale of the improvement in the labour market: only two years ago, building was 40th and starting salaries still have not regained their 2008 level. But, at fewer than four applications to the place and entry qualifications among the lowest in the *Guide*, the subject is surely a good bet once more.

University College London (UCL) has overtaken Loughborough to top this year's table. UCL, whose Project Management for Construction degree is the only one in the table to register average entry grades of more than 400 points, also has the best scores for research and graduate prospects. There is less variation in entry grades than in most subjects: two-thirds of the universities average between 300 and 400 points. Satisfaction rates are similarly bunched. While Edinburgh Napier was again well clear of the rest in the National Student Survey – Coventry was the only other university to top 90 per cent satisfaction – only four universities slipped below 70 per cent on this measure.

The building table is dominated by post-1992 universities, although older foundations take the top three places. Glasgow Caledonian is the highest-placed, in fourth, with Plymouth, South Wales and Robert Gordon also making the top ten. Of the 75 institutions planning to offer courses in this area in 2015, however, a significant proportion are colleges, many of them focusing on part-time degrees and Higher National Diplomas. Courses in this category include surveying and building services engineering, as well as construction.

Employed in professional job:	72%	Employed in non-professional job and studying:	0%
Employed in professional job and studying:	3%	Employed in non-professional job:	11%
Studying:	3%	Unemployed:	10%
Average starting professional salary:	£22,479	Average starting non-professional salary:	£15,948

Building	Research quality %	Entry standards	Student satisfaction %	Graduate prospects %	Overall rating
1 University College London	48.3	404	89.3	95.2	100.0
2 Loughborough	41.7	367	84.5	95.1	94.1
3 Reading	40.0	352	82.2	93.3	91.4
4 Glasgow Caledonian	30.0	375	82.3	82.5	86.6
5 Heriot-Watt	26.7	388	80.9	84.4	86.5
6 Plymouth	25.0	324	87.0	82.7	84.1
7 Nottingham	20.0	369	77.5	88.4	83.4
8 South Wales	23.3	325	84.1	81.4	82.2
9 Robert Gordon	16.7	326	80.2	89.5	81.3
10 Ulster	31.7	314	83.5	72.3	80.9
11 Westminster	33.3	328	78.8	73.0	80.6
12 Sheffield Hallam	18.3	301	86.2	80.7	79.9
13 Northumbria	20.0	345	76.7	81.9	79.7
14 Edinburgh Napier	15.0	328	94.7	65.3	79.1
15 Salford	38.3	328	71.5	70.1	78.3
16 Nottingham Trent	10.0	288	82.6	88.7	77.9
17 Aston	18.3	319	72.9	87.0	77.8
18 Liverpool John Moores	30.0	299	80.9	69.4	77.6
19 Anglia Ruskin		325	89.3	77.9	76.5
20 West of England	18.3	311	74.7	80.3	76.0
21 Oxford Brookes		352	79.5	80.6	75.1
22 Coventry		308	90.4	72.1	74.1
23 Brighton	13.3	277	79.1	75.2	72.7
24 Central Lancashire	16.7	324	82.6	54.4	71.4
25 Greenwich	20.0	240	76.7	72.5	70.7
26 Portsmouth		280	77.1	81.4	70.3
27 Kingston		267	76.6	79.6	68.8
28 Bolton	20.0		64.6	71.4	67.0
29 Leeds Metropolitan		256	68.7	72.6	63.0
30 Birmingham City		289	63.7	70.5	62.4
31 London South Bank		221	76.2	64.7	61.4
32 Southampton Solent		172	64.2	72.0	56.3

Business Studies

The various branches of business and management are among the most popular subjects in higher education. Even without the many dual or combined Honours degrees that are common for both of the main areas, there were more than 130,000 applications in 2013. Numbers are still down on the years before £9,000 fees were introduced, but early figures for 2014 suggest that the recovery is continuing.

Management is the more competitive field, attracting nearly six applications for every place in 2013, one more than for business studies. The subjects are the biggest recruiters in

Business Studies cont

many of the new universities, but some of the most famous business schools are absent from this ranking because they do not offer undergraduate courses. Manchester Business School provides Manchester's undergraduate courses.

Cambridge has taken first place back from Oxford, having lost it only last year. Neither Oxford's Said Business School nor Cambridge's Judge School of Management qualify for the table, being exclusively postgraduate institutions, so both universities are assessed on courses offered by other faculties. Cambridge does not publish separate entry scores for business and its undergraduates in this field did not respond to the National Student Survey in sufficient numbers for a satisfaction rate to be compiled, so its rise is due entirely to an improved score for graduate prospects. It already led on research. Imperial College actually produced the best grades in the 2008 Research Assessment Exercise, but does not have enough undergraduates in this area to qualify for the table.

Oxford has by far the highest entry standards in the table and Loughborough, in fifth place, has the most satisfied students. Although it is the only university to win the approval of 90 per cent of final-year undergraduates, satisfaction levels are generally high. Only three of the 116 universities dropped below 70 per cent in the 2014 National Student Survey. More than half of the institutions in one of our biggest tables are modern universities, but only five appear in the top 50. Robert Gordon is the highest-placed, at 42nd. Business and management filled twice as many places in Clearing as any other subject in 2013.

Employment scores are extremely variable, ranging from 96 per cent at Durham to less than 32 per cent at bottom-placed Bolton. Overall, business and management fare less well than might be expected in the employment table, dropping to 49th this year. Those who secure graduate-level jobs do better in comparison with those from other subjects, however. The average starting salary of £22,144 is just outside the top 20, and the £16,565 average for non-professional jobs is nearly in the top ten for graduates who find themselves in that position.

Employed in professional job:	49%	Employed in non-professional job and studying:	1%
Employed in professional job and studying:	3%	Employed in non-professional job:	28%
Studying:	6%	Unemployed:	13%
Average starting professional salary:	£22,144	Average starting non-professional salary:	£16,565

Business Studies		Research quality %	Entry standards	Student satisfaction %	Graduate prospects %	Overall rating
1	Cambridge	48.3			88.1	100.0
2	Oxford	43.3	581	84.6	83.7	98.1
3	Bath	43.3	466	88.1	91.2	97.6
4	Warwick	41.7	519	84.1	86.8	95.9
5	Loughborough	30.0	414	91.0	89.5	94.2
6	St Andrews	26.7	539	84.5	81.8	92.4
=7	Cardiff	46.7	397	87.0	74.6	92.3
=7	King's College London	43.3	490	82.6	76.0	92.3
=7	Lancaster	41.7	445	83.4	83.9	92.3
10	London School of Economics	43.3	500	78.3	83.5	91.4
11	Strathclyde	38.3	509	85.2	62.5	90.9

12	Exeter	30.0	448	85.5	81.3	90.5
13	Leeds	36.7	438	83.6	77.7	89.8
14	Nottingham	36.7	418	82.5	76.0	88.2
15	Surrey	23.3	403	87.2	77.9	87.8
16	Durham	28.3	439	75.3	96.2	86.3
17	Birmingham	31.7	415	76.8	90.4	86.1
18	Aston	30.0	385	82.8	75.2	85.5
19	Newcastle	23.3	418	81.0	81.7	85.2
20	Kent	25.0	370	84.0	76.7	84.8
=21	East Anglia	21.7	383	85.6	72.0	84.6
=21	Heriot-Watt	21.7	407	85.2	68.4	84.6
23	Manchester	38.3	422	77.4	69.8	84.4
=24	City	28.3	462	76.5	70.1	83.0
=24	SOAS, London	16.7	396	85.5	67.6	83.0
26	Sussex	30.0	392	78.4	74.6	82.9
=27	Aberdeen	20.0	423	80.7	72.7	82.8
=27	University College London		492	81.6	82.0	82.8
29	Bristol	10.0	456	82.9		82.2
30	York	23.3	409	79.0	71.2	81.7
31	Edinburgh	23.3	458	74.8	74.6	81.5
=32	Reading	23.3	396	79.0	69.4	80.9
=32	Royal Holloway	28.3	390	80.0	61.2	80.9
34	Keele	21.7	363	81.1	70.0	80.8
35	Glasgow	25.0	449	74.9	69.6	80.7
36	Liverpool	23.3	392	79.5	66.0	80.5
37	Sheffield	30.0	389	72.3	78.8	79.8
38	Southampton	28.3	411	69.9	83.7	79.6
39	Stirling	20.0	395	79.0	64.1	79.1
40	Leicester	28.3	368	74.0	74.2	78.9
41	Bradford	25.0	316	81.0	64.7	78.8
=42	Bangor	31.7	315	81.2	55.3	78.7
=42	Robert Gordon	16.7	385	75.4	80.1	78.7
=42	Salford	22.8	322	84.7	53.1	78.7
45	Queen's, Belfast	28.3	376	76.6	62.6	78.6
46	Portsmouth	15.0	319	80.4	75.9	78.3
47	Coventry	6.7	291	85.8	73.0	78.2
48	Nottingham Trent	13.3	332	80.7	72.4	77.9
=49	Brunel	21.7	329	81.7	56.7	77.4
=49	Oxford Brookes	11.7	372	81.5	61.6	77.4
=51	De Montfort	18.3	297	83.9	58.3	77.3
=51	Essex	25.0	315	80.1	59.5	77.3
53	Northumbria	6.7	361	81.0	69.3	77.0
54	Lincoln	6.7	320	81.7	72.5	76.6
55	Sheffield Hallam	11.7	325	84.0	55.5	76.2
56	Dundee		374	84.5	58.8	76.1
57	Hull	18.3	298	82.1	56.7	75.9
58	Central Lancashire	13.3	334	84.2	47.9	75.6

Business Studies cont		Research quality %	Entry standards	Student satisfaction %	Graduate prospects %	Overall rating
=59	Edinburgh Napier	5.0	353	82.9	58.6	75.5
=59	Harper Adams		312		77.8	75.5
61	Northampton	8.3	264	85.6	60.4	75.2
62	Huddersfield	10.0	332	79.6	64.8	75.1
63	Bournemouth	13.3	335	77.6	66.6	75.0
=64	Brighton	28.3	310	75.4	59.2	74.9
=64	Falmouth		273	77.6	94.1	74.9
66	Bath Spa		291	84.9	64.9	74.6
67	Queen Mary, London	28.3	399	72.5	50.0	74.5
=68	Buckingham		320	81.4	69.2	74.3
=68	Chester		295	82.8	69.3	74.3
=68	Swansea	20.0	324	72.8	72.1	74.3
=71	Liverpool John Moores	1.7	316	85.6	53.6	74.2
=71	Manchester Metropolitan	15.0	333	76.2	65.0	74.2
73	Birmingham City	11.7	298	83.6	49.7	73.9
74	Winchester		313	86.4	50.9	73.7
75	Hertfordshire	15.0	352	76.5	56.0	73.4
=76	Glasgow Caledonian	8.3	366	77.2	52.8	72.2
=76	Kingston	21.7	287	79.5	43.4	72.2
=76	Ulster	15.0	297	81.8	42.6	72.2
=76	West of England	10.0	324	74.3	68.6	72.2
80	Plymouth	13.3	288	79.4	52.5	71.9
81	South Wales	8.3	325	81.1	42.0	71.1
=82	Gloucestershire	3.3	264	77.1	71.6	70.9
=82	Leeds Trinity		221	81.0	70.7	70.9
84	Edge Hill		286	85.5	40.4	70.2
85	Worcester		294	79.1	59.5	70.1
86	Westminster	13.3	330	75.8	45.4	69.8
87	Abertay	5.0	291	77.2	57.7	69.7
88	West of Scotland	13.3	282	77.7	46.7	69.5
=89	Queen Margaret, Edinburgh	1.7	324	77.0	53.9	69.2
=89	Staffordshire	15.0	219	80.7	44.8	69.2
91	Chichester		258	81.4	52.5	69.0
92	Greenwich	10.0	307	79.1	37.9	68.9
93	Anglia Ruskin		241	84.1	45.8	68.8
94	Canterbury Christ Church		256	79.9	55.1	68.5
95	London South Bank	10.0	203	83.4	39.9	68.3
=96	Middlesex	13.3	274	78.5	38.4	68.2
=96	Royal Agricultural University		282	74.5	66.3	68.2
98	Buckinghamshire New	6.7	234	80.3	47.6	68.1
99	Southampton Solent		279	78.1	54.2	68.0
100	Teesside	11.7	295	75.0	45.3	67.7
101	Roehampton		259	79.7	48.8	67.3

102	Derby		284	77.6	49.9	67.1
103	St Mary's, Twickenham		253	79.1	50.1	66.9
104	Cumbria		256	81.9	39.7	66.8
105	Leeds Metropolitan	6.7	256	72.7	57.8	66.1
106	Sunderland		279	77.4	45.1	65.9
107	Aberystwyth	13.3	298	67.6	56.6	65.7
=108	University of the Arts London		318	74.4	46.6	65.6
=108	York St John		259	74.4	57.3	65.6
=110	East London		258	78.2	39.7	64.6
=110	Glyndŵr		234	72.5	62.8	64.6
112	West London		230	77.3	44.6	64.0
113	Bedfordshire	5.0	196	79.2	36.9	63.8
114	Cardiff Metropolitan	3.3	295	70.0	43.1	62.3
115	London Metropolitan	5.0	231	69.3	44.7	60.3
116	Bolton	3.3	251	71.8	31.9	59.7

Celtic Studies

Only 135 students started full-time Celtic studies degrees in 2013, making it one of the smallest categories in the *Guide*. But the number of universities in our table is back up to ten this year and 14 plan to run degree courses in 2015, either in Celtic Studies or one of the Celtic languages. Applications had been rising until the switch to higher fees, but there was a drop of more than 20 per cent in 2013 and the wider languages group has seen a further decline this year.

The ranking is split between four universities from Wales, which naturally major in Welsh, and the remaining six, which focus on Irish or Gaelic studies. Ironically, it is the only one from England that tops the table for the third year in a row. Cambridge's average entry grades are nearly 100 points ahead of its nearest rival and it recorded by far the best results in the 2008 Research Assessment Exercise, when almost half of its submission was judged to be world-leading. Second-placed Bangor, which has the most satisfied students, takes over the leadership of the group from Wales. Glasgow has resumed its lead in Scotland on rejoining the table, and Ulster remains ahead of Queen's, Belfast.

The small numbers make for extremely volatile results from year to year, especially for graduate prospects. In the 2013 *Guide*, only 5 per cent of graduates were unemployed, for example. This year the figure is 15 per cent. Yet Celtic Studies remains among the top 40 subjects for positive destinations because 40 per cent of graduates went on to postgraduate courses. Only physics saw a higher proportion. The story is not as positive where graduate salaries are concerned: the £18,326 average in graduate-level jobs was in the bottom ten of the 66 subject groupings. Students seem to enjoy their courses: of those with enough responses in the National Student Survey to compile a score, only Liverpool failed (by a fraction of a point) to satisfy at least 80 per cent of their final-year undergraduates.

Employed in professional job:	24%	Employed in non-professional job and studying:	2%
Employed in professional job and studying:	1%	Employed in non-professional job:	21%
Studying:	37%	Unemployed:	15%
Average starting professional salary:	£18,326	Average starting non-professional salary:	£13,324

Celtic Studies	Research quality %	Entry standards	Student satisfaction %	Graduate prospects %	Overall rating
1 Cambridge	55.0	533	87.9	73.9	100.0
2 Bangor	25.0	411	92.0	90.9	94.9
3 Aberystwyth	38.3	403	87.0	78.3	92.1
4 Cardiff	28.3	441	85.7	85.7	91.5
5 Glasgow	26.7		88.9	74.1	90.7
6 Swansea	35.0	319	87.6	76.9	88.7
7 Ulster	48.3	290	89.0	29.6	85.3
8 Queen's, Belfast	16.7	367	81.7	62.7	81.0
9 Liverpool	26.7		79.4	48.4	77.6
10 Highlands and Islands	8.3	351		33.3	75.2

Chemical Engineering

Only dentists earn more than chemical engineering graduates, according to the latest salary survey. With average starting salaries in professional jobs only just below £30,000, even medicine cannot compete. Indeed, even those in "non-professional" jobs earn more than £20,000 – a higher figure than the average for high-skilled jobs in more than half of the 66 subject groupings. Not that many chemical engineers are in this position: only 1 per cent start out in such jobs, although the 12 per cent unemployment rate is just above the norm. Perhaps not surprisingly, applications jumped by almost a third in 2013, when universities filled an additional 600 places. Chemical engineering is still not as popular as some other branches of the discipline, but it is closing the gap.

Cambridge tops the table for the 13th year in a row and has much the highest entry standards, the best employment record, and shares the top research score with second-placed Imperial College. Both universities had 30 per cent of their work rated as world-leading in the 2008 Research Assessment Exercise. Cambridge and Imperial were both ranked by QS among the top six universities in the world for chemical engineering in 2014. The most satisfied students were at third-placed Bath, while the West of Scotland was the highest-placed of three post-1992 universities in the table.

Although only 22 universities appear in the ranking, 35 are planning to offer chemical engineering in 2015. They include specialist options such as renewable energy engineering at Ulster and oil, gas and energy management at Coventry.

Degree courses normally demand chemistry and maths A levels or their equivalent and often physics as well. Four out of five chemical engineers come with A levels or equivalent qualifications, and average entry grades are the highest for any engineering subject – all but five of the 22 universities in the table average more than 400 points at entry. This helps produce engineering's largest proportion of Firsts and 2:1s. Most courses offer industrial placements in the final year and lead to Chartered Engineer status.

Employed in professional job:	62%	Employed in non-professional job and studying:	1%
Employed in professional job and studying:	1%	Employed in non-professional job:	7%
Studying:	17%	Unemployed:	12%
Average starting professional salary:	£29,582	Average starting non-professional salary:	£20,577

Chemical Engineering	Research quality %	Entry standards	Student satisfaction %	Graduate prospects %	Overall rating
1 Cambridge	48.3	641	91.0	93.3	100.0
2 Imperial College	48.3	627	89.4	86.9	97.2
3 Bath	25.0	469	94.1	90.2	88.6
4 Birmingham	35.0	488	88.7	86.2	88.4
5 Nottingham	41.7	442	83.5	88.2	86.6
6 Leeds	40.0	423	87.4	84.7	86.5
7 Heriot-Watt	31.1	426	89.1	86.8	85.5
8 Manchester	45.0	490	76.0	86.0	85.1
9 Edinburgh	28.3	507	81.0	90.2	84.6
10 Surrey	35.0	435	85.1	82.8	84.0
11 Loughborough	36.7	464	81.8	82.6	83.9
12 Sheffield	28.3	445	87.5	82.0	83.5
13 Newcastle	26.7	448	82.8	90.4	83.0
14 Swansea	36.7	330	84.0	87.8	81.5
15 Strathclyde	16.7	500	79.7	88.0	80.0
16 Queen's, Belfast	18.3	415	87.0	82.5	79.7
17 University College London	35.0	507	75.1	70.5	78.9
18 Aberdeen	31.7	437	69.9	92.1	78.2
19 Aston	18.3	366	78.3	61.5	69.0
20 West of Scotland	16.7	350	80.6	58.3	68.4
21 Teesside	8.3	364	79.6	52.9	64.9
22 London South Bank	23.3	285	73.3	56.3	64.0

Chemistry

Only a few years ago, chemistry was considered an endangered subject, with courses closing even at leading universities. In 2015, however, 95 universities and colleges plan to offer the subject, as student demand continues to rise. The introduction of £9,000 fees did not affect this trend and applications grew by another 10 per cent in 2013, when almost 5,000 students started undergraduate courses. For many, chemistry remains the classic science and forensic science has become an attractive alternative. Some courses demand maths as well as chemistry, and most successful candidates for the leading universities take more than one science at A level. Forensic science covers aspects of biology, physics, mathematics and statistics, as well as chemistry.

Cambridge has maintained its substantial lead at the top of the table with the highest entry standards and the best research grades. Durham's high student satisfaction rate has helped to keep it in second place, ahead of Oxford, but the most satisfied students of all are at Central Lancashire, in 34th. The best employment record is at Bradford, in 19th position overall. There are good employment scores throughout most of the ranking, with only five universities seeing less than 60 per cent of their chemists go into professional jobs or further study. More than a third of 2013 graduates continued on full-time postgraduate courses, helping to keep chemistry in the top 20 for overall graduate employment. It is a little lower

Chemistry cont

in the comparison of starting salaries, but still close to the average for all graduates.

Chemistry is old university territory, with only one post-1992 institution, Nottingham Trent, in the top 30. The number of modern universities in the table has almost doubled this year, however, with Brighton, Central Lancashire and De Montfort all in the top 40. Entry grades are generally high: only four of the 53 universities in the table average less than 300 points on the UCAS tariff and seven average more than 500 points. Nearly nine out of ten undergraduates have A levels or their equivalent.

Employed in professional job:	37%	Employed in non-professional job and studying:	1%
Employed in professional job and studying:	3%	Employed in non-professional job:	13%
Studying:	34%	Unemployed:	12%
Average starting professional salary:	£21,821	Average starting non-professional salary:	£15,180

Chemistry	Research quality %	Entry standards	Student satisfaction %	Graduate prospects %	Overall rating
1 Cambridge	53.3	665	87.4	86.6	100.0
2 Durham	35.0	572	90.0	83.9	93.7
3 Oxford	45.0	618	82.5	82.6	93.1
4 Warwick	35.0	456	91.9	83.6	91.2
5 St Andrews	43.3	503	86.2	81.8	91.1
6 Edinburgh	43.3	508	83.3	84.4	90.4
7 York	35.0	479	90.0	81.7	90.3
8 Imperial College	38.3	550	81.2	85.8	89.9
9 Bristol	41.7	476	88.0	77.3	89.5
10 Nottingham	48.3	454	85.9	76.9	89.2
11 Sheffield	33.3	432	88.9	79.0	87.3
12 Manchester	35.0	429	86.5	80.7	86.9
13 Sussex	23.3	403	88.9	86.6	86.3
14 Strathclyde	30.0	450	87.4	78.2	86.1
15 Bath	23.3	451	84.8	87.4	85.8
16 Birmingham	26.7	425	88.4	80.1	85.6
17 Southampton	26.7	441	87.0	80.5	85.5
18 Queen's, Belfast	18.3	411	90.8	81.7	85.0
19 Bradford	28.3	292	88.3	88.7	84.5
20 Surrey	33.3	425	81.7	82.3	84.4
21 Leeds	36.7	436	82.1	77.3	84.2
22 Heriot-Watt	23.3	434	90.7	72.1	84.1
23 Cardiff	26.7	388	83.8	85.8	83.8
24 Liverpool	36.7	401	81.8	78.7	83.5
25 Loughborough	8.3	364	91.5	86.8	83.1
26 Glasgow	30.0	490	79.7	76.2	82.8
27 University College London	31.7	510	80.7	69.2	82.3
28 East Anglia	21.7	422	89.4	69.5	82.0
29 Nottingham Trent	28.3	301	88.0	73.7	80.4

30 Aberdeen	16.7	459	76.7	86.8	80.3
31 Keele	23.3	355	87.8	71.0	80.0
32 De Montfort	18.3	306	84.9	82.1	79.1
33 Newcastle	18.3	405	79.8	75.9	77.6
34 Central Lancashire	13.3	324	96.3	57.1	77.3
=35 Hull	20.0	333	83.6	72.4	76.8
=35 Leicester	16.7	375	84.3	69.2	76.8
37 Bangor	21.7	309	80.1	79.0	76.6
38 Reading	8.3	351	88.4	69.0	76.2
39 Aston	18.3	357	81.1	65.8	74.1
40 Brighton	18.3	319	79.9	68.7	73.1
41 Plymouth	14.7	314	86.9	55.3	72.0
42 Queen Mary, London	21.0	381	80.3	51.8	71.0
43 Huddersfield	8.3	280	84.5	64.1	70.8
44 Northumbria	13.3	332	80.1	57.0	69.2
45 Teesside		350	77.5	70.0	69.0
46 Manchester Metropolitan	10.0	315	78.0	63.5	68.7
47 Liverpool John Moores		317	76.2	74.4	68.6
48 Sheffield Hallam	8.3	305	76.0	68.2	68.3
49 Kent		309	76.4	71.3	67.6
50 South Wales		321	77.5	64.1	66.5
51 University of the Arts London		290		64.3	66.0
52 Greenwich		325	78.0	58.3	65.3
53 Kingston		263	72.4	71.0	64.2

Civil Engineering

Civil engineering has not shared in the recovery seen in other branches of the discipline in the last two years. It suffered more than the other areas when fees went up to £9,000 a year and both applications and enrolments continued to decline in 2013. Concerns about the state of the construction industry may be to blame, but they are not borne out by the latest employment figures: civil engineering is in the top ten for starting salaries in graduate-level jobs and for overall employment. This is reflected in the institutional table, where a quarter of the 52 universities saw at least nine out of ten leavers go straight into graduate-level jobs or on to postgraduate study. The best rate was at Surrey, just ahead of Cambridge, the perennial leader overall in civil engineering.

There are high student satisfaction rates, too, throughout the table. Greenwich, in 35th place, has the best score on this measure, fractionally ahead of Ulster, which is only four places higher in the table. Only five universities failed to satisfy at least three-quarters of final-year undergraduates. Entry rates are far more variable, however. Cambridge entrants averaged almost 650 points, nearly three times the total of some universities in the table. Fewer than half of all undergraduates are admitted with A levels, reflecting the large numbers of mature students who are upgrading their qualifications. Some of the top degrees in civil engineering are four-year courses leading to an MEng; others are sandwich courses incorporating a period at work. The leading departments will expect physics and maths A levels, or their equivalent.

Civil Engineering cont

The top four in the table are unchanged since the last edition of the *Guide*, with Imperial College narrowing the gap slightly on Cambridge, which had the best grades in the last Research Assessment Exercise. Both universities are ranked in the top ten in the world in this subject by QS. Aberdeen has made the most progress since last year, breaking into the top ten, rising ten places and becoming the leader in Scotland. Almost half of the universities in the table are post-1992 institutions. Nottingham Trent is the highest-placed, at 27th, and is joined in the top 30 by Plymouth and Coventry.

Employed in professional job:	66%	Employed in non-professional job and studying:	1%
Employed in professional job and studying:	2%	Employed in non-professional job:	9%
Studying:	12%	Unemployed:	10%
Average starting professional salary:	£24,524	Average starting non-professional salary:	£18,265

Civil Engineering	Research quality %	Entry standards	Student satisfaction %	Graduate prospects %	Overall rating
1 Cambridge	60.0	647	91.0	97.0	100.0
2 Imperial College	58.3	574	89.2	87.7	94.0
3 Bath	40.0	499	85.7	92.6	87.7
4 Southampton	43.3	497	82.0	95.2	87.5
5 Cardiff	46.7	430	87.7	90.6	87.4
6 Sheffield	41.7	467	86.0	89.3	86.3
7 Surrey	35.0	433	85.5	97.1	85.9
8 Newcastle	43.3	418	85.5	90.6	85.4
9 Swansea	55.0	370	79.4	94.6	84.9
10 Aberdeen	31.7	434	82.9	96.6	84.0
11 Loughborough	31.7	410	87.8	91.3	83.8
12 Dundee	38.3	387	88.1	87.0	83.5
13 Bristol	43.3	514	73.6	91.4	83.2
14 Nottingham	45.0	440	79.6	86.2	82.5
15 Manchester	36.7	432	85.6	83.5	82.3
16 Warwick	36.7	422	82.4	88.1	82.0
17 Heriot-Watt	21.7	415	87.0	91.2	81.5
18 Edinburgh	28.3	463	78.0	93.8	81.2
19 Glasgow	28.3	484	80.3	86.7	80.8
20 Exeter	25.0	435	85.2	86.5	80.7
21 Leeds	25.0	416	88.5	82.9	80.5
22 Liverpool	32.1	400	81.1	85.7	79.1
23 University College London	28.3	535	71.2	87.9	78.7
24 Queen's, Belfast	38.3	392	79.7	79.3	77.7
25 Birmingham	28.3	418	76.3	87.0	77.1
26 Strathclyde	16.7	451	81.3	83.0	76.6
27 Nottingham Trent	10.0	277	91.4	88.1	75.9
28 Plymouth	25.0	305	87.8	77.3	75.3
29 Coventry	6.7	329	91.8	81.0	74.9

30 Salford	38.3	321	81.0	72.4	74.1
31 Ulster		278	92.6	85.3	73.6
32 Bradford	21.7	300	86.9	75.0	73.3
33 South Wales	23.3		82.4	75.9	73.0
34 Brunel		356	91.7	75.8	72.7
35 Greenwich	15.0	293	93.0	63.6	71.0
36 Liverpool John Moores		299	85.2	84.4	70.7
37 Derby		263	82.2	91.7	70.4
=38 Anglia Ruskin		270	85.2	85.7	70.2
=38 Edinburgh Napier	13.3	328	81.1	76.3	70.2
40 West of Scotland		330	87.8	75.0	70.0
41 Glasgow Caledonian		343	82.4	80.8	69.7
42 Teesside		394	83.0	68.0	67.8
43 City	21.7	372	74.3	66.7	67.6
44 Portsmouth		312	79.5	80.4	67.4
45 Bolton	15.0	220	84.5	70.0	67.0
=46 Brighton	13.3	278	76.0	73.0	65.6
=46 Leeds Metropolitan		229	79.4	83.0	65.6
48 Kingston	11.7	302	78.0	66.9	65.0
49 East London		274	86.4	65.3	64.9
50 Abertay		300	62.9	81.3	60.0
51 West of England		303	63.3	79.2	59.7
52 London South Bank	23.3	200	75.9	51.7	59.1

Classics and Ancient History

Competition for places in classics has eased a little over the last two years as applications have declined and the number of places increased. But entry standards remain high: only one of the 22 universities in this year's table averages less than 330 points. Independent schools dominate provision of Latin and Greek at A level, producing some of the highest average grades of any subjects. However, most universities offering classics teach the subject from scratch, as well as to more practised students.

There is never much between Oxford and Cambridge in classics and ancient history, but Cambridge retains top place with the highest scores in the table for research and entry grades. Third-placed Exeter has the top employment score, while Warwick, in fourth, boasts the most satisfied students. Satisfaction rates are universally high: only two universities failed (by a maximum of 1.5 percentage points) to satisfy three-quarters of final-year undergraduates in the latest edition of the National Student Survey. But the subject does not quite live up to its reputation as a magnet for IT companies and management consultants, who value the logic and precision demanded of classicists. Although graduates' average starting salaries in 2013 were in the top half of the table, classics was only just inside the top 40 for the proportion going straight into professional jobs or on to further study.

St Andrews remains the leader in Scotland, while Swansea is the only representative of Wales. Roehampton is the only post-1992 university in the ranking. Several universities teach the subjects as part of a modular degree scheme, but not as a degree in its own right, while most providers now broaden their offering with degrees in classical studies or classical

Classics and Ancient History cont

civilisation that range beyond language. Almost a third of graduates opt for postgraduate courses, but only about the same proportion go straight into graduate jobs.

Employed in professional job:	31%	Employed in non-professional job and studying:	4%
Employed In professional Job and studying:	3%	Employed in non-professional job:	22%
Studying:	25%	Unemployed:	14%
Average starting professional salary:	£21,723	Average starting non-professional salary:	£14,790

Classics and Ancient History	Research quality %	Entry standards	Student satisfaction %	Graduate prospects %	Overall rating
1 Cambridge	53.3	587	91.1	82.7	100.0
2 Oxford	50.0	574	89.7	75.8	96.6
3 Exeter	40.0	464	90.4	83.6	92.4
4 Warwick	38.3	447	92.0	77.4	90.9
5 Durham	38.3	535	87.0	69.5	89.8
6 St Andrews	30.0	492	88.5	78.6	89.1
7 University College London	41.7	531	79.2	71.9	86.7
8 King's College London	41.7	453	85.4	63.7	85.4
9 Birmingham	30.0	412	86.8	66.3	82.7
10 Newcastle	21.7	402	89.6	65.7	81.9
11 Nottingham	25.0	420	84.9	67.3	81.1
12 Manchester	35.0	410	81.4	60.7	79.6
13 Royal Holloway	18.3	406	84.7	67.0	78.9
14 Glasgow	15.0	430	89.8	52.8	78.8
15 Bristol	31.7	448	73.5	73.6	78.7
=16 Leeds	13.3	410	80.5	61.2	74.4
=16 Liverpool	23.3	400	80.6	52.1	74.4
=16 Reading	23.3	355	85.1	48.6	74.4
=16 Swansea	11.7	330	86.1	62.2	74.4
20 Edinburgh	21.7	470	74.0	51.8	73.0
21 Kent	6.7	353	81.6	59.2	71.1
22 Roehampton		287	85.9	26.2	62.5

Communication and Media Studies

A combination of £9,000 fees and poor employment prospects seemed to have brought about the decline long predicted for courses in communication and media studies by critics in the media itself. But a 17 per cent increase in applications for media studies in 2013 more than compensated for the previous year's drop and, while journalism did not share growth on this scale, this year the demand for media subjects as a whole has been back to the level seen before the fees went up.

The division of jobs into professional and non-graduate fields of employment hits communication and media studies harder than most other subjects. Academics in the field argue that it is normal for students completing media courses to take "entry level" work that is not classified as a graduate job. Nevertheless, the subjects are in the bottom five of the employment league, with 15 per cent unemployment, and in the bottom seven for graduate starting salaries.

Communication and media studies are mainly the preserve of the new universities, but older universities have been moving in and now monopolise the top ten. Warwick has retained top place and shared the best research score with Westminster, which is again the leading post-1992 university, despite slipping out of the top ten this year. Student satisfaction has improved: Southampton has the most satisfied students and two other universities topped 90 per cent in the 2014 National Student Survey, while only one dipped below 60 per cent.

Inevitably, the employment scores are lower. Sheffield is well ahead of the field with more than eight out of ten graduates going straight into professional jobs or staying on for a postgraduate course. Of the remaining 88 institutions, only Kent and Loughborough managed positive destinations for three-quarters of its graduates and the rate was half that at a dozen universities. Entry scores remain modest at most universities. Although no institution averages less than 200 points, almost half registered averages below 300 points in 2013. The highest is 474 points at Strathclyde, in equal 21st place.

Employed in professional job:	41%	
Employed in professional job and studying:	1%	
Studying:	5%	
Average starting professional salary:	£18,270	

Employed in non-professional job and studying:	2%	
Employed in non-professional job:	36%	
Unemployed:	15%	
Average starting non-professional salary:	£14,725	

Communication and Media Studies	Research quality %	Entry standards	Student satisfaction %	Graduate prospects %	Overall rating
1 Warwick	70.0	469	86.8	56.9	100.0
2 Exeter	45.2	435	88.0	64.1	95.7
3 Lancaster	43.3		88.6	66.7	94.9
4 Sheffield	21.7	439	84.9	81.7	94.6
5 Cardiff	55.0	403	82.6	63.9	93.3
6 Southampton	38.3	399	94.7	54.0	92.9
7 King's College London	55.0	459	82.5	52.2	92.8
8 Newcastle	23.3	438	92.7	60.0	92.6
9 Loughborough	31.7	379	83.9	75.2	91.1
10 East Anglia	63.3	423	81.0	48.5	90.8
11 Leicester	46.3	376	81.1	63.0	89.0
12 Westminster	70.0	344	78.1	56.4	88.8
13 Royal Holloway	38.3	390	84.6	59.0	88.7
14 Leeds	26.7	397	83.2	68.3	88.6
15 Queen Mary, London	40.0	407	83.3	53.7	87.8
16 Lincoln	33.3	346	84.8	66.3	87.6
17 Goldsmiths, London	56.7	383	75.2	46.0	83.6
18 Kent		425	73.8	80.0	83.3
19 Coventry	23.3	300	89.7	57.0	82.9

Communication and Media Studies cont	Research quality %	Entry standards	Student satisfaction %	Graduate prospects %	Overall rating
20 Nottingham Trent	40.0	326	82.5	52.0	82.6
=21 Liverpool		400	84.7	60.0	82.0
=21 Strathclyde		474	76.2	62.5	82.0
23 Surrey	13.3	388	77.0	66.9	81.9
24 Swansea	18.3	345	84.4	57.6	81.7
25 Stirling	30.0	410	75.4	50.5	81.0
26 Sussex	35.0	382	75.8	50.4	80.7
27 Birmingham City	40.0	317	78.3	54.2	80.6
28 Bournemouth	26.7	363	74.2	61.7	80.3
29 Central Lancashire	21.7	306	80.0	62.9	79.7
30 De Montfort	36.7	291	81.3	52.0	79.5
31 West of England	30.0	333	79.7	47.5	78.2
32 Oxford Brookes		340	85.3	56.7	77.8
33 Robert Gordon		364	79.5	62.1	77.7
34 Keele		350	83.3	56.3	77.2
35 Brunel	18.3	347	83.7	40.6	76.6
36 Portsmouth	17.4	285	84.8	48.7	76.0
37 Northumbria	23.8	348	77.6	44.6	75.7
38 Huddersfield	0.0	303	83.1	58.9	75.4
39 Sheffield Hallam	16.7	296	84.9	42.7	74.8
40 Leeds Metropolitan	28.3	266	77.0	53.7	74.7
41 Roehampton	15.0	264	83.6	48.8	73.8
=42 Bath Spa	13.3	328	80.8	42.9	73.7
=42 Hull	25.0	296	80.6	40.7	73.7
44 Edinburgh Napier		389	77.6	46.0	73.4
=45 City		394	66.3	64.4	73.2
=45 Ulster	31.7	297	79.1	37.0	73.2
=47 Glyndŵr		284	76.5	64.6	72.7
=47 West of Scotland	16.7	322	78.1	42.7	72.7
=49 Chester		266	83.7	54.4	72.5
=49 Glasgow Caledonian	15.0	395	69.4	45.3	72.5
=51 Bangor		288	82.5	52.4	72.4
=51 Teesside		270	83.9	52.9	72.4
=53 Gloucestershire	0.0	291	84.0	48.6	72.2
=53 Sunderland	31.7	304	75.5	38.4	72.2
55 Queen Margaret, Edinburgh	20.0	335	78.7	33.3	71.6
56 Queen's, Belfast		365	82.6	34.9	71.5
=57 Bradford	10.0	286	75.5	54.0	71.3
=57 Chichester		252	90.5	40.9	71.3
59 Brighton	15.0	302	76.4	43.2	70.5
60 Winchester	15.0	312	76.1	40.9	70.2
=61 Liverpool John Moores		324	76.1	49.0	70.1
=61 Middlesex	15.0	278	76.1	46.6	70.1

63 Derby	30.0	274	80.7	28.1	70.0
64 Falmouth		255	79.2	54.4	69.6
=65 Kingston	10.0	296	74.5	47.5	69.5
=65 Southampton Solent		340	74.1	47.6	69.5
=67 Northampton		252	80.0	53.0	69.4
=67 Staffordshire	11.7	263	75.4	50.5	69.4
69 St Mary's, Twickenham		270	78.4	52.2	69.3
70 East London	40.0	249	71.7	38.9	69.2
71 York St John		292	78.6	47.1	69.1
=72 Leeds Trinity		262	80.7	47.3	68.7
=72 Worcester		271	77.9	50.6	68.7
74 St Mark and St John		275	78.0	48.4	68.3
75 Manchester Metropolitan	13.3	330	72.7	37.4	68.1
76 Anglia Ruskin		246	86.7	37.3	68.0
77 Bedfordshire	23.3	209	78.5	40.1	67.5
=78 Canterbury Christ Church		270	74.0	52.3	67.1
=78 London Metropolitan	23.3	239	72.4	43.9	67.1
80 Salford	26.7	351	62.5	37.8	66.9
81 South Wales	16.7	318	71.8	32.7	66.3
82 Greenwich	3.3	284	79.1	34.0	65.9
83 University of the Arts London		278	65.9	58.4	65.1
=84 Aberystwyth		304	73.1	38.2	64.4
=84 University for the Creative Arts		269	67.2	55.0	64.4
86 Edge Hill		291	74.6	33.8	63.2
87 West London	6.7	227	60.0	61.3	61.7
88 London South Bank	23.3	223	72.9	22.1	60.2
89 Cumbria		226	82.3	19.3	59.5
90 Buckinghamshire New		248	57.4	43.0	54.8

Computer Science

Computer science saw the biggest increase in enrolments of any major subject in 2014, having attracted the strongest growth in applications a year earlier. Demand for the subject began to take off in 2010 after years of decline, but did not survive the move to higher fees. Now it seems that the various courses in the computing field are once again seen as a natural route into a rewarding career. Although unemployment is still high, at 15 per cent, the latest survey showed six out of ten graduates going straight into professional roles and the subject was up to 14th in the salary league, averaging £23,700 in graduate-level jobs.

Oxford, which slipped to fourth in last year's table, has supplanted Cambridge in first place this year. It has the highest entry standards and good scores on the all the other measures. Cambridge registered the best grades in the 2008 Research Assessment Exercise, when 45 per cent of the university's research was considered world-leading. But the most satisfied students were at fourth-placed St Andrews, which for the second year in a row also achieved one of the few 100 per cent employment scores in any subject.

Entry standards are spread more widely than in most subjects, average scores on the UCAS tariff ranging from more than 600 points at Oxford and Cambridge to less than 250 at

Computer Science cont

nine of the 100 universities. Some of the leading universities demand maths at A level, or the equivalent, while others want computing or computer science.

More than 100,000 students applied for places in computer science in 2014, however. The most competitive area was the small field of artificial intelligence, where there were only 60 places in 2013, while the strongest growth has been in computer games courses, where applications grew by almost 50 per cent in a year. More than 200 institutions, including a large number of further education colleges, are offering courses at undergraduate level in 2015.

Employed in professional job:	59%	
Employed in professional job and studying:	1%	
Studying:	8%	
Average starting professional salary:	£23,699	

Employed in non-professional job and studying:	1%	
Employed in non-professional job:	16%	
Unemployed:	15%	
Average starting non-professional salary:	£15,890	

Computer Science	Research quality %	Entry standards	Student satisfaction %	Graduate prospects %	Overall rating
1 Oxford	50.0	647	91.2	90.2	100.0
2 Cambridge	60.0	632	83.2	97.4	98.7
3 Imperial College	51.7	574	86.7	95.1	96.5
4 St Andrews	30.0	513	93.4	100.0	94.7
5 Birmingham	45.0	434	92.2	90.7	92.7
6 Southampton	51.7	462	83.0	94.8	90.8
7 Glasgow	46.7	434	88.2	86.5	90.0
8 Durham	35.0	530	84.1	92.7	89.7
9 Manchester	48.3	443	86.8	84.3	89.4
10 Edinburgh	51.7	491	81.8	85.6	89.2
11 Warwick	31.7	507	85.5	92.0	88.9
12 University College London	50.0	518	78.1	90.3	88.6
13 Bath	41.7	480	82.7	88.6	87.8
14 Bristol	43.3	493	76.9	95.3	86.8
15 Swansea	40.0	334	87.8	93.2	86.5
16 Leeds	43.3	422	85.3	79.8	85.9
17 Newcastle	36.7	408	84.4	87.0	85.1
18 Liverpool	45.0	403	80.2	86.7	84.3
19 Loughborough	28.3	373	87.9	87.4	84.2
20 Sheffield	31.7	419	80.7	92.6	83.5
21 Nottingham	46.7	401	77.3	88.0	83.2
22 Lancaster	43.3	419	78.8	83.2	83.0
23 East Anglia	35.0	395	85.3	76.4	82.6
24 Heriot-Watt	30.0	421	85.1	77.2	82.5
25 York	41.7	454	75.5	85.6	82.4
26 Royal Holloway	38.3	366	84.4	77.3	82.0
27 Strathclyde	26.7	434	80.6	87.6	81.9
28 King's College London	30.0	421	81.4	82.2	81.5

29	Kent	31.7	378	79.4	92.4	81.4
30	Surrey	23.3	397	82.0	90.1	81.3
31	Queen's, Belfast	30.0	382	81.1	87.8	81.2
32	Cardiff	36.7	390	78.5	85.7	81.0
33	Essex	31.7	330	85.9	78.8	80.7
34	Aston	18.3	366	85.7	82.0	79.6
35	Dundee	31.7	351	88.0	62.2	79.1
=36	Aberdeen	36.7	397	75.4	82.7	78.9
=36	Leicester	35.0	373	77.4	82.8	78.9
=38	Lincoln	26.7	344	83.6	77.5	78.5
=38	Sussex	36.7	381	74.2	86.6	78.5
40	Plymouth	41.7	318	81.8	70.1	78.3
41	Salford	31.7	367	84.4	61.2	77.4
42	Hull	13.3	326	86.6	78.3	77.0
43	Aberystwyth	40.0	299	78.2	77.7	76.9
=44	Brunel	30.0	347	76.9	77.4	75.6
=44	City	28.3	392	76.3	73.5	75.6
=44	Reading	13.3	349	78.2	90.6	75.6
47	Robert Gordon	18.3	347	80.8	74.7	74.7
48	Goldsmiths, London	33.3	302	82.0	62.2	74.5
49	Nottingham Trent	10.0	299	84.9	77.4	74.3
50	Queen Mary, London	41.7	379	67.2	79.6	74.2
51	Bangor	26.7	267	79.2	78.5	73.8
52	Ulster	25.0	313	79.0	69.4	73.0
=53	Bournemouth	15.0	339	75.3	84.6	72.9
=53	Edinburgh Napier	10.1	332	85.5	63.6	72.9
55	Coventry	13.5	289	83.7	71.3	72.8
56	Edge Hill		289	90.1	67.5	72.7
=57	Liverpool John Moores	20.0	325	81.5	63.1	72.4
=57	West of England	21.7	324	73.9	81.9	72.4
59	De Montfort	22.5	300	77.3	73.8	72.0
60	Abertay		369	80.1	77.0	71.8
61	Central Lancashire		349	81.9	74.9	71.7
62	Oxford Brookes	26.7	427	71.2	62.5	71.4
63	Keele		381	81.7	67.4	71.1
=64	Brighton	28.3	284	74.2	74.0	71.0
=64	Teesside	25.0	362	78.9	51.9	71.0
66	Portsmouth	11.7	309	82.9	62.6	70.8
67	Hertfordshire	25.0	315	76.9	63.7	70.7
68	Northumbria		334	82.3	69.0	70.2
=69	Northampton		286	85.3	66.7	69.8
=69	Sheffield Hallam	11.7	298	80.0	67.1	69.8
71	Stirling	18.3	391	69.8	72.3	69.7
72	Middlesex	18.3	253	82.9	58.6	69.6
73	Huddersfield	11.7	320	77.5	66.9	69.1
74	Bradford	18.3	285	77.9	64.0	69.0
=75	Chester		297	82.7	67.7	68.9

	Research quality %	Entry standards	Student satisfaction %	Graduate prospects %	Overall rating
=75 Staffordshire	10.0	297	80.7	62.3	68.9
77 Sunderland	11.7	330	77.6	63.3	68.8
=78 Derby		324	76.3	76.5	68.1
=78 Glyndŵr	16.7	329	77.7	54.8	68.1
80 South Wales	16.7	321	74.0	65.3	67.9
81 Greenwich	6.7	307	83.7	51.1	67.8
=82 Birmingham City		316	79.6	64.2	67.1
=82 Manchester Metropolitan	15.0	328	73.0	64.6	67.1
84 Anglia Ruskin		242	83.6	62.0	66.5
85 Gloucestershire		262	78.5	70.2	66.0
86 Glasgow Caledonian	5.0	318	75.7	62.2	65.7
87 London South Bank	13.3	205	83.8	45.6	64.8
88 Cardiff Metropolitan		288	74.7	68.3	64.4
89 Worcester		266	76.7	63.1	63.7
90 West of Scotland	10.0	293	75.4	49.2	63.1
91 Southampton Solent		239	76.0	63.9	62.6
=92 Bedfordshire	10.0	218	74.8	55.5	61.6
=92 Leeds Metropolitan		254	73.9	62.1	61.6
=94 Bolton		299	77.7	44.0	61.4
=94 Kingston	15.0	260	69.4	57.4	61.4
96 Canterbury Christ Church		245	69.9	70.1	60.7
97 Westminster	11.7	265	71.7	49.0	60.5
98 West London	5.0	225	75.3	50.0	59.9
99 East London		233	78.5	43.2	59.6
100 London Metropolitan	3.3	205	77.5	44.1	58.9
101 Buckinghamshire New		222	72.7	50.0	57.4

Creative Writing

Creative writing – or imaginative writing, as it is known by UCAS – has been one of the unheralded growth areas of higher education in recent years. No fewer than 88 universities and colleges are offering full-time undergraduate courses in the subject starting in 2015. Less than half that number appear in the first subject table for creative writing to be published in *The Times and Sunday Times Good University Guide* because many of the courses are small and/or part of a joint honours programme. It is paired with subjects as diverse as ceramics, business and biology, but more normally with English. More than 3,000 applications were received in 2013, however – 20 per cent more than in 2008.

Warwick tops the inaugural table, with the highest entry grades and one of the best research scores. Birmingham is only a fraction of a point behind and is the only university to see more than 70 per cent of graduates go straight into professional jobs or onto postgraduate courses in 2013. Employment is, perhaps not surprisingly, the Achilles heel of creative writing when compared with other subjects. It has the highest unemployment rate of any subject – 18 per cent – and is in the bottom two overall, with less than 30 per cent of graduates starting out in professional jobs. Average salaries for those who did find a professional job were the lowest in any subject and the only one below £17,000. Two-thirds of the universities with enough graduates to compile an employment score saw less than half of their graduates go into professional employment or further study.

With fewer than four applications to the place, entry standards are generally low – only five universities averaged more than 400 points on the UCAS tariff. The table is largely composed of post-1992 universities, although the top seven are older foundations. De Montfort is the highest-placed modern university and tied with Nottingham for the best performance in the 2008 Research Assessment Exercise. The best satisfaction rate – an impressively high 97.6 per cent – was at Westminster, the only other modern university to appear in the top ten.

Employed in professional job:	27%	
Employed in professional job and studying:	2%	
Studying:	12%	
Average starting professional salary:	£16,903	

Employed in non-professional job and studying:	3%
Employed in non-professional job:	38%
Unemployed:	18%
Average starting non-professional salary:	£14,276

Creative Writing	Research quality %	Entry standards	Student satisfaction %	Graduate prospects %	Overall rating
1 Warwick	45.0	518	77.2		100.0
2 Birmingham	36.7	418	82.7	78.9	99.6
3 Queen's, Belfast	45.0	390	87.2		97.4
4 Royal Holloway	41.7	442	82.9		97.0
5 Nottingham	46.7	377	81.8	67.3	96.3
6 East Anglia	35.0	467	84.5	53.5	95.1
7 Lancaster	33.3	479	76.1		91.9
8 De Montfort	46.7	292	80.5	58.3	88.2
9 Bangor	25.0	319	83.2	59.4	85.1
10 Westminster	6.7	306	97.6	46.4	82.5
11 Hull	25.0	301	84.1	48.5	81.3
12 Bath Spa	13.3	343	83.7	51.9	81.1
=13 Liverpool John Moores	13.3	330	85.8	46.7	79.8
=13 Winchester	15.0	342	94.0	29.0	79.8
15 Chester	10.0	289	84.2	57.6	79.1
16 Aberystwyth	20.0	343	76.5	48.2	78.2
17 Birmingham City	10.0	277	88.9		76.7
18 Manchester Metropolitan	21.7	311	80.1	38.7	75.8
19 Gloucestershire	15.0	316	83.9	36.1	75.4
20 Northampton	5.0	281	89.1		75.1
21 Brunel	25.0	360	87.9	10.0	74.8
22 Portsmouth		313	80.2	54.3	74.5
23 Bedfordshire	23.3	219	83.9		74.2
24 St Mary's, Twickenham	13.3	297	75.9	49.1	73.7
25 Middlesex	15.0	261	81.7		72.6

Creative Writing cont

	Research quality %	Entry standards	Student satisfaction %	Graduate prospects %	Overall rating
26 Kingston	20.0	280	71.9	47.6	72.2
27 Cumbria	3.3	212	92.5		71.8
28 Bolton	3.3	242	85.0	44.2	71.0
29 Plymouth	16.7	323	70.6	39.1	70.4
30 Chichester	8.3	266	79.6	41.6	70.2
31 Central Lancashire	6.7		80.0	39.0	70.1
32 Bournemouth		339	67.6	54.5	69.6
33 Greenwich	8.3	341	65.7	47.4	69.0
34 South Wales	23.3	300	67.3	36.7	68.6
35 Derby		281	81.8	36.2	68.1
36 Staffordshire		220	82.1	46.5	68.0
37 Edge Hill	6.7	330	75.1	26.9	66.5
38 St Mark and St John	0.0	199	87.5		66.2
39 Southampton Solent		318	70.6	37.5	64.8
40 Sheffield Hallam	13.3	321	62.6	33.8	63.6
41 London South Bank		218	69.8	28.8	56.2

Dentistry

The average starting salaries of graduates in dentistry fell in the latest survey but, as in the last two years, it was the only subject to average more than £30,000. There is no figure for non-graduate jobs because virtually everyone who completes a degree goes on to become a dentist, so the subject is also in the top two for employment. None of the 14 undergraduate dental schools had less than 97 per cent of graduates going into professional jobs or further study. This measure is not used to determine positions so as not to exaggerate the impact of tiny numbers delaying their entry into the profession. Even so, for the third year in a row, there was small drop in applications in 2013.

Most degrees last five years, although several universities offer a six-year option for those without the necessary scientific qualifications. The number of places has been increased in recent years to tackle shortages in the profession, but there are still nearly ten applications to the place – more than in any subject except medicine. Entry standards are correspondingly high: none of the schools averages less than 460 points and the top six are all over 500. Most demand chemistry and biology, and some also demand maths or physics.

Scores in the subject are so close that the ranking changes frequently, but Glasgow has maintained its lead over King's College London at the top. Glasgow leads on student satisfaction, where it again boasts an unusually high score. However, it has been overhauled by Dundee, in fifth place, for the highest entry scores. Manchester recorded the best performance in the 2008 Research Assessment Exercise. Plymouth is the first post-1992 university to enter the ranking in its own right, having previously partnered Exeter in the Peninsula Medical and Dental School. The two universities went their own ways in 2013 and Plymouth alone now offers dentistry. It will be joined in future *Guide*s by Central Lancashire, which opened a purpose-built dental school in 2007, but does not yet have sufficient data to be ranked.

		Employed in non-professional job and studying:	0%
Employed in professional job:	91%		
Employed in professional job and studying:	7%	Employed in non-professional job:	1%
Studying:	0%	Unemployed:	2%
Average starting professional salary:	£30,395	Average starting non-professional salary:	..

Dentistry	Research quality %	Entry standards	Student satisfaction %	Graduate prospects %	Overall rating
1 Glasgow	30.0	531	98.4	99.4	100.0
2 Queen Mary, London	41.7	507	91.0	97.6	97.7
=3 Manchester	45.0	501	86.6	97.5	96.0
=3 Newcastle	30.0	519	91.9	99.2	96.0
5 Dundee	23.3	572	84.8	97.7	95.8
6 King's College London	43.3	505	84.8	98.6	95.2
7 Queen's, Belfast	25.0	484	96.4	100.0	93.6
8 Sheffield	33.3	485	89.8	98.9	93.0
9 Cardiff	31.7	496	84.8	98.0	91.2
10 Bristol	33.3	492	84.4	100.0	91.1
11 Plymouth	11.7		96.7	100.0	90.8
12 Birmingham	26.7	492	86.9	100.0	90.5
13 Liverpool	20.0	461	96.4	99.3	90.1
14 Leeds	33.3	484	82.9	97.4	89.7

Drama, Dance and Cinematics

Drama has become one of the most popular subjects in UK higher education, with cinematics and photography not far behind. The three main subjects in this table attracted more than 90,000 applications between them in 2013, a slight improvement on the previous year but still not on the scale experienced before fees reached £9,000 a year. Universities have been rebalancing their intakes to reflect changes within the group, which have seen drama recover more strongly than the other subjects. In 2013, more places were filled in drama than before the fees went up, but cinematics was still 400 places down on 2010, the last year unaffected by the changes.

There are still more than six applications to the place in drama, although the ratio is now below 5:1 in cinematics and photography. The subjects' popularity has never been reflected in high entry grades. Although 13 of the 93 universities and colleges in the table average more than 400 points at entry, none reaches 500 and 19 universities have averages of less than 300 points. Warwick, which has the highest entry grades, resumes the leadership of the table after a single year's break, taking over from Exeter. Cardiff Metropolitan, at 25th and the top university in Wales, has the most satisfied students. Queen Mary, University of London, had much the best results in the 2008 Research Assessment Exercise and has moved up to second this year. Roehampton's research in dance achieved an even higher score, but it was not sustained over the whole group of subjects in this category. The majority of institutions offering drama, dance or cinematics are post-1992 universities, but only Coventry made the top 20.

Drama, Dance and Cinematics cont

Birmingham, in fifth place, had the best of a generally low set of employment scores. Surrey was the only other institution to see more than 70 per cent of graduates go straight into professional jobs or start a postgraduate course and the proportion was below 50 per cent at more than half of the universities in the ranking. The subjects are in the bottom six for employment, with 40 per cent of graduates starting out in low-level jobs. They are lower still for salaries in professional jobs, with an average of only £17,300 in 2013. As in other performing arts, freelancing and periods of temporary employment are common for new graduates. Standards of performance may be influential in the selection process for dance and drama, but drama courses at leading universities are likely to require English literature A level.

Employed in professional job:	39%	Employed in non-professional job and studying:	2%
Employed in professional job and studying:	2%	Employed in non-professional job:	38%
Studying:	7%	Unemployed:	13%
Average starting professional salary:	£17,308	Average starting non-professional salary:	£14,177

Drama, Dance and Cinematics	Research quality %	Entry standards	Student satisfaction %	Graduate prospects %	Overall rating
1 Warwick	48.3	491	90.9	63.9	100.0
2 Queen Mary, London	63.3	466	91.8	56.1	99.6
3 Exeter	48.3	435	94.0	67.8	98.9
4 Sheffield	38.3	400	89.3	69.8	93.2
5 Birmingham	31.7	411	82.1	79.3	92.1
6 Lancaster	43.3	393	85.3	68.5	91.6
7 Manchester	58.3	395	87.3	54.0	91.4
8 Glasgow	55.0	478	83.4	43.7	91.3
9 Kent	46.7	381	85.7	65.5	90.8
10 Surrey	33.3	365	85.0	77.9	90.4
11 Leeds	36.7	413	88.0	55.5	88.9
12 Royal Holloway	48.3	410	78.7	59.5	88.1
13 Bristol	55.0	444	66.2	65.0	87.7
14 York	55.0	439	71.1	56.5	87.2
15 Essex	25.0	366	93.9	56.5	86.5
16 Sussex		428	94.5	58.8	86.4
17 Edinburgh	50.0	410	75.7	52.9	85.3
18 Reading	38.3	368	86.1	53.8	85.1
19 Coventry	23.3	380	84.4	61.7	84.4
20 Nottingham	31.7	364	87.0	54.6	84.1
21 East Anglia		468	90.5	47.1	83.8
22 Loughborough	23.3	411	76.9	62.5	83.3
23 Central School of Speech and Drama	28.3	360	80.0	61.3	82.0
24 Middlesex	31.7	330	83.8	56.6	81.1
25 Cardiff Metropolitan		302	95.2	65.3	80.5
26 Roehampton	46.0	312	81.5	51.9	80.4

27 De Montfort	30.0	339	83.9	49.8	79.4
28 Lincoln	10.0	334	83.1	64.5	79.0
29 Arts University Bournemouth	3.3	339	79.7	69.2	77.8
30 Royal Conservatoire of Scotland		323	83.3	68.2	77.4
31 Manchester Metropolitan	13.3	379	80.4	49.0	76.8
32 Queen's, Belfast	28.3	368	82.6	37.2	76.7
33 Hull	25.0	333	83.8	43.7	76.2
=34 Aberdeen	31.7		78.6	44.4	75.7
=34 Chichester	13.3	337	85.5	46.8	75.7
=34 Goldsmiths, London	35.0	345	75.2	45.8	75.7
37 Northampton	8.3	292	90.5	49.7	74.9
38 Birmingham City		336	83.3	56.4	74.8
=39 Bath Spa		361	82.1	51.5	74.4
=39 Brighton	45.0	316	75.5	39.9	74.4
41 Chester	13.3	298	83.3	52.9	74.0
42 Nottingham Trent		356	83.0	49.0	73.8
43 Edinburgh Napier		370	78.6	51.6	73.5
44 Brunel	23.3	328	83.3	37.1	73.4
45 Central Lancashire		333	82.7	52.8	73.3
46 Aberystwyth	40.0	322	72.8	42.3	73.2
47 Hertfordshire	8.3	362	76.9	47.2	72.7
48 Winchester	15.0	345	78.5	42.5	72.3
49 West of England		339	79.1	53.2	72.2
50 Gloucestershire		290	85.1	54.3	72.1
51 Falmouth		300	74.1	68.5	72.0
52 Huddersfield		335	78.8	53.2	71.8
53 Northumbria		364	81.7	41.2	71.4
54 East London	15.0	364	73.9	41.5	71.1
55 Norwich University of the Arts		295	80.3	56.4	70.9
=56 Kingston	15.0	329	79.4	39.3	70.7
=56 Westminster		309	84.2	46.8	70.7
58 Liverpool John Moores		356	82.5	38.1	70.4
59 Bangor		277	82.6	54.8	70.3
60 Portsmouth	3.3	330	78.4	46.6	70.1
61 Derby		305	82.7	45.6	69.4
62 Bolton		314	84.9	40.0	69.3
63 Plymouth	20.5	353	75.7	30.4	69.1
64 St Mary's, Twickenham		322	79.3	45.1	68.9
65 Leeds Metropolitan		268	81.0	53.0	68.5
66 West of Scotland		344	81.5	35.5	68.4
67 Sunderland	8.3	289	84.9	36.2	68.3
68 Bedfordshire	23.3	265	80.7	35.2	67.7
69 Ulster		308	89.5	28.1	67.5
70 South Wales	13.3	322	70.2	44.7	67.4
71 Bournemouth		388	61.7	51.8	67.2
72 University of the Arts London		348	67.3	51.3	67.0
73 Sheffield Hallam		327	78.2	38.9	66.9

	Research quality %	Entry standards	Student satisfaction %	Graduate prospects %	Overall rating
74 University for the Creative Arts		318	71.9	50.0	66.8
=75 Canterbury Christ Church		282	84.4	30.4	66.6
=75 Greenwich		342	73.9	41.1	66.6
77 Teesside		299	82.8	33.8	65.7
78 Staffordshire	11.7	265	82.1	34.0	65.6
=79 Cumbria		294	87.9	26.6	65.5
=79 Edge Hill		329	77.3	35.2	65.5
=81 Salford	10.0	392	59.7	39.6	65.1
=81 Southampton Solent		317	76.0	38.2	65.1
83 Anglia Ruskin		294	77.5	38.0	64.3
84 London Metropolitan	8.3		74.8	35.7	63.8
85 York St John	15.0	305	63.9	44.3	63.7
86 Queen Margaret, Edinburgh	0.0	361	61.5	43.2	62.9
87 West London		292	61.2	56.6	62.3
88 Worcester		307	72.0	35.6	61.9
=89 Glyndŵr		265	72.7	43.6	61.8
=89 London South Bank		248	76.8	41.0	61.8
91 Bishop Grosseteste		263	77.7	34.4	61.3
92 Newman		263	82.0	23.1	59.9
93 Buckinghamshire New		274	60.7	37.2	55.3

East and South Asian Studies

Degrees in these subjects attracted fewer than 500 new students in 2013, most taking either Japanese or Chinese. The subjects are afforded extra protection because of their small size and their economic and cultural importance, but the low numbers make for exaggerated swings in the ranking. Cardiff, which was joint top in the last edition of the *Guide*, is not in this year's table because it did not have enough students entering or graduating for reliable scores to be compiled. Although only 11 universities appear in the table, 37 are offering undergraduate courses in Chinese or Chinese studies in 2015, and 23 in Japanese.

Numbers may well grow in future years, with the clamour for more interaction with China and India, but non-European languages have been among the hardest hit by increased fees. Chinese has now overtaken Japanese in terms of enrolments, but fewer than 200 students began degrees in either subject in 2013. There has been modest growth in applications for Chinese, but demand for Japanese has dropped by almost a third since £9,000 fees were introduced and the number of applications per place is down from nine to six. Applications and enrolments in South Asian studies is lower still, with only 40 students beginning degrees in 2013.

Oxford retains top position, which until last year had been the property of Cambridge since the table was first compiled. Oxford has the most satisfied students, but Cambridge – now fourth – has marginally higher entry grades. The School of Oriental and African Studies, in second place, produced the best results in the 2008 Research Assessment Exercise, while the top employment score is at third-placed Edinburgh. Like last year, East and South Asian Studies have the third highest unemployment rate of any subject (16 per cent this year), but they are not in the bottom 20 for overall graduate prospects. Most undergraduates learn their chosen language from scratch, although universities expect to see evidence of potential in other modern language qualifications.

Employed in professional job:	45%	Employed in non-professional job and studying:	1%
Employed in professional job and studying:	2%	Employed in non-professional job:	21%
Studying:	15%	Unemployed:	16%
Average starting professional salary:	£19,258	Average starting non-professional salary:	£16,220

East and South Asian Studies

	Research quality %	Entry standards	Student satisfaction %	Graduate prospects %	Overall rating
1 Oxford	35.0	549	88.0	76.7	100.0
2 SOAS, London	41.7	451	80.2	61.2	90.0
3 Edinburgh	18.3	493	78.2	79.2	88.2
4 Cambridge	26.7	555	70.5	74.6	87.7
5 Nottingham	16.7	390	80.2	78.4	84.8
6 Leeds	18.3	428	80.6	57.0	80.5
7 Sheffield	13.3	399	72.1	64.8	75.7
8 Manchester	18.3	409	69.9	58.3	74.6
9 Westminster	16.7	305	77.0		74.3
10 Oxford Brookes		343	82.5	50.5	70.6
11 Central Lancashire		289	69.6	57.0	63.8

Economics

Economics is in the top five for graduate starting salaries, reflecting the value that employers place on a subject that they see combining the skills of the sciences and the arts. Although it is lower for overall employment rates, the subject is still comfortably in the top 25. Its reputation as a highly marketable degree helped economics to withstand the impact of higher fees better than most subjects. The numbers starting degrees dropped in 2012, recovered in 2013 and look to have improved again this year. Competition for places remains stiff, with approaching seven applications for every degree place.

Many of those considering a degree in economics underestimate the mathematical skills required. Most of the leading universities demand maths at A level or its equivalent as part of offers that are consistently high. Entry standards in this year's table reflect this, with the top six universities all averaging over 550 points – the equivalent of more than four As at A level and another at AS level. Another five have averages over 500 points. There is a wider spread of entry scores this year, however, as seven more universities have joined the table. The bottom six all have averages of less than 250 points.

Top place in economics has changed for the third year in a row. Oxford and Cambridge had swapped places last year, but now Warwick leads for the first time with high scores across the board. Cambridge, which shares second place with Oxford, still has the highest

Economics cont

entry standards and the best employment record, but is well behind Warwick for student satisfaction and research. All three of the leading universities were eclipsed by fourth-placed London School of Economics and also by University College London, in fifth, in the 2008 Research Assessment Exercise (RAE). Like last year, the most satisfied students are at Coventry, which is the leading post-1992 university and would have been higher than 38th place in the table if it had entered the RAE in this category.

Employed in professional job:	50%	Employed in non-professional job and studying:	1%
Employed in professional job and studying:	7%	Employed in non-professional job:	15%
Studying:	13%	Unemployed:	13%
Average starting professional salary:	£26,283	Average starting non-professional salary:	£16,604

Economics	Research quality %	Entry standards	Student satisfaction %	Graduate prospects %	Overall rating
1 Warwick	58.3	566	87.9	87.4	100.0
=2 Cambridge	45.0	637	80.8	95.2	97.3
=2 Oxford	58.3	589	84.6	81.2	97.3
4 London School of Economics	71.7	576	78.5	86.5	97.1
5 University College London	68.3	556	79.5	84.0	95.9
6 Exeter	38.3	481	83.2	86.2	90.6
7 Nottingham	48.3	506	78.8	84.3	90.2
=8 Bath	43.3	504	76.0	92.2	89.4
=8 Surrey	31.7	418	90.5	76.4	89.4
10 Strathclyde	38.3	502	88.4	64.7	89.2
=11 Bristol	48.3	505	78.1	80.0	88.8
=11 Durham	28.3	560	78.8	87.6	88.8
13 East Anglia	31.7	409	90.4	74.7	88.6
14 Lancaster	41.7	451	82.1	80.1	88.3
15 Kent	35.0	393	87.4	77.7	87.8
16 Leeds	36.7	450	82.7	79.6	87.5
17 Queen Mary, London	48.3	407	80.0	80.9	87.1
18 Essex	58.3	349	86.7	63.1	87.0
=19 Edinburgh	40.0	476	77.5	83.3	86.8
=19 Heriot-Watt	21.7	385	92.2	73.5	86.8
21 Sheffield	33.3	435	84.5	75.2	86.4
22 Aberdeen	35.0	439	80.6	79.8	85.7
23 York	37.1	454	77.0	83.0	85.2
=24 Cardiff	46.7	417	76.9	78.3	84.7
=24 Leicester	36.7	379	85.0	70.8	84.7
26 Birmingham	31.7	447	77.1	81.9	83.8
=27 Aston	30.0	391	83.4		83.0
=27 St Andrews	28.3	527	72.9	81.5	83.0
29 Newcastle	23.3	441	82.3	72.3	82.8
30 Southampton	40.0	458	76.1	71.3	82.6

31 Royal Holloway	40.0	402	79.1	68.6	82.0
32 Loughborough	18.3	415	81.9	76.5	81.8
33 Reading	23.3	360	81.0	79.0	81.1
34 City	25.0	420	81.6	65.8	80.5
35 Glasgow	41.7	471	71.4	69.2	80.0
=36 Manchester	43.3	430	71.8	71.3	79.9
=36 Sussex	26.7	396	79.5	70.3	79.9
38 Coventry		299	97.0	60.3	79.8
39 Swansea	30.0	313	76.6	84.5	79.7
40 Salford	13.3	312	87.5		78.8
=41 Bradford	23.1	281	88.4	60.5	78.7
=41 Buckingham		359	82.4	84.2	78.7
43 Queen's, Belfast	28.3	379	81.0	61.0	78.4
44 Liverpool	23.3	395	76.9	72.2	78.1
45 Keele	21.7	358	80.6	66.8	77.6
46 Nottingham Trent	13.3	322	86.1	64.2	77.5
=47 Liverpool John Moores	1.7		86.2	68.2	77.3
=47 Stirling	30.0	368	81.0	56.3	77.3
49 Portsmouth	15.0	313	80.7	74.8	76.9
=50 Brunel	26.7	329	83.2	56.4	76.8
=50 Hull	18.3	302	84.6	63.0	76.8
52 Greenwich	10.0	305	90.4	53.4	76.4
53 Ulster		302	85.9	68.9	75.4
54 SOAS, London	20.0	442	68.8	75.7	75.1
55 Staffordshire	15.0		80.2	61.9	74.1
56 Birmingham City	11.7	263	84.5	61.5	73.9
57 West of England	10.0	331	77.9	69.2	73.6
=58 De Montfort		286	83.6	68.0	73.4
=58 Dundee	18.3	337	77.8	61.0	73.4
60 Central Lancashire	13.3	319	81.9	53.9	72.6
61 Hertfordshire	15.0	333	77.5	60.7	72.3
62 Sheffield Hallam	11.7	317	79.8	59.1	72.2
63 Oxford Brookes		323	81.2	57.3	70.6
64 Plymouth	13.3	260	81.3	51.1	69.8
65 Northampton	8.3	229	85.1	48.3	69.4
66 Aberystwyth	13.3	301	73.6	60.5	68.8
67 Leeds Metropolitan		291	78.5	59.6	68.6
68 Manchester Metropolitan	3.3	306	75.0	62.5	68.3
69 London Metropolitan	11.7	200	82.2	45.2	66.8
70 East London		226	84.5	44.9	66.7
71 Middlesex		230	83.7	38.8	64.9
72 Anglia Ruskin		231	80.3	43.8	64.1
73 Kingston	10.0	248	74.0	48.4	63.9

Education

The education table is generally assumed to be about teacher training, and in terms of applications, it is. But the number of places labelled by UCAS as Academic Studies in Education is actually much higher. That is because entry to the BEd courses that train teachers at undergraduate level is highly competitive, with seven applications to the place. The chances of winning a place on the other education courses, which include early years qualifications, as well as those for youth work and outdoor education, is more than twice as good. That balance may alter as rising rolls in primary schools fuel the demand for teachers. The BEd remains the most common route into primary teaching, whereas alternatives such as the Postgraduate Certificate in Education, Teach First and the Government's new Schools Direct programme have limited the demand for undergraduate training at secondary level.

Education is the only ranking that still contains teaching scores – because teacher training assessments are carried out by Ofsted at English universities. Sixteen universities, including five from outside the top 30 tie for the best scores from the inspections. Cambridge maintains a clear lead in the table with entry standards that are more than 80 points ahead of its nearest challenger and much the best research grades. The Cambridge course is an example of those that do not offer Qualified Teacher Status, but combines the academic study of education with other subjects.

Coventry, in ninth place, has the most satisfied students, but is not the top post-1992 university. That distinction goes to West of Scotland for the third year in a row.

Satisfaction levels are high generally, not only among the final-year undergraduates who complete the National Student Survey, but also in the early stage of careers. Three years after graduation, those with education degrees were among the most satisfied at work and least inclined to wish they had taken a different subject. Employment scores at different universities reflect to some extent the variations in demand for new staff between primary and secondary schools as well as between different parts of the UK. Universities that specialise in primary training are at an advantage at the moment in terms of employment. Glasgow and Aberdeen, both of which have a primary focus at undergraduate level, each topped 97 per cent on this measure, but four universities were below 50 per cent.

Some of the best-known education departments are absent from the table because they offer only postgraduate courses. The University of London's Institute of Education, which is ranked top in the world in this field by QS and achieved the top grades in the 2008 research assessments, is one example; Oxford and King's College London, which ran it close, are others.

Education	Research quality %	Teaching quality/5	Entry standards	Student satisfaction %	Graduate prospects %	Overall rating
1 Cambridge	41.7	4.0	519	85.1	83.9	100.0
2 Durham	31.7	4.0	437	87.6	87.5	96.2
3 Glasgow	16.7		411	89.9	97.7	95.0
4 Stirling	28.3		411	82.6	92.6	92.8
5 Manchester	31.7	4.0	394	91.5	61.8	92.1
6 Dundee	10.0		390	91.3	90.7	91.5
7 West of Scotland	13.3		337	93.4	92.3	91.1

8	East Anglia	26.7	4.0	426	84.9	69.0	90.6
9	Coventry	13.9			94.0	75.0	90.0
10	Strathclyde	13.3		407	85.1	88.0	89.3
11	York	30.0	3.0	399	89.1	76.5	88.6
12	Canterbury Christ Church	18.3	4.0	338	84.9	89.1	88.5
13	Leeds	33.3	3.0	386	90.8	69.1	88.3
14	Brighton	18.3	4.0	332	85.9	85.9	88.2
=15	Edinburgh	25.0		428	72.6	95.2	87.8
=15	Manchester Metropolitan	31.7	4.0	341	81.9	75.7	87.8
17	Birmingham	21.7	4.0	390	79.7	78.5	87.3
18	Birmingham City	11.7	4.0	330	88.2	78.9	86.6
19	Northumbria		4.0	383	87.0	81.3	86.3
20	Aberdeen	11.7		405	76.4	97.2	85.7
21	Keele	31.7	3.5	383	81.6	62.6	85.0
22	Cardiff	35.0		357	81.2	62.7	84.9
=23	Huddersfield	8.3	3.5	327	90.8	79.4	84.7
=23	Sunderland	8.3	3.5	331	88.2	85.5	84.7
25	Brunel	8.3	3.5	334	89.1	81.0	84.5
26	Reading	16.7	3.5	339	85.7	77.3	84.3
27	Winchester	16.7	3.5	334	88.0	71.7	84.2
28	St Mary's, Twickenham	3.3	4.0	310	84.0	89.7	83.9
29	Oxford Brookes	13.3	3.5	410	80.3	72.1	83.4
30	Sheffield	23.3	3.0	377	82.6		83.1
=31	Chichester		4.0	318	84.4	81.4	82.5
=31	Worcester		4.0	330	86.9	71.4	82.5
=33	Sheffield Hallam	11.7	3.3	319	86.1	79.4	82.0
=33	Warwick	33.3	3.8	378	72.4	59.6	82.0
35	Chester	5.0	3.8	309	85.2	77.4	81.9
36	Edge Hill	1.7	4.0	315	82.0	81.2	81.5
37	Bangor	16.7		310	85.3	68.0	81.1
38	Derby		4.0	311	87.0	65.3	80.7
39	Liverpool John Moores	6.7	3.5	353	86.1	62.1	80.6
40	York St John	0.0	3.3	310	86.1	86.0	80.3
41	Glyndŵr	1.7		319	89.5	67.5	80.1
=42	Hull	11.7	3.3	314	85.1	67.5	79.5
=42	Kingston	8.3	3.5	278	86.6	71.3	79.5
44	Bath Spa	5.0	4.0	307	79.6	72.1	79.4
45	Gloucestershire	15.0	3.8	301	79.1	67.7	79.3
46	Plymouth	16.7	3.5	293	82.5	65.0	79.0
47	Hertfordshire	6.7	3.0	349	79.0	84.2	78.5
48	Bishop Grosseteste	3.3	3.5	286	84.3	70.6	77.7
49	West of England	8.3	3.8	332	71.8	76.9	77.4
50	Northampton	8.3	3.0	299	84.9	69.1	76.9
51	Leeds Metropolitan	6.7	3.0	282	83.0	77.5	76.4
52	Leeds Trinity		3.0	305	83.4	77.7	76.2
53	Roehampton	13.3	3.0	312	81.6	62.8	76.0
54	Bolton	5.0			79.1	75.0	75.9

	Research quality %	Teaching quality/5	Entry standards	Student satisfaction %	Graduate prospects %	Overall rating
55 Greenwich	6.7	3.3	323	77.2	67.4	75.3
56 Cumbria	1.7	3.0	312	79.9	70.9	75.1
57 Newman	8.3	3.0	307	80.5	66.9	75.0
58 Bedfordshire		3.0	253	86.1	73.5	74.6
59 Cardiff Metropolitan	0.0		320	85.7	51.8	74.4
60 Goldsmiths, London	16.7	3.0	293	78.5	61.5	74.3
61 Middlesex		3.0	281	77.8	86.8	74.2
62 Nottingham Trent		3.0	322	83.1	60.3	74.0
63 South Wales	6.7		316	81.4	53.7	73.9
64 Aberystwyth			295	81.2	63.5	73.4
65 Portsmouth		3.5	294	78.5	57.3	72.6
66 Anglia Ruskin		3.0	254	81.1	71.2	72.0
67 Ulster	15.0		290	80.8	41.3	71.9
68 St Mark and St John	1.7	2.0	269	83.9	85.3	71.8
69 Central Lancashire	1.7		323	78.7	54.8	71.7
=70 De Montfort			303	79.9	53.3	70.9
=70 East London	11.7	3.0	262	83.2	41.3	70.9
72 London Metropolitan	23.3	3.0	236	74.5	48.3	69.4
73 Teesside			298	78.6	37.0	66.4

Employed in professional job:	56%	Employed in non-professional job and studying:		2%
Employed in professional job and studying:	2%	Employed in non-professional job:		22%
Studying:	12%	Unemployed:		6%
Average starting professional salary:	£21,176	Average starting non-professional salary:		£14,333

Electrical and Electronic Engineering

The demand for places in electrical and electronic engineering has taken longer to recover from the introduction of higher fees than was the case in other branches of the discipline. But there was a small increase in applications and enrolments in 2013 and this seems set to continue this year. Some natural applicants have been diverted into courses such as computer games design and, at fewer than five applications to the place, selection is less competitive than in most other branches of engineering. Nevertheless, only mechanical courses attract more students. The subject is in the top 20 for employment prospects and the top ten for salaries in graduate-level jobs – both positions that have improved since the last edition of the *Guide*.

Surrey has narrowed Cambridge's lead in electrical and electronic engineering this year, but it is still substantial. Cambridge has by far the best research grades and a lead of 90 points (over Imperial College) on entry standards. York, in 14th place, is top for student satisfaction, just ahead of Heriot-Watt and Bath, while Aberdeen registered a rare 100 per cent employment score in 2013. Coventry has become the highest-placed post-1992 institution, just outside the top 30, in a subject where old universities predominate.

Most of the top courses demand maths and physics at A level, or the equivalent, but the table displays a big divide in entry standards. Cambridge, Imperial College and University College London average more than 500 points, but there are five universities with averages of less than 250 points. There are also wide variations in employment rates and the gap between those in professional jobs and lower-level employment is among the widest of any subject, at almost £9,000. Nearly three-quarters of graduates go straight into professional jobs or continue their studies, but the 13 per cent unemployment rate is above the average for all subjects.

Employed in professional job:	58%	Employed in non-professional job and studying:	1%
Employed in professional job and studying:	2%	Employed in non-professional job:	14%
Studying:	12%	Unemployed:	13%
Average starting professional salary:	£24,639	Average starting non-professional salary:	£15,801

Electrical and Electronic Engineering	Research quality %	Entry standards	Student satisfaction %	Graduate prospects %	Overall rating
1 Cambridge	60.0	647	84.8	97.0	100.0
2 Surrey	43.3	488	89.6	93.8	91.3
3 Southampton	38.3	499	88.8	96.1	90.4
4 Imperial College	38.3	557	85.9	90.4	89.9
5 Leeds	46.7	419	88.7	89.0	88.3
6 Glasgow	35.0	480	88.4	89.0	87.1
7 Bath	36.7	447	91.9	84.0	87.0
8 University College London	36.7	527	85.7	82.6	86.7
9 Strathclyde	26.7	493	86.8	91.6	85.1
10 Sheffield	32.7	396	89.9	91.9	84.8
11 Manchester	40.0	433	86.0	81.7	84.2
12 Heriot-Watt	25.0	421	92.0	86.3	83.4
13 Birmingham	26.7	405	88.4	91.8	82.7
14 York	25.0	412	92.2	81.0	82.1
=15 Aberdeen	31.7	458	75.6	100.0	81.6
=15 Loughborough	30.0	365	87.8	89.9	81.6
17 Newcastle	30.0	407	83.0	90.1	80.8
18 Bristol	28.3	435	81.2	88.1	80.1
19 Bangor	43.3	299	88.0	75.0	79.9
20 Exeter	25.0	435	83.1	86.5	79.7
21 Queen's, Belfast	33.3	396	82.4	81.1	79.2
22 Essex	33.3	348	79.4	95.0	78.9
23 Edinburgh	28.3	460	76.1	86.1	78.2
24 Nottingham	28.3	402	80.5	80.2	77.0
25 Liverpool	28.3	381	80.6	82.8	76.8
26 Reading	16.7	368	87.7	82.5	76.4
27 Cardiff	23.3	337	85.5	83.1	76.2
=28 Brunel	20.0	341	83.6	77.8	73.4
=28 City	21.7	375	87.9	59.5	73.4
30 Kent	23.3	251	88.1	76.2	72.9

Electrical and Electronic Engineering	Research quality %	Entry standards	Student satisfaction %	Graduate prospects %	Overall rating
31 Coventry	20.0	308	86.2	74.0	72.7
32 Huddersfield	15.0	327	86.7	73.5	72.1
33 Staffordshire	20.0	285	81.3	85.7	72.0
34 Aston	18.3	338	75.1	90.2	71.4
35 Sheffield Hallam	15.0	298	83.0	79.2	70.5
36 Derby		322	86.0	87.7	70.4
=37 Hull	13.3		86.1	66.7	70.2
=37 Swansea	16.7	327	78.2	81.8	70.2
=37 West of England	25.0	335	70.1	87.7	70.2
40 Robert Gordon	10.0	401	72.3	90.2	70.0
41 Liverpool John Moores	33.3	332	74.3	65.7	69.9
42 South Wales	18.7	333	83.5	63.6	69.8
43 Salford	31.7	321	78.3	58.2	69.4
44 Portsmouth	11.7	299	76.9	90.3	69.0
45 Hertfordshire	26.7	319	81.4	55.3	68.8
46 Sussex	26.7		69.3	81.5	68.6
47 Central Lancashire	10.0	338	81.2	68.9	67.6
48 Northumbria	20.0	360	75.4	62.5	67.0
=49 Queen Mary, London	26.7	374	66.3	69.0	66.5
=49 Ulster		280	80.6	88.9	66.5
51 Brighton	26.7		84.0	33.3	64.7
52 Bolton		293	85.3	59.2	63.1
53 Plymouth	10.0	281	78.9	61.2	62.8
54 London South Bank	23.3	231	82.4	43.2	62.7
55 Glasgow Caledonian	6.7	349	70.5	67.4	61.7
56 Manchester Metropolitan	11.7	322	69.9	66.7	61.6
57 Bradford	3.3	276	77.4	67.5	61.4
58 De Montfort	15.0	296	71.8	60.0	61.2
59 Southampton Solent		233	82.5	63.6	60.6
60 Teesside		323	79.3	52.6	60.0
61 Bedfordshire	10.0	200	84.3	47.1	59.6
62 Kingston	15.0	241	73.2	57.7	59.4
63 Birmingham City		312	72.5	60.1	57.9
64 Greenwich		286	77.4	52.5	57.7
65 Westminster	5.0	299	67.6	56.7	55.8
66 Anglia Ruskin		200	71.8	54.8	52.5

English

Degrees in English are a perennial favourite of university applicants, despite the fact that they never feature among the top 50 subjects for employment prospects or starting salaries in professional jobs. Applications and enrolments dropped slightly in 2013, but English remained among the top six choices for a degree. The table is one of the largest in the *Guide*, with six more universities joining this year, and entry standards are high at the leading institutions. Six of them average more than 500 points on the UCAS tariff.

Oxford's three-year run at the top of the table came to a spectacular end last year, as it dropped to sixth. It is back up to third this year, but still well behind top-placed Cambridge, which has a fractionally better employment score than Durham, in second place. Durham also has the highest entry standards, while Teesside, just outside the top 50, has the most satisfied students. York, in 11th place, produced the best results in the 2008 Research Assessment Exercise, when three-quarters of its work was judged to be world-leading or internationally excellent. The table is dominated by older universities, with only Coventry and De Montfort, of the post-1992 institutions, appearing in the top 40.

Just under 30 per cent of English graduates continue their studies, while almost a third go into graduate-level jobs. Unemployment is only slightly above average for all subjects, but more than a third of all graduates start out in lower-level jobs. Employment rates have improved since the last edition of the *Guide*, but only Cambridge and Durham saw eight out of ten graduates go straight into graduate-level work or further study. English has produced consistently good scores in the National Student Survey, however. In the results published in 2014, only four of the 105 universities in the table failed to satisfy at least three-quarters of the final-year undergraduates.

Employed in professional job:	30%	Employed in non-professional job and studying:	4%
Employed in professional job and studying:	3%	Employed in non-professional job:	30%
Studying:	21%	Unemployed:	12%
Average starting professional salary:	£18,483	Average starting non-professional salary:	£14,554

English	Research quality %	Entry standards	Student satisfaction %	Graduate prospects %	Overall rating
1 Cambridge	48.3	565	87.9	81.6	100.0
2 Durham	40.0	572	87.6	81.5	98.5
3 Oxford	48.3	551	89.5	72.6	98.3
4 Exeter	51.7	479	89.9	68.7	95.8
5 St Andrews	46.7	524	84.5	78.3	95.5
6 University College London	41.7	527	82.1	70.9	91.4
=7 Nottingham	46.7	466	83.2	72.1	91.3
=7 Southampton	38.3	430	89.2	68.9	91.3
9 Leeds	45.0	465	84.7	66.9	90.6
10 Newcastle	40.0	455	85.3	70.5	90.5
11 York	55.0	494	78.1	69.9	90.2
12 Sheffield	38.3	446	87.9	64.8	90.1
13 Royal Holloway	41.7	421	87.0	66.2	89.7
14 Edinburgh	50.0	495	81.3	62.8	89.5
15 Manchester	45.0	439	86.5	61.5	89.4
16 Lancaster	33.3	459	84.0	72.3	89.0
=17 East Anglia	35.0	460	88.0	60.1	88.8
=17 Glasgow	46.7	472	82.7	62.3	88.8

English cont

	Research quality %	Entry standards	Student satisfaction %	Graduate prospects %	Overall rating
19 Birmingham	36.7	419	82.9	75.2	88.4
20 Queen Mary, London	50.0	444	82.4	62.4	88.3
21 Cardiff	43.3	423	84.4	65.1	88.2
=22 Kent	41.7	384	86.4	65.8	88.0
=22 Sussex	31.7	423	88.1	64.2	88.0
24 Warwick	45.0	512	78.1	65.6	87.9
25 Loughborough	23.3	403	88.0	68.3	86.7
26 Leicester	30.0	411	84.5	69.8	86.5
27 Queen's, Belfast	45.0	383	87.4	53.4	86.2
28 Aberdeen	41.7	445	83.5	54.4	85.5
29 Bristol	36.7	485	74.8	72.9	85.2
30 Reading	38.3	371	86.5	55.2	84.4
31 Keele	23.3	398	87.1	61.3	84.3
32 Dundee	21.7	421	90.0	51.9	84.2
33 Liverpool	41.7	417	79.5	59.9	83.5
34 Swansea	26.7	345	81.5	76.2	83.4
35 King's College London	33.3	484	76.4	60.8	82.6
36 Coventry	6.7	288	93.9	61.4	81.5
37 Aston	10.0	353	85.2	69.7	81.2
38 De Montfort	46.7	293	84.5	50.6	81.1
39 Buckingham		325	89.5	69.2	80.7
40 Strathclyde	25.0	446	83.9	43.8	80.1
41 Brunel	25.0	346	86.2	51.7	80.0
42 Edinburgh Napier	10.0	368	89.0	52.9	79.9
43 Bangor	25.0	296	84.0	62.2	79.6
44 Stirling	25.0	377	84.5	48.1	79.2
=45 Roehampton	18.3	288	88.7	55.2	79.1
=45 West of England	13.3	340	88.0	53.7	79.1
47 Portsmouth	25.0	311	85.6	53.2	78.9
48 Lincoln		331	87.5	63.7	78.5
49 Essex	25.0	347	82.4	54.0	78.4
50 Chester	10.0	319	88.0	55.9	78.3
51 Northampton	5.0	281	93.9	49.0	78.0
52 Teesside		289	96.2	46.0	77.9
53 Sunderland	20.0	303	89.0	43.3	77.3
54 Cumbria	3.3	240	95.2	49.0	77.1
55 Surrey		424	79.9	61.7	76.6
56 Bath Spa	13.3	335	85.2	49.5	76.3
57 Oxford Brookes	16.7	353	83.6	47.9	76.2
=58 Hertfordshire	21.7	349	82.0	48.3	76.1
=58 Hull	25.0	332	82.2	47.0	76.1
=58 Northumbria	11.7	358	84.1	49.4	76.1
61 Edge Hill	6.7	327	87.8	48.3	76.0

62	Falmouth		302	90.1	50.6	75.9
63	Goldsmiths, London	31.7	368	75.4	51.9	75.7
64	Southampton Solent		272	91.7	49.6	75.5
=65	Newman		293	83.5	66.3	75.4
=65	Plymouth	16.7	309	83.6	50.7	75.4
67	Liverpool John Moores	13.3	316	87.3	42.2	75.1
68	Aberystwyth	20.0	340	79.9	50.3	74.8
69	Gloucestershire	15.0	301	84.6	47.8	74.7
70	Bishop Grosseteste	0.0	237	86.3	62.9	74.4
=71	Anglia Ruskin	30.0	261	83.9	41.5	74.3
=71	Bolton	3.3	238	88.3	54.7	74.3
73	Manchester Metropolitan	21.7	334	79.4	48.6	74.2
74	Central Lancashire	6.7	353	84.6	44.7	74.1
75	Nottingham Trent	25.0	292	81.9	44.6	74.0
76	York St John	3.3	305	85.5	49.4	73.5
=77	Cardiff Metropolitan		302	85.5	51.9	73.4
=77	Greenwich	8.3	299	87.0	42.0	73.4
79	St Mary's, Twickenham	13.3	288	83.7	46.6	73.2
80	Sheffield Hallam	13.3	328	82.3	44.2	73.1
81	Birmingham City	10.0	298	81.1	53.3	72.9
82	Bournemouth		353	85.9	40.3	72.6
83	Chichester	8.3	297	84.4	44.3	72.4
=84	Huddersfield	10.0	343	75.5	58.0	72.3
=84	Worcester	11.7	296	82.6	46.2	72.3
86	Bedfordshire	23.3	207	90.0	30.6	72.2
87	Winchester		334	79.9	54.5	71.8
88	Westminster	6.7	306	82.1	47.4	71.7
89	Canterbury Christ Church	6.7	270	85.1	43.1	71.3
=90	Kingston	20.0	286	75.4	53.5	71.1
=90	Leeds Trinity	11.7	249	83.3	45.7	71.1
92	Middlesex	15.0	247	80.0	49.8	70.7
93	East London		248	86.8	43.7	70.4
94	South Wales	23.3	308	76.7	41.3	70.3
95	Ulster	15.0	300	83.4	31.2	70.0
96	Glyndŵr		271		51.5	69.7
=97	Bradford	11.7	296	74.6	53.9	69.4
=97	Brighton	15.0	323	76.6	42.2	69.4
99	St Mark and St John	0.0	267	88.3	32.6	69.3
100	Leeds Metropolitan		256	82.7	45.4	68.7
101	Derby		343	83.3	22.5	66.4
102	Salford	18.3	333	68.5	45.0	66.2
103	Staffordshire	11.7	215	77.5	42.7	65.8
104	London Metropolitan		234	77.8	46.4	65.2
105	London South Bank		241	74.0	31.5	59.6

Food Science

Only 550 students started courses classified by UCAS as Food and Beverage Studies in 2013, but this still represented a 14 per cent increase on the previous year and 30 per cent more than enrolled before £9,000 fees were introduced. Degrees range from professional cookery to food manufacturing and nutrition. The subject has dropped 12 places in the employment table this year, but this was due to a decline in the numbers staying on for postgraduate degrees rather than a worsening of employment rates. More than half of those completing courses go straight into professional jobs and the unemployment rate is among the 20 lowest in all subjects.

King's College London remains the clear leader in Food Science, with Surrey now in second place. King's has the highest entry grades, the best employment record and managed the top grades in the 2008 Research Assessment Exercise (RAE), when two-thirds of its submission in nutritional sciences was considered world-leading or internationally excellent. Coventry has the most satisfied students and is one of three post-1992 institutions in the top 10. But the most spectacular progress has been made by Glasgow Caledonian, which jumps from twelfth place to fifth and becomes the leading modern university, even though it did not enter the RAE in this subject. Most of the 35 institutions in the ranking are new universities, although higher entry standards and research grades ensure that their older counterparts fill the top four places.

Entry standards have been rising – none of the universities in this year's ranking averages less than 270 points – but there were still little more than three applications per place in 2013. Almost a third of entrants to food science courses arrive with alternative qualifications to A levels. The subject has dropped into the bottom half of the table for salaries in graduate-level jobs, as the average slipped from just above to just below £21,000 in 2013.

Employed in professional job:	50%	Employed in non-professional job and studying:	2%
Employed in professional job and studying:	3%	Employed in non-professional job:	24%
Studying:	10%	Unemployed:	11%
Average starting professional salary:	£20,965	Average starting non-professional salary:	£15,434

Food Science	Research quality %	Entry standards	Student satisfaction %	Graduate prospects %	Overall rating
1 King's College London	41.7	452	76.3	95.1	100.0
2 Surrey	33.3	415	83.1	88.8	96.0
3 Nottingham	30.0	399	87.3	84.0	94.3
4 Leeds	31.7	408	84.9	80.0	93.6
5 Glasgow Caledonian		437	88.6	76.9	86.7
6 Reading	21.7	348	81.8	87.0	86.5
7 Heriot-Watt	16.7			81.8	86.3
8 Coventry		348	96.9	85.5	85.6
9 Queen's, Belfast	13.3	355	86.0	83.7	85.4
10 Hertfordshire		342	82.2	92.3	80.7
11 Newcastle	18.3	371	67.8	82.1	80.2
12 Ulster	11.7	315	88.5	72.3	80.1
13 Chester	5.0	320	84.0	86.5	80.0

14 Robert Gordon		402	88.3	58.1	79.6
=15 Harper Adams	8.3	321	79.3	87.5	79.4
=15 Queen Margaret, Edinburgh		358	85.8	75.4	79.4
17 Liverpool John Moores	11.7	307	92.1	64.9	79.3
18 Sheffield Hallam		327	91.7	67.7	77.7
19 Leeds Metropolitan		329	85.5	71.2	76.2
20 Brighton	18.3		81.5	52.6	75.4
21 Bath Spa		316	90.0	62.7	75.0
22 Bournemouth		291	90.2	66.7	74.1
23 Northumbria	10.9	326	78.8	60.0	73.8
24 Plymouth	3.3	330	80.1	64.3	73.4
25 Central Lancashire		355	78.5	61.1	72.8
26 Westminster	15.0	312	79.0	53.5	72.7
27 Cardiff Metropolitan	8.3	300	80.9	60.8	72.2
28 Lincoln	6.7		77.0	60.9	70.8
29 Manchester Metropolitan	10.0	315	78.8	49.5	70.3
30 Huddersfield		274	80.8	67.1	69.2
31 Roehampton		289	75.9	66.7	68.2
32 Kingston		313	89.4	33.3	67.6
33 St Mary's, Twickenham		288	78.1	49.8	65.0
34 London Metropolitan	1.7		56.9	79.6	63.7
35 Abertay	3.3	297	60.9	66.7	63.6

French

Languages have suffered a well-publicised decline in recent years – enrolments were dropping before the introduction of £9,000 fees and the process has accelerated since. But the predictions of widespread departmental closures have proved wide of the mark: 73 universities (surprisingly, no colleges) are offering full-time undergraduate courses in or including French for 2015. Only 530 started degrees in French in 2013, but another 2,775 opted for broader modern language courses. French remains the most popular language at degree level, attracting more than 3,000 applications in 2013, but a continuing decline at A level suggests more tough times ahead.

However, entry standards remain relatively high. In spite of the falling numbers, there are almost six applications to the place in 2013, when more than half of the 47 universities in the table averaged more than 400 points. Perhaps not surprisingly, nine out of ten undergraduates enter with A levels or their equivalents, although some universities will teach the language from scratch, especially as part of joint degrees.

Cambridge has overtaken Oxford, the leader for the last five years, thanks mainly to much higher entry grades. Its lead is the smallest possible. Oxford achieved the best grades in the 2008 Research Assessment Exercise, while third-placed Durham has the top score for graduate prospects. Coventry has the most satisfied students – almost 96 per cent of them – despite only just holding down a place in the top 40. Satisfaction ratings are generally high: only Salford, which has since announced the closure of its language courses, failed to satisfy at least three-quarters of final-year undergraduates. Portsmouth has regained the position of leading post-1992 university, but just fails to make the top 30 this year.

French has retained its place among the top 30 subjects for employment, but has dropped

French cont

six places in the comparison of graduate starting salaries. The unemployment rate has stabilised after a big increase last year, but a £250 drop in average salaries has left it outside the top 40 on that measure. No university managed an employment rate of 85 per cent in 2013, but only four universities dropped below 50 per cent.

Employed in professional job:	44%	Employed in non-professional job and studying:	2%
Employed in professional job and studying:	3%	Employed in non-professional job:	20%
Studying:	18%	Unemployed:	12%
Average starting professional salary:	£19,664	Average starting non-professional salary:	£15,912

French	Research quality %	Entry standards	Student satisfaction %	Graduate prospects %	Overall rating
1 Cambridge	31.7	592	91.6	80.7	100.0
2 Oxford	41.7	543	88.5	81.6	99.9
3 Durham	26.7	536	87.0	84.3	94.9
4 Southampton	38.3	433	93.2	71.1	94.7
5 King's College London	38.3	454	88.3	75.8	94.1
6 St Andrews	26.7	519	89.9	72.7	92.8
7 Warwick	35.0	470	87.6	71.5	92.2
8 Exeter	26.7	469	90.6	75.2	92.1
9 Bath	21.7	457	88.5	82.8	90.9
10 Newcastle	26.7	435	89.0	78.4	90.8
11 Sheffield	33.3	417	87.2	72.0	89.7
12 Queen's, Belfast	20.0	405	94.8	72.6	89.2
13 Leeds	28.3	437	86.6	71.1	88.3
14 University College London	25.0	490	82.3	75.9	88.1
15 Nottingham	31.7	434	83.8	70.9	87.6
16 Birmingham	21.7	425	85.3	80.2	87.4
17 Manchester	26.7	438	84.0	69.9	86.1
18 Edinburgh	25.0	488	81.2	64.6	84.6
19 Leicester	8.3	406	89.5	79.3	84.5
20 Kent	26.7	365	86.6	67.9	84.3
21 York		466	84.7	86.6	83.4
=22 Aberdeen	31.7	454	76.5	66.0	83.3
=22 Cardiff	25.0	417	81.9	68.1	83.3
24 Stirling	13.3	393	86.4	74.5	82.8
25 Glasgow	25.0	498	77.5	62.6	82.5
26 Lancaster	15.0	433	80.0	78.3	82.3
27 Liverpool	23.3	381	83.2	67.5	82.0
28 Royal Holloway	25.0	397	85.0	58.4	81.8
=29 Heriot-Watt	16.7	446	79.0	73.6	81.6
=29 Queen Mary, London	25.0	376	88.6	53.3	81.6
31 Portsmouth	25.0	318	83.2	68.6	80.5
32 Bristol	15.0	461	77.6	69.4	79.8

33	Swansea	15.0	334	79.6	79.6	78.8
34	Reading	28.3	343	74.8	70.8	78.6
=35	Aberystwyth	25.0	315	79.8	66.7	78.1
=35	Hull	25.0	313	84.5	57.0	78.1
37	Aston	10.0	376	83.0	62.4	76.2
38	Edinburgh Napier		367	89.3	61.4	75.9
39	Coventry		257	95.9	62.5	75.7
40	Nottingham Trent	10.0	305	86.3	54.9	73.5
=41	Oxford Brookes	15.0	333	84.6	47.9	73.4
=41	Strathclyde		467	77.6	61.4	73.4
43	Bangor		295	87.9	60.2	72.2
44	Ulster	11.7	294	77.7	63.6	71.3
45	Sussex		393	85.4	47.3	71.2
46	Chester		298	75.6	80.3	70.9
47	Manchester Metropolitan	6.7	339	83.6	45.2	69.8
48	Salford	12.5		73.9	59.6	69.0
49	Westminster	8.3	308	84.9	36.8	67.8

General Engineering

Although they still do not attract as many applications as the established specialist branches of engineering, the general courses have enjoyed stronger growth than the others in recent years. The numbers starting courses in the general engineering category rose by 15 per cent when £9,000 fees arrived in 2012, while other parts of the discipline were in decline, and there was further growth of 9 per cent in 2013. One reason for its success may be that general engineering has become a fixture in the top four of the graduate salaries table, with those in professional jobs averaging more than £26,000 a year. The subject has fallen four places in the overall employment table this year, but is still in the top 15.

Cambridge has maintained its lead over Imperial College at the top of the table, with the highest entry standards and the top grades in the 2008 Research Assessment Exercise, when 45 per cent of the university's work was classified as world-leading. A 97 per cent success rate would normally secure the leadership of the employment measure as well, but Lincoln achieved the rare feat of full employment among its 2013 graduates. Lincoln would have been higher than 17th in the table if it had entered the 2008 Research Assessment Exercise. As it is, twelfth-placed Liverpool John Moores has the distinction of being the highest-placed modern university.

The best of a generally high set of scores in the 2014 National Student Survey was at Central Lancashire, just outside the top 20. As in the specialist branches of engineering, there is an enormous spread of entry grades, from almost 650 points at Cambridge to only 159 at Bolton. Like other engineering degrees, most of the general courses at leading universities will require both maths and physics at A level, with further maths, design technology and/or computing welcome additions. But there were fewer than four applications per place in 2013, making admissions the least competitive in the engineering disciplines.

General Engineering cont

Employed in professional job:	63%	Employed in non-professional job and studying:	1%
Employed in professional job and studying:	3%	Employed in non-professional job:	8%
Studying:	12%	Unemployed:	13%
Average starting professional salary:	£26,362	Average starting non-professional salary:	£16,906

General Engineering	Research quality %	Entry Standards	Student satisfaction %	Graduate prospects %	Overall rating
1 Cambridge	60.0	647	83.1	97.0	100.0
2 Imperial College	41.7	578	88.8	76.9	91.5
3 Durham	26.7	569	85.7	87.1	88.4
4 Warwick	36.7	493	77.7	90.0	85.4
5 Oxford	45.0	593	73.7	77.7	85.1
6 Heriot-Watt	25.0	446	87.2		84.8
7 Exeter	25.0	435	85.6	86.5	84.1
8 Cardiff	35.5	415	87.7	70.0	83.2
9 Nottingham	41.7		82.5	72.2	83.1
10 Swansea	36.7	336	76.8	86.7	79.9
11 Liverpool	35.4	434	77.7	75.0	79.7
12 Liverpool John Moores	33.3	354	83.1	69.2	78.4
13 Aberdeen	31.7	412	75.7		77.8
14 Lancaster	23.3	391	80.4		77.5
15 Bournemouth	16.7	305	80.1	91.8	77.0
16 West of England	25.0	341	75.3	85.7	76.0
17 Lincoln		372	78.0	100.0	75.5
18 Queen Mary, London	21.7	395	76.0	75.9	74.5
19 Edinburgh Napier	13.3	339	76.8	83.6	73.3
20 London South Bank	23.3	219	82.6	72.2	72.8
21 Central Lancashire	10.0	310	91.1	56.3	72.3
22 Leicester	25.0	370	64.8	83.2	70.8
23 Glasgow Caledonian	6.7	310	77.2	79.5	70.0
24 Bolton	15.0	159	84.5		69.2
25 City	21.7	329	74.3	53.8	66.4
26 Bradford	17.3	279	73.0		66.3
27 De Montfort	13.3		80.0	54.5	66.0
28 Ulster		295	76.7	68.4	64.9
29 Sheffield Hallam	15.0	283	69.6	68.5	64.7

Geography and Environmental Sciences

Geography and environmental sciences continue to benefit from strong interest in "green" issues among prospective students. Applications and enrolments for geography grew again in 2013. Perhaps surprisingly, it was environmental science that saw a modest decline, while it was human and social (rather than physical) geography that attracted the biggest increases.

The subjects' attractions do not seem to be related to career prospects since geography and environmental science are only just in the top 50 in the employment table. They fare better in the comparison of earnings, with the average starting salary in professional jobs rising by almost £1,000 between 2012 and 2013, but the subjects are still outside the top 30.

There have been big changes at the top of the table this year, with Cambridge dropping from first to fifth despite recording high scores across the board. Durham has taken over at the top, with Oxford, Cardiff and Bristol also overtaking Cambridge. Cardiff has the most satisfied students, while the London School of Economics, in sixth place, has the best graduate prospects. Cambridge still has the highest entry standards and shared the top scores in the 2008 Research Assessment Exercise with Durham, Bristol and Oxford. Coventry is the only post-1992 university in the top half of the table.

Satisfaction ratings were generally good in the 2014 National Student Survey, but employment scores in the latest table are mediocre. No university saw nine out of ten graduates go straight into professional jobs or onto postgraduate courses, and the proportion dropped below half at 19 universities. Physical geography courses may give preference to candidates with a science or maths A level in addition to geography, while for environmental science, most of the leading universities will ask for two from biology, chemistry, maths, physics and geography at A level or the equivalent.

Employed in professional job:	35%	Employed in non-professional job and studying:	3%
Employed in professional job and studying:	3%	Employed in non-professional job:	27%
Studying:	20%	Unemployed:	13%
Average starting professional salary:	£21,252	Average starting non-professional salary:	£14,803

Geography and Environmental Sciences	Research quality %	Entry standards	Student satisfaction %	Graduate prospects %	Overall rating
1 Durham	43.3	542	85.8	83.2	100.0
2 Oxford	43.3	529	88.2	79.5	99.9
3 Cardiff	37.8	367	96.6	82.7	97.5
4 Bristol	43.3	492	84.2	82.5	97.0
5 Cambridge	43.3	555	81.0	79.2	96.9
6 London School of Economics	36.7	487	84.3	86.8	96.3
7 St Andrews	33.3	491	88.8	71.3	94.2
8 East Anglia	39.0	454	86.9	64.8	91.4
9 Exeter	33.3	441	84.9	73.7	90.6
10 Manchester	31.7	419	89.9	66.3	90.3
11 Nottingham	33.3	428	85.3	73.0	90.2
12 Glasgow	22.2	473	85.4	76.9	90.1
=13 Lancaster	33.3	448	85.0	69.9	90.0
=13 Royal Holloway	35.0	391	92.7	60.4	90.0
15 Sheffield	36.7	430	86.0	66.3	89.8
16 Southampton	35.0	429	83.4	73.1	89.6
17 Swansea	30.0	367	87.1	74.5	88.3
18 Loughborough	23.3	385	89.1	71.9	87.8
19 Dundee	30.0	405	90.1	59.2	87.6

Geography and Environmental Sciences cont	Research quality %	Entry standards	Student satisfaction %	Graduate prospects %	Overall rating
=20 Leeds	40.0	431	79.9	66.6	87.4
=20 Newcastle	25.0	410	84.9	74.0	87.4
=20 Queen Mary, London	41.7	376	84.4	63.5	87.4
23 York	26.7	401	85.2	71.3	86.9
24 Birmingham	28.3	426	79.2	75.7	86.2
25 King's College London	36.7	414	78.6	69.8	86.0
26 Aberdeen	23.3	455	80.8	70.3	85.6
27 Reading	37.6	370	79.9	69.0	85.0
28 Edinburgh	31.7	473	77.2	63.9	84.8
29 Sussex	31.7	405	82.5	59.1	83.8
30 Liverpool	25.0	406	82.3	58.6	81.9
31 Leicester	20.0	393	83.6	61.4	81.6
32 Hull	28.3	310	87.6	56.3	81.3
33 University College London	38.3	499	59.9	76.2	81.2
34 Aberystwyth	35.0	335	81.7	56.0	80.7
35 Coventry	6.7	318	94.0	60.0	80.6
36 Bradford	30.0		78.6	59.7	79.3
37 Highlands and Islands	16.7	348		64.3	79.2
38 Queen's, Belfast	23.3	352	84.2	53.3	79.1
39 Sunderland	3.3		88.8	63.5	79.0
40 Stirling	16.7	405	77.5	64.8	78.8
41 Chester	3.3	305	88.5	66.0	77.8
42 Keele		353	85.9	65.8	77.4
43 Plymouth	21.4	305	83.8	53.8	76.7
44 Northampton	7.7	258	92.8	50.0	75.3
45 Ulster	16.7	268	87.7	49.3	75.0
46 Portsmouth	13.3	295	85.7	51.1	74.6
47 West of England	6.7	321	82.3	60.6	74.5
48 Sheffield Hallam	30.0	320	78.3	44.6	74.1
49 Brighton	13.3	290	84.5	50.8	73.7
50 Gloucestershire	5.0	272	89.5	50.5	73.5
51 Oxford Brookes		321	83.8	57.9	72.9
52 Hertfordshire		306	88.0	47.5	72.0
53 Bangor		285	84.7	57.5	71.9
54 Worcester	3.3	289	86.4	46.9	71.2
55 Northumbria		342	83.9	47.3	71.1
56 Manchester Metropolitan	16.5	321	78.1	45.5	70.8
57 Derby		315	89.4	37.9	70.7
58 Bath Spa	5.0	275	86.5	45.0	70.6
59 Liverpool John Moores		311	88.3	40.0	70.5
60 South Wales		327	86.2	41.1	70.2
61 Edge Hill	1.7	260	85.5	50.9	70.1
62 Bournemouth	21.7	304	76.8	36.8	68.6

63 Kingston	13.3	267	76.8	49.8	68.3
64 Staffordshire		231	81.3	58.0	68.0
65 St Mary's, Twickenham		267	79.1	52.7	66.9
66 Strathclyde	6.7		83.6	35.1	66.8
67 Canterbury Christ Church		267	80.8	48.0	66.7
68 Nottingham Trent	1.7	285	81.1	39.1	65.7
69 Salford	13.3	268	69.5	48.0	63.9
70 Southampton Solent		225	78.2	44.7	62.8
71 Leeds Metropolitan		266	74.1	46.7	62.6
72 Cumbria		265	74.7	44.9	62.5
73 Central Lancashire		290	68.4	51.5	61.7

Geology

There has been a surge in interest in geology since £9,000 fees were introduced and more students have opted for what they see as marketable degrees. Applications have increased by almost 20 per cent since 2010, the last year unaffected by the changes in fees. The supply of places has not kept pace, with only 200 added in three years. As a result, although there are only just over five applications to the place, entry standards are high. Table-topping Cambridge recorded its normal astronomical entry grades (665 points in 2013) and another five of the 29 universities in the table topped 500 points. Some of the leading universities expect candidates to have two scientific or mathematical subjects at A level, or the equivalent.

Graduate salaries and the prospect of an international career may be behind the subject's growing popularity. Geology is in the top 20 in the salary table, despite a drop of nearly £1,500 in the average paid in professional jobs compared with 2012. The subject is lower in the overall employment table, with a relatively high unemployment rate of 15 per cent. Only 40 per cent of graduates went straight into professional jobs in 2013, but there is always a high take-up for postgraduate degrees. Almost 30 per cent took this route in 2013.

Cambridge has extended its lead over Imperial College, benefiting from the best performance in the 2008 Research Assessment Exercise, as well as the highest entry standards. Imperial again has the best of a generally high set of scores in the 2014 National Student Survey. Its 98.5 per cent satisfaction rating followed a score of 99 per cent last year – both among the best in any subject – and even Derby, two places off the bottom of the table, managed 91 per cent after recording 92 per cent in 2013. Fourth-placed St Andrews has much the best employment record, as the only university to see more than 90 per cent of graduates gain a professional job or go on to further study. Plymouth is again the highest-placed of seven post-1992 universities in the ranking.

Employed in professional job:	38%	Employed in non-professional job and studying:	1%
Employed in professional job and studying:	2%	Employed in non-professional job:	17%
Studying:	26%	Unemployed:	15%
Average starting professional salary:	£22,319	Average starting non-professional salary:	£14,698

Geology

	Research quality %	Entry standards	Student satisfaction %	Graduate prospects %	Overall rating
1 Cambridge	56.7	665	87.4	86.6	100.0
2 Imperial College	40.0	540	90.5	85.7	93.8
3 Oxford	51.7	603	75.2	82.0	90.4
4 St Andrews	33.3	488	80.7	94.5	86.0
5 Bristol	41.7	474	88.7	69.4	83.6
6 Durham	33.3	502	81.6	83.2	83.3
7 University College London	43.3	459	74.2	80.0	81.6
8 Liverpool	35.0	406	89.9	74.3	80.9
9 East Anglia	40.0	400	87.4	71.0	80.4
10 Royal Holloway	36.7	361	85.7	79.7	80.0
11 Southampton	36.7	410	80.2	79.6	79.7
12 Leeds	33.3	411	89.9	71.4	79.6
13 Glasgow	21.7	509	90.0	70.0	78.7
14 Manchester	36.7	408	86.1	69.2	78.6
15 Edinburgh	33.3	524	73.7	72.4	78.0
16 Birmingham	31.7	412	81.2	77.3	77.7
17 Leicester	28.3	412	91.9	67.7	77.6
18 Aberdeen	26.7	417	76.0	86.0	77.0
19 Cardiff	33.3	364	81.7	71.6	75.1
20 Exeter	15.0	409	84.2	77.3	73.1
21 Plymouth	21.4	307	88.6	62.3	68.8
22 Bangor	26.7	272	81.2	53.3	63.9
23 Portsmouth	18.3	295	79.4	59.1	63.0
24 Keele		342	89.9	55.3	61.1
25 Brighton	13.3	268	82.6	54.5	60.2
26 Aberystwyth		343	85.4	56.3	59.9
27 Derby		284	91.1	50.3	58.1
28 Kingston		289	56.5	82.8	55.5
29 South Wales		291	52.4	59.2	47.0

German

German has suffered more than other European languages from the decline in the numbers taking courses in the sixth-form, or even earlier. But applications and enrolments seemed to have stabilised – albeit at a low level – in 2013. Only just over 200 students began degrees, although many others are learning the language as part of a broader degree. The introduction of £9,000 fees undoubtedly contributed to falling numbers, but there has been a worldwide decline in the language that has been worrying the German government, as well as academic linguists. Courses in the language will be available at more than 50 universities in 2015, but only about half are offering single Honours in the language.

Cambridge makes it nine years in a row as the leader in German, while Durham has moved up from fourth place to become the nearest challenger. Cambridge has much the highest entry standards, with Durham boasting the best employment prospects. The most

German

	Research Quality %	Entry standards	Student satisfaction %	Graduate prospects %	Overall rating
1 Cambridge	35.0	592	91.6	80.7	100.0
2 Durham	33.3	536	87.0	84.2	96.5
3 Oxford	35.0	541	88.4	73.7	94.5
4 Warwick	25.0	477	92.2	81.8	93.8
5 Newcastle	28.3	438	90.7	83.0	93.1
6 Southampton	38.3	427	90.2	72.5	92.0
7 Exeter	28.3	469	90.6	75.2	91.7
=8 Birmingham	30.0	433	86.5	79.3	90.2
=8 King's College London	36.7	448	82.4	77.9	90.2
=8 St Andrews	33.3		81.7	80.5	90.2
11 University College London	35.0	487	82.1	72.8	89.3
12 Edinburgh	33.3	473	89.0	60.5	87.9
=13 Leeds	33.3	433	88.0	65.8	87.6
=13 Swansea	23.3		89.7	71.0	87.6
15 Bristol	26.7	448	82.7	77.3	87.3
16 Bath	21.7	437	85.5	78.4	87.2
17 Manchester	31.7	433	83.6	60.3	83.3
18 Sheffield	16.7	427	89.4	65.3	83.2
=19 Glasgow	18.3	513	70.4	79.1	81.7
=19 Heriot-Watt	16.7	446	79.0	74.6	81.7
=19 Nottingham	20.0	400	83.4	69.7	81.7
=22 Lancaster	15.0	452	80.5	71.4	81.1
=22 Queen's, Belfast	8.3		92.4	65.1	81.1
24 Cardiff	25.0	397	77.5	71.4	80.7
25 Portsmouth	25.0	295	84.6	68.6	79.8
26 Liverpool	21.7	394	78.4	69.7	79.5
27 Queen Mary, London	16.7	361	84.7		79.0
28 Reading	16.7	325	83.3	65.2	76.7
29 Aberdeen	8.3	463	78.5		76.5
30 Royal Holloway	31.7	382	76.6	52.7	75.8
31 Kent	10.0	372	80.1	65.5	75.0
32 Hull		303	85.7	71.4	74.3
33 Bangor		285	88.0	68.4	73.8
34 Aston	10.0	339	76.0	71.3	73.6
35 Manchester Metropolitan	6.7	359	87.6	50.0	72.3
36 Aberystwyth	25.0	300	74.9	58.8	72.2
37 Salford	12.5		75.9	63.1	71.2
38 Nottingham Trent		262	86.3	55.2	68.1

Employed in professional job:	43%	Employed in non-professional job and studying:	2%
Employed in professional job and studying:	4%	Employed in non-professional job:	20%
Studying:	19%	Unemployed:	12%
Average starting professional salary:	£19,442	Average starting non-professional salary:	£15,159

satisfied students are outside the top 20, at Queen's, Belfast, fractionally ahead of fourth-placed Warwick. Most universities scored well in the 2014 National Student Survey; only two failed to satisfy at least 75 per cent of final-year undergraduates. Southampton had the best results in the 2008 Research Assessment Exercise, while Portsmouth is by far the highest-placed of just three post-1992 universities in the ranking.

Despite the recruitment difficulties in German departments, entry standards are relatively high, especially at the leading universities. At nearly two-thirds of the universities in the table, entrants average at least 400 points. As in other modern languages, career prospects are reasonable: the subject is just outside the top 30 for the proportion of graduates going into professional jobs or onto postgraduate courses. However, starting salaries in professional jobs have dropped for the second year in a row, making a reduction of more than £1,500 since the 2013 *Guide*. Most universities in the table offer German from scratch as part of a languages package, as well as catering for those who took the subject at A level.

History

History showed that it had withstood the impact of £9,000 fees by recording a 6 per cent increase in applications and even larger growth in enrolments in 2013. Early figures suggest that the trend has continued this year. Yet the subject is in the bottom 20 for employment, with more graduates starting out in non-professional jobs than those categorised as professional occupations. There was a £700 drop in average starting salaries in the professional jobs taken by historians in the last year, taking the subject into the bottom half of the table, but surveys suggest that they often rise to the top later in their careers.

Durham and Cambridge have been taking it in turns to lead the history table for the last five years, and they have swapped again in this edition. Cambridge leads with the highest entry standards and shares the best research score with University College London. In fact, Imperial College's work on the history of science won the top grade in the 2008 Research Assessment Exercise (RAE), but history is not an undergraduate subject at Imperial so it does not appear in this table. The most satisfied students are at Brunel, which only just makes the top 50 because it did not enter the RAE in history. Satisfaction levels are high throughout the ranking: it is one of the few subjects in which every university managed at least a 70 per cent approval rating.

The older institutions continue to dominate the table: only Oxford Brookes, of the modern universities, appears in the top 30, with Huddersfield and Chester joining it in the top 40. Average entry scores have dropped slightly since last year. Although seven universities top 500 points – the equivalent of more than four As at A level – six universities, compared with only one last year, average less than 250 points. Employment scores are less variable than in the last *Guide*, but almost 40 institutions saw less than half of those graduating in 2013 go into professional jobs or start postgraduate courses by the end of the year.

Employed in professional job:	29%	Employed in non-professional job and studying:	4%
Employed in professional job and studying:	3%	Employed in non-professional job:	29%
Studying:	22%	Unemployed:	13%
Average starting professional salary:	£20,045	Average starting non-professional salary:	£14,818

History

	Research quality %	Entry standards	Student satisfaction %	Graduate prospects %	Overall rating
1 Cambridge	48.3	579	89.1	79.9	100.0
2 Durham	33.3	553	93.1	81.8	98.7
3 St Andrews	33.3	533	89.4	74.6	94.2
4 Oxford	46.7	552	82.6	75.5	94.0
=5 Exeter	33.3	471	90.9	76.1	93.4
=5 Warwick	45.0	487	85.3	76.8	93.4
7 London School of Economics	45.0	507	83.3	75.3	92.5
8 York	35.0	495	87.1	72.0	91.5
9 Sheffield	45.0	468	86.2	65.4	90.9
10 Southampton	43.3	438	86.7	68.4	90.5
=11 King's College London	36.7	487	85.3	70.3	90.1
=11 University College London	48.3	515	78.7	72.2	90.1
=13 Glasgow	36.7	497	86.6	60.4	89.1
=13 Kent	46.7	396	86.6	65.4	89.1
15 Leeds	31.7	472	88.3	63.5	88.9
16 Queen Mary, London	40.0	441	86.0	65.5	88.8
17 East Anglia	33.3	436	90.2	59.4	88.3
18 Lancaster	28.3	450	86.2	71.0	87.7
19 Birmingham	33.3	424	84.2	74.2	87.5
20 Royal Holloway	33.3	433	87.4	61.0	86.9
=21 Manchester	37.1	428	84.1	63.8	86.2
=21 Sussex	38.3	409	86.2	59.4	86.2
=23 Liverpool	46.7	413	83.7	55.7	85.9
=23 Newcastle	23.3	445	85.4	70.8	85.9
25 Essex	46.7	377	86.7	49.0	85.1
26 Aberdeen	40.0	432	83.7	54.9	84.8
27 Queen's, Belfast	30.0	366	91.3	53.2	84.7
=28 Keele	31.7	384	87.1	60.0	84.5
=28 SOAS, London	40.0	389	82.3	63.7	84.5
30 Oxford Brookes	38.3	355	88.1	53.2	84.2
=31 Leicester	30.0	388	85.7	61.7	83.8
=31 Nottingham	26.7	448	81.7	67.0	83.8
33 Edinburgh	36.7	504	77.3	58.9	83.4
34 Bristol	28.3	474	75.3	77.1	83.3
35 Cardiff	21.7	429	85.7	59.6	82.9
36 Swansea	26.7	338	86.8	63.7	82.5
37 Huddersfield	18.3	344	88.4	62.4	81.5
38 Reading	23.3	366	86.3	58.0	81.2
39 Chester	25.0	311	86.2	60.7	80.3
40 Strathclyde	16.7	454	83.4	52.6	79.7
41 Loughborough		381	86.2	71.8	79.4
42 Bangor	26.7	298	88.5	50.1	79.3
43 Teesside	23.3	296	90.0	48.6	79.2

	Research quality %	Entry standards	Student satisfaction %	Graduate prospects %	Overall rating
44 Hull	31.7	354	81.9	52.1	78.8
45 Lincoln	13.3	335	87.6	57.8	78.7
46 Portsmouth	25.0	312	84.0	58.0	78.5
47 Winchester	28.3	315	85.3	48.1	78.0
48 Brunel		352	94.7	44.5	77.7
49 West of England	16.7	335	88.7	44.0	77.2
50 Hertfordshire	40.0	344	73.4	59.1	76.7
51 Dundee	31.7	353	85.3	32.1	76.5
52 Bath Spa	18.3	292	89.2	42.0	76.0
53 Roehampton	18.3	274	87.4	48.9	75.8
54 Cumbria	6.7		91.9	38.6	75.5
55 Coventry		283	92.6	50.0	75.4
=56 Edge Hill	15.0	265	89.9	42.9	75.0
=56 Stirling	26.7	386	78.0	45.6	75.0
58 Northampton	16.7	256	89.1	44.4	74.9
59 Anglia Ruskin	33.3	236	87.4	34.2	74.8
60 Sunderland	21.7	290	86.8	39.2	74.6
61 Northumbria	6.7	359	84.2	50.4	74.4
62 Central Lancashire	18.3	320	84.4	43.0	74.3
63 Goldsmiths, London	16.7	360	79.3	52.5	74.1
64 Brighton	45.0	263	77.2	42.1	73.9
65 Liverpool John Moores	5.0	333	89.0	36.0	73.0
66 Manchester Metropolitan	6.7	312	84.2	50.1	72.8
67 Sheffield Hallam	16.7	312	86.0	34.0	72.7
68 Ulster	28.3	291	82.7	34.2	72.6
=69 De Montfort	15.0	281	82.5	49.1	72.4
=69 South Wales	23.3	307	82.2	37.5	72.4
71 Glyndŵr		236	89.3	51.9	72.3
72 Chichester	10.0	278	87.2	38.8	71.8
73 Derby		297	93.1	29.1	71.7
=74 Gloucestershire	11.7	308	82.5	39.3	70.5
=74 Highlands and Islands	8.3	281	81.4	50.0	70.5
76 Bradford	11.7	317	75.7	56.9	70.4
77 St Mary's, Twickenham		293	87.7	38.6	70.3
78 Greenwich	18.3	298	83.3	29.7	70.1
79 Staffordshire		238	86.6	47.9	69.9
=80 Aberystwyth	21.7	325	74.5	44.4	69.5
=80 Canterbury Christ Church	10.0	273	84.7	35.6	69.5
82 Westminster	5.0	295	84.0	35.8	68.8
83 East London		245	78.4	64.0	68.6
84 Plymouth	8.3	280	81.6	40.2	68.5
=85 Newman	0.0	273	87.7	31.0	68.1
=85 Nottingham Trent	13.3	283	76.8	46.2	68.1

87 Bishop Grosseteste		240	76.8	64.8	67.6
88 Leeds Trinity	11.7	223	77.7	46.0	66.2
89 York St John		297	80.9	36.3	65.9
90 Leeds Metropolitan		260	80.2	38.0	64.6
91 Kingston	13.3	258	74.1	38.5	64.0
92 Salford	11.7		72.4	47.3	63.9
93 Worcester	0.0	285	76.6	38.4	63.4

History of Art, Architecture and Design

The Courtauld Institute, an independent college of the University of London based in Somerset House, is the only specialist institution to top any of our league tables. It describes itself as "one of the world's pre-eminent centres for the study of the history of art" and its performance in our subject table begins to back up that claim. It has jumped from ninth place to top the table for the history of art, architecture and design, with the most satisfied students and strong scores on the other measures. The Courtauld, which has only 155 undergraduates, was the perennial leader of this table in the early years of the century, but its ranking had slipped in the last two years.

East Anglia, which enjoyed a big rise last year retains its second place, while Oxford, last year's leader, falls to third. Cambridge, which has dropped to sixth, has the highest entry standards, while eighth-placed Birmingham has the best employment score and is the only university to see 80 per cent of graduates go straight into professional jobs or postgraduate training. The subjects are in the bottom ten for salaries in graduate-level jobs, but somewhat higher for overall employment. More than a quarter of graduates continue their studies, but three in ten start out in low-level employment.

The numbers starting courses in the history of art, architecture and design fell in 2013, in common with other branches of history. But more than 40 universities are offering degrees in the subjects – often in combination with other disciplines – for 2015. Entry standards are high: only two universities in the table average less than 330 points. Glasgow produced the best grades in the 2008 Research Assessment Exercise, when 85 per cent of its work was classified as world-leading or internationally excellent. The subjects are mainly the preserve of older universities, but four post-1992 institutions appear in this year's table. Oxford Brookes, where 13 different combinations are available in addition to the single Honours course, is the highest-placed of them.

History of Art, Architecture and Design	Research quality %	Entry standards	Student satisfaction %	Graduate prospects %	Overall rating
1 Courtauld	53.3	476	92.1	71.0	100.0
2 East Anglia	56.7	421	90.0	69.5	97.0
3 Oxford	46.7	553	82.4	68.8	95.3
4 York	53.3	421	88.5	67.8	95.1
5 St Andrews	35.0	483	89.8	69.2	94.5
6 Cambridge	26.7	555	88.2	65.2	93.6
7 Glasgow	58.3	467	86.7	52.6	93.5

History of Art, Architecture and Design
cont

	Research quality %	Entry standards	Student satisfaction %	Graduate prospects %	Overall rating
8 Birmingham	43.3	409	83.9	81.7	92.8
9 University College London	46.7	502	78.7	**73.5**	92.3
10 Sussex	53.3	406	86.2	60.9	91.6
11 Kent	46.7	332	87.0	77.2	91.4
12 Manchester	53.3	408	85.2	57.3	90.3
13 SOAS, London	36.7	431	82.3	69.8	88.6
14 Warwick	33.3	447	85.2	61.6	88.3
15 Leeds	31.7	411	87.6	59.7	87.5
16 Essex	41.7		86.9	44.8	86.1
17 Edinburgh	30.0	486	76.2	70.8	85.9
18 Reading	30.0	338	86.9	65.0	85.1
19 Nottingham	38.3	393	81.5	56.2	83.9
20 Leicester	20.0	396	85.8	55.3	82.4
21 Bristol	25.0	458	73.7	63.6	80.6
22 Goldsmiths, London	30.0	408	78.9	53.4	80.5
=23 Aberdeen	31.7		83.7	44.2	80.3
=23 Oxford Brookes	28.3	333	88.1	42.9	80.3
25 Brighton	45.0	294	78.3	43.8	77.0
26 Plymouth	21.7	269	81.6	60.7	76.6
27 Manchester Metropolitan	21.7	359	84.2	28.0	74.2
28 Aberystwyth	11.7		74.5	42.4	66.7

Employed in professional job:	35%	Employed in non-professional job and studying:		3%
Employed in professional job and studying:	3%	Employed in non-professional job:		27%
Studying:	20%	Unemployed:		12%
Average starting professional salary:	£18,491	Average starting non-professional salary:		£15,083

Hospitality, Leisure, Recreation and Tourism

This group of subjects covers a variety of courses directed towards management in the leisure and tourism industries, mainly delivered at modern universities. It remains in the top 20 for applications, but does surprisingly poorly in the graduate employment market, given the size of the sectors it serves. The group has only escaped from the bottom two in the employment table because the two new subjects added to the *Guide* have entered in lower positions. The subjects do better in the salaries table, finishing in the top 50, but more than 40 per cent of graduates start out in low-level jobs.

The numbers starting courses in 2013 rose, even though applications had dropped for the second year in succession. Entry standards are low, but seem to have risen at some of the leading universities. Although second-placed Exeter is the only one averaging more than 400 points on the UCAS tariff, nine others (compared with five last year) have averages of more than 350 points. Only eight institutions in the table are pre-1992 universities, but they include the top two. Surrey, with its 40-year reputation in hotel and tourism management, remains clear at the head of the table. It had the best grades in the 2008 Research Assessment Exercise (RAE) and the top score in the 2014 National Student Survey. Fifth-placed Birmingham again has the best employment record but, like Exeter, did not enter the RAE in this category. Only 15 of the 54 universities and colleges in the table did.

More than 70 universities and colleges are offering courses in one of more of the hospitality, leisure, recreation and tourism subjects in 2015. Satisfaction rates are invariably high: only four universities failed to achieve at least 70 per cent approval in the 2014 survey, although Surrey was the only one to top 90 per cent. Central Lancashire, in third place, has overtaken Sheffield Hallam to become the leading post-1992 university. They are joined in the top ten by Manchester Metropolitan, Chester and Hertfordshire.

Employed in professional job:	40%	Employed in non-professional job and studying:	2%
Employed in professional job and studying:	1%	Employed in non-professional job:	40%
Studying:	4%	Unemployed:	13%
Average starting professional salary:	£19,265	Average starting non-professional salary:	£15,861

Hospitality, Leisure, Recreation and Tourism	Research quality %	Entry standards	Student satisfaction %	Graduate prospects %	Overall rating
1 Surrey	23.3	394	91.9	57.4	100.0
2 Exeter		448	85.5	81.3	89.6
3 Central Lancashire	21.7	340	82.5	46.6	88.3
4 Sheffield Hallam	18.3	332	83.6	52.9	87.6
5 Birmingham		362	88.7	87.1	87.4
6 Stirling	20.9		78.8	53.1	86.6
7 Manchester Metropolitan	15.0	333	82.4	54.2	85.1
8 Chester	11.7	302	86.5	57.3	83.9
9 Salford	13.3	369	84.8	35.0	83.3
10 Hertfordshire	15.0	351	79.1	46.8	82.8
11 Bournemouth	13.3	331	78.6	57.1	82.6
=12 Brighton	18.3	298	81.7	40.4	81.8
=12 Plymouth	14.1	291	85.6	45.8	81.8
14 Oxford Brookes		376	82.9	63.6	80.1
15 Robert Gordon		375	83.4	57.7	79.0
=16 Lincoln		313	84.1	65.3	77.3
=16 West of England	6.7	326	83.8	42.5	77.3
18 Huddersfield		310	88.1	53.2	76.5
=19 Arts University Bournemouth		317	79.3	69.6	75.9
=19 Manchester		372	76.6	61.0	75.9
21 Sunderland	13.3	275	81.4	30.5	74.8
22 Cardiff Metropolitan	11.7	307	73.7	42.7	74.3
23 Coventry		289	81.7	60.7	73.5
24 Northampton		277	87.0	48.5	72.9
25 University of the Arts London		383	72.7	52.4	72.7
26 East London		283	81.9	56.6	72.4
27 Chichester		272	84.7	52.9	72.3

	Research quality %	Entry standards	Student satisfaction %	Graduate prospects %	Overall rating
28 Edinburgh Napier		354	77.2	47.4	72.2
29 Derby		317	82.8	42.7	71.9
30 Portsmouth		270	81.9	56.4	71.6
31 Winchester		317	82.0	36.3	70.0
32 Southampton Solent		285	77.2	52.2	69.0
33 Leeds Metropolitan		278	76.5	55.2	68.9
34 St Mary's, Twickenham		270	82.7	40.9	68.6
=35 Falmouth		263	67.9	76.5	68.2
=35 Ulster		292	81.1	37.0	68.2
37 Greenwich		326	74.1	43.8	68.1
38 Middlesex		295	76.9	43.8	67.7
39 Gloucestershire		280	74.3	53.8	67.6
40 Westminster		303	81.9	24.4	66.6
41 Bedfordshire	10.0	194	75.6	37.2	66.1
42 West of Scotland		311	76.3	32.6	65.9
43 Buckinghamshire New		228	80.7	43.1	65.5
44 Queen Margaret, Edinburgh		283	73.5	42.4	64.9
45 South Wales		320	65.4	49.7	64.5
46 Highlands and Islands		240	69.4	61.1	64.2
47 West London		232	77.2	40.3	63.3
48 Canterbury Christ Church		266	72.6	38.7	62.5
49 Liverpool John Moores		276	72.4	27.6	60.6
50 Staffordshire		219	73.0	40.8	60.4
51 Anglia Ruskin		245	77.6	18.8	59.6
52 London Metropolitan		268	65.3	35.7	58.2
53 London South Bank		196	73.2	35.9	58.0
54 Aberystwyth		259	72.9	17.4	57.7

Iberian Languages

Spanish is still gaining on French as the most popular language at degree level, following
its rise at school level. But the numbers are small: although applications and enrolments for
Spanish stabilised in 2013, fewer than 400 students started courses. The table also includes
Portuguese, but not a single student embarked on a degree in the language in 2013. Just four
had done so the previous year, but Portuguese will still be available – either alone or as part
of a modern languages degree – at 22 universities in 2015.

Cambridge has maintained a considerable lead over Durham at the top of the table, with
Oxford still in third place. Cambridge has the highest entry standards, but Coventry, although
outside the top 30 overall, has the most satisfied students. Like last year, Stirling has the best
employment record, but this time Lancaster is only a fraction of a point behind. Nottingham
and Manchester tied for the best performance in the 2008 Research Assessment Exercise.

Only seven of the 46 institutions in the ranking are post-1992 universities, but this is still more than last year. Portsmouth, with its lengthy pedigree in language teaching and research, is the only one in the top 30, although Coventry and Northumbria are not far behind. There are high levels of student satisfaction in most universities: only two failed to satisfy at least 70 per cent of final-year undergraduates. Entry standards have been rising: half of the universities in the table average over 400 points and five have averages of more than 500. Iberian languages have improved their positions, relative to other subjects, for both overall employment and average salaries in graduate jobs. The languages are now in the top 30 for the proportion of graduates going into professional jobs or beginning postgraduate courses and average salaries had risen by more than £1,000 between 2012 and 2013.

Employed in professional job:	45%
Employed in professional job and studying:	4%
Studying:	19%
Average starting professional salary:	£20,603

Employed in non-professional job and studying:	2%
Employed in non-professional job:	20%
Unemployed:	11%
Average starting non-professional salary:	£16,051

Iberian Languages	Research quality %	Entry standards	Student satisfaction %	Graduate prospects %	Overall rating
1 Cambridge	43.3	592	91.6	80.7	100.0
2 Durham	35.0	536	87.0	84.2	94.3
3 Oxford	30.0	555	88.0	77.3	92.2
4 Newcastle	26.7	435	90.4	86.8	90.1
5 Southampton	38.3	442	84.9	81.9	89.8
6 St Andrews	28.3	509	82.5	83.6	89.1
7 Exeter	25.0	469	90.6	75.2	87.8
8 Leeds	33.3	429	85.4	77.3	86.8
9 Manchester	45.0	422	84.4	67.9	86.7
10 Bath	21.7	452	87.7	81.0	86.5
11 Leicester	20.0	405	93.4	78.7	86.0
12 Queen's, Belfast	28.3	401	95.5	64.9	85.3
13 Sheffield	35.0	397	86.3	69.2	84.1
14 Stirling	13.3	396	86.6	87.7	83.3
15 Nottingham	45.0	409	78.7	66.0	83.1
16 King's College London	37.5	456	83.0	56.5	82.2
17 Lancaster	15.0	415	78.8	87.5	81.0
18 University College London	21.7	469	74.7	79.2	80.8
19 Kent	11.7	381	88.0	78.4	80.1
20 Queen Mary, London	36.7	359	81.4	65.8	79.9
=21 Birmingham	20.0	390	78.7	82.2	79.8
=21 Glasgow	13.3	509	76.0	75.8	79.8
=23 Bristol	16.7	461	75.0	76.2	78.4
=23 Edinburgh	26.7	457	73.2	69.5	78.4
=25 Aberystwyth	25.0	340	83.1	69.7	77.7
=25 Heriot-Watt	16.7	446	79.0	69.3	77.7
=25 Strathclyde	6.7	479	76.9	78.1	77.7
28 Aberdeen	21.7	440	85.7	53.8	77.5

	Research quality %	Entry standards	Student satisfaction %	Graduate prospects %	Overall rating
29 Portsmouth	25.0	295	84.6	68.6	76.2
30 Swansea	21.7	348	75.8	73.3	74.8
31 Coventry		271	97.6	69.0	74.1
32 Aston	10.0	336	88.3	63.0	73.7
33 Northumbria		334	88.3	71.9	73.3
=34 Bangor	11.7	292	89.1	63.3	72.8
=34 Cardiff	25.0	411	68.5	65.6	72.8
36 Royal Holloway	25.0	367	69.3	65.5	71.4
37 East Anglia		395	89.2	54.5	71.3
38 Sussex		399	88.9	54.1	71.2
39 Liverpool	26.7	380	74.1	51.8	70.7
40 Hull		319	91.3	59.1	70.4
41 Salford	12.5		75.4	59.8	67.3
42 Nottingham Trent		292	86.3	55.6	66.1
43 Manchester Metropolitan	6.7	341	81.6	48.5	65.9
44 Chester		287	75.2	67.9	64.4
45 Ulster	3.3	288	77.3	58.1	63.6
46 Westminster		304	79.0	45.7	60.5

Italian

Small numbers can make for exaggerated swings in some subject tables, and Italian is a case in point. Both applications and enrolments halved in 2013, but since there were fewer than 50 of either in 2012, linguists will hope that the latest figures represent a blip. Many more students will have included Italian in broader language degrees or as one or more modules in another subject, and 40 universities are continuing to offer the language in 2015. Most students have no previous knowledge of Italian, although they are likely to have taken another language at A level.

Inevitably, the graduate employment statistics have also been subject to considerable year-on-year variation. Average starting salaries in professional jobs had dropped by more than £1,000 in last year's *Guide*, for example, whereas they are up by over £1,500 this time. Yet Italian has dropped 12 places is the overall employment table. The unemployment rate is up by 4 percentage points and there is an even larger decline in the proportion staying on for postgraduate courses.

For the second year in succession, Cambridge has extended its already considerable lead over Oxford at the top of the table. Cambridge registered the top grades in the 2008 Research Assessment Exercise, when 80 per cent of its submission was judged to be world-leading or internationally excellent. It also has the highest entry grades and the most satisfied students. Durham, in third place, has the best employment record. There are only three post-1992 universities left in the table, with Portsmouth the clear leader.

Entry standards remain surprisingly high, given the small numbers of applicants. Five of the 20 universities in the ranking average more than 500 points at entry and more than two-thirds top 400 points. There is a high response rate and scores have generally been good in the National Student Survey. Only one university failed to satisfy at least seven out of ten final-year undergraduates taking Italian.

Employed in professional job:	44%	Employed in non-professional job and studying:	2%
Employed in professional job and studying:	3%	Employed in non-professional job:	21%
Studying:	14%	Unemployed:	15%
Average starting professional salary:	£20,374	Average starting non-professional salary:	£16,128

Italian	Research quality %	Entry standards	Student satisfaction %	Graduate prospects %	Overall rating
1 Cambridge	56.7	592	91.6	80.7	100.0
2 Oxford	40.0	533	85.6	68.6	88.0
3 Durham	11.7	536	87.0	84.2	86.9
4 Exeter	18.3	469	90.6	75.2	85.2
5 Birmingham	26.7		85.4	74.7	84.4
6 Warwick	40.0	448	83.5	69.3	84.1
7 Bristol	31.7	443	79.8	77.4	82.6
8 Manchester	31.7	432	85.1	67.9	82.2
9 Bath	21.7	433	84.5	75.5	81.8
10 University College London	28.3	488	75.6	78.3	81.6
=11 Leeds	41.7	410	86.3	56.9	81.1
=11 Reading	38.3	337	88.7	64.6	81.1
13 Glasgow	13.3	523	80.3		78.6
14 Edinburgh	8.3	495	82.5	68.7	78.2
15 Portsmouth	25.0	295	84.6	68.6	75.8
16 St Andrews	13.3	520	66.8	78.2	75.2
17 Manchester Metropolitan	6.7	359	87.6	50.0	70.4
18 Royal Holloway	16.7	408	80.0	49.0	70.3
19 Cardiff	25.0	382	72.8	54.9	69.4
20 Nottingham Trent		296	86.3	55.2	67.4

Land and Property Management

Graduates in land and property management who found professional jobs in 2013 enjoyed the biggest rise in average salaries of any subject, compared with the previous year. It had taken until then to regain the level achieved in 2009, but the new £22,722 average has taken land and property management into the top 20 for all subjects. Almost two-thirds of graduates go straight into professional jobs, but the subjects have dropped out of the top 20 for "positive destinations" this year. The table confirms the high employment rates: 98 per cent of graduates at second-placed Reading found high-level work or continued to study, and the rate was almost 94 per cent at fourth-placed Birmingham City, the leading post-1992 institution, which also has the most satisfied students.

But the table also reflects falling intakes: three universities (a third of the total number)

Land and Property Management cont

that had enough new students to compile entry scores last year no longer did in 2013. Even top-placed Cambridge did not have sufficient responses in the National Student Survey to compile a satisfaction rating. It did have by far the highest entry standards, however, and the best grades in the 2008 Research Assessment Exercise.

The table is less than half the size of a decade ago, with no representatives from Scotland or Wales, but more than 20 universities and colleges are offering courses in this area in 2015. They include degrees in woodland ecology and conservation, property investment and management, and countryside management, as well as the real estate degrees that are the largest recruiters.

The subjects have acquired a reputation for recruiting disproportionate numbers from independent schools, but property firms have donated more than £500,000 to support a "Pathways to Property" scheme to try to widen participation. Those who take the courses appear to enjoy the experience: no university in the table recorded less than 75 per cent satisfaction in the 2014 National Student Survey.

Employed in professional job:	65%	Employed in non-professional job and studying:	1%
Employed in professional job and studying:	0%	Employed in non-professional job:	14%
Studying:	5%	Unemployed:	15%
Average starting professional salary:	£22,722	Average starting non-professional salary:	£15,430

Land and Property Management	Research quality %	Entry standards	Student satisfaction %	Graduate prospects %	Overall rating
1 Cambridge	45.0	569		86.9	100.0
2 Reading	36.7	384	78.5	98.0	90.2
3 Sheffield Hallam	30.0	313	84.1	75.4	87.9
4 Birmingham City	15.0	271	85.3	93.8	87.1
5 Ulster	31.7		80.0	76.8	86.9
6 Nottingham Trent	10.0	300	80.2	87.8	82.1
7 Greenwich	20.0		83.0	42.9	79.7
8 Westminster	11.7	297	75.1	73.9	76.5
9 Queen's, Belfast	16.7		76.5	55.4	74.8

Law

There were more than 100,000 applications to study law in 2013 – the first time that this milestone had been reached and something that only nursing can match. While other subjects suffered from the introduction of higher fees, law managed small increases in both applications and enrolments in 2012 and grew more sharply in the following year and again in 2014. Entry standards reflect the subject's popularity: only in medicine do so many universities make such testing demands. Ten of the 100 universities in the table average more than 500 points and more than a third have average entry scores of over 400 points. However, so many universities now offer law that it was still possible to find one (Bedfordshire) where the average was below 200 points in 2013.

Cambridge has held on to the top place it regained from Oxford last year. Its entry grades are just one point higher than Oxford's and neither university could match the results achieved by the London School of Economics in the 2008 Research Assessment Exercise (RAE). Once again, the most satisfied students are not at one of the leading universities in the table. Anglia Ruskin did best in the 2014 National Student Survey and would have finished higher than 60th if it had entered the RAE in law. Oxford Brookes is the highest-placed post-1992 university and the only one in the top 30. Glasgow has the best record for graduate destinations, but is overtaken by Edinburgh as top in Scotland.

Aspiring solicitors in England go on to take the Legal Practice Course, while those aiming to be barristers take the Bar Vocational Course, so it is no surprise that 40 per cent of all law graduates are engaged in postgraduate study six months after completing a degree. Note that in Scotland, most law courses are based on the distinctive Scottish legal system, which also has different professional qualifications. The 11 per cent unemployment rate is the average for all subjects, but law has dropped out of top 30 for early career employment prospects, and there are some surprisingly low scores at universities towards the bottom of the ranking. Average starting salaries are only just in the top 50, partly because of training salaries in law firms and also because only about half of all law graduates find their way into the profession.

Employed in professional job:	28%	Employed in non-professional job and studying:	6%
Employed in professional job and studying:	5%	Employed in non-professional job:	22%
Studying:	29%	Unemployed:	11%
Average starting professional salary:	£19,598	Average starting non-professional salary:	£15,739

Law	Research quality %	Entry standards	Student satisfaction %	Graduate prospects %	Overall rating
1 Cambridge	36.7	587	91.2	87.4	100.0
2 Oxford	46.7	586	86.5	85.2	98.7
3 Durham	41.7	557	85.0	86.0	96.1
=4 London School of Economics	55.0	552	78.9	82.9	94.2
=4 Nottingham	41.7	491	86.2	83.2	94.2
6 University College London	48.3	549	80.9	81.6	93.7
7 Edinburgh	38.3	521	80.7	86.2	91.7
=8 Glasgow	28.3	535	80.1	87.8	90.1
=8 Queen Mary, London	33.3	499	85.2	74.1	90.1
10 Kent	41.7	393	85.3	79.1	89.9
11 Bristol	28.3	485	83.8	80.7	89.3
12 Aberdeen	15.0	482	86.1	84.5	88.8
=13 King's College London	26.7	555	79.9	79.8	88.4
=13 Newcastle	13.3	481	87.0	82.2	88.4
15 East Anglia	16.7	429	90.1	76.6	88.2
=16 Cardiff	36.7	420	83.6	76.1	87.9
=16 Leeds	28.3	467	84.0	76.3	87.9
18 Reading	33.3	432	85.0	73.2	87.8
19 Queen's, Belfast	36.7	423	83.1	74.5	87.4
20 Strathclyde	33.3	523	77.6	78.4	87.1

Law cont

	Research quality %	Entry standards	Student satisfaction %	Graduate prospects %	Overall rating
21 Lancaster	18.3	445	86.3	75.9	86.5
=22 Birmingham	30.0	428	81.2	79.1	86.0
=22 Manchester	23.3	436	83.6	77.5	86.0
=22 Surrey	13.3	409	87.9	78.1	86.0
25 SOAS, London	18.3	434	85.8	71.7	85.0
=26 Leicester	16.7	398	83.1	83.1	84.5
=26 Warwick	21.7	505	78.7	76.5	84.5
28 Oxford Brookes	21.7	379	88.0	67.4	84.4
29 Sussex	21.7	409	86.0	68.0	84.2
30 Dundee	20.0	439	83.3	71.1	83.8
31 York		476	85.0	79.1	83.7
32 Exeter	21.7	484	76.4	79.4	83.1
33 Keele	23.3	379	82.6	74.6	83.0
34 Southampton	20.0	443	80.9	73.1	82.9
35 Portsmouth	15.0	329	84.9	80.8	82.7
36 Aston	30.0	386	81.2	69.2	82.6
37 Sheffield	26.7	427	79.7	69.4	82.3
38 Robert Gordon	1.7	402	84.2	82.2	82.0
39 Heriot-Watt		409	86.1	76.8	81.9
40 Brunel	20.0	381	85.3	64.4	81.8
41 Salford	6.7	344	89.5	68.6	81.5
42 Edinburgh Napier	1.7	377	91.0	63.5	81.2
43 Liverpool	25.0	412	77.5	74.0	81.1
44 Swansea	18.3	346	80.0	80.7	80.9
45 Huddersfield		378	88.2	70.7	80.8
=46 Brighton	28.3	322	80.6	72.4	80.7
=46 Chester		310	90.8	72.2	80.7
48 Essex	20.0	343	83.9	66.3	80.2
49 Stirling	16.7	407	79.0	72.0	79.8
50 Buckingham		324	83.3	85.9	79.7
51 Lincoln	3.3	332	87.0	71.6	79.6
52 Manchester Metropolitan	15.0	348	81.7	71.7	79.3
53 Abertay	6.7	328	85.9	68.2	78.8
54 Nottingham Trent	3.3	329	84.6	71.9	78.1
55 Ulster	31.7	325	85.0	45.4	78.0
56 Central Lancashire	5.0	320	83.4	72.7	77.6
=57 De Montfort	6.7	322	87.0	60.5	77.5
=57 West of England	10.0	331	80.8	73.2	77.5
59 Coventry	1.7	291	85.0	73.6	77.3
60 Anglia Ruskin		253	93.8	55.8	77.2
=61 Bangor		286	87.1	68.0	76.9
=61 City	15.0	360	77.8	70.3	76.9
63 Hull	18.3	370	79.0	62.2	76.8

64	Northumbria		376	83.0	66.5	76.7
65	Teesside		323	88.7	58.1	76.6
66	Greenwich	1.7	325	91.0	48.5	76.3
67	Bradford	25.0	320	76.4	67.0	76.1
=68	Gloucestershire		288	88.3	60.0	75.8
=68	Middlesex	5.0	282	84.3	66.9	75.8
70	Hertfordshire	15.0	347	76.2	69.9	75.4
71	Aberystwyth	15.0	340	75.5	69.7	74.8
72	Glasgow Caledonian	5.0	426	80.8	53.0	74.7
=73	Derby		310	82.2	67.9	74.5
=73	Liverpool John Moores		338	83.9	59.4	74.5
75	Bournemouth	0.0	339	78.0	72.9	74.0
76	Plymouth	15.0	316	83.8	46.6	73.9
77	Westminster	11.7	329	75.6	69.3	73.8
78	Northampton		265	86.3	55.8	73.0
=79	Bedfordshire		198	88.9	55.8	72.5
=79	Birmingham City		286	80.8	65.9	72.5
81	Sheffield Hallam	1.7	323	80.6	56.1	71.6
82	Buckinghamshire New		236	85.5	52.8	71.0
83	London South Bank		214	86.3	53.5	70.9
84	Cumbria		239	83.3	57.8	70.8
85	East London	15.0	258	79.1	52.7	70.7
=86	Edge Hill		280	85.2	46.4	70.6
=86	Winchester		342	80.1	52.1	70.6
88	Staffordshire		283	78.6	60.9	70.0
89	St Mary's, Twickenham		260	78.7	59.7	69.1
90	Leeds Metropolitan		272	77.3	61.7	69.0
91	London Metropolitan	3.3	216	78.6	60.5	68.6
92	Roehampton		260	85.0	40.0	68.5
=93	Bolton		258	75.8	60.5	67.4
=93	Kingston	3.3	303	74.0	56.2	67.4
95	South Wales	5.0	306	75.5	50.3	67.3
96	West London		261	76.3	57.8	67.2
97	Southampton Solent	0.0	227	75.0	55.8	64.9
=98	Canterbury Christ Church		269	77.7	39.2	64.1
=98	Sunderland	0.0	288	75.6	42.1	64.1
100	West of Scotland	0.0	287	72.6	34.4	60.4

Librarianship and Information Management

Average starting salaries for graduates in librarianship and information management have dropped by more than £1,300 since the last *Guide* but are still in the top 20 for all subjects. It is safe to assume that few of them are in public libraries. In fact, most of the courses in this category concern broader information services; there are only four full-time undergraduate courses in librarianship in the UK, and two of them are Foundation degrees. Throughout information services, only 110 students started undergraduate courses in 2013 and just six universities had enough students in this area to qualify for the table.

Librarianship and Information Management cont

Loughborough has taken back the leadership, having surrendered it to Sheffield in the 2014 *Guide* after a four-year spell at the top. Loughborough has the highest entry standards, at little more than 350 points, as well as the most satisfied students and the best employment record. Sheffield has the best score for research, although King's College London actually produced the top results in the 2008 Research Assessment Exercise, but does not have the undergraduate courses necessary to appear in the table. Liverpool John Moores, which did not have enough students to qualify for last year's table, has re-entered as the leading post-1992 university.

The small numbers in this field can make for big swings, even in the national statistics. But graduate prospects vary considerably among the six universities in the ranking. More than 80 per cent of Loughborough's graduates went straight into professional jobs or started postgraduate courses but, for the second year in a row, the proportion at Aberystwyth was below 15 per cent. Overall, the subjects are just below half way in the employment league. A respectable 56 per cent find professional work, but less than 10 per cent take a postgraduate qualification, full or part-time.

Employed in professional job:	56%	Employed in non-professional job and studying:	1%
Employed in professional job and studying:	0%	Employed in non-professional job:	22%
Studying:	8%	Unemployed:	12%
Average starting professional salary:	£22,899	Average starting non-professional salary:	£15,536

Librarianship and Information Management	Research quality %	Entry standards	Student satisfaction %	Graduate prospects %	Overall rating
1 Loughborough	28.3	357	85.3	81.7	100.0
2 Sheffield	41.7	337	84.2	72.0	97.9
3 Liverpool John Moores	11.7		82.6	60.0	91.5
4 Northumbria	6.7	345	75.9	67.4	89.4
5 Manchester Metropolitan	6.7	320	74.9	48.1	83.4
6 Aberystwyth	23.3		70.4	12.8	81.7

Linguistics

Linguistics has fared much better than might have been expected since the introduction of £9,000 fees. The numbers starting degrees in 2013 jumped by 25 per cent, following a big increase in applications, and more than 60 universities and colleges are offering the subject in 2015, eight more than in the current year. There are still not much more than four applications for each place, but entry standards are comparatively high. Only one of the 25 universities in the table averages (just) less than 300 points and most are above 400 points.

Cambridge is top in linguistics for the third year in a row, extending its lead over Edinburgh. But, like last year, there is considerable movement in other positions. Oxford is up two places to third, with the best graduate prospects, while Sheffield has the most satisfied students and has jumped seven places and fourth. Queen Mary, University of London, the leader in linguistics a decade ago but now in 18th place, tied with Cardiff for the best grades in the 2008 Research Assessment Exercise. The University of the West of England remains the highest-placed modern university.

The numbers going straight into professional jobs after completing a degree in linguistics had improved a little at the time of the latest survey, in 2013, but still accounted for less than 40 per cent of all graduates. The subject has slipped to 53th in the latest employment ranking, largely because of a fall in the numbers continuing their studies. No university in the table had an 80 per cent success rate in graduate destinations. Linguistics is no longer in the bottom ten for graduate salaries, however. A rise of £800 in the average in professional jobs has taken it close to the top 50 subjects on this measure.

Employed in professional job:	34%	Employed in non-professional job and studying:	3%
Employed in professional job and studying:	4%	Employed in non-professional job:	31%
Studying:	16%	Unemployed:	13%
Average starting professional salary:	£18,919	Average starting non-professional salary:	£15,120

Linguistics	Research quality %	Entry standards	Student satisfaction %	Graduate prospects %	Overall rating
1 Cambridge	30.0	593	87.9	73.7	100.0
2 Edinburgh	40.0	516	82.4	68.7	95.8
3 Oxford	20.0	544	86.7	78.1	95.0
4 Sheffield	33.3	422	93.2	64.2	92.8
=5 Cardiff	43.3	420	86.6	62.7	92.7
=5 University College London	30.0	448	87.0	73.5	92.7
7 Lancaster	28.3	443	82.8	75.0	90.5
8 Newcastle	23.3	401	86.1	75.4	88.4
9 York	35.0	411	83.5	61.1	87.5
10 Kent	26.7	415	87.2	58.4	85.7
11 Leeds	20.0	439	79.0	64.6	82.7
12 Manchester	25.0	417	84.8	52.7	82.5
13 Essex	36.7	324	83.3	54.2	81.9
14 SOAS, London	18.3		78.1	60.6	77.5
15 West of England	21.7	335	88.9	45.3	77.3
16 Bangor	15.0	320	80.4	64.7	76.0
17 Ulster	23.3	308	83.7	49.0	75.3
18 Queen Mary, London	43.3	401	52.8	57.0	74.5
19 Aberdeen		429	80.5	56.8	73.7
20 Hertfordshire	21.7	351	81.9	40.1	73.3
21 King's College London		442	72.4	64.7	73.0
22 York St John		297	90.5	45.2	68.8
23 Salford	15.0	313	73.2	39.0	64.8
24 Brighton	3.3	332	77.6	40.5	64.3
25 Westminster	6.7	304	79.1	37.3	63.9

Materials Technology

Courses in this table cover four distinct areas: materials science, mining engineering, textiles technology and printing, and marine technology. The various subjects are highly specialised and attract relatively few applicants, but are beginning to recruit more strongly after a dip when £9,000 fees were introduced. Although only 275 students started courses in materials technology itself in 2013, that represented a 20 per cent increase on the previous year. The leading universities demand chemistry and sometimes also physics, maths or design technology at A level or its equivalent.

Cambridge enjoys one of the biggest leads in any subject for the materials group. It has much the highest entry standards and a big lead in research. Only 5 per cent of the university's submission was considered less than world-leading or internationally excellent in the 2008 Research Assessment Exercise. Imperial College remains fractionally ahead of Oxford in second place, while fifth-placed Swansea has both the most satisfied students and a rare 100 per cent score for graduate prospects. De Montfort is the highest-placed of six post-1992 universities in the lower section of the ranking, which now contains no universities from Scotland or Northern Ireland.

Materials technology has dropped into the bottom half of the employment table, but is still in the top 12 for salaries in graduate-level jobs. A £4,000 rise in average earnings took the subjects into the top ten last year and it appeared this might be a blip arising from the small numbers involved. But even after an £400 drop in 2013, materials graduates were averaging more than £24,000 in professional roles. Almost a quarter of graduates continue their studies, either full or part-time, and a high unemployment rate in last year's *Guide* is now close to the average for all subjects.

Employed in professional job:	44%	Employed in non-professional job and studying:	2%
Employed in professional job and studying:	2%	Employed in non-professional job:	22%
Studying:	19%	Unemployed:	12%
Average starting professional salary:	£24,289	Average starting non-professional salary:	£16,625

Materials Technology	Research quality %	Entry Standards	Student satisfaction %	Graduate prospects %	Overall rating
1 Cambridge	58.3	665	84.8	86.6	100.0
2 Imperial College	31.7	542	86.1	88.5	90.2
3 Oxford	43.3	608	81.3	75.0	89.9
4 Loughborough	36.7	376	89.0	89.8	87.7
5 Swansea	30.0	316	89.6	100.0	86.6
6 Sheffield	31.7	418	82.0	80.6	82.2
7 Queen Mary, London	28.3	381	88.6	69.6	81.1
8 Exeter	15.0	416	76.6	91.2	77.5
9 Manchester	40.0	416	74.0	64.3	76.5
10 Birmingham	35.0	407	67.9	84.8	76.3
11 Leeds	40.0		72.7	66.2	75.5
12 De Montfort	13.3	331	86.2	67.3	74.0
13 Manchester Metropolitan	10.0		75.7	83.3	72.7

14 Sheffield Hallam	15.0			278	77.1		66.3
15 Huddersfield				365	72.1	47.3	60.0
16 Buckinghamshire New				317	69.8	42.4	56.1
17 London Metropolitan	0.0				70.2	47.2	54.9

Mathematics

The average entry qualifications of mathematicians starting a degree at Cambridge in 2013 were the highest there has ever been for any subject in the *Guide*, at 680 points, the equivalent of four A* grades at A level and two As at AS level. Entrants to the other leading universities were almost as well-qualified: eight of the top ten in the table average more than 500 points and the top three more than 600. The scores are boosted by the fact that most successful candidates for the leading universities have taken two A levels in the subject, as well as two or three others. But the table also covers the widest spread of entry scores in any subject, with London Metropolitan averaging only 176 points in 2013.

Applications and enrolments have recovered from a modest decline when higher fees were introduced in 2012, the numbers starting degrees increasing by more than 5 per cent in 2013. Maths is often cited as one of the subjects most likely to lead to a lucrative career, and the earnings table seems to bear this out. Although starting salaries in graduate jobs fell in 2013, the £24,000 average was still close to the top ten subjects. Maths is also in the top 20 for the proportion of graduates going straight into professional jobs or becoming postgraduate students, as almost one in three does. Employment scores in the table reflect this, with around half of the 69 universities recording positive destinations for at least 75 per cent of their graduates.

Cambridge has held onto the lead over Oxford that it established last year, registering the best employment score in the table, as well as the highest entry standards. However, the most satisfied students were at Nottingham Trent, in 42th place, with Greenwich, one place lower in the table, the nearest challenger. Sheffield Hallam is the top-performing post-1992 university and is joined in the top 40 by Portsmouth and Coventry. There are separate research scores for the three main strands of mathematics. Imperial College achieved the best grades in pure maths, while Oxford was top for statistics and shared the leading position with Cambridge in applied maths.

Mathematics	Research quality % Pure Mathematics	Research quality % Applied Mathematics	Research quality % Statistics	Entry standards	Student satisfaction %	Graduate prospects %	Overall rating
1 Cambridge	45.0	45.0	45.0	680	85.7	91.9	100.0
2 Oxford	48.3	45.0	56.7	642	83.7	85.7	97.2
=3 Imperial College	55.0	35.0	41.7	604	84.1	86.7	95.0
=3 Warwick	50.0	40.0	40.0	575	84.8	86.8	95.0
5 Bath	36.7	36.7	33.3	548	87.4	85.8	93.4
6 Durham	33.3	35.0	20.0	612	86.8	83.5	93.2
7 St Andrews	15.0	40.0	26.7	569	85.7	90.7	92.5

Mathematics cont

	Research quality % Pure Mathematics	Research quality % Applied Mathematics	Research quality % Statistics	Entry standards	Student satisfaction %	Graduate prospects %	Overall rating
8 Lancaster	23.3		30.0	483	87.8	80.6	88.7
9 Bristol	43.3	40.0	40.0	526	78.5	81.4	88.3
10 Dundee		21.7		375	92.8	82.1	87.4
11 Surrey		33.3		433	85.1	79.9	87.0
12 Nottingham	26.7	35.0	36.7	499	83.3	75.5	86.7
13 Keele		30.0		378	91.9	70.4	86.2
14 Birmingham	28.3	21.7		459	85.7	80.8	86.1
15 Loughborough	25.0	23.3		429	89.0	77.1	86.0
16 Glasgow	28.3	23.3	26.7	499	83.5	78.7	85.8
17 Exeter	25.0	26.7		480	83.1	80.9	85.7
18 Heriot-Watt	40.0	31.7	21.7	450	84.1	77.7	85.4
19 Southampton	20.0	33.3	31.7	470	81.1	81.1	85.1
20 University College London	33.3	23.3	23.3	544	80.4	76.1	84.9
21 East Anglia	30.0	18.3		422	90.4	68.3	84.5
22 Newcastle	15.0	30.0	25.0	459	84.0	78.1	84.3
23 London School of Economics	18.3		28.3	547	77.5	80.8	83.7
24 Strathclyde		23.3	20.0	454	83.3	77.8	83.3
25 Cardiff	16.7			460	82.7	79.3	82.1
26 Aberdeen	35.0			418	83.8	61.8	81.9
=27 King's College London	36.7	31.7		470	81.4	62.7	81.8
=27 Manchester	33.3	36.7	31.7	476	79.1	66.1	81.8
29 Edinburgh	40.0	31.7	21.7	531	71.4	77.3	81.7
=30 Leeds	25.0	28.3	38.3	459	79.0	72.4	81.4
=30 Leicester	23.3	18.3		388	80.4	85.4	81.4
=30 Queen's, Belfast	18.3			421	83.5	77.2	81.4
33 Sheffield	28.3	21.7	26.7	470	79.6	72.4	81.2
34 Sheffield Hallam	11.7	11.7	11.7	331	91.1	74.9	80.9
35 Sussex		23.3		425	81.0	75.0	80.8
36 Portsmouth		35.0		288	84.5	69.6	80.6
37 York	21.7	23.3		463	77.2	77.5	80.2
38 Reading		16.7	15.0	363	87.5	71.4	80.1
39 Swansea	16.7			361	83.2	79.7	79.8
40 Coventry	6.7	6.7		309	90.1	78.3	79.4
41 Stirling		16.7		385	82.8	75.4	79.2
42 Nottingham Trent	13.3	13.3	13.3	327	94.8	56.6	78.7
43 Greenwich			13.3	300	94.2	59.5	78.4
=44 Hertfordshire	28.3			318	83.0	65.7	78.0
=44 Northumbria		20.0		353	83.9	68.3	78.0
46 Kent	11.7	21.7	35.0	351	75.9	80.0	77.9
47 Brunel		23.3	26.7	346	84.0	63.0	77.7
48 Chester		5.0		278	90.2	74.0	77.1
49 Edge Hill				345		83.6	77.0

#	University							
50	South Wales		6.7		352	87.0	68.7	76.4
51	Aston	18.3	18.3	18.3	369	79.1	71.0	76.0
52	Brighton		5.0		297	90.1	66.9	75.8
53	Liverpool John Moores				305	88.8	71.4	75.2
54	Royal Holloway	8.3			401	81.5	67.6	74.9
55	Plymouth		8.3	10.9	326	88.1	59.1	74.8
56	Liverpool	21.7	30.0	11.7	403	74.5	64.3	74.4
57	Oxford Brookes		3.3		354	89.1	57.8	74.1
58	Aberystwyth	16.7			351	81.1	57.6	72.9
59	Manchester Metropolitan	18.3			322	79.3	62.1	72.7
60	Queen Mary, London	26.7	23.3	20.0	389	70.0	65.3	71.6
61	City		10.0		379	80.1	53.4	70.4
62	Derby				287	83.1	66.0	70.2
63	Bolton				266	84.2	61.8	69.2
64	Central Lancashire				377	86.3	41.2	68.3
65	Kingston				271	82.6	60.5	68.1
66	West of England		3.3		317	75.5	63.4	67.0
67	Essex				359	84.1	41.0	66.5
68	London Metropolitan	18.3		11.7	176	80.4	45.9	64.5
69	Staffordshire		0.0		236		51.6	60.4

Employed in professional job:	41%	Employed in non-professional job and studying:	2%
Employed in professional job and studying:	7%	Employed in non-professional job:	15%
Studying:	23%	Unemployed:	12%
Average starting professional salary:	£24,075	Average starting non-professional salary:	£16,260

Mechanical Engineering

Mechanical engineering is by far the biggest branch of engineering, attracting twice as many applicants as any of the other subjects. Indeed, it is comfortably inside the top 20 for all degree choices. The introduction of higher fees has only increased the subject's popularity: there was a 10 per cent rise in the number of students starting courses in 2013 and applications are up again this year.

It is not hard to see why. Throughout the economic downturn, mechanical engineering was among the top ten subjects for early career prospects and for starting salaries in graduate-level employment. Two-thirds of graduates go straight into such jobs and only one in ten has to settle for a lower-level role. Most of the leading universities demand maths – preferably with a strong component of mechanics – and another science subject (usually physics) at A level or its equivalent.

Cambridge has extended its lead over Imperial College at the top of table. Cambridge, which is ranked third in the world in mechanical engineering by QS, has by far the highest entry standards, research grades and employment score. Once again, the top score in the National Student Survey is to be found much further down the table. That distinction goes to Dundee, in 33rd place, where 95 per cent of final-year undergraduates were satisfied with their course. Liverpool John Moores is the highest-placed post-1992 university in the table, just outside top 20.

Mechanical Engineering cont

High satisfaction scores are spread through most of the ranking, with only five universities failing to win the approval of at least 70 per cent of final-year undergraduates. Entry scores are also rising, with seven universities averaging more than 500 points and only one, compared with six two years ago, averaging less than 250 points. Nationally, there are over six applications to the place. There are four additional universities in the table this year, but not all of the newcomers have enough students taking mechanical engineering to compile entry scores.

Employed in professional job:	66%	
Employed in professional job and studying:	2%	
Studying:	11%	
Average starting professional salary:	£26,076	

Employed in non-professional job and studying:	1%	
Employed in non-professional job:	10%	
Unemployed:	10%	
Average starting non-professional salary:	£17,671	

Mechanical Engineering	Research quality %	Entry standards	Student satisfaction %	Graduate prospects %	Overall rating
1 Cambridge	60.0	647	83.5	97.0	100.0
2 Imperial College	46.7	581	84.6	90.0	92.2
3 Bristol	40.0	524	85.7	92.2	89.1
4 Sheffield	45.0	486	84.5	93.2	89.0
5 Leeds	38.3	440	91.6	90.3	87.3
6 Bath	25.0	514	94.5	87.4	86.4
7 Nottingham	41.7	467	85.0	86.1	85.6
8 Birmingham	36.7	437	85.5	94.6	85.5
9 Loughborough	36.7	448	84.4	90.9	84.5
10 Surrey	35.0	452	87.8	87.3	84.4
11 Southampton	30.0	479	83.4	94.4	84.2
12 Cardiff	35.0	419	86.0	87.4	82.5
13 Strathclyde	26.2	502	81.9	89.6	82.1
14 Manchester	36.7	436	83.5	84.7	82.0
15 Heriot-Watt	25.0	444	89.8	86.0	81.6
16 Newcastle	31.7	424	82.1	90.8	81.2
17 Warwick	36.7	439	78.4	87.0	80.8
18 Lancaster	23.3	467	77.7	95.8	80.0
19 Liverpool	35.4	413	82.3	82.4	79.7
20 Edinburgh	28.3	510	72.6	88.0	79.0
21 Liverpool John Moores	33.3	326	88.6	84.1	78.7
22 Queen's, Belfast	31.7	385	81.4	84.9	77.9
23 Exeter	25.0	435	80.1	86.5	77.7
24 Aberdeen	31.7	430	72.2	89.2	77.2
=25 Brunel	23.3	378	89.8	77.2	76.3
=25 Glasgow	21.7	466	80.0	80.6	76.3
=25 Robert Gordon	10.0	404	85.9	93.6	76.3
28 Swansea	21.7	339	85.2	90.2	76.1
29 University College London	31.7	525	72.4	69.4	75.4

30 Coventry	7.4	344	92.7	86.9	74.1
31 Sussex	26.7	367	74.5	88.2	74.0
32 Aston	18.3	364	84.5	81.6	73.5
33 Dundee		400	95.1	76.7	72.1
34 City	21.7	348	86.8	69.0	71.3
=35 Greenwich	43.3	314	81.1	57.2	71.0
=35 Sunderland	10.0	283	89.0	86.2	71.0
=37 Derby		294	92.3	89.3	70.6
=37 Portsmouth	18.3	302	84.6	79.2	70.6
39 Huddersfield	15.0	355	76.5	86.6	70.4
40 West of England	25.0	346	72.5	79.8	69.6
=41 Queen Mary, London	21.7	414	77.8	65.9	69.5
=41 Salford	23.3		71.2	82.0	69.5
43 Harper Adams		319	86.4	88.4	69.0
44 De Montfort	20.0	266	82.4	77.8	68.5
45 Hertfordshire	26.7	329	76.3	70.2	68.4
46 Bradford	20.0	292	71.6	87.5	68.0
47 Northumbria	20.0	354	74.3	74.1	67.6
48 Teesside		337	87.3	78.6	67.3
49 Central Lancashire		379	91.1	65.9	66.9
50 Oxford Brookes		448	83.3	65.1	66.3
51 Staffordshire	20.0	276	76.8	74.6	65.8
52 Ulster		291	77.7	91.7	65.5
=53 Brighton	26.7	307	66.9	73.8	64.9
=53 Plymouth	8.3	314	79.8	74.5	64.9
55 Manchester Metropolitan	11.7	335	78.6	69.0	64.8
56 Hull	13.3	310	76.2	73.2	64.5
57 Sheffield Hallam	15.0	282	76.9	70.7	63.6
58 London South Bank	23.3	252	77.4	54.2	60.6
59 Glasgow Caledonian	6.7	338	74.0	65.0	60.5
60 West of Scotland		324	77.0	68.4	60.1
61 Anglia Ruskin		223	83.5	71.4	59.7
62 South Wales	23.3		56.8	75.0	59.6
63 Birmingham City		276	71.2	79.2	59.0
64 Kingston	11.7	296	65.3	57.4	55.1
65 Bolton	15.0		64.8	35.0	46.0
66 Glyndŵr	15.0		49.2	56.5	45.8

Medicine

There are more than 11 applications for every place in medicine – easily the highest ratio in any subject and all the more remarkable since candidates can only apply to four medical schools. Entry standards are correspondingly fearsome: only two of the 31 schools averaged less than 500 points in 2013 and neither of them was more than 13 points adrift of this mark. Nearly all schools demand chemistry and most biology. Physics or maths is required by some, either as an alternative or addition to biology. Universities will want to see evidence of

Medicine cont

commitment to the subject through work experience or voluntary work. Almost all schools interview candidates, and several use one of the two specialist aptitude tests (*see* chapter 1).

In spite of the highly selective nature of the subject, medicine is among the top four for applications, attracting yet more candidates in 2013. The subject carries unique prestige and is also the perennial leader in the employment table. Employment scores for individual schools are no longer used in the ranking (although they are still shown for guidance) to avoid small differences distorting positions in a subject where virtually all graduates become junior doctors or researchers. Ten schools reported full employment in 2013, and only two dropped below 95 per cent. Strangely, they were the top two in the table: Oxford and Cambridge. Indeed, Oxford is the first school for many years to dip below 90 per cent on this measure.

Medicine	Research quality %	Entry standards	Student satisfaction %	Graduate prospects %	Overall rating
1 Oxford	47.6	607	95.4	89.1	100.0
2 Cambridge	51.9	650	79.2	94.3	98.6
3 Imperial College	40.5	584	83.4	99.1	91.4
4 University College London	42.7	587	79.6	99.8	90.9
5 Queen Mary, London	37.1	548	87.9	99.4	89.2
6 Aberdeen	36.2	547	88.4	100.0	89.0
7 Edinburgh	44.3	577	73.3	99.5	88.2
8 St Andrews	23.3	554	90.4	98.2	86.6
9 Newcastle	27.9	535	87.6	100.0	85.4
=10 Dundee	24.1	542	87.2	98.8	84.7
=10 Leeds	27.5	530	87.1	100.0	84.7
12 Glasgow	28.1	560	79.4	100.0	84.4
13 Birmingham	29.3	554	79.5	99.9	84.2
=14 Exeter	22.8	515	91.7	99.7	83.8
=14 Keele	14.8	534	94.0	100.0	83.8
=14 Manchester	33.4	524	81.7	99.6	83.8
=14 Plymouth	22.8	515	91.7	99.7	83.8
18 Hull-York Medical School	32.3	510	81.7	99.0	82.4
=19 Bristol	29.2	515	81.7	100.0	81.9
=19 Southampton	28.9	500	85.2	100.0	81.9
21 Cardiff	22.7	531	82.5	99.8	81.5
22 East Anglia	18.3	542	83.2	98.6	81.4
23 Brighton and Sussex Medical School	15.0	492	93.2	99.6	80.2
24 Queen's, Belfast	21.6	516	81.3	99.2	79.5
25 Sheffield	23.2	526	75.9	100.0	78.8
26 Leicester	20.1	528	75.3	99.8	77.8
27 Warwick	21.9		75.9	100.0	77.4
28 Nottingham	15.2	542	74.6	99.5	77.3
29 St George's, London	18.7	512	74.8	100.0	75.9
30 King's College London	29.6	526	63.2	99.4	75.8
31 Liverpool	26.7	487	69.4	99.8	74.1

The top two have been the same for the last five years, but there is some movement in other leading positions: Imperial College has taken third place from Edinburgh, which is no longer the top university in Scotland for medicine. Aberdeen, in sixth place, now enjoys that distinction. Oxford's lead over Cambridge has narrowed, but it still has the most satisfied students in the table. Cambridge has the highest entry standards and the best research grades. In the 2008 Research Assessment Exercise, at least 80 per cent of its work was considered world-leading or internationally excellent in all but one of the eight specialisms in which it submitted work. Universities were able to submit research in up to 12 areas (called units of assessment, UoA). Full details can be seen for UoA 1–9, 12, 14 and 15 at **www.rae.ac.uk/results.**

Undergraduates have to be prepared to work long hours, particularly towards the end of the course, which will usually be five years long. But student satisfaction is generally high: only in the bottom two schools did the approval rating drop below 70 per cent. The early career rewards are high: only dentistry and chemical engineering bettered medicine's average starting salaries in 2013. The figures for Exeter and Plymouth, in joint 14th place, relate to the Peninsula Medical School, which was run jointly by the two universities. The school has now separated and applications should be made to the University of Exeter Medical School or Plymouth University Peninsula Medical School.

Employed in professional job:	93%	Employed in non-professional job and studying:	0%
Employed in professional job and studying:	1%	Employed in non-professional job:	0%
Studying:	5%	Unemployed:	1%
Average starting professional salary:	£28,548	Average starting non-professional salary:	..

Middle Eastern and African Studies

There were reports of increased interest in Middle Eastern studies around the time of the Arab Spring, but only 114 students started courses in 2013 – one more than the previous year – and non-European languages suffered the biggest decline of any subject area this year. The subjects enjoy some official protection because they are classed as "vulnerable". But there were only 55 applications for African studies, with a mere 15 students enrolling, although several universities are offering courses in African languages and/or culture in 2015.

Cambridge's lead over Durham at the top of the table is much narrower this year. Durham has the highest entry standards and again boasts the best employment record, while fourth-placed Birmingham has the most satisfied students. Oxford, which remains in third place, achieved the best grades in the 2008 Research Assessment Exercise, when 40 per cent of its submission was regarded as world-leading. This year's table contains no universities from outside England and only one (Westminster) from the post-1992 sector.

The small numbers inevitably make for big swings even in the national statistics. Only one subject has a higher unemployment rate than the 17 per cent recorded for Middle Eastern and African Studies in 2013. But even this was better than last year's 24 per cent. Yet the subjects remain in the top 50 starting salaries in professional jobs. Applicants for courses in Arabic or African languages are not expected to have previous knowledge of the language, although they would normally be expected to demonstrate an aptitude for learning other languages.

Middle Eastern and African Studies

	Research quality %	Entry standards	Student satisfaction %	Graduate prospects %	Overall rating
1 Cambridge	48.3	533	87.9	73.9	100.0
2 Durham	35.0	557	87.1	87.2	98.5
3 Oxford	50.0	526	88.0	61.7	97.4
4 Birmingham	33.3		88.9	69.4	90.5
5 Edinburgh	40.0	451	68.9	84.4	87.0
6 SOAS, London	36.7	398	70.9	75.0	82.2
7 Exeter	23.3	425	75.6	73.8	79.9
8 Manchester	30.0	401	73.8	44.4	73.5
9 Leeds		366	79.5	75.4	70.3
10 Westminster		281	76.7	44.9	58.2

Employed in professional job:	35%	Employed in non-professional job and studying:	3%
Employed in professional job and studying:	7%	Employed in non-professional job:	20%
Studying:	18%	Unemployed:	17%
Average starting professional salary:	£19,302	Average starting non-professional salary:	£17,390

Music

Music has well and truly recovered from the impact of introducing £9,000 fees. Applications were up by 20 per cent and new enrolments by a remarkable 46 per cent in 2013. One effect has been that the number of applications per place has dropped from more than five to less than four. Entry grades are relatively low at most universities – 14 average less than 300 UCAS points – although music grades and the quality of auditions are more significant. Nine out of ten degree applicants come with A levels and most university departments expect music to be among them, although they may accept a distinction or merit in Grade 8 music exams. The character of courses varies considerably, from the practical and vocational programmes in conservatoires to the more theoretical degrees in some of the older universities, and everything from creative sound design and new media to sonic arts elsewhere. No fewer than 186 universities and colleges are offering courses in 2015.

Oxford is back at the top of the table after a single year's absence. Cambridge, in third, shared highest entry grades with Durham, only one point ahead of last year's leader, Manchester, which is second. Royal Holloway, in fifth place, had the best grades in a high-scoring set of research assessments, with no less than 90 per cent of its research considered world-leading or internationally excellent. Derby has the most satisfied students, despite finishing outside the top 40 with one of the lowest employment scores in the table. Huddersfield is the leading post-1992 university, just outside the top 20.

The Royal College of Music has the best employment score, just ahead of the Royal Academy. It is noticeable that the specialist institutions do far better than most university departments on this measure. While the specialists (including the Birmingham Conservatoire, part of Birmingham City) produced five of the seven best employment scores, 17 universities saw fewer than half of their graduates go straight into professional jobs or further training. Music does better than the other performing arts in the employment table, although it is still in the bottom half. The 11 per cent unemployment rate is no worse than the average for all subjects, but 30 per cent of leavers were in non-graduate occupations six months after graduation. Only creative writing had lower average salaries for graduates who found employment classified as professional.

Employed in professional job:	39%	Employed in non-professional job and studying:	3%
Employed in professional job and studying:	4%	Employed in non-professional job:	27%
Studying:	16%	Unemployed:	11%
Average starting professional salary:	£17,118	Average starting non-professional salary:	£14,299

Music

	Research quality %	Entry standards	Student satisfaction %	Graduate prospects %	Overall rating
1 Oxford	58.3	529	90.5	87.6	100.0
2 Manchester	61.7	543	89.1	78.2	98.4
3 Cambridge	58.3	544	78.3	80.2	93.5
4 Birmingham	61.7	444	82.6	86.3	92.6
5 Royal Holloway	70.0	487	80.9	67.8	91.1
6 Sheffield	56.7	402	93.9	72.1	91.0
7 Glasgow	45.0	488	85.9	75.2	90.1
8 Edinburgh	35.0	470	88.6	77.1	88.8
9 King's College London	58.3	470	73.6	81.6	88.1
10 Nottingham	45.0	435	85.4	77.2	87.7
11 York	58.3	397	85.5	72.9	87.6
12 Durham	40.0	544	76.2	75.2	87.5
13 Newcastle	50.0	437	84.1	72.2	87.0
14 Surrey	35.0	470	86.1	70.4	86.0
15 Southampton	60.0	399	78.2	75.6	85.4
16 Queen's, Belfast	46.7	377	89.1	68.9	84.8
17 City	41.7	386	89.9	65.4	83.6
18 Royal Academy of Music	40.0	317	81.5	94.6	83.5
19 Bangor	40.0	325	90.0	72.4	82.1
20 Royal College of Music	26.7	309	84.6	95.5	81.8
21 Bristol	35.0	458	74.2	72.9	80.8
22 Huddersfield	38.3	337	87.8	69.7	80.7
23 Leeds	35.0	462	79.8	60.9	80.5
24 Goldsmiths, London	43.3	356	81.7	69.6	79.9
25 Keele	35.0	361	87.4	63.9	79.5
26 Cardiff	33.3	405	80.0	68.4	79.2
27 Sussex	35.0	403	80.4	65.3	78.9
28 Birmingham City	23.3	327	83.3	84.2	78.7
29 Bath Spa	16.7	369	88.2	69.9	78.0
30 Royal Conservatoire of Scotland	23.3	399	73.9	82.8	77.8
31 Lancaster	43.3	364	77.8	63.6	77.1
32 Royal Northern College of Music	15.0	345	76.0	88.2	75.7
33 Brunel	25.0	328	93.4	47.8	74.5

Music cont

	Research quality %	Entry standards	Student satisfaction %	Graduate prospects %	Overall rating
34 Hull	16.7	354	89.3	54.4	73.9
35 Oxford Brookes	21.7	345	88.3	50.8	73.2
36 Brighton	45.0	268	88.5	41.6	72.0
37 Middlesex		298	90.4	67.6	71.4
38 West London	3.3	302	83.1	73.7	70.6
=39 Edinburgh Napier	1.7	397	85.2	51.7	70.5
=39 Liverpool	26.7	395	76.5	47.1	70.5
41 SOAS, London	50.0		71.5	47.2	70.3
42 Ulster	10.0	329	88.9	49.2	69.8
43 Aberdeen	20.0	400	74.0	52.4	69.6
44 Hertfordshire	8.3	341	82.2	55.6	68.7
45 Derby		351	94.5	35.9	68.1
46 Anglia Ruskin	8.3	276	79.1	70.2	67.8
47 Northampton	8.3	272	88.4	51.5	67.0
48 Chester	13.3	312	80.6	52.7	66.9
49 Manchester Metropolitan		338	80.4	58.3	66.7
50 Chichester		335	81.2	56.9	66.6
51 Gloucestershire		259	88.0	59.4	66.4
=52 Coventry	23.3	336	72.2	52.1	66.3
=52 De Montfort	28.3	315	78.5	41.0	66.3
54 Plymouth	25.0	268	79.4	50.5	66.0
55 Central Lancashire		348	80.8	50.8	65.5
56 Salford	8.3	341	75.3	52.1	64.8
=57 Cumbria		359	83.1	37.8	63.9
=57 Westminster	15.0	293	70.6	61.0	63.9
59 South Wales		334	69.3	65.4	63.4
60 East Anglia	13.3		72.2	52.0	62.2
61 Canterbury Christ Church	16.7	294	75.5	43.3	62.1
62 Sunderland	8.3	291	78.5	44.8	61.9
=63 Falmouth		283	71.9	60.5	60.8
=63 Southampton Solent		306	82.4	37.3	60.8
65 York St John	15.0	263	71.9	47.2	59.6
66 East London		302	71.3	52.6	59.5
67 Buckinghamshire New		277	78.7	42.6	59.1
68 West of Scotland		353	70.9	35.4	57.6
69 Liverpool John Moores		311	75.6	30.3	56.4
70 London South Bank		222	73.8	48.1	55.6
71 University of the Arts London		239	62.4	62.5	54.9
72 Kingston	3.3	315	61.3	46.1	54.8
73 Kent		333	42.1	59.3	49.8

Nursing

Nursing attracts more than twice as many applications as any other subject. There has been phenomenal growth since the move towards an all-graduate profession, with the number of applications passing 100,000 for the first time in 2008 and reaching 200,000 by 2011. Demand rose again in 2013 and, in spite of extra provision, there were over nine applications for every place. Even so, entry requirements are low. Although just one university, compared with eight last year, averaged less than 250 points, only the top two in the table have averages of more than 400 points.

At the top of the table Glasgow has slightly extended the lead over Edinburgh that it established last year. Glasgow has the most satisfied students, while Edinburgh has the highest entry standards. Manchester, which has moved up seven places to third this year, produced the best grades in the 2008 Research Assessment Exercise, with 85 per cent of its submission considered world-leading or internationally excellent. South Wales just pips Northumbria to the highest position among the post-1992 universities, finishing in the top ten. Just over a third of the institutions in the table are pre-1992 universities, although they fill the top eight places.

Five universities, compared with eleven two years ago, achieved full employment in 2013, and all but three saw more than 90 per cent go straight into professional jobs. The perfect scores were at Liverpool, Manchester Metropolitan, Keele, De Montfort and Derby. The subject remains in the top three for employment prospects, but is only just in the top 20 in the earnings league, with average starting salaries just above £22,500.

Almost two-thirds of the students arrive without A levels, many of them upgrading other health-related qualifications. A quarter of those who join pre-registration programmes drop out, but the rate is nearer 10 per cent thereafter.

Nursing	Research quality %	Entry standards	Student satisfaction %	Graduate prospects %	Overall rating
1 Glasgow	30.0	422	95.6	94.4	100.0
=2 Edinburgh	41.7	500	78.1	89.5	97.5
=2 Liverpool	20.0	366	91.8	100.0	97.5
4 Manchester	61.7	375	77.7	95.2	97.3
5 Ulster	53.3	328	86.2	96.0	97.0
6 Nottingham	31.7	364	85.1	98.7	96.4
7 Southampton	58.3	353	73.4	98.8	96.3
8 Leeds	36.7	388	78.5	98.0	95.9
9 South Wales	18.3	378	88.6	96.7	95.2
10 Cardiff	25.0	375	81.6	98.6	94.8
11 Northumbria	26.7	360	85.6	96.7	94.7
12 King's College London	23.3	383	79.4	98.8	94.4
13 Queen Margaret, Edinburgh		365	93.3	98.7	94.3
14 Surrey	1.7	396	86.7	98.7	93.9
=15 East Anglia	20.0	369	80.1	99.4	93.7
=15 Huddersfield		372	91.6	97.9	93.7
17 Glyndŵr	8.3		90.5	98.5	93.4

Nursing cont

	Research quality %	Entry standards	Student satisfaction %	Graduate prospects %	Overall rating
=18 Portsmouth		380	90.2	97.0	93.2
=18 York	46.7	352	70.6	97.8	93.2
20 Manchester Metropolitan	10.0	331	87.6	100.0	93.1
21 Swansea	18.3	335	83.2	98.1	92.2
22 Keele		333	88.9	100.0	92.1
23 Birmingham		376	83.0	99.3	92.0
=24 Bournemouth	20.0	325	83.8	97.1	91.7
=24 City	43.3	323	81.5	91.8	91.7
=24 West of England	16.7	353	79.1	98.3	91.7
27 De Montfort	16.7	309	81.6	100.0	91.3
28 Coventry		332	92.8	95.6	91.1
29 Central Lancashire	23.3	343	82.7	93.4	90.9
30 Edge Hill	13.3	328	87.3	94.3	90.5
31 Hertfordshire	35.0	319	73.6	97.0	90.4
32 Sheffield Hallam	18.3	324	84.1	94.0	90.0
=33 Glasgow Caledonian	30.0	318	82.1	92.0	89.8
=33 West London	20.0	290	81.9	97.6	89.8
35 Derby		293	87.2	100.0	89.7
=36 Oxford Brookes		343	86.1	95.7	89.6
=36 Salford	20.0	352	74.2	96.2	89.6
38 Birmingham City		341	81.7	98.0	89.3
39 Teesside		330	84.6	96.9	89.2
40 Stirling	30.0	271	81.2	95.4	89.0
=41 Leeds Metropolitan		299	89.3	95.9	88.7
=41 Staffordshire		328	82.1	97.8	88.7
43 Liverpool John Moores	16.7	334	76.1	95.2	88.3
44 Chester	5.0	314	81.1	97.2	88.2
=45 Bradford	18.3	328	78.8	93.0	88.1
=45 Greenwich	13.3	300	87.7	91.7	88.1
47 Plymouth	16.7	312	75.8	96.7	88.0
=48 Bangor		307	80.6	99.0	87.9
=48 Northampton		326	79.2	98.1	87.9
=50 Essex		276	91.2	94.6	87.5
=50 Hull		351	82.2	93.1	87.5
52 Edinburgh Napier	16.7	284	79.8	95.7	87.4
53 Cumbria		311	77.9	98.1	86.8
54 Kingston/St George's, London	25.0	288	70.3	97.0	86.6
55 Worcester		273	84.9	96.5	86.4
56 Canterbury Christ Church		292	79.1	98.0	86.2
=57 Bedfordshire		262	83.2	98.0	86.1
=57 Dundee	23.3	237	80.4	95.2	86.1
59 Queen's, Belfast	20.0	295	72.4	94.6	85.6
60 Brighton	5.0	315	68.1	98.7	85.0

61 Anglia Ruskin		273	78.1	97.7	84.9
62 Abertay		266	87.6	91.2	84.3
63 Robert Gordon		300	76.6	91.8	82.8
64 London South Bank	15.0	271	65.7	95.4	82.0
65 Lincoln		321	61.9	95.2	80.9
66 Buckinghamshire New	3.3	272	74.0	90.6	80.6
67 West of Scotland		258	78.1	82.8	76.8
68 Middlesex	15.0	282	81.2	72.7	76.2

Employed in professional job:	91%	Employed in non-professional job and studying:	0%
Employed in professional job and studying:	3%	Employed in non-professional job:	2%
Studying:	2%	Unemployed:	3%
Average starting professional salary:	£22,580	Average starting non-professional salary:	£15,207

Other Subjects Allied to Medicine

This table was shorn of two of the most popular subjects in the group when physiotherapy and radiography were given rankings of their own. But taken together, the remaining subjects still recruit more students than the totals for most other tables.

Those subjects include audiology, complementary therapies, counselling, health services management, health sciences, nutrition, occupational therapy, optometry, ophthalmology, orthoptics, osteopathy, podiatry and speech therapy. Only ophthalmics managed increased enrolments when £9,000 fees arrived, but both applications and enrolments for the group as a whole improved in 2013 and again this year.

Since the removal of physiotherapy and radiography, traditional universities no longer monopolise the upper reaches of the table, but they still occupy nine of the top ten places. Aston, which is famously strong in ophthalmics, remains the leader. But Leeds, which has moved up from fifth place and has one of the two top research scores, could hardly be closer. University College London is the other research star, while Robert Gordon, in equal 17th place, has the most satisfied students. Cambridge, which is restricted to fourth place because it did not enter the 2008 Research Assessment Exercise in this category, has average entry grades that are 176 points ahead of its nearest challenger, Dundee.

For the second year in a row, Abertay achieved a rare 100 per cent employment record from its degree in food, nutrition and health, despite finishing just outside the top 20. Glasgow Caledonian is the highest-placed post-1992 university in sixth position. The choice of specialism naturally affects graduate employment rates, which range from better than 90 per cent positive destinations at 11 universities to less than 60 per cent at nine others. Overall, the subjects are in the top 20 for employment prospects, with only 10 per cent unemployed six months after graduating. They are lower in the comparison of salaries in professional jobs, but still in the top 30.

Employed in professional job:	57%	Employed in non-professional job and studying:	2%
Employed in professional job and studying:	4%	Employed in non-professional job:	16%
Studying:	11%	Unemployed:	10%
Average starting professional salary:	£21,328	Average starting non-professional salary:	£13,935

Other Subjects Allied to Medicine	Research quality %	Entry standards	Student satisfaction %	Graduate prospects %	Overall rating
1 Aston	26.7	425	93.5	98.9	100.0
2 Leeds	36.7		86.5	97.5	99.0
3 Surrey	33.3	487	84.1		96.6
4 Cambridge		665	87.4	86.6	96.5
5 Manchester	30.0	433	88.8	86.0	95.5
6 Glasgow Caledonian	30.0	420	84.8	91.2	93.9
7 Cardiff	31.7	441	79.8	96.2	93.6
8 University College London	36.7		82.8	86.1	93.5
9 Newcastle	30.0	461	86.2	77.5	93.2
10 Lancaster	33.3	435	86.5	73.3	92.2
11 Portsmouth	28.3		89.0	75.0	91.8
12 Hertfordshire	26.0	369	83.0	98.1	91.5
13 City	18.3	403	86.8	90.8	91.3
14 Oxford Brookes	16.7	382	89.4	86.4	90.5
15 Liverpool	20.0	349	93.1	78.7	90.3
16 Swansea	31.7	368	81.0	90.3	90.0
=17 Kingston	11.7		88.9	87.5	89.9
=17 Robert Gordon	10.0	370	95.5	78.8	89.9
19 Dundee	23.3	489	84.1	70.0	89.7
20 Nottingham Trent	30.0			70.6	88.6
21 Abertay	3.3		84.8	100.0	87.7
22 Sheffield	30.0	424	82.4	68.5	87.5
23 Strathclyde	30.0	480	74.0	78.9	87.4
24 Kent	16.7	387	91.8	65.9	87.2
25 East Anglia	5.0	436	88.4	75.5	86.5
26 Warwick	28.3	460	79.5	65.7	86.2
27 Southampton	8.3	409	83.1	85.3	85.5
28 West of England	31.7	356	80.0	74.8	85.3
29 Exeter	30.0	452	70.8	80.0	84.7
30 Anglia Ruskin	8.3	280	86.8	94.0	84.5
=31 Brunel	15.0	352	86.4	73.9	84.2
=31 Manchester Metropolitan	12.7	365	87.4	71.9	84.2
33 Ulster	31.0	346	83.9	59.4	83.4
34 Bradford	16.2	375	77.5	85.0	83.0
35 Brighton	5.0	333	81.4	95.1	82.9
36 Nottingham	20.0	351	89.2	55.6	82.8
37 South Wales	0.0	357	81.8	93.4	82.4
38 Birmingham		416	85.2	74.3	82.3
39 Northampton	6.7	301	87.5	77.2	81.4
40 Reading		435	84.4	68.9	81.3
41 Bournemouth		335	85.0	83.8	81.1
=42 Central Lancashire	13.3	344	85.7	64.4	80.8
=42 Cumbria	0.0	318	88.7	76.3	80.8

=42 Northumbria	13.3	386	83.2	63.1	80.8
=42 Salford	15.0	365	81.0	70.3	80.8
46 Teesside	6.7	339	87.4	68.0	80.7
=47 King's College London	15.0		76.3	84.6	80.6
=47 York St John	1.7	340	83.3	82.8	80.6
49 Sheffield Hallam	8.3	317	85.8	72.9	80.5
50 Plymouth	3.3	338	82.6	82.5	80.4
51 Coventry	6.7	308	85.7	75.1	80.1
52 Queen Margaret, Edinburgh	1.7	386	79.5	79.6	79.5
53 Essex		330	87.5	71.2	79.4
54 Huddersfield		323	86.9	73.4	79.3
55 Hull	33.3		82.1	44.5	79.0
56 Cardiff Metropolitan	8.3	319	84.1	69.5	78.8
57 Derby		349	88.7	61.5	78.6
=58 Canterbury Christ Church	1.7	294	87.3	72.4	78.5
=58 West of Scotland	23.3	312	83.7	53.3	78.5
=60 Chester	5.0	304	85.8	70.0	78.4
=60 Greenwich		307	87.4	71.2	78.4
62 Birmingham City		365	85.2	66.0	78.3
63 Liverpool John Moores	11.7	341	80.7	64.6	77.5
=64 Glyndŵr	8.3	394	82.6	53.3	77.2
=64 Lincoln	3.3	321	83.1	70.5	77.2
66 Middlesex	13.3	327	80.7	63.1	77.0
67 Edinburgh Napier	6.7		79.6	71.9	76.3
68 St Mark and St John		316		73.1	75.9
69 East London	16.7	262	82.4	59.7	75.4
70 Westminster	18.3	288	71.7	78.7	75.3
71 Leeds Metropolitan	3.3	281	80.5	68.5	73.7
72 St Mary's, Twickenham		293	77.8	72.2	72.7
73 De Montfort	11.7	304	70.8	67.3	71.1
74 Staffordshire	1.7	200	82.6		69.0
75 Bedfordshire		234	72.1	78.6	68.5
76 London Metropolitan	13.3		72.8	51.9	67.3
77 Bolton		251	77.1	54.5	66.5
78 Newman		304	76.4	46.4	66.3

Pharmacology and Pharmacy

A Government-commissioned inquiry is deciding whether to reduce the number of places in pharmacy, but it is hard to imagine that any such decision would be implemented in 2015. Pharmacology is not part of the inquiry, which is focusing on the growth in the numbers taking the MPharm course, the only direct route to professional registration as a pharmacist. The qualification is now offered at 29 institutions, compared with 12 in 2002, with another dozen running a BSc in the subject. Unlike medicine and dentistry, recruitment in the subjects has never been controlled centrally, but there has been concern about the growing numbers who fail to secure a place on a pre-registration year. The problem does not yet

Pharmacology and Pharmacy cont

manifest itself in our employment table, which has pharmacology and pharmacy in fifth place, with an unemployment rate of 4 per cent that is bettered only by medicine, dentistry and nursing.

There is certainly no sign of a decline in the subjects' popularity: applications and enrolments both grew again in 2013, when there were almost seven applications for every place. Departments in England are evenly split between those specialising in pharmacy and pharmacology. Only four cover both. While the MPharm degree takes four years, pharmacology is available either as a three-year BSc or as an extended course. Most degrees require chemistry and another science or maths at A level or the equivalent. Partly because of the training structure for pharmacists, the subjects are not in the top 40 in the earnings league: averaging less than £20,000 in professional-level jobs.

Cambridge remains top of the table, where the university's normal high entry standards make the difference: they are 150 points ahead of the rest. Students give the subjects attract high satisfaction ratings, especially in Northern Ireland. Ulster produced an unusually high (98 per cent) score in the 2014 National Student Survey, with Queen's, Belfast, which has moved up to second place in the table, the nearest challenger. Nottingham, which has dropped to third, has the best research score. Three universities, compared with seven last year, saw all their graduates go into professional jobs or further study. They were Reading, Central Lancashire and Kent.

Employed in professional job:	77%	Employed in non-professional job and studying:	1%
Employed in professional job and studying:	6%	Employed in non-professional job:	5%
Studying:	8%	Unemployed:	4%
Average starting professional salary:	£19,763	Average starting non-professional salary:	£16,821

Pharmacology and Pharmacy	Research quality %	Entry standards	Student satisfaction %	Graduate prospects %	Overall rating
1 Cambridge	33.3	665	87.4	86.6	100.0
2 Queen's, Belfast	28.3	429	95.5	99.1	94.9
3 Nottingham	50.0	488	78.3	96.6	93.9
4 East Anglia	28.3	471	90.6	96.9	93.7
5 Bath	33.3	481	82.8	97.4	91.5
6 Manchester	43.3	444	81.6	93.2	91.3
7 Cardiff	28.3	452	87.2	97.8	91.2
8 Leeds	30.0	405	94.1	83.3	90.8
9 Aston	26.7	438	87.6	99.4	90.7
10 King's College London	28.3	431	88.1	90.3	89.5
11 Strathclyde	28.3	511	78.8	95.4	88.9
12 University College London	36.1	474	76.8	94.3	88.2
=13 Bristol	28.3	452	82.8	88.6	87.3
=13 Dundee	38.3	493	84.4	58.1	87.3
=13 Kent	15.5	379	91.8	100.0	87.3
=16 Keele	5.0	425	92.5	99.0	86.6
=16 Newcastle	33.3	375	87.0	83.3	86.6

=16 Reading	21.7	393	86.1	100.0	86.6
19 Robert Gordon		480	90.0	99.1	86.2
=20 Brighton	18.3	365	88.3	97.7	85.2
=20 Ulster		392	98.3	90.0	85.2
22 De Montfort	18.3	394	86.2	90.5	84.1
=23 Bradford	28.3	390	79.0	94.8	83.7
=23 Portsmouth	28.3	351	84.0	89.3	83.7
25 Liverpool	30.2	413	82.1	73.2	83.0
26 Leicester	16.7	437	86.8	73.5	82.8
27 Glasgow	28.3	452	74.8	85.2	82.4
28 Edinburgh	43.3		77.9	62.5	81.8
29 Liverpool John Moores	11.7	393	81.1	98.1	80.8
30 Huddersfield	8.3	403	81.9	97.9	80.7
31 Central Lancashire	13.3	406	76.7	100.0	79.8
32 Aberdeen	16.7	424	82.2	71.4	79.5
33 Hertfordshire	15.0	364	77.5	94.6	78.0
34 Glasgow Caledonian	13.3	358	89.5	53.3	76.3
35 Sunderland	6.7	345	74.4	97.7	73.7
36 Greenwich	11.7	333	82.0	65.8	73.0
37 Kingston	11.7	302	75.4	78.5	70.4
38 Queen Margaret, Edinburgh		341	86.1	45.5	68.6
39 East London		282	87.4	46.2	66.9
40 London Metropolitan		258	85.1	34.3	62.5

Philosophy

The demand for places in philosophy stabilised in 2013, following a serious decline when £9,000 fees were introduced. Seventy universities are offering the subject in 2015. The level of competition has eased since it was one of the most selective subjects in the arts and social sciences only three years ago, but still seven universities average more than 500 points at entry and the figure is above 400 at more than half of the institutions in the table. Relatively few philosophy undergraduates studied the subject at A level – indeed, Bristol warns that even an A in the subject is "not necessarily evidence of aptitude for philosophy at university". Degrees can require more mathematical skills than many candidates expect, especially when there is an emphasis on logic in the syllabus.

Oxford has extended its lead over Cambridge at the top of the table. It has the highest entry standards in the table, but University College London, in eighth place, produced the best results in the 2008 Research Assessment Exercise, when three-quarters of its submission was rated world-leading or internationally excellent. The University of the West of England again has much the most satisfied students and is the top post-1992 university, having broken into the top 20 this year. Philosophers are generally satisfied with their courses: only four universities had an approval rating below 75 per cent in the 2014 National Student Survey.

Graduate employment is more of a problem, however. Cambridge was the only university to see 80 per cent of philosophers go straight into professional jobs or onto postgraduate courses in 2013. At 15 universities, fewer than half of the graduates were in this position. Philosophy remains just in the bottom 20 subjects in the employment table, but salaries for

Philosophy cont

those who do find professional-level jobs are in the top 25, following a rise of more than £1,000 in the average since the 2012 survey. A high proportion – almost three in ten – stay on as postgraduates, whether full or part-time, but little more than a third of graduates go straight into professional jobs.

Employed in professional job:	32%	Employed in non-professional job and studying:	4%
Employed in professional job and studying:	3%	Employed in non-professional job:	24%
Studying:	22%	Unemployed:	16%
Average starting professional salary:	£21,869	Average starting non-professional salary:	£14,838

Philosophy	Research quality %	Entry standards	Student satisfaction %	Graduate prospects %	Overall rating
1 Oxford	45.0	594	85.8	77.6	100.0
2 Cambridge	42.7	588	80.8	83.3	97.6
3 King's College London	48.3	455	90.3	72.9	97.2
4 St Andrews	51.7	505	85.5	68.3	95.9
5 London School of Economics	45.0	512	80.8	76.6	93.7
6 Exeter	31.7	445	88.4	75.8	92.8
7 Bristol	41.7	480	82.9	70.7	91.8
8 University College London	55.0	526	71.1	74.3	90.1
9 Durham	28.3	532	81.4	69.9	89.8
10 Sheffield	46.7	439	82.9	60.4	89.0
11 Essex	38.3	366	87.7	65.1	88.5
12 Southampton	16.7	406	90.6	69.9	88.2
13 York	28.3	464	83.6	67.7	88.1
14 Newcastle	26.7	402	87.6	67.4	87.8
15 Nottingham	36.7	412	81.6	68.2	86.9
16 Birmingham	18.3	404	84.3	76.0	86.1
17 Edinburgh	35.0	488	75.3	69.1	85.8
18 Warwick	28.3	509	78.3	63.6	85.7
19 West of England	5.0	334	97.5	61.9	85.3
20 Leeds	35.0	413	82.4	58.2	84.7
21 Sussex	26.7	426	84.4	57.9	84.6
22 Kent	18.3	381	86.8	65.7	84.4
23 East Anglia	15.0	423	85.6	64.4	84.2
24 Lancaster	20.0	413	81.9	70.4	84.1
25 Glasgow	21.7	460	87.8	45.4	84.0
26 Reading	45.0	372	81.9	50.7	83.4
27 Stirling	40.0	375	84.0	44.8	82.4
28 Manchester	21.7	428	80.2	62.5	82.2
29 Cardiff	13.3	405	80.4	69.8	81.4
30 Queen's, Belfast	25.0	376	88.2	41.6	81.0
31 Keele	16.7	369	82.7	64.3	80.8
32 Dundee	21.7	382	90.5	32.6	79.8

33 Aberdeen	8.3	439	84.2	45.8	78.4
34 Oxford Brookes	0.0	326	90.5	49.3	77.0
35 Hertfordshire	11.7	347	84.4	48.1	76.3
36 Hull	15.0	310	82.7	51.2	75.3
37 Brighton	45.0	256	78.9	37.2	74.2
38 Central Lancashire		309	86.5	46.0	73.2
39 Royal Holloway		393	73.6	63.4	72.6
40 Liverpool	8.3	395	73.0	50.5	71.2
41 Manchester Metropolitan	16.7	310	78.8	36.2	70.0
42 Staffordshire	6.7	258	79.0	53.3	69.9
43 Anglia Ruskin		214	91.3	33.8	69.8
44 Roehampton		268	86.4	34.8	69.1
45 St Mary's, Twickenham		289	78.9	48.1	68.4
46 Bath Spa		308	82.2	34.7	68.1
47 Heythrop College	1.7	356	73.6	42.9	66.9

Physics and Astronomy

The long decline in the numbers taking physics in the sixth-form and university was being reversed before higher fees arrived, and the recovery has not been knocked off course. The numbers starting physics degrees went up by 50 per cent in six years and there were further increases in applications and enrolments in 2013. The "Brian Cox effect" has been credited with the recent boom in popularity, in recognition of the engaging Manchester University professor's many television appearances. There are now more applications for physics than for chemistry – almost six for every place. Astronomy and astrophysics degrees are even more selective and are being offered by over 30 universities in 2015.

Physics and Astronomy	Research quality %	Entry standards	Student satisfaction %	Graduate prospects %	Overall rating
1 Cambridge	38.3	665	87.4	86.6	100.0
2 Birmingham	33.3	555	91.1	87.9	97.0
3 Bath	36.7	512	89.7	90.1	96.9
=4 Lancaster	40.0	521	94.7	76.4	96.7
=4 St Andrews	38.3	555	90.2	82.0	96.7
6 Durham	33.3	621	85.8	84.4	95.5
7 Oxford	31.7	631	84.2	86.7	95.1
8 Imperial College	35.0	603	81.9	87.7	94.6
9 Nottingham	38.3	501	87.0	78.0	92.4
10 Manchester	31.7	560	86.8	80.0	92.2
11 Warwick	26.7	551	82.9	88.5	90.8
12 Exeter	30.0	476	84.2	89.3	90.6
13 Sheffield	33.3	457	89.1	78.2	90.3
14 Glasgow	33.3	492	84.2	81.9	90.1
15 Sussex	30.0	436	87.8	85.3	89.9

	Research quality %	Entry standards	Student satisfaction %	Graduate prospects %	Overall rating
16 Bristol	31.7	490	83.1	82.5	89.1
17 Surrey	25.0	435	81.2	95.5	87.9
18 Edinburgh	35.0	523	76.1	80.5	87.4
19 Leicester	28.3	407	88.2	80.4	87.2
20 Southampton	28.3	455	84.4	81.2	87.1
21 Cardiff	20.0	461	87.1	85.3	86.7
22 Liverpool	31.7	425	84.3	77.4	86.2
23 University College London	33.3	513	77.5	75.7	85.8
24 Hertfordshire	28.3	374	88.4	76.5	85.1
25 Queen's, Belfast	23.3	418	85.0	83.2	85.0
26 York	28.3	443	84.1	71.9	83.9
27 Heriot-Watt	28.3	425	83.7	72.2	83.2
28 Leeds	26.7	447	80.0	77.7	83.1
29 Aberdeen	31.7	423	72.9	83.8	82.7
30 Strathclyde	16.7	423	87.5	74.2	81.3
31 Nottingham Trent	28.3	313	94.1	59.7	81.1
32 Kent	26.5	325	87.3	70.0	80.6
33 Queen Mary, London	27.4	401	85.5	62.3	80.1
34 King's College London	23.3	466	80.0	68.5	79.9
35 Royal Holloway	25.0	414	82.0	65.9	79.0
36 Loughborough	26.7	390	79.9	68.5	78.7
37 Keele	16.7	354	88.8	66.0	77.4
38 Swansea	23.3	363	77.8	73.0	77.0
39 Hull	20.0	344	89.8	57.4	76.3
40 Central Lancashire	16.7	365	73.2	80.0	74.5
41 Salford	23.3	333	82.7	58.5	74.2
42 Aberystwyth	10.0	330	78.8	75.6	72.4
43 Dundee		383	89.7	62.1	71.5
44 West of Scotland	6.7	332	65.4		58.7

Employed in professional job:	36%	Employed in non-professional job and studying:	1%
Employed in professional job and studying:	5%	Employed in non-professional job:	9%
Studying:	36%	Unemployed:	13%
Average starting professional salary:	£24,523	Average starting non-professional salary:	£14,308

   Entry scores are correspondingly high. No fewer than 13 universities, led by top-placed Cambridge, average more than 500 points at entry and four top 600. Lancaster, which shares fourth place with St Andrews, has the most satisfied students and achieved the best of surprisingly modest scores in the 2008 Research Assessment Exercise. For the second year in a row, Surrey has the best graduate prospects, with Bath the only other university where 90 per cent of those completing courses were in professional jobs or continuing their studies six months after graduation. Physics and astronomy are just outside the top 10 for starting salaries, averaging just £24,500. The subjects are only a little lower in the overall comparison of graduate prospects, with 42 per cent taking postgraduate courses, either full or part-time.

Most universities demand physics and maths at A level for both physics and astronomy, as well as good grades overall. Only three of the 44 universities in the table are post-1992 institutions: Hertfordshire is the highest-placed at 24th. Just one undergraduate in five is female and a similarly small proportion arrives without A levels or their equivalent. About 5 per cent transfer to other courses or drop out, usually at the end of the first year, but well over half of those who remain get firsts or 2:1s.

Physiotherapy

Not long ago, unemployment among newly graduated physiotherapists had become a cause for concern because opportunities in the labour market had not kept pace with growth in higher education courses. The subject has continued to increase in popularity but it is now in the top ten subjects for graduate prospects, with 88 per cent of those completing courses in physiotherapy going straight into professional jobs. The Chartered Society of Physiotherapy accredits degrees at all 35 institutions offering the subject in the UK, two of which did not have enough entrants and/or graduates to appear in this table. Most of the leading courses demand biology A level or equivalent, but some may also want another science or maths.

The ranking is in its second year, the subject having appeared previously as part of the table for "other subjects allied to medicine". Like last year, Cardiff emerges at the top, although Keele is now its nearest challenger and the only university with a 100 per cent employment record. Cardiff and the University of the West of England tied for the best grades in the 2008 Research Assessment Exercise, but the standard in physiotherapy was lower than in most other subjects. Entry standards at most of the leading universities are relatively low, but they are closely bunched. Robert Gordon has the highest average score, at 479 points, but only Cumbria averages less than 350 points.

Two-thirds of the universities in the table are post-1992 institutions, and they hold their own against their older counterparts. Robert Gordon, in third place, is one of six modern universities in the top ten. Satisfaction levels are high. Although none can match the 98.7 per cent rate at Leeds Metropolitan, nine other universities satisfied at least 90 per cent of final-year undergraduates. Employment scores within the table are equally impressive: more than half of the universities saw at least nine out ten leavers find professional jobs or start postgraduate courses within six months of graduation. The average starting salary in professional roles was just outside the top 20 for all subjects, at just over £22,000.

Physiotherapy	Research quality %	Entry standards	Student satisfaction %	Graduate prospects %	Overall rating
1 Cardiff	31.7	461	94.5	97.0	100.0
2 Keele	23.3	424	91.7	100.0	95.7
3 Robert Gordon	10.0	479	96.4	93.6	95.4
4 Glasgow Caledonian	30.0	424	90.0	90.3	93.6
5 Oxford Brookes	16.7	431	88.2	95.3	91.8
6 Nottingham	20.0	422	86.9	95.0	91.5
7 Northumbria	13.3	436	88.5	93.4	90.7

	Research quality %	Entry standards	Student satisfaction %	Graduate prospects %	Overall rating
8 West of England	31.7	415	82.2	88.9	90.3
9 East London	10.7		85.1	85.2	90.0
10 Liverpool	20.0	416	86.5	91.7	89.9
=11 Brunel	15.0	416	94.4	86.3	89.7
=11 King's College London	15.0	475	82.1	88.5	89.7
13 East Anglia	5.0	425	94.8	91.7	89.6
14 Sheffield Hallam	8.3	424	89.8	94.2	89.5
15 Bradford	16.7	366	93.6	93.8	89.2
16 Queen Margaret, Edinburgh	1.7	472	85.4	92.0	88.5
17 Birmingham		435	87.2	96.6	88.0
18 Coventry	6.7	402	92.9	90.3	87.5
19 Leeds Metropolitan	3.3		98.7	83.7	87.0
20 Huddersfield		444	88.3	88.5	86.3
21 Teesside	6.7	384	90.7	91.9	86.2
22 Manchester Metropolitan	13.5	416	82.6	83.6	84.3
23 Hertfordshire		395	88.1	89.9	83.7
24 Brighton	5.0	356	89.2	91.3	83.4
25 Salford	15.0	388	87.8	78.7	83.2
26 York St John	1.7	375	89.0	88.7	82.8
27 Plymouth	3.3	377	79.8	91.8	81.1
28 Bournemouth		365	83.9	90.0	80.5
29 Central Lancashire	13.3	355	85.2	79.3	80.1
30 Kingston/St George's, London	11.7	390	71.5	86.3	79.3
31 Ulster	31.0	385	77.9	65.3	79.2
32 Southampton	8.3	430	67.5	82.8	78.4
33 Cumbria	0.0	320	84.2	73.9	72.6

Employed in professional job:	86%	Employed in non-professional job and studying:	0%
Employed in professional job and studying:	2%	Employed in non-professional job:	6%
Studying:	1%	Unemployed:	4%
Average starting professional salary:	£22,013	Average starting non-professional salary:	£14,047

Politics

The boom that politics courses had been enjoying before the introduction of £9,000 fees seems to have returned. A slump in 2012 was followed by increases of more than 6 per cent in both applications and enrolments in the following year and another rise in 2014. There were still almost six applications for every place in 2013 and correspondingly high entry scores at the leading universities. Seven of the top ten average more than 500 points and only five of the 75 universities in this year's table fall below 250 points. More than 100 universities and colleges are offering courses at undergraduate level in 2015.

The top two remain unchanged, with Oxford in first place. It has the highest entry grades, ahead of Cambridge in second place. Sheffield, which has dropped to fourth, shares the best score from the 2008 Research Assessment Exercise with Essex, which is now outside the top ten. Coventry has much the most satisfied students, but Huddersfield is again the highest-placed post-1992 university and the only one in the top 30. Satisfaction scores in politics were generally high in the 2014 National Student Survey: only three universities failed to satisfy at least 70 per cent of their final-year undergraduates.

Employment scores are less impressive: politics is just inside the top 40 for the proportion of graduates going straight into professional jobs or continuing their studies. Durham, in sixth place, had the best employment record in 2013, but only four other universities registered more than 80 per cent positive destinations and 13 were below 50 per cent. Nationally, unemployment is above average at 14 per cent. More than a quarter of all politics graduates take postgraduate courses, but almost the same proportion start their careers in low-level employment. Starting salaries in professional jobs are only just in the top 30 of the 66 subject groupings.

Employed in professional job:	38%	Employed in non-professional job and studying:	3%
Employed in professional job and studying:	3%	Employed in non-professional job:	22%
Studying:	20%	Unemployed:	14%
Average starting professional salary:	£21,628	Average starting non-professional salary:	£15,866

Politics	Research quality %	Entry standards	Student satisfaction %	Graduate prospects %	Overall rating
1 Oxford	43.3	582	85.7	79.7	100.0
2 Cambridge	30.0	546	85.6	81.7	95.9
3 University College London	35.0	551	84.1	78.2	95.6
4 Sheffield	55.0	448	82.9	73.2	95.0
5 Exeter	31.7	462	87.5	82.2	94.5
6 Durham	26.7	518	84.6	84.6	94.2
7 Warwick	33.3	504	85.0	78.0	94.0
8 St Andrews	21.7	542	86.4	76.3	92.7
9 London School of Economics	40.0	545	74.9	79.3	91.6
10 Bath	21.7	463	84.4	83.4	90.6
11 Essex	55.0	349	84.8	63.5	90.3
12 York	25.0	453	82.0	78.9	88.6
13 SOAS, London	30.0	492	81.5	67.8	88.2
14 Newcastle	23.3	411	86.9	71.1	87.6
15 Nottingham	26.7	425	80.4	75.4	86.3
16 Glasgow	25.0	486	83.3	61.1	86.2
17 Bristol	20.0	461	78.0	78.5	85.2
18 Birmingham	18.3	410	79.2	83.8	85.0
19 Loughborough	20.0	369	84.3	74.9	84.8
20 Lancaster	10.0	424	85.1	74.4	84.5
21 Cardiff	25.0	392	78.8	77.4	84.2
22 Kent	11.7	360	87.0	75.8	84.1
23 Manchester	30.0	420	77.4	67.2	83.2

Politics cont

	Research quality	Entry standards	Student satisfaction %	Graduate prospects %	Overall rating
24 Queen Mary, London	18.3	418	81.9	67.4	82.9
25 Reading	18.3	347	85.9	67.7	82.0
26 Brunel	11.7	358	90.6	61.1	82.6
=27 Keele	16.7	366	89.5	56.4	82.3
=27 Surrey	13.3	386	89.1	57.9	82.3
=27 Sussex	29.1	396	82.1	56.7	82.3
30 Huddersfield	0.0	325	90.5	74.8	81.8
31 Southampton	13.3	402	80.2	74.2	81.7
=32 Aberystwyth	48.3	330	78.2	52.7	81.5
=32 Hull	18.3	350	85.4	63.2	81.5
34 Coventry	6.7	257	95.0	65.5	81.4
35 Royal Holloway	13.3	363	83.0	71.6	81.3
=36 Aston	10.0	342	86.7	69.0	81.2
=36 East Anglia	15.0	420	82.8	61.9	81.2
38 Strathclyde	10.0	470	84.5	52.5	80.4
39 King's College London	25.0	479	71.9	65.0	80.3
40 Leicester	8.3	388	83.9	65.7	80.0
41 Edinburgh	25.0	487	69.0	69.2	79.9
42 Queen's, Belfast	23.3	380	82.1	53.6	79.5
43 City		371	84.8	69.9	78.9
44 Leeds	8.3	428	77.2	70.1	78.6
45 Aberdeen	11.7	447	75.4	67.7	78.5
46 Swansea	10.0	352	78.8	74.2	78.3
=47 Oxford Brookes	6.7	341	83.4	65.0	77.5
=47 West of England	5.0	310	89.5	56.5	77.5
=49 Dundee	16.7	354	86.4	44.9	77.3
=49 Portsmouth	25.0	290	85.1	48.8	77.3
51 Liverpool	5.0	415	78.7	62.4	76.3
52 Chester		258	90.0	57.7	75.0
53 Nottingham Trent		279	88.4	57.8	74.8
54 De Montfort	10.0	279	86.7	50.6	74.6
55 Stirling	8.3	384	80.3	51.6	74.4
=56 East London		244	87.9	61.8	74.2
=56 Lincoln	10.0	305	81.4	57.9	74.2
58 Northumbria	15.0	347	76.2	56.8	73.7
59 Brighton	45.0	289	74.6	36.8	73.3
60 Bradford	26.7	265	68.2	71.3	72.7
61 Winchester		307	87.6	46.7	72.6
62 Ulster	18.3	289	81.8	39.8	71.6
=63 Goldsmiths, London	16.7	294	78.3	49.1	71.5
=63 Manchester Metropolitan	6.7	322	81.6	47.4	71.5
65 Plymouth	19.5	273	77.6	50.1	71.4
66 Westminster	10.0	285	79.9	50.0	70.7

67 Leeds Metropolitan		235	84.7	54.9	70.4
68 London Metropolitan	10.0	201	80.8	55.5	69.7
69 Northampton		226	85.8	46.2	68.6
70 Greenwich	0.0	284	83.3	38.9	67.4
71 Canterbury Christ Church		239	80.5	50.0	66.9
72 Central Lancashire	1.7		81.2	40.3	66.6
73 Kingston	10.0	279	72.0	47.0	65.2
74 Sheffield Hallam		300	77.7	40.2	65.0
75 Salford	11.7	329	66.0	43.6	63.1

Psychology

Psychology is the biggest table in the *Guide*, having added three more universities this year. A drop in the demand for places after the introduction of £9,000 fees is becoming a distant memory; the number of applications almost reached 100,000 in 2013, when there was a 12 per cent increase in the numbers starting psychology degrees. The popularity of the subject endures in spite of poor performances in the graduate employment market: it is in the bottom ten for the proportion of graduates with "positive destinations", and the bottom 15 for average starting salaries in professional-level jobs. More than 40 per cent of graduates begin their careers in low-level jobs.

Psychology	Research quality %	Entry standards	Student satisfaction %	Graduate prospects %	Overall rating
1 Cambridge	51.7	665	85.6	81.7	100.0
2 Bath	48.3	512	95.3	77.4	98.1
3 Oxford	50.0	564	81.6	70.2	91.1
4 University College London	45.0	516	87.0	66.3	90.3
5 Glasgow	33.3	510	86.2	74.6	89.3
6 Birmingham	43.3	439	86.8	72.8	88.9
7 Durham	30.0	492	82.9	72.3	85.7
8 York	35.0	468	88.9	58.4	85.5
9 Surrey	20.0	448	90.4	66.5	84.5
10 Exeter	28.3	455	86.0	67.4	84.4
11 St Andrews	35.0	517	79.2	67.0	84.2
12 Cardiff	40.0	445	82.7	63.1	83.7
13 Southampton	30.0	420	85.7	68.2	83.6
14 Newcastle	20.0	449	90.1	62.3	83.3
15 Bristol	26.7	482	83.7	64.0	82.9
16 Birkbeck	40.0	254	83.1	84.6	82.8
17 Warwick	25.0	474	86.1	60.2	82.6
18 Bangor	35.0	321	89.6	64.0	82.3
19 Loughborough	36.7	399	84.6	61.0	81.9
20 Kent	20.0	413	84.1	71.7	81.3
21 Nottingham	26.7	440	82.0	66.0	81.1

Psychology cont

		Research quality %	Entry standards	Student satisfaction %	Graduate prospects %	Overall rating
22	Royal Holloway	33.3	451	82.9	56.4	80.9
23	Sussex	30.0	431	82.9	60.0	00.4
=24	Leeds	23.3	422	81.8	61.7	78.6
=24	Strathclyde	10.0	462	86.5	57.7	78.6
=26	Reading	26.7	404	80.8	59.9	77.7
=26	Sheffield	30.0	444	78.8	56.3	77.7
28	Stirling	8.3	416	88.6	56.2	77.4
=29	Aston	26.7	380	84.4	54.1	77.3
=29	East Anglia	5.0	429	90.1	53.9	77.3
31	Lancaster	20.0	435	76.0	69.3	77.2
32	Lincoln	11.7	351	86.7	64.9	77.1
33	Essex	25.0	358	85.0	54.2	76.5
34	Dundee	15.0	385	85.4	55.0	75.7
35	City	20.0	374	83.7	54.1	75.3
36	Aberdeen	20.0	424	79.4	55.5	75.1
37	Portsmouth	8.3	339	84.9	62.5	74.4
38	Leicester	8.3	402	82.8	56.8	74.0
39	Queen Margaret, Edinburgh		326	90.8	56.4	73.8
40	Manchester	23.0	429	75.9	53.7	73.5
41	Edinburgh	30.0	483	67.5	57.0	73.3
42	Manchester Metropolitan	17.4	337	84.7	50.1	73.0
43	Heriot-Watt	1.7	414	79.9	62.5	72.9
44	Nottingham Trent	5.0	329	88.3	53.0	72.7
45	Swansea	15.0	364	75.1	66.8	72.5
46	Keele	8.3	382	82.8	53.3	72.4
47	York St John	0.0	311	84.8	64.0	72.0
=48	Coventry	6.2	313	81.4	64.0	71.6
=48	Queen's, Belfast	13.3	386	78.9	53.3	71.6
50	Bath Spa	1.7	314	86.9	55.0	71.2
51	West of Scotland		323	88.5	50.6	71.0
=52	Chester	5.0	308	85.7	54.0	70.9
=52	Goldsmiths, London	23.3	325	78.7	50.9	70.9
=52	Plymouth	13.3	328	82.2	51.6	70.9
55	Liverpool	13.3	400	76.1	54.3	70.8
=56	Brunel	15.0	356	81.2	47.0	70.5
=56	Central Lancashire	10.0	339	83.6	48.7	70.5
58	West of England	16.7	374	76.5	52.9	70.4
59	Aberystwyth	5.0	327	85.8	49.1	70.3
=60	Abertay	5.0	350	80.9	54.9	70.0
=60	Hertfordshire	13.3	355	78.4	52.4	70.0
62	De Montfort		306	87.7	50.4	69.9
63	Birmingham City		290	88.3	50.0	69.6
64	Teesside		311	88.4	46.1	69.3

=65	Bournemouth	15.0	326	82.1	44.1	69.2
=65	Middlesex	3.3	320	79.3	60.4	69.2
67	Northumbria	8.3	375	79.1	48.8	69.0
68	Bradford	23.3	293	76.5	52.0	68.9
69	Leeds Trinity	0.0	269	87.3	50.3	68.4
70	Oxford Brookes	8.3	369	76.7	51.7	68.3
71	Staffordshire	10.0	274	85.9	43.0	68.1
72	Queen Mary, London	20.0	377	71.4	50.7	68.0
73	Hull	15.0	315	76.5	51.6	67.8
74	Greenwich	5.0	301	87.3	38.5	67.6
75	Anglia Ruskin	18.3	262	82.7	41.6	67.4
76	Sunderland	1.7	281	88.1	40.7	67.2
=77	Edinburgh Napier	1.7	365	83.2	38.8	67.0
=77	Roehampton	6.7	282	82.1	48.5	67.0
=77	West London	0.0	267	82.1	55.9	67.0
80	Ulster	11.7	298	87.4	30.0	66.8
=81	Edge Hill		297	87.8	39.0	66.7
=81	Salford	15.0	329	78.0	42.4	66.7
83	East London	6.7	258	86.5	40.7	66.6
84	Huddersfield		313	78.2	55.8	66.5
85	Liverpool John Moores	11.7	338	77.6	43.1	66.2
86	Glyndŵr		252	75.1	66.7	65.5
87	Cumbria		214	84.8	50.0	65.1
88	Gloucestershire	3.3	294	85.2	35.2	65.0
89	Westminster	5.0	303	77.7	47.8	64.9
90	Chichester	10.0	284	82.0	36.2	64.6
=91	Brighton	11.7	307	75.4	44.5	64.3
=91	Southampton Solent		284	80.7	45.9	64.3
=93	Cardiff Metropolitan	8.3	268	81.7	38.6	64.2
=93	Glasgow Caledonian	3.3	416	74.4	38.3	64.2
=93	Winchester		344	76.1	47.2	64.2
=96	Leeds Metropolitan		307	81.8	38.3	63.7
=96	South Wales	3.3	327	76.9	43.1	63.7
98	Newman		304	78.3	45.5	63.6
=99	Bolton	1.7	263	75.2	52.6	62.7
=99	Derby	3.3	289	76.7	44.7	62.7
=99	Northampton		288	80.2	40.3	62.7
102	Sheffield Hallam	3.3	332	73.2	44.2	62.2
103	Canterbury Christ Church		286	78.8	39.1	61.6
104	London Metropolitan	3.3	264	71.3	53.1	61.1
105	St Mary's, Twickenham		275	76.5	41.8	60.7
106	Kingston	6.7	277	72.0	44.1	60.4
107	Bedfordshire		217	81.5	37.7	60.3
=108	Buckinghamshire New		257	78.2	36.3	59.6
=108	London South Bank	6.7	266	74.8	36.6	59.6
110	Worcester		296	68.4	45.5	58.0

Psychology cont

Most undergraduate programmes are accredited by the British Psychological Society, which ensures that key topics are covered, but the clinical and biological content of courses still varies considerably. Some universities require maths and/or biology A levels among three high-grade passes, but others are much less demanding. The contrast is obvious in the ranking, with 33 universities averaging more than 400 points at entry but with 13 below 270 points. Cambridge, which remains top of the table, has an entry score 100 points more than any of its rivals and also had the best grades in the 2008 Research Assessment Exercise, when 80 per cent of research considered world-leading or internationally excellent.

Bath has narrowed the gap on Cambridge and achieved the highest ratings in the 2014 National Student Survey, when four other universities also satisfied at least 90 per cent of final-year undergraduates. This year Birkbeck joined the top two in the table is seeing three-quarters of their psychology graduates go straight into professional jobs or join postgraduate courses. Lincoln is again the highest-placed post-1992 university, despite dropping 14 places in the table. University College London has made the most progress at the top of the table, rising four places to fourth, while Surrey has gone up 11 places to break into the top ten.

Employed in professional job:	27%	Employed in non-professional job and studying:	5%
Employed in professional job and studying:	4%	Employed in non-professional job:	36%
Studying:	16%	Unemployed:	12%
Average starting professional salary:	£18,773	Average starting non-professional salary:	£14,622

Radiography

Only medicine, dentistry and nursing had a better employment record than radiography in 2013. More than nine out of ten graduates went straight into professional jobs, although their average salaries were outside the top 20 in the earnings table. Courses are divided into diagnostic and therapeutic specialisms. Diagnostic courses usually involve two years of studying anatomy, physiology and physics followed by further training in sociology, management and ethics, and the practice and science of imaging. The therapeutic branch covers much of the same scientific content in the first year, but follows this with training in oncology, psycho-social studies and other modules. Degrees require at least one science subject, usually biology, among three A levels or the equivalent.

The table is in its second year, radiography having been listed previously among "other subjects allied to medicine" in the *Guide*. A total of 25 universities expect to offer the subject in 2015, two more than the number in this edition of the table, which is headed for the second time by Exeter. There is plenty of movement in other positions, however. Leeds has moved up four places to second, while Sheffield Hallam has jumped ten places to sixth. Leeds achieved the best of a low set of grades in the 2008 Research Assessment Exercise. More than half of the universities in table are post-1992 institutions, led by Robert Gordon in third place, which has the most satisfied students.

Employment scores are high, with 16 universities seeing more than nine out of ten graduates go straight into professional jobs. Four institutions managed full employment in 2012, but only Bangor has repeated the feat in the new table. Exeter has the highest entry grades and is one of only three universities to average more than 400 points on the UCAS tariff. However, scores are tightly bunched: only two universities average less than 320 points.

Employed in professional job:	89%	Employed in non-professional job and studying:	0%
Employed in professional job and studying:	2%	Employed in non-professional job:	3%
Studying:	2%	Unemployed:	5%
Average starting professional salary:	£22,286	Average starting non-professional salary:	£19,150

Radiography	Research quality	Entry standards	Student satisfaction %	Graduate prospects %	Overall rating
1 Exeter	30.0	410	88.5	98.9	100.0
2 Leeds	36.7	389	86.8	95.7	98.2
3 Robert Gordon	10.0	393	93.8	97.8	97.4
4 Portsmouth	28.3	362	90.5	95.9	96.9
5 Glasgow Caledonian	30.0	409	83.9	93.1	96.0
6 Sheffield Hallam	8.3	367	90.5	97.3	94.1
7 Liverpool	20.0	357	83.3	98.7	93.1
8 West of England	31.7	343	81.6	95.9	92.7
9 Teesside	6.7	354	91.5	89.4	90.7
=10 Cardiff	31.7	341	75.8	96.6	90.4
=10 City	18.3	349	88.0	87.6	90.4
12 Bangor		403	76.4	100.0	89.7
13 Cumbria	0.0	351	87.0	93.0	88.8
14 Ulster	27.2	375	86.5	74.5	88.1
15 Bradford	16.7	332	80.0	91.2	87.1
16 Queen Margaret, Edinburgh	1.7	349	82.5	92.7	87.0
17 Derby		353	82.7	91.3	86.5
18 Salford	15.0		81.8	87.2	86.2
19 Hertfordshire		339	83.3	89.8	85.5
20 Kingston/St George's, London	11.7	280	87.9	87.5	85.4
21 Birmingham City		344	79.0	92.6	84.9
22 London South Bank	15.0	323	79.5	85.9	84.2
23 Canterbury Christ Church	1.7	260	84.5	90.2	82.1

Russian and Eastern European Languages

While most tables in the *Guide* have grown this year, Russian and Eastern European languages has lost two more universities, leaving it with little more than half the number it contained ten years ago. Only ten had enough students entering in 2013 for a reliable entry score to be compiled for this measure. Just 55 students started courses – ten fewer than in 2012. Nevertheless, 19 universities – the same number as last year – intend to offer courses in 2015. The small numbers inevitably make for exaggerated swings in statistics. Two years ago, Russian was among the top ten subjects for starting salaries in graduate-level jobs; now it is outside the top 30, although still ahead of other languages. Last year, Russian had a 22 per cent unemployment rate, the worst in any subject, but now it is down to 14 per cent and the subjects are in the top half of the employment table.

Cambridge and Oxford have swapped places at the top of the table for the third year in a row. Cambridge's lead could not be smaller, although it again has the highest entry standards and the most satisfied students. Oxford tied with Manchester for the best performance in Russian and Eastern European languages in the 2008 Research Assessment Exercise. For the second year in a row, Bristol has much the best employment score, but is restricted to eighth place. Portsmouth is the sole representative of the post-1992 universities and there are no institutions from Wales or Northern Ireland.

Most undergraduates learn the language from scratch. Despite the small numbers, entry standards remain high throughout the table: the top three all average more than 500 points and only two universities are below 400 points on the UCAS tariff. Satisfaction levels are also high. Nearly every university in the table satisfied at least three-quarters of its final-year undergraduates.

Employed in professional job:	43%	Employed in non-professional job and studying:	3%
Employed in professional job and studying:	3%	Employed in non-professional job:	17%
Studying:	20%	Unemployed:	14%
Average starting professional salary:	£21,031	Average starting non-professional salary:	£14,126

Russian and East European Languages	Research quality %	Entry standards	Student satisfaction %	Graduate prospects %	Overall rating
1 Cambridge	35.0	592	91.6	80.7	100.0
2 Oxford	46.7	568	88.0	80.6	99.9
3 Durham	16.7	536	86.9	84.2	91.7
4 Exeter	23.3	469	90.6	75.2	90.9
5 Manchester	46.7		84.3	59.4	90.2
6 Birmingham	28.3		85.5	65.2	87.0
7 Sheffield	40.0	429	83.1	65.4	86.9
8 Bristol	30.0	425	77.1	88.1	86.2
9 Nottingham	33.3	386	76.6	83.2	84.2
10 University College London	21.7	488	77.1	73.9	83.3
11 Queen Mary, London	26.7		84.8	37.5	77.5
12 Portsmouth		295	84.9	68.6	74.2
13 Leeds	8.3	476	71.6	57.8	72.9
14 Glasgow	1.7		81.5	52.6	71.7

Social Policy

There is less competition for places in social policy than in any of the 66 subject groupings featured in this chapter. In 2013, there were only three applications for every place, a fraction less than in the previous year. Yet entry standards are by no means the lowest: while only five universities average more than 400 points on the UCAS tariff, just two of those with enough students to compile a score dropped below 250 points. The table contains six more universities than last year, although that is still six fewer than in the 2013 *Guide*. More than 1,500 students started courses in 2013 – a small increase on the previous year – and 74 universities and colleges are offering the subject for 2015.

The London School of Economics (LSE) has lost the lead in social policy for the first time since the table was published more than 15 years ago, dropping to fourth place with the lowest student satisfaction in the ranking. Leeds, which shared first place last year, has also been overtaken by Bristol. The new leader again has the best graduate prospects, although

Social Policy	Research quality %	Entry standards	Student satisfaction %	Graduate prospects %	Overall rating
1 Bristol	33.3	417	86.1	79.7	100.0
2 Leeds	45.0	413	85.3	69.0	99.9
3 Kent	43.3	356	85.4	67.9	96.4
4 London School of Economics	60.0	413	68.9	71.6	94.7
5 Glasgow	27.5		84.3	67.2	92.3
6 Nottingham	23.3	351	82.4	77.6	91.3
7 Keele	31.7	369	87.3	47.6	90.4
8 Bath	48.3	406	74.6	51.4	90.0
9 West of Scotland	20.0		86.6	61.9	89.8
10 York	38.3	363	78.2	61.3	89.6
11 Loughborough	31.7	365	83.0	54.1	89.1
12 Sheffield Hallam	30.0	394	84.2	44.9	88.7
13 Bolton	18.3		84.0	60.5	86.8
14 Swansea	26.7	334	79.5	62.0	86.0
15 Stirling	25.0		86.2	44.1	85.8
16 Edinburgh	41.7	457	73.1	33.3	85.7
=17 Birmingham	30.0	378	72.4	64.4	85.3
=17 Sheffield	35.0	367	77.3	48.5	85.3
19 Leicester	13.9		83.9	58.7	84.6
20 Cardiff	35.0	358	78.3	37.9	83.1
21 Queen's, Belfast	31.7	367	80.1	34.4	82.9
22 Ulster	26.7	287	88.5	33.3	82.2
23 Aston	10.0	334	78.0	65.9	81.5
24 Northampton		275	88.8	46.2	77.7
25 London Metropolitan	23.3	247	78.8	48.6	77.1
26 Lincoln	15.0	289	80.0		76.5
27 Plymouth	21.7		78.8	36.2	76.3
28 Anglia Ruskin	13.3	177	87.1	44.9	74.9
29 Salford	20.0	342	72.9	36.8	74.8
30 Brighton	11.7	297	77.1	44.8	74.7
31 Canterbury Christ Church		273	75.7	59.0	72.8
32 Aberystwyth		297	81.3	27.3	70.0
33 Birmingham City	10.0	257	71.7	48.0	69.7

Employed in professional job:	34%	Employed in non-professional job and studying:		4%
Employed in professional job and studying:	3%	Employed in non-professional job:		32%
Studying:	14%	Unemployed:		13%
Average starting professional salary:	£19,918	Average starting non-professional salary:		£15,089

even its score was below 80 per cent on this measure. Nationally, the subject is just outside the bottom ten for employment, with more than a third of graduates starting out in low-level jobs. It does better in the comparison of starting salaries in graduate-level jobs. The average of almost £20,000 in 2013 was just outside the top 40 subjects.

The highest entry standards are at Edinburgh, but the university is well outside the top ten because only a third of its social policy graduates found professional jobs or started postgraduate programmes within six month of completing their course. Northampton has the most satisfied students, but is in the bottom ten, partly because it did not enter the Research Assessment Exercise in this subject. The LSE achieved by far the best grades in those assessments.

Social Work

Applications for social work degrees have dropped by more than a quarter since 2010, the last year unaffected by the transition to higher undergraduate fees. But the subject remains a popular choice, with more than 12,500 students starting courses in 2013 – an increase of more than 10 per cent on the previous year. The combination of falling demand and increasing provision has seen the number of applications per place drop from more than seven in 2010 to less than five in 2013. Surprisingly, however, the new table sees a rise in entry standards, with five universities averaging more than 400 points, compared with one last year, and only five slipping below 250 points, when there were 16 last year. Another surprise is social work's continued presence among the top 15 subjects for starting salaries in professional jobs. Almost 60 per cent of graduates secure such jobs, but the subject is only midway in the overall employment table.

Once again, there are big changes in the table, and none of the top 40 occupies the same position as last year. Bath, which has the best research score, has regained the lead it lost to Sussex in the 2014 *Guide*. Sussex has dropped to eighth, while Leeds and Swansea have moved up to second and third respectively. The highest entry grades are at East Anglia, but nine of the top 20 universities did not have enough students for reliable scores to be compiled on this measure. Bristol has the most satisfied students, a fraction ahead of Strathclyde.

The University of the West of England (UWE) could not quite match its 100 per cent employment record of last year, but it did not miss by much. With over 98 per cent of graduates going straight into professional jobs or continuing their studies, it was still the leader on graduate prospects. There is wide variation in the employment scores. While Swansea, second on this measure, managed almost 97 per cent positive destinations, this figure was below 40 per cent at two institutions. Bolton overtook UWE as the highest-placed post-1992 university, and both are joined in the top 20 by Middlesex.

Employed in professional job:	56%	Employed in non-professional job and studying:	1%
Employed in professional job and studying:	3%	Employed in non-professional job:	22%
Studying:	6%	Unemployed:	11%
Average starting professional salary:	£23,643	Average starting non-professional salary:	£14,747

Social Work

	Research quality %	Entry standards	Student satisfaction %	Graduate prospects %	Overall rating
1 Bath	48.3	419	86.8	78.7	100.0
2 Leeds	45.0	396	90.1	73.1	97.9
3 Swansea	26.7		86.6	96.7	95.6
4 Lancaster	33.3	396	85.3	85.1	95.1
5 Queen's, Belfast	31.7	367	87.5	86.8	94.4
6 Sheffield	35.0		82.6	87.8	93.4
7 Birmingham	30.0	356	85.3	85.5	91.8
8 Sussex	30.0	369	83.0	85.1	91.4
9 Bristol	33.3	411	90.4	56.3	91.3
10 York	38.3	416	74.4	79.3	91.1
11 Glasgow	16.7		88.8	88.5	90.3
12 Stirling	25.0		82.7	89.3	90.0
13 Strathclyde	16.7		90.3	82.5	89.3
14 Bolton	18.3		85.8	88.9	89.2
15 East Anglia	25.0	446	79.5	70.2	89.1
16 Nottingham	23.3		83.1	81.8	87.1
17 West of England	8.3	360	81.2	98.6	87.0
18 Kent	43.3	291	76.4	79.6	86.2
19 Keele	31.7		76.3	81.8	86.1
20 Middlesex	20.0		83.5	81.6	86.0
21 Edinburgh	41.7	396	67.3	70.8	85.4
22 Coventry	11.7	335	86.6	79.4	84.3
23 Robert Gordon		322	88.8	90.9	84.0
24 Teesside		391	86.3	77.9	83.7
25 Huddersfield	21.7	306	85.3	72.8	83.3
26 Manchester Metropolitan	10.0	329	84.9	74.7	81.5
27 Nottingham Trent	30.0	302	85.1	56.5	81.4
28 Hull	20.0	345	73.7	79.3	81.2
29 West of Scotland	20.0	385	78.8	56.9	80.4
30 Anglia Ruskin	13.3	290	82.5	80.0	80.3
31 Ulster	26.7	299	81.8	63.0	80.2
32 Lincoln	15.0	318	75.1	83.4	79.8
=33 Northumbria	15.0	354	83.1	58.7	79.6
=33 Sheffield Hallam	18.3	295	83.1	68.7	79.6
=35 De Montfort	13.3	303	81.6	74.8	79.4
=35 Manchester	25.0		76.8	68.4	79.4
=35 Salford	20.0	410	70.7	62.4	79.4
38 Dundee	15.0	330	76.3	75.5	79.1
39 Central Lancashire	20.0	320	82.4	57.8	78.5
40 Southampton Solent		320	80.5	84.5	78.4
41 Brunel	15.0	317	77.4	70.7	77.7
42 Portsmouth		343	72.9	89.6	77.3
43 Winchester		301	89.7	64.8	76.8

	Research quality %	Entry standards	Student satisfaction %	Graduate prospects %	Overall rating
=44 Birmingham City	10.0	312	75.6	75.0	76.1
=44 Goldsmiths, London	18.3		70.5	70.7	76.1
=44 Oxford Brookes		368	71.1	82.0	76.1
47 Bradford	23.3	292	75.1	64.5	76.0
48 Northampton		317	83.2	66.7	75.0
49 Brighton	11.7	327	80.1	56.0	74.9
50 Plymouth	21.7	314	69.9	66.5	74.8
51 Cardiff Metropolitan		236	85.1	77.8	73.9
=52 Bedfordshire	20.0		73.7	61.7	73.2
=52 Derby		258	84.1	71.7	73.2
54 Sunderland		303	85.4	56.7	72.8
=55 Buckinghamshire New		296	76.0	75.6	72.6
=55 Essex		256	85.7	66.7	72.6
57 South Wales	18.3	284	78.0	51.8	72.3
58 West London		222	85.2	73.7	72.1
59 London South Bank	30.0		62.6	67.7	72.0
60 Staffordshire		286	76.3	73.7	71.7
61 Liverpool John Moores		334	83.2	48.9	71.6
62 Chester	5.0	300	69.6	76.1	71.3
63 Hertfordshire	5.0	319	64.4	80.0	71.0
64 London Metropolitan	23.3	239	71.3	63.0	70.7
=65 Bangor	13.3	283	74.3	55.0	69.8
=65 Glyndŵr	6.7	254	75.6	67.3	69.8
67 East London	11.7	258	72.9	63.6	69.3
68 St Mark and St John		215	82.9	66.5	68.8
=69 Gloucestershire	3.3	271	67.7	77.1	68.5
=69 Newman		303	85.0	39.9	68.5
71 Greenwich		253	82.1	56.2	68.2
72 Chichester		284	75.7	57.4	67.2
73 Canterbury Christ Church		258	80.5	51.2	66.4
74 Leeds Metropolitan		255	76.6	57.2	65.9
75 Worcester		258	68.2	67.0	64.5
76 Edge Hill	5.0	283	76.3	36.9	63.8
77 Cumbria		237	72.5	60.1	63.6

Sociology

Sociology has escaped from last place in the employment table only because two new subjects have come in below it. Almost 60 per cent of those graduating in 2013 were in low-level jobs or unemployed at the end of the year. Yet, apart from a single year's decline when £9,000 fees were introduced, the demand for places has been rising since the start of the decade. There was a 6 per cent increase in the number of students starting courses in

2013, although the competition for places remained more modest than in most of the social sciences.

Cambridge remains well clear in first place, despite uncharacteristically low grades for research. The sociology panel for the 2008 assessments was no respecter of reputations: neither Cambridge nor the London School of Economics is among the top 15 universities on this measure. But Cambridge has entry grades that are nearly 100 points ahead of Edinburgh, its nearest challenger, and it also has the best employment score. Birmingham was the only other university to see more than 80 per cent of its sociologists go straight into professional jobs or continue their studies. Indeed, second-placed Bath, which has the best research score, was the only other one to top 70 per cent for employment.

Queen's, Belfast, in 20th place, has the most satisfied students, just ahead of Ulster and Chester, which are both much further down the table. Portsmouth is the highest-placed post-1992 university, and the only one in the top 30. More than 120 universities are offering courses starting in 2015. They include subjects such as criminology, urban studies, women's studies and some communication studies, as well as sociology itself, and a large number of institutions teach the subject as part of a combined studies or modular programme. The subject's low standing in the employment ranking is not repeated in the comparison of graduate earnings. It is out of the bottom 20 this year after a rise of nearly £1,000 in average starting salaries in graduate-level jobs.

Employed in professional job:	28%	Employed in non-professional job and studying:	4%
Employed in professional job and studying:	2%	Employed in non-professional job:	41%
Studying:	13%	Unemployed:	13%
Average starting professional salary:	£19,652	Average starting non-professional salary:	£15,246

Sociology	Research quality %	Entry standards	Student satisfaction %	Graduate prospects %	Overall rating
1 Cambridge	31.7	546	85.6	81.7	100.0
2 Bath	48.3	416	85.5	76.6	96.8
3 Southampton	46.7	381	89.7	57.7	93.3
4 Surrey	38.3	401	87.7	63.0	92.4
5 Warwick	38.3	428	82.3	65.8	90.9
6 Durham	30.0	429	83.9	68.7	90.8
7 Kent	43.3	365	83.3	67.8	90.3
8 York	40.0	378	84.3	61.9	89.4
9 Lancaster	43.3	396	81.8	60.6	89.1
=10 Leeds	45.0	386	80.6	62.5	88.8
=10 Loughborough	31.7	364	86.1	64.8	88.8
12 Manchester	46.7	391	84.0	50.5	88.7
13 Exeter	31.7	408	86.5	52.9	88.2
14 Keele	31.7	415	87.5	44.4	87.3
15 Sussex	35.0	380	84.4	56.0	87.2
16 Birmingham	13.3	380	82.3	81.4	86.9
=17 Aberdeen	28.3	426	78.2	67.8	86.6
=17 Edinburgh	38.3	453	77.6	54.4	86.6

Sociology cont

		Research quality %	Entry standards	Student satisfaction %	Graduate prospects %	Overall rating
19	Newcastle	26.7	354	83.9	66.9	86.4
20	Queen's, Belfast	31.7	348	91.0	43.3	86.3
21	Essex	43.3	361	84.4	44.4	85.6
22	Sheffield	35.0	352	83.4	56.4	85.5
23	Glasgow	20.0	413	83.9	57.2	85.3
24	East Anglia	25.0	446	82.3	49.0	85.0
25	Leicester	16.7	370	85.3	60.7	84.4
26	Bristol	23.3	438	76.8	61.2	83.7
27	Nottingham	23.7	360	82.6	59.5	83.6
=28	Portsmouth	25.0	323	85.0	51.9	82.1
=28	Stirling	25.0	388	84.2	42.0	82.1
30	Aston	10.0	327	87.9	57.8	82.0
31	Huddersfield	8.3	252	88.2	68.8	81.1
32	Robert Gordon	5.0	351	84.2	63.1	80.9
=33	Goldsmiths, London	43.3	326	79.5	39.4	80.0
=33	London School of Economics	28.3	434	70.2	58.7	80.0
35	Coventry		281	88.7	64.3	79.9
36	Cardiff	35.0	365	74.2	49.3	78.9
37	Chester	5.0	290	90.3	47.2	78.5
38	Bradford	23.3	281	82.2	48.5	77.4
39	Edinburgh Napier	3.3	358	80.7	54.3	76.8
40	Brunel	23.3	307	82.9	38.2	76.7
41	Royal Holloway	21.7	351	78.8	41.8	76.5
42	East London	20.0	257	85.4	38.6	75.5
43	Abertay		321	80.6	58.5	75.4
44	Roehampton	13.3	265	85.3	42.1	75.1
45	West of England	5.0	335	81.5	46.8	75.0
=46	Northampton		262	89.5	43.5	74.9
=46	Strathclyde	6.7		83.7	44.7	74.9
48	Glasgow Caledonian	11.2	384	79.3	36.6	74.8
49	Northumbria	15.0	348	79.2	39.0	74.6
50	Salford	22.3	289	80.5	38.6	74.4
51	Oxford Brookes		363	78.7	50.5	74.2
52	Hull	20.0	305	78.5	41.6	74.0
53	Lincoln		319	79.4	54.6	73.7
54	Brighton	14.4	289	78.7	45.0	73.0
=55	City	25.0	367	68.6	45.5	72.6
=55	St Mary's, Twickenham		263	80.1	58.3	72.6
=57	Bangor		284	80.1	54.2	72.5
=57	Ulster		280	90.5	26.6	72.5
=59	Greenwich		299	85.2	36.7	72.4
=59	Westminster		279	86.0	38.5	72.4
=61	Bedfordshire	20.0	209	85.3	32.7	72.1

=61 Canterbury Christ Church		252	84.6	46.1	72.1
63 Nottingham Trent		293	81.7	44.9	71.9
64 Manchester Metropolitan	15.0	317	77.9	35.9	71.8
65 Middlesex		297	82.5	40.9	71.6
=66 Liverpool	13.3	384	72.7	37.5	71.5
=66 Plymouth	15.0	280	78.8	39.0	71.5
68 Birmingham City	10.0	296	77.4	43.2	71.1
69 Teesside	11.7	274	81.0	34.3	70.7
70 Sunderland		282	82.3	38.7	70.3
71 Anglia Ruskin		246	82.8	41.7	69.8
72 Central Lancashire		314	79.0	38.1	69.5
73 Staffordshire	11.7	230	78.5	42.6	69.3
74 De Montfort	13.3	277	75.7	39.5	69.2
75 Bath Spa		293	78.2	41.8	69.0
76 Worcester		279	79.4	40.9	68.9
77 Liverpool John Moores		290	79.9	33.0	67.9
78 South Wales		288	78.8	35.7	67.8
79 Leeds Metropolitan		242	81.2	37.0	67.6
=80 Gloucestershire		280	77.2	39.3	67.3
=80 Sheffield Hallam		297	77.6	35.0	67.3
82 Kingston	10.0	269	74.3	38.8	67.1
83 Winchester		306	81.0	22.9	67.0
84 Edge Hill		293	74.4	39.3	66.2
=85 Buckinghamshire New		241	75.7	44.1	65.8
=85 Derby		276	74.5	40.6	65.8
=85 London South Bank		216	80.9	34.9	65.8
88 London Metropolitan		238	75.5	39.6	64.5

Sports Science

Sports science has been one of the big growth areas of UK higher education over the past decade – so much so that it has had its own table for the last six years. Although there was a substantial drop in applications with the introduction of higher fees in 2012, both applications and enrolments recovered strongly in 2013 and there was further growth this year. Sports and exercise science remains on the verge of the top ten subjects at degree level. The subject covers more than 40 specialisms, from sports therapy to equestrian sport studies and marine sport technology. Many courses contain more science and less physical activity than candidates may expect. Essex, for example, requires maths or one of the sciences at A level. Many universities now offer sports scholarships for elite performers, but most are not tied to a particular course and, officially at least, do not mean that the normal entry requirements are waived.

All the universities at the top of the table have excellent sports facilities and successful teams, but it is their performance in research and sports degree courses that counts here. Birmingham has taken over from Durham at the top of the table, with Bath up from fourth to second place, only a fraction of a point off the lead and with the highest entry standards. Birmingham ties for the top research score with fourth-placed Loughborough, the most

Sports Science

	Research quality %	Entry standards	Student satisfaction %	Graduate prospects %	Overall rating
1 Birmingham	36.7	398	88.5	77.8	100.0
2 Bath	21.7	437	92.6	75.2	99.8
3 Durham	30.0	434	89.7	73.3	99.6
4 Loughborough	36.7	424	86.0	76.6	99.5
5 Exeter	18.3	426	91.5	75.4	97.9
6 Portsmouth	28.3	353	89.4	68.4	93.7
7 Edinburgh	25.0	412	79.7	80.6	93.5
8 Leeds	16.7	416	88.4	62.6	91.8
9 Bangor	18.3	308	93.8	65.6	90.8
=10 Kent	25.0	379	80.9	72.0	90.3
=10 Robert Gordon		357	92.6	74.3	90.3
12 Hertfordshire	15.0	361	87.2	66.7	89.1
13 Glasgow	31.7	429	82.0	48.5	88.8
14 Liverpool John Moores	33.3	358	83.2	56.9	88.6
15 Chester	11.7	287	91.5	71.9	88.5
16 Cardiff Metropolitan	11.7	362	88.5	64.3	88.4
17 Lincoln		338	91.4	70.8	87.8
18 Stirling	23.3	391	80.9	61.0	87.5
19 Leeds Metropolitan	23.3	343	85.2	60.2	87.4
20 Essex	16.7	391	82.8	60.9	86.9
21 East Anglia		427	84.7	64.3	86.6
22 Huddersfield		303	86.4	82.9	86.4
23 Brunel	21.7	359	82.6	59.3	86.0
24 Coventry	5.0	317	86.7	71.4	85.5
25 Middlesex		280	90.6	74.5	85.4
26 Brighton	18.3	347	80.6	66.0	85.3
=27 Chichester	10.0	317	87.5	64.4	85.2
=27 Sheffield Hallam	18.3	368	82.8	57.2	85.2
29 Glyndŵr		329	88.7	63.1	83.7
30 Salford	15.0	347	81.1	61.4	83.5
31 Hull	3.3	347	88.8	54.8	83.3
32 Oxford Brookes		343	89.9	55.0	82.9
=33 Aberdeen	13.3	403	81.8	47.0	82.4
=33 Derby		338	89.3	55.0	82.4
35 Ulster	13.3	342	84.5	51.1	82.0
=36 Nottingham Trent	0.0	353	81.9	63.2	81.1
=36 Staffordshire	6.7	276	89.2	55.7	81.1
38 Newman	0.0	336	85.2	58.9	81.0
39 Gloucestershire	3.3	326	83.2	59.5	80.3
=40 Central Lancashire		358	87.0	47.7	80.0
=40 Swansea	0.0	290	80.9	73.0	80.0
42 Bournemouth		330	81.1	64.4	79.8
=43 Heriot-Watt	15.0		79.1	58.5	79.7

=43 Northumbria	10.0	383	79.1	49.2	79.7
=45 Northampton		277	87.1	59.9	79.3
=45 Southampton Solent		305	84.6	59.8	79.3
47 East London		327	84.8	54.9	79.2
=48 Bedfordshire	10.0	247	83.5	61.5	78.8
=48 Worcester		319	80.9	63.3	78.8
50 Greenwich		338	83.1	54.3	78.6
51 Cumbria		267	86.1	60.7	78.5
52 St Mary's, Twickenham	3.3	297	79.9	64.5	78.3
53 South Wales	10.0	315	80.3	53.7	78.2
54 Kingston		277	88.4	52.1	78.1
55 Abertay		300	81.1	62.0	77.7
56 Bishop Grosseteste		287	81.0	64.4	77.5
=57 Bolton		297	80.8	61.9	77.3
=57 Roehampton	0.0	277	80.0	67.2	77.3
59 Edge Hill		335	87.6	39.4	77.1
60 Aberystwyth	5.0	307	84.5	46.4	77.0
=61 Leeds Trinity		305	82.6	52.9	76.3
=61 York St John	0.0	311	77.0	63.7	76.3
63 Sunderland	13.3	327	79.8	42.2	76.2
64 West of England		307	77.3	63.1	76.1
65 Canterbury Christ Church	6.7	265	85.7	46.2	76.0
66 Manchester Metropolitan	12.7	320	74.9	53.0	75.9
67 St Mark and St John	0.0	288	81.3	56.5	75.7
68 Edinburgh Napier		341	80.5	46.0	75.0
69 West of Scotland		286	81.9	52.6	74.9
70 London South Bank	11.7	214	84.1	50.0	74.8
=71 Plymouth		302	86.7	37.7	74.5
=71 Winchester		292	79.1	55.8	74.5
73 Anglia Ruskin		192	86.3	55.4	73.5
74 Teesside		328	76.5	50.3	73.3
75 London Metropolitan		283	74.7	62.0	73.1
76 Buckinghamshire New	1.7	226	75.9	52.1	68.8

Employed in professional job:	38%	Employed in non-professional job and studying:	3%
Employed in professional job and studying:	4%	Employed in non-professional job:	31%
Studying:	14%	Unemployed:	9%
Average starting professional salary:	£18,554	Average starting non-professional salary:	£14,139

famous name in university sport and the leader of the table until last year. Bangor, in ninth place, has the most satisfied students, while the best employment record is at Huddersfield, just outside the top 20. Portsmouth is the highest-placed modern university, in sixth place, and it is joined in the top ten by Robert Gordon.

Sports science is just inside the top 50 subjects for graduate prospects and just outside for starting salaries in professional jobs. Only 9 per cent of 2013 graduates were unemployed at the end of the year, one of the lowest rates outside the medical subjects, but more than a third of graduates started out in low-level work.

Theology and Religious Studies

The table for theology and religious studies shows its fifth change of leadership in as many years. Durham has regained the top position that it lost to Cambridge last year, while Oxford (another previous leader) has moved up to second. Durham produced the best results in the 2008 Research Assessment Exercise, when two-thirds of its work was considered world leading or internationally excellent. But Oxford has the highest entry grades and Exeter, despite slipping four places to sixth, the most satisfied students. Competition is particularly keen in Scotland, which has four of the top 12 universities, led by St Andrews, which shares third place with Cambridge this year.

By no means all graduates go into the church, but the vocation has helped to maintain relatively healthy employment records up to now. The two subjects are well inside the top 40 in both the employment and earnings tables. Nearly a third of those completing courses take postgraduate degrees, either full or part-time. St Andrews recorded the best employment score in 2013, with nearly 86 per cent of graduates finding professional jobs or continuing their studies, but two universities dropped below 40 per cent on this measure.

More than 1,000 students began degrees in theology or religious studies in 2013, but this represented the second successive decline in enrolments. It was already one of the least competitive subjects in the arts and social sciences, with little more than four applications to the place. This is not reflected in the entry grades, however. The top three in the table all average more than 500 points and another eleven top 400, while only one university has an average of less than 250 points. Of the 37 institutions in the table, 14 are post-1992 universities, but Cumbria and St Mary's, Twickenham are the only ones to reach the top half of the ranking, Cumbria jumping up from bottom last year.

Theology and Religious Studies	Research quality %	Entry standards	Student satisfaction %	Graduate prospects %	Overall rating
1 Durham	48.3	513	88.0	84.5	100.0
2 Oxford	41.7	537	86.8	80.2	97.7
=3 Cambridge	43.3	528	86.7	80.1	97.6
=3 St Andrews	30.0	485	92.7	85.7	97.6
5 Edinburgh	40.0	453	87.5	78.6	94.1
6 Exeter	23.3	429	95.1	75.8	92.9
7 Birmingham	30.0	406	89.0	77.0	90.5
8 Sheffield	35.0	400	83.5	82.9	89.8
9 Bristol	25.0	443	81.4	81.7	87.6
10 Aberdeen	36.7	413	83.1	67.9	86.8
11 Nottingham	33.3	382	80.7	78.8	86.2
12 Glasgow	21.7	476	86.1	60.0	85.4
13 Lancaster	28.3	448	76.7	76.9	84.8
=14 Kent	20.0	366	88.5	69.4	84.6
=14 Manchester	38.3	380	84.5	59.3	84.6
16 Leeds	25.0	426	88.5	52.5	83.9
17 Cumbria	8.3		91.9	60.3	81.8

18 St Mary's, Twickenham	20.0	307	87.1	64.0	80.3
19 Cardiff	15.0	381	82.3	68.1	80.2
20 SOAS, London	31.7	344	77.8	66.7	79.8
21 Chester	10.0	301	82.7	79.9	79.2
22 Bangor	13.3		88.9	53.7	78.9
23 Queen's, Belfast		357	88.9	63.6	78.4
24 King's College London	28.3	433	70.5	60.7	76.8
25 Winchester	3.3	309	88.1	60.0	76.1
26 Newman		269	89.2	60.0	74.4
27 Chichester	5.0	231	90.5		74.2
28 Bath Spa	3.3	313	86.7	54.4	74.1
29 Heythrop College	3.3	316	82.6	61.4	73.6
30 Roehampton	10.0	289	85.5	51.4	73.3
31 Canterbury Christ Church	6.7	287	83.1	59.0	73.0
32 Highlands and Islands	3.3		81.2	60.0	72.1
33 Gloucestershire	13.3	267	89.6	35.4	71.7
34 York St John	1.7	279	84.9	51.3	70.7
35 Stirling	13.3		84.9	36.5	70.4
36 South Wales		280	76.9	53.3	66.3
37 Leeds Trinity	13.3	275	68.2	53.6	64.5

Employed in professional job:	34%	Employed in non-professional job and studying:	3%
Employed in professional job and studying:	4%	Employed in non-professional job:	23%
Studying:	25%	Unemployed:	10%
Average starting professional salary:	£20,606	Average starting non-professional salary:	£15,421

Town and Country Planning and Landscape

There was a small rise in applications for courses in town and country planning in 2013, but the numbers actually enrolling were down for the fifth year in a row. The demand for places began to decline after the 2008 recession, but there were signs of a recovery before the introduction of £9,000 fees. The main growth is in landscape and garden design, although it is less than half the size of the other planning courses in terms of applications and enrolments. Across both areas, there are only four applications to the place.

Cambridge continues to have a big lead in the table, with the best research grades and entry standards that are more than 100 points higher than the nearest challenger. Of the other universities with enough entrants to compile a reliable score, only University College London, in ninth place, averages more than 400 points, although there is also just one where the average is below 250. Competition was tight in the 2008 Research Assessment Exercise: Cambridge had the most work placed in the top two categories, but Sheffield – which has dropped from second to fifth this year – had a higher proportion judged to be world-leading. Cardiff, which has taken over second place, has the most satisfied students, while Gloucestershire, in eighth is the top post-1992 institution.

Employment scores are just inside the top 20 for all subjects, although they were in the top ten only five years ago. Starting salaries in professional-level jobs are back in the top 30 after a rise of nearly £1,200 in the average between 2012 and 2013. Reading, which registered

Town and Country Planning and Landscape cont

100 per cent employment scores for five years in a row, did not have enough graduates in 2013 for a score to be included in the new table. The best graduate prospects were at the Royal Agricultural University.

Employed in professional job:	55%	
Employed in professional job and studying:	5%	
Studying:	11%	
Average starting professional salary:	£21,451	

Employed in non-professional job and studying:	2%
Employed in non-professional job:	15%
Unemployed:	12%
Average starting non-professional salary:	£15,865

Town and Country Planning and Landscape	Research quality %	Entry standards	Student satisfaction %	Graduate prospects %	Overall rating
1 Cambridge	45.0	569	84.3	86.9	100.0
2 Cardiff	41.7	377	91.6	86.8	95.1
3 Newcastle	38.3	362	86.6	89.5	91.8
4 Reading	36.7	395	82.2		88.5
5 Sheffield	42.2	362	81.7	78.7	87.5
=6 Aberdeen	33.3			78.2	87.3
=6 Heriot-Watt	30.0		83.4	83.3	87.3
8 Gloucestershire	16.7		85.8	90.0	86.8
9 University College London	33.3	455	79.0	73.1	86.2
10 Loughborough	41.7	364	84.2	67.6	85.9
11 Manchester Metropolitan	15.0		87.8	84.6	85.7
12 Northumbria	20.0	334	87.5	82.8	84.8
13 Oxford Brookes	16.7	362	83.0	84.9	83.4
14 Liverpool	23.3		85.1	74.2	83.1
15 Manchester	33.3	371	81.0	69.1	82.8
16 Queen's, Belfast	16.7	337	87.8	76.5	82.7
17 Birmingham	23.3	396	77.5	80.0	82.3
18 West of England	19.5	327	82.4	80.5	81.2
19 Dundee	16.7		82.4	76.2	79.7
20 Royal Agricultural University	5.0	336	80.2	90.5	79.4
21 Edinburgh	40.0	396	66.6		78.9
22 Nottingham Trent	10.0	289	80.7	83.2	77.1
23 Birmingham City	15.0	303	83.8	68.4	76.8
24 Glasgow Caledonian	30.0	368	73.9	60.0	75.9
25 Leeds Metropolitan		280	86.9	65.5	72.9
26 Westminster	11.7	255	85.4	56.7	71.8
27 Sheffield Hallam	30.0	247	71.6	49.0	67.0
28 Ulster		270	73.2	56.6	63.2

Veterinary Medicine

Only medicine itself has higher entry standards than veterinary medicine, where successful candidates had an average of 526 points in 2013. Just two of the seven schools in the table – one of which was top-placed Nottingham – averaged less than 500 points, and there were more than nine applications for every place. An eighth veterinary school opened in 2013 at the University of Surrey, but it will be several years before there are enough data to include it in this table. Nottingham was the last newcomer, opening in 2006, and it is already enjoying its third year as the top school. It again has the best rating for student satisfaction and was not far behind second-placed Edinburgh in the 2008 Research Assessment Exercise. Cambridge has much the highest entry grades, but remains in third place.

Veterinary medicine is another of the rankings in which employment scores have been removed from the calculations that determine universities' positions. The scores are still shown in the table, but the review group of academic planners consulted on the *Guide* agreed that employment rates in the subject were so tightly bunched that small differences could distort the overall ranking. Veterinary medicine has been a fixture in the top five for both graduate destinations and starting salaries in professional jobs, but no longer features in either. Indeed, the subject is down to eighth in the earnings table, despite average salaries of almost £25,000 in 2013.

Applications rose in 2013, but the number of places is centrally controlled. Most courses demand high grades in chemistry and biology, with some accepting physics or maths as one alternative subject. Cambridge and the Royal Veterinary College also set applicants a specialist aptitude test that is used by a number of medical schools. Few candidates win places without evidence of practical commitment to the subject through work experience, either in veterinary practices or laboratories. The norm for veterinary science degrees is five years, but the Cambridge course takes six years and both Bristol and Nottingham offer a "pre-veterinary" year. Both Edinburgh and the Royal Veterinary College run four-year courses for graduates. There are no degrees in the subject in Wales or Northern Ireland, or in the post-1992 universities, although a number of them and several colleges offer veterinary nursing.

Veterinary Medicine	Research quality %	Entry standards	Student satisfaction %	Graduate prospects %	Overall rating
1 Nottingham	30.0	496	88.8	94.4	100.0
2 Edinburgh	31.7	542	82.2	94.6	98.7
3 Cambridge	18.3	620	81.9	92.2	97.7
4 Royal Veterinary College	25.0	513	78.7	87.0	92.1
5 Bristol	13.3	512	85.2	82.1	91.9
6 Liverpool	18.3	475	85.3	97.2	91.8
7 Glasgow	21.7	524	78.1	93.2	91.0

Employed in professional job:	87%	Employed in non-professional job and studying:	0%
Employed in professional job and studying:	1%	Employed in non-professional job:	5%
Studying:	2%	Unemployed:	5%
Average starting professional salary:	£24,934	Average starting non-professional salary:	£14,500

The universities that topped the subject tables in *The Times and Sunday Times Guide*

	First place	Second place	Third place
Accounting and Finance	Warwick	Strathclyde	Lancaster
Aeronautical and Manufacturing Engineering	Cambridge	Imperial College	Leeds
Agriculture and Forestry	Newcastle	Reading	Queen's, Belfast
American Studies	Manchester	Warwick	Birmingham
			Sussex
Anatomy and Physiology	Cambridge	Oxford	University College London
Animal Science	Nottingham	West of England	Royal Veterinary College
Anthropology	Cambridge	Oxford	London School of Economics
			St Andrews
Archaeology	Durham	Oxford	Cambridge
Architecture	Bath	Sheffield	Edinburgh
Art and Design	Oxford	Glasgow	Lancaster
Biological Sciences	Cambridge	Oxford	York
Building	University College London	Loughborough	Reading
Business Studies	Cambridge	Oxford	Bath
Celtic Studies	Cambridge	Bangor	Aberystwyth
Chemical Engineering	Cambridge	Imperial College	Bath
Chemistry	Cambridge	Durham	Oxford
Civil Engineering	Cambridge	Imperial College	Bath
Classics and Ancient History	Cambridge	Oxford	Exeter
Communication and Media Studies	Warwick	Exeter	Lancaster
Computer Science	Oxford	Cambridge	Imperial College
Creative Writing	Warwick	Birmingham	Queen's, Belfast
Dentistry	Glasgow	Queen Mary, London	Manchester
			Newcastle
Drama, Dance and Cinematics	Warwick	Queen Mary, London	Exeter
East and South Asian Studies	Oxford	SOAS London	Edinburgh
Economics	Warwick	Cambridge	
		Oxford	
Education	Cambridge	Durham	Glasgow
Electrical and Electronic Engineering	Cambridge	Surrey	Southampton
English	Cambridge	Durham	Oxford
Food Science	King's College London	Surrey	Nottingham
French	Cambridge	Oxford	Durham
General Engineering	Cambridge	Imperial College	Durham
Geography and Environmental Sciences	Durham	Oxford	Cardiff
Geology	Cambridge	Imperial College	Oxford
German	Cambridge	Durham	Oxford
History	Cambridge	Durham	St Andrews
History of Art, Architecture and Design	Courtauld Institute	East Anglia	Oxford
Hospitality, Leisure, Recreation and Tourism	Surrey	Exeter	Central Lancashire
Iberian Languages	Cambridge	Durham	Oxford

	First place	Second place	Third place
Italian	Cambridge	Oxford	Durham
Land and Property Management	Cambridge	Reading	Sheffield Hallam
Law	Cambridge	Oxford	Durham
Librarianship and Information Management	Loughborough	Sheffield	Liverpool John Moores
Linguistics	Cambridge	Edinburgh	Oxford
Materials Technology	Cambridge	Imperial College	Oxford
Mathematics	Cambridge	Oxford	Imperial College Warwick
Mechanical Engineering	Cambridge	Imperial College	Bristol
Medicine	Oxford	Cambridge	Imperial College
Middle Eastern and African Studies	Cambridge	Durham	Oxford
Music	Oxford	Manchester	Cambridge
Nursing	Glasgow	Edinburgh	Manchester
Other Subjects Allied to Medicine	Aston	Leeds	Surrey
Pharmacology and Pharmacy	Cambridge	Queen's, Belfast	Nottingham
Philosophy	Oxford	Cambridge	King's College London
Physics and Astronomy	Cambridge	Birmingham	Bath
Physiotherapy	Cardiff	Keele	Robert Gordon
Politics	Oxford	Cambridge	University College London
Psychology	Cambridge	Bath	Oxford
Radiography	Exeter	Leeds	Robert Gordon
Russian and East European Languages	Cambridge	Oxford	Durham
Social Policy	Bristol	Leeds	Kent
Social Work	Bath	Leeds	Swansea
Sociology	Cambridge	Bath	Southampton
Sports Science	Birmingham	Bath	Durham
Theology and Religious Studies	Durham	Oxford	Cambridge St Andrews
Town and Country Planning and Landscape	Cambridge	Cardiff	Newcastle
Veterinary Medicine	Nottingham	Edinburgh	Cambridge

The top university for each subject covered in *The Times and Sunday Times Guide*

Cambridge	Aeronautical and Manufacturing Engineering	**Warwick**	Accounting and Finance
	Anatomy and Physiology		Communication and Media Studies
	Anthropology		Creative Writing
	Biological Sciences		Drama, Dance and Cinematics
	Business Studies		Economics
	Celtic Studies		
	Chemical Engineering	**Durham**	Archaeology
	Chemistry		Geography and Environmental Sciences
	Civil Engineering		Theology and Religious Studies
	Classics and Ancient History		
	Education	**Bath**	Architecture
	Electrical and Electronic Engineering		Social Work
	English		
	French	**Glasgow**	Dentistry
	General Engineering		Nursing
	Geology		
	German	**Nottingham**	Animal Science
	History		Veterinary Medicine
	Iberian Languages		
	Italian	**Aston**	Other Subjects Allied to Medicine
	Land and Property Management		
	Law	**Birmingham**	Sports Science
	Linguistics		
	Materials Technology	**Bristol**	Social Policy
	Mathematics		
	Mechanical Engineering	**Cardiff**	Physiotherapy
	Middle Eastern and African Studies		
	Pharmacology and Pharmacy	**Courtauld Institute**	History of Art, Architecture and Design
	Physics and Astronomy		
	Psychology	**Exeter**	Radiography
	Russian and East European Languages		
	Sociology	**King's College London**	Food Science
	Town and Country Planning and Landscape		
		Loughborough	Librarianship and Information Management
Oxford	Art and Design		
	Computer Science	**Manchester**	American Studies
	East and South Asian Studies		
	Medicine	**Newcastle**	Agriculture and Forestry
	Music		
	Philosophy	**Surrey**	Hospitality, Leisure, Recreation and Tourism
	Politics		
		University College London	Building

6 Making Your Application

In an era when there are relatively few interviews and more candidates each year achieve high A-level grades, what goes on your UCAS form is becoming more and more important – too important, many would say. The art of conveying knowledge of, and enthusiasm for, your chosen subject – preferably with supporting evidence from your school or college – can make all the difference.

Too many people take their eye off the ball when actually applying for a higher education place. Surprising numbers of applicants each year spell their own name wrongly, or enter an inaccurate date of birth, or the wrong course code. And that is to say nothing of the damage that can be done in the personal statement and teachers' references. While UCAS will decode misspelt names, other errors in grammar or spelling present admissions officers with an easy starting point in cutting applications down to a more manageable number.

There was talk of a new application system, with only two choices and later deadlines. But, for the moment, applicants will continue to have five course choices, and to make decisions well before they have their results. You do not have to take advantage of all five – some people make only a single application, perhaps because they do not want to leave home or they have very particular requirements – but you will give yourself the best chance of success if you go for the maximum.

A number of relatively minor changes were made to UCAS procedures for entry in 2014, but no more are planned for 2015. Perhaps the most important recent change allowed candidates to submit a new personal statement if their initial applications are unsuccessful and they use the UCAS Extra process. This and other changes are outlined below.

The application process

Most applications for full-time higher education courses go through UCAS, although specialist admissions bodies still handle applications to the music conservatoires (Conservatoires UK Admissions Service: **www.cukas.ac.uk**). The trend is towards the UCAS model even among specialist providers, however: recruitment to nursing and midwifery diploma and degree courses in Scotland switched to the UCAS system in 2010, and the art and design courses that used to recruit using the separate "Route B" scheme have also moved to the main system.

Some universities that have not filled all their places, even during Clearing, will accept direct applications up to and sometimes after the start of the academic year, but UCAS is both the official route and the only way into the most popular courses.

Since 2006, all UCAS applications have been made online. The Apply electronic system is accessed via the UCAS website and is straightforward to use. For those who do not have the internet at home and prefer not to use school or college computers, the UCAS website lists libraries all over the UK where you can make your application. Apply is available 24 hours a day, and, when the time comes, information on the progress of your application may arrive at any time.

Registering with Apply

The first step in the process is to register. If you are at a school or college, you will need to obtain a "buzzword" from your tutor or careers adviser – it is used when you log on to register. It links your application to the school or college so that the application can be sent electronically to your referee (usually one of your teachers) for your reference to be attached. If you are no longer at a school or college, you do not need a "buzzword", but you will need details of your referee. More information is given on the UCAS website.

To register, go to the UCAS website and click on "Apply". The system will guide you through the business of providing your personal details and generating a username and password, as well as reminding you of basic points, such as amending your details in case of a change of address. You can register separate term-time and holiday addresses – a useful option for boarders, who could find offers and, particularly, the confirmation of a place, going to their school when they are miles away at home. Remember to keep a note of your username and password in a safe place.

Throughout the process, you will be in sole control of communications with UCAS and your chosen universities. Only if you nominate a representative and give them your unique nine-digit application number (sent automatically by UCAS when your application is submitted), can a parent or anyone else give or receive information on your behalf, perhaps because you are ill or out of the country.

Improved video guides on the application process are available on the UCAS website. Once you are registered, you can start to complete the Apply screens. The sections that follow cover the main screens.

Personal details

This information is taken from your initial registration, and you will be asked for additional information, for example, on ethnic origin and national identity, used to monitor equal

---

The main screens to be completed in UCAS Apply

» Personal details and some additional non-educational details for UK applicants.

» Student finance, a section for UK-resident applicants.

» Your course choices.

» Details of your education so far, including examination results and examinations still to be taken.

» Details of any jobs you have done.

» Your personal statement.

» A reference from one of your teachers.

» Payment details (applications cost £23, or £12 to apply to just one course).

» A declaration that you confirm that the information is correct and that you will be bound by the UCAS rules.

opportunities in the application process. UK students will also be asked to complete a student finance section designed to speed up your loan application when you make it later in the process.

Choices

In most subjects, you will be able to apply to a maximum of five universities and/or colleges. The exceptions are medicine, dentistry and veterinary science, where the maximum is four, but you can use your fifth choice as a back-up to apply for a different subject.

The other important restriction concerns Oxford or Cambridge, because you can only apply to one or the other; you cannot apply to both Oxford and Cambridge in the same year, nor can you apply for more than one course. For both universities you may need to take a written test (see pages 20–21) and submit examples of your work, depending on the course selected. In addition, for Cambridge, you will be asked to complete a Supplementary Application Questionnaire once the university has received your application from UCAS. The deadline for Oxbridge applications – and for all medicine, dentistry and veterinary science courses – is 15 October. For all other applications the deadline is 15 January (or 24 March for some specified art and design courses).

Most applicants use all five choices. But if you do choose fewer than five courses, you can still add another to your form up to 30 June, as long as you have not accepted or declined any offers. Nor do you have to choose five different universities if more than one course at the same institution attracts you – perhaps because the institution itself is the real draw and one course has lower entrance requirements than the other. Universities are not allowed to see where else you have applied, or whether you have chosen the same subject elsewhere. But they will be aware of multiple applications within their own institution. Remember that it is more difficult to write a convincing personal statement if it has to cover two subjects.

For each course you select, you will need to put the UCAS code on the form – and you should check carefully that you have the correct code and understand any special requirements that may be detailed on the UCAS description of the course. It does not matter what order you enter in your choices as all your choices are treated equally. You will also need to indicate whether you are applying for a deferred entry (for example, if you are taking a gap year – see page 209).

Education

In this section you will need to give details of the schools and colleges you have attended, and the qualifications you have obtained or are preparing for. The UCAS website gives plenty of advice on the ways in which you should enter this information, to ensure that all your relevant qualifications are included with their grades. While UCAS does not need to see qualification certificates, it can double-check results with the examination boards to ensure that no-one is tempted to modify their results.

In the Employment section that follows add details of any paid jobs you have had (unpaid or voluntary work should be mentioned in your personal statement).

Personal statement

As the competition for places on popular courses has become more intense, so the value attached to the personal statement has increased. Admissions officers look for a sign of potential beyond the high grades that growing numbers of applicants offer. Many (but not all) academics responsible for admissions value success in extracurricular activities such as drama, sport or the Duke of Edinburgh's Award scheme. But your first priority should be to demonstrate an interest in and understanding of your chosen subject beyond the confines of the exam syllabus.

This is not easy in a relatively short statement that can readily sound trite or pretentious. You should resist any temptation to lie, particularly if there is any chance of an interview. A claim to have been inspired by a book that you have not read will backfire instantly under questioning and, even without an interview, experienced academics are likely to see through grandiose statements that appear at odds with a teacher's reference.

Genuine experiences of after-hours clubs, lectures or visits – better still, work experience or actual reading around the syllabus – are much more likely to strike the right note. If you are applying for medicine, for example, any practical work experience or volunteering in medical or caring settings should be included. Take advice from teachers and, if there is still time before you make your application, look for some subject-related activities that will help fill out your statement.

Admissions officers are also looking for evidence of character that will make you a productive member of their university and, eventually, a successful graduate. Taking responsibility in any area of school or college life suggests this – leading activities outside your place of learning even more so. Evidence of initiative and self-discipline is also valuable, since higher education involves much more independent study than sixth-formers are used to.

Your overall aim in writing your personal statement is to persuade the admissions officer to pick yours out from the piles of applications. That means trying to stand out from an often rather dull and uniform set of statements based around the curriculum and the more predictable sixth-form activities. Everyone is going to say they love reading, for example; narrow your interest down to an area of (real) interest. Don't be afraid to include the unusual, but bear in mind that an academic's sense of humour may not be the same as yours.

Give particular thought to why you want to study your chosen subject – especially if it is not one you have taken at school or college. You need to show that your interests and skills are well-suited to the course and, if it is a vocational degree, that you know how you envisage using the qualification. Admissions officers want to feel that you will be committed to their subject for the length of the course, which could be three, four or even five years, and capable of achieving good results.

Your school or college should be the best source of advice, since they see personal statements every year, but there are others. The UCAS website has a useful checklist of themes that you may wish to address, while sites such as **www.studential.com** also provide tips. But do not fall into the trap of cutting and pasting from the model statements included on such sites – both UCAS and individual universities have software that will spot plagiarism immediately. In one year, no fewer than one in 20 applicants came to grief in this way. Plagiarists of this type are unlikely to be disqualified, but they destroy the credibility of their application.

UCAS top ten personal statement tips

1 Express interest in the subject and show real passion.
2 Go for a strong opening line to grab the reader's attention.
3 Relate outside interests to the course.
4 Think beyond university.
5 Get the basics right.
6 Don't try to sound too clever.
7 Take time and make it your best work.
8 Don't leave it until the last minute – remember the 15 January deadline!
9 Get a second opinion.
10 Honesty is the best policy.

Try not to cram in more than the limited space will allow – admissions officers will have many statements to go through, and judicious editing may be rewarded. As long as you write clearly – preferably in paragraphs and possibly with sub-headings – it will be up to you what to include. It is a *personal* statement. But consider the points listed below and make sure that you can answer all the questions raised. Once you have completed your statement show it to others you trust. It is really important to have others read your statement before submitting it – sometimes things that are clear to you may not be to fresh eyes.

The Apply system allows 4,000 characters (including spaces) or 47 lines for your statement. While there is no requirement to fill all the space, it should not look embarrassingly short. Indeed, from 2014, your statement will have to be at least 1,000 characters long. It is hard to believe that many candidates could not rustle up 200 words to support their application, but presumably significant numbers were not doing so. UCAS recommends using a word-processing package to compile the statement before pasting it into the application system. This is because Apply will time-out after 35 minutes of inactivity, so there is a danger of losing valuable material. Working offline also has the advantage of leaving you with a copy and making it easier to show it to others.

References

Hand in hand with your personal statement goes the reference from your school, college or, in the case of mature students, someone who knows you well, but is not a friend or family member. From 2014, even referees who are not your teachers will be encouraged to predict your grades, although they will be allowed to opt out of this process. Whatever the source, the reference has to be independent – you are specifically forbidden to change any part of it if you send off your own application – but that does not mean you should not try to influence what it contains.

Most schools and colleges conduct informal interviews before compiling a reference, but it does no harm to draw up a list of the achievements that you would like to see included, and ensure your referee knows what subject you are applying for. Referees cannot know every detail of a candidate's interests and most welcome an aide-memoire.

The UCAS guidelines skirt around the candidate's right to see his or her reference, but it does exist. Schools' practices vary, but most now show the applicant the completed reference. Where this is not the case, the candidate can pay UCAS £10 for a copy, although at this stage it is obviously too late to influence the contents. Better, if you can, to see it before it goes off, in case there are factual inaccuracies that can be corrected.

Key points to consider in writing your personal statement

» What attracts you to this subject (or subjects, in the case of dual or combined honours)?

» Have you undertaken relevant work experience or voluntary activities, either through school or elsewhere?

» Have you taken part in other extra-curricular activities that demonstrate character – perhaps as a prefect, on the sports field or in the arts?

» Have you been involved in other academic pursuits, such as Gifted and Talented programmes, widening participation schemes, or courses in other subjects?

» Which aspects of your current courses have you found particularly stimulating?

» Are you planning a gap year? If so, explain what you intend to do and how it will affect your studies. Some subjects – notably maths – actively discourage a break in studies.

» What other outside interests might you include that show that you are well-rounded?

Timetable for applications for university admission in 2015

2014

May onwards	Find out about courses and universities. Attend open days.
early July	Registration starts for UCAS Apply.
mid September	UCAS starts receiving applications.
15 October	Final day for applications to Oxford and Cambridge, and for all courses in medicine, dentistry and veterinary science.

2015

15 January	Final day for all other applications from UK and EU students including all art and design courses except those which have a 24 March deadline (specified in UCAS Course Search).
16 January–30 June	New applications continue to be accepted by UCAS, but only considered by universities if the relevant courses have vacancies.
25 February	Start of applications through UCAS Extra.
24 March	Final day for applications to art and design courses that specify this date.
31 March	Universities should have sent decisions on all applications received by 15 January.
6 May	Final day by which applicants have to decide on their choices if all decisions received by 31 March (exact date for each applicant will be confirmed by UCAS). **If you do not reply to UCAS, they will decline your offers.**
7 May	UCAS must have received all decisions from universities if you applied by 15 January.
4 June	Final day by which applicants have to decide on their choices if all decisions received by 7 May .
25 June	Final day by which applicants have to decide on their choices if all decisions received by 4 June.
1 July	Any new application received from this date held until Clearing starts.
2 July	Final day for applications through UCAS Extra.
16 July	Universities must give decisions on all applications submitted by 30 June. You must make a decision on these offers by 23 July.
4 August	SQA results published. Scottish Clearing starts.
13 August	GCE results published. Full Clearing and Adjustment starts.
31 August	Adjustment closes.
21 September	Last day UCAS will accept applications for courses about to start.
30 September	Clearing vacancy service closes. Contact universities directly about vacancies.
21 October	Last date by which a university can accept you through Clearing.

Timing

The general deadline for applications through UCAS is 15 January, but even those received up to 30 June will be considered if the relevant courses still have vacancies. After that, you will be limited to Clearing, or an application for the following year. In theory – and usually in practice – all applications submitted by the January deadline are given equal consideration. But the best advice is to get your application in early: before Christmas, or earlier if possible. Applications are accepted from mid-September onwards, so the autumn half-term is a sensible target date for completing the process. Although no formal offers are made before the deadline, many admissions officers look through applications as they come in and may make a mental note of promising candidates. If your form arrives with the deadline looming, you may appear less organised than those who submitted in good time; and your application may be one of a large batch that receives a more cursory first reading than the early arrivals. Under UCAS rules, last-minute applicants should not be at a disadvantage, but why take the risk?

Next steps

Once your application has been processed by UCAS, you will receive a welcome letter or email confirming your choices and summarising what will happen next. The letter will contain a reminder of your identification number and the username and password that you used to apply. These will also give you access to "Track", the online system that allows you to follow the progress of your application. Check all the details carefully: you have 14 days to contact UCAS to correct any errors. Universities can make direct contact with you through Track, including arranging interviews.

After that, it is just a matter of waiting for universities to make their decisions, which can take days, weeks or even months, depending on the university and the course. Some obviously see an advantage in being the first to make an offer – it is a memorable moment to be reassured that at least one of your chosen institutions wants you – and may send their response almost immediately. Others take much longer, perhaps because they have so many good applications to consider, or maybe because they are waiting to see which of their applicants withdraw when Oxford and Cambridge make their offers. Universities are asked to make all their decisions by the end of March, and most have done so long before that.

Interviews

Unless you are applying for a course in health or education that brings you into direct contact with the public, the chances are you will not have a selection interview. For prospective medics, vets, dentists or teachers, a face-to-face assessment of your suitability will be crucial to your chances of success. Likewise in the performing arts, the interview may be as important as your exam grades. Oxford and Cambridge still interview applicants in all subjects, and a few of the top universities see a significant proportion. But the expansion of higher education has made it impractical to interview everyone, and many admissions experts are sceptical about interviews.

What has become more common, however, is the "sales" interview, where the university is really selling itself to the candidate. There may still be testing questions, but the admissions staff have already made their minds up and are actually trying to persuade you to accept an offer. Indeed, you will probably be given a clear indication at the end of the interview that an offer is on its way. The technique seems to work, perhaps because you have invested time and nervous energy in a sometimes lengthy trip, as well as acquiring a more detailed impression of both the department and the university.

The difficulty can come in spotting which type of interview is which. The "real" ones require lengthy preparation, revisiting your personal statement and reading beyond the exam syllabus. Impressions count for a lot, so dress smartly and make sure that you are on time. Have a question of your own ready, as well as being prepared to give answers.

While you would not want to appear ignorant at a "sales" interview, lengthy preparation might be a waste of valuable time during a period of revision. Naturally, you should err on the side of caution, but if your predicted grades are well above the standard offer and the subject is not one that normally requires an interview, it is likely that the invitation is a sales pitch. It is still worth going, unless you have changed your mind about the application.

Offers

When your chosen universities respond to your application, there will be one of three answers:

» Unconditional Offer (U): This is a possibility only if you applied after satisfying the entrance requirements – usually if you are applying as a mature student, while on a gap year, after resitting exams or, in Scotland, after completing Highers.
» Conditional Offer (C): The university offers a place subject to you achieving set grades or points on the UCAS tariff.
» Rejection (R): You do not have the right qualifications, or have lost out to stronger competition.

If you have chosen wisely, you should have more than one offer to choose from, so you will be required to pick your favourite as your firm acceptance – known as UF if it was an unconditional offer and CF if it was conditional. Candidates with conditional offers can also accept a second offer, with lower grades, as an Insurance choice (CI). You must then decline any other offers that you have.

You do not have to make an Insurance choice – indeed, you may decline all your offers if you have changed your mind about your career path or regret your course decisions. But most people prefer the security of a back-up route into higher education if their grades fall short. You must be sure that your firm acceptance is definitely your first choice because you will be allocated a place automatically if you meet the university's conditions. It is no good at this stage deciding that you prefer your Insurance choice because UCAS rules will not allow a switch.

The only way round those rules, unless your results are better than your highest offer (see Adjustment, below), is through direct contact with the universities concerned. Your firm acceptance institution has to be prepared to release you so that your new choice can award you a place in Clearing. Neither is under any obligation to do so but, in practice, it is rare for a university to insist that a student joins against his or her wishes. Admissions staff will do all they can to persuade you that your original choice was the right one – as it may well have been, if your research was thorough – but it will almost certainly be your decision in the end.

UCAS Extra

If things do go wrong and you receive five rejections, that need not be the end of your higher education ambitions. From the end of February until the end of June, you have another chance through UCAS Extra, a listing of courses that still have vacancies after the initial round of offers. Extra is sometimes dismissed (wrongly) as a repository of second-rate courses. In fact, even in the boom years for applications, most Russell Group universities still have courses listed in a wide variety of subjects.

You will be notified if you are eligible for Extra and can then select courses marked as available on the UCAS website. In order to assist students who choose different subjects after a full set of rejections in their original application, you will be able to submit a new personal statement for Extra. Applications are made, one at a time, through UCAS Track. If you do not receive an offer, or you choose to decline one, you can continue applying for other courses until you are successful. About half of those applying through Extra normally find a place. Nearly 8,000 were successful this way in 2013.

Results Day

Rule Number One on results day is to be at home, or at least in easy communication – you cannot afford to be on some remote beach if there are complications. The day is bound to be stressful, unless you are absolutely confident that you achieved the required grades – more of a possibility in an era of modular courses with marks along the way. But for thousands of students Track has removed the agony of opening the envelope or scanning a results noticeboard. On the morning of A-level results day, the system informs those who have already won a place on their chosen course. You will not learn your grades until later, but at least your immediate future is clear.

If you get the grades stipulated in your conditional offer, the process should work smoothly and you can begin celebrating. Track will let you know as soon as your place is confirmed and the paperwork will arrive in a day or two. You can phone the university to make quite sure, but it should not be necessary and you will be joining a long queue of people doing the same thing.

If the results are not what you hoped – and particularly if you just miss your grades – you need to be on the phone and taking advice from your school or college. In a year when results are better than expected, some universities will stick to the letter of their offers, perhaps refusing to accept your AAC grades when they had demanded ABB. Others will forgive a dropped grade to take a candidate who is regarded as promising, rather than go into Clearing to recruit an unknown quantity. Admissions staff may be persuadable – particularly if there are extenuating personal circumstances, or the dropped grade is in a subject that is not relevant to your chosen course. Try to get a teacher to support your case, and be persistent if there is any prospect of flexibility.

One option, if your results are lower than predicted, is to ask for papers to be re-marked, as growing numbers do each year. The school may ask for a whole batch to be re-marked, and you should ensure that your chosen universities know this if it may make the difference to whether or not you satisfy your offer. If your grades improve, the university will review its decision, but if by then it has filled all its places, you may have to wait until next year to start the course.

If you took Scottish Highers, you will have had your results for more than a week by the time the A-level grades are published. If you missed your grades, there is no need to wait for A levels before you begin approaching universities. Admissions staff at English universities may not wish to commit themselves before they see results from south of the border, but Scottish universities will be filling places immediately and all should be prepared to give you an idea of your prospects.

Adjustment

If your grades are better than those demanded by your first-choice university, there is now an opportunity to "trade up". Introduced in 2009, the Adjustment Period runs from when you receive your results until 31 August and you can only use it for five 24-hour periods during that period, so there is no time to waste. First, go into the Track system and click on "Register for Adjustment" and then contact your preferred institutions to find another place. If none is available, or you decide not to move, your initial offer will remain open. The number of students switching universities in this way more than doubled in 2012. Although the total slipped back slightly in 2013, there were still 1,220 successful candidates. The process has become as established part of the system and, without the previous restrictions on the number of students they could recruit, many leading universities see it as a good source of talented undergraduates. UCAS does not publish a breakdown of which universities take part – some, such as Oxford and Cambridge, simply do not have places available – but it is known that many students successfully go back to institutions that had rejected them at the initial application stage. Even if you are eligible for Adjustment, you may decide to stick with the offer you have, but it is worth at least exploring your options.

Clearing

If you do not have a place on Results Day, there will still be plenty of options through the UCAS Clearing scheme. More than 57,000 people – about one successful applicant in nine – found a place through this route in 2013 and the numbers rose again in 2014. With recruitment restrictions lifted, universities that used to regard their absence from Clearing as a point of pride are appearing in the vacancy lists. It is likely that this trend will accelerate in 2015, as more universities seek to expand, particularly in arts, social science and business subjects.

Although the most popular courses may still fill up quickly, many remain open up to and beyond the start of the academic year. And, at least at the start of the process, the range of courses with vacancies is much wider than in Extra. Most universities will list some courses, and most subjects will be available somewhere.

Clearing runs from A-level Results Day until the end of September, matching students without places to full-time courses with vacancies. As long as you are not holding any offers and you have not withdrawn your application, you are eligible automatically. You will be sent a Clearing number via Track to quote to universities.

Now it is just a matter of trawling through the lists on the UCAS website, and elsewhere, before making a direct approach to the university offering the course that appeals most, and where you have a realistic chance of a place – do not waste time on courses where the standard offer is far above your grades. Universities run Clearing hotlines and have become adept at dealing with a large number of calls in a short period, but you can still spend a long time on the phone at a time when the most desirable places are beginning to disappear. If you can't get through send an email setting out your grades and the course that interests you.

The best advice is to plan ahead and not to wait for Results Day to draw up a list of possible Clearing targets. Many universities publish lists of courses that are likely to be in Clearing on their websites from the start of August. Think again about some of the courses that you considered when making your original application, or others at your chosen universities that had lower entrance requirements. But beware of switching to another subject simply because you have the right grades – you still have to sustain your interest and be capable of succeeding over three or more years. Many of the students who drop out of degrees are those who chose the wrong course in a rush during Clearing.

In short, you should start your search straight away if you do find yourself in Clearing, and act decisively, but do not panic. You can make as many approaches as you like, until you are accepted on the course of your choice. Remember that if you changed your personal statement for applications in Extra, this will be the one that goes to any universities that you approach in Clearing, so it may be difficult to return to the subjects in your original application.

Most of the available vacancies will appear in Clearing lists, but some of the universities towards the top of the league tables may have a limited number of openings that they choose not to advertise – either for reasons of status or because they do not want the administrative burden of fielding large numbers of calls to fill a handful of places. If there is a course that you find particularly attractive – especially if you have good grades and are applying late – it may be worth making a speculative call. Sometimes a number of candidates holding offers drop grades and you may be on the spot at the right moment.

What are the alternatives?

If your results are lower than expected and there is nothing you want in Clearing, there are several things you can do. The first is to resit one or more subjects. The modular nature of most courses means that you will have a clear idea of what you need to do to get better grades. You can go back to school or college, or try a "crammer". Although some colleges have a good success rate with re-takes, you have to be highly focused and realistic about the likely improvements. Some of the most competitive courses, such as medicine, may demand higher grades for a second application, so be sure you know the details before you commit yourself.

Other options are to get a job and study part-time, or to take a break from studying and return later in your career. The part-time route can be arduous – many young people find a job enough to handle without the extra burden of academic work. But others find it just the combination they need for a fulfilling life. It all depends on your job, your social life and your commitment to the subject you will study. It may be that a relatively short break is all that you need to rekindle your enthusiasm for studying. Many universities now have a majority of mature students, so you need not be out of place if this is your chosen route.

Taking a gap year

The other popular option is to take a gap year. In most years, about 7 per cent of applicants defer their entry until the following year while they travel, or do voluntary or paid work. A whole industry has grown up around tailor-made activities, many of them in Asia, Africa or Latin America. Some have been criticised for doing more for the organisers than the underprivileged communities that they purport to assist, but there are programmes that are useful and character-building, as well as safe. Most of the overseas programmes are not cheap, but raising the money can be part of the experience.

Various organisations can help you find voluntary work. Some examples include vInspired (**www.vinspired.com**), Lattitude Global Volunteering (**www.lattitude.org.uk**) and Volunteer Africa (**www.volunteerafrica.org**). Voluntary Service Overseas (**www.vso.org.uk**) works mainly with older volunteers but has an offshoot, run with five other volunteering organisations, International Citizen Service (**www.volunteerics.org**), that places 18–25 year olds around the world.

The alternative is to stay closer to home and make your contribution through organisations like Community Service Volunteers (**www.csv.org.uk**) or to take a job that will make higher education more affordable when the time comes. Work placements can be casual or structured, such as the Year in Industry Scheme (**www.etrust.org.uk**). Sponsorship is also available, mainly to those wishing to study science, engineering or business. Buyer beware: we cannot vouch for any of these and you need to be clear whether the aim is to make money or to plump up your CV. If it is the second, you may end up spending money, not saving it.

Many admissions staff are happy to facilitate gap years because they think it makes for more mature, rounded students than those who come straight from school. The longer-term benefits may also be an advantage in the graduate employment market. Both university admissions officers and employers look for evidence that candidates have more about them than academic ability. The experience you gain on a gap year can help you develop many of the attributes they are looking for, such as interpersonal, organisational and teamwork skills, leadership, creativity, experience of new cultures or work environments, and enterprise..

There are subjects – maths in particular – that discourage a break because it takes too long to pick up study skills where you left off. From the student's point of view, you should also bear in mind that a gap year postpones the moment at which you embark on a career. This may be important if your course is a long one, such as medicine or architecture.

If you are considering a gap year, it makes sense to apply for a deferred place, rather than waiting for your results before applying. The application form has a section for deferments. That allows you to sort out your immediate future before you start travelling or working, and leaves you the option of changing your mind if circumstances change.

Useful websites
The essential website for making an application is, of course, that of UCAS:
www.ucas.com/how-it-all-works/undergraduate/filling-your-application
For applications to music conservatoires: **www.cukas.ac.uk**
For advice on your personal statement:
**www.ucas.com/students/how-it-all-works/undergraduate/filling-your-application/
    your-personal-statement**
www.studential.com

Gap years
To help you consider options and start planning: **www.gapadvice.org**
For links to volunteering opportunities in the UK: **www.do-it.org.uk**
For links to many gap year organisations: **www.yearoutgroup.org**
See also page 211.

7 University Tuition Fees

Only two universities in England – University College Birmingham and Sunderland – will charge less than £9,000 for all their courses in 2015–16. But the actual fees charged in England, let alone other parts of the UK, will vary much more widely than media reporting might suggest. The average fee for UK and European Union undergraduates, when all forms of financial support are taken into account, will be £8,280. It will range from £7,451 at Sunderland to £8,879 at Middlesex. Some further education colleges will still be offering average fees of less than £6,000 after accounting for financial support.

This *Guide* quotes the higher headline fees because only a minority of students will qualify for reductions, usually by virtue of family income or their academic performance. But even these will vary according to whether you are from inside or outside the EU, studying full-time or part-time, and whether you are taking a Foundation degree or an Honours programme. Non-European medical students may pay as much as £35,000 a year, Britons taking part-time Foundation degrees as little as £3,500. But all the attention has been focused on full-time Honours degrees for British and other EU undergraduates because those are the courses for which the maximum fees shot up to £9,000 in 2012.

£9,000 fee now the norm

Student numbers dropped in the first year of higher fees, but prospective students now appear to have resigned themselves to the new charges. Both applications and enrolments recovered in 2013 and have increased further this year – even among mature students, whose numbers have been down until now. There is little sign that applicants are basing their choices on the marginal differences in fee levels at different universities. Concern remains, however, over the impact on part-time courses and, in years to come, on the numbers prepared to continue to postgraduate study.

Most readers of *The Times and Sunday Times Good University Guide* will be choosing full-time undergraduate or Foundation degree courses. The fees for 2015–16 are listed alongside each university's profile in chapter 14 and access agreements for universities in England, including full details of bursaries and scholarships, are on the website of the Office for Fair Access (OFFA). Institutions in Scotland, Wales and Northern Ireland will continue to have lower charges for their own residents, but will charge varying amounts to students from other parts of the UK. Only those living in Scotland and studying at Scottish universities will escape all fees, although there will be reduced fees for those living and studying in Wales and Northern Ireland.

No one living in the UK will pay more than the £9,000 maximum introduced in 2012. Inflation is eating into tuition fee income – now a big part of universities' finances – and there is no longer any significant incentive to keep fees down. The number of bursaries and scholarships offered to reduce the burden on new students will fall since OFFA has suggested that such initiatives do little to attract students from low-income households. OFFA's evidence pre-dated £9,000 fees so may no longer be correct, but universities have acted on its advice and the Government has switched its National Scholarship Programme from an undergraduate to a postgraduate scheme.

With most of the institutions that have resisted charging £9,000 for some or all of their courses in previous years now raising their charges, the average headline fee for 2015–16 will rise by 1.2 per cent to just above £8,700. But the reductions in bursaries and fee waivers will mean that the average after allowing for all forms of financial support will go up by 3 per cent. For most students, that increase will not matter because they would not have qualified for the various benefits in any case.

Variations among universities

The lowest full-time fee at an English university in 2015–16 will be £3,500 a year, charged for the small number of Foundation degrees in education and theology at York St John University. But even there, honours degree students will pay £9,000. At 44 university-level institutions, every course will cost £9,000 and at several others the only exceptions will be during work placements or years abroad.

Many universities will continue to devote a substantial proportion of the income they receive from higher fees to access initiatives, whether in the form of bursaries or outreach activities. In the case of the London School of Economics, half of all of its fee income above £6,000 will be spent in this way. The lowest proportion will be 10 per cent at Wolverhampton.

These measures appear to be having some success in attracting students from disadvantaged backgrounds. Early enrolment figures for 2014–15 showed an 8 per cent increase on the previous year in the numbers from the lowest socio-economic classes, as the gap between rich and poor began to close to some extent. Students who do not qualify for university bursaries may prefer that a larger proportion of the income will be spent on teaching them.

Even if it is closer to business as usual than many universities dared hope in the run-up to such a dramatic hike in fees, that does not mean that financial considerations will be completely irrelevant to the decision-making process. In the current economic circumstances, students will want to keep their debts to a minimum and are bound to take the cost of living into account. They will also want the best possible career prospects and may choose their subject accordingly.

Alternative options

Some further education colleges will offer substantial savings on the cost of a degree, or Foundation degree, but they tend to have very local appeal, generally in a limited range of vocational subjects. Similarly, the private sector may be expected to compete more vigorously in future, following the success of two-year degrees at the University of Buckingham and BPP University in particular. Most will continue to undercut the traditional universities, although Regent's University, one of the latest to be awarded that title, has been charging around £15,000 and the New College of the Humanities, also in London, £17,814. Like other private institutions, both are yet to set fees for 2015–16.

Impact on subject and university choice

There is little evidence yet that fee levels have more than a marginal influence on choices of university. Many candidates appear to have decided that the possibility of repaying £27,000, rather than perhaps £25,000, over an extended period is not going to affect their preferences.

Higher fees have had an impact on students' choices of subject, however. Although predictions that old universities and/or vocational subjects would prosper at the expense of the rest have been shown to be too simplistic: some arts subjects have suffered and some science courses have prospered. Yet for many young people, the options have not changed. If you want to be a doctor, a teacher or a social worker, there is no alternative to higher education. And, while there are now more options post A level, it remains to be seen whether they offer the same promotion prospects as a degree.

Only four of the 20 UCAS subject groups (surprisingly including maths and law) did not attract increased applications in 2014. But 12 of the 20 are yet to return to the level of applications enjoyed in 2011, the last year before the fees went up. The areas that have seen significant increases are health subjects, biological and physical sciences, engineering and computing – not a social science or arts subject among them.

It is enrolments that matter in the end, however, and here the pattern is slightly different. Languages – ancient and modern, European and non-European – have suffered particularly, but the social sciences have seen modest growth, in spite of lower applications. Computer science is up by almost 20 per cent since 2011 and engineering is up significantly over the same period. Only languages had filled fewer places than in 2013 – 13 per cent fewer in the case of non-European languages and literature.

It will take time to detect whether the new fees regime brings about more fundamental changes in subject choice, starting at A level or the equivalent, if not before that. Sixth formers studying English, history and French cannot suddenly switch to a chemistry degree. There were signs in schools, well before the fees went up, of a renaissance in the sciences.

There is little doubt that applicants are looking more carefully at future career prospects when choosing a degree, but they have decided (rightly or wrongly) that some careers are more secure, or more lucrative, than others. Applications for law remain buoyant and medicine is holding its own, despite a long and now much more expensive training. But architecture and building are down both in terms of applications and enrolments, compared with 2011.

With no real pattern yet established, those hoping to start courses in 2015 would be unwise to jump to conclusions about levels of competition in different subjects, or between whole universities. A drop in applications may mean less competition for places, or it may lead universities to close courses and possibly even intensify the race for entry. The only reliable forecast is that competition for places on the most popular courses will remain stiff, just as it has been since before students paid any fees.

Getting the best deal

There will still be a certain amount of variation in fees and student support packages in 2015–16, so it will be possible to shop around, particularly if your family income is low. But remember that the best deal, even in purely financial terms, is one that leads to a rewarding career. By all means compare the full packages offered by individual universities, but consider whether marginal differences in headline fees really matter as much as the quality of the course and the likely advantages it will confer in the employment market. Higher career earnings will soon account for more than £3,000 in extra fees to be repaid over 30 years. It is all a matter of judgement – Scottish students can save themselves £27,000 by opting to study north of the border. That is a very different matter to the much smaller saving that is available to students in England, particularly if the Scottish university is of comparable quality to the alternatives elsewhere.

Those who are eligible for means-tested bursaries may not be able to afford to ignore the financial assistance they offer. No one has to pay tuition fees while they are a student, but you still have to find thousands of pounds in living costs to take a full-time degree. In some cases, bursaries may make the difference between being able to afford higher education and having to pass up a potentially life-changing opportunity. Some are worth up to £3,000 a year, although most are less generous than this, often because large numbers of students qualify for an award.

Some scholarships are even more valuable, and are awarded for sporting and musical prowess, as well as academic achievement. Most scholarships are not means-tested, but a few are open only to students who are both high performers academically and from low-income families.

How the new fees work

What follows is a summary of the position for British students in summer 2014. While there are substantial differences between the four countries of the UK, there is one important piece of common ground. Up-front payment of fees is not compulsory, as students can take out a fee loan from the Student Loans Company to cover them (see chapter 8). This is repayable in instalments after graduation, when earnings reach £21,000 for English students, a threshold set by the Government.

With undergraduate fees remaining at a maximum of £9,000, the most you can borrow to pay fees will also stay at £9,000, with lower sums set for private colleges and part-time study. There are different levels of fees and support for UK students who are not from England. Students from other EU countries will pay the same rate as home students in the UK nation in which they study. Those from outside the EU are not affected by the changes, and may well have to pay quite a lot more than home and European students. The latest information on individual universities' fees at the time of going to press is listed at the end of this chapter and alongside their profiles in chapter 14.

With changes, large or small, becoming almost an annual occurrence, it is essential to consult the latest information provided on the websites of the relevant Government agencies.

Fees in England

In England, the maximum tuition fee for full-time undergraduates from the UK or anywhere in the European Union will be £9,000 a year in 2015–16. Most courses will demand fees of £9,000, or close to it, in order to recoup the money removed from their Government grants and leave room for further investment and student support.

In many public universities, the lowest fees will be for Foundation degrees and Higher National Diplomas. Although some universities have chosen to charge the same for all courses, in many universities and further education colleges, these two-year courses will remain a cost-effective stepping stone to a full degree or a qualification in their own right. Those universities that offer extended work placements or a year abroad, as part of a degree course, will charge much less than the normal fee for the "year out". The maximum fees for a placement year is 20 per cent of the full tuition fee and for a year abroad, 15 per cent.

Fees in Scotland

At Scottish universities and colleges, students from Scotland and those from other EU countries outside the UK pay no fees directly. The universities' vice-chancellors and principals have appealed for charges to be introduced at some level to save their institutions from falling behind their English rivals in financial terms, but Alex Salmond, Scotland's First Minister, famously declared that the "rocks will melt with the sun" before this happens. This is regarded as an election promise from which he would find it hard to draw back.

Students whose home is in Scotland and are who studying at a Scottish university apply to the Student Awards Agency for Scotland (SAAS) to have their fees paid for them. Note, too, that three-year degrees are rare in Scotland, so most students can expect to pay four years of living costs.

Students from England, Wales and Northern Ireland studying in Scotland will pay fees at something like the level that applies in England and will have access to finance at similar levels to those available for study in England. Several Scottish universities are offering a "free" fourth year to bring their total fees into line with English universities, but Edinburgh and St Andrews are charging £9,000 in all four years of their degree courses.

Fees in Wales

Welsh universities have, in previous years, applied a range of fees up to £9,000, but by 2015–16 most have opted for £9,000. Students who live in Wales will be able to apply for a Tuition Fee Loan as well as a Tuition Fee Grant, wherever they study. The grant is intended to pay fees beyond £3,685 a year in 2014–15. The 2015–16 arrangements have not been announced at the time of writing.

Tuition Fees

The figures below show the maximum fees that can be charged.

Domicile of student   Location of institution

	England	Scotland	Wales	Northern Ireland
England[1]	£9,000	£9,000[2]	£9,000	£9,000
Scotland	£9,000	No fee	£9,000	£9,000
Wales[3]	£3,685	£3,685[2]	£3,685	£3,685
Northern Ireland	£9,000	£9,000[2]	£9,000	£3,685[4]
European Union	£9,000	No fee	£9,000	£3,575
Other international	Variable	Variable	Variable	Variable

1 Figures for 2015–16.
2 Note that Honours degrees in Scotland take four years and some universities charge £9,000 a year. Figures for 2014–15.
3 Welsh-domiciled students are entitled to a tuition fee grant for any fees above £3,685 wherever they study in the UK (2014–15; figure for 2015–16 not announced at time of going to press).
4 Figure for 2014–15; figures for 2015–16 not announced at time of going to press.

Fees in Northern Ireland

The two universities of Northern Ireland are charging local students £3,685 a year for 2014–15. Students can receive a fee loan to postpone paying this until their earnings are above £16,910 a year. For students from elsewhere in the UK, the fee is currently £6,000 a year at Ulster, still good value compared to much English provision, and £9,000 at Queen's, Belfast. The arrangements for 2015–16 have not been announced at the time of writing.

Useful websites

With changes, large or small, becoming almost an annual occurrence, it is essential to consult the latest information provided by Government agencies. It is worth checking the following websites for the latest information:

England: **www.gov.uk/student-finance** and **www.sfengland.slc.co.uk**

Wales: **www.studentfinancewales.co.uk**

Scotland: **www.saas.gov.uk**

Northern Ireland: **www.studentfinanceni.co.uk**

University tuition fees for UK/EU and international students

England

The fees given for UK/EU undergraduates are those for **2015–16**. The fees shown are for full degrees and do not include the sometimes lower fees charged for Foundation degrees or for Foundation years (Year 0). The International student fees are for **2014–15**. Please check university websites for the most recent information.

	Undergraduate fees UK / EU students 2015–16	Undergraduate fees International students 2014–15
Anglia Ruskin	£9,000	£9,800–£10,300
Arts University Bournemouth	£9,000	£12,510
Aston	£9,000	£13,000–£16,000
Bath	£9,000	£13,700–£17,400
Bath Spa	£9,000	£10,905–£11,665
Bedfordshire	£9,000	£9,750
Birkbeck	£9,000	£13,000
Birmingham	£9,000	£12,565–£16,565; £16,565–29,085 (medicine)
Birmingham City	£9,000	£10,500–£11,800; £14,900 (Conservatoire and acting)
University College Birmingham	£8,558	£9,100
Bishop Grosseteste	£9,000	£10,000
Bolton	£9,000	£11,250
Bournemouth	£9,000	£9,500–£12,500
Bradford	£9,000	£11,000–£13,100
Brighton	£9,000	£11,220–£13,220; £26,100 (medicine)
Bristol	£9,000	£14,750–£17,750
		£17,750–£33,000 (dentistry, medicine, veterinary medicine)
Brunel	£9,000	£14,250–£16,000
Buckingham	£12,750[1]	£17,289[1]; £35,000 (medicine)
Buckinghamshire New	£9,000	£9,500
Cambridge	£9,000	£15,063–£22,923; £36,459 (medicine)[2]
Canterbury Christ Church	£9,000	£9,710
Central Lancashire	£9,000	£10,950–£11,950; £35,000 (medicine)
Chester	£9,000	£10,700
Chichester	£9,000	£9,950–£11,350
City	£9,000	£12,000–£15,000
Coventry	£8,331–£9,000	£10,950–£12,444 (Coventry); £10,375–£11,040 (London)
Cumbria	£9,000	£10,500–£14,965
De Montfort	£9,000	£11,250–£11,750
Derby	£8,500–£9,000	£10,445–£11,010
Durham	£9,000	£14,000–£17,900
East Anglia	£9,000	£12,900– £15,900; £27,500 (medicine)
East London	£9,000	£10,400
Edge Hill	£9,000	£10,950
Essex	£9,000	£11,950–£13,950
Exeter	£9,000	£15,000–£17,500; £17,500–£29,500 (medicine)
Falmouth	£9,000	£11,500–£12,225
Gloucestershire	£9,000	£10,500

	Undergraduate fees UK / EU students 2015–16	Undergraduate fees International students 2014–15
Goldsmiths	£9,000	£12,100–£16,700
Greenwich	£9,000	£10,350
Harper Adams	£9,000	£10,000
Hertfordshire	£9,000	£10,100
Huddersfield	£9,000	£12,000–£13,000
Hull	£9,000	£12,000–£14,400; £25,420 (medicine)
Imperial	£9,000	£22,950–£26,000; £35,000 (medicine)
Keele	£9,000	£12,000–£14,500; £24,100 (medicine)
Kent	£9,000	£12,450–£14,860
King's College London	£9,000	£15,200–£19,570; £19,570–£36,050 (medicine and dentistry)
Kingston	£9,000	£11,000–£13,300
Lancaster	£9,000	£13,270–£16,640; £22,500 (medicine)
Leeds	£9,000	£12,900–£16,500; £18,450–£30,700 (medicine and dentistry)
Leeds Metropolitan	£9,000	£9,500
Leeds Trinity	£9,000	£9,500–£11,000
Leicester	£9,000	£13,395–£16,525; £16,525–£33,655 (medicine)
Lincoln	£9,000	£11,798–£13,648
Liverpool	£9,000	£13,400–£16,800; £29,950 (dentistry and medicine)[3]
Liverpool Hope	£9,000	£10,800
Liverpool John Moores	£9,000	£11,000–£12,000
London Metropolitan	£9,000	£10,000
London School of Economics	£9,000	£16,392
London South Bank	£9,000	£10,500
Loughborough	£9,000	£13,750–£17,300
Manchester	£9,000	£14,000–£18,000; £18,000–£33,000 (medicine)
Manchester Metropolitan	£9,000	£10,250–£18,000
Middlesex	£9,000	£10,700
Newcastle	£9,000	£12,075–£15,490; £15,490–£28,670 (medicine and dentistry)
Newman	£9,000	£9,700
Northampton	£9,000	£10,500–£11,500
Northumbria	£9,000	£11,200–£13,200
Norwich University of the Arts	£9,000	£12,000
Nottingham	£9,000	£13,470–£17,340; £18,270–£31,750 (medicine) £17,340–£25,270 (veterinary medicine)
Nottingham Trent	£9,000	£11,500–£12,000
Oxford	£9,000	£14,415–£21,220; £16,545–£29,225 (medicine)[4]
Oxford Brookes	£9,000	£11,900–£13,670
Plymouth	£9,000	£11,500; £17,500–£32,000 (medicine)
Portsmouth	£9,000	£11,000–£12,500
Queen Mary	£9,000	£13,250–£19,900; £19,900–£30,400 (medicine)
Reading	£9,000	£13,230–£16,500
Roehampton	£9,000	£11,500
Royal Agricultural University	£9,000	£10,000
Royal Holloway	£9,000	£12,900–£14,600
St Mark and St John	£9,000	£9,400–£10,350

	Undergraduate fees UK / EU students 2015–16	Undergraduate fees International students 2014–15
St Mary's, Twickenham	£9,000	£9,900
Salford	£9,000	£11,090–£12,800
SOAS London	£9,000	£15,320
Sheffield	£9,000	£13,390–£17,470; £17,470–£31,580 (medicine)
Sheffield Hallam	£9,000	£11,500–£12,400
Southampton	£9,000	£13,290–£16,320; £16,320–£31,500 (medicine)
Southampton Solent	£9,000	£10,080–£11,140
Staffordshire	£9,000	£10,000
Sunderland	£8,250–£8,750	£9,500
Surrey	£9,000	£13,665–£14,550
Sussex	£9,000	£13,750–£17,000; £26,100 (medicine)
Teesside	£9,000	£10,450
University of the Arts London	£9,000	£15,180
University College London	£9,000	£15,200–£20,100; £29,900 (medicine)
University for the Creative Arts	£9,000	£11,030–£11,490
Warwick	£9,000	£15,070–£19,220; £17,595–£30,650 (medicine)
West London	£9,000	£9,950
West of England	£9,000	£10,750–£11,750
Westminster	£9,000	£11,750
Winchester	£9,000	£10,800–£13,400
Wolverhampton	£9,000	£10,700
Worcester	£9,000	£10,920
York	£9,000	£14,340–£18,660; £25,420 (medicine)
York St John	£9,000	£9,500–£11,500

1 Courses starting in January 2015. Note that courses only lasts two years (eight terms).
2 Plus Cambridge College fees (£5,500–£6,500). UK & EU students who are eligible for tuition fee support not liable for College fees.
3 For 2015–16.
4 Plus Oxford College fees (£6,725). UK & EU students who are eligible for tuition fee support not liable for College fees.

Wales

For **2015–16**, universities can to charge up to £9,000, with the Welsh Assembly paying fees above £3,685 (2014–15) for Welsh students.

Aberystwyth	£9,000	£10,500–£12,000

	Undergraduate fees UK / EU students 2015–16	Undergraduate fees International students 2014–15
Bangor	£9,000	£11,000–£12,800
Cardiff	£9,000	£13,500–£18,000; £17,000–£29,800 (medicine and dentistry)
Cardiff Metropolitan	£9,000	£9,700; £11,400 (podiatry)
Glyndŵr	£7,400–£8,450[1]	£8,950–£9,450[2]
South Wales	£9,000	£11,300
Swansea	£9,000	£11,750–£14,000
Trinity St David (UWTSD)	£9,000	£9,000

1 Figures for 2014–15.
2 Includes accommodation for the first year of study (£7,450 with no accommodation).

Scotland

In **2014–15** there are no fees for Scottish and EU students, but there are fees for students from elsewhere in the UK. As Scottish Honours degrees are 4 years in length, the cost of some degrees in Scotland for students from the rest of the UK will be higher than in England, although some universities have put a maximum cap on charges to maintain equality with English fees. There is some financial support from the universities specifically for students from the rest of the UK. Please consult university websites for the fees to be charged in **2015–16**, as arrangements have not been announced at time of writing. The fees for International students are for **2014–15**.

	Fees for Scottish students and eligible non-UK EU students 2014–15[1]	Fees for students from elsewhere in the UK 2014–15	Undergraduate fees International students 2014–15
Aberdeen	No fee	£9,000[2]	£12,600–£15,700; £27,800 (medicine)
Abertay	No fee	£7,000	£10,500
Dundee	No fee	£9,000[2]	£10,700–£15,500; £18,600–£31,500 (medicine and dentistry)
Edinburgh	No fee	£9,000	£15,250–£20,050 £23,450–£45,400 (medicine) £28,450 (veterinary studies)
Edinburgh Napier	No fee	£6,630	£10,690–£12,410
Glasgow	No fee	£6,750 £9,000[3]	£13,750–£17,250 £17,250–£31,250[3]
Glasgow Caledonian	No fee	£7,000[4]	£10,200–£14,500
Heriot Watt	No fee	£9,000	£12,280–£15,490
Highlands and Islands	No fee	£7,740–£9,000[5]	£8,700–£10,320[6]
Queen Margaret	No fee	£6,750	£10,170–£12,090
Robert Gordon	No fee	£5,000–£8,500	£10,500–£13,500
St Andrews	No fee	£9,000	£16,230–£24,500 (medicine)
Stirling	No fee	£6,750	£11,000–£13,100
Strathclyde	No fee	£9,000[7]	£12,000–£15,900
West of Scotland	No fee	£7,250	£10,300–£10,815

1 For all eligible students, SAAS will pay fees of £1,820 direct to the universities
2 Capped at £27,000 for most 4-year courses
3 Medicine, dentistry, veterinary science
4 Capped at £25,000 for 4-year courses
5 Capped at £23,200–£27,000 for 4-year courses
6 Online access for students with no Scottish term-time address: £4,860–£5,760
7 Capped at £27,000 for all courses

Northern Ireland

For **2014–15** there will be different fees for students resident in Northern Ireland and students coming from other parts of the UK. There is some financial support from the universities specifically for students from the rest of the UK. Please consult university websites for the fees to be charged in **2015–16**, as arrangements were announted at the time of writing.

	Fees for Northern Irish students and eligible non-UK EU students 2014–15	Fees for students from elsewhere in the UK 2014–15	Undergraduate fees International students 2014–15
Queen's Belfast	£3,685	£9,000	£12,650–£16,225 £16,750–£31,590 (medicine) £25,654 (dentistry)
Ulster	£3,685	£6,000	£10,110

8 The Cost of Studying

Anyone reading this *Guide* already knows that they need to think hard about how they will pay for their higher education. But they do not always realise that there are two quite different timescales to consider: in the short term the calculations are all about affordability, while the long term is more about value for money. Most commentary on the subject conflates the two, focusing on the total debt that the average student will have at graduation. Although an intimidating figure and one that should not be ignored by those contemplating a degree, it has little to do with whether you can afford three or more years as an undergraduate.

Affordability

While the introduction of £9,000 fees has added enormously to graduates' debts, it has made no difference to the amount of money you will need as a student. That calculation is about bridging the gap between a maintenance loan, which is England will be worth up to £5,740 (or £8,009 in London) in 2015–16, and the real cost of living. With hall fees topping £5,000 a year at some universities, there will be a gap, but this was so before the fees went up. Through a combination of parental help, part-time employment and – for those from less affluent homes – grants (of up to £3,387 in England) and bursaries, most students find a way to make ends meet. Grants have the great virtue that you don't have to pay them back. The only problem is that this means complex calculations on sources of financial support, fee levels, the length of courses and the cost of living at different universities. With many families feeling the pinch, it has never been more important to get it right.

How well you can live on these sums will vary from person to person. But most people will need to gather together all the resources they can just to survive. Analysis by the National Union of Students suggests that it is not possible to get by on student loans and grants alone. Savings, earnings, and help from family and friends have to be added to the pot. The information provided here will help you understand how big your pot needs to be, and what you can expect to be added and taken away from it. But it takes careful budgeting to avoid adding credit card debt to the income-contingent variety offered by the Government and repaid (or not) over 30 years.

Value for money

Only when you are sure you can cope with the costs of student life should you move on to the longer-term question of whether your chosen degree will be worth repaying £40,000 or more in student loans. Even in purely financial terms, there are too many uncertainties to be sure of the answer. You may never earn enough (£21,000 a year) to be required to repay any of it – although no one goes to university with those expectations and very few will be in that position. Or your degree may help you land such a well-paid job that university was cheap at the price. Most graduates will be somewhere in the middle, and the system is too new for any to have experienced the impact of loan repayments of 9 per cent of salary above £21,000 for such an extended period of up to 30 years.

Most surveys suggest that, on average, a degree is still a worthwhile investment in terms of future salary expectations, even after adding in the amount you might have earned while you were at university. A study by London Economics for the million+ group of post-1992 universities put the average graduate premium at £115,000 over a working lifetime. But averages can be deceiving: more recent research suggested that almost half of the graduates of post-1992 universities were earning less than young people who took higher apprenticeships.

This *Guide* should help to fill in some of the detail on employment rates on different courses at different universities. Salary data by course is available on the Unistats website, but no one can be certain of salary prospects over an entire career, possibly spanning a number of employment fields. Many satisfying jobs are open only to graduates, while in others the vast majority of new entrants have degrees.

Even before higher fees arrived, graduates and current students still on courses owed more than £40 billion between them in England alone, making them a major component of the public finances. Virtually all of this debt was in the form of income-contingent loans. The money was owed by 3.8 million borrowers, of whom 2.5 million were earning enough to make repayments, making the average debt just over £10,000 per person. Those figures are rising rapidly and current students expect to graduate with debts of between £20,000 and £40,000, according to Sodexo's 2014 survey.

Planning your finances

This chapter will focus on the costs while at university and the support that is available to get you through your undergraduate years. Like maximum fees, national student support schemes are the responsibility of the devolved UK administrations. There are separate sections for Northern Ireland, Wales and Scotland that follow the advice given for English students below. Where the rates for 2015–16 had not been announced when this book went to press, the figures quoted are for 2014–15.

With changes, large or small, becoming almost an annual occurrence, it is essential to consult the latest information provided by Government agencies. It is worth checking the following websites for the latest information:

» England: **www.gov.uk/student-finance** and **www.sfengland.slc.co.uk**
» Wales: **www.studentfinancewales.co.uk**
» Scotland: **www.saas.gov.uk**
» Northern Ireland: **www.studentfinanceni.co.uk**

Student loans and grants for English students

Around 80 per cent of students take out a student loan, and it is not difficult to see why. The UK Border Agency, which had to decide whether incoming international students can support themselves, reckoned that a single student needs £1,000 a month to live in London, although prices are lower elsewhere in the UK. If you don't take out a loan to cover your fees and living costs, you will have to pay for them up front. Most students find it impossible to cover everything on savings and earnings alone and would require significant family support to cover the difference. The only reasons to consider paying your fees up front might be if your parents are offering to meet the costs, or if a university is offering a discount if you do so.

Experts such as Martin Lewis, who writes regularly on student finance, agree that student loans are a good deal compared with other forms of borrowing. In particular, he counsels against using family savings to pay fees upfront, especially since the Government's own estimates suggest that most graduates will not repay the whole amount that they borrow.

There are two types of student loan – one to cover the cost of tuition fees and another to help you cover the cost of living.

Tuition fees loan

You can borrow up to the full amount needed to cover the cost of your tuition fees wherever you study in the UK and it is not dependent upon your household income.

Tuition fees loans for part-time students

The most that universities or colleges can charge for part-time courses is between £4,500 and £6,750 a year for 2015–16. They cannot charge more than 75 per cent of the full-time course fee. New part-time students will be able to apply for a tuition fee loan that is not dependent on household income or on age, which has led to some courses having a surprising number of pensioner students. Eligibility depends on the "intensity" of the course being at least 25 per cent of a full-time course. This measure works by comparing the course to a full-time equivalent. So if a course takes six years to complete and the full-time equivalent takes three, the intensity will be 50 per cent.

Maintenance loan

The second type of student loan, a maintenance loan, is means-tested. The amount you can borrow depends on a number of factors, including your family income, where you intend to study, and whether you expect to be living at home.

Although you are legally an adult, your student finance options depend heavily on your family income, frequently termed "household income", which in practice means your mother's and father's earning power. If your parents are separated, divorced or widowed, then only the income of the parent with whom you normally live will be assessed. However, if that parent has married again, entered into a civil partnership, or has a partner of the opposite sex, then both their incomes will be taken into account.

For 2015 entry, the maximum loan for those living at home is £4,565, for students living away from home outside London, £5,740, and for those living away from home in London £8,009. You can even get £6,820 for a year studying abroad as part of a UK course. Final-year students receive less than those in earlier years. Sixty-five per cent of the maintenance loan is available to you regardless of your family circumstances, while the remaining 35 per cent is means-tested. Note, too, that there is extra cash available for future teachers, social workers and healthcare workers, including doctors and dentists.

Maintenance loans for mature students

Mature students (those who are married, over the age of 25, or have supported themselves for at least three years before entering university) are assessed for loan and grant entitlements on their own income plus that of their spouse or partner. Grants are also available for those with children, for single parents, and for students with adult dependents. Further support is available for students with children through the Childcare Grant, the Parents' Learning Allowance, the Adult Dependants' Grant and Child Tax Credit system. You have to be under 60 to receive a living cost loan if you are studying full-time. But remember that the student finance system is mainly open only to people taking a degree for the first time, and funding for graduates taking a similar level of qualification to one they have already completed is problematic.

Maintenance grant

Students from less affluent families can apply for a maintenance grant from the Government. Those on full-time courses are entitled to a full grant of £3,387 if their household income is £25,000 or less, or a partial grant if their household income is between £25,000 and £42,620. Grants are paid into the student's bank account at the beginning of each term. When you apply for tuition-fee and maintenance loans, you will automatically be assessed for any maintenance grants. One important rule to bear in mind is that for every £1 you receive in maintenance grant, the amount you can borrow in student loans falls by £1. Thus, it is not possible to have both a full grant and a maximum student loan. See the table below.

Repaying loans

Full-time students will begin accumulating interest during their course and will start repaying in the April after graduation, if they earn over £21,000. They will then pay 9 per cent of their income above £21,000, but repayments will stop during any period in which annual income falls below the threshold. Repayments are normally taken automatically through tax and National

---

Maintenance grant and loan example for a first-year English student 2015

The mixture of grant and loan for a first-year English student in 2015–16 who is studying full-time and living away from home (but not in London). The maximum loan is £5,740, payable when the household income is £42,875. The loan thereafter declines to a minimum of £3,731 by £62,143. The maximum loan for those living at home is £4,565 and for those living away from home in London is £8,009.

Household income	Non-repayable grant	Maintenance loan	Total
£25,000 and below	£3,387	£4,047	£7,434
£30,000	£2,441	£4,520	£6,961
£35,000	£1,494	£4,993	£6,487
£40,000	£547	£5,467	£6,014
£42,620	£50	£5,715	£5,765
£42,875	£0	£5,740	£5,740
£45,000	£0	£5,519	£5,519
£50,000	£0	£4,998	£4,998
£55,000	£0	£4,476	£4,476
£60,000	£0	£3,955	£3,955
£62,143 and above	£0	£3,731	£3,731

Department for Business, Innovation and Skills

Insurance. If the loan has not been paid off after 30 years, no further repayments will be required.

During the repayment period, the amount of interest will vary according to how much you earn. If you earn less than £21,000, interest will be at the rate of inflation as measured by the Retail Price Index; between £21,000 and £41,000 you will be charged inflation plus up to 3 per cent; and if you earn over £41,000, interest will be at inflation plus the full 3 per cent. The Government website set up to guide prospective students through these arrangements includes a repayments calculator based on starting salaries for a range of careers, at **www. gov.uk/student-finance.** At the time of writing, the interest rate was 6.6 per cent for courses that started in 2012. Anyone earning £25,000 a year would face monthly repayments of £30 a month. If you are on £60,000, the sum rises to £292 a month, a fair bite even from that healthy paycheque. By the time you graduate, the interest rate will probably have changed and the repayment threshold may have risen, if only by inflation.

Student loans and grants for Northern Ireland students

Maintenance loans vary from a maximum of £3,750 for students living at home, £4,840 for those studying away from home, all the way to £6,780 for those studying in London (and only 25 per cent of the loan is means-tested). There are also extra sums for people doing courses longer than 30 weeks a year, worth up to £108 a week if you are in London. Tuition fee loans are available for the full amount of tuition fees, regardless of where you study in the UK. For 2014–15 maintenance grants range from £3,475 for students with household incomes of £19,203 or below, to zero if the figure is £41,066 or above. Your maximum loan is reduced by the size of any grant you receive. Loan repayments of 9 per cent of salary start one your income reaches £16,910 and interest is calculated on the retail price index or 1 per cent above base rate, whichever is lowest. The loan will be cancelled after 25 years.

As in England, there are also special funds for people with disabilities and other special needs, and for those with children or adult dependants. There are modest special bursaries of up to £2,000 for students studying in the Republic of Ireland, who also have their fees paid by their local Education and Library Board.

Student loans and grants for Welsh students

For 2014–15, the maximum maintenance loan is £4,027 for students living at home, £5,202 for those living away from home, £6,202 for a year studying abroad, and £7,288 for those living in London (and only 25 per cent of the loan is means-tested). Tuition fee loans are available to cover the first £3,685 of your tuition fees. The remainder of your fees are covered by a non-means-tested grant of up to £5,315. Repayment of loans starts once your income reaches £21,000. Interest repayments and the length of loan is as for England (see above).

In addition, students in Wales are also able to apply for Welsh Government Learning Grants of up to £5,161. They will be scaled according to household income, which in 2014–15 ranged from £18,370 for a full grant to £50,020 for the smallest payment of £50. The loan you can get is reduced by 50p for every £1 of grant you receive up to £2,575. As in England, there are also special funds for people with disabilities and other special needs, and for those with children or adult dependants.

Student loans and grants for Scottish students

The Scottish Government has a commitment to a minimum income of £7,500 a year for students from poorer backgrounds, not bad in a setting where tuition is also free. Students from a family with an income below £17,000 can get a £1,750 Young Students' Bursary (YSB) as well as a loan of £5,750. This bursary does not have to be repaid. It tapers off to zero for family incomes of £34,000, at which point the maximum loan also falls from £5,750 to £4,750. The loan does not vary in size depending on whether you live at home or where you are studying in the UK. Higher loans but more limited bursaries are available for "independent" students, those who are married, mature or without family support. Note that you must be under 50 when you first apply for a loan. Repayment of the loan starts when your income reaches £16,910 and repayments will continue until the loan is paid off, with any outstanding amount being cancelled after 35 years.

As in England, there are also special funds for people with disabilities and other special needs, and for those with children or adult dependants. No tuition fee loans are required by Scottish students studying in Scotland but such loans are available for Scottish students studying elsewhere in the UK.

Living in one country, studying in another

As each of the countries of the UK develops its own distinctive system of student finance, the effects on students leaving home in one UK nation to go and study in another have become knottier. UK students who cross borders to study pay the tuition fees of their chosen university and are eligible for a fee loan, and maybe a partial grant, to cover them. They are also entitled to apply for the scholarships or bursaries on offer from that institution. Any maintenance loan or grant will still come from the awarding body of their home country. If you are in this position, you must check with the authorities in your home country about the funding you are eligible for.

Funding timetable

It is vital that you sort out your funding arrangements before you start university. Each funding agency has its own arrangements, and it is very important that you find out the exact details from them. The dates below give general indications of key dates.

March/April

» Online and paper application forms become available from funding agencies.
» You must contact the appropriate funding agency to make an application.
» Complete application form as soon as possible. At this stage select the university offer that will be your first choice.
» Check details of bursaries and scholarships available from your selected universities.

May/June

» Funding agencies will give you details of the financial support they can offer.
» Last date for making an application to ensure funding is ready for you at the start of term (exact date varies significantly between agencies).

August

» Tell your funding agency if the university or course you have been accepted for is different from that originally given them.

September

» Take letter confirming funding to your university for registration.
» After registration, the first part of funds will be released to you.

European Union laws stipulate that EU students from outside the UK must be charged the same tuition fees as those paid by nationals of the country where they are studying, rather than the higher fees paid by students from outside the EU. They can also apply for a fee loan and may be considered for some of the scholarships and bursaries offered by individual institutions. Only students who have been living and studying in the UK for at least three years can apply for a maintenance loan or grant. If you haven't, then you will need to apply for such assistance from the authorities in your own country. Tuition fee rules for non-UK European Union students are the same in Scotland as for Scottish students – that is, they do not have to pay tuition fees. There are also no fees to pay for exchange students coming to the UK, including those on the Socrates Programme.

Applying for support

English students should apply for grants and loans through Student Finance England, Welsh students through Student Finance Wales, Scottish students through the Student Awards Agency for Scotland, and those in Northern Ireland through Student Finance NI or their Education and Library Board. You should make your application as soon as you have received an offer of a place at university. Maintenance loans are usually paid in three instalments a year into your bank or building society account. European Union students from outside the UK will usually be sent an application form for tuition fee loans by the university that has offered them a place.

University scholarships and bursaries

As well as taking out student loans for both tuition and living costs, you can shop around for university bursaries, scholarships and other sponsorship packages, and seek out supplementary support to which you may be entitled. There may be reductions for a range of other groups, including local students, which vary widely from university to university and which are usually detailed on university web sites. Some examples are given alongside the university profiles in chapter 14 and the full details of the financial support offered by all universities in England are listed in the access agreements published on the website of the Office for Fair Access (**www.offa.org.uk**).

Although English universities scaled back their support for 2015–16, there is still a bewildering variety of bursaries and scholarships on offer at UK universities. Some awards are guaranteed depending on your financial circumstances, while scholarships are available through open competition. In general, bursaries that provide students with the money to make ends meet at university have (rightly) proved more popular than fee waivers giving relief from repayments that may stretch over 30 years. Some universities offer eligible students the choice of accommodation discounts, fee waivers or cash. Most also have hardship funds for those who find themselves in financial difficulties.

Do take note of the application procedures for scholarships and bursaries, as these vary from institution to institution, and even from course to course within individual institutions. There may be a deadline you have to meet to apply for an award. In some cases the university will work out for you whether you are entitled to an award by referring to your funding agency's financial assessment. If your personal circumstances change part-way through a course, your entitlement to a scholarship or bursary may be reviewed.

If you feel you still need more help or advice on scholarships or bursaries, you can usually find it on a university's website or in its prospectus. Some institutions also maintain a helpline. Some questions you will need answered include whether the bursary or scholarship is automatic or conditional and, if the latter, when you will find out whether your application has been successful. For some awards, you won't know whether you have qualified until you get your exam results. Another obvious question is how the scholarship or bursary on offer compares with awards made by another university you might consider applying to. Watch out for institutions that list entitlements that others don't mention, but which you would get anyway.

Students with disabilities

Extra financial help is available to disabled students studying on a part-time basis through Disabled Students' Allowances, which are paid in addition to the standard student finance package. They are available for help with education-related conditions such as dyslexia, and for other physical and mental disability. They do not depend on income and do not have to be repaid. The cash is available for extra travel costs, equipment and to pay helpers. The maximum for a non-medical helper is £20,725 a year, or £15,543 a year for a part-time student. The scheme is being altered for 2016–17 in England, with universities picking up a greater share of cost. Details were not available at time of writing so you must check for updates.

Further sources of income

If you are feeling daunted by the potential costs, you can take some comfort from this section, which outlines just some of the ways you can raise additional funds.

Taking a gap year

Gap years (see chapter 6) have become increasingly popular both for travelling and to earn some money to help pay for higher education. Many students will simply want to travel, but others will be more focused on boosting the bank balance in preparation for life as a student. Work opportunities can be structured or casual. An example of the structured variety is the Year in Industry Scheme (**www.etrust.org.uk**).

Further support

There are various types of support available for students in particular circumstances, other than the main loans, grants and bursaries.

» Undergraduates in financial difficulties can apply for help to their university's student hardship fund. These are allocated by universities to provide support for anything from day-to-day study and living costs to unexpected or exceptional expenses. The university decides which students need help and how much money to award them. These funds are often targeted at older or disadvantaged students, and finalists who are in danger of dropping out. The sums range up to a few thousand pounds, are not repayable and do not count against other income.

» Students with children can apply for a Childcare Grant, worth £150.23 a week if you have one child and £257.55 a week if you have two or more children under 15, or under 17 with special needs; and a Parents' Learning Allowance, for help with course-related costs, of between £50 and £1,523 a year.

» Any students with a partner, or another adult family member who is financially dependent on them, can apply for an Adult Dependants' Grant of up to £2,668 a year.

If you do not qualify for any of this kind of financial support you may still be able to apply for a Professional and Career Development Loan available from certain banks, in partnership with the National Careers Service. Students on a wide range of vocational courses can borrow from £300 to £10,000 at a fixed rate of interest to fund up to two years of learning, but the loans cannot be used for first full-time degrees.

Part-time work

The need to hold down a part-time job during term time is now a fact of life for more than half of students. Students from a working-class background are more likely to need to earn while they learn.

If you need to earn during term time, it is important to try to ensure that you do not work so many hours that it starts to affect your studies. A survey by the NUS found that 59 per cent of students who worked felt it had an impact on their studies, with 38 per cent missing lectures and over a fifth failing to submit coursework because of their part-time jobs. You may find that new universities are better geared-up to cope with working students than more traditional institutions.

Student employment agencies, which can now be found on many university campuses, can help you get the balance right. These introduce employers with work to students seeking work, sometimes even offering jobs within the university itself. But they also abide by codes of practice that regulate both minimum wages and the maximum number of hours worked in term time (typically 15 hours a week). It is worth thinking how much paid work is enough. In a 2012 survey, Lloyds TSB found that 49 per cent of students said they had taken on paid work, and a quarter of those employed in term time say it had a negative effect on their studies.

Some firms, such as the big supermarkets, offer continuing part-time employment to their school part-time employees when they go to university. Some students make use of their expertise in areas like web design to earn some extra money, but most take on casual work in retail stores, restaurants, bars and call centres.

Most students, including those who don't work during term time, get a job during vacations. A Government survey found that 86 per cent of students in their second year of study or above worked during their summer vacation. Most of this kind of work is casual, but some is formalised in a scheme like STEP (**www.step.org.uk**) or may be part of a sponsorship programme. Many vacation jobs are fairly mundane, but it is possible to find more interesting work. Some students broaden their experience by working abroad, others work as film extras, do tutoring, or do a variety of jobs at big events such as festivals. It is also a good idea to try to use the summer holidays to get some work experience in a field that has some relevance to your career aspirations. Even if you don't get paid, this can significantly enhance your chances of finding employment after graduation.

What you will need to spend money on

Living costs

Even in 2012–13, the NUS estimated that a student living in London would have an average cost of living of £13,388, not including tuition fees, books or equipment. Although the sums are lower outside the capital (the NUS estimated £12,056 living costs outside London in 2012), even these can readily outstrip student grants, loans and bursaries. Little surprise, then, that a growing number of students are choosing to work while studying, or to live at home and study at a local university. However, even this option is not necessarily cheap, once travel to and from the university is taken into account.

Certain costs are unavoidable. You have to have a roof over your head, eat enough, clothe yourself, and probably do a certain amount of travelling. But the cost of even these essential items can be cut down significantly through a mixture of shopping around and careful budgeting. If you set aside a certain amount of money a week for food, you will find it goes much further if you keep takeaways and ready-meals to a minimum, and stick to a shopping list when you go to a supermarket. Some catering outlets at your university or in the students' union may well offer good value meals, but probably the most economical way to eat is to cook and share meals with fellow students with whom you may be living in a shared house. Make sure you make full use of student travel cards and other offers and facilities available locally to help you cut the cost of travel. In certain locations, a bicycle is a very worthwhile investment (as is buying a lock for it).

If you can keep your essential costs down, you will have more money for what you would probably prefer to spend your money on – going out and personal items. Most students spend a proportion of their budget on socialising, and this is certainly an important part of the university experience. You can have plenty of fun and keep your leisure costs down by making the most of your student union's facilities and events.

The latest version of an annual survey of student life by the company Sodexo suggests that half of all students have altered their eating and socialising habits for lack of money. One in five say they spend nothing at all on socialising, while three-quarters spend less than £20 a week. A third of students claim not to drink alcohol at all and 40 per cent limit their drinking to one night a week. It is not just leisure that is being cut back: 65 per cent of students claim to spend nothing on books in a typical week.

Studying costs

The latest NUS survey estimated that the average student spent about £1,000 a year on costs associated with course work and studying, mainly books and equipment. The amount you spend will be determined largely by the nature of your course and what you study. Additional financial support may be available for certain expenditure, but this is unlikely to cover you fully for spending on books, stationery, equipment, fieldwork or electives. A long reading list could prove very expensive if you tried to buy all of the required books brand new. Find out as soon as possible which books are available either in your university library or local libraries. Another approach is to buy books second-hand from students who no longer need them. Your students' union or your university may run second-hand book sales or offer a service helping students to buy and sell books.

Other costs

Keep any other costs you may incur as low as possible. This may sound trite, but it is easy to let "other costs" get out of hand to the extent that they start to eat into your budget for day-to-day living. Mobile phone bills are a case in point: nearly two-thirds of students in the Sodexo survey were spending £20 a week on them. Look at your previous bills, or think carefully about your usage, and then shop around for the best deal to cover what you need. Extras like downloading games or music, or sending pictures, can add significantly to your bill. Most of all, try to avoid getting tied up with an expensive and inflexible contract.

Overdrafts and credit cards

"Other costs" it is best to avoid are the more expensive forms of debt. Many banks offer free overdraft facilities for students, but if you go over that limit without prior arrangement, you can end up paying way over the odds for your borrowing. Credits cards can be useful if managed properly. The best way to manage a credit card is to set up a direct debit to pay off your balance in full every month, which means you will avoid paying any interest. One of the worst ways is just paying the minimum charge each month, which can cost you a small fortune over a long period. If you are the kind of person who spends impulsively and doesn't keep track of your spending, you are probably better off without a credit card. That way, you can't spend money you don't have.

Insurance

One kind of additional spending that can actually end up saving you money is getting insurance cover for your possessions. Most students arrive at university with laptops and other goodies such as digital cameras, mobile phones and iPods, not to mention bikes, that are tempting to petty thieves. It is estimated that around a third of students fall victim to crime at some point during their time at university. If you shop around, you should be able to get a reasonable amount of cover for these kinds of items without its costing you an arm and a leg. It may also be possible to add this cover cheaply to your parents' domestic contents policy.

Planning your budget

University websites, the National Union of Students and many other sites offer guidance on preparing a budget, usually with the basic headings provided for you to complete. First, list all your likely income (grants, bursaries, loans, part-time work, savings, parental support) and then see how this compares with what you will spend. Try to be realistic, and not too optimistic, about both sides of the equation. With care, you will end up either only slightly in the red, or preferably far enough in the black for you to be able to afford things you would really like to spend your money on.

Above all, keep track of your finances so that your university experience isn't ruined by money worries, or finding you can't go to the ball because the cash machine has eaten your card. Spreadsheets make doing this simpler, and it is one skill you can learn at college that you are definitely going to need for the rest of your life.

If all else fails, your campus almost certainly has a student money adviser who is a member of NASMA, the National Association of Student Money Advisers. You can find them via **www.nasma.org.uk**. NASMA reports that some students, especially those with children or whose family circumstances force them to drive to university, are noticing steep inflation right now. However, the bargains available in student shops can mean that you might not experience the painful price rises that newspaper headlines suggest are affecting the bulk of consumers.

NASMA's Jo Gibson says that many student advisers spend time helping people with low levels of basic financial awareness and planning ability. In addition, they have noticed that students are increasingly likely to spend money they cannot afford on TV and online gambling, so make sure to avoid this temptation.

She adds that the overall pattern of student finance is a complex one. For example, university hardship funds have been cut, but the fact that child benefit is not taken into account for housing benefit has been good for students with children. The message is: stay informed and you might get through university in better financial shape than you had imagined.

Useful websites

For the basics of fees, loans, grants and other allowances:
www.gov.uk/student-finance
www.gov.uk/browse/education/student-finance

UCAS provides helpful advice: **www.ucas.com/how-it-works/studentfinance**

For England, visit Student Finance England : **www.sfengland.slc.co.uk**
Office for Fair Access: **www.offa.org.uk**
For Wales, visit Student Finance Wales: **www.studentfinancewales.co.uk**
For Scotland, visit the Student Awards Agency for Scotland: **www.saas.gov.uk**
For arrangements for Scottish students studying in the UK or EU, and for students from the rest of the UK studying in Scotland:
www.scotland.gov.uk/Topics/Education/UniversitiesColleges/16640/financial-help.
For Northern Ireland, visit Student Finance Northern Ireland: **www.studentfinanceni.co.uk**

All UK student loans are administered by the Student Loans Company: **www.slc.co.uk**

For guidance on the tax position of students, visit HM Revenue and Customs:
www.hmrc.gov.uk/students

NHS Student Bursaries for students on pre-registration health professional and social work training courses: **www.nhsbsa.nhs.uk/students**

For finding out about availability of scholarships: **www.scholarship-search.org.uk**

9 Finding Somewhere to Live

Students spend almost three times as much on rent as any other area of expenditure, according to a recent survey, so it is vital to make the right choice of accommodation. It would be a key decision whatever the financial implications because where you live will have an impact on your whole university experience.

Particularly in your first year – and especially if it is your first time away from home – you are likely to be happier and more successful academically in accommodation of reasonable quality, preferably in a setting that helps you meet other students. Of course, whatever you choose has to be affordable, but if your budget will stand it, that may mean a hall of residence or university flat.

Term-time type of accommodation of full-time and sandwich students

	2012/13
University maintained property	18.4%
Private-sector halls	6.1%
Parental/guardian home	19.4%
Own residence	15.3%
Other rented accommodation	29.9%
Other	4.6%
Not known	6.2%
HESA 2014 (adapted)	

The number of students seeking somewhere to live has risen in all parts of the UK over recent years, and this growth means that the search for reasonably priced and acceptable housing has become tougher. The property bubble may have burst, but rents have continued to rise, particularly in the student market. The latest accommodation survey by the National Union of Students (NUS) showed no sign of average rents dropping even when £9,000 fees prompted a decline in student numbers. Unlike some private landlords, universities generally did not reduce charges, even where they had empty rooms. The union reported a 25 per cent increase in rents in the three years ending in 2012–13 and Family Investments reported another 25 per cent increase when numbers recovered in 2013–14. The rents for university accommodation quoted in chapter 14 also show another increase this year.

The NUS stressed the importance of accommodation issues in its 2014 research report *Homes Fit for Study*. It showed that housing is a generally tricky area of student life, exacerbated by the collision between business-minded landlords and panicky students who are entering the murky and unfamiliar world of property rental for the first time. The results can include rushed, poor decisions, hefty advance payments to secure property, and a low level of attention to important topics such as household Energy Performance Certificates or safe boiler operation. The same survey shows that a majority of students in rented accommodation have had to cope with mice, slugs, mould, freezing cold, or all of these. So it is worth putting some effort into basic decisions on this subject.

Living at home

Although student loan repayments start only after graduation, many undergraduates are understandably cautious about the debts they run up, so the option of avoiding big accommodation charges is a tempting one for those who are attracted by a local university. The pattern of recent applications shows that the trend towards studying at home is accelerating, and there is no reason to think that this will change in the near future. Indeed it may be a permanent shift, given the rising costs of student housing and the willingness of many young people to live with their parents well into their twenties.

The proportion of students living at home grew from 13 per cent to 18 per cent in three years before undergraduate fees went up, according to the latest Sodexo University Lifestyle Survey. This figure includes mature students, many of whom live at home because of their family circumstances. They may have children, dependent parents, or partners who are not keen to move. They may even be living in their own homes, not their parents'. Among younger students, women are more likely than men to stay at home: 20 per cent of them do, compared to 15 per cent of men. Asian women are particularly likely to take this option. Home study is also four times more common at post-1992 universities than older institutions, again reflecting the larger numbers of mature students at the newer universities and a generally younger and more affluent student population at the older ones.

For those considering studying from home, there are important considerations, of which the relationship with your parents and the availability of quiet space are the most obvious ones. You will still be entitled to a maintenance loan, although it will be a maximum of £4,565 In England, rather than £5,740 if you were living away from home. There may be advantages in terms of academic work if the alternative involves shopping, cooking and cleaning, as well as the other distractions of a student flat. The downside is that you may miss out on a lot of the student experience, especially the social scene and the opportunity to make new friends. There is no evidence that students living at home do any worse academically. You can always move out at a later date if you think you are missing out – many initially home-based students do in their second year.

Living away from home

Most of those who can afford it still see moving away to study as integral to the rite of passage that student life represents. Some have little option if, in spite of the expansion of higher education, the course they want is not available locally. Others are happy to travel to secure their ideal place and widen their experience.

For the lucky majority, the search for accommodation will be over quickly because the university can offer a place in one of its halls of residence or self-catering flats. The choice may come down to the type of accommodation and whether or not to do your own cooking. But for others, there will be an anxious search for a room in a strange city.

Going to university will oblige those who take the "away" route to think for the first time about the practicalities of living independently. This can make the decision about where to live – in terms of location and the type of accommodation – doubly difficult. It may even influence your choice of university, since there are big differences across the sector and the country in the cost and standard of accommodation, and in its availability.

How much will it cost?

A survey by student accommodation providers UNITE shows that cost is the biggest single concern relating to student housing for students and university applicants alike, ahead of issues such as comfort and security. The same survey showed that over 80 per cent of students regard their own accommodation as reasonably priced, but the NUS found enormous variations. While those living in London were paying more than £150 a week, average rents in Northern Ireland were still under £85 week and in Wales under £95. And these averages conceal a vast range of actual rents, particularly in London.

There is undoubtedly a growing luxury end to the student market, even while others live in much cheaper, often sub-standard, accommodation. Most universities with a range of accommodation find that their most expensive rooms fill up first, and that students appear to have higher expectations. Almost half of all the rooms in the NUS survey had en-suite facilities. The downside of this trend is that there can be fewer university-owned places available at the lowest price band, which is also the one where rents have seen the biggest percentage rises. Privately run blocks, which the union blames for pushing up prices, tend to be well-appointed as well as popular. The NUS estimates that private owners accounted for 79 per cent of the 18,607 new student housing spaces that became available in 2013.

Generally speaking, the cost of student accommodation is highest in London and the southeast of England, and lower in the Midlands and North of England, Wales, Scotland and Northern Ireland. But even within those regions there is considerable variation. Renting in new blocks of flats – and especially those that are en-suite – is often more expensive than sharing a house with friends, but sharing is a lot more common after the first year.

It is important to remember that both your living costs and your potential earnings should be factored into your calculations when deciding where to live. While living costs in London are by far the highest, potential part-time earnings are nearly double those in other parts of the country.

The choices you have

No longer are you faced with a straightforward choice between a university hall of residence and a poor-quality rented house. The NUS puts accommodation into 16 categories, ranging from luxurious university halls to a bedsit in a shared house. The choices include:

» University hall of residence, with individual study bedrooms and a full catering service. Many will have en-suite accommodation.
» University halls, flats or houses where you have to provide your own food.
» Private, purpose-built student accommodation.
» Rented houses or flats, shared with fellow students.
» Living at home.
» Living as a lodger in a private house.

This chapter will provide you with more information to help you decide where you would like to live and whether you can afford it.

Making your choice

Finance is not the only factor you should consider when deciding where to live. It is worth investing time to find the right place, and to avoid the false economy of choosing somewhere cheap, where you may end up feeling depressed and isolated. Most students who drop out of university do so in the first few months, when homesickness and loneliness can be felt most acutely.

Being warm and well fed is likely to have a positive effect on your studies. Perhaps for these reasons, most undergraduates in their first year plump for living in university halls, which offer a convenient, safe and reliable standard of accommodation, along with a supportive community environment. If meals are included, this extra adds further peace of mind both for students and their parents. The NUS survey found that the difference in cost between full board and self-catering is £45–75 a week on average, not unreasonable for two hot meals a day. But nowadays most are self-catering, with groups of students sharing a kitchen. The sheer number of students – especially first years – in halls also makes this form of accommodation an easy way of meeting people from a wide range of courses and making friends. Again, the UNITE survey shows that many students have what they regard as a disappointingly low level of connection to their housemates and to the other students on their course.

Wherever you choose to live, there are some general points you will need to consider, such as how safe the neighbourhood seems to be, and how long it might take you to travel to and from the university, especially during rush hour. A recent survey of travel time between term-time accommodation and the university found that most students in London can expect a commute of at least 30 minutes and often over an hour, while students living in Wales are usually much less than 30 minutes away from their university. Be sure to make use of any local or national Student Travel Card and any university or students' union transport system that may be provided to help you get back to your accommodation cheaply and safely.

In chapter 14, we provide details of what accommodation each university offers, covering the number of places, the costs, and policy towards first-year students.

What universities offer

You might think that opting to live in university accommodation is the most straightforward choice, especially since first-year students are invariably given priority in the allocation of places in halls of residence, and it is possible to arrange university accommodation in advance and at a distance. Searching for private housing can often be a matter of having to be in the right place at the right time. However, you may still need to select from a range of options, because some universities will have a variety of accommodation on offer. You will need to consider which best suits your pocket and your preferred lifestyle.

New university accommodation

At the top end of the market, partnerships between universities and private firms have begun to lead the way in recent years. Private organisations such as UPP, UNITE plc and Liberty Living have been paid by universities to build and manage some of the most luxurious student accommodation the UK sector has ever seen. Rooms in these complexes are nearly always en suite and include facilities such as your own phone line, satellite TV and internet access. Shared kitchens are top-quality and fitted out with all the latest equipment.

This kind of accommodation naturally comes at a higher price, but offers the advantages of flexibility both in living arrangements and through a range of payment options. Overall, according to the NUS survey, higher education institutions charged average weekly rents of £118.49 for their own accommodation and £119.83 for rooms managed by private companies under contract, while private providers operating outside institutional links charged an average of £140.07. Private companies have invested more than £5 billion in new student flats in recent years, continuing to do so even while the recession brought the rest of the construction business to a halt.

Halls of residence

Many new or recently refurbished university-owned halls offer a standard of accommodation that is not far short of the privately built residences. This is partly because rooms in these halls can be offered to conference delegates during vacations. Even though these halls are also at the pricier end of the spectrum, you will probably find that they are in great demand, and you may have to get your name down quickly to secure one of the fancier rooms. That said, you can often get a guarantee of some kind of university accommodation if you give a firm acceptance of an offered place by a certain date in the summer. If you have gained your place through Clearing, this option might have gone, although rooms in private halls might still be on offer at this stage.

While a few halls are single-sex, most are mixed, and often house over 500 students. They are therefore great places for making friends and becoming part of the social scene. One possible downside is that they can also be noisy places where it can be difficult at times to get down to some work. The more successful students learn, before too many essay deadlines and exams start to loom, to get the balance right between all-night partying and escaping to the library for some undisturbed study time. Remember that some libraries, especially new ones, are now open 24 hours a day. If you feel in need of either personal or study support, it is often at hand either through a counselling service or from fellow students.

The most important features in student accommodation

Reasonably priced	80%
Wi-Fi	70%
To be clean	66%
Location within walking distance to campus	64%
To be fully inclusive of bills	59%
Secure entry	52%
To be able to make the room my own	51%
To have my own bathroom	45%
To be modern and high quality	36%
To have temperature controllable heaters	35%

From UNITE Student Experience Survey 2014

University self-catering accommodation

An alternative to halls, now offered by most universities, are smaller, self-catering properties fitted out with a shared kitchen and other living areas. Students looking for a more independent and flexible lifestyle often prefer this option. Remember that if you choose this kind of university housing, you will be responsible for feeding yourself, and you may also have heating and lighting bills to pay. University properties are often on campus or nearby, so travel costs should not be a problem.

Catering in university accommodation

Many universities have responded to a general increase in demand from students for a more independent lifestyle by providing more flexible catering facilities. A range of eateries, from fast food outlets to more traditional refectories, can usually be found on campus or in student villages. Students in university accommodation may be offered pay-as-you-eat deals as an alternative to full-board packages.

What after the first year?

After your first year of living in university residences you may well wish, and will probably be expected, to move out to other accommodation. The main exceptions are the collegiate universities – particularly Oxford and Cambridge – which may allow you to stay on in college halls for another year or two, and particularly for your final year. Students from outside the EU are also sometimes guaranteed accommodation. At some universities, such as Loughborough, where there is a sufficiently large stock of residential accommodation, it is not uncommon for students to move back in to halls for their final year.

Practical details

Whether or not you have decided to start out in university accommodation, you will probably be expected to sign an agreement to cover your rent. Contract lengths vary. They can be for around 40 weeks, which includes the Christmas and Easter holiday periods, or for just the length of the three university terms. These term-time contracts are common when a university uses its rooms for conferences during vacations, and you will be required to leave your room empty during these weeks. It is therefore advisable to check whether the university has secure storage space for you to leave your belongings. Otherwise you will have to make arrangements to take all your belongings home or to store them privately between terms. International students may be offered special arrangements by which they can stay in halls during the short vacation periods. Organisations like **www.hostuk.org** can arrange for international students to stay in a UK family home at holiday times such as Christmas.

Parental purchases

One option for affluent families is to buy a house or flat and take in student lodgers. This might not be the safe bet it once appeared, but it is still tempting for many parents. The Sodexo University Lifestyle Survey for 2014 found that 7 per cent of students live in houses owned by their own or fellow students' parents. Those who are considering this route tend to do so from their first year of study to maximise the return on the investment.

Being a lodger or staying in a hostel

A small number of students live as a lodger in a family home, an option most frequently taken up by international students. The usual arrangement is for a study bedroom and some meals to be provided, while other facilities such as the washing machine are shared. Students with particular religious affiliations or those from certain countries may wish to consider living in a hostel run by a charity catering for a specific group. Most of these can be found in London. The Sodexo survey found that this option was growing in popularity.

Renting from the private sector

More than a third of students live in privately rented flats or houses, again according to the Sodexo survey. Every university city or town is awash with such accommodation, available via agencies or direct from landlords. Indeed, this type of accommodation has grown to the point where so-called "student ghettoes", in which local residents feel outnumbered have become hot political issues in some cities. Into this traditional market in rented flats and houses have come the new private-sector complexes and residences, often created in partnership with universities, adding to the private-sector options. Some are on university campuses, but others are in city centres and usually open to students of more than one university. Examples can be seen online; some sites are listed at the end of this chapter.

While there are always exceptions, a much more professional attitude and approach to managing rented accommodation has emerged among smaller providers, thanks to a combination of greater regulation and increasing competition. Nevertheless, it is wise to take certain precautions when seeking out private residences.

How to start looking for rented property

Contact your university's accommodation service and ask for its list of approved rented properties. Some have a Student Accommodation Accreditation Scheme, run in collaboration with the local council. To get onto an approved list under such schemes, landlords must show they are adhering to basic standards of safety and security, such as having an up-to-date gas and electric safety certificate. University accommodation officers should also be able to advise you on any hidden charges. For instance, you may be asked to pay a booking or reservation fee to secure a place in a particular property, and fees for references or drawing up a tenancy agreement are sometimes charged. The practice of charging a "joining fee", however, has been outlawed. It would be wise to speak to older students with first-hand experience of renting in the area. Certain companies in the area will often be notorious among second and third years and you can try to avoid them. In addition to websites and accommodation services designed for students, you can also use sites such as Gumtree that cater for the population at large.

Making a choice

Once you have made an initial choice of the area you would like to live in and the size of property you are looking for, the next stage is to look at possible places. If you plan to share, it is important that you all have a look at the property. If you will be living by yourself, take a friend with you when you go to view a property, since he or she can help you assess what you see objectively, and avoid any irrational or rushed on-the-spot decisions. Don't let yourself be pushed into signing on the dotted line there and then. Take time to visit and consider a number of options. It is often helpful to spend some time in the area in which you may be living, so you can check out the local facilities, transport and the general environment at various times of the day and different days of the week.

If you are living in private rented accommodation, it is likely that at least some of your neighbours will not be students. Local people often welcome students, but resentment can build up, particularly in areas of towns and cities that are dominated by student housing. It is important to respect your neighbours' rights, and not to behave in an anti-social manner.

Preparing for sharing

The people you are planning to share a house with may have some habits that you find at least mildly irritating. How well you cope with some of the downsides of sharing will be partly down to the kind of person you are – where you are on the spectrum between laid back and highly strung – but it will help a lot if you are co-habiting with people whose outlook on day-to-day living is not too far out of line with your own. Some students sign for their second year houses as early as November. While it is good to be ahead of the rush, you may not yet have met your best friends at this stage. If you have not selected your own group of friends, universities and landlords can help by taking personal preferences and lifestyle into account when grouping tenants together. You can make this task easier if you give full details about yourself when filling in accommodation application forms.

Potential issues to consider when deciding whether to move into a shared house include whether any of the housemates smoke or own a loud musical instrument. It will also be important to sort out broadband arrangements that will work for everyone in the house, and that you will be able to arrange access to the university system. UNITE's student survey for 2014 found that 13 per cent of students are unhappy with the Wi-Fi at their accommodation, whose low capacity threatens their studies and their social lives alike. It is also a good idea to agree a rota for everyone to share in the household cleaning chores from the start. Otherwise it is almost certain that you will live in a state of unhygienic squalor or that one or two individuals will be left to clear up everyone else's mess.

The practical details about renting

It is a good idea to ask whether your house is covered by an accreditation scheme or code of standards. Such codes provide a clear outline of what constitutes good practice as well as the responsibilities of both landlords and tenants. Adhering to schemes like the National Code of Standards for Larger Student Developments compiled by Accreditation Network UK (**www. anuk.org.uk**) may well become a requirement for larger properties, including those managed by universities, now that the Housing Act is in force.

At the very least, make sure that if you are renting from a private landlord, you have his or her telephone number and home address. Some can be remarkably difficult to contact when repairs are needed or deposits are due to be returned.

Multiple occupation

If you are renting a private house it may be subject to the 2004 Housing Act in England and Wales (similar legislation applies in Scotland and Northern Ireland). Licenses are compulsory for all private Houses in Multiple Occupation (HMOs) with three or more storeys and that house five or more unrelated residents. The provisions of the Act also allow local authorities to designate whole areas in which HMOs of all sizes must be licensed. The good news is that these regulations can be applied in sections of university towns and cities where most students live. This means that a house must be licensed, well-managed and must meet various health and safety standards, and its owner subject to various financial regulations. The bad news is that this could lead to a reduction in the number and range of privately rented properties on the market, or an increase in rental prices.

Tenancy agreements

Whatever kind of accommodation you go for, you must be sure to have all the paperwork in order and be clear about what you are signing up to before you move in. If you are taking up residence in a shared house, flat or bedsit, the first document you will have to grapple with is a tenancy agreement or lease offering you an "assured shorthold tenancy". Since this is a binding legal document, you should be prepared to go through every clause with a fine-tooth comb. Remember that it is much more difficult to make changes or overcome problems arising from unfair agreements once you are a tenant than before you become one.

You would be well advised to seek help in the likely event of your not fully understanding some of the clauses. Your university accommodation office or students' union is a good place to start – they should know all the ins and outs, and have model tenancy agreements to refer to. A Citizens Advice Bureau or Law Advice Centre should also be able to offer you free advice. In particular, watch out for clauses that may make you jointly responsible for the actions of others with whom you are sharing the property. If you name a parent as a guarantor to cover any costs not paid by you, they may also be liable for charges levied on all tenants for damage that was not your fault. A rent review clause could allow your landlord to increase the rent at will, whereas without such a clause, they are restricted to one rent rise a year. Make sure you keep a copy of all documents, and get a receipt (and keep it somewhere safe) for anything you have had to pay for that is the landlord's responsibility.

Contracts with private landlords tend to be longer than for university accommodation. They will frequently commit you to paying rent for 52 weeks of the year. Leaving aside the cost, there are probably more advantages than disadvantages to this kind of arrangement. It means you don't have to move out during vacation periods, which you might have to in university halls. You can store your belongings in your room when you go away (but don't leave anything really valuable behind if you can help it). You may be able to negotiate a rent discount for those periods when you are not staying in the property. The other advantage, particularly important for cash-strapped students, is that you have a base from which to find work and hold down a job during the vacations. Term dates are also not as dictatorial as they might be in halls; if you rent your own house then you can come back when you wish.

Deposits

On top of the agreed rent, you will need to provide a deposit or bond to cover any breakages or damage. This will probably set you back the equivalent of another month's rent. The deposit should be returned, less any deductions, at the end of the contract. However, be warned that disputes over the return of deposits are common, with the question of what constitutes reasonable wear and tear often the subject of disagreements between landlord and tenant. To protect students from unscrupulous landlords who withheld deposits without good reason, the 2004 Housing Act introduced a National Tenancy Deposit Scheme under which deposits are held by an independent body. This is designed to ensure that deposits are fairly returned, and that any disputes are resolved swiftly and cheaply.

Inventories and other paperwork

You should get an inventory and schedule of condition of everything in the property. This is another document that you should check very carefully – and make sure that everything listed is as described. Write on the document anything that is different. The NUS even suggests taking photographs of rooms and equipment when you first move in (setting the correct date on your camera), to provide you with additional proof should any dispute arise when your contract ends and you want to get your deposit back. If you are not offered an inventory, then make one of your own. You should have someone else witness and sign this, send it to your landlord, and keep your own copy. Keeping in contact with your landlord

---

Security in rented accommodation

Students in private housing are twice as likely to be burgled as those in university halls. When looking at accommodation, use this NUS security checklist:

» Check that the front and back doors are fitted with five-lever mortise locks in addition to standard catch locks.

» Make sure the door to your room has a lock, and always lock up when you leave it, especially for long periods such as during vacations.

» Check the locks and catches on accessible windows, especially those at ground-floor level.

» Before you move in, try to talk to neighbours about how safe the area is and whether there have been many instances of burglary.

» Ask your landlord to ensure that all previous tenants and holders of keys no longer have copies.

» If you find a property that you like but have some security concerns, discuss these with the letting agency or landlord.

throughout the year and developing a good relationship with him or her will also do you no harm, and may be to your advantage in the long run.

You should ask your landlord for a recent gas safety certificate issued by a qualified CORGI engineer, a fire safety certificate covering the furnishings, and a record of current gas and electricity meter readings. Take your own readings of meters when you move in to make sure these match up with what you have been given, or make your own records if the landlord doesn't supply this information. This also applies to water meters if you are expected to pay water rates (although this isn't usually the case).

Finally, students are not liable for Council Tax. If you are sharing a house only with other full-time students, then you will not have to pay it. However, you may be liable to pay a proportion of the Council Tax bill if you are sharing with anyone who is not a full-time student. You may need to get a Council Tax exemption certificate from your university as evidence that you do not need to pay Council Tax.

Safety and security

Once you have arrived and settled in, remember to take care of your own safety and the security of your possessions. You are particularly vulnerable as a fresher, when you are still getting used to your new-found independence. This may help explain why a fifth of students are burgled or robbed in the first six weeks of the academic year. Take care with valuable portable items such as mobile phones, tablet computers and laptops, all of which are tempting for criminals. Ensure you don't have them obviously on display when you are out and about and that you have insurance cover. If your mobile phone is stolen, call your network or 08701 123123 to immobilise it. Students' unions, universities and the police will provide plenty of practical guidance when you arrive. Following their advice will reduce the chance of you becoming a victim of crime, and help you to enjoy living in the new surroundings of your chosen university town.

Useful websites

For advice on a range of housing issues, visit: **www.nus.org.uk/en/student-life/housing-advice** The Shelter website has separate sections covering different housing regulations in England, Wales, Scotland and Northern Ireland: **www.shelter.org.uk**

As examples of providers of private hall accommodation, visit: **www.upp-ltd.com**, **www.unite-students.com** or **www.libertyliving.co.uk**

There are a number of sites that will help you find accommodation and/or potential housemates, including:
www.accommodationforstudents.com
http://uk.easyroommate.com
www.studentpad.co.uk
www.let4students.com
www.studentbunk.com
http://student.spareroom.co.uk

10 Sporting Opportunities

Two-thirds of students now take part in sport of some sort while at university – a far cry from the days when physical exercise on campus was simply not cool. Indeed, more than half play sport at least once a week and nearly a third say that sports facilities were influential in their choice of university. Both in elite sport and the everyday recreation and fitness activities that are the experience of most students, the opportunities are greater than ever before.

Over the past decade in particular, there has been unprecedented expansion and upgrading of facilities all over the country. Such has been the scale of investment that some of the biggest multi-sports developments have been on university campuses, where facilities nationally are said to be worth an astonishing £20 billion. As a result, half of all universities were chosen as pre-Olympics training bases for Great Britain squads and 30 hosted other nations' teams in the run-up to the 2012 Games.

If the students and alumni of UK universities and colleges had been a team at the London Games, they would have finished fifth in the medals table. And they repeated their successes in 2014 at the Commonwealth Games and European Championships. Adam Gemili, of the University of East London, was already the British Universities and Colleges Sport (BUCS) Sportsman of the Year after winning Gold in the 100m at the BUCS Outdoor Athletics event before going on to win silver at the Commonwealth Games and gold in the 200m at the European Championships. Isobel Pooley, of Nottingham University, became the Commonwealth silver medallist after establishing herself as the BUCS indoor and outdoor high jump champion, and Great Britain Men's Rugby Sevens Team retained their title as World University Champions in Brazil.

Naturally, most students will never aspire to such heights, but may still welcome the chance to use top-grade facilities. Until recently, sport was a side issue at best for most students choosing universities. It still does not rate with the quality of course or the location of the university in the list of most applicants' priorities, but you only have to look at the investment in campus facilities to know that universities themselves think it is important.

Research for the BUCS suggests that at least 1.7 million students take part in regular physical activity, from gym sessions to competitive individual or team sports. There are good reasons, beyond fitness, for doing so, according to the BUCS research. In 2013, graduates who had played and/or volunteered in sport were found to be earning between £4,264–£5,616 more than those who did not, and were 25 per cent less likely to have experienced unemployment. Nine out of ten employers thought that participation in university sport helped to develop valuable skills and strengths in potential employees.

Some specialist facilities may be reserved at times for elite (often international) performers, but all universities are conscious of the need for wider access. Surveys show that two-thirds of sessions at university sports facilities are taken by students, roughly a quarter by the local community and the rest by staff.

Sporting opportunities

Being a full-time student offers unrivalled opportunities to discover and play a vast range of sports. Many universities still encourage departments not to schedule lectures and seminars on Wednesday afternoons, to give students free time for sport. Even those who spend long hours in the laboratory have more time for leisure activities as a student than they will be able to spare later in life. There are student-run clubs for all the major sports and – particularly at the larger universities – a host of minor ones. Or you can content yourself with high-quality gyms, with staff on hand to devise personalised training regimes and run popular activities such as zumba and pilates. The cost varies widely between universities, and membership fees can represent a large amount to lay out at the start of the year, but most provide good value if you are going to be a regular user.

More and more students want to keep fit, even if they do not play competitive sport, and universities have joined a race of their own to provide the best facilities. Sport may still be a secondary consideration for most applicants, but particularly good (or particularly poor) facilities can sometimes tip the balance.

Sport for all

For most universities, it is in the area of "sport for all" that most attention has been focused. Beginners are welcomed and coaching provided in a range of sports, from ultimate Frisbee to tai-chi, that would be difficult to match outside the higher education system. Check on university websites to see whether your usual sport is available, but do not be surprised if you come across a new favourite when you have the opportunity to try out something different as a student. Many universities have programmes designed to encourage students to take up a new sport, with expert coaching provided.

All universities are conscious of the need to provide for a spread of ability. Sports scholarships for elite performers are now commonplace, but there will be plenty of opportunities, too, for beginners. University teams demand a hefty commitment in terms of training and practice sessions – often several times a week – and in many sports standards are high. University teams often compete in local and national leagues.

For those who do not aspire to such heights, or whose interests are primarily social, there are thriving internal, or intramural, leagues. These provide opportunities for groups from halls of residence or faculties, or even a group of friends, to form a team and participate on a regular basis. A recent BUCS survey found 41,000 participants in the intramural programmes of 41 institutions. The largest programme was at the University of Brighton, where more than 6,000 students were playing sports ranging from football, rugby and badminton to softball, orienteering and fencing. Nor is university sport a male preserve – student teams were among the pioneers in mixed sport and are still strong in areas such as women's cricket, football and rugby. In 2010–11, more than a third of the teams entered in national leagues – nearly 4,300 of them –were female.

At 32 institutions in London, there are extra opportunities through the London

Universities Sport League. There are now 375 teams – male, female and mixed – competing at a variety of levels in14 different sports. A BUCS initiative that started in 2012, the leagues are intended to reach students and include sports that are not in the main national competitions.

First-year sport

Halls of residence and university-owned flats will often have their own sports teams. At some universities, these are part of the intramural network of leagues, while others have separate arrangements for first years. In such cases, a Sports Captain, elected the year previously as part of the Junior Common Room, takes responsibility for organising trials and picking the teams, as well as arranging fixtures for the year. Hall sport is a great way of meeting like-minded people from your accommodation and over the course of the years, friendly rivalries often develop with other halls or flats. Generally there will be teams for football (both five- and 11-a-side), hockey, netball, cricket, tennis, squash, badminton and even golf. If your lodgings are smaller then don't worry, they are often twinned with similar flats to enable as many first-year students as possible to get involved in freshers' sport.

Other opportunities

You may even end up wanting to coach, umpire or referee – and this is another area in which higher education has much to offer. Many university clubs and sports unions provide subsidised courses for students to gain qualifications that may be of use to the individual in later life, as well as benefiting university teams in the short term. Or you might want to try your hand at some sports administration, with an eye to your career. In most universities there is a sports (or athletic) union, with autonomy from the main students' union, which organises matches and looks after the wider interests of those who play. There are plenty of opportunities for those seeking an apprenticeship in the art of running a club, or larger organisation. Southampton Solent University, for example, deploy students on volunteer coaching placements in more than 70 local schools. These placements increase a university's community engagement as well as enhancing student employability with minimal investment.

Universities that excel

A few universities are known particularly for sport – Exeter and Loughborough men's teams play national Premier League hockey, for example, while Bath and Northumbria both have teams in the Netball Super League. The University of London women's volleyball team has won the English Volleyball Championships, and "Team Bath" have tasted success in the FA Cup as a university team. Several of this elite group had a head start as former physical education colleges. Loughborough is probably the best-known of them, but Leeds Metropolitan and Brunel are others with a similar pedigree. Other universities with different traditions, such as Bath and East Anglia, also have a variety of outstanding facilities, while the likes of Stirling and Cardiff Metropolitan have the same in a narrower range of sports.

As in so much else, Oxford and Cambridge are in a category of their own. The Boat Race and the Varsity Match (in rugby union) are the only UK university sporting events with a big popular following – although there are varsity matches in several university cities that have become big occasions for students – and there is a good standard of competition in other sports. But you should not assume that success in school sport will be a passport to an Oxbridge place, for the days of special consideration for sporty undergraduates appear to be long since over.

Representative sport

Competitive standards have been rising in university sport, as have the numbers taking part in it. More than 6,500 students competed in 11 sports at the 2014 BUCS Nationals in Sheffield. The British Universities and Colleges Sport (BUCS: **www.bucs.org.uk**) runs competitions in almost 50 sports, and ranks participating institutions based on the points earned in the competitive programme. Over 4,700 teams compete in BUCS leagues, making the organisation the largest provider of league sport across Europe. More than a third of those teams are female and many others mixed. There is also international competition in a number of sports, and the World Student Games have become one of the biggest occasions in the international sporting calendar.

BUCS is the national organisation for higher education sport in the UK, providing a comprehensive, multi-sport competition structure and managing the development of services and facilities for participative, grass-roots sport and healthy campuses, through to high-performance elite athletes. Its mission is to raise the profile of student sport and drive the university sport agenda by influencing government and key stakeholders in the sector.

University sports facilities

Even the smallest university should provide reasonable indoor and outdoor sports facilities – a sports hall, modern gym equipment and outdoor pitches (usually including an all-weather surface and floodlights). Many will also have a swimming pool and extras such as climbing walls, but some smaller universities make arrangements for students to use local sports centres and clubs when it is not feasible to provide for minority sports. The same goes for the really expensive sports, like golf, which is usually the subject of an arrangement with one or more local clubs that give students a discount. Specialist facilities, like boat houses and climbing huts, obviously depend on location, but the most landlocked university is likely to have a sailing club that organises regular activities away from campus, and a skiing club that runs at least annual trips to the mountains.

Many of the larger universities have spent millions of pounds improving their sports facilities, sometimes in partnership with local authorities or national sporting bodies. University campuses are ideal locations for national coaching centres, and many have been established in recent years. Although elite coaching generally takes place in closed sessions, students can occasionally find themselves rubbing shoulders with star players.

It is estimated that close to £500 million has been spent on new or upgraded sports facilities at UK universities over the past decade, and planned investment for the next three years will add at least £170 million to this figure. Universities now boast a significant proportion of the UK's 50-metre pools, for example, and more are planned to follow the recent opening at the University of Surrey. Other innovative schemes include Leeds Metropolitan's development of the Headingley cricket and rugby league grounds, providing teaching space for students during the week and improved facilities for players and spectators on match days.

Beyond scrutinising the prospectus for the extent of university facilities, there are two important questions to ask: how much do they cost and where are they? Neither is easy to track down on the average university website.

How much?

University prospectuses tend to major on the quality of the sports facilities without being as forthcoming about the prices. Students who are used to free (if inferior) facilities at school often get a nasty surprise when they find that they are expected to pay to join the Athletic Union and then pay again to use the gym or play football. Because most university sport is subsidised, the charges are reasonable compared to commercial facilities, but the best deal may require a considerable outlay at the start. Some campus gyms and swimming pools now charge more than £300 a year, for example, which is still considerably cheaper than paying per visit if you intend to use the facilities regularly (and provides an incentive to carry on doing so). Some universities are offering sports facility membership as part of the £9,000 fee, but most offer a variety of peak and off-peak membership packages – some for the entire length of your course.

Outdoor sports are usually charged by the hour, although clubs will also charge a membership fee. You may be required to pay up to £60 for membership of the Athletic Union (although not all universities require this). Fees for intramural sport are seldom substantial; teams will usually pay a fee for the season, while courts for racket sports tend to be marginally cheaper per session than in other clubs.

How far away?

The other common complaint by students is that the playing fields are too far from the campus – understandable in the case of city-centre universities, but still aggravating if you have to arrange your own transport. This is where campus universities have a clear advantage. For the rest, there has to be some trade-off between the quality of outdoor facilities and the distance you have to travel to use them. But universities are beginning to realise that long journeys depress usage of important (and expensive) facilities, and some have tried to find suitable land closer to lectures and halls of residence. Indoor sports centres should all be within easy reach.

Sport as a degree subject

Sports science and other courses associated with sport had seen consistent increases in applications until the imposition of higher fees. The subject is in the top dozen in terms of popularity, with more than 58,000 applications at degree level in 2013. The demand for places had recovered from a decline in 2012. A separate ranking for the subject is on page 189. If you are hoping to be rewarded with an academic qualification for three years on the sports field, you will be disappointed because there is serious science involved. However, sport is a growing employment field and one that demands qualifications like any other.

Other degrees in the sports area are more closely focused on management, with careers in the leisure industry in mind – golf course management, for example, has proved popular with students despite being a target of those who see anything beyond the traditional academic portfolio as "dumbing down". The question is not whether the courses are up to standard, but whether a less specialised one will offer more career flexibility if a decline in popularity for the particular sport limits future opportunities.

Sports scholarships

The number and range of sports scholarships have expanded just as rapidly as courses in the subject, but the two are usually not connected. Sports scholarships are for elite performers, regardless of what they are studying – indeed, they exist at universities with barely any degrees in the field. Imported from the USA, scholarships now exist in an array of sports. At Birmingham University, for example, there are specialist golf awards (as there are at ten other universities) and a scholarship for triathletes, as well as others open to any sport.

The value of scholarships varies considerably – sometimes according to individual prowess. The Royal and Ancient scholarships for golfers, for example, range from £500 for promising handicap golfers to £10,000 for full internationals, and are available at 11 universities. All of them demand that you meet the normal entrance requirements for your course and maintain the necessary academic standards, as well as progressing in your sport. In practice, most departments will be flexible about attendance and deadlines, as long as you make your requests well in advance.

Many sports scholarships offer benefits in kind, in the form of coaching, equipment or access to facilities. The Government-funded Talented Athlete Scholarship Scheme (TASS), which is restricted to students at English universities who have achieved national recognition at under-18 level and are eligible to represent England in one of 40 different sports, is one such example. Winning Students is a similar scheme in Scotland. Some 200 current or former TASS athletes took part in the London Olympics, 44 of them winning a medal. The scholarships are worth £3,500 a year and can be put towards costs such as competition and training costs, equipment or mentoring. Further details are available at **www.tass.gov.uk**.

Part-time work

University sports centres are an excellent source of term-time (and out-of-term) employment. You may also be trained in first aid, fire safety, customer care and risk assessment – all useful skills for future employment. The experience will help you secure employment in commercial or local authority facilities – and even for jobs such as stewarding at football grounds and music venues. Most universities also have a sabbatical post in the Athletic Union or similar body, a paid position with responsibility for organising university sport and representing the sporting community within the university.

University sporting facilities

Different students look for different things from their sport while at university and the table that follows gives an initial guide to what's on offer at different institutions and, where appropriate, their various campuses.

The table is based on a detailed survey of university sport undertaken by BUCS in early 2012 and updated in 2013. The information in the table relates only to the facilities and services that universities provide centrally for all their students and does not include any facilities there may be in halls of residence or colleges.

The table contains a mix of factual information and "1–5" rankings, with five dots the best and one dot the worst. If there is no dot there is no facility. All the ratings take account of the number of students at each university, or on each campus, so they provide comparative information. The information in the table includes:

» The university's overall BUCS ranking and number of teams in BUCS competitions. Teams get points each year for their success in inter-university competitions and BUCS uses them to compile an annual league table. Some multi-site universities (eg, Manchester Metropolitan) have a BUCS ranking for each of their campuses, others (eg, Cumbria) have only one.
» The type of pool, if any (25m, 50m or other) at each university and the extent of its availability to students. The availability rating takes account of the extent to which the pool may be reserved for outside users, for example by a local swimming club or squad.
» Ratings for the range and availability of indoor dry sports facilities, such as sports halls,

dance studios, squash courts and fitness gyms, derived from the total at-one-time capacity of the facilities and number of students. The more dots in the "Range" column, the more extensive the facilities in relation to the student population. A significant difference in the rating for range and availability indicates that while facilities exist, students may have restricted access to them.

» The total number of fitness training machines, plus an asterisk if the university's fitness facilities are accredited under the Inclusive Fitness Initiative (IFI) by the English Federation of Disability Sport. However, note that the IFI scheme does not operate in Northern Ireland, Scotland or Wales.

» Ratings for the range and availability of outdoor grass and artificial pitches and tennis or netball courts.

» The number of sports with intramural competitions.

» The availability of taught or instructor-led classes.

» The number of sports scholarships or bursaries available; they may be any mix of funding and free access to facilities or elite athlete support services.

» The number of different forms of support for achieving sporting excellence, such as coaching, sports psychology, nutritional advice, access to sports medicine or specialist strength and conditioning training.

University sports websites are given in the university profiles (chapter 14).

University sporting facilities

Name	BUCS Ranking 2013–14	Teams in BUCS Leagues	Swimming pool	Availability of pools	Range of indoor dry sports facilities	Availability of indoor dry sports facilities
Aberdeen	34	53	Other	•	•••••	••••
Abertay	96	15			••	•••
Aberystwyth	65	21	Other	••	•••••	•••••
Anglia Ruskin	75	1			•••	•••
Arts University, Bournemouth	-	No information available				
Aston	98	25	Other	•	•••••	••••
Bangor	68	35			•••	••••
Bath	4	71	50m	•••••	•••	••••
Bath Spa	119	No information available				
Bedfordshire	74	6			•••••	•••••
Birmingham	3	65	25m	•••	••	••
Birmingham City	128	No information available				
University College Birmingham	125	No information available				
Bishop Grosseteste	141	No information available				
Bolton	131	No information available				
Bournemouth	30	32			•	••
Bradford	86	29	25m	•	•••••	••••
Brighton (Brighton)	37	40			•••	••
Brighton (Eastbourne)	37	40	25m	••	•••••	•••••
Bristol	11	48			••	•
Brunel	31	No information available				
Buckingham	-	0			•••••	•••••
Buckinghamshire New	85	No information available				
Cambridge	14	37			•••••	••••
Canterbury Christ Church	79	No information available				
Cardiff	22	57			•••••	•••••
Cardiff Metropolitan	12	37			•	•
Central Lancashire	53	31			••	•••
Chester (Chester)	90	No information available				
Chester (Warrington)	130	No information available				
Chichester	52	29			•••••	•••••
City	93	13			•	•
Coventry	55	31			••	•••
Creative Arts	145	No information available				
Cumbria (Ambleside)	116	0			••••	•••••
Cumbria (Carlisle)	116	3			•	•
Cumbria (Lancaster)	116	13			•	••
Cumbria (Penrith)	116	2			•••••	•••••
Cumbria (Preston)	116	0			•	•••
De Montfort	82	30			•	•
Derby	58	27			••	••
Dundee	44	39	25m	•••	•••	••••
Durham	2	61			••••	•••
East Anglia	47	26	50m			
East London	63	0			•	•
Edge Hill	87	30			•••	•••

Fitness machines	Number of winter pitches	Availability of winter pitches	Outdoor courts	Availability of outdoor courts	Sports with intramural competitions	Availability of taught classes	Sports scholarships/ bursaries	Forms of elite athlete support
200	•••••	•••••	•	•	1	•••••	29	6
35					1	•	0	10
76	••••	••••	•••••	•••••	1	•••••	30	5
20					3	••••	25	0
103	••••	•••	•	••	0	••	6	2
93	•••	•••	••	••	6	•••	10	0
101*	••••	•••	••••	•••	2	•••	39	10
19	•••	•••	•••	•••	6	•	67	2
90*	••••	••••	•	•	6	•••••	67	10
55					10	•••	55	9
100*	••	•	•••	•••	17	•••	8	0
88	•••	•••	••••	••••	8	•	30	10
47	••••	••••	•••••	•••••	7	••••	30	10
100	••••	•••	••••	•	9	••	26	10
16	••	••			1	•••••	0	0
470					19	••	15	5
90	••	•••	•	••	3	••	60	9
55	•	•	•	•	2	•	28	6
108	••	•	••••	••••	1	••••	12	8
28	•••••	•••••	•••	•••	2	•	16	3
0					5	••	0	0
86	••	••			10	••	65	10
0	•	•			0	••	0	0
21					0	••	10	7
17	•••	•••			0	•	10	7
15	•••••	•••••			5		10	7
0	••	••	••••	•	0	•	0	8
90					6	•	0	0
37	•	•	••	••	0		6	10
125	••	••	•••	•••	8	•••••	12	10
242	•••••	•••••	••••	••••	20	•••	45	10
80							0	0
10					6	•	22	10
56	••••	•••			0	••••	18	10

Name	BUCS Ranking 2013–14	Teams in BUCS Leagues	Swimming pool	Availability of pools	Range of indoor dry sports facilities	Availability of indoor dry sports facilities
Edinburgh	5	71	25m	•••	•••••	••••
Edinburgh Napier	72	13			••	•••
Essex	45	64			••••	••••
Exeter	6	58	25m	•••	•••••	•••••
Falmouth	116	0			•••	••••
Glasgow	26	36	25m	•••••	••	•
Glasgow Caledonian	94	18			•	•
Gloucestershire	40	46			•••••	•••••
Glyndŵr	120	No information available				
Goldsmiths	133	8			••••	•
Greenwich	118	13			•	••
Harper Adams	106	18			•••••	•••••
Heriot-Watt	59	28			•••	•••
Hertfordshire	54	33	25m	••••	•••	•••
Highlands and Islands	114	No information available				
Huddersfield	97	16			•	•
Hull	67	48			•	••
Imperial College	18	48	25m	•••••	•••••	•••••
Keele	70	25			••••	•••••
Kent	46	41			•	•
King's College London	39	57			••	••
Kingston	84	26			•	•
Lancaster	41	41	25m	••••	••••	••••
Leeds	15	70	25m	••••	•••	••
Leeds Metropolitan	9	66	Other	••	•••	•••
Leeds Trinity	122	15			••••	•••••
Leicester	50	34			••••	••
Lincoln	69	34			••	••
Liverpool	33	81	25m	••••	••	•••
Liverpool Hope	105	No information available				
Liverpool John Moores	66	No information available				
London Metropolitan	127	No information available				
LSE	64	No information available				
London South Bank	99	No information available				
Loughborough	1	66	50m	•••••	•••••	••••
Manchester	10	77	50 m	•••	••	••
Manchester Metropolitan (MMU)	42	29			••••	•••
MMU (Cheshire)	-	0			•••••	•••••
Middlesex	81	19			••	••
Newcastle	16	69			••	••••
Newman	142	No information available				
Northampton	80	No information available				
Northumbria	8	68	25m	•	•••••	•••
Nottingham	7	72	25m	•••••	•••	••••
Nottingham Trent	17	44			•••	••
Oxford	13	No information available				
Oxford Brookes	51	35	25m	••	••••	••
Plymouth	35	23			•	•
Portsmouth	32	51			••	•••

Fitness machines	Number of winter pitches	Availability of winter pitches	Outdoor courts	Availability of outdoor courts	Sports with intramural competitions	Availability of taught classes	Sports scholarships/ bursaries	Forms of elite athlete support
266	••	••	•	••	11	••••	278	10
57					0	•	4	1
88	•••	••••	•••	•••	20	•••	7	10
125	•••••	•••••	•••••	•••••	16	•••••	60	10
40			•••	•••	2	••••	6	3
145	•••	•••	••••	••••	4	•••••	38	4
110					0	•••••	18	5
40*	•••••	•••••	•••••	•••••	4	•••••	18	10
113	•	•	••	••	3	••••	0	0
38*	•	•	•••	•••	0		0	3
22	•••••	•••••	•••••	•••••	0	••••	1	1
51	••••	••••	•••	••••	5	•••••	41	6
102*	•••••	•••••	•••	•••	2	•••	20	10
26					3	••	0	0
53*	•••	••	•••	•••	2	•	0	10
242	•••••	•••••	••	•••	7	••••	44	10
57	•••	•••	•	•	1	••••	0	2
110					9		51	9
32	••	•••	••	••	0	•	0	1
40	•	•	••	•	3	•	8	10
90	•••	••••	••	•••	16	•••••	0	0
221*	•	••	••	••	17	•••	35	10
169	•••	••••	•••	••••	4	•	52	10
16	••••	•••••	•••	•••	8	••••	0	3
96	••	••	••••	••••	13	•••	5	4
44*	••••	••••	••	••	5	••	15	7
92	•••	••••	••	••	7	••••	40	10
233	•••••	•••••	•••••	•••••	45	••••	135	10
105	•	•	•	••	12	•••	40	8
178*			•	•	0		0	10
50	•••••	•••••	•••••	•••••	3		0	10
78			•	•	8	••	43	10
108	••	•••	••	••	7	••	32	9
240	•••	•••			0		100	10
184	•••	••••	•••••	•••••	8	•••	35	10
140	••••	••••	••	••	4	•••	50	10
107	•••	•••	•••••	•••••	5	••••	25	8
43					10	••	20	6
96	•	•	••	••	13	•••••	15	6

Name	BUCS Ranking 2013–14	Teams in BUCS Leagues	Swimming pool	Availability of pools	Range of indoor dry sports facilities	Availability of indoor dry sports facilities
Queen Margaret	109	7			•••••	•••••
Queen Mary	56	34			•••	••
Queen's, Belfast	110	No information available				
Reading	43	51			••••	••••
Robert Gordon	76	22	25m		••••	•••
Roehampton	102	23			•••	•••••
Royal Holloway	60	46			•••	•••
St Andrews	28	51			•••	•••
St Mark and St John (Marjon)	71	19	25m	••	•••••	•••••
St Mary's, Twickenham	61	No information available				
Salford	88	22	25m	••	•	•
SOAS	140	No information available				
Sheffield	20	56	25m	••••	••	•
Sheffield Hallam	24	46			•	•
South Wales (Newport)	107	11			•••	••••
South Wales (Pontiprydd)	48	31			••••	••••
Southampton	21	57	25m			
Southampton Solent	77	17			•••••	•••••
Staffordshire	89	38			•••••	•••
Stirling	23	41	50m	•••••	••••	•••••
Strathclyde	57	0	Other	•	••	•
Sunderland	83	20			••	••
Surrey	36	40	50m	•••••	•••••	•••••
Sussex	49	30			•••	••
Swansea	27	No information available				
Swansea Metropolitan	132	No information available				
Teesside	91	26			••	••
Trinity Saint David	111	No information available				
Ulster	129	0			•	•
University College London	25	66			•	•
University of the Arts London	113	No information available				
West of England, Bristol	29	39			••	•
West of England, Hartpury	73	No information available				
Warwick	20	3	25 m	••••	••••	•••
West London	135	No information available				
West of Scotland	108	No information available				
Westminster	91	No information available				
Winchester	101	No information available				
Wolverhampton	103	18			•	•
Wolverhampton (Walsall)	103	18	25 m	•	•••••	•••••
Worcester	62	38			••••	••••
York	38	55	25 m	•••	•••	•••
York St John	95	26			•	••

Fitness machines	Number of winter pitches	Availability of winter pitches	Outdoor courts	Availability of outdoor courts	Sports with intramural competitions	Availability of taught classes	Sports scholarships/ bursaries	Forms of elite athlete support
50					0	•••••	0	0
70	•	•			4	•••	0	2
103	•••	•••	••••	••••	3	•••••	40	7
98*			••••	••••	0	••••	20	9
37*	•	•	••••	••••	0		23	10
48	••	••	•••••	•••••	0		28	4
45	•••••	•••••	•••••	•••••	14	••••	15	8
45	•••••	•••••	•••••	•••••	3	•••••	5	4
46	•	•			0	•	0	6
140	••	••			0		27	5
98	•	•	•	•	5	•••	36	10
35	•	•	•••	••••	3	••••	15	10
134	••••	••••			7	•••	24	9
140					11			
175	••••	••	•	•	20	•••	28	10
68	•••••	•••••	•••••	•••••	2	••	0	10
86	••••	••••	••••	••••	3	•••••	91	8
97	•	••			3	•••	44	5
60					0		10	10
110	•••••	•••••	••••	••••	0		14	10
103	•••	••	•••	•••	5	•••	27	4
50*	••	••			3	••••	12	10
45	••	••			2	•	0	9
75*	•	•	•	•	3	••	26	7
100*	•	•			5	••	19	10
98*	••••	••••	••	•	7	••••	No	9
17					7	••	0	10
38	••••	••••	••••	••••	7	••••	30	10
60	•••••	••••			1	••	27	10
71*	•••	••	•••••	•••••	14	•	13	4
18	••	•••			0		1	9

11 What Parents Should Do

There is no right or wrong extent for a parent to be involved with their children's higher education – everything comes down to individual relationships. But there is no doubt that, in general, parents have become more engaged in the selection and application processes, and even in monitoring the student experience. The introduction of £9,000 fees was meant to make the student responsible for his or her higher education – including paying for it – but parents are making as big a financial contribution as ever and are every bit as focused on the outcome.

That is because most parents are paying towards students' living costs, not their tuition. Maintenance loans may be larger than they were, but few students will get by on the £5,740 available to most undergraduates outside London. And those who can are often anxious to spare their children yet more debt on top of the cost of tuition. Surprising numbers of students from affluent families are not taking out loans at all, and are relying instead on support from parents or sometimes grandparents. Up to half the students at some leading universities are doing without Government maintenance loans, although throughout England, well over 80 per cent are taking them up.

Parental involvement starts well before student days, however, and is by no means limited to money. For those in the know, it begins when teenagers are choosing A levels, or even GCSEs, to keep their degree options open. Certainly, parents are encouraged by many schools and colleges to play an active role in the process of choosing a course. At the most basic (but vital) level, this means keeping an eye on deadlines, but it is also about acting as a sounding board and doing some of your own research to guide your child towards the right university and course.

Open days are now organised with parents, as well as prospective students, in mind. Often it is the parents (usually mothers) who ask the most direct and practical questions, sometimes to the embarrassment of their children. But most of today's sixth-formers and college students seem happy to have their parents' help and advice – even if they do not take it in the end. Research by the Knowledge Partnership consultancy found that more than half of the parents of first-year undergraduates felt they had exerted some influence on their children's choices of university and course, although only about 7 per cent characterised this as "a lot".

Once the choices have been made and the necessary obstacles cleared, most parents' only involvement is financial. But growing numbers now want to play their part in ensuring that their children get value for money at university. This chapter looks at where to draw the line between constructive involvement and unwelcome interference.

Nearly all students are adults, and university offers an environment where they can begin to make their own decisions and develop as individuals. A good starting point is to offer advice only when it is sought, and to leave direct contact with university administrators and academics to the student. Of course, throughout the *Guide*, all references to parents apply equally to guardians and step-parents.

Student finance and parental involvement

Hundreds of thousands of students – particularly mature students – pay their own way through university. Many undergraduates of all ages supplement their income with term-time and vacation jobs. But every survey shows that families play an important (and growing) role where students move straight from school to higher education. The Knowledge Partnership research suggested that at least half of parents were meeting part or all of the costs of accommodation, food, clothing and books.

Those from the poorest households will be eligible for grants to supplement maintenance loans and may well receive additional bursaries from their university. Even these benefits are being scaled back, while others have to apply for income-assessed loans which carry the expectation of a family contribution towards living expenses. This applies particularly to students in Scotland, whose tuition is free, but who have to make do with less generous loans. A frank discussion on what the family can afford is essential before the student leaves home. It is all too easy for a young person who has never had to budget for themselves to get into financial difficulties in the social whirl that is the first term of a degree course. In the worst cases, this can lead to excessive term-time employment to keep up with spiralling debts and pressures that contribute towards a student dropping out.

"Helicopter parents"

Universities have found that anxious mothers and fathers are more inclined than ever to question what their children are getting for their now substantial fees. There have been stories of parents challenging not just the amount and quality of tuition, but even the marking of essays and exams. The phenomenon, first reported in the USA, has given rise to the phrase "helicopter parents" – so called because they hover over their children's education when they should be letting go. No one wants to think of themselves in that category, but it is not surprising – or reprehensible – that parents are taking more of an interest. Many more of today's parents have been to university themselves, so have the knowledge and confidence to offer advice, both in choosing where and what to study, and in the decisions facing students at university.

One of the reasons that some then overstep the mark is that they are shocked that the amount of teaching and size of seminar groups are not what they recall from their own "free" higher education. The new fees are meant to herald improvements in the student experience, including more contact hours, but these have been marginal in most universities so far. It may be that fewer and larger seminars are here to stay in the arts and social sciences, where almost all state support has been withdrawn, and more learning opportunities will be provided online.

An associated reason for greater parental involvement is that family relationships have changed. Many teenage applicants are glad to accept a lift to an open day to get a second opinion on a university and their prospective course. They are also more likely than previous generations of students to come home at the weekend – or to live there in the first place – and to air any grievances.

Laying the ground

The first thing any parent can do to smooth the path to university is to be encouraging about the value of higher education. Ideally, this should have started long before the application process, but it is especially important at this point. Now that student debt has become a frequent media topic and the economic downturn has hit graduate employment prospects, it is only natural for sixth-formers and others to have second thoughts about higher education.

The lure of a regular wage packet will be tempting, should one be available, and there are plenty of young people who are not suited to full-time higher education. More big companies are choosing to employ promising 18-year-olds, rather than rely entirely on graduate recruitment, and there has been a rapid expansion of apprenticeships. Even after the years of enormous university expansion, most people still do not go to university. Nevertheless, those who are capable of going generally do not regret the decision. Many people look back on their student days as the best period of their life, as well as the one that shaped their personality and their career. Time as a student should still pay off for the individual in terms of lifetime earnings, as well as personal development. A little reassurance at this stage may make all the difference.

Making the choice

Any parent wants to help a son or daughter through the difficult business of choosing where and what to study. How big a role you play will depend on a number of factors, not the least of which is the extent to which your advice is wanted. In the end, it is the student's decision, and you can do no more than offer relevant information. One important factor is the quality of advice available at school or college. If this is good, parental involvement should be marginal. But often that is not the case, and you may have to call on other resources, including your own research. A second factor is your own level of expertise: you may have opinions about particular universities or subjects, but are they up to date and based on evidence? Try not to give advice that is coloured by memories of your own student days. That was probably a quarter of a century ago, and higher education has changed out of all recognition in the intervening years. Avoid second-hand opinions gleaned through the media or dinner party gossip. You may think that some subjects are a sure-fire route to lucrative employment, while others are shunned by employers, but are you right? And do you really know the strengths and weaknesses of more than 100 universities? The tables in chapters 2 and 4 offer a reality check, but even they cannot take account of the differences within institutions. The subject tables in chapter 5 show that the best graduate employment rates are often not at the obvious universities.

Above all, do not try to rewind your own career decisions through your children. The fact that you enjoyed – or hated – a subject or a university does not mean that they will. You may have always regretted missing out on the chance to go to Oxbridge or to become a brain surgeon, but they have their own lives to lead. Students who switch courses or drop out frequently complain that they were pressured into their original choice by their parents.

Check that choices are being made for sensible reasons, not on the basis of questionable gossip or trivial criteria. But beyond that, you should stay in the background unless there is a very good reason to play a more substantive role. Make a point of looking for important aspects of university life that the applicant might miss. Security, for example, usually does not feature near the top of a teenager's list of priorities; likewise other practical issues, such as the proximity of student accommodation to lectures, the library and the students' union.

Many universities now publish guides specifically for parents and put on programmes for them at Open Days. The latter may be a way of separating prospective applicants from their more demanding "minders", but the programmes themselves can be interesting and informative. Do not worry that you will be an embarrassment by attending Open Days – thousands of parents do so, and you may add a critical edge to the proceedings. Like prospectuses, Open Days are part of the sales process, and it is easy for a sixth-former to be carried away by the excitement surrounding a lively university. You are much more likely to spot the defects – even if they are ignored in the final decision.

Finding a place

UCAS publishes its own guide for parents, offering useful tips and outlining the deadlines that applicants will have to meet. The school should be on top of the timing and offering the necessary advice, but there is no harm in providing a little back-up, especially on parts of the process that take time and thought, such as writing the personal statement. There is little a parent can do as the offers and/or rejections come rolling in, other than to be supportive. If the worst happens and there are five rejections, you may have to start the advice process all over again for a new round of applications through UCAS Extra. If so, a cool head is even more necessary, but the same principles apply.

Results day

Then, before you know it, results day is upon you. Make sure you are at home, rather than in some isolated holiday retreat. Your son or daughter needs to have access to instant advice at school or college, and to be able to contact universities straight away if Clearing or Adjustment is required. And your moral support will be much more effective face to face, rather than down a telephone line. Whatever happens, try not to transmit the anxiety that you will inevitably be feeling to your son or daughter, especially if the results are not what was wanted. It is easy to make rash decisions about re-sitting exams or rejecting an insurance offer in the heat of the moment. Try to slow the process down and encourage clear and realistic thinking. Make sure you know in advance what might be required, such as where to access Clearing lists, and if Clearing or Adjustment is being used, you will need to be on hand to offer advice and help with visits to possible universities. Clearing or Adjustment is all but over in a week, so the agony should be short-lived.

Before they go

Little more than a month after the tension of results day, everything should be ready for the start of term. Unless your son or daughter is one of the growing band choosing to stay at home to study, there will be forms to fill in to secure university accommodation, as well as student loans to sort out and registration to complete. You can perform useful services, like supplying recipe books if the first year is to be spent in self-catering accommodation, but now is the time for independence to become reality. Make sure that important details like insurance are not forgotten, but otherwise stand clear.

Then it is just a matter of agreeing a budget, assuming you are in a position to make a financial contribution. How large that contribution is will depend on family circumstances and your attitude to independent living. Some parents want to ensure that their children leave university debt-free; others could never afford to do that. The important thing is that students and parents know where they stand.

After they've left

Any new student is going to be nervous if he or she is leaving home for the first time and having to settle into a strange environment. But in most cases it is not going to last long because everyone is in the same boat and freshers' weeks hardly leave time for homesickness. In any case, they will not want to let their apprehension show. The people who are most likely to be emotional are the parents – especially if they are left with an empty nest for the first time. It can take a while to get used to an orderly, quiet house after all those years of mayhem.

Resist any temptation to decorate their bedroom and turn it into an office – it is more common than you might think, and psychologists say it can do lasting damage to family relationships. Keep in touch by phone, text or email, but try not to pry. You're not going to be told everything anyway – which is probably just as well. They will be back soon enough and, just as you were getting used to having the place to yourself, a weekend visit or the Christmas vacation will remind you of how things used to be. If things are not going smoothly at university, this may be the time for more reassurance – more students drop out at Christmas of their first year than at any other time.

Lastly, do not become a helicopter parent. Your son or daughter may well seek your advice if they are dissatisfied with the course, their accommodation or some other aspect of university life. By all means, give advice, but leave them to sort the problem out. Universities will cite the Data Protection Act, in any case, to say they can only deal with students, not parents. What they really mean is that students are adults and should look after themselves.

Useful websites

Many universities have sections on their websites for parents of prospective students. UCAS has a Parents section and a guide on its website: **www.ucas.com/sites/default/files/ucas-parent-guide-2015-entry_3.pdf**

To find out more about open days, visit: **www.opendays.com**

12 Coming to the UK to Study

All around the world, more and more young people are choosing to study outside their own country – the numbers doubled to more than 4 million between 2000 and 2012, and show every sign of continuing to grow. Sometimes this is because their home universities are poorly regarded, or just full. In other cases it is to master a different language, experience another culture or take the first step on an international career ladder.

The UK is one of the prime destinations of choice for those seeking to broaden their horizons, attracting 11 per cent of all international students. Only the USA, with its vast higher education system, has more. Global surveys have shown that UK universities are seen as offering high quality in a relatively safe environment. And, while the UK is seen as an expensive place to study and visa regulations have become a growing obstacle, courses that are relatively short by international standards cut the overall costs and speed progress into the employment market.

UK universities have been popular among international students for many years, although their "market share" has dropped as countries such as Australia and Germany have competed aggressively. Numbers have stalled in 2014, but the decline has been mostly among further education colleges and private institutions, rather than universities. Both applications and enrolments from outside the UK at undergraduate level rose in 2013.

Both EU students (who pay the same fees as their British counterparts) and those from the rest of the world (who pay considerably more) have shared in the boom. Beyond the EU, where the new fees do not apply, applications were up by 5 per cent in 2013. When postgraduates are included, by far the largest numbers continue to come from China, with Malaysia, Hong Kong, Cyprus, Germany and France next at undergraduate level.

Universities in the UK continue to be extremely proactive in the recruitment of international students, participating in international fairs and sometimes opening their own offices in target countries. The fees such students pay is the obvious motivation, but universities also value the cultural richness that a diverse international intake contributes to student life.

Why study in the UK?

Aside from the strong reputation of UK degree courses and the opportunity to be taught and immerse yourself in English, research shows that most graduates are handsomely rewarded when they return home. A report from the Department for Business, Innovation and Skills (BIS) shows that UK graduates earn much higher salaries than those who studied in their own country. The starting salaries of UK graduates in China and India were more than twice as high as those for graduates educated at home, while even those returning to the USA enjoyed a salary premium of more than 10 per cent.

Some premium is to be expected – you are likely to be bright and highly motivated if you are prepared to uproot yourself to take a degree. And, unless they have government scholarships, most students have to be from a relatively wealthy background to afford the fees and other expenses of international study. A higher salary will probably be a necessity to compensate for the cost of the course. But the scale of increase demonstrated in the report suggests that a UK degree remains a good investment. Three years after graduation, 95 per cent of the international graduates surveyed were in work or further study. More than 90 per cent had been satisfied with their learning experience and almost as many would recommend their university to others.

A popular choice

Nearly all UK universities are cosmopolitan places that welcome international students in large numbers. Recent surveys by i-graduate, the student polling organisation which also produced the BIS report, put the country close behind the USA among the world's most

The top countries for sending international students to the UK

EU countries (top 20)		%	Non-EU Countries (top 20)		%
Cyprus (EU)	7,404	10.2	China	33,272	25.8
Germany	6,483	8.9	Malaysia	11,191	8.7
France	6,378	8.8	Hong Kong	10,499	8.1
Ireland	5,723	7.9	Nigeria	6,027	4.7
Romania	5,032	6.9	India	5,967	4.6
Bulgaria	5,007	6.9	Singapore	4,586	3.6
Greece	4,694	6.5	United States of America	4,334	3.4
Lithuania	4,537	6.3	Saudi Arabia	4,103	3.2
Italy	3,622	5.0	Norway	3,519	2.7
Poland	3,405	4.7	Pakistan	2,996	2.3
Spain	3,159	4.4	Canada	2,813	2.2
Sweden	2,435	3.4	Korea (South)	2,329	1.8
Belgium	1,803	2.5	Bangladesh	2,190	1.7
Latvia	1,759	2.4	Vietnam	2,079	1.6
Finland	1,367	1.9	Sri Lanka	1,868	1.4
Netherlands	1,351	1.9	Russia	1,790	1.4
Portugal	1,156	1.6	Switzerland	1,629	1.3
Slovakia	954	1.3	United Arab Emirates	1,590	1.2
Austria	940	1.3	Brunei	1,511	1.2
Estonia	854	1.2	Kenya	1,343	1.0
All EU students	72,511		All non-EU students	128,987	

Note: First degree non-UK students .

attractive study destinations. International students now make up over 17 per cent of all students at UK universities and colleges. More full-time postgraduates – the fastest-growing group – come from outside the UK than within it. In many UK universities you can expect to have fellow students from over 100 countries.

More than 90 per cent of international students declare themselves satisfied with their experience of UK universities in i-graduate surveys, although they are less sanguine in the National Student Survey and more likely than UK students to make official complaints. Nevertheless, satisfaction increased by 8 percentage points in four years, according to i-graduate, reflecting greater efforts to keep ahead of the global competition. International students are particularly complimentary about students' unions, multiculturalism, teaching standards and places of worship. Their main concerns tend to be financial, with the UK considered the second-most expensive study location in the world (after the USA), partly because of a lack of employment opportunities (in one survey, only 56 per cent were satisfied with the ability to earn money while studying).

One way round this in a growing number of countries is to take a UK degree through a local institution or a full branch campus of a UK university. Indeed, there are now almost as many international students taking UK degrees in their own country as there are in Britain, 320,000 of them outside the EU. The numbers grew by 70 per cent in a decade and are likely to rise further if the UK Government prevents universities increasing the number of students coming to Britain.

Where to study in the UK

The vast majority of the UK's universities and other higher education institutions are in England. Of the 131 universities profiled in this *Guide*, 106 are in England, 15 in Scotland, 8 in Wales and 2 in Northern Ireland. Fee limits in higher education for UK and EU students are determined separately in each administrative area, which in some cases has brought benefits for EU students. All undergraduates from other EU countries are charged the same fees as those from the part of the UK where their chosen university is located, so EU students currently pay no tuition fees in Scotland, for example.

Within the UK, the cost of living varies by geographical area. Although London is the most expensive, accommodation costs in particular can also be high in many other major cities. You should certainly find out as much as you can about what living in Britain will be like. Further advice and information is available through the British Council at its offices worldwide, at more than 60 university exhibitions that it holds around the world every year, or at its Education UK website (**www.educationuk.org**). Another useful website for international students is provided by the UK Council for International Student Affairs (UKCISA) at **www.ukcisa.org.uk**.

Universities in all parts of the UK have a worldwide reputation for high quality teaching and research, as evidenced in global rankings such as those shown on pages 52–54. They maintain this standing by investing heavily in the best academic staff, buildings and equipment, and by taking part in rigorous quality assurance monitoring. The main regulatory bodies include the Quality Assurance Agency for Higher Education (QAA), higher education funding councils for each country of the UK, and the Office for Standards in Education, all of which publish reports on their websites. Professional bodies also play an important role, and there is an Independent Adjudicator for Higher Education who handles student complaints that have not been resolved by universities' own internal procedures.

Although many people from outside the UK associate British universities with Oxford and Cambridge, in reality most higher education institutions are nothing like this. Some universities do still maintain a traditional culture, but most are modern institutions that place at least as much emphasis on teaching as on research and offer many vocational programmes, often with close links with business, industry and the professions. The table below shows the universities that are most popular with international students at undergraduate level. Although some of those at the top of the lists are among the most famous names in higher education, others achieved university status only in the last 20 years.

What subjects to study?

One of the reasons for such diversity is that strongly vocational courses are favoured by international students. Many of these in professional areas such as architecture, dentistry or medicine take one or two years longer to complete than most other degree courses. Traditional first degrees are mostly awarded at Bachelor level (BA, BEng, BSc, etc.) and last three to four years. There are also some "enhanced" first degrees (MEng, MChem, etc.) that take four years to complete. The relatively new Foundation degree programmes are almost all vocational and take two years to complete as a full-time course, with an option to study for a further year to gain a full degree. The table on the next page shows the most popular subjects studied by international students. Remember, though, that you need to consider the details of any university course that you wish to study and to look at the ranking of that university in our main league table in chapter 4 and in the subject tables in chapter 5.

The universities most favoured by EU and non-EU students

Institution (top 20)	EU students	Institution (top 20)	Non-EU students
Aberdeen	2,070	Manchester	4,776
Glasgow	1,925	University College London	3,576
Edinburgh	1,710	Nottingham	3,285
Middlesex	1,563	University of the Arts London	3,197
Essex	1,504	Edinburgh	3,031
Coventry	1,469	Liverpool	2,977
London Metropolitan	1,457	Coventry	2,517
University of the Arts London	1,425	Sheffield	2,504
Manchester	1,415	Warwick	2,367
Westminster	1,325	Imperial College	2,349
University College London	1,272	Sunderland	2,274
King's College London	1,257	Sheffield Hallam	2,178
Portsmouth	1,191	St Andrews	1,990
Kent	1,187	Southampton	1,903
Kingston	1,151	Exeter	1,894
Edinburgh Napier	1,126	Portsmouth	1,881
Imperial College	1,030	Hertfordshire	1,846
Cambridge	985	Leeds	1,834
Warwick	952	Northumbria	1,739
Ulster	929	Leicester	1,721

English language proficiency

The universities maintain high standards partly by setting demanding entry requirements, including proficiency in English. For international students, this usually includes a score of 6 or 7 in the International English Language Testing System (IELTS), which assesses English language ability through listening, speaking, reading and writing tests. Under visa regulations introduced in 2011, universities are able to vouch for a student's ability in English. This proficiency will need to be equivalent to an "upper intermediate" level (level B2) of the CEFR (Common European Framework of Reference) for studying at an undergraduate level.

There are many private and publicly funded colleges throughout the UK that run courses designed to bring the English language skills of prospective higher education students up to the required standard. However, not all of these are Government approved. Some private organisations such as INTO (**www.into.uk.com**) have joined with universities to create centres running programmes preparing international students for degree-level study. The British Council also runs English language courses at its centres around the world.

Tougher student visa regulations were introduced in 2012. Although universities' international students should not be denied entry to the UK, as long as they are found to have followed immigration rules, some lower-level preparatory courses taken by international students have been affected. It is, therefore, doubly important to consult the

The most popular subjects for international students

Subject	EU students	Non–EU students	Total students	% of all international students
Business studies	10,829	25,661	36,490	18.1
Accounting	2,394	14,050	16,445	8.2
Law	3,736	8,439	12,175	6.0
Economics	2,594	6,939	9,533	4.7
Computing	3,855	5,023	8,878	4.4
Art and design	3,399	4,919	8,318	4.1
Electrical and electronic engineering	1,357	5,539	6,896	3.4
Mechanical engineering	1,567	4,611	6,178	3.1
Politics	3,410	2,763	6,173	3.1
Biological sciences	2,685	2,789	5,474	2.7
Mathematics	1,346	4,016	5,362	2.7
Psychology	2,865	2,164	5,029	2.5
Communications and media studies	2,605	2,254	4,859	2.4
Civil engineering	1,494	3,027	4,521	2.2
Medicine	970	3,363	4,333	2.2
Hospitality, leisure, recreation and tourism	1,889	2,361	4,250	2.1
Architecture	1,986	1,989	3,975	2.0
Drama, dance and cinematics	2,019	1,333	3,352	1.7
Pharmacy and pharmacology	762	2,528	3,290	1.6
Other subjects allied to medicine	1,338	1,513	2,852	1.4

Note: First degree non-UK students

official UK government list of approved institutions (web address given at the end of this chapter) before lodging an application.

How to apply

You should read the information below in conjunction with that provided in chapter 6, which deals with the application process in some detail.

Some international students apply directly to a UK university for a place on a course, and others make their applications via an agent in their home country. But most applying for a full-time first degree course do so through the Universities and Colleges Admissions Service (UCAS). If you take this route, you will need to fill in an online UCAS application form at home, at school or perhaps at your nearest British Council office. There is lots of advice on the UCAS website about the process of finding a course and the details of the application system (**www.ucas.com/how-it-all-works/international**).

Whichever way you apply, the deadlines for getting your application in are the same. For those applying from within an EU country, application forms for most courses starting in 2015 must be received at UCAS by 15 January 2015. Note that applications for Oxford and Cambridge and for all courses in medicine, dentistry and veterinary science have to be received at UCAS by 15 October 2014, while some art and design courses have a later deadline of 24 March 2015.

If you are applying from a non-EU country to study in 2015, you can submit your application to UCAS at any time between 1 September 2014 and 30 June 2015. Most people will apply well before the 30 June deadline to make sure that places are still available and to allow plenty of time for immigration regulations, and to make arrangements for travel and accommodation.

Entry and employment regulations

Visa regulations have been the subject of frequent controversy in the UK and many new rules and regulations have recently been introduced, often hotly contested by universities. The Government was criticised for increasing visa fees, doubling the cost of visa extensions, and ending the right to appeal against a refusal of a visa.

It also introduced a points system for entry – known as Tier 4 – which came into effect in 2009. Under this scheme, prospective students can check whether they are eligible for entry against published criteria, and so assess their points score. Universities are also required to provide a Confirmation of Acceptance for Study to their international student entrants and they must have "Highly Trusted" status on the Register of Sponsors. Prospective students have to demonstrate that, as well as the necessary qualifications, they have English language proficiency and enough money for the first year of their specified course. This includes the full fees for the first year and living costs of £1,020 per month for the duration of the course, up to a maximum of nine months, if studying in inner London (£820 per month elsewhere in London and the rest of the UK). Under the new visa requirements, details of financial support are checked in more detail than before.

All students wishing to enter the UK to study are required to obtain entry clearance before arrival. The only exceptions are British nationals living overseas, British overseas territories citizens, British Protected persons, British subjects, and non-visa national short-term students who may enter under a new Student Visitor route. Visa fees have been increased again and the details of the regulations have been reviewed by the UK Border Agency. You can find more about all the latest rules and regulations for entry and visa requirements at **www.gov.uk/browse/visas-immigration/study-visas**.

The rules and regulations governing permission to work vary according to your country of origin and the level of course you undertake. If you are from a European Economic Area (EEA) country (the EU plus Iceland, Liechtenstein and Norway) or Switzerland, you do not need permission to work in the UK, although you will need to be ready to show an employer your passport or identity card to prove you are a national of an EEA country. Students from outside the EEA who are here as Tier 4 students are allowed to work part-time for up to 20 hours a week during term time and full-time during vacations. These arrangements apply to students on degree courses; stricter limits were introduced in 2010 for lower-level courses. If you wish to stay on after you have graduated, you can apply for permission under Tier 2 under the new points-based immigration system, but you will need a sponsor and the work must be considered "graduate level", commanding a salary of at least £20,500. The latest reforms abolished the Tier 1 two-year post-study period for graduates who do not have such a sponsor. They will be required to apply for a new visa from scratch. Full details are on the Home Office study visas website above.

A new Graduate Entrepreneur Scheme will enable up to 1,000 graduates to remain in the UK longer than others if they have developed "world class innovative ideas or entrepreneurial skills". Successful applicants, who will be selected by their university, will be allowed to stay in the UK for 12 months, with the possibility of a further 12-month extension.

Bringing your family

Since 2010, international students on courses of six months or less have been forbidden to bring a partner or children into the UK, and the latest reforms extend this prohibition to all undergraduates except those who are government sponsored. Postgraduates will still be able to bring dependants to the UK and most universities can help to arrange facilities and accommodation for families as well as for single students. The family members you are allowed to bring with you are your husband or wife, civil partner (a same-sex relationship that has been formally registered in the UK or your home country) and dependent children.

If you are a national of any country outside the EEA, your family will be subject to immigration policy. Those who are eligible to bring dependants will need to show that they can support them financially, arrange appropriate accommodation, and that they will leave the UK when the student has finished his or her studies. Such family members will usually be able to study (children under 16 are required to attend full-time education), and any over the age of 16 should be able to work as long as you have permission to stay for over 12 months and are following a degree or Foundation degree course. You can find out more about getting entry clearance for your family at **www.ukcisa.org.uk/**.

Support from British universities

Support for international students is more comprehensive than in many countries, and begins long before you arrive in the UK. Many universities have advisers in other countries. Some will arrange to put you in touch with current students or graduates who can give you a first-hand account of what life is like at a particular university. Pre-departure receptions for students and their families, as well as meet-and-greet arrangements for newly arrived students, are common. You can also expect an orientation and induction programme in your first week, and many universities now have "buddying" systems where current students are assigned to new arrivals to help them find their way around, adjust to their new surroundings and make new friends. Each university also has a students' union that organises social, cultural and sporting events and clubs, including many specifically for international students. Both the university and the students' union are likely to have full-time staff whose job it is to look after the welfare of students from overseas.

International students also benefit from free medical and subsidised dental and optical care and treatment under the UK National Health Service, plus access to a professional counselling service and a university careers service.

At university, you will naturally encounter people from a wide range of cultures and walks of life. Getting involved in student societies, sport, voluntary work, and any of the wide range of social activities on offer will help you gain first-hand experience of British culture, and, if you need it, will help improve your command of the English language.

Useful websites

The British Council, with its dedicated Education UK site designed for those wishing to find out more about studying in the UK:
www.educationuk.org
The UK Council for International Student Affairs (UKCISA) provides a wide range of information on all aspects of studying in the UK:
www.ukcisa.org.uk
UCAS, for full details of courses available and an explanation of the application process:
www.ucas.com/how-it-all-works/international
For the latest information on entry and visa requirements, visit the UK Border Agency:
www.gov.uk/browse/visas-immigration/study-visas
Register of Sponsors for Tier 4 educational establishments:
www.gov.uk/government/publications/register-of-licensed-sponsors-students
For a general guide to Britain, available in many languages:
www.visitbritain.com

13 Applying to Oxbridge

Oxbridge (as Oxford and Cambridge are called collectively) not only dominates UK higher education; the two universities are recognised as among the best in the world, regularly featuring among the top five in global rankings. But that is not why they merit a separate chapter in this *Guide*.

The two ancient universities have different admissions arrangements to the rest of the higher education system. Although part of the UCAS network, they have different deadlines from other universities, you can only apply to one or the other, and selection is in the hands of the colleges rather than the university centrally. Most candidates apply to a specific college, although you can make an open application if you are happy to go anywhere.

There have been reforms to the admissions system at both universities in recent years, in order to make the process more user-friendly to those who do not have school or family experience to draw upon. In particular, the business of choosing a college has been intimidating for many prospective applicants. Candidates are now distributed around colleges more efficiently, regardless of the choices they make initially.

There is little to choose between the two universities in terms of entrance requirements, and a formidable number of successful applicants have the maximum possible grades. However, that does not mean that the talented student should be shy about applying: both have fewer applicants per place than many less prestigious universities, and admissions tutors are always looking to extend the range of schools and colleges from which they recruit. For those with a realistic chance of success, there is little to lose except the possibility of one wasted space out of five on the UCAS application.

Overall, there are about five applicants to every place at Oxford and Cambridge, but there are big differences between subjects and colleges. As the tables in this chapter show, competition is particularly fierce in subjects such as medicine and English, but those qualified to read geology or classics have a much better chance of success. The pattern is similar to that in other universities, although the high degree of selection (and self-selection) that precedes an Oxbridge application means that even in the less popular subjects the field of candidates is certain to be strong.

The two universities' power to intimidate prospective applicants is based partly on myth. Both have done their best to live down the *Brideshead Revisited* image, but many sixth-formers still fear that they would be out of their depth there, academically and socially. In fact, the state sector produces nearly 58 per cent of entrants to Oxford and Cambridge, and the dropout rate is lower than at almost any other university. The "champagne set" is still present and its activities are well publicised, but most students are hard-working high achievers with the same concerns as their counterparts on other campuses. A joint poll by the two universities' student newspapers showed that undergraduates were spending much of their time in the library or worrying about their employment prospects, and relatively little time on the river or even in the college bar.

State school applicants

Both universities and their student organisations have put a great deal of effort into trying to encourage applications from state schools, and many colleges have launched their own campaigns. Such has been the determination to convince state school pupils that they will get a fair crack of the whip that a new concern has grown up of possible bias against independent school pupils. In reality, however, the dispersed nature of Oxbridge admissions rules out any conspiracy. Some colleges set relatively low standard offers to encourage applicants from the state sector, who may reveal their potential at interview. Some admissions tutors may give the edge to well-qualified candidates from comprehensive schools over those from highly academic independent schools because they consider theirs the greater achievement in the circumstances. Others stick with tried and trusted sources of good students. The independent sector still enjoys a degree of success out of proportion to its share of the school population.

Choosing the right college

Simply in terms of winning a place at Oxford or Cambridge, choosing the right college is not quite as important as it used to be. Both universities have got better at assessing candidates' strengths and finding a suitable college for those who either make an open application or are not taken by their first-choice college.

Cambridge: The Tompkins Table 2014

College	2014	2013	College	2014	2013
Trinity	1	1	St John's	16	13
Pembroke	2	2	Sidney Sussex	17	19
Trinity Hall	3	3	Corpus Christi	18	16
Jesus	4	6	Fitzwilliam	19	20
Emmanuel	5	4	Robinson	20	22
Churchill	6	5	St Catharine's	21	9
Queens'	7	7	Newnham	22	23
Clare	8	11	Girton	23	21
Christ's	9	8	Homerton	24	26
Magdalene	10	15	Wolfson	25	25
Downing	11	12	Murray Edwards	26	24
Peterhouse	12	10	Hughes Hall	27	27
Selwyn	13	18	St Edmund's	28	29
King's	14	14	Lucy Cavendish	29	28
Gonville and Caius	15	17			

At Oxford, subject tutors from around the university put candidates into bands at the start of the selection process, using the results of admissions tests as well as exam results and references. Applicants are spread around the colleges for interview and may not be seen by their preferred college if the tutors think their chances of a place are better elsewhere. Almost a quarter of successful candidates are offered places by a college other than the one they applied to.

Cambridge relies on the "pool", which gives the most promising candidates a second chance if they were not offered a place at the college to which they applied. Those placed in the pool are invited back for a second round of interviews early in the new year. The system lowers the stakes for those who apply to the most selective colleges – in 2013 about 21 per cent of offers came via the pool. Cambridge still interviews more than 80 per cent of applicants, whereas the new system at Oxford has resulted in more immediate rejections in some subjects. In medicine, fewer than a third of Oxford's applicants are interviewed, while in biochemistry almost all were.

However, most Oxbridge applicants still apply direct to a particular college, not only to maximise their chances of getting in, but because that is where they will be living and socialising, as well as learning. Most colleges may look the same to the uninitiated, but there are important differences. Famously sporty colleges, for example, can be trying for those in search of peace and quiet.

Thorough research is needed to find the right place. Even within colleges, different admissions tutors may have different approaches, so personal contact is essential. The tables in this chapter give an idea of the relative academic strengths of the colleges, as well as the varying levels of competition for a place in different subjects. But only individual research will suggest where you will feel most at home. For example, women may favour one of the few remaining single-sex colleges (Murray Edwards, Newnham and Lucy Cavendish at Cambridge). Men have no such option.

Oxford: The Norrington Table 2014

College	2014	2013	College	2014	2013
Merton	1	4	Christ Church	16	17
St John's	2	3	St Hugh's	17	23
Worcester	3	11	Keble	18	27
New	4	1	Brasenose	19	8
Wadham	5	19	Balliol	20	10
Jesus	6	14	St Hilda's	21	20
Hertford	7	18	St Peter's	22	22
Harris Manchester	8	5	Oriel	23	9
Magdalen	9	6	University	24	25
Lincoln	10	7	Mansfield	25	15
Trinity	11	2	Lady Margaret Hall	26	30
St Catherine's	12	21	Somerville	27	29
St Anne's	13	12	St Edmund Hall	28	16
Corpus Christi	14	24	Queen's	29	26
Exeter	15	28	Pembroke	30	13

Oxford applications and acceptances by course

Arts	Applications		Acceptances		Acceptances to Applications %	
	2013	2012	2013	2012	2013	2012
Ancient and Modern History	81	74	14	13	17.3	17.6
Archaeology and Anthropology	101	106	20	23	19.8	21.7
Classical Archaeology and Ancient History	67	85	19	17	28.4	20
Classics	293	330	123	127	42	38.5
Classics and English	30	29	8	5	26.7	17.2
Classics and Modern Languages	23	33	8	7	34.8	21.2
Computer Science and Philosophy	23	26	9	8	29	30.8
Economics and Management	1,192	1,107	84	94	7	8.5
English	1,142	1,268	240	245	21	19.3
English and Modern Languages	117	149	18	17	15.4	11.4
European and Middle Eastern Languages	28	36	8	6	28.6	16.7
Fine Art	189	174	28	21	14.8	12.1
Geography	371	416	77	85	20.8	20.4
History	1,029	1,012	246	227	23.9	22.4
History and Economics	99	87	13	13	13.1	14.9
History and English	89	86	7	10	7.9	11.6
History and Modern Languages	87	81	16	17	18.4	21
History and Politics	279	303	39	46	14	15.2
History of Art	137	130	12	14	8.8	10.8
Law	1,302	1,226	196	187	15.1	15.3
Law with Law Studies in Europe	317	301	31	29	9.8	9.6
Mathematics and Philosophy	90	92	16	19	17.8	20.7
Modern Languages	573	567	189	179	33	31.6
Modern Languages and Linguistics	72	77	27	25	37.5	32.5
Music	221	218	70	76	31.7	34.9
Oriental Studies	168	159	48	41	28.6	25.8
Philosophy and Modern Languages	51	64	13	18	25.5	28.1
Philosophy and Theology	118	92	28	24	23.7	26.1
Physics and Philosophy	146	123	16	18	11	14.6
Philosophy, Politics and Economics (PPE)	1,640	1,726	232	260	14.1	15.1
Theology	91	105	28	40	30.8	38.1
Theology and Oriental Studies	4	8	1	1	25	12.5
Total Arts	**10,178**	**10,290**	**1,884**	**1,912**	**18.5**	**18.6**

The findings in the Tompkins Table (see page 270) are not officially endorsed by Cambridge University itself. However, since 2007 we have been able to publish the "official" Norrington Table from Oxford. Sanctioned or not, both tables give an indication of where the academic powerhouses lie – information which can be as useful to those trying to avoid them as to those seeking the ultimate challenge. Although there can be a great deal of movement year by year, both tables tend to be dominated by the rich, old foundations. Both tables are

Oxford applications and acceptances by course cont

Sciences	Applications		Acceptances		Acceptances to Applications %	
	2013	2012	2013	2012	2013	2012
Biochemistry	399	386	90	101	22.6	26.2
Biological Sciences	428	390	111	108	25.9	27.7
Biomedical Sciences	193	213	33	33	17.1	15.5
Chemistry	638	546	180	181	28.2	33.2
Computer Science	147	139	23	25	15.6	18
Earth Sciences (Geology)	116	154	34	34	29.3	22.1
Engineering Science	720	666	157	156	21.8	23.4
Engineering, Economics and Management	100	106	10	9	10	8.5
Experimental Psychology	212	327	50	64	23.6	19.6
Human Sciences	155	135	31	28	20	20.7
Materials Science (including MEM)	79	133	33	36	41.8	27.1
Mathematics	917	950	161	172	17.6	18.1
Mathematics and Computer Science	119	117	28	24	23.5	20.5
Mathematics and Statistics	172	160	22	13	12.8	8.1
Medicine	1,471	1,511	149	155	10.1	10.3
Physics	1,011	916	173	167	17.1	18.2
Psychology and Philosophy	161	102	29	15	18	14.7
Total Sciences	**7,038**	**6,951**	**1,314**	**1,321**	**18.7**	**19**
Total Arts and Sciences	**17,216**	**17,241**	**3,198**	**3,233**	**18.6**	**18.8**

Note: the dates refer to the year in which the acceptances were made

compiled from the degree results of final-year undergraduates. A first is worth five points; a 2:1, four; a 2:2, three; a third, one point. The total is divided by the number of candidates to produce each college's average.

In both universities, teaching for most students is based in the colleges. In practice, however, in the sciences this arrangement holds good only for the first year. One-to-one tutorials, which are Oxbridge's traditional strength for undergraduates, are by no means universal. Teaching groups remain much smaller than in most universities, and the tutor remains an inspiration for many students.

The applications procedure
Both universities have set a UCAS deadline of 15 October 2014 for entry in 2015. You may also need to take a written test and submit examples of your work – the exact requirements vary depending on the course you select, so check this carefully. See pages 20–21 for details of assessment tests, which are now being used for an increasing number of subjects. In addition, once Cambridge receives your UCAS form, you will be asked to complete an online Supplementary Application Questionnaire (SAQ). The deadline for this will be 22 October 2014 in most cases. For international applications to Cambridge you must also submit a Cambridge Online Preliminary Application (COPA), by 20 September or 15 October 2014;

Cambridge applications and acceptances by course

	Applications		Acceptances		Acceptances to Applications %	
Arts, Humanities and Social Sciences	**2013**	**2012**	**2013**	**2012**	**2013**	**2012**
Anglo-Saxon, Norse and Celtic	57	57	30	25	52.6	43.9
Archaeology and Anthropology	–	140	–	56	–	40.9
Architecture	395	456	41	45	10.4	9.9
Asian and Middle Eastern Studies	113	135	40	41	35.4	30.4
Classics	155	153	70	71	45.2	46.4
Classics (4 years)	54	40	18	14	33.3	35.0
Economics	1,206	1,328	156	171	12.9	12.9
Education	95	75	36	29	37.9	38.7
English	718	743	199	210	27.7	28.3
Geography	309	262	97	101	31.4	38.5
History	637	591	190	199	29.8	33.7
History of Art	77	104	22	26	28.6	25.0
Human, Social and Political Sciences	877	–	198	–	22.6	–
Land Economy	215	228	50	48	23.3	21.1
Law	933	1,021	212	215	22.7	21.1
Linguistics	109	91	30	34	27.5	37.4
Modern and Medieval Languages	388	476	168	178	43.3	37.4
Music	146	142	59	53	40.4	37.3
Philosophy	258	245	53	48	20.5	19.6
Politics, Psychology and Sociology	–	669	–	104	–	15.5
Theology and Religious Studies	110	105	50	43	45.5	41.0
Total Arts, Humanities and Social Sciences	**6,852**	**7,061**	**1,719**	**1,725**	**25.1**	**24.4**
Science and Technology	**2013**	**2012**	**2013**	**2012**	**2013**	**2012**
Computer Science	521	394	86	84	16.5	21.3
Engineering	1,927	1,862	294	331	15.3	17.8
Mathematics	1,360	1,382	234	253	17.2	18.3
Medical Sciences	1,867	1,897	260	302	16.9	12.8
Natural Sciences	2,860	2,670	619	675	21.6	25.3
Psychological and Behavioural Sciences	382	–	64	–	16.8	–
Veterinary Medicine	416	435	74	66	17.8	15.2
Total Science and Technology	**9,333**	**8,640**	**1,652**	**1,712**	**17.7**	**19.8**
Total	**16,185**	**15,701**	**3,371**	**3,437**	**20.8**	**21.9**

Note: the dates refer to the year in which the acceptances were made.
Mathematics includes mathematics and mathematics with physics. Medical sciences includes medicine and the graduate course in medicine.
The Tripos courses in chemical engineering, management studies and manufacturing engineering can be taken only after Part 1 in another subject. Applications and acceptances for these courses are recorded under the first year subjects taken by the applicants involved.

check the Cambridge website for full details.

You may apply to either Oxford or Cambridge (but not both) in the same admissions year, unless you are seeking an Organ award at both universities. Interviews take place in December for those short-listed (for international applicants, Cambridge hold some interviews overseas while Oxford holds some interviews over the internet, though medicine interviewees must come to Oxford). Applicants to Oxford will receive either a conditional offer or a rejection by Christmas, while in Cambridge the news arrives early in the new year.

For more information about the application process and preparation for interviews, visit **www.study.cam.ac.uk/undergraduate** and **www.ox.ac.uk/admissions/undergraduate**.

Oxford College Profiles

Balliol

Oxford OX1 3BJ   01865 277777   www.balliol.ox.ac.uk

Undergraduates: 382   Postgraduates: 305   undergrad.admissions@balliol.ox.ac.uk

Famous as the *alma mater* of many prominent post-war politicians, Balliol has maintained a strong presence in university life and is usually well represented in the Union and most other societies. Academic standards are formidably high, as might be expected in the college of Wyclif and Adam Smith, and usually falls in the top ten of the Norrington Table. Library facilities are good and include the Taylor law library. Balliol began admitting overseas students in the 19th century and has cultivated an attractively cosmopolitan atmosphere. Most undergraduates are offered guaranteed accommodation in college for their first and final years. Graduate students are usually lodged in the Graduate Centre at Holywell Manor, ten minutes' walk from the main site. Balliol is strong in rugby, football and rowing and has a thriving music and drama scene. "Doug's lunches", organised by the Dean, bring a steady stream of interesting speakers to Balliol throughout the term. Hall food is good quality and the JCR has its own cafeteria.

Brasenose

Oxford OX1 4AJ   01865 277510 (admissions)   www.bnc.ox.ac.uk

Undergraduates: 370   Postgraduates: 192   admissions@bnc.ox.ac.uk

Brasenose may not be the most famous Oxford college, but it makes up for its discreet image with an advantageous city-centre position, nestled beside the stunning Radcliffe Camera. The *alma mater* of David Cameron, Brasenose was one of the first colleges to admit women in the 1970s, and now usually has a near-even split within each year. BNC, as the college is often known, has a strong rugby reputation, having won the rugby cuppers 14 times over the years. Named after the door knocker on the 13th-century Brasenose Hall, the college has a pleasant, intimate ambience which most find conducive to study. Law, PPE, medicine and modern history are traditional strengths, and competition for places in these subjects is intense. The library is open 24 hours a day and there is a separate law library. Sporting standards are as high as at many much larger colleges and BNC's rowing club is one of the oldest in the university. The college puts on a successful annual Arts Week. The annexe at Frewin Court means nearly all undergraduates can live in, and many postgraduates can also live in the St Cross Building. College rooms vary in quality but are priced accordingly.

Christl Church

Oxford OX1 1DP   01865 276181 (admissions)   www.chch.ox.ac.uk
Undergraduates: 423   Postgraduates: 164   admissions@chch.ox.ac.uk

The college, founded by Cardinal Wolsey in 1525, boasts the largest quad in Oxford, complete with an ornamental pond full of Japanese koi carp, donated by the Empress of Japan. Around half of offers tend to be made to state school pupils, which leaves Christ Church among the highest proportion of private school students. However, the student-run Ambassadors scheme set up in September 2013 is helping the college shake its public school image and endeavours to improve access opportunities. Despite the college usually ranking in the top ten of the Norrington Table, academic pressure is relatively relaxed. The magnificent 18th-century library is one of the best in Oxford and is supplemented by a separate law library. Christ Church has its own art gallery, which holds over 2,000 works of mainly Italian Renaissance art. Recent sporting strengths are found in netball and football, and the river is close by for the aspiring oarsman. Accommodation for all three years is rated by college undergraduates as excellent and includes flats off Iffley Road as well as a number of beautifully panelled shared sets (double rooms) in college. Christ Church food is highly regarded and a three-course dinner (served daily) is exceptionally cheap. The college bar has recently been refurbished. The chapel is also the cathedral of the Diocese of Oxford – England's smallest medieval cathedral. The constant stream of tourists is mildly disruptive to collegiate life.

Corpus Christi

Oxford OX1 4JF   01865 276693 (admissions)   www.ccc.ox.ac.uk
Undergraduates: 249   Postgraduates: 93   admissions.office@ccc.ox.ac.uk

Corpus, one of Oxford's smallest colleges, is naturally overshadowed by its Goliath-like neighbour, Christ Church, but makes the most of its intimate, friendly atmosphere and exquisite beauty. Although the college has only around 350 students including postgraduates, it has an admirable library open 24 hours a day. Academic expectations are high and English, Classics, PPE and medicine are especially well-established. Corpus is able to offer accommodation to all its undergraduates, one of its many attractions to those seeking a smaller community in Oxford. Rooms in the new, off-site Lampl building are modern and en suite. Many of the older rooms are due to be refurbished from early 2015. The college is also one of the most generous with bursaries, giving travel, book and vacation grants at an almost unparalleled level across the university. Scholars are particularly well rewarded. The MBI Al-Jaber Auditorium is a large, modern and pleasant space built into a bastion of the medieval city wall and is used for music and drama, as well as for parties, art exhibitions, seminars and lectures. Corpus's drama company, the Owlets, is highly regarded in Oxford. The college sports grounds are shared with University College, but sporting success is relatively limited.

Exeter

Oxford OX1 3DP   01865 279648 (academic secretary)   www.exeter.ox.ac.uk
Undergraduates: 333   Postgraduates: 203   admissions@exeter.ox.ac.uk

Exeter is the fourth oldest college in the university and was founded in 1314 by Walter de Stapeldon, Bishop of Exeter. *Alma mater* to J.R.R. Tolkien, Alan Bennett and Philip Pullman, Exeter is full of history. Nestling between the High Street and Broad Street, it could hardly be more central. Most undergraduates are guaranteed three years of college accommodation, although many second year students currently live out. Graduate students are housed off-site on the Exeter House campus. Work has begun on a new 90-room quad on the former site of Ruskin College, on the edge of the city centre. The Rector, Frances Cairncross, the former managing editor of *The Economist,* has created a new dynamic at the college, with regular, high-profile speaker events and the only college careers service. Among an array of societies, the John Ford Society exists to fund dramatic ventures; the Fortescue Society to talk about the law; the PPE Society to bring in high-profile speakers. The College puts something back into the local community through its own Vacation project titled EXVAC, a student-run scheme that raises funds through sponsorship and takes children from disadvantaged backgrounds on holiday during the Easter vacation.

Harris Manchester

Oxford OX1 3TD   01865 271009 (admissions tutor)   www.hmc.ox.ac.uk

Undergraduates: 85   Postgraduates: 91   enquiries@hmc.ox.ac.uk

Founded in Manchester in 1786 to provide education for non-Anglican students, Harris Manchester finally settled in Oxford in 1889 after spells in both York and London. A full university college since 1996, its central location with fine buildings and grounds in Holywell Street is very convenient for the Bodleian, although the college itself does have an excellent library. Harris Manchester admits only mature students to read for both undergraduate and graduate degrees, predominantly in the arts. All students must be 21 or older, though the average age has come down slightly in recent years. There are also groups of visiting students from American universities and students training for the ministry. Most members live in and all meals are provided – indeed the college encourages its members to dine regularly in hall. Food is among the finest in Oxford. The college has few sporting facilities (a croquet lawn and a college punt), but members can use two central Oxford gyms without charge and can play sport for other college or university teams. Other outlets include the college Drama Society and the chapel, a focal point for many students.

Hertford

Oxford OX1 3BW   01865 279404 (admissions)   www.hertford.ox.ac.uk

Undergraduates: 400   Postgraduates: 188   admissions@hertford.ox.ac.uk

Though tracing its roots to the 13th century, Hertford is determinedly modern. It was one of the first colleges to admit women (in 1975). Hertford also helped set the trend towards offers of places conditional on A levels, which paved the way for the abolition of the entrance examination (now being replaced by subject specific aptitude tests). It is popular with state school applicants, and is one of the least stuffy colleges, with a reputation for attracting students from a broad range of backgrounds. The college lacks the grandeur of Magdalen, of which it was once an annex, but has its own architectural trademark in the Bridge of Sighs. It is also close to the History Faculty library (Hertford's neighbour) and the Bodleian library. Its proximity to the King's Arms and the Turf Tavern, two of Oxford's most popular pubs, bolsters the already vibrant social scene. Accommodation has improved, thanks in part to the Abingdon House and Warnock House complex close to the Thames near Folly Bridge, and the college can now lodge all of its undergraduates at any one time, often at subsidised rates, albeit in disparate parts of the city.

Jesus

Oxford OX1 3DW   01865 279721 (admissions)   www.jesus.ox.ac.uk
Undergraduates: 339   Postgraduates: 182   admissions.officer@jesus.ox.ac.uk

Jesus, the only Oxford college to be founded in the reign of Elizabeth I, suffers from something of an unfair reputation for insularity. Its students, whose predecessors include T.E. Lawrence and Harold Wilson, describe it as "friendly but gossipy" and shrug off the legend that all its undergraduates are Welsh. Close to most of Oxford's main facilities, Jesus has three compact quads, the second of which is especially enticing in the summer. The college's JCR is well-equipped. Sporting success has tailed off in recent years, but the college has a symphony orchestra shared with St Peter's. Accommodation is almost universally excellent and relatively inexpensive. Self-catering flats in north and east Oxford have enabled every graduate to live in throughout his or her Oxford career. The range of accommodation available to undergraduates is similarly good and is available for the full length of any course. The new Ship Street Centre contains 33 en-suite rooms for first-year students and a lecture theatre. The college's Cowley Road development, next to the college's sports ground, was described by the students' union as "some of the plushest student housing in Oxford".

Keble

Oxford OX1 3PG   01865 272711 (admissions)   www.keble.ox.ac.uk
Undergraduates: 431   Postgraduates: 226   college.office@keble.ox.ac.uk

Keble is one of Oxford's most distinct colleges, built of brick in unmistakably extravagant Victorian Gothic style. Keble was founded in 1870 with the intention of making Oxford education more accessible, and the college remains proud of "the legacy of a social conscience". With around 450 undergraduates, Keble is one of the biggest colleges in Oxford, and with guaranteed college accommodation for most undergraduates for three years, its vibrant community spirit provides Keble students with a coveted social life. Graduates are housed in the Acland site on Banbury Road, a two-minute walk from the main college. It is strong in the sciences, where it benefits from easy access to the Science Area, the Radcliffe Science Library and the Mathematical Institute. The college's sporting record remains exemplary, with the rugby and netball teams regularly dominating university competitions in addition to a high proportion of students playing university-level sport. Sport does by no means dominate Keble undergraduate life, however, with its thriving music and drama societies, which make use of the modern O'Reily Theatre. The college hall, where students wishing to dine must wear gowns six nights a week, is one of the most impressive in the university.

Lady Margaret Hall

Oxford OX2 6QA   · 01865 274310 (admissions)   www.lmh.ox.ac.uk
Undergraduates: 405   Postgraduates: 184   admissions@lmh.ox.ac.uk

Lady Margaret Hall, Oxford's first college for women, has been co-educational since 1978 and now enjoys an equal gender balance. For many students, LMH's comparative isolation – the college is three-quarters of a mile north of the city centre – is a real advantage, ensuring a clear distinction between college life and university activities, and a refuge from tourists. For others it means a long journey to central library facilities, and an even longer journey to the university sports facilities on Iffley Road, shared with Trinity College. Although the neo-Georgian architecture is not to everyone's taste, the college's beautiful gardens back onto the Cherwell River, allowing LMH to have its own punt house and 12 acres of land. The construction of a front courtyard, with new teaching facilities and postgraduate accommodation, should be completed in late 2015. Accommodation is guaranteed for first, second and third years since the opening of the Pipe Partridge building, which also houses a new JCR, dining hall and lecture theatre. There are tennis courts on site and it has become a leading rowing college. It has long been one of Oxford's centres for student drama.

Lincoln

Oxford OX1 3DR   01865 279836 (admissions)   www.lincoln.ox.ac.uk
Undergraduates: 299   Postgraduates: 327   admissions@lincoln.ox.ac.uk

Small, central Lincoln cultivates a lower profile than many other colleges with comparable assets. The college's 15th-century buildings and beautiful library – a converted Queen Anne church – combine to produce a delightful environment in which to spend three years. The college's relaxed atmosphere is justly celebrated and city-centre accommodation is provided by the college for all undergraduates throughout their careers. Graduate students have their own centre a few minutes' walk away in Bear Lane and at the EPA Science Centre close to the university science area. Finalists live in a recently refurbished complex on Museum Road, by Keble and the University Parks. Lincoln's small size and self-sufficiency have led to the college being accused of insularity. Lincoln's food is outstanding, among the best in the university. The college admires its chef so much that it commissioned a portrait of him for the hall. Sporting achievement is impressive for a college of this size, but tends to fall short of larger colleges that have more players to choose from.

Magdalen

Oxford OX1 4AU   01865 276063 (admissions)   www.magd.ox.ac.uk
Undergraduates: 411   Postgraduates: 159   admissions@magd.ox.ac.uk

Perhaps the most beautiful Oxbridge college, Magdalen is known around the world for its tower, its deer park and its May morning celebrations. The college has shaken off its public school image to become a truly cosmopolitan place, with a large intake from overseas and one of the highest proportion of state school pupils. The college is consistently high in the Norrington Table. Library facilities are excellent, especially in history and law. First-year students are accommodated in the Waynflete Building and are allocated rooms in subsequent years by ballot. Undergraduates can be housed in college for the full length of their course. Rents are not cheap compared to other colleges, but there is always financial help on offer. Magdalen is also conveniently placed between the city centre and east Oxford, where there is a plethora of pubs and restaurants and a lively music scene. The college bar is one of the best in Oxford and backs out onto a riverside terrace from which the students can go punting. Magdalen is well suited to creative individuals with a successful film society, drama society and choir. In recent years the college has become particularly strong at rowing.

Mansfield

Oxford OX1 3TF   01865 270920 (admissions)   www.mansfield.ox.ac.uk
Undergraduates: 211   Postgraduates: 97   admissions@mansfield.ox.ac.uk

An Oxford college since 1995, Mansfield's attractive site is fairly central, close to the libraries and the University Parks. With just over 200 undergraduates, the community is close-knit. The less intimidating atmosphere of Mansfield is, perhaps helped by its strong representation of state-school students; among the highest ratio in the university. First and third years live in college accommodation, either on-site or in an annex in east Oxford, while second-years have to find their own accommodation. Fundraising efforts are underway to build additional accommodation on-site to house all undergraduates. The library is open 24 hours and the JCR is among the largest of any college. Sports grounds are shared with Merton and the croquet lawn is one of the best in Oxford. In recent years the college has produced many student journalists and contributes many performers to theatre and music productions. The American Institute backs onto its gardens, evidence of the strong links between Mansfield and the USA, which is reflected by some 35 visiting students annually. It also spearheads the Oxford FE Initiative, which encourages applications to the university from further education colleges.

Merton

Oxford OX1 4JD   01865 276299 (admissions)   www.merton.ox.ac.uk
Undergraduates: 299   Postgraduates: 281   admissions@admin.merton.ox.ac.uk

Founded in 1264 by Walter de Merton, Bishop of Rochester and Chancellor of England, Merton is one of Oxford's oldest and most prestigious colleges. Quiet and beautiful, with the oldest quad in the university, Merton has high academic expectations of its undergraduates, normally reflected in its position at or near the top of the Norrington Table. The medieval library is the envy of many other colleges. Owing to the college's wealth, accommodation is some of the cheapest in the university, of a good standard and offered to students for all three years. Merton's food is well priced and among the best in the university; formal Hall is served six times a week at a low price. Merton's many diversions include the Merton Floats, its dramatic society, the Neave Society (politics), an excellent Christmas Ball and the peculiar Time Ceremony, which was set up in the seventies as a spoof tradition to "maintain the integrity of the space-time continuum during the transition from British Summer Time to GMT". Sports facilities are excellent, although participation tends to be more important than the final score.

New College

Oxford OX1 3BN   01865 279512 (admissions)   www.new.ox.ac.uk
Undergraduates: 441   Postgraduates: 291   admissions@new.ox.ac.uk

New College is actually rather old (founded in 1379 by William of Wykeham), large and much more relaxed than most expect when first confronting its daunting facade. It is a bustling place, as proud of its excellent music and its bar as of its academic prestige. The college was fourth in the Norrington Table in 2014, having topped it the previous year. Traditionally poor at attracting state-school students, the college has been making particular efforts to change this, inviting applications from schools that have never sent candidates to Oxford. All first, second and fourth-year students can live in college and almost all of the third-years who want to live in usually can. The college's library facilities are impressive. The sports ground is nearby and includes good tennis courts. Women's sport is particularly strong, especially on the river. A sports complex, named after Brian Johnston, opened in 1997, at St Cross Road . The sheer beauty of New College remains one of its principal assets and the college gardens are a memorable sight in the summer, especially the other-worldly Mound in the heart of the college. The Commemoration Ball, held every three years, is a highlight of Oxford's social calendar.

Oriel

Oxford OX1 4EW   01865 276522 (admissions)   www.oriel.ox.ac.uk

Undergraduates: 305   Postgraduates: 176   admissions@oriel.ox.ac.uk

In spite of its reputation as a rower's paradise, Oriel is a friendly, centrally located college with a strong sense of identity. The college is traditionally described as having "a strong crew spirit" reflecting its traditions on the river, and the Oriel crew regained their position as Head of the River in 2014. Academically, it tends to inhabit the middle reaches of the Norrington Table. The well-stocked library is open 24 hours a day. Oriel's sporting reputation is certainly deserved and sports other than rowing are well catered for with an impressive sports ground, squash courts and two gyms a short cycle ride away from the city centre. Accommodation is of variable quality, but Oriel can provide rooms for the duration of the course – be it three years or four – for those students who require them. Extensive accommodation is provided one mile away off the Cowley Road and at the Island Site on Oriel Street. The college also offers a lively drama society, the Oriel Lions, who put on a Shakespearian production each summer in the front quad. Eight choral scholarships and two organ scholarships underpin the college's successful chapel choir, one of the best mixed choirs in Oxford.

Pembroke

Oxford OX1 1DW   01865 276412 (admissions)   www.pmb.ox.ac.uk

Undergraduates: 366   Postgraduates: 190   admissions@pmb.ox.ac.uk

Tucked away off St Aldate's, Pembroke is a welcoming and inclusive community with an improving state-school intake, thanks to its access schemes. The college is historically poor financially, but by no means shy when awarding undergraduate scholarships and prizes. It has Fellows and lecturers in almost all the major university subjects. Pembroke is now able to accommodate all undergraduates after a new extension opened in October 2012, and the Sir Geoffrey Arthur building on the river, ten minutes' walk from the college, offers excellent facilities; in addition to 100 student rooms there is a concert room, computer room and a multi-gym. College food is among the most expensive in Oxford and students have to pre-pay for a minimum of six dinners per week, which discourages Pembroke students from eating elsewhere; good for maintaining Pembroke's renowned community feel but poor for establishing inter-college relationships. Rowing is strong, with Pembroke men's crew positioned second on the river, behind Oriel, and the women's crew fourth in their division. Squash and tennis courts are available at the nearby sports ground.

Queen's

Oxford OX1 4AW   01865 279161   www.queens.ox.ac.uk

Undergraduates: 342   Postgraduates: 122   admissions@queens.ox.ac.uk

Despite being one of the most striking sights of the High Street, Queen's is one of Oxford's least dynamic colleges. Its academic record is average, usually occupying the lower end of the Norrington Table. Modern languages, chemistry and mathematics are reckoned among the strongest subjects. The library is as beautiful as it is well stocked. All students are offered accommodation, first years being housed in modernist annexes in east Oxford, and the college has converted a large number of rooms into en-suite facilities. Queen's can be insular and is largely apolitical, but has a strong college enthusiasm for sport, particularly rugby and netball. The college also has an excellent mixed choir, an orchestra and puts on a summer musical in the gardens. The college's beer cellar is one of the most popular in the university and the JCR facilities are also better than average. An annual dinner commemorates a student who is said to have fended off a bear by thrusting a volume of Aristotle into its mouth. Postgraduates are accommodated in St Aldate's House, a modern building close to the centre of town.

St Anne's

Oxford OX2 6HS   01865 274840 (admissions)   www.st-annes.ox.ac.uk

Undergraduates: 430   Postgraduates: 295   enquiries@st-annes.ox.ac.uk

Architecturally uninspiring (a Victorian row with concrete "stack-a-studies" dropped into their back gardens), St Anne's makes up in community spirit what it lacks in awesome grandeur. One of the largest colleges, it has an above average proportion of state-school students. A women's college until 1979, it has an excellent library, which is now open 24 hours and is very well-stocked; it is rich in law, Chinese and medieval history texts. The college has recently had a strong presence in the university journalism scene, and its rugby team won the most recent cuppers competition. Students also enjoy close proximity to the beautiful University Parks. Accommodation is guaranteed to all undergraduates, and the college also operates an equalisation scheme which gives grants to students wishing to live out. The college is situated to the north of the city centre. Three new accommodation blocks contain 150 student rooms, including four for disabled students, while the older rooms have been refurbished. Half of all rooms are en suite.

St Catherine's

Oxford OX1 3UJ   01865 271703 (admissions)   www.stcatz.ox.ac.uk

Undergraduates: 487   Postgraduates: 298   admissions@stcatz.ox.ac.uk

Arne Jacobsen's modernist design for "Catz", one of Oxford's youngest and largest undergraduate colleges, has attracted much attention as the most striking contrast in the university to the lofty spires of Magdalen and New College. Close to the law, English and social science faculties, the university science area and the pleasantly rural Holywell Great Meadow, St Catherine's is a lot closer to the city centre than it feels. The well-liked Wolfson library is open till midnight on most days. Rooms are small but tend to be warmer than in other, more venerable, colleges, and are now available on site for first, second and third years. There is an excellent theatre, as well as an on-site punt house, gym and squash courts. The college is host to the Cameron Mackintosh Chair of Contemporary Theatre, whose incumbents have included Meera Syal, Kevin Spacey, Arthur Miller and Sir Ian McKellen. St Catherine's has one of the best JCR facilities in Oxford.

St Edmund Hall

Oxford OX1 4AR   01865 279011 (admissions)   www.seh.ox.ac.uk

Undergraduates: 427   Postgraduates: 248   admissions@seh.ox.ac.uk

St Edmund Hall – "Teddy Hall" – has one of Oxford's smallest college sites but also one of its most populous. The college offers students the chance to live in its medieval quads right in the heart of the city. With the male/female ratio nearly equal, the college is shedding its image as a home for "hearties", and the authorities have gone out of their way to tone down younger members' rowdier excesses. Nonetheless, the sporting culture is still vigorous, winning the mixed Lacrosse cuppers in 2014 and coming runner-up to St Anne's in the rugby cuppers. Academically, Teddy Hall tends to yo-yo between the middle and the bottom of the Norrington Table. It hosts three annual prizes for journalism, including a £500 award for a student from St Edmund Hall. College accommodation is reasonable and can be offered for three years, either on the main site or in three annexes, one near the University Parks, and two on Iffley Road, where many of the rooms have private bathrooms.

St Hilda's

Oxford OX4 1DY   01865 286620 (admissions)   www.st-hildas.ox.ac.uk

Undergraduates: 406   Postgraduates: 163   college.office@st-hildas.ox.ac.uk

October 2008 marked a milestone for St Hilda's and the university as a whole, as the college welcomed its first mixed sex intake. Although the college, founded in 1893, lasted more than 100 years as an all-female institution, the governing body voted in 2006 to admit men. There are now equal numbers of males and females. The college has long languished at the lower end of the Norrington Table. Like the other originally female colleges, St Hilda's boasts an impressive library, which is particularly well-stocked for English. The college has beautiful riverside gardens, allowing students to go punting from the college site, and is close to the lively social scene in multi-ethnic east Oxford. Accommodation is guaranteed to first years and finalists and the common room and student-run bar have been renovated and enlarged with improved disabled access. Many of the rooms offer some of the best river views in Oxford, with the city's spires as a backdrop. The standard of food is high, yet all students living on-site have access to kitchens. St Hilda's commitment to music is particularly strong and its facilities world class.

St Hugh's

Oxford OX2 6LE   01865 274910 (admissions)   www.st-hughs.ox.ac.uk

Undergraduates: 443   Postgraduates: 290   admissions@st-hughs.ox.ac.uk

One of the lesser-known colleges, St Hugh's was criticised by students in 1986 when it began admitting men. There is now an equal male/female ratio, a better balance than at most Oxford colleges. Like Lady Margaret Hall, St Hugh's picturesque setting is a bicycle ride from the city centre. It is an ideal college for those seeking a place to live and study away from the madding crowd, and is well liked for its pleasantly bohemian atmosphere and beautiful gardens. Academic pressure remains comparatively low. St Hugh's guarantees accommodation to undergraduates for all three years, although the standard of rooms is variable. Sport, particularly football, is taken quite seriously. As the college enjoys extensive grounds compared to most colleges, there is space for a croquet lawn and tennis courts. Following a £10-million donation from a Hong Kong businessman, the Dickson Poon building for the university's China Centre opened in September 2014 with the aim of bringing together academics who share interests related to China. The building also provides 63 en-suite student bedrooms, a new lecture theatre, a 200 seat dining area, and a dedicated library that will provide a permanent home for books from the Bodleian Library's China Collection.

St John's

Oxford OX1 3JP   01865 277317 (admissions)   www.sjc.ox.ac.uk

Undergraduates: 393   Postgraduates: 223   admissions@sjc.ox.ac.uk

St John's is one of Oxford's powerhouses, excelling in almost every field and boasting arguably the most beautiful gardens in the university. Founded in 1555 by a London merchant, it is Oxford's wealthiest college, and makes the most of its resources by providing guaranteed college accommodation at a subsidised rate for all its undergraduates in addition to generous annual book grants and prizes. Academic standards are high, with English, chemistry and history among the traditional strengths, and all students benefit from the impressive library. The college is usually challenging for the top spot in the Norrington Table. However, the emphasis on academia tends to limit the St John's social scene despite its close proximity to some of Oxford's best-known pubs: the Eagle and Child and the Lamb and Flag. St John's has a strong sporting tradition with a particular strength in women's rowing; the first VIII claiming the Head of the River title in 2013 and narrowly missing out to Wadham in 2014. The college is also well represented in the Oxford Union. As befits such an all-round strong college, entry is fiercely competitive.

St Peter's

Oxford OX1 2DL   01865 278863 (admissions)   www.spc.ox.ac.uk
Undergraduates: 344   Postgraduates: 149   admissions@spc.ox.ac.uk

Opened as St Peter's Hall in 1929, St Peter's has been an Oxford college since 1961. Its medieval, Georgian and 19th-century buildings are in the city centre and close to most of Oxford's main facilities. Though still young, St Peter's is well-represented in university life and has pockets of academic excellence, despite being towards the bottom of the Norrington Table; history tutoring is particularly good. Accommodation is offered to students in their first and third years, varying from traditional rooms in college to new purpose-built rooms a few minutes' walk away. The college's facilities are impressive, including one of the university's best JCRs and a popular student bar. The college has a proud sporting heritage, being particularly strong at rugby and rowing. St Peter's is known as one of Oxford's most vibrant colleges socially. It is strong in acting, journalism and music.

Somerville

Oxford OX2 6HD   01865 270619 (admissions)   www.some.ox.ac.uk
Undergraduates: 402   Postgraduates: 131   secretariat@some.ox.ac.uk

Named after Mary Somerville, one of the best-known female scientists of the nineteenth century, Somerville college only admitted females until 1994, when it went co-educational. The male/female ratio is now equal. The college's atmosphere appears to have survived the momentous change. The college, *alma mater* to chemistry graduate Margaret Thatcher, has an average state-school representation. Accommodation, including 30 small flats, is of a reasonable standard, and was supplemented recently by a 68-room building, so that all first, third and fourth-year students can live in, as well as around three-quarters of second-years. There are kitchens in all college buildings, but hall food is towards the cheaper end of the university. Sport is strong at Somerville and the women's rowing eight usually finishes near the head of the river. The college's sports facilities include football, rugby, hockey and cricket pitches and tennis courts and are shared with Wadham and St Hugh's. The library is open 24 hours a day and is the second largest college library as well as one of the most beautiful in Oxford. The college also has an active music society and a strong drama presence.

Trinity

Oxford OX1 3BH   01865 279860 (admissions)   www.trinity.ox.ac.uk
Undergraduates: 297   Postgraduates: 114   admissions@trinity.ox.ac.uk

Architecturally impressive and boasting beautiful lawns (which you can actually walk on), Trinity is one of Oxford's least populous colleges, admitting some 80 undergraduates each year. It is ideally located, beside the Bodleian, Blackwell's bookshop and the White Horse pub, a short stroll from the University Parks and the town centre. Trinity has shaken off its reputation for apathy, and whilst members are active in all walks of university life, the college has its own debating and drama societies, as well as sharing a fierce rivalry with neighbouring Balliol. Usually, all undergraduates are given a room on the main site in their first and second years, with the majority of third and fourth years living in a purpose-built block a mile and a half north of the main site. Students rate the food highly for both its quality and price. Trinity's Commemoration Ball, held once every three years, has one of the biggest budgets in Oxford and is a popular event.

University

Oxford OX1 4BH   01865 276959 (admissions)   www.univ.ox.ac.uk
Undergraduates: 374   Postgraduates: 208   admissions@univ.ox.ac.uk

University is the first Oxford college to be able to boast a former student in the Oval Office as the former President Clinton was a Rhodes Scholar at University in the late 1960s. The college is probably Oxford's oldest – a claim fought over with Merton. Academic expectations are high and the college prospers in most subjects. Accommodation is guaranteed to undergraduates for all three years, with third years lodged in an annexe in north Oxford about a mile and a half from the college site on the High Street, although the vast majority of third years choose to live out in rented accommodation. Sport is strong with the men's badminton team being crowned 2014 cuppers champions and the college having the highest participation in the summer eights regatta of any other college (though participation is emphasised over the end result). Students from the state sector can benefit from a generous bursary scheme, and Univ's access programme is among the best in Oxford.

Wadham

Oxford OX1 3PN   01865 277545 (admissions)   www.wadham.ox.ac.uk
Undergraduates: 436   Postgraduates: 118   admissions@wadh.ox.ac.uk

Founded by Dorothy Wadham in 1609, Wadham is known in about equal measure for its progressive and liberal atmosphere and its leftist politics. The JCR – or student union as it has rebranded itself – is famously dynamic and politically active, although the breadth of political opinion is greater than its left-wing stereotype suggests. The college is very strong on admitting students from state schools, owing to its successful Student Ambassador Scheme. Its gardens are beautiful, hosting Shakespearian performances each summer and the somewhat rough-hewn chapel is similarly memorable. The college has a good 24-hour library. Accommodation is guaranteed in first year and at least one further year. Graduates are either offered accommodation in "Merifield", the college's modern development of shared flats in Summertown or choose to live in private accommodation. Journalism, music and drama play an important part. Highlights in the social calendar are Queer Festival, a riotous celebration of LGBTQ culture, and Wadstock, the college's open-air spring music festival. The women's rowing team are currently Head of the River.

Worcester

Oxford OX1 2HB   01865 278391 (admissions)   www.worc.ox.ac.uk
Undergraduates: 413   Postgraduates: 161   admissions@worc.ox.ac.uk

Worcester is to the west of Oxford what Magdalen is to the east: a spacious contrast to the urban rush of the city centre. The college's rather mediocre exterior conceals a delightful environment, including some striking Baroque architecture, extensive gardens and a lake.

The dramatic society makes use of the beautiful grounds, with a notable sell-out performance of *The Merchant of Venice* performed on the lake last year. The 24-hour library is strongest in the arts. Accommodation, guaranteed for two years and provided for the majority of third years, varies in quality from ordinary to conference standard in the Canal Building. More en-suite accommodation, next to the new gym, is also available. Sport plays an important part in college life, as befits the only college with playing fields on site. Worcester is a noted powerhouse in men's football. Worcester boasts good quality and reasonably priced formal halls, available four nights a week, with a Michelin star chef every Wednesday. Like Magdalen and New, it is home to the Commemoration Ball once every three years, a highlight of the Oxford social calendar.

Cambridge College Profiles

Christ's

Cambridge CB2 3BU   01223 334983 (admissions)   www.christs.cam.ac.uk

Undergraduates: 409   Postgraduates: 208   admissions@christs.cam.ac.uk

Christ's is the *alma mater* of some of Cambridge's most illustrious alumni including John Milton and Charles Darwin and has maintained its learned reputation, maintaining a top 10 position in the Tompkins Table in recent years. Its strength is in natural science and maths, but is also well known for its Visual Arts Centre. The modern gallery and performance space, the Yusuf Hamied theatre, is used by a buzzing amateur dramatic society. One of the major attractions of Christ's for students is its proximity to the centre of town and to the natural science and geography faculties. Accommodation is all within college or just behind it on Jesus Lane and is spread between the old-world splendour of First and Second Court and modern rooms in New Court. Just over 40 per cent of the rooms are en suite and the newer ones have private balconies. The college playing fields, about a ten-minute cycle ride, are shared with St Catharine's. Sport flourishes and the Christ's football team has won Cuppers more times than any other college. The renovated swimming pool in the 17th-century Fellows Garden is a popular place to cool off during summer exam season.

Churchill

Cambridge CB3 0DS   01223 336202 (admissions)   www.chu.cam.ac.uk

Undergraduates: 480   Postgraduates: 290   admissions@chu.cam.ac.uk

The college may not be renowned for its splendour but Churchill students do enjoy spacious grounds and some of the best facilities in Cambridge, including a new gym, a theatre-cum-cinema and a modern music room. It has squash and tennis courts and grass pitches on site and a strong reputation for rowing. The college provides accommodation for all students for the first three years of their undergraduate degree. Work on a new court of 70 undergraduate rooms will soon be finished. Some students, however, do move out to be nearer to the centre, as Churchill is about a 15-minute cycle to town and to most lecture halls. It was the first all-male college to welcome female students in 1972, and is proud of its modern attitude. Students are allowed to walk on the grass (a rarity on Cambridge's hallowed lawns) and don't wear academic gowns when dining formally in hall. Dame Athene Donald became the college's first female Master in 2014. It has been in the Tompkins Table top 10 for the past seven years. With a founding remit to address the "national need for scientists and engineers and to forge links with industry", it is more science-focused than many colleges.

Clare

Cambridge CB2 1TL   01223 333246 (admissions)   www.clare.cam.ac.uk

Undergraduates: 504   Postgraduates: 312   admissions@clare.cam.ac.uk

Cambridge's second oldest college, tucked between King's and Trinity Hall, has bright, clean architecture and is popular with students for being a quiet haven with lovely gardens on along the Cambridge "Backs". It is also popular for its music scene, which ranges from a renowned college choir to live music in the bar. The college has squash courts on site, but the rest of the college's sports facilities are 15 minutes away by bike and are shared with Peterhouse and Clare Hall. What it lacks in sports pitches, it makes up for in accommodation. The newest development, Lerner Court, which was opened in 2009, provides en-suite undergraduate accommodation and is popular with arts students for its proximity to the faculties on Sidgwick Site. Next door to Lerner, Memorial Court provides more first-year accommodation and boasts its own computer facilities, common room and music room as well as the college library. Some prefer living a little further from college in "Clare Colony", about ten minutes cycle from the main site near Magdalene. Clare is currently one of the most gender equal colleges and, unsurprising given its beauty and centrality, received the highest number of applications in the last admissions cycle.

Corpus Christi

Cambridge CB2 1RH   01223 338056 (admissions)   www.corpus.cam.ac.uk

Undergraduates: 223   Postgraduates: 223   admissions@corpus.cam.ac.uk

The only Oxbridge college to have been founded by townspeople, Corpus is one of the smallest colleges in Cambridge, giving it an intimate atmosphere. Some students find this claustrophobic, while others enjoy its situation on Trumpington Street, close to the Sidgwick Site for arts students and the Downing Site for sciences, as well as the town centre. Corpus is strong on arts and is home to not one, but two libraries. The Taylor Library, the main one for undergraduates, was opened in 2008, while the older Parker Library holds the college's collection of rare books and manuscripts. The college has a policy of partly allocating rooms based on exam results – a rule not much loved by students. All undergraduates do have the option of living in college accommodation for all three years of their degree either in the historic courts or in nearby hostels, which are comfortable with particularly good kitchens. Sports facilities are just over a mile away on the Leckhampton site, though many college teams are collaborative ventures with Christ's and King's due to the small undergraduate numbers. Drama, on the other hand, is strong and the Corpus playroom was refurbished in 2011.

Downing

Cambridge CB2 1DQ   01223 334826 (admissions)   www.dow.cam.ac.uk

Undergraduates: 425   Postgraduates: 271   admissions@dow.cam.ac.uk

Downing is a breath of fresh air with its spacious quadrangle and neo-Classical architecture, designed by William Wilkins in 1800. Though it is not far from town and backs onto the Downing site where many of the science faculties are, it feels far from the Cambridge hustle and bustle. Its founding premise was for students to study law and it still remains strong in this subject though its forte has spread into engineering and medicine too. Downing has a fearsome reputation on the river where it often wins inter-college competitions known as "Bumps", and has an on-site gym as well as tennis, netball and squash courts. The bar has been refurbished and a new accommodation block was unveiled in July 2014. Generally, student accommodation is of very high standard, with first and third years housed on site and second year accommodation a short walk away. For the less sporty, Downing has an active cultural scene with a much used 120-seater theatre, the popular Blake Society (named after popular alumnus Quentin Blake) hosting talks, tours and workshops, and a new chapel organ.

Emmanuel

Cambridge CB2 3AP   01223 334290 (admissions)   www.emma.cam.ac.uk

Undergraduates: 430   Postgraduates: 220   admissions@emma.cam.ac.uk

Founded in the 1584 with a Puritan ethic (one of the earliest alumni was John Harvard of Harvard University fame), Emmanuel prides itself on a friendly atmosphere, which really does extend beyond the prospectus jargon. It has a strong academic reputation and is regularly near the of the Tompkins Table. As one of the wealthier colleges, "Emma" provides cheaper accommodation than most colleges and offers many generous grants for travel, books and welfare. It is also the only college to provide an in-college laundry service as part of the rent. First and third years live either in college or in Georgian houses along its edge, overlooking one of Cambridge's biggest green spaces, Parker's Piece. Second years live in rooms a maximum ten-minute cycle ride from college. The award-winning Emmanuel chefs serve up heavily subsidised food, which is reliably good. Sports pitches are a ten-minute cycle ride away and the college fields a number of sports teams that are more inclusive than competitive, though the college does have a strong boat club. The gender balance in Emmanuel is nearly 50:50, and the college welcomed Dame Fiona Reynolds as its first female master in 2013.

Fitzwilliam

Cambridge CB3 0DG   01223 332030 (admissions)   www.fitz.cam.ac.uk
Undergraduates: 492   Postgraduates: 288   admissions@fitz.cam.ac.uk

"Fitz" can lay claim to occupying the highest point in Cambridge: the top of their most recent building work, a library which opened in 2010 after £5-million investment. Designed by award-winning architect Edward Cullinan, it has state-of-the-art IT facilities and is open 24 hours a day, seven days a week. With just over 400 rooms in college and a further 167 in houses nearby, all undergraduates are comfortably accommodated. Amid the rather stark buildings are lovely gardens. The college café is a popular place to work or catch-up with friends. Fitzwilliam was originally established in 1869 in order to widen access to the university, although the college currently has one of the lower percentages of state school applicants. As home to the most drinking societies of any college and an impressive array of sports teams, Fitz enjoys something of a party reputation. The sports teams also achieve highly on the pitch and there are well-kept sports facilities close by for football, rugby, cricket, hockey and tennis, as well as a gym. It is not the most academic of colleges, coming 19th in the 2014 Tompkins Table, yet a fifth of all students graduated with a first.

Girton

Cambridge CB3 0JG   01223 338972 (admissions)   www.girton.cam.ac.uk
Undergraduates: 502   Postgraduates: 220   admissions@girton.cam.ac.uk

Girton is a hidden gem. Since few except Girton students make the 15-minute cycle up the Huntingdon Road, its lawns, orchard and majestic red brick buildings remain a haven of peace and quiet. It also means that Girton's 50 acres of grounds can provide some of the best facilities of all colleges including, uniquely, an indoor swimming pool (newly refurbished), a gym, tennis, squash and basketball courts, and a new sports pavilion that opened in 2013. The library is one of the largest of all the colleges and Girton also has a strong artistic bent, housing its own museum, which dates from the involvement of the Pre-Raphaelites at its foundation, and a choir, which regularly makes recordings. Second years can live closer to town in Wolfson Court, where any student can go for lunch if they don't have time to get back to the college between lectures. All other students have space to live in reasonably priced rooms on campus. Although it was originally an all-female college (and has always had a female 'Mistress'), since opening its doors to men in 1977, Girton's student body has become just over half male. The college has the highest number of female Fellows of any co-ed college.

Gonville and Caius

Cambridge CB2 1TA   01223 332440 (admissions)   www.cai.cam.ac.uk
Undergraduates: 540   Postgraduates: 253   admissions@cai.cam.ac.uk

Gonville and Caius (pronounced "keys") is a tucked away just off Cambridge's market square. It was founded in 1348 as Gonville Hall, which makes it one of the oldest colleges, although it was re-founded in its current state in 1557. Entering through its Porter's Lodge is an old-world experience and the stunning student library in the Cockerell Building was once the University Library. Caius has held on to a somewhat old-fashioned reputation. Gowns are required in hall every night of the week, whether students are attending the "informal" early hall or the later "formal" hall. Both are three-course meals preceded by a Latin grace read by one of the fellows. Harvey Court, renovated in 2011, provides 100 en-suite rooms to undergraduates, while next door the £13-million Stephen Hawking building offers another 75 en suite rooms. Both are a five minute walk from the college across the Backs. The rest of the accommodation is tucked into the college's small but stunning historic courts or a ten-minute cycle ride away near the station. The Harvey Court complex is also home to a well-equipped gym and the college has a strong rowing reputation.

Homerton

Cambridge CB2 8PH   01223 747252 (admissions)   www.homerton.cam.ac.uk
Undergraduates: 629   Postgraduates: 695   admissions@homerton.cam.ac.uk

Despite being situated in Cambridge since the 1890s (the college was founded in London), Homerton has only been part of the university for 37 years and officially a college since 2010. It is the largest of all the Cambridge colleges with over 1,100 students. Unusually for a mixed Cambridge college it has a ratio of roughly 60:40 women to men. Originally a teacher training college, it is still home to those taking the PGCE course (which accounts for around a fifth of the student body), However, Homerton does offer the full range of subjects. Many students comment on the college's location near the station, a 15-minute cycle ride from the town centre. Its relative newness and large site mean that students enjoy an experience more akin to a campus university. Its grounds host two large halls of residence where students are accommodated for three years of undergraduate study, as well as squash courts, football pitches, a rugby-training strip and croquet lawn. Homerton also boasts a vast range of societies and some eclectic musical provision with college instruments ranging from harpsichords to marimbas. Academically, Homerton hovers towards the lower end of the scale but it makes up for this in extra-curricular excellence.

Hughes Hall

Cambridge CB1 2EW   01223 334897 (admissions)k   www.hughes.cam.ac.uk
Undergraduates: 100   Postgraduates: 500   admissions@hughes.cam.ac.u

Starting as a small institution for women training to be teachers with just 14 students in its first intake, Hughes Hall is the oldest of the five graduate colleges in Cambridge and also welcomes mature undergraduate applications. Named after its first principal, Elizabeth Hughes, who travelled widely abroad, it follows her precedent by welcoming one of the most internationally diverse communities of any college. All students (now both male and female) are over the age of 21 and Hughes has a mature approach to social life with a range of famous speakers, well-attended theatrical events and garden parties in their spacious grounds near the University sports centre, Fenners. It may be due to its location that Hughes is one of the sportiest colleges, often providing Blues in rowing and other sports. Accommodation is provided within college for all single undergraduates and affiliated students throughout their course, but family accommodation is harder to secure. A new library was built in 2008, although most postgraduate students tend to gravitate toward their faculties. Students like the location on the cosmopolitan Mill Road.

Jesus

Cambridge CB5 8BL 01223 339455 (admissions) www.jesus.cam.ac.uk
Undergraduates: 465 Postgraduates: 332 undergraduate-admissions@jesus.cam.ac.uk
Jesus' extensive grounds, backed by Jesus Green on one side and the town centre on the other, make it the envy of other colleges. Although a high performer academically, it is also known for sporting prowess. With football, rugby and cricket pitches in college, as well as ten tennis courts and three squash courts, this reputation is no surprise. Having one of the largest undergraduate bodies helps. Other extra-curricular activities abound: the college has an extensive collection of sculpture spread throughout the grounds, and is home to the university's Visual Arts Society. Jesus is near the famous ADC theatre, home of the Cambridge Footlights with its much-loved bar, and prides itself on an extensive annual May Ball, which is particularly popular with first-years. Despite being one of the bigger colleges, teaching provision is excellent, with a high ratio of Fellows to students and all the benefits of being one of Cambridge's wealthiest colleges. Accommodation is available within the grounds for all first years and half of the third-year students, while all other students live in well-appointed college houses across the road.

King's

Cambridge CB2 1ST 01223 331255 (admissions) www.kings.cam.ac.uk
Undergraduates: 403 Postgraduates: 282 undergraduate.admissions@kings.cam.ac.uk
Think of Cambridge and as likely as not King's College will come to mind. Around the world people listen to the carols from its famous chapel every Christmas Eve and tourists (when permitted) throng the grounds. Originally founded in 1441 for boys from Eton College, it has completely thrown off the traditionalist image and is known across the university for its leftist leanings. A favourite debate among students is whether or not the hammer and sickle flag should remain hanging above the bar. It has also done away with many of the traditions associated with Cambridge life, including gowns, the Fellows' "High Table" in hall and room allocation based on academic achievement. It has the highest intake of state sector students (nearly three quarters in the last admissions cycle) and it is active in trying to attract students from disadvantaged backgrounds. The college was also among the first of the all-male colleges to admit women. King's students are also proud of their anti-May Ball, the "King's Affair", which has been known to attract queues two hours long for tickets. King's boasts an extensive library of 130,000 volumes and the highest ratio of Fellows to students.

Lucy Cavendish

Cambridge CB3 0BU 01223 330280 (admissions) www.lucy-cav.cam.ac.uk
Undergraduates: 144 (women only) Postgraduates: 226 lcc-admissions@lists.cam.ac.uk
Lucy Cavendish is not just the only college for mature female students in Cambridge; it is unique for this in the UK as a whole. Although all students are over 21, the age mix is diverse with some 20 per cent over the age of 40 and some in their 60s. "Lucy", as it is fondly known,

is one of the smallest colleges and has a close knit community. It is one of the "hill colleges", a ten-minute cycle from town up the Huntingdon Road and a short walk from the Maths faculty, Veterinary faculty and the Sidgwick Site for arts subjects. It is not a social hub – the bar is only open three nights a week – but many appreciate this as it fosters a supportive working environment. It also means that Lucy students are often more socially active on a university-wide level. Accommodation is provided for all students either in college or in houses nearby. For sportier women, the college shares a boathouse with Hughes Hall, which won the 2014 Pegasus Cup for most successful boathouse, and there is a well-equipped gym. The college is particularly strong on the medical side but also has a good reputation for English, with a well-regarded annual fiction prize.

Magdalene
Cambridge CB3 0AG   01223 332135 (admissions)   www.magd.cam.ac.uk
Undergraduates: 320   Postgraduates: 206   admissions@magd.cam.ac.uk

Magdalene is one of Cambridge's oldest colleges and one of its most traditional. Students outside the college know it for its triennial white-tie ball, and its candlelit formal dinner which, currently priced at just £4.95, is one of the cheapest in Cambridge. Its beautiful situation on the river (it has the longest river frontage of any college) helps it to live up to many a Cambridge cliché. Magdalene was the last all-male college to admit women in 1988, though these days the gender balance is more or less equal. Rowing and rugby are strong, and the college shares sports grounds with the equally sporty St John's. It also has its own Eton fives court. On the musical side, the Magdalene choir sing twice weekly in the stunning chapel, and the college offers a number of choral, music and organ scholarships. Cripps Court, which was completed in 2005, has a 140-seat auditorium where concerts are regularly held. About 60 undergraduate rooms are in Cripps while the rest of the accommodation is either in other areas of college or close by in its 21 houses and hostels. It has climbed its way back up the Tompkins Table under the new mastership of former Archbishop of Canterbury, Rowan Williams.

Murray Edwards
Cambridge CB3 0DF   01223 762229 (admissions)   www.murrayedwards.cam.ac.uk
Undergraduates: 360 (women) Postgraduates: 188 admissions@murrayedwards.cam.ac.uk

After a £30 million endowment and a new name in 2008, Murray Edwards, which was previously known as "New Hall", is finally getting used to its new identity though it is still occasionally referred to by its old name. One of three female-only colleges in Cambridge, Murray Edwards enjoys a less stridently feminist reputation than the other two. It tends to be in the lower half of the Tompkins Table. Murray Edwards is known for being a friendly, relaxed place with airy modern buildings and informal gardens. Since 2012, members of the college have been able to have their own allotments if they wish. Strong on the sporting front, the college fields teams in everything from croquet to ultimate Frisbee and often provides the university teams with players. Unlike many colleges, Murray Edwards does not have a chapel or any religious stance. It has the second largest collection of contemporary women's art in the world and an onsite art studio with dark room facilities. While many students like to get out of college to socialise, they do put on popular events including a summer garden party. Accommodation is comfortable and 40 per cent of new rooms are en suite.

Newnham

Cambridge CB3 9DF   01223 335783 (admissions)   www.newn.cam.ac.uk
Undergraduates: 380 (women)   Postgraduates: 264   admissions@newn.cam.ac.uk

The first college to be set up for women to allow them to attend lectures at Cambridge, Newnham is proud of its past and boasts a stellar line up of alumni including Sylvia Plath, Emma Thompson, Germaine Greer and Mary Beard. It is the largest women-only college and has an all-female fellowship. Sports teams are enthusiastic, if not always high achieving, and the college has a well-used arts centre called "The Old Labs". Weekly lunchtime recitals are held in term time. Unusually for a Cambridge college, Newnham has no chapel, so the college choir joins up with neighbouring Selwyn to sing. The 18-acre grounds mean that all sports pitches and tennis courts are on site alongside gardens whose tranquil lawns are a favourite of students in summer. All students can live in college and take advantage of three common rooms. They can also make use of one of the largest college libraries. Newnham is best known for its strength in arts subjects — not a surprise as the lecture halls of Sidgwick are a minute from the college doors.

Pembroke

Cambridge CB2 1RF   01223 338154 (admissions)   www.pem.cam.ac.uk
Undergraduates: 444   Postgraduates: 260   adm@pem.cam.ac.uk

Tucked into the corner of Pembroke and Trumpington Streets, the grounds of Pembroke are an oasis in the midst of the city bustle. With a stunning chapel – Christopher Wren's first commission – and a 17th-century library, Pembroke is one of Cambridge's most beautiful colleges. After Clare, it is the most popular college with prospective applicants. It is gradually shaking off a traditionalist image. Men and women have nearly reached parity (53 per cent male last year) and the state to independent school ratio sticks at around 60:40. The conventional Cambridge sports of rowing and rugby are strong, but the arts are increasingly becoming a feature of college life. Pembroke has ranked in the top five of the Tompkins Table for the past four years, and is traditionally strong in sciences. It helps that it is a two-minute walk from the main science faculties. Accommodation is of variable quality. While many undergraduates can live in college, second years and some third years live out in pokey college hostels. Freshers live in the recently refurbished Foundress Court, where rooms are spacious and modern.

Peterhouse

Cambridge CB2 1RD   01223 338223 (admissions)   www.pet.cam.ac.uk
Undergraduates: 279   Postgraduates: 162   admissions@pet.cam.ac.uk

Peterhouse is both the smallest and the oldest undergraduate college and is often perceived as traditionalist and elite. However, this image belies a college that has one of the highest percentages of state school students and a male to female ratio of 60:40. Some find the small bounds of the college suffocating but the size of the student body (around 80 undergraduates are admitted per year) means that rooms are generally large and at most ten minutes' walk from the college. The college is particularly strong in the arts and performs highly in Arts Tripos, but it has limited provision for scientists. This can pull it down the Tompkins Table, although in recent years it has hit the top half. Beyond lectures, Peterhouse has a rich array of societies ranging from politics to drama, science and music. However, with not many undergraduates to choose from and sports pitches shared with two other colleges, it is not known for its sport. Peterhouse students tend to be an eclectic lot and the cosy bar is much enjoyed. The candle-lit formal and triennial white-tie ball are also very Cantabrigian treats.

Queens'

Cambridge CB3 9ET   01223 335540 (admissions)   www.queens.cam.ac.uk
Undergraduates: 511   Postgraduates: 496   admissions@queens.cam.ac.uk

Although Queens' has one of the largest undergraduate bodies, on-site accommodation for three years means that Queens' students all know each other well. Walnut Tree Court and Old Court are as idyllic as their names sound and have rooms highly sought-after by third years. Most first years are housed across the famous Mathematical Bridge, designed by Sir Isaac Newton, in the less quaint and much noisier Cripps Court, also home to the spacious and popular bar. A large student body means many student societies. Drama is strong and the Fitzpatrick Hall is well-equipped for productions. Sport ranges from a strong rowing team to a tiddlywinks club, and recent building projects include a multi-gym, three squash courts and provision for badminton and table tennis. These complement the spacious sports ground they share with Robinson just under a mile away. Queens' is particularly strong in the sciences with plenty of engineers and medics in the undergraduate ranks. Over 60 per cent of the intake comes from the state sector and generally around half of the intake is female.

Robinson

Cambridge CB3 9AN   01223 339143 (admissions)   www.robinson.cam.ac.uk
Undergraduates: 386   Postgraduates: 172   apply@robinson.cam.ac.uk

Robinson is probably best known for its austere red brick architecture, which has led some to dub it "the car park". The bricks conceal excellent facilities – a large auditorium, gardens and lake, the popular Red Brick Café and an outstanding chapel organ. Founded just over 40 years ago, Robinson's youthful atmosphere is also an unpretentious one. It typically accepts around 60 per cent of its intake from state schools and a quarter of the fellows are women. Rooms are comfortable and spacious, although rents are the highest of any college and some students bemoan the lack of travel grants to undertake studies abroad. On the plus side, the food is inexpensive and has been named amongst the best in Cambridge by *Varsity*, the student newspaper. The sports grounds (shared with Queens', Selwyn and Kings) are less than a mile from the main site and the proximity to university rugby ground attracts a sporty student body. Academically, it has been languishing in the second half of the Tompkins Table in recent years, but the college is close to the University Library and a five-minute walk from the arts faculties of the Sidgwick Site.

St Catharine's

Cambridge CB2 1RL   01223 338319 (admissions)   www.caths.cam.ac.uk
Undergraduates: 430   Postgraduates: 220   undergraduate.admissions@caths.cam.ac.uk

Although not among the best known of Cambridge colleges, "Catz" has one of the larger student bodies. It occupies a prominent position on King's Parade and dates from the 15th century. It has not one but two libraries, on the belief of its original benefactor, Robert Woodlark, that books were central to learning. First-year rooms are all provided on site with a few en suite, while in second year, students move out to the popular flats in the St Chad's complex, close to the arts faculties. Third years move back into college with a pick of the best rooms, some of which are extensive, and a preference is given to those who performed well in exams. It is known for its football squad and is the only college in the university to have all-weather hockey pitch. Catz has also provided Blues rowers and manages to field a surprising number of sports teams that vary in talent. In June 2013 the McGrath Centre, which houses an auditorium, a new student bar and common room, was completed.

St Edmund's

Cambridge CB3 0BN   01223 336086 (admissions)   www.st-edmunds.cam.ac.uk
Undergraduates: 122   Postgraduates: 343   admissions@st-edmunds.cam.ac.uk

With a student body coming from over 50 different countries, St Edmund's can claim to be the most international of the Cambridge colleges. Not far from the city centre to the northwest, it is the most central of the graduate colleges and also the sportiest. The Blues rugby and rowing team line-ups regularly feature a substantial number of "Eddies" students. The gym, which was refurbished three years ago, is well equipped. This was part of a development plan that saw the opening of three new accommodation blocks, including the Brian Heap Building whose dining room, kitchens and en-suite facilities put its rooms in high demand. St Edmund's is one of the most flexible of colleges for accommodation with a number of small maisonettes for couples and students with children, and a good number of rooms for students with physical disabilities. It has an unpretentious atmosphere – there is no high table for fellows in the dining hall, for example – and unique among all the Cambridge colleges, St Edmund's has a Catholic chapel. Social life is vibrant for a primarily graduate college.

St John's

Cambridge CB2 1TP   01223 338703 (admissions)   www.joh.cam.ac.uk
Undergraduates: 543   Postgraduates: 354   admissions@joh.cam.ac.uk

While not always academically brilliant – it has maintained a middling position in recent years' Tompkins Table – St John's is known for stunning grounds, beautiful architecture (including the famous Bridge of Sighs), excellent facilities, a vibrant if laddish social life and for excelling on the sports field. The college grounds straddle the River Cam which becomes blocked by punts on the night of the famous St John's May Ball, as those without tickets crowd into boats to watch the fireworks display. The chapel is home to a strong musical tradition and singers from all over the university audition for places in the John's choir. It is one of the biggest colleges, but this has not enabled it to throw off its largely "posh boy" public school reputation. It has one of the lowest ratios of women to men, and has a state school intake of just over half. Accommodation is of a high standard and under a new system, Johnians are allowed to keep their rooms year round (as opposed to moving out during the holidays). Thanks to a large endowment, Johns students can also enjoy generous grants for things like travel. Food is also well regarded and invitations to John's formal are coveted university-wide.

Selwyn

Cambridge CB3 9DQ   01223 335896 (admissions)   www.sel.cam.ac.uk
Undergraduates: 377   Postgraduates: 200   admissions@sel.cam.ac.uk

Although some students complain that Selwyn is "miles" from town amenities, it is, in fact, tucked just behind the university's Sidgwick Site, a position enhanced by its lovely gardens. The location is also ideal for arts and humanities students whose faculty lecture halls are next door. As one of the first colleges to admit women, it has maintained a nearly gender equal balance and was the first college to appoint a female head porter. Accommodation for all students is either in the imposing red brick buildings in college or in Cripps Court over the road, which is currently undergoing a £13-million refurbishment and will reopen in December 2014. A couple of hostels (essentially large houses) are also available for second and third years and are a popular choice. Sports are strongly promoted through the Hermes and Sirens Club, longstanding male and female sports clubs, which fund bursaries and various teams. Planning permission has been granted for a new boathouse. For other sports, the college shares facilities with King's. Selwyn tends towards the middle of the academic rankings and is better known for its Winter Ball – a high point on the Cambridge social calendar.

Sidney Sussex

Cambridge CB2 3HU   01223 338872 (admissions)   www.sid.cam.ac.uk
Undergraduates: 348   Postgraduate: 239   admissions@sid.cam.ac.uk

As one of the smaller colleges, Sidney has an almost familial atmosphere, where students all tend to know each other. Some like this while others find it a bit much, and Sidney students are certainly active outside of college. Sidney's location in the centre of town is a draw and accommodation is split between hostels around town and rooms in college. Perhaps the most coveted rooms are those in Garden Court, which have enormous bay windows. Although Sidney faces onto Sidney Street, it is only a short walk down to Jesus Green and the boathouse on the other side of the Cam. For all other sports, the college shares a sports ground with Christ's, a ten-minute cycle away. It is also a very short distance from Cambridge's main theatre and home to the Footlights, the ADC, and plays are also put on in the quiet gardens behind Front Court in summer. Sidney has an award-winning catering team who have taken the top prize in the annual university-wide culinary competition three times in the past five years. Academically, the college tends toward the middle of the Tompkins Table.

Trinity

Cambridge CB2 1TQ   01223 338422 (admissions)   www.trin.cam.ac.uk
Undergraduates: 696   Postgraduates: 364   admissions@trin.cam.ac.uk

Trinity is big in all ways. It is the richest Cambridge college, it has the largest number of Nobel-prize winning alumni and it also has the biggest undergraduate population, of whom about two thirds are men. With an endowment almost as big as all the other colleges put together, it can afford to fund generous travel grants and maintains its facilities well. Scholars have first choice of rooms, but most rooms are large and nearly half are en suite so there isn't much concern about this prioritising. Accommodation is also among the cheapest in Cambridge as it is heavily subsidised. In the latest results, Trinity topped the Tompkins Table for the fourth year in a row and over 42 per cent of students graduated with a first – the highest ever achieved. It also won this year's University Challenge competition. Food is excellent and one kind benefactor gave Trinity its own ice cream chef. Sports are strong, and the college provides a gym on site as well as hockey, tennis, netball, rugby, football, basketball and cricket pitches a short walk away. With all the grandeur, it may not be a surprise that the number of students from the state sector has been historically low, hovering at around 40 per cent.

Trinity Hall

Cambridge CB2 1TJ   01223 332535 (admissions)   www.trinhall.cam.ac.uk
Undergraduates: 380   Postgraduates: 263   admissions@trinhall.cam.ac.uk

Glorying in the nickname "Tit Hall", this small college is one of Cambridge's oldest. Thanks to its size, students enjoy living in a close community right on the river with a two-minute walk to town in one direction and a short cycle ride over a notoriously bumpy bridge to the University Library in the other. It is best known for its strength in the Law Tripos but is an academic all-rounder coming in the top three in the Tompkins Table for the past three years. For such a small college, it is a hive of activity, with its own newspaper, *Hallmark*, and one of the better college drama groups, the Preston Society. Sports are strong and they are proud of their sporting alumni including Olympic and Commonwealth medal winning cyclist Emma Pooley. The Refurbishment of the Dining Hall was completed in April 2014 and plans for a new boathouse are underway. All undergraduates are provided with accommodation for all years of their course, and rents are very reasonable. The Wychfield Site, with its 90 en-suite rooms and pretty gardens is an especially popular choice. Most students continue to be housed in older accommodation in college.

Wolfson

Cambridge CB3 9BB   01223 335918   www.wolfson.cam.ac.uk
Undergraduates: 135   Postgraduates: 576   ugadministrator@wolfson.cam.ac.uk

Originally founded as University College in 1965, Wolfson became known by its current name following a generous grant from the Wolfson Foundation. It was opened to host the influx of academics to Cambridge in the post-war years and is primarily for graduate students. However, it also welcome around 170 mature or affiliated undergraduates and is one of the few colleges to offer part-time study. Like Hughes Hall, it has an internationally diverse community. The atmosphere is different to many Cambridge colleges as it does not uphold many of the university's better known customs like having a Fellows' table in hall. Not one of the most beautiful colleges architecturally, it does boast tranquil and well-tended gardens. Its location out of town adds to the peaceful atmosphere, although some gripe that it is nearer to the M11 than to Cambridge. In reality, it is a 20-minute walk from the centre of town. There is a packed cultural calendar including lunchtime talks and many language classes. Accommodation is functional rather than glamorous. Most students can be accommodated, either the "old" (1970s) blocks or "new" (1990s) buildings, and there is some space for couples.

14 University Profiles

This chapter provides profiles of every university that appears in *The Times and Sunday Times* league table. In addition there are profiles for Norwich University of the Arts and the Royal Agricultural University, both created as universities in 2013 but which could not fairly be compared with generalist universities included in the league table, and the two major suppliers of part-time degrees, the Open University and Birkbeck College. There are also profiles for those institutions which did not release data for use in the table. However, we do not have separate profiles for specialist colleges and medical schools, such as the Royal College of Music (**www.rcm.ac.uk**) and St George's, University of London medical school (**sgul.ac.uk**), or institutions that only offer postgraduate degrees, such as Cranfield University (**www.cranfield.ac.uk**) and London Business School (**www.lbs.ac.uk**). Their omission is no reflection on their quality, simply a function of their particular roles. A number of additional institutions with degree-awarding powers are listed at the end of the book with their contact details.

Comments on campus facilities apply to the universities' own sites only. Newer universities, in particular, operate "franchised" courses at further education colleges, which are likely to have lower levels of provision. Prospective applicants should check out the library and social facilities before accepting a place away from the parent institution.

The profiles contain valuable information about each university. You can find contact details, including the postal address, the telephone number for admission enquiries, email or web addresses for admissions and prospectus enquiries, web addresses for the university, the students' union and for sports facilities, and any university grouping that the institution is affiliated to (Russell Group, etc.). In addition, each profile provides information under the following headings:

» **The Times and Sunday Times rankings** For the overall ranking, the figure in bold refers to the university's position in 2015 and the figure in brackets to 2014. All the information listed is taken from the main league table. See chapter 4 for explanations and the sources of the data.
» **Undergraduates** The first figure is for full-time undergraduates. The second figure (in brackets) gives the number of part-time undergraduates. The figures are for 2012–13, and are the most recent provided by Higher Education Statistics Agency (HESA).

» **Postgraduates** The first figure is for full-time postgraduates. The second figure (in brackets) gives the number of part-time postgraduates. The figures are for 2012–13, and are the most recent provided by HESA.

» **Mature students** The percentage of undergraduate entrants who were 21 or over at the start of their studies in 2013. The figures are from UCAS (except for Buckingham and Birkbeck, which are for 2012–13, as calculated by HESA).

» **International students** The number of undergraduate overseas students (both EU and non-EU) as a percentage of full-time undergraduates. The figures relate to 2012–13, and are based on HESA data.

» **Applications per place** The number of applicants per place for 2013 as calculated by UCAS.

» **From state-school sector** The number of young full-time first-degree entrants from state schools or colleges in 2012–13 as a percentage of total young entrants. The figures are published by HESA.

» **From working-class homes** The number of young full-time first-degree entrants in 2012–13 whose parental occupations are skilled, manual, semi-skilled or unskilled (NS-SEC classes 4–7) as a percentage of total young entrants. The figures are published by HESA.

» **Accommodation** The information was obtained through a survey made of all university accommodation services, and their help in compiling this information is gratefully acknowledged.

Undergraduate fees and bursaries

Details of tuition fees and financial support for students starting in 2015–16 are given wherever possible. Tuition fees for international students refer to 2014–15. For Scotland and Northern Ireland the figures refer to 2014–15, while for Wales details of government support for students are for 2014–15, as figures for 2015–16 were not available at the time this book went to press. It is of the utmost importance that you check university websites for the latest information. In England the Office for Fair Access (**www.offa.org.uk**) publishes "Access Agreements" for every English university. Each agreement outlines the university's plans for fees, financial support and measures being taken to widen access to that university and to encourage students to complete their courses. The agreements are available on the OFFA website. In the summary given on the profile pages:

» **RUK** describes students from the Rest of the UK at Scottish and Northern Irish universities. Fees and financial support given by universities differs from those available to students resident in Scotland or Northern Ireland.

» **Household income** is the income that comes into a student's home before tax (but after a few allowances have been taken). For a young student, this will tend to be the parental income, for married and mature students, this will be all the income coming into his or her home.

Universities also offer a variety of scholarships and bursaries, for example, in particular subjects or to help people from particular places. There is not space in this book to give full details of such awards, and, again, you are advised to check university websites for details.

University of Aberdeen

Academic assessors were highly complimentary about Aberdeen in the university's latest quality audit, praising the "transformative" effect of curriculum reforms, the quality of online learning resources, personal tutoring and employability initiatives. Established in 1495, Aberdeen is the UK's fifth oldest university. It has been enjoying record demand for places since the adoption of "Sixth Century Courses", which include cross-disciplinary degrees such as risk in society, sustainability and the digital society. Even on traditional degree programmes, students can try out three or four subjects before committing themselves at the end of their first or even second year. The modular system is so flexible that the majority of students change their intended degree before graduation. The aim is to give graduates broader knowledge and more intellectual flexibility. The university added 100 academic posts to deliver the new courses, as well as strengthening its research.

Applications increased in 2013, but Aberdeen had to cut its intake of undergraduates by almost 40 per cent to keep within Scottish government limits. There should be more places available in 2015. The university is offering a range of scholarships to international students, each worth a year's free tuition, and undertaking not to raise fees in mid-course to ensure the cosmopolitan character of its campus. Roughly half of its students study medicine, science or engineering, half the arts or social sciences.

A new £22-million Aquatic Centre, with 50-metre pool, opened this year, completing the Aberdeen Sports Village, which has been built in partnership with the city council and sportscotland. The first phase opened in 2009 and has produced some of the best sports facilities at any university in the UK. It is just one of a number of big capital projects in recent years, including a futuristic library costing £57 million. Named after the Principal who commissioned it, the Sir Duncan Rice Library was chosen as one of the 12 best new buildings in Scotland, and collected an award from the Royal Institute of British Architects. Student services had already been transformed and the redeveloped Butchart Centre has given the Students' Association a new social focus on campus. The university expects to invest £377 million on capital projects by 2019.

Aberdeen registered some good results in the 2008 Research Assessment Exercise, when more than half of the work submitted was judged to be world-leading or internationally excellent. Health services research and theology, divinity and religious studies produced the best results in the UK, while computer science and informatics,

---

King's College
Aberdeen AB24 3FX

01224 272090/91 (admissions)
sras@abdn.ac.uk
www.abdn.ac.uk
www.ausa.org.uk
Affiliation: none

ABERDEEN
Edinburgh
Belfast
London
Cardiff

The Times and Sunday Times Rankings

Overall Ranking: **44** (last year: 40)

Student satisfaction:	=84	80.4%
Research quality:	34	20.7%
Entry standards:	18	444
Student–staff ratio:	=37	15.5
Services & facilities/student:	36	£1,859
Expected completion rate:	=87	82.5%
Good honours:	=42	71.0%
Graduate prospects:	34	74.3%

anthropology, English and history also did particularly well. Research income grew by more than a third over five years, cementing Aberdeen's ambitions to be recognised among the top 100 universities in the world.

The university established the English-speaking world's first chair in medicine and has produced its share of advances since. The Institute of Medical Sciences, which has brought together all Aberdeen's work in this area, boasts high quality laboratory facilities. Another £20 million was invested in the Suttie Centre, a teaching and learning centre for medical education and clinical skills. Education is now also considered among Aberdeen's strengths, while biological sciences have developed considerably in recent years, becoming second only to the social sciences in terms of size. Biomedicine is particularly strong, and the university's links with the oil industry show in geology's high reputation.

Today's university is a fusion of two ancient institutions which came together in 1860. The original King's College buildings are the focal point of an appealing campus, complete with cobbled main street and some sturdily handsome Georgian buildings, about a mile from the city centre. Medicine is at Foresterhill, a 20-minute walk away, Buses link the two sites with the Hillhead residential complex. Almost a third of all students come from the north of Scotland, but the one in six from England and the 120 nationalities from further afield are generally prepared for Aberdeen's remote location and, although the winters are long, the climate is warmer than the uninitiated might expect. Transport links are good. Students find the city lively and welcoming, but expensive: the JobLink service provides a good selection of part-time employment.

The students' centre in The Hub brings together dining and retail outlets with support services, including the accommodation office and the careers service. The university's ICT network has over 1,500 computers for student use. All new undergraduates are guaranteed housing – an important benefit in a city with the highest rents in Scotland. Aberdeen is also one of four Scottish universities collaborating in a new initiative to promote spin-out companies.

Undergraduate Fees and Bursaries

» Fees for Scottish and EU students 2014–15   No fee
» Fees for Non-Scottish UK (RUK) students for 2014–15   £9,000
  capped at a maximum of £27,000 regardless of course length,
  with the exception of enhanced degrees and medicine.
» Fees for international students 2014–15   £12,600–£15,700
  Medicine   £27,800
» Entrance scholarships available for Scottish students.
» For RUK students: £2,000 accommodation bursary in year 1.
  Access scholarships: household income below £20K, £3,000
  for three years; household income £20K–£30K, £2,000 for
  three years. Merit scholarships (AAB at A level or equivalent)
  excluding medicine, £3,000 for four years.

Students

Undergraduates:	**10,640**	**(1,250)**
Postgraduates:	**2,145**	**(1,285)**
Mature students:	**15.2%**	
International students:	**22.8%**	
Applications per place:	**11.8**	
From state-sector schools:	**79.5%**	
From working-class homes:	**21.5%**	
Satisfaction with students' union	**64%**	

For detailed information about sports facilities:
www.abdn.ac.uk/sportandexercise

Accommodation

Number of places and costs refer to 2014–15
University-provided places: about 2,531
Percentage catered: 12%
Catered costs: £149–£164 a week (39 weeks).
Self-catered costs: £90–£142 a week (39–51 weeks).
First-year students are guaranteed accommodation.
International students: as above.
studentaccomm@abdn.ac.uk
www.abdn.ac.uk/accommodation/

Abertay University

Sony chose Abertay as the site for the largest teaching laboratory in Europe for its PlayStation consoles – such is the international reputation the university has established in computer arts and games design. Abertay opened Europe's first research centre dedicated to computer games and digital entertainment, and more recently established a centre for research into systems pathology. It remains the only UK university with official accreditation for both computer games technology and computer arts: the university hosts the first Interactive Media Academy in the UK and also the first national Centre for Excellence in Computer Games Education. Its courses hold five of only twelve degree accreditations in these areas awarded by Skillset, the Government-sponsored training council for the creative industries.

The university is upgrading its own IT facilities to match, investing £3 million this year in an extensive programme of software upgrades and hardware replacement across the campus, including a new Wi-Fi network. Abertay has one of the highest ratios of PC-per-student in Britain, providing almost one computer for every four students.

But the university is not just about computer games. Abertay launched Scotland's first degrees in bioinformatics, biotechnology and ethical hacking, and now claims to be a leader for teaching and research in environmental science. A series of specialist research centres has been established in areas as diverse as urban water systems, bioinformatics, earth systems and environmental sciences. The latest are in Sustainability Assessment, Visualisation and Enhancement, and Food and Innovation. Environmental sciences, urban water engineering and intelligent systems engineering produced the best scores in the 2008 research assessments. Those for law and psychology were the best at any post-1992 Scottish university.

Based in the centre of Dundee, all the university's teaching and learning buildings are within five minutes' walk of each other. They are modern and functional, such as the innovative White Space facility, the university's flagship creative learning and working environment, where students study alongside industry professionals who are working on real commercial or broadcast projects. A new graduate school provides dedicated study space for postgraduates, as well as training and professional development opportunities.

The university doubled in size during the 1990s and has grown to around 5,500 since tuition fees were abolished for Scottish students. Most are based in Dundee, but Abertay's degrees are also taught as far away as Malaysia and China. The university

---

Bell Street
Dundee DD1 1HG

01382 308080
sro@abertay.ac.uk
www.abertay.ac.uk
www.uadsa.com
Affiliation: million+

The Times and Sunday Times Rankings

Overall Ranking: **106** (last year: 105)

Student satisfaction:	105	78.8%
Research quality:	=84	3.0%
Entry standards:	=69	330
Student–staff ratio:	107	21.3
Services & facilities/student:	73	£1,436
Expected completion rate:	117	73.2%
Good honours:	=72	64.3%
Graduate prospects:	81	61.1%

enjoyed big increases in applications in the early years of this decade, but there was a 15 per cent drop in 2013, when a number of Scottish institutions saw a similar decline. Actually enrolment fell by only 120.

Abertay has been gradually improving its position in *The Times and Sunday Times* league table. Its strength has been in graduate employment figures that are comfortably in the top half of the table. There have been occasional suggestions that Abertay might merge with neighbouring Dundee University – most recently in 2011 – but it is now firmly on an independent path.

Entrance requirements have been rising, although for most courses other than high-demand areas such as computer games, they are still modest. Well-qualified A-level students are eligible for direct entry into second year.

Degrees are predominantly vocational, with more subjects being added every year. Food and consumer sciences, creative sound production, and digital forensics are recent examples. All courses can be taken on a part-time basis, and new programmes aim to offer students the chance to spend at least 30 per cent of their time in industry.

Undergraduates take a maximum of eight core modules a year plus options, completing a Certificate of Higher Education after one year, a diploma after two, an ordinary degree after three, or honours in four years. The dropout rate

has been improving and is now one in ten – considerably better than average for its courses and entry qualifications. Abertay is piloting problem-based and work-based approaches to learning, focusing on real-world issues and teamwork rather than sitting in conventional lectures.

New premises for the £5-million Business Prototyping Project to support the UK's creative industries opened in 2011. The university also hosts the Dundee Academy of Sport, launched in partnership with Dundee and Angus College – a venture using sport as a vehicle for learning across the school curriculum and throughout life.

Dundee has seen considerable investment recently. The city has a large student population and the cost of living is modest. A 500-bed student village opened in 2010, lifting pressure on housing sufficiently to allow all first-years to be guaranteed accommodation.

Undergraduate Fees and Bursaries

» Fees for Scottish and EU students 2014–15   No fee
» Fees for Non-Scottish UK (RUK) students for 2014–15   £7,000
» Fees for international students 2014–15   £10,500
» Academic merit or personal achievement in music or sport scholarships, £1,500 a year.
» For RUK students: household income below £27K, annual bursary £1,750; household income £17K–£24K, £1,000; household income £24K–£34K, £500. Merit award of £1,000 for RUK students with ABB at A level or above.

Students

Undergraduates:	**4,125**	**(290)**
Postgraduates:	**260**	**(155)**
Mature students:	**30.2%**	
International students:	**10.4%**	
Applications per place:	**5**	
From state-sector schools:	**93.6%**	
From working-class homes:	**34.7%**	
Satisfaction with students' union	**66%**	

For detailed information about sports facilities:
www.sport.abertay.ac.uk/

Accommodation

Number of places and costs refer to 2014–15
University-provided places: 668
Percentage catered: 0%
Self-catered costs: £59.00–£112.31 a week (38, 42 or 51 weeks).
All new entrants (home and international) guaranteed accommodation if conditions are met. Early bird discount available (some residential restrictions).
Free bus travel for students living in Alloway Halls.
residences@abertay.ac.uk
www.abertay.ac.uk/studying/accommodation

Aberystwyth University

Aberystwyth has doubled the investment it is planning in its residences and teaching and research facilities, taking total spending to £100 million. The first students have moved into new residences close to the existing student village and within walking distance of the Penglais and Llanbadarn campuses. They provide self-catering accommodation for 1,000 students in flats for six or eight, with a central hub that houses social and learning facilities. The Llanbadarn Centre has been reconfigured and refurbished to provide improved teaching accommodation for management, business, law and information studies and a new innovation and research campus is due to open in 2015 at Gogerddan. An upland agricultural research centre is being developed near Aberystwyth, while the original Old College Building is to be redeveloped as an arts centre, with postgraduate accommodation and study space.

The attractive seaside location remains a draw for applicants and there had been strong growth in the demand for places over several years before the fees went up. Although the oldest of the Welsh universities, Aberystwyth has long prided itself on a modern outlook: it was among the pioneers of the modular degree system and allowed students flexibility between subjects even before that. Uniquely in the UK, every student is offered the opportunity of a year's work experience in commerce, industry or the public sector, either at home or abroad. Those who have taken advantage of the scheme have achieved better than average degrees and enhanced their employment prospects. Welsh-medium teaching is thriving, with more courses available in the language.

Aberystwyth has set itself the goal of becoming one of the top 30 universities in the UK and the top 250 in the world by 2017. It is a tall order where *The Times and Sunday Times* league table is concerned: an 11-place drop has taken it to its lowest-ever position of 93rd. The university's strategic plan emphasises the student experience. The university has done well in the International Student Barometer, which compares Aberystwyth favourably with other institutions – not only in Wales, but the UK as a whole. Nevertheless, applications were down 9 per cent in 2013, in spite of the fee concessions offered to Welsh students, who make up about a third of Aber's intake, although there was only a small drop in the numbers taking up places.

Over 90 per cent of the undergraduates come from state schools or colleges – a higher proportion than the mix of subjects would imply – but the proportion of entrants from working-class homes was only 30 per cent in the latest survey. The

Penglais
Aberystwyth
Ceredigion SY23 3FL

01970 622021 (admissions)
ug-admissions@aber.ac.uk
www.aber.ac.uk
www.abersu.co.uk
Affiliation: none

The Times and Sunday Times **Rankings**
Overall Ranking: **93** (last year: 82)

Student satisfaction:	111	77.9%
Research quality:	=35	20.3%
Entry standards:	71	325
Student–staff ratio:	=92	20.0
Services & facilities/student:	106	£1,167
Expected completion rate:	=59	86.1%
Good honours:	=82	63.2%
Graduate prospects:	113	52.8%

projected dropout rate of less than 10 per cent is one of the lowest in Wales. A Student Welcome Centre continues to offer advice on everything from money problems to learning difficulties long after undergraduates have enrolled.

Recent developments include a building on the main Penglais campus for the Institute of Biological, Environmental and Rural Sciences, which serves more than 1,000 undergraduate and research students and has a remit to look for creative solutions to some of the major challenges facing the world in sustainable land use, climate change, renewable energy, and the security of food and water supplies. The Institute, which has a link with Bangor University, has over 300 staff and an annual budget in excess of £25 million, making it one of the largest groups of scientists and support staff working in this field in Europe. Aber has the widest range of land-related courses in the UK.

Entrance scholarships and bursaries are available in a range of subjects, even though Welsh students have been spared the full impact of higher fees. Aber boasts one of higher education's most informative websites and also publishes a special guide for parents. There is 24-hour access to the computer network, and the four university libraries are complemented by the National Library of Wales. International politics produced the best results in the 2008 research assessments, when computer science was the leader in Wales, while geography and earth sciences, Welsh, and theatre, film and television also did well.

Aberystwyth town is compact and travel to other parts of the UK slow, so applicants should be sure that they will be happy to spend three years or more in a tight-knit community. The students' guild is the largest entertainment venue in the region. The seaside town of 25,000 people was voted the best university location in Wales and eighth in the UK in one survey. There is plenty of out-of-season accommodation to supplement the university's extensive stock. Sports facilities are good and well used, and include a 400-metre running track, 50 acres of playing fields, a new 3G pitch, refurbished swimming pool, a climbing wall and specialist outdoor facilities for water sports.

Undergraduate Fees and Bursaries

- » Fees for UK/EU students for 2015–16 £9,000
- » Year abroad £1,350
- » Placement year £700
- » Welsh Assembly non-means-tested grant to pay fees above £3,685 (2014–15) for Welsh students.
- » Fees for international students 2014–15 £10,500–£12,000
- » For all UK students: household income less than £18,371, a bursary of £1,100 a year; sliding scale to £34,090, £950–£700; £400 bursary in year 1 for those in university accommodation.
- » Entrance scholarships and subject-linked bursaries available, from £500 to £1,200 a year.

Students

Undergraduates:	8,035	(1,805)
Postgraduates:	1,090	(685)
Mature students:	13.2%	
International students:	13.5%	
Applications per place:	3.9	
From state-sector schools:	93.7%	
From working-class homes:	30%	
Satisfaction with students' union	56%	

For detailed information about sports facilities:
www.aber.ac.uk/sportscentre/

Accommodation

Number of places and costs refer to 2014–15
University-provided places: 3,750
Percentage catered: 15%
Catered costs: £94.20 (twin) – £116.20 (single) a week (32 or 38 weeks).
Self-catered costs: £78.40 (twin) – £133.00 (single) a week (38 or 50 weeks).
First years are guaranteed accommodation if conditions are met.
International: guaranteed for those classed as overseas for fees.
accommodation@aber.ac.uk;
www.aber.ac.uk/en/accommodation/

Anglia Ruskin University

Even before it became a university, Anglia Ruskin had strong links with employers, involving them in course design and delivery. Now Harrods, Barclays, UPS, Vision Express, Specsavers, Volvo, the RAF and British Army are among the employers whose staff take the university's courses. And the university's business-facing approach helps to produce average graduate starting salaries 10 per cent above the national average, at £23,000. Among its latest initiatives are a £6-million business innovation centre, which includes a Startup Lab for Anglia Ruskin students to test and develop their ideas.

Anglia Ruskin is one of the largest universities in Eastern England, with over 30,000 students, including part-timers. The two main campuses are at Cambridge and Chelmsford, some 40 miles apart with a smaller campus at Peterborough and University Centres in Harlow, King's Lynn and Peterborough. The university has invested £122 million in the last five years in the latest learning environments, including the £35-million redevelopment of the Cambridge campus and two buildings dedicated to Health and Social Care in Chelmsford. It plans to spend another £98 million over the next five years, beginning with the development of a new £9-million site five minutes' walk from the East Road campus, in Cambridge. A new Health Building is already open, as well as a Music Therapy Centre. The remainder of the site should be ready by Autumn 2015.

Anglia Ruskin was the last university to retain a polytechnic title, discarding it in 2005. The former APU took the name of John Ruskin, who founded the Cambridge School of Art, which evolved into Anglia Ruskin. It has since acquired the former Homerton College School of Health Studies in Cambridge, after a long period of partnership, and opened the £9.3-million University Centre Harlow with Harlow College, Britain's oldest journalism school. In Chelmsford, the 22-acre Rivermead campus boasts an impressive business school and a sports hall, as well as the £15-million Marconi Building for law students. Recent additions include a new health and social care building with counselling rooms, simulated hospital wards, operating theatres and a complementary medicine suite.

The university has a history of providing innovative courses: the BOptom (Hons) is the only qualification of its kind in the UK and the Hearing Aid Audiology course was among the first to lead directly to registration. Paramedic Science is the latest addition. Among the specialist study facilities are an eye clinic, forensic science laboratories, a music therapy clinic, multimedia language laboratories, a human

Chelmsford Campus:
Bishop Hall Lane,
Chelmsford CM1 1SQ
Cambridge Campus:
East Road,
Cambridge CB1 1PT
0845 271 3333 (enquiries)
answers@anglia.ac.uk
www.anglia.ac.uk
www.angliastudent.com
Affiliation: million+

The Times and Sunday Times Rankings
Overall Ranking: **110** (last year: 110)

Student satisfaction:	=34	83.4%
Research quality:	=102	1.7%
Entry standards:	119	252
Student–staff ratio:	=116	23.0
Services & facilities/student:	=96	£1,279
Expected completion rate:	=87	82.5%
Good honours:	118	51.6%
Graduate prospects:	91	58.5%

energetic sports science laboratory, and a mock courtroom. Electronic networking and a central administration mean that key academic facilities are available throughout all campuses.

Nearly all the students attended state schools or colleges and almost 40 per cent are from working-class homes. The projected dropout rate had improved in the latest survey, and is significantly better than the national average for its subjects and entry grades. Each undergraduate has an adviser to help compile a degree package which looks at the chosen subject from different points of view to maximise future job prospects. Three-quarters of the full-time undergraduate leavers who find jobs in the UK stay in East Anglia. The university has an innovative scheme placing graduates with the region's small firms – usually the companies that are least likely to take on those emerging from higher education.

Anglia Ruskin stresses its green credentials and was the first UK university to sign the Rio+20 Declaration of Higher Education Institutions. Its Global Sustainability Institute, established in 2011, is building an international reputation for its research on behaviour change, resource scarcity and climate finance, and Anglia Ruskin is aiming to make sustainability an important part of every student's experience. Only 71 academics were entered for the Research Assessment Exercise in 2008, but almost a third of their work was considered world-leading or internationally excellent. All but one of the nine subject areas had some top-rated research, with history, English and psychology producing the best grades. Psychology produced the best results among the post-1992 universities.

The social scene varies between the campuses. There is limited collaboration with Cambridge University on the Cambridge Centre for Cricketing Excellence, and a base for Anglia Ruskin's Rowing Club. The university's flourishing programme to encourage sporting participation is particularly successful at elite level in judo. Sports facilities in Cambridge are being improved with the addition of a new pavilion, and both grass and artificial pitches, including one 3G surface. In the past, some students have found Chelmsford's social scene underwhelming, but it is said to be improving, and neither main base is far from London by train.

Undergraduate Fees and Bursaries

- » Fees for UK/EU students 2015–16 £9,000
- » Foundation degree £7,500
- » Undergraduate courses at associated colleges £6,000–£8,500
- » Fees for international students 2014–15 £9,800–£10,300
- » Household income below £25K, £800 study-related services each year.
- » Household income below £42.6K, £400 of study-related services each year.

Students

Undergraduates:	**13,210**	**(4,440)**
Postgraduates:	**1,800**	**(1,625)**
Mature students:	**30.4%**	
International students:	**11.8%**	
Applications per place:	**4.5**	
From state-sector schools:	**96.3%**	
From working-class homes:	**39.6%**	
Satisfaction with students' union	**66%**	

For detailed information about sports facilities:
www.anglia.ac.uk/sport

Accommodation

Number of places and costs refer to 2014–15
University-provided places: Cambridge, 708 plus 1,237 referral rooms; Chelmsford, 511
Percentage catered: 0%
Self-catered costs: Cambridge: £84–£165 a week; Chelmsford: £107–£114 a week.
Most first years are accommodated. Distance restrictions apply.
International students: conditions and deadline apply.
essexaccom@anglia.ac.uk; cambaccom@anglia.ac.uk
www.anglia.ac.uk/housing

Arts University Bournemouth

The new Arts University Bournemouth (AUB) made its debut in *The Times and Sunday Times* league table last year in the top half of the ranking, above all of its peers in the latest wave of universities and among the highest-placed of those established in the last 25 years. Unlike other arts-based institutions, it scores well in the National Student Survey and in terms of graduate employment. The combination – and the new title – is proving popular: a healthy increase in applications allowed the university to increase the size of the undergraduate intake by 18 per cent in 2013.

Awarded university status in 2012, the former Arts University College Bournemouth has some 3,000 students based on a single campus. It has operated as a specialist institution since 1885 and is now one of only 15 higher education institutions in the UK devoted solely to the study of art, design and media. AUB is one of four arts universities in our table because it offers a sufficiently wide portfolio of courses to qualify for inclusion. There are degrees in acting, architecture, dance, event management and film production, as well as art and design subjects. The university describes its courses as having a "highly practical streak" designed to give students an edge in a competitive creative world.

The campus in Wallisdown, which straddles Bournemouth and Poole, was opened in the 1980s by the Princess Royal, who returned in 2007 to open University House, the current flagship building. The Gallery showcases work by students and other contemporary artists, hosting talks, events and film nights to support the exhibition programme. There is also an Enterprise Pavilion (eP) on campus to develop, attract and retain new creative businesses in the South West. The purpose-built library has over 50,000 books covering a wide range of art, design, media and performance subjects, with a further collection of more than 45,000 e-books and over 300 specialist journal titles, many of which are available online. The Museum of Design in Plastics is located in the library and holds over 12,000 artefacts of predominantly 20th- and 21st-century mass-produced design and popular culture. The items are selected specifically to support the academic courses taught at the university. Laser cutting machinery and a 3-D printer feature among the high-tech equipment available to students.

More than a third of the undergraduates are from working-class homes and 96 per cent attended state schools or colleges – both figures close to the national average for AUB's subjects and entry qualifications. The low dropout rate is a point of particular pride – at only 5 per cent, it is half the

---

Wallisdown
Poole
Dorset BH12 5HH

01202 533011
hello@aub.ac.uk (enquiries)
www.aub.ac.uk
http://aubsu.co.uk
Affiliation: GuildHE

The Times and Sunday Times Rankings

Overall Ranking: **59** (last year: =52)

Student satisfaction:	=59	82.3%
Research quality:	=117	0.3%
Entry standards:	68	331
Student–staff ratio:	=26	14.9
Services & facilities/student:	120	£640
Expected completion rate:	=37	90.4%
Good honours:	86	62.6%
Graduate prospects:	61	66.2%

university's benchmark figure. Students and staff work in partnership on an innovative programme of professional practice and research, with different disciplines encouraged to work together. The academics include many with experience in, and continuing engagement with, the creative industries, while the careers service provides students with subject-specific and generic advice on future employment. Industry liaison groups and visiting tutors keep the university abreast of developments in the creative industries, while alumni return regularly as lecturers. Students are encouraged to join the university's European Exchange programme to study abroad.

AUB was a university college for only three years, having been given degree awarding powers in 2008. It now boasts a Skillset Media Academy in partnership with Bournemouth University, offering eight accredited courses in animation, film and digital media production, photography, make-up for media and performance, graphic design and model-making. The two universities also bid successfully to become a Screen Academy, through which Skillset recognises excellence in film and the broader screen-based media, providing some students with access bursaries. The most recent audit of the university by the Quality Assurance Agency resulted in the highest possible grade, commending the

academic standards and highlighting a number of features of good practice.

The university has fewer than 600 places in its halls of residence and gives priority in their allocation to overseas students and those with disabilities or other medical conditions. There is plenty of privately rented accommodation in the area, for which the average rent in 2013–14 was £85 a week in a shared house. The university keeps a register of approved housing at the **www.aubstudentpad.com** website and runs accommodation days in July and August for current and prospective students to find potential housemates. Bournemouth has a large and cosmopolitan student population and one of the most vibrant club scenes outside London. The capital is less than two hours away and is easily reached by regular train and coach services or via good motorway links. Bournemouth and Southampton both have international airports providing good value flights to more than 50 destinations.

Undergraduate Fees and Bursaries

» Fees for UK/EU students 2015–16	£9,000
» Year abroad	£1,000
» Fees for international students 2014–15	£12,510
» Course material fee waived for all students.	
» Household income below £25K, £200 progression scholarship at Level 6.	

Students

Undergraduates:	**2,750**	**(40)**
Postgraduates:	**45**	**(30)**
Mature students:	**10.5%**	
International students:	**12.3%**	
Applications per place:	**5.2**	
From state-sector schools:	**96.5%**	
From working-class homes:	**34.4%**	
Satisfaction with students' union	**67%**	

For detailed information about sports facilities:
http://aucbsu.co.uk/sports

Accommodation

Number of places and costs refer to 2014–15
University-provided places: 560
Percentage catered: 0%
Self-catered costs: £110 (single en suite); £115(double, en suite); £139 (single studio); £130 (double studio) a week.
Priority is given to students with medical conditions/disabilities.
International students have priority.
studentadvice@aub.ac.uk
http://aub.ac.uk/plan-visit-apply/accommodation/

University of the Arts London

Arts subjects – and institutions – suffered disproportionately from the introduction of £9,000 fees. But the University of the Arts London (UAL) saw a strong recovery in the demand for places in 2013, with a 5 per cent increase in applications and a bigger undergraduate intake. UAL is the biggest specialist art and design university in Europe, a federation of six colleges that also cover fashion and media, most of which are world-famous in their own right.

Five of the colleges originally came together as the London Institute in 1989 and became a university 15 years later. Almost 20,000 students are spread through 14 sites around central London. A global reputation attracts more than 3,200 international students and 1,500 from other EU countries. The five colleges became six when Wimbledon College of Arts joined in 2006, bringing an international reputation in theatre design and the UK's largest school of theatre. The founding members, which continue to use their own names and enjoy considerable autonomy, were Camberwell College of Arts, Central Saint Martins, Chelsea College of Arts, London College of Fashion and London College of Communication (formerly the London College of Printing). The university offers one Foundation course across Camberwell, Chelsea and Wimbledon.

Big changes were already under way before the change of title was agreed: a £70-million development next door to the Tate Gallery produced prestigious new premises for Chelsea College, with extensive workshop facilities, studios and a new library. Another £32 million was spent on new headquarters for the College of Communication at the Elephant and Castle, south of the Thames, where a Special Archives and Collections Centre includes the archives of the filmmaker Stanley Kubrick. The college has Film Academy status. London's largest open-air art gallery was launched in 2008 on the Parade Ground at the heart of the Chelsea College, and final-year students' work is also showcased online at a virtual degree show. The university hopes to consolidate the London College of Fashion's three East London sites, but there are no detailed plans yet.

The biggest project of all has brought Central Saint Martins together on one site for the first time, moving to the new King's Cross development. The £200-million campus is based on a Grade II listed former granary, which accommodates a new School of Performing Arts as well as the college's existing art, fashion and design courses. There is a 350-seat public theatre, studios and rehearsal spaces, as well as four levels

---

272 High Holborn
London WC1V 7EY

0207 514 6197 (admissions)
admissions@arts.ac.uk
www.arts.ac.uk
www.suarts.org
Affiliation: none

The Times and Sunday Times **Rankings**
Overall Ranking: **85** (last year: =77)

Student satisfaction:	**123**	73.4%
Research quality:	**=35**	20.3%
Entry standards:	**=53**	343
Student–staff ratio:	**=78**	18.7
Services & facilities/student:	**60**	£1,562
Expected completion rate:	**56**	87.1%
Good honours:	**=72**	64.3%
Graduate prospects:	**109**	55.0%

of workshops, studios and exhibition space, with facilities for students from across the university. The new building was voted the world's best higher education building in 2012.

An inability, shared by most arts-based institutions, to match the high levels of student satisfaction seen at generalist universities holds UAL back in our league table. Overall satisfaction levels fell in the 2014 National Student Survey, leaving the university at the bottom on this measure. Published assessments have barely done justice to the eminence of the colleges, although the 2008 Research Assessment Exercise saw half of the university's submission rated as world-leading or internationally excellent. All the colleges make good use of visiting lecturers, who keep students abreast of developments in their field. The university has also been running weekend classes and summer schools in an attempt to broaden the intake. The proportion of undergraduates from working-class homes is just under 30 per cent, while 95 per cent come from state schools or colleges. Almost three-quarters of the undergraduates are female. The latest survey showed a sharp rise in the dropout rate, but this followed a succession of improvements. At 12 per cent, it is still close to the national average for the university's courses and entry grades.

Students have access to the largest art and design specialist careers centre in the country, in the Student Enterprise and Employability Service, while the pioneering Emerging Artists Programme continues to support graduates in the early years of their careers. The university holds the only recruitment festival tailored to the needs of creative graduates, providing access to hundreds of industry professionals for networking opportunities and advice.

The colleges vary considerably in character and facilities, although a single students' union serves them all. The university's student hub provides a central place for students to work, socialise and share ideas, as well as being the location for student services such as housing and careers. The university is not overprovided with residential accommodation, although there are 13 residences spread around the colleges, providing more than 3,000 beds. House-hunting workshops help those who have to rely on an expensive private housing market. The university owns no sports facilities, although it has arranged student discounts with a number of providers.

Undergraduate Fees and Bursaries
» Fees for UK/EU students 2015–16 £9,000
» Fees for international students 2014–15 £15,180
» Household income below £25K, minimum of £1,000 each year.
» Range of scholarships available.
» Check the university's website for the latest information.

Students		
Undergraduates:	13,560	(425)
Postgraduates:	2,315	(745)
Mature students:	23.2%	
International students:	39.4%	
Applications per place:	6.6	
From state-sector schools:	95.6%	
From working-class homes:	29.5%	
Satisfaction with students' union	56%	
For detailed information about sports facilities:		
www.suarts.org/groups#club-society#sport		

Accommodation
Number of places and costs refer to 2014–15
University-provided places: 3,051
Percentage catered: 0%
Self-catered costs: £99–£264 a week.
First-year students are offered accommodation if conditions are met.
Priority for disabled students and those from outside London.
International students: guaranteed if conditions met.
accommodation@arts.ac.uk
www.arts.ac.uk/study-at-ual/accommodation/

Aston University

Aston has been bulldozing the last of the 1970s buildings from its early days as a university, to create a landscaped centre to the campus that symbolises a new era. Only one university has enjoyed stronger growth in the demand for places over the last two years and none has seen a bigger rise in student satisfaction. The applications boom enabled Aston to take 17 per cent more undergraduates in 2013, almost half of them coming with ABB or better at A level. Many are attracted by a consistently good graduate employment record – the university's main selling point. Seven out of ten students have a work placement, often abroad, and the target is 100 per cent.

Small and lively, set in the heart of Birmingham, the university has remained resolutely specialist in business, science and technology, languages and social science, concentrating on the sandwich degrees which have served its graduates so well in the employment market. Even after considerable growth in recent years, in 2013–14 there were still only 11,000 students – 9,200 of them undergraduates. With the Government's relaxation of recruitment controls, the aim is to grow to 13,000 by 2017. By then, Aston expects to open a privately funded medical school and to launch new undergraduate programmes such as applied physics.

The university has been concentrating on improving the student experience and boosting research performance with the eventual aim of becoming a top ten university. The new MyAston mobile app allows all students to access course materials and other information remotely and at a time of their own choosing. Over 70 per cent signed up for the service in the first six months. The completion of the Aston Student Villages provides 3,000 en-suite rooms on campus. They are part of a £215-million programme of improvements. An impressive new library opened in 2010. The Woodcock Sport Centre, which includes a Grade II listed swimming pool, followed in 2011 and has since acquired a new sports hall with indoor courts and team sports facilities. More chemistry and chemical engineering laboratories have been provided and £16.5 million spent on the European Bio Energy Research Centre.

Once a college of advanced technology, Aston remains strong in engineering and the sciences, although the highly rated business school accounts for almost half of the students. A £20-million extension to the business school has seen an increase in staff from 80 to over 120. New undergraduates are offered 12 online study skills modules before the formal start of their course. Aston has also introduced a free programme of language tuition for all

---

Aston Triangle
Birmingham B4 7ET

0121 204 4444 (course enquiries)
ugenquiries@aston.ac.uk
www.aston.ac.uk
www.astonunion.com
Affiliation: none

The Times and Sunday Times **Rankings**
Overall Ranking: **=34** (last year: =29)

Student satisfaction:	=24	84.0%
Research quality:	50	13.3%
Entry standards:	42	381
Student–staff ratio:	=44	16.2
Services & facilities/student:	49	£1,735
Expected completion rate:	30	91.6%
Good honours:	30	75.2%
Graduate prospects:	26	77.1%

students, covering six languages from Arabic to Portuguese, as part of its efforts to help boost employability further. More than a quarter of first-year students use the service.

There is a wide range of joint honours programmes for those who prefer not to specialise. Almost nine out of ten Aston graduates – far more than the national average – go straight into jobs, often returning to the scene of work placements. The tuition fee for the placement year is set at £1,000, and most students are paid by their host company. At the forefront of employer-led degrees, the university was awarded £1.6 million to set up a Foundation Degree Centre to establish new courses and explore other ways of delivering qualifications.

The projected dropout rate has improved considerably in recent years and, at 7 per cent, is well ahead of the national average for Aston's subjects. The intake is diverse, with more than 40 per cent of the undergraduates coming from working-class homes. Six out of ten undergraduates come from outside the West Midlands, around a fifth of them from outside the UK.

Business and management led the way in the 2008 Research Assessment Exercise, with health subjects also producing good grades. New research centres have since been established in enterprise, healthy ageing, Europe, and neuroscience and child development. The £6-million Aston Brain Centre opened in 2011, combining research and teaching in a single unique facility. Research funding is at record levels, with the new Aston Institute for Photonics Research proving particularly successful.

Residential places are guaranteed for first years and overseas students. Recent developments have helped to place Aston among the top dozen universities in the People and Planet Green League of sustainability for the past three years. It has been given "Platinum Eco Campus" status for demonstrating a lasting commitment to sustainability. The renamed Aston Students' Union remains active, both socially and in student welfare matters.

Undergraduate Fees and Bursaries

» Fees for UK/EU students 2015–16 £9,000
» Fees for international students 2014–15 £13,000–£16,000
» Household income below £25K, at least 500 awards of £1,000 university accommodation discount in year 1, £1,000 fee discount for placement year, progression scholarships of £500 cash or £500 fee or university accommodation discount in years 2 and 4.
» Household income below £35K, £500 cash or £500 fee or university accommodation discount each year.
» For all Home/EU students, £1,000 placement year scholarship as cash or fee waiver.
» Excellence scholarships (AAB at A level or equivalent), £1,000 fee waiver, accommodation discount or cash in year 1 and placement year, £500 in years 2 and 4.
» Check the university's website for the latest information.

Students

Undergraduates:	7,280	(595)
Postgraduates:	1,335	(780)
Mature students:	9.2%	
International students:	21.7%	
Applications per place:	5.1	
From state-sector schools:	93.1%	
From working-class homes:	42.9%	
Satisfaction with students' union	62%	

For detailed information about sports facilities:
www.aston.ac.uk/prospective-students/sport/

Accommodation

Number of places and costs refer to 2014–15
University-provided places: 3,017
Percentage catered: 0%
Self-catered accommodation: £116–£129 (42 weeks); £113–£126 (45 weeks); £107–£120 (51 weeks).
First years are guaranteed accommodation if they fulfil requirements and apply by the deadline.
International fee-paying students: as above.
accom@aston.ac.uk
www.aston.ac.uk/study/accommodation/

Bangor University

Bangor featured in the top 20 universities in *Times Higher Education* magazine's 2014 student experience survey, scoring well for helpful staff, good security and accommodation. The small North Wales city has been rated as among the cheapest in the UK in which to study and the standard of university accommodation has been rated in the top 10. A Peer Guiding scheme, where second and third year students mentor new students and arrange social activities for them, is one of the largest schemes in the country. Such features are reflected in consistently high student satisfaction scores, which has seen Bangor reach the top 50 in *The Times and Sunday Times* league table this year, even with relatively modest entry standards and low spending on student services.

The university estate has been re-developed, with the addition of a £5-million environmental sciences building, while a £3.5-million Cancer Research Institute is attracting specialists of international repute. A combination of private funds and a £5-million European grant was used to establish a new Business Management Centre on a waterfront site. A £40-million Arts and Innovation Centre is due to open in 2014, forming a bridge between the university's upper campus and the nearby science site. The centre will focus on science, technology and the creative arts, and will include a theatre, studio, cinema, lecture theatres, exhibition spaces, bar and café. Improved sports facilities such as the new Dome and new student accommodation that includes studio apartments and townhouses are among the latest developments.

Bangor's community focus dates back to a 19th-century campaign which saw local quarrymen putting part of their weekly wages towards the establishment of a college. The School of Lifelong Learning continues the tradition with courses across North Wales, but the university has also built a worldwide reputation in areas such as environmental studies and ocean sciences. Like Swansea and Aberystwyth, it left the University of Wales to assert its independence, taking the title of Bangor University and awarding its own degrees.

Bangor merged with a nearby teacher training college, Coleg Normal, in 1996, and that site is now part of the university. The 23 academic schools are grouped into five colleges. All schools are within walking distance of each other, apart from the School of Ocean Sciences, which is two miles away in Menai Bridge. The 2008 research assessments identified some world-leading work in all Bangor's 19 subject areas. The university claimed the grades for accounting and finance to be the best in the UK, with electronic engineering second and

---

Bangor
Gwynedd LL57 2DG

01248 388484 (admissions)
admissions@bangor.ac.uk
www.bangor.ac.uk
www.undeb.bangor.ac.uk
Affiliation: none

The Times and Sunday Times **Rankings**
Overall Ranking: **50** (last year: 56)

Student satisfaction:	=11	85.4%
Research quality:	=45	16.0%
Entry standards:	=91	305
Student–staff ratio:	=63	17.8
Services & facilities/student:	105	£1,169
Expected completion rate:	68	85.1%
Good honours:	=89	61.2%
Graduate prospects:	59	66.6%

both sports science and Welsh in the top ten in their respective subjects.

The university is an expanding centre for Welsh-medium teaching. Although a majority of students come from outside Wales – there is a strong link with Ireland, for example – around 20 per cent of the students speak the language and one of the halls of residence is for Welsh-speakers. Bangor also has a flourishing international exchange programme. Undergraduate students are offered a study abroad option to give them the international experience many employers are now looking for. The International Experience Programme gives students the option of studying overseas for one extra year in a wide variety of destinations in Europe, North America, Australia and the Far East.

Almost 95 per cent of the students come from state schools or colleges, and more than a third are from working-class homes. For 2015 entry, the university is offering scholarships and bursaries worth over £3.7 million, which range from merit awards based on pre-entry examinations, to sports scholarships and excellence awards in several subject areas. The university's Talent Opportunities Programme, which operates in schools across North Wales, targets potential applicants from lower socio-economic families, who have little or no history of going on to university.

There is a strong focus on student support including a pioneering dyslexia unit, which offers individual and group support throughout students' courses. The Study Skills Centre, which opened in 2013, helps with the transition to university and provide continuing academic support. In addition, the Bangor Employability Award (BEA) has been introduced to enhance students' career prospects by accrediting co-curricular and extra-curricular activities such as volunteering and part-time work that are valued by employers.

The university is rated the "greenest" in Wales and is in the top 20 in an international league table of environmentally friendly institutions. The city is little more than a stone's throw from Snowdonia with its attractions for sports enthusiasts. Social life for most students is concentrated on the students' union, which has around 150 clubs and societies, covering a range of interests, activities and sports.

Undergraduate Fees and Bursaries

» Fees for UK/EU students 2015–16   £9,000
» Welsh Assembly non-means-tested grant to pay fees above £3,685 (2014–15) for Welsh students.
» Fees for international students 2014–15   £11,000–£12,800
» Bangor Bursary: household income below £25K, £1,500 a year; household income £25K–£40K, £750 a year. Welsh-medium study bursaries.
» Scholarships include Excellence Scholarships (up to £5,000) in some subjects and Merit Scholarships (up to £3,000), awarded on Entrance Scholarship examinations.

Students

Undergraduates:	7,315	(1,145)
Postgraduates:	1,940	(960)
Mature students:	18.2%	
International students:	11.4%	
Applications per place:	4.6	
From state-sector schools:	94.5%	
From working-class homes:	35.1%	
Satisfaction with students' union	69%	

For detailed information about sports facilities: www.bangor.ac.uk/brailsford

Accommodation

Number of places and costs refer to 2014–15
University-provided places: around 2,450
Percentage catered: 0%
Self-catered costs: £71–£100 (standard); £105–£127 (en-suite or larger rooms) a week (40–42 weeks UG contract).
All first-year students are guaranteed places.
International UG students: as above.
halls@bangor.ac.uk;
www.bangor.ac.uk/accommodation

University of Bath

Until this year Bath had been climbing *The Times and Sunday Times* league table and it continues to go from strength to strength in terms of popularity. There has been a 12 per cent rise in applications in 2014, repeating the previous year's increase and far outpacing the national average. The demand for places is strong both in the UK and overseas, and those who win places generally do not regret it: Bath had the top score in the 2013 National Student Survey, and almost repeated the feat this year, when 93 per cent were satisfied overall.

With its origins as a technological university established in the 1960s, Bath is still a relatively small institution with a high proportion of postgraduates. The modern campus on the edge of Bath cannot live up to the magnificence of the city's architecture, but the 200-acre site has pleasant grounds, with academic, recreational and residential facilities in close proximity. The university is rated among the top 20 in the world in the GreenMetric environmental ranking. The sports facilities are outstanding and were used as a training base in sports as diverse as athletics, judo, swimming and beach volleyball in the run up to London 2012. The university's Sports Training Village was chosen to host the Paralympics GB team ahead of the Games

and will do so again before Rio 2016. Eleven alumni and athletes who train at the university won medals at the Games. Over 1,500 students compete regularly at every level from regional leagues to national tournaments.

The university is in the midst of a four-year £150-million capital programme to provide new teaching and research space, student accommodation and a new arts centre. Additional teaching accommodation for 2,000 students opened in 2013 and is connected to the main campus parade by a "skywalk" bridge. A £43-million student accommodation complex providing 708 additional en-suite bedrooms in 75 flats was available for 2014 entrants. The new Centre for the Arts opens at the end of 2014 and contains a theatre, performance and rehearsal studios, a gallery and teaching facilities. Two more academic buildings are due to open by September 2015, one for engineering and the other for psychology. In addition, the university is refurbishing the central 1 West building, which will have new learning facilities, computer laboratories, research facilities and offices.

The Claverton campus features a modern student centre and a dedicated centre for postgraduates. The sports facilities were already among the best in Britain before the addition of a £35-million training village, funded with Lottery money. There is a 50-metre swimming pool, indoor running

---

Claverton Down
Bath BA2 7AY

01225 383019 (admissions)
ask-admissions@bath.ac.uk
www.bath.ac.uk
www.bathstudent.com
Affiliation: none

The Times and Sunday Times Rankings
Overall Ranking: **10** (last year: 7)

Student satisfaction:	=2	87.1%
Research quality:	=23	23.3%
Entry standards:	=9	489
Student–staff ratio:	=48	16.6
Services & facilities/student:	40	£1,784
Expected completion rate:	11	95.2%
Good honours:	15	80.2%
Graduate prospects:	3	85.4%

track, multipurpose sports hall, eight indoor tennis courts, an indoor jumps and throws hall, air pistol and fencing sale, a judo dojo and a simulated bobsleigh track. There is even a skeleton start area, as used by Lizzy Yarnold, the 2014 Olympic gold medallist, and her predecessor Amy Williams. The university pioneered sports scholarships more than 20 years ago and there will be a range of them available for 2015.

Research is Bath's greatest strength: 60 per cent of the work submitted for the 2008 Research Assessment Exercise was judged to be world-leading or inter nationally excellent. Social work and social policy, business and management, physics, maths and pharmacy did particularly well, but there were good results in a number of areas. The university's research grants and contracts portfolio is worth £117 million. Most degree courses have a practical element, and assessors have praised the university for the work placements it offers. Most undergraduates take courses with placements or a period of study abroad, which helps to produce consistently outstanding graduate employment figures. Bath has become the first UK university to join the Magalhaes Network of leading universities from Latin America, the Caribbean and the EU, opening up new opportunities for engineering and architecture students. Student entrepreneurship is actively encouraged

through a number of initiatives and projects. Recent additions to the portfolio of courses include integrated undergraduate master's degrees in sport and exercise science and also in psychology, which can be taken over four years, or five with a placement. There is also a new suite of management degrees and a BSc in biomedical sciences, with input from specialists in biology and biochemistry, health and pharmacy and pharmacology. New programmes in physics and astrophysics are planned for 2015.

A quarter of the undergraduates were educated at independent schools. Many take advantage of the nightlife of Bristol, with its combined student population of more than 60,000, which is only a few minutes away by public transport. The popular students' union has a Gold Best Bar None award for the management of its bar and nightclub, and has also been commended for its provision for international students. The university's support services include a new virtual learning environment and centralised provision of advisory services.

Undergraduate Fees and Bursaries

» Fees for UK/EU students 2015–16 £9,000
» Franchised Foundation degree £7,500
» Fees for international students 2014–15 £13,700–£17,400
» Household income £20K or below and other criteria, £3,000 cash each year (including unpaid placement or overseas study year).
» Range of scholarships and bursaries available.

Students

Undergraduates:	**10,215**	**(370)**
Postgraduates:	**2,185**	**(2,295)**
Mature students:	**2.7%**	
International students:	**21.9%**	
Applications per place:	**7.4**	
From state-sector schools:	**74.0%**	
From working-class homes:	**16.8%**	
Satisfaction with students' union	**84%**	

For detailed information about sports facilities:
www.bathstudent.com/sport

Accommodation

Number of places and costs refer to 2014–15
University-provided places: 4,086
Percentage catered: 23%
Catered cost: £163–£200 a week.
Self-catered cost: £60 (shared) – £145 (en-suite single) a week.
First years guaranteed accommodation if conditions are met, and applications received by 1 July.
International students: as above. Exchange students are housed on a reciprocal basis.
www.bath.ac.uk/accommodation/

Bath Spa University

Bath Spa is focusing on creativity, culture and enterprise, and hoping to expand its international reputation with a series of imaginative initiatives. The university has helped to found the Global Academy of Liberal Arts (GALA), bringing together a number of universities from around the world. It has also established Bath Spa Global, which will see the first 60 students admitted to a new International First Year in 2014. The programme will provide additional support to help international students to integrate within the UK education system before they progress to full degree programmes. They will receive language tuition, academic instruction and information on UK history and culture, as well as the opportunity to become involved in local community projects. There will also be a Bath Spa Global School of Business and Entrepreneurship, offering one of the few degree programmes in Europe to combine design thinking with global business, entrepreneurship and creativity. The university hopes to recruit 15 per cent of its students from overseas in 2015.

All students can collect a Global Citizenship award by completing a module that covers a range of cross-cutting issues with relevance to all subjects in the arts, humanities and sciences. There are four-year Integrated Masters courses in a number of creative subjects – a relatively unusual model in the arts and humanities, but one that offers advantages to students in terms of funding and progression opportunities. Bath Spa is building a reputation for expertise in the field of creative computing, with several new courses coming online, ranging from software development to gaming, and a growing number of PhD students joining the new Centre for Creative Computing.

The university is far from new, although it was awarded the title only in 2005. The history of its predecessor colleges goes back 160 years, and it boasts some famous alumni, including Body Shop founder Anita Roddick and Turner Prize winner Sir Howard Hodgkin. The university's Newton Park headquarters, four miles outside the World Heritage city of Bath, is in grounds landscaped by Capability Brown in the 18th century, with a handsome Georgian manor house owned by the Duchy of Cornwall as its centrepiece.

Newton Park is the base for all students except those taking art and design subjects, and provides a study environment where historic buildings blend sympathetically with modern facilities. A £70-million development completed in 2014, provides impressive new study facilities for students, particularly in the field of digital arts. By contrast, the Creative Writing Centre is

---

Newton Park
Newton St Loe
Bath BA2 9BN

01225 875875 (enquiries)
enquiries@bathspa.ac.uk
www.bathspa.ac.uk
www.bathspasu.co.uk
Affiliation: million+

The Times and Sunday Times **Rankings**
Overall Ranking: **70** (last year: 70)

Student satisfaction:	=42	83.0%
Research quality:	=84	3.0%
Entry standards:	67	332
Student–staff ratio:	=92	20.0
Services & facilities/student:	113	£1,046
Expected completion rate:	=54	87.3%
Good honours:	=42	71.0%
Graduate prospects:	104	56.4%

housed in the 14th-century gatehouse, a scheduled ancient monument. As part of the new development an additional 550 study bedrooms will be provided in a new student village on campus.

A second campus at Sion Hill, in Bath itself, houses the Bath School of Art and Design. It has recently undergone a £6-million redevelopment and boasts facilities that are among the most modern in the country. The university also has a postgraduate centre at Corsham Court, a 16th-century manor house near Chippenham, and is establishing a specialist Bath Spa Institute for Education at Hartham Park in Corsham, offering a range education study and research opportunities. About a third of the students are postgraduates, including a large cohort training to be teachers.

Bath Spa is currently enjoying an increase in undergraduate applications above the national average. Results in the National Student Survey have been good, especially for teaching quality. Students like the "small and friendly" atmosphere. Half of the subjects in which the university entered the 2008 Research Assessment Exercise (art and design, communication, cultural and media studies, English, history and music) were judged to have some world-leading work. The appointment of some high profile professors (such as Fay Weldon and Gavin Turk) has strengthened the university's profile for both research and teaching in key areas such as creative writing and art and design.

Despite a setting that would seem to be a magnet for applicants from independent schools, almost 95 per cent of the home intake is state-educated and approaching 40 per cent are from working-class homes. Two-thirds of the students are female, reflecting the arts and social science bias in the curriculum, and a quarter are over 25. The latest projected dropout rate of less than 9 per cent is better than the national benchmark for the university's courses and entry grades. Currently about 90 per cent of first years who are eligible for university accommodation are offered places, but more halls are being built so that a higher percentage will be housed.

The university is proud of its environmental record and has been successful in the People and Planet Green League. Sports facilities are not extensive, but a new gym in the students' union has improved them, and some of the university's sports teams do well in local competitions.

Undergraduate Fees and Bursaries
» Fees for UK/EU students 2015–16 — £9,000
» Franchised Foundation and first degrees — £7,500–£9,000
» Placement year — £1,800
» Fees for international students 2014–15 — £10,905–£11,655
» Household income below £25K, 320 bursaries with priority criteria: £1,000 cash in years 1 and 2, £1,500 in year 3.

Students

Undergraduates:	**5,120**	**(245)**
Postgraduates:	**810**	**(1,690)**
Mature students:	**13.1%**	
International students:	**3%**	
Applications per place:	**6.3**	
From state-sector schools:	**94.4%**	
From working-class homes:	**38.4%**	
Satisfaction with students' union	**61%**	

For detailed information about sports facilities:
www.bathspasu.co.uk/et

Accommodation
Number of places and costs refer to 2014–15
University provided places: 1,523 in halls; 33 in Accredited Independent Housing
Percentage catered: 0%
Self catered: £93.00– £157 a week (40–51 weeks).
First years are housed provided requirements are met. Residential restrictions apply.
International students (first year of study): students with a disability or medical condition have priority.
http://thehub.bathspa.ac.uk/services/housing

University of Bedfordshire

Bedfordshire launched an attractive new campus in Milton Keynes in 2013 to add to its main bases in Luton and Bedford. But applications still dropped by 15 per cent and the undergraduate intake was 1,000 lower than in the boom year of 2011. University Campus Milton Keynes, which is a partnership with the local authority, opened with 100 students taking engineering, technology, health and business courses. It will expand with the fastest growing city in the UK, but the bulk of the students will still be on the university's town-centre site in Luton, where a new £46-million library is due to open before the 2015 entrants arrive.

Bedfordshire has spent £180 million on its six campuses since the university changed its identity in 2006, when the former Luton University took over De Montfort's campus in Bedford. Another £120 million has been committed for a range of projects over the next few years. A new campus centre opened in Luton in 2010, with teaching and exhibition space as well as the students' union, information desks and a careers and employment centre. A £40-million student halls complex with en-suite facilities, phone and high-speed internet access, a Postgraduate and Continuing Professional Development Centre and a well-equipped media arts centre have followed.

The Bedford campus, in a leafy setting 20 minutes' walk from the town centre, has a new campus centre comprising a 280-seat auditorium and a students' union, as well as an accommodation block for 500 students. Further redevelopment is planned. The campus is home to the Education and Sport Faculty, with 3,273 students, making it the UK's largest provider of physical education teacher training, as well as a national centre for other subjects at primary and secondary level. Another 1,000 students take subjects such as performing arts, law and business management.

The Putteridge Bury campus, a neo-Elizabethan mansion on the outskirts of Luton, doubles as a management centre and conference venue, as well as an academic teaching space. It is home to the Bedfordshire and Hertfordshire Postgraduate Medical School, which is run in partnership with Hertfordshire and Cranfield universities. Nursing and midwifery students in the growing Faculty of Health and Social Sciences are based at the Butterfield Park campus near Luton, or at the Oxford House development in Aylesbury, Buckinghamshire. Placements are available at a wide range of hospitals, including Stoke Mandeville, Wycombe General Hospital, Luton and Dunstable, and Bedford.

Bedfordshire's courses are largely vocational. The portfolio of two-year

---

University Square
Luton
Bedfordshire LU1 3JU

01234 400400
admissions@beds.ac.uk
www.beds.ac.uk
www.bedssu.co.uk
Affiliation: million+

***The Times and Sunday Times* Rankings**
Overall Ranking: **108** (last year: 115)

Student satisfaction:	=68	81.9%
Research quality:	=102	1.7%
Entry standards:	123	225
Student–staff ratio:	=102	20.9
Services & facilities/student:	72	£1,440
Expected completion rate:	90	82.3%
Good honours:	121	50.7%
Graduate prospects:	88	59.3%

Foundation degrees has been scaled back, but a range of subjects from animal management to web design and software development are provided through partner colleges in a wide range of towns and cities across the East of England. The university pioneered electronic assessment, with more than 10,000 students in disciplines from accountancy to biology tested by computer. Bedfordshire was also awarded a national centre of excellence in personal development planning and employability, aiming to link student learning with life after university. The university celebrated much-improved results in the 2008 Research Assessment Exercise, registering at least some world-leading work in earth systems and environmental science, social work, social policy and administration, sport, tourism and leisure, English language and literature, and communications, cultural and media studies. Bedfordshire was awarded the Queen's Anniversary Prize in 2013 for applied research on child exploitation, which influenced new safeguarding policy and practice.

Almost all of Bedfordshire's entrants are from state schools and 46 per cent come from working-class backgrounds. Around a third of the undergraduates are 21 or over on entry and about the same proportion take part-time courses. Clearing numbers have dropped from nearly one in three to under one in ten, and the projected dropout rate has improved considerably. Although it was over 16 per cent in the last survey, that was better than the national average for the university's courses and entry qualifications. Around one in five students are from outside the EU, many of them taking postgraduate courses. Bedfordshire has see-sawed in our league table, partly because it has struggled in the National Student Survey, although its scores rose in 2014, when 84 per cent of final-year undergraduates were satisfied overall.

Both Luton and Bedford have their share of pubs, clubs and restaurants, and London is not far away. Bedford's impressive sports facilities are expected to have a role in the 2015 Rugby World Cup. The university broke into the top 20 in the People and Planet Green League in 2013, scoring highly for its reduction in carbon emissions, and is Fairtrade accredited.

Undergraduate Fees and Bursaries

» Fees for UK/EU students 2015–16   £9,000
» Foundation degree   £6,000
» Fees for international students 2014–15   £9,750
» Welcome package of £350 (£500 if from partner colleges) for university services.
» Household income below £25K, welcome package plus flexible payment £150, year 1; £300, years 2 and 3.
» Range of other scholarships and bursaries available.
» Check the university's website for the latest information.

Students

Undergraduates:	**11,575**	**(2,615)**
Postgraduates:	**3,465**	**(2,665)**
Mature students:	**28.9%**	
International students:	**12.8%**	
Applications per place:	**4.8**	
From state-sector schools:	**98.3%**	
From working-class homes:	**45.7%**	
Satisfaction with students' union	**71%**	

For detailed information about sports facilities:
www.beds.ac.uk/sportbeds

Accommodation

Number of places and costs refer to 2014–15
University-provided places: about 2,530
Percentage catered: 0%
Self-catered costs: £97–£166 a week.
First years cannot be guaranteed a place, but help is available to find alternative housing in the private sector.
International students: as above.
www.beds.ac.uk/studentlife/accommodation
Bedford and Luton campuses: info@studentvillagebeds.com

Birkbeck, University of London

Birkbeck has seen the biggest increases in both applications and enrolments of any university in the last two years, as it has expanded its portfolio of three-year, evening-taught degrees. Applications rose by 38 per cent in 2013 alone, and the numbers taking the "intensive part-time" courses have trebled since 2011–12. Young applicants, in particular, appreciate the opportunity to combine daytime work with evening study and believe it will give them a head start in their chosen career when they graduate. There will be more than 50 three-year degrees available in 2015, in addition to the four-year part-time programmes that are Birkbeck's traditional fare. They will range from arts and social science degrees to biomedicine, business and management, psychology, English, environment, law, and language and economics programmes.

London's leading provider of part-time higher education, Birkbeck expanded beyond its Bloomsbury base for the first time in 2013. Since 2005 it had offered courses in Stratford, East London, but now shares a new five-storey building with the University of East London, offering courses in law, business and subjects tailored for the creative industries. University Square Stratford is the first shared project of its kind in the capital. Facilities include a 300-seat lecture theatre, learning centre, student support centre and seminar rooms for 3,400 students. Courses will be available either on the traditional or intensive model.

Birkbeck now has its own degree-awarding powers, but is remaining part of the University of London. The college has reorganised into a smaller number of "super-schools", increased its recruitment activity and set about improving the student experience. The strategy brought the college a leadership award. Recruitment to part-time courses nationally was hit hard by the Labour Government's removal of funding for graduates returning to take a different qualification. As in other institutions, there has been a further decline since higher fees were introduced. Fees for most of the three-year degrees are £9,000 a year, with a pro-rata reduction for four-year courses. Bursaries and fee waivers are available for students with low household incomes.

Birkbeck does not appear in the overall ranking of universities published in this *Guide* because it cannot be compared fairly with other institutions on some of the measures. But the college has become an increasingly popular and prestigious choice for Londoners of all ages. Courses are tailored to the employment market. For example, a new BSc in applied accounting and business is run in collaboration with

---

Malet Street
Bloomsbury
London WC1E 7HX

020 7631 6000 (general enquiries)
contact via website
www.bbk.ac.uk
www.birkbeckunion.org
Affiliation: none

The Times and Sunday Times **Rankings**
The available data do not match the data used to rank the other full-time universities, so Birkbeck could not be included in the league table this year.

the Institute of Chartered Accountants in England and Wales, allowing trainee accountants to combine work and study to gain their qualifications at a substantially lower cost and much sooner than if they took a degree before completing their professional qualification. Birkbeck graduates enjoy high average starting salaries, partly because many of them are mature students returning to already successful careers.

The college encourages applications from people without traditional qualifications and draws 44 per cent of its undergraduate intake from low socio-economic groups. In 2012, it received a national award for promoting and supporting women in the fields of science, technology, engineering, mathematics and medicine. Students apply for Birkbeck's three-year courses through UCAS, but the college takes direct applications for its four-year programmes. Applicants who have taken A level or an equivalent qualification recently are made offers based on the UCAS tariff, but others assessed by the college on the basis of interviews and/or short tests. The My Birkbeck Student Centre acts as a front door to all the college's student support services, from help in choosing courses and submitting applications to information about financial support and study skills.

Founded in 1823, Birkbeck now has over 17,000 students. Nine out of ten academics at the college are researchers as well as teachers. More than half of the work submitted to the 2008 Research Assessment Exercise was considered world-leading or internationally excellent. Earth Sciences, psychology, history, classics and archaeology, and history of art, film and visual media were rated in the top five nationally. Its research strength has helped Birkbeck to a place just outside the top 200 universities in the world, according to the 2013 *Times Higher Education* rankings.

Birkbeck is located close to the University of London's main facilities, including its excellent and underused students' centre. Almost £20 million has been spent consolidating the college's buildings and bringing them under one roof. Bloomsbury is easily accessible by public transport and cycle routes. Most Birkbeck students live in the capital, but full-time students looking for housing can apply to the University of London Housing Service.

Undergraduate Fees and Bursaries

» Fees for full-time UK/EU students 2015–16 — £9,000
» Fees for international students 2014–15 — £13,000
» Full-time students with household income below £20K, £1,500 as fee waiver or cash bursary; £1,125 for four-year part-time students; £750 for six-year part-time students.
» Full-time students with household income of £20K–£25K, £1,000 as fee waiver or cash bursary; £750 for four-year part-time students; £500 for six-year part-time students.
» Part-time students with household income of £25K–£40K, pro-rata bursary of £1,000.

Students

Undergraduates:	855	(10,635)
Postgraduates:	1,120	(3,855)
Mature students:	73.2%	
International students:	6.1%	
Applications per place:	2.1	
From state-sector schools:	89.2%	
From working-class homes:	44.3%	
Satisfaction with students' union	63%	

For detailed information about sports facilities:
www.student-central.co.uk/activities/sportssocs

Accommodation

Number of places and costs refer to 2014–15

The university has a limited number of places in the intercollegiate halls of residence, and these are normally reserved for full-time international students.

Catered costs: £165.55 (small single) – £194.60 (standard single); £136.85 (twin); £231.00–£238.70 (en-suite single); £176.50 (en-suite twin) a week.

www.bbk.ac.uk/mybirkbeck/services/facilities/accommodation
www.bbk.ac.uk/prospective/international/accommodation

University of Birmingham

Birmingham was one of the big winners in the Government's relaxation of controls on the recruitment of students with ABB or better at A level. Having promised unconditional offers for applicants in a dozen subjects who were predicted better than three As, the university took 750 more students in 2013 than in the previous year. Just over a third of those who received unconditional offers took up places. The initiative was one of the factors that brought Birmingham the title of *The Times and Sunday Times* University of the Year for 2013–14. The scheme was extended to 33 subjects, from African studies and anthropology to social work in 2014, and is expected to continue in 2015.

Birmingham was the original "redbrick" university. The 230-acre campus in leafy Edgbaston is dominated by a 300-foot clock tower, one of the city's best-known landmarks, and boasts its own station. Dentistry is located in the city centre, while part of the School of Education is in Selly Oak, a mile from the Edgbaston campus. Drama is also located there, along with the BBC Drama Village, which is part of a strategic alliance between the university and the corporation. Vice-Chancellor Sir David Eastwood said on his appointment that he wanted the university to be the "best of the rest" outside Oxbridge and the top London colleges, and a series of initiatives in teaching and research are taking the university in the right direction. One of them has seen Birmingham partner with the University of Nottingham on a series of projects, mainly in research.

The university's enduring reputation is based on its research, with 16 per cent of the work submitted for the Research Assessment Exercise regarded as world-leading. Birmingham took satisfaction from the broad range of subjects in which it produced good results, with music, physics, computer science, mechanical engineering, European studies, primary care, cancer sciences, psychology and law all doing well. Birmingham is the hub for a national STEM programme to promote interest in science, technology, engineering and maths among young people and enhance higher level skills in the workplace. It has also become the first link in a chain of Cancer Research UK Centres, while a £60-million fundraising campaign launched in 2009 will support projects ranging from research into brain injury, ageing and clean energy to scholarships and a centre for heritage and cultural learning.

The university is part way through a long-term programme of investment. Work has started on a new library and cultural hub that will embrace new and emerging technologies for an enhanced student

---

Edgbaston
Birmingham B15 2TT

0121 415 8900 (admissions)
admissions@bham.ac.uk
www.birmingham.ac.uk
www.guildofstudents.com
Affiliation: Russell Group

The Times and Sunday Times **Rankings**

Overall Ranking: **15** (last year: 16)

Student satisfaction:	=51	82.8%
Research quality:	=21	24.0%
Entry standards:	=21	439
Student–staff ratio:	23	14.5
Services & facilities/student:	11	£2,375
Expected completion rate:	=13	94.2%
Good honours:	=11	81.1%
Graduate prospects:	4	84.3%

experience. A new sports centre will boast Birmingham's first 50-metre swimming pool. The new Student Services Hub will see part of the redbrick Aston Webb Building remodelled to house a number of different services including employability, careers and a 400-seat lecture theatre. The facility will be ready for the 2015 entry. Recent developments have included a student facilities building at the medical school and a new home for sport and exercise sciences, as well as refurbished student accommodation and a new music building.

Birmingham's 25,000 full-time students include 4,000 from 150 different countries. Three-quarters of them undertake work experience as part of their course. The university encourages interdisciplinary study, for example allowing undergraduates to combine technology with subjects ranging from Latin or modern Greek to the management of floods and other natural disasters. There has also been £3.5-million investment in an employability initiative which will include internships and mentoring by some of the university's most successful alumni.

The university stepped up its efforts to widen participation following the introduction of £9,000 fees. In 2015, around 1,500 new students are expected to benefit from its package of enhanced financial support for those from lower income backgrounds. The Access to Birmingham (A2B) scheme, which encourages students from the West Midlands whose families have little or no experience of higher education to apply to university, will be extended to students outside the Midlands.

Most of the halls and university flats are conveniently located in an attractive parkland setting near the main campus. There are more than 4,200 university-owned beds, and accommodation in the private sector is also plentiful. The campus is less than three miles from the city centre, but the area has plenty of shops, pubs and restaurants. With its own nightclub among the facilities on campus, some students do not even stray that far, but the city is acquiring a growing reputation among the young. Some 40 per cent of Birmingham graduates make the city their home.

Student facilities on campus are on a par with the best in the country, and include a medical practice. An outdoor pursuits centre is by Coniston Water in the Lake District. The Active Lifestyles Programme attracts 4,000 students to 150 different courses.

Undergraduate Fees and Bursaries

» Fees for UK/EU students 2015–16   £9,000
» Placement year   £1,350
» Fees for international students 2014–15   £12,565–£16,565
   Medicine   £16,565–£29,085
» Household income up to £36K, around 1,500 Chamberlain Awards of £1,000–£2,000 a year, with priority to care leavers and those with lowest household income.

Students

Undergraduates:	17,530	(1,250)
Postgraduates:	7,360	(4,555)
Mature students:	8.1%	
International students:	10.9%	
Applications per place:	6.8	
From state-sector schools:	78.6%	
From working-class homes:	22.4%	
Satisfaction with students' union	67%	

For detailed information about sports facilities:
www.sport.bham.ac.uk

Accommodation

Number of places and costs refer to 2014–15
University-provided places: 4,279
Percentage catered: 33%
Catered costs: £118–£179 a week.
Self-catered costs: £83–£144 a week.
All first years are guaranteed housing (subject to conditions).
International students: as above.
living@contacts.bham.ac.uk
www.birmingham.ac.uk/undergraduate/accommodation

Birmingham City University

Birmingham City followed the example of its neighbouring university by introducing unconditional offers in a range of subjects for highly qualified applicants in 2014. The university increased its undergraduate intake by almost 800 students in 2013 and has seen further growth in the demand for places in 2014. Candidates must have three Bs at AS level or a DDM profile in BTEC and make the university their first choice.

Birmingham City opened the first phase of its expanded city centre campus in 2013. Situated next to Millennium Point and opposite the newly opened Eastside City Park, the £125-million development will become the university's main base, helping to create a Learning Quarter in Eastside. The first phase houses design-related courses from Birmingham Institute of Art and Design (BIAD) and the whole of Birmingham School of Media. Construction is under way on the second phase, which will house business, law, social science and English courses, as well as a new library, IT and student support facilities from September 2015. A third phase of development, set to open in 2017, will create additional teaching space at both the City Centre and City South campuses. A new building for Birmingham Conservatoire will also open at the City Centre Campus in 2017, when it will move from the Convention Centre. The Conservatoire is one of the university's best-known features, together with the School of Jewellery, which is part of BIAD, the largest institute of its kind outside London.

The university has been remodelling its estate for some time, and now has four sites in and around the city centre, plus one in the north and another in the south of Birmingham. City North, until recently the main base, will close in 2017. Millennium Point already houses computing and engineering, as well as Birmingham School of Acting. The City South campus, in Edgbaston, has been refurbished for the Faculty of Health, with a prize-winning library, IT suites, teaching facilities and recreational space. Meanwhile, the Bournville campus, which occupies part of the Cadbury Village, hosts a new college for overseas students to support BCU's international ambitions. Birmingham City University International College, which provides preparatory courses for undergraduate and postgraduate programmes, is a joint venture with global education provider Navitas Ltd.

Birmingham City has thrived since adopting its new name in 2007. The switch from the previous identity as the University of Central England was designed to emphasise the university's location, reinforce its close relationship with the city

---

City North Campus
Birmingham B42 2SU

0121 331 5595 (enquiries)
access via website
www.bcu.ac.uk
www.bcusu.com
Affiliation: million+

The Times and Sunday Times Rankings

Overall Ranking: **=91** (last year: =91)

Student satisfaction:	80	81.0%
Research quality:	=92	2.3%
Entry standards:	=80	317
Student–staff ratio:	106	21.2
Services & facilities/student:	59	£1,563
Expected completion rate:	85	82.8%
Good honours:	=80	63.3%
Graduate prospects:	75	63.0%

and give the university a stronger identity. The university enjoys strong links with business and the professions. As a pioneer in green technology, it is attracting support from national and regional partners to help support a green economy with the potential to create thousands of jobs. There is a strong emphasis on making graduates "job-ready", with support schemes and work placements among a raft of initiatives designed to help develop skills and knowledge for the workplace. High-powered visiting lecturers and an innovative i-learning strategy contribute to this agenda, with students having access to learning tools such as Shareville – a virtual town where students can engage with real-life scenarios.

The prize-winning Student Academic Partners scheme has spawned a formal agreement between the university and the students' union to improve the student experience. Internal student surveys have led to the introduction of internet tutorials in engineering and new help with research for law and social science undergraduates. Teacher education courses consistently produce among the best scores in Ofsted inspections.

Almost 45 per cent of the students come from working-class homes and 97 per cent were state educated. Six out of ten come from the West Midlands, many from ethnic minorities. The dropout rate has been improving and now matches the national average for the university's courses and entry grades. Birmingham City is working with schools in the region to encourage more young people to go on to higher education. Many students enter through the network of associated further education colleges, which run foundation and access programmes.

The university has been increasing its portfolio of high-tech degree courses such as electronic commerce, communications and network engineering, and electronic systems. The 2008 Research Assessment Exercise recorded some world-leading work in all seven areas covered by the university's submission. In art and design, 30 per cent were given the top grade, placing Birmingham City in the top ten for the subject. Most research is applied, with an accent on employment in the region.

University accommodation is guaranteed for first years whose homes are outside Birmingham. The city's student scene is highly rated and has become a draw for many young applicants.

Undergraduate Fees and Bursaries

» Fees for UK/EU students 2015–16	£9,000
» Placement year	no fee
» Foundation degree	£6,000
» Fees for international students 2014–15	£10,500–£11,800
	£14,900 (Conservatoire and acting)
» 15% of additional fee income to be spent on additional access and student success measures.	

Students

Undergraduates:	**15,275**	**(3,240)**
Postgraduates:	**1,815**	**(1,755)**
Mature students:	**25.6%**	
International students:	**7.0%**	
Applications per place:	**5.3**	
From state-sector schools:	**97.0%**	
From working-class homes:	**45.7%**	
Satisfaction with students' union	**68%**	

For detailed information about sports facilities:
www.bcusu.com/sports

Accommodation

Number of places and costs refer to 2014–15
University-provided places: 2,485
Percentage catered: 0%
Self-catered costs: £98 (standard) – £132 (extra large) a week (40– 51 weeks).
Accommodation guaranteed for first years if conditions are met.
International students are guaranteed accommodation.
accommodation@bcu.ac.uk
http://bcu.ac.uk/student-info/accommodation

University College Birmingham (UCB)

University College Birmingham (UCB) chose not to change its name when full university status arrived in 2013, but it has still felt the benefits of official recognition of its quality: applications are up 17 per cent this year. UCB is unique among UK universities in having more than a third of its students taking further education programmes. For that reason, it is concerned that it would be at a disadvantage in league tables and has again instructed the Higher Education Statistics Agency not to release its data, so it does not appear in our main league table or any of the subject tables. UCB is the largest of the dozen universities established when the criteria for university status changed. There are more than 5,500 higher education students and nearly 2,500 taking further education courses.

The new university traces its history back more than 100 years, to the foundation of a Municipal Technical School offering cookery and household science courses. Several different titles followed until it became a university college in 2007 and received degree awarding powers, although some degrees are still accredited by the University of Birmingham. The core subjects are hospitality, tourism, business, sport and education. The most recent Ofsted inspection rated the further education provision as outstanding, while 100 per cent of students in the most recent exit survey rated their postgraduate teacher training as good or better. UCB has an international reputation in hospitality and tourism, with about a third of the students coming from outside the UK.

UCB is based in Birmingham city centre, close to the International Convention Centre, Symphony Hall and Central Library, as well as the main shopping areas. The main campus is at Summer Row, with New Street train station a five-minute walk away. UCB is investing £50 million on new teaching facilities in Birmingham's historic Jewellery Quarter – just a short walk from the main campus in Summer Row. The four-storey first phase of the development, which has been funded from within the university's reserves, opens in September 2014. It features dedicated facilities for undergraduate and postgraduate study, a 24-hour flexible learning centre, three lecture theatres, teaching rooms, IT facilities and a café. Phase Two will see the development of a new campus for further education students, which may allow new subjects to be added. Existing specialist teaching facilities include high-quality training kitchens, commercial training restaurants, full bakery and a product development kitchen.

Summer Row
Birmingham B3 1JB

0121 604 1040 (admissions)
admissions@ucb.ac.uk
www.ucb.ac.uk
www.ucbsu.com
Affiliation: GuildHE

Edinburgh
Belfast
BIRMINGHAM
Cardiff
London

The university focuses on giving students an advantage in the highly competitive graduate job market. Many courses include a full- or half-year industrial placements, including overseas opportunities in the USA, Hong Kong, Canada and Europe. As well as arranging placements, the Careers and Employability Centre team provides students with support to develop skills such as communication, teamwork, problem solving and time management through work experience, workshops, volunteering, part-time and seasonal work. There are strong relationships with employers, including a job-shop service which is accessible 24 hours a day. The university is investing more than £150,000 in a new service to boost graduate employability, and the Unitemps Office provides employment opportunities to students during their studies.

UCB has one of the most socially diverse student bodies in the country – 56 per cent are from a black and minority ethnic background. Student ambassadors promote further and higher education to young people from a range of backgrounds. Over 97 per cent of the undergraduates are state educated and more than half come from the four poorest socio-economic groups. There are fee waivers for students from low-income families. The university has done well in the National Student Survey, generally recording satisfaction rates that are in the top quartile for the UK as a whole. Retention rates for some groups are good, but the projected overall dropout rate of more than 20 per cent remains significantly worse than the national average for UCB's courses and entry qualifications.

More than 1,000 students can be accommodated in UCB's halls of residence, and accommodation can be offered to all years and programmes of study. The Maltings halls are ten minutes' walk from UCB and Cambrian Hall is only 150 yards from the main campus. Both offer among the best value in the Midlands. The Spa, at Richmond House on Newhall Street, offers hairdressing salons, beauty therapy suites, sports therapy clinic, a multi-gym, and fitness assessment suite. There is also a gym and sports hall at the Maltings site, which are open on weekday evenings and at weekends. Two restaurants staffed by the university's students are open to the public, as well as to students and staff.

Undergraduate Fees and Bursaries

- » Fees for UK/EU students 2015–16 £8,558
- » Placement year no fees
- » Fees for international students 2014–15 £9,100
- » English students with household income below £16,190, £1,060 fee waiver each year.
- » In addition, £1,060 fee waiver each year for students previously on a full-time FE programme at UCB in 2014/15.
- » For students from selected colleges a £1,060 fee waiver for year 1.
- » Check the university's website for the latest information.

Students

Undergraduates:	**3,315**	**(1,090)**
Postgraduates:	**485**	**(75)**
From state-sector schools:	**97.7%**	
From working-class homes:	**51.5%**	
Satisfaction with students' union	**67%**	

For detailed information about sports facilities:
www.ucb.ac.uk/facilities/gym-and-sports.aspx

Accommodation

Places and costs refer to 2014–15

University-provided places: 1,074

Percentage catered: 0%

Self-catered costs: £78 (shared); £90 (standard); £97 (en suite); £151 (twin) (42 weeks).

Priority is given to disabled students (new and returning) and new full-time students by application date.

International students: guaranteed housing if application received by mid June.

www.ucb.ac.uk/facilities/accommodation/home.aspx

Bishop Grosseteste University

Bishop Grosseteste (BGU) made its debut in *The Times and Sunday Times* league table below the other institutions awarded university titles in 2013 and the volume of applications dropped by 9 per cent. But rankings for student satisfaction and graduate prospects among the top half of all universities should provide firm foundations for the future. BGU maintained the size of its intake in 2013, despite the lower demand for places, and is planning "controlled expansion" and a more international outlook. Almost 100 courses cover a range of arts and social sciences, but teacher training still dominates. Ofsted rates the courses for primary teachers as "Excellent" and those for secondary as "Good". The university has been allocated 50 places to train teachers of children aged up to nine years old on programmes leading to the new Early Years Teacher Status introduced by the Government to raise the status and quality of the early years workforce. The new courses will mean that, for the first time, Bishop Grosseteste will train teachers of every age group, including adults.

Based on an attractive, leafy campus in uphill Lincoln, not far from the gothic cathedral and castle, Bishop Grosseteste celebrated 150 years of teacher training in 2012. With only 2,000 students, the former university college used to be too small to become a university, but a change of rules allowed it to take the title at last. Named after a theologian and scholar who was bishop of Lincoln in the 13th century, BGU is still proudly associated with the Church of England, although it welcomes students of all faiths and none. It describes itself as a Church university within the Anglican tradition.

The campus has a friendly, welcoming feel. The campus entrance and reception area has been remodelled at a cost of £250,000. Other recent developments have seen the campus theatre equipped with a new digital projection system, surround sound and fully refurbished seating to double as a cinema which can also stage theatrical productions. The Venue is now home to the Lincoln Film Society and is open to staff, students and the public. The library has been extended and given a new name: the Cornerstone Building. It is now home to the Student Support and Learning Advice teams, as well as Library Services. The students' union building has had a major refit and new teaching and learning spaces added. The university spent another £6.5 million in 2013 upgrading accommodation and learning spaces, and providing a new restaurant. A new complex of flats has replaced an older hall of

---

Lincoln LN1 3DY

01522 527347 (reception)
admissions@bishopg.ac.uk
www.bishopg.ac.uk
www.bgsu.co.uk
Affiliation: GuildHE,
Cathedrals Group

The Times and Sunday Times Rankings

Overall Ranking: **=102** (last year: =106)

Student satisfaction:	=26	83.9%
Research quality:	=117	0.3%
Entry standards:	112	279
Student–staff ratio:	122	30.2
Services & facilities/student:	123	£446
Expected completion rate:	29	92.0%
Good honours:	107	57.0%
Graduate prospects:	=57	67.0%

residence, and together with the extensive refurbishment of an existing hall, has brought the number of campus rooms to more than 200.

More than a third of the undergraduates are from working-class families and approaching a quarter come from areas of low participation in higher education – one of the largest proportions at any university. The projected dropout rate, at only 8 per cent, is significantly better than the national average for BCU's subjects and entrance qualifications. The university is divided into two schools. The School of Teacher Development offers undergraduate and postgraduate training courses, as well as conducting research. The School of Culture, Education and Innovation covers a dozen disciplines and offers courses as diverse as sport with mathematics and applied drama with music. A popular new psychology degree, which attracted twice the target enrolment when it was introduced in 2013, has been awarded accreditation by the British Psychological Society. In 2015, students will be able to study the visual arts in combination with a number of subjects, including drama, English or education. Archaeology with history will be another new offering.

Business development is among the priorities identified in the new university's strategic plan. A business start-up centre has opened on campus and is proving popular with new businesses and entrepreneurs. BG Futures differs from other incubation centres by emphasising the university's values of equality and diversity. The university generally produces good graduate employment figures and has secured European funding to support 50 paid graduate internships for small and medium-sized businesses based within the city boundaries.

The university also took on a purpose-built student accommodation with 79 additional rooms close to the campus in 2013. The Sport and Fitness Centre has a sports hall which can cater for a variety of different sporting activities and fitness classes and a well-appointed fitness suite. Ten acres of sports fields are close by. The city of Lincoln is one of the fastest-growing in the UK, with relatively low living costs. It may not compete with the big conurbations for youth culture, but it has a growing student population and a range of bars and nightclubs to serve it.

Undergraduate Fees and Bursaries

» Fees for UK/EU students 2015–16   £9,000
» Foundation degree   £6,750
» Fees for international students 2014–15   £10,000
» BGU Learning Fund awards of up to £2,000 a year, awarded by application after registration.
» Household income below £25K, bursary of £550 (Honours degree), £415 (Foundation degree).
» Check the university's website for the latest information.

Students

Undergraduates:	1,715	(20)
Postgraduates:	305	(375)
Mature students:	29.2%	
International students:	0%	
Applications per place:	3	
From state-sector schools:	97.8%	
From working-class homes:	36.8%	
Satisfaction with students' union	60%	

For detailed information about sports facilities:
www.bishopg.ac.uk/?_id=10236

Accommodation

Places and costs refer to 2014–15
University-provided places: 218 on campus; 79 off campus.
Percentage catered: 0%
Self-catered costs: £95.00–£125.00 a week (33 or 44 weeks).
Priority is given to disabled and new full-time students on a first come, first served basis.
International students: limited accommodation is available.
www.bishopg.ac.uk/?_id=10432

University of Bolton

Bolton has become the first university in the UK, if not the world, to host a professional motor racing team. This apparently unlikely development is just one of a series of initiatives that is enlivening a university that some critics expected to struggle in the era of £9,000 fees. Applications did drop by a worrying 13 per cent in 2013, but Bolton still maintained the size of its intake. Although there are only around 11,000 students, including some in partner colleges in several Asian countries, the university is not planning to expand. There is now a single campus in the town centre, as well as a branch campus in the United Arab Emirates. The Ras al-Khaimah campus opened in 2008, offering a range of undergraduate and postgraduate courses identical to those taught at Bolton. The £1-million development near Dubai is designed to take 700 students. Students at Bolton have the opportunity to study in the UAE for part of their degree course.

The university has spent more than £40 million on its Bolton campus. The rationalisation of sites in the town has provided additional and enhanced teaching space, facilities to interact with industry and a new students' union. In 2013, the university launched the Bolton Business School, which hosts business, law and accountancy courses, along with the Centre of Islamic Finance. The school includes a £100,000 law court for students to develop their advocacy skills. The purpose-built Centre for Advanced Performance Engineering (CAPE), which is run in conjunction with a motorsports company, is the base for the race team. New degree courses in automotive performance engineering and motorsport technology are being taught at CAPE. Students work and learn alongside engineers and mechanics from the team, as well as the university's mechanical engineering lecturers.

Continuing the university's focus on combining academic learning with industry-led practice, Bolton has also partnered with the owners of ten dental practices in the North of England. A state-of-the-art practice has opened on the university campus and the company is sponsoring new clinical simulation facilities in Bolton One, the university's £31-million health, leisure and research facility for students and the local community. The university is launching a range of dental courses with input and support from its partner in September 2014. There will be degrees in advanced dental nursing and dental hygiene and therapy, and a Diploma of Higher Education for clinical dental technicians. Other building projects include a new £10-million technical college for 600 students aged between 14 and 19.

The university traces its roots back

Deane Road

Bolton BL3 5AB

01204 903903 (applications)
enquiries@bolton.ac.uk
www.bolton.ac.uk
www.ubsu.org.uk
Affiliation: million+

The Times and Sunday Times **Rankings**

Overall Ranking: **120** (last year: 119)

Student satisfaction:	**100**	79.1%
Research quality:	**=94**	2.0%
Entry standards:	**=115**	276
Student–staff ratio:	**=90**	19.9
Services & facilities/student:	**117**	£927
Expected completion rate:	**119**	71.9%
Good honours:	**122**	50.6%
Graduate prospects:	**99**	57.4%

190 years to one of the country's first three mechanics institutes. In spite of an international dimension that also includes Botswana, Malaysia, China, Zambia, Malawi and Vietnam, it sees itself as primarily a regional institution. The student population is one of the most ethnically diverse in the UK, with around a quarter of British students coming from ethnic minority communities. The university exceeds all the access measures designed to widen participation in higher education: nearly half of the undergraduates are from working-class homes and the proportion from areas without a tradition of higher education is among the highest in the UK. The downside is that, despite successive big improvements, the projected dropout rate remains significantly higher than the national average for Bolton's courses and entry qualifications, at nearly 20 per cent.

Bolton is not a research-driven university, but it has been accredited for research degrees for more than a decade. About 1,400 of the students are postgraduates, taking qualifications up to and including PhDs. Engineering, architecture and the built environment, social work and social policy all contained some world-leading research in the 2008 assessments. An institute for research and innovation in materials was the first of a series of "knowledge exchange zones". Institutes for educational cybernetics and

renewable energy and environmental technologies have followed, as well as a research centre for health and wellbeing.

The building programme at the Deane campus has included a design studio and three floors of teaching and learning space where students work on actual briefs for companies seeking design solutions, an Innovation Factory housing, among others, special effects laboratories and a product design studio. Within this development is a new social learning zone which includes students' union offices, advice centre, bar and social facilities, plus a computer access room. Bolton One boasts a 25-metre swimming pool and sports complex that includes a gym, dance studio, sports courts and climbing wall, as well as health service facilities. Well over a third of the undergraduates are 21 or over at entry. The 700 residential places are reasonably priced and go a long way towards meeting the demand for accommodation.

Undergraduate Fees and Bursaries

- » Fees for UK/EU students 2015–16: £9,000
- » Placement year £500
- » Foundation year £4,500
- » Courses at partner colleges £5,400–£9,000
- » Fees for international students 2014–15 £11,250
- » Grant of £500 each year for students from partner colleges.
- » Vice Chancellor's Award, up to £15,000, for most outstanding and academically gifted students (max. three awards a year).
- » Range of other scholarships and bursaries available.

Students

Undergraduates:	**4,205**	**(1,920)**
Postgraduates:	**455**	**(715)**
Mature students:	**38%**	
International students:	**6.4%**	
Applications per place:	**3.9**	
From state-sector schools:	**99.4%**	
From working-class homes:	**48.7%**	
Satisfaction with students' union	**57%**	

For detailed information about sports facilities:
http://bolton.ac.uk/Sport/Home.aspx

Accommodation

Number of places and costs refer to 2014–15
University-provided places: 700
Percentage catered: 0%
Self-catered costs: £2,983 (38 weeks); £78.50 a week.
All first years are generally accommodated.
International students: accommodation is secured for these students.
accomm@bolton.ac.uk
www.bolton.ac.uk/Students/AdviceAndSupport/StudentAccommodation/Home.aspx

Bournemouth University

While other universities are pouring money into bricks and mortar, Bournemouth is investing £1 million a year to support projects that will improve its teaching and research by bringing the two closer together. It describes its Fusion fund as promoting "the combination of inspirational teaching, world-class research and the latest thinking in the professions which creates a continuous and fruitful exchange of knowledge that stimulates new ideas, learning and thought leadership." One project has seen staff and students in the School of Tourism collaborating on research into the social impact of festivals. Fusion is the latest manifestation of a change of approach from a university that once gloried in the absence of traditional academic disciplines. It appointed 150 academics in three years to "foster the development of an academically led culture". The approach won official approval in 2013, when the Quality Assurance Agency made Bournemouth the first university to receive its new "commended" grade, the highest possible.

Not that the university is neglecting its two Bournemouth area campuses. A new, £22-million academic building is scheduled to open on the Talbot Campus, in Poole, in 2016. More than £10 million has been committed to a new student centre on the campus, where 80 per cent of the university's 17,000 students are taught. It will open in 2015. The Lansdowne Campus is less than two miles away in the town centre and will be the site of the new Bournemouth International College, which is due to open in September 2015, providing preparatory courses for overseas students. It also houses the School of Health and Social Care, and serves as the centre of postgraduate study for the Business School. The university is expanding postgraduate opportunities, promising up to 100 doctoral places each year until 2018, many of them fully funded.

Every undergraduate is promised a work placement, typically 40 weeks in length. An independent survey published in 2013 showed that Bournemouth had the highest proportion of graduates (almost 90 per cent) with some form of work experience on their CV – a feature that invariably translates into good graduate employment prospects. The retail management degree, for example, notched up eight successive years of full employment. Like the university's position in our league table, student recruitment has seesawed in recent years, but enrolments were up by 500 students in 2013. The university's performance in the National Student Survey has improved, but a poor year for graduate employment has contributed to a 21-place drop in our table.

Virtually all students take up the offer of

Fern Barrow
Talbot Campus
Poole
Dorset BH12 5BB

01202 961916 (enquiries)
askBUenquiries@
   bournemouth.ac.uk
www.bournemouth.ac.uk
www.subu.org.uk
Affiliation: University Alliance

The Times and Sunday Times **Rankings**
Overall Ranking: **88** (last year: 67)

Student satisfaction:	**110**	78.1%
Research quality:	**=70**	4.3%
Entry standards:	**=63**	336
Student–staff ratio:	**=110**	21.6
Services & facilities/student:	**83**	£1,372
Expected completion rate:	**=54**	87.3%
Good honours:	**71**	64.5%
Graduate prospects:	**=71**	63.6%

personal development planning, both online and with trained staff, while 1,400 first years also take advantage of peer-assisted learning, receiving advice and mentoring from more experienced undergraduates. Bournemouth has been increasing its use of education technology, for example to enable its part-time students to study from home or the workplace and reduce the amount of time they need spend on campus. In the 2008 Research Assessment Exercise, eight of the ten subject areas contained at least some world-leading research, with art and design and communication, cultural and media studies producing the best grades. Only three universities showed more improvement in overall grades.

Bournemouth has particular strengths in media subjects and boasts the National Centre of Computer Animation, a field in which the university was awarded a Queen's Anniversary Prize in 2012. State-of-the-art equipment includes a motion capture facility for real-time animation, which is used in teaching and available for use by outside companies. The university was designated as England's only centre for excellence in media practice. Bournemouth claims a number of firsts in its portfolio of courses, notably in the areas of tourism, media-related programmes and conservation. Degrees in public relations, retail management, script-writing and tax law were all ahead of their time. Foundation degrees are delivered in five further education colleges in Dorset and Somerset, as well as on the main campus. They support the needs of business in the creative arts, media and tourism. Top-up courses are available for those who wish to turn their qualification into an Honours degree.

The southern seaside location and the subject mix attract more middle-class students than at most new universities, although 93 per cent attended state schools. The campuses are served by a subsidised bus service and students are discouraged from bringing cars. The students' union's Old Fire Station bar is among many nightlife options. Sports facilities have been improving and in 2012 there was a complete refurbishment of the gym suite, with the addition of a new multipurpose large studio.

There is a wide range of accommodation: students based in halls of residence in Poole enjoy a millionaire's view of the harbour. The university finished on the verge of the top ten in the 2013 People and Planet Green League of environmental performance.

Undergraduate Fees and Bursaries

- » Fees for UK/EU students 2015–16 £9,000
- » Placement year £790
- » Foundation degree £6,000
- » Fees for international students 2014–15 £9,500–£12,500
- » Around 400 bursaries of £2,000 in year 1. Priority to those from low-income families or low-participation areas.
- » Care leaver's bursary of £6,000 Year 1, £5,000 Years 2 and 3.

Students

Undergraduates:	**12,220**	**(2,785)**
Postgraduates:	**1,625**	**(1,340)**
Mature students:	**20.9%**	
International students:	**7.5%**	
Applications per place:	**5.1**	
From state-sector schools:	**93.2%**	
From working-class homes:	**30.2%**	
Satisfaction with students' union	**77%**	

For detailed information about sports facilities:
http://studentportal.bournemouth.ac.uk/things/sportbu/

Accommodation

Number of places and costs refer to 2014–15

University-provided places: about 3,200 (2,817 in halls; 383 head tenancy)

Percentage catered: 0%

Self-catered costs: £100–£145 (single); £135–£155 (studio) a week including bus pass.

The university expects to offer all first years a place to live. Residential restrictions apply.

International students: guaranteed if conditions are met.

www.bournemouth.ac.uk/accommodation/

University of Bradford

Bradford was the first university outside London to offer part-time degrees, and around a quarter of the undergraduates are mature students – only three pre-1992 institutions have more. Other distinctive features include the world-renowned Peace Studies department and its pioneering record on green issues. But Bradford has slipped below a number of younger universities in *The Times and Sunday Times* league table and is now one of the lowest-ranked of its peer group. Applications dropped by more than 10 per cent in 2013, although there was only a small decline in the numbers actually enrolling.

The university pulled off something of a coup in 2013 with the appointment as vice-chancellor of Professor Brian Cantor, the former Vice-Chancellor of the University of York. Professor Cantor oversaw major expansion at York, with the establishment of a new campus and took the university into the Russell Group, but he faces different challenges at Bradford. Perhaps the major advantage at undergraduate level is the vocational slant of the courses and the accent on work experience and placements, which regularly place Bradford well up the employment tables.

The university has been a leading light in the green movement in higher education, with its "ecoversity" programme addressing issues of sustainable development in all the university's practices, including the curriculum. The most visible sign was the opening in 2011 of The Green, a sustainable student village catering mainly for 1,000 first-year and international students. The development, which won a Green Gown award for sustainability in 2012 and the Best Student Housing prize the following year, is part of a £70-million modernisation plan that includes a £7-million investment in new and upgraded teaching facilities. Bradford was in the top ten in the People and Planet Green League of universities' environmental performance for 2013. A major refurbishment of the library made carbon savings by maximising insulation and natural ventilation, attracting another Green Gown award, while the "edible campus" project allows gardeners to improve the inner-city site and to monitor biodiversity. Bradford has reduced its carbon footprint by 30 per cent since 2005 and is well on the way to meeting its target of a 50 per cent reduction by 2020.

More than half of the undergraduates are from working-class homes – the biggest proportion at any of the older universities. Around 15 per cent of the university's students are from overseas, many of them taught in partner institutions in Singapore, Brunei, Malaysia, Pakistan and India. Nearer home, there are alliances with a

---

Richmond Road
Bradford
West Yorkshire BD7 1DP

0800 073 1225 (freephone)
course-enquiries@bradford.ac.uk
www.bradford.ac.uk
www.ubuonline.co.uk
Affiliation: University
  Alliance

The Times and Sunday Times Rankings
Overall Ranking: **76** (last year: =84)

Student satisfaction:	=95	79.3%
Research quality:	54	10.0%
Entry standards:	=77	320
Student–staff ratio:	=75	18.6
Services & facilities/student:	75	£1,426
Expected completion rate:	78	83.6%
Good honours:	=66	65.8%
Graduate prospects:	40	72.4%

number of further education colleges to help boost participation in a region where it is well below the national average. The colleges offer Foundation degrees in areas such as public sector administration, community justice, engineering technology and enterprise in IT. Perhaps the best known is in health and social care, where the university was already expanding opportunities locally, bringing about a fourfold increase in enrolments by young women from South Asian families.

The relatively small, lively campus is close to the city centre. Health students moved into a new state-of-the-art facility on campus in 2011, leaving only the highly rated management school on a different site. It is two miles away in a 14-acre parkland setting. Improvements on The City Campus in recent years have included upgraded laboratories for chemical and forensic science, and new sports facilities including a gym and climbing wall and an improved sports hall. There is also a distinctive four-storey Atrium, which has brought together all student support services in a single, open-plan social space, and "Student Central", which houses the students' union.

A separate online portal is available to applicants and new students to smooth their transition to higher education. Computer-assisted learning is increasing in many subjects, making use of unusually extensive IT provision and a new wireless network.

Some courses feature online assessment and the use of laptops in lectures. The human studies programme, which combines psychology, literature and sociology with philosophy, is an imaginative construct that is proving attractive to students. Some 80 per cent of the work submitted for the 2008 Research Assessment Exercise was placed in the top two categories, although more than a third of the academics were not entered. Social work and social policy, politics, civil engineering and pharmacy produced the best results.

Places in halls are reasonably priced and all have internet connections. Rents for private housing are among the lowest in any university city in 2014. The university has particularly good provision for disabled students, who account for 6 per cent of the university population. Bradford's senior management group includes the Director of Student Success to ensure that the student voice is heard in future developments.

Undergraduate Fees and Bursaries

» Fees for UK/EU students 2015–16	£9,000
» Foundation degree	£6,000
Clinical science	£9,000
» Placement year	£900
» Fees for international students 2014–15	£11,000–£13,100
» Household income below £30K, £500 each year with conditions.	
» Academic scholarship of £2,000, year 1; £1,500 years 2 and 3, with conditions.	

Students

Undergraduates:	**9,160**	**(1,260)**
Postgraduates:	**1,040**	**(1,735)**
Mature students:	**24%**	
International students:	**14.9%**	
Applications per place:	**4.9**	
From state-sector schools:	**95.3%**	
From working-class homes:	**51.3%**	
Satisfaction with students' union	**77%**	

For detailed information about sports facilities:
www.bradford.ac.uk/unique/

Accommodation

Number of places and costs refer to 2014–15
University-provided places: 1,051
Percentage catered: 0%
Self-catered costs: £89.00 – £108.41 a week (42-week contracts).
All first-year undergraduate students are guaranteed accommodation (terms and conditions apply).
International students: as above.
accommodation@bradford.ac.uk
www.bradford.ac.uk/student/accommodation/

University of Brighton

Brighton has become the first post-1992 university to raise money from the bond markets to fund campus improvements. It has spent more than £100 million on new buildings and equipment in the last decade. In the latest project, £29 million is being invested in updating teaching facilities on the Moulsecoomb campus, where another new building houses pharmacy and biosciences. A third academic building and £40 million of student accommodation is planned for the campus. A similar amount has been committed to halls of residence and support facilities in nearby Varley Park. In addition, a new academic building has opened in Hastings and facilities for the Faculty of Arts are being expanded on the Grand Parade Campus, in Brighton, which also hosts the Design Council's national archive. The developments have helped the university to fifth place in the People and Planet Green League, with praise for its approach to sustainability in the curriculum. Brighton has set itself a target of reducing carbon emissions by half in five years.

The university is among the top 30 in the UK for the volume of applications it receives. The demand for places has risen in 2014 after two years of decline, with engineering, computing, applied psychology and criminology among the subjects showing increases. More than nine out of ten courses include a placement or the option of a sandwich year. The four-year fashion textiles degree, for example, offers work placements in the USA, France and Italy, as well as Britain. Degrees are designed in collaboration with employers, and the majority are accredited or recognised by professional associations. There are well-established mentoring, entrepreneurship and volunteering schemes for students to develop themselves outside the classroom.

Brighton came of age as one of the first new universities to be awarded a medical school, but is equally well known for imaginative regional initiatives. Its campus in Hastings, which focuses on digital and broadcast media, runs a number of schemes to draw people from the region into higher education. The £28.5-million medical school, run jointly with Sussex University, is training 128 doctors a year. Brighton was already heavily engaged in other health subjects, such as nursing and midwifery. The medical school's headquarters, on Brighton's Falmer campus, has also provided a new base for applied social sciences, such as criminology and applied psychology. The two universities have been collaborating since Brighton was a polytechnic, and there is a joint research building for science policy and management studies.

There are 21,000 students on five campuses. The School of Education, as well

Mithras House
Lewes Road
Brighton BN2 4AT

01273 600900 (switchboard)
admissions@brighton.ac.uk
www.brighton.ac.uk
www.bsms.ac.uk
www.brightonsu.com
Affiliation: none

The Times and Sunday Times **Rankings**
Overall Ranking: **82** (last year: 76)

Student satisfaction:	94	79.4%
Research quality:	55	9.7%
Entry standards:	79	319
Student–staff ratio:	=70	18.3
Services & facilities/student:	111	£1,118
Expected completion rate:	=75	84.2%
Good honours:	=57	67.3%
Graduate prospects:	=62	65.8%

as languages and literature students, moved into a new building on the Falmer campus, which now also boasts a £7.3-million sports centre. The university's wealth of teaching facilities are designed to build real-life skills, and include a radio station and TV studio, a podiatry hospital, a physiotherapy clinic, flight simulator, rapid prototyping facilities, industrial textile rooms and a clinical skills and simulation suite for nursing students. At Eastbourne there is a new library and extensive leisure and sports facilities, which attracted the Swedish tennis team for its pre-Olympic preparations. Sport science laboratories and 354 en-suite residential places have been added, and improvements made to the learning resources centre, lecture theatres and refectory.

Brighton was again one of the top new universities in the last Research Assessment Exercise. Art and design produced the best results, with two-thirds of the work submitted considered world-leading or internationally excellent. Business management, sports studies and mechanical and aeronautical engineering also did well. Brighton's strengths in art and design – recognised in the award of national teaching centres in design and creativity – have been at the forefront of the university's popularity. But the university also has a growing reputation in areas such as sport and hospitality, as well as scoring well in teacher education rankings.

The university has a cosmopolitan air, with more overseas students and a more middle-class UK intake than most post-1992 universities. Among the efforts to widen participation are progression partnerships with six primary and over 50 secondary schools and colleges in the South East of England, where students are guaranteed offers for Brighton courses, as well as financial support from the university. Over 2,000 students applied from Compact partnership schools in 2014, the first full year of operation. The university also holds a Charter Mark for its commitment to care leavers and has a higher-than-average number of disabled students. Over a quarter of the full-time undergraduates are 21 or over on entry. Students have a personal tutor and there is an award-winning student services department. Most like Brighton's lively social scene, despite the high cost of living for those not in hall. Eastbourne is also popular, and both towns offer plentiful accommodation to supplement the university's stock.

Undergraduate Fees and Bursaries

» Fees for UK/EU students 2015–16	£9,000
» Foundation degrees at partner colleges	£7,000–£7,500
» Placement year	£1,000
» Fees for international students 2014–15	£11,220–£13,220
Medicine	£26,100
» Student support for 2015–16 to be announced. It will be based on cash, discounted university services, tuition fee waivers.	

Students

Undergraduates:	**14,190**	**(2,965)**
Postgraduates:	**1,895**	**(2,265)**
Mature students:	**27.1%**	
International students:	**11.7%**	
Applications per place:	**6.4**	
From state-sector schools:	**93.4%**	
From working-class homes:	**30.1%**	
Satisfaction with students' union	**59%**	

For detailed information about sports facilities:
www.brighton.ac.uk/sportbrighton

Accommodation

Number of places and costs refer to 2014–15
University-provided places: 2,104; 300 in private sector university-managed houses or flats.
Percentage catered: 53%
Catered costs: £138–£164 a week.
Self-catered costs: £104–£150 a week.
First years have priority for housing if conditions are met.
International students: guaranteed accommodation if conditions met.
accommodation@brighton.ac.uk
www.brighton.ac.uk/living-here

University of Bristol

Increasing the size of Bristol's intake by more than 1,000 students has helped to attract even more applicants. Already the most oversubscribed multi-faculty university in Britain, it saw the demand for places grow by another 9 per cent in 2013. The university seized the opportunity to expand when recruitment restrictions were lifted for the brightest applicants. There are now more than 14,000 undergraduates, although Bristol remains among the smallest institutions in the Russell Group. The university's official strategy is to "stay relatively compact and nurture the collegial atmosphere that makes it a true community as well as an ambitious and challenging place to be."

Bristol has long been favoured by independent schools as a natural alternative to Oxbridge. To broaden the intake, departments may make slightly lower offers to the most promising applicants from the bottom 40 per cent of schools and colleges at A level. Over 500 students came from such schools in 2013, and one entrant in seven came from a low socio-economic group. The university has spent more than £15 million since 2006 on recruiting and supporting students from disadvantaged backgrounds. Some 600 local students take the Access to Bristol course while at school or college, for example, and receive a substantial bursary if they go on to a Bristol degree and their family income is less than £25,000. Even the proportion of mature students has risen at a time when it is falling nationally. Nevertheless, 40 per cent of entrants in 2012 came from independent schools, the highest proportion outside Oxbridge.

The university has a powerful academic reputation – the QS rankings for 2014 again placed it in the top 30 in the world. Entry standards are high and Bristol continued to live up to expectations in the last Research Assessment Exercise, when almost two-thirds of the work submitted was rated in the top two categories. Epidemiology and public health, health services research, chemistry, mathematics, drama, mechanical engineering and economics produced the best results. There are 33 Fellows of the Royal Society and similar numbers in other learned societies. The latest research development saw the opening in 2013 of an £18-million Centre for Power Electronics that will focus on delivering the underpinning science and engineering behind many low-carbon technologies.

The university celebrated its centenary in 2009 and launched a fundraising campaign with a £100-million target. The previous campaign helped the university to create new chairs and embark on a number of building projects, including a

---

Senate House
Tyndall Avenue
Bristol BS8 1TH

0117 928 9000 (switchboard)
ug-admissions@bristol.ac.uk
www.bristol.ac.uk
www.ubu.org.uk
Affiliation: Russell Group

The Times and Sunday Times Rankings
Overall Ranking: **19** (last year: 15)

Student satisfaction:	=84	80.4%
Research quality:	=7	29.7%
Entry standards:	12	483
Student–staff ratio:	=21	14.1
Services & facilities/student:	27	£2,030
Expected completion rate:	10	95.5%
Good honours:	10	83.1%
Graduate prospects:	11	80.2%

well-appointed centre for the highly rated chemistry department. Both chemistry and medical sciences were chosen to house national teaching and learning centres, and the university was also awarded four centres to train doctoral scientists and engineers. The largest estate investment programme in the university's history is currently underway, with £200 million of projects due to be completed by 2016. A £54-million Life Sciences Building was completed this year, providing new teaching and research facilities for biological sciences and a range of related disciplines. A new hall of residence at Stoke Bishop has added 320 places, ensuring that the university continues to guarantee accommodation for all first years. A rolling programme of refurbishment is underway to modernise the existing halls.

An impressive sports complex with a well-equipped gym has been developed at the heart of the university precinct, where the careers centre has also been refurbished. The students' union houses one of the city's biggest live music venues as well as a café, bars, theatre and swimming pool. A £31-million refurbishment and redesign will be complete this year, providing more space for community activities, an extended café bar, student societies and sports clubs. The students' union has raised its game partly because of the intense competition. Bristol possesses a vibrant youth culture and, as one of the country's most prosperous cities, offers job opportunities to students and graduates alike. The university merges into the centre, its famous gothic tower dominating the skyline from the junction of two of the main shopping streets. Despite its hills, Bristol is England's first Cycling City and was chosen by *The Sunday Times* as the best city in the UK in which to live. It will also be European Green Capital for 2015. Most students enjoy life in Bristol, although the high cost of living can be a drawback. The dropout rate is among the lowest in Britain, and one student in five stays in the city after graduation. Parts of the city suffer from the same security concerns as any big conurbation, but the university won a police-approved Secured Environments award for its crime protection work.

Undergraduate Fees and Bursaries

- » Fees for UK/EU students 2015–16 £9,000
- » Placement year/overseas study year £1,350
- » Fees for international students 2014–15 £14,750–£17,750
  Dentistry, medicine, veterinary medicine £17,750–£33,000
- » Students with household income below £25K, bursary of £2,000; household income £25K–£30K, £1,500; household income £30K–£35K, £1,250; household income £35K–£40K, £750; household income £40K–£42.6K, £500.
- » For students in the Access to Bristol scheme, £9,000 fee waiver in year 1 plus eligible for Access to Bristol annual maintenance bursary of £3,750.
- » Range of other scholarships and bursaries available.
- » Check the university's website for the latest information.

Students

Undergraduates:	**13,565**	**(475)**
Postgraduates:	**4,055**	**(1,375)**
Mature students:	**5.9%**	
International students:	**15%**	
Applications per place:	**8.2**	
From state-sector schools:	**59.4%**	
From working-class homes:	**14.3%**	
Satisfaction with students' union	**40%**	

For detailed information about sports facilities:
www.bris.ac.uk/sport

Accommodation

Number of places and costs refer to 2014–15
University-provided places: about 5,123
Percentage catered: 35%
Catered costs: £118.16 (shared room) – £175.70 a week.
Self-catered costs: £72.03 (shared room) – £172.00 a week.
First years are guaranteed one offer of accommodation provided conditions are met.
International students: accommodation is guaranteed provided conditions are met.
www.bristol.ac.uk/accommodation/

Brunel University

Brunel was voted the university offering the best student experience in London in *Times Higher Education*'s annual survey, 16 places above the next institution from the capital and in the top 30 nationally. Students liked the high quality, convenient facilities at one of London's few campus universities, and were particularly complimentary about the sports facilities and library, which recently moved to 24-hour opening. Brunel has spent more than £350 million on its campus over recent years, with the library and now world-class sports facilities attracting much of the investment. The latest major construction project was the £30-million Eastern Gateway Building that opened in 2012, providing new teaching and research facilities, a large auditorium, a café and an art gallery. There have been many new and refurbished social, teaching and residential facilities, and more green spaces for students to enjoy. The programme has transformed the campus, which retains its original 1960s architecture but with the addition of striking new buildings and landscaping.

The university is also changing academically. The eight schools are being replaced by three colleges (business, arts and social sciences; engineering, design and physical sciences; and health and life sciences). There will be three autonomous interdisciplinary research institutes to encourage academics from different subjects to work together and produce innovative courses and research projects. The highest-profile example has been the establishment of the first Centre for Comedy Studies Research, launched by Brunel alumni Jo Brand and Lee Mack. A new Educational Excellence Centre will encourage innovative teaching and the use of technology in the classroom, while another new unit will nurture students' business skills and exploit the university's research. Brunel tries to enhance graduates' employment prospects through work placements and the inclusion in degree courses of skills modules, such as oral and written communication, business and computer literacy.

The latest strategic plan sets the goal of confirming the university's standing in the top third of UK higher education, making stronger connections between teaching and research, and further improving the quality of students' experience. Brunel scored well in its last audit by the Quality Assurance Agency. There has been significant growth in courses focusing on new technologies such as multimedia design and broadcast media, as well as health and social care. Other innovations include creative writing, professionally accredited journalism, sonic arts, aviation engineering and pilot studies, motorsport engineering and games design.

Substantial investment in research

Kingston Lane

Uxbridge

Middlesex UB8 3PH

01895 265265 (admissions)

contact via website

www.brunel.ac.uk

http://brunelstudents.com

Affiliation: none

The Times and Sunday Times **Rankings**

Overall Ranking: **47** (last year: 46)

Student satisfaction:	20	84.4%
Research quality:	=42	17.0%
Entry standards:	49	352
Student–staff ratio:	=53	16.9
Services & facilities/student:	45	£1,741
Expected completion rate:	61	86.0%
Good honours:	79	63.4%
Graduate prospects:	85	60.0%

centres and academic recruitment produced significant improvements in the last Research Assessment Exercise, when Brunel registered one of the biggest increases in the numbers of staff entered. Almost nine out of ten academics were assessed, compared with barely more than six out of ten in 2001. With 43 per cent of the work submitted judged to be world-leading or internationally excellent, the outcome was a 54 per cent increase in Brunel's research allocation from the Higher Education Funding Council for England. The extra money was invested in 40 senior academic posts. Benjamin Zephaniah took up his first academic position as Chair of Creative Writing, and Will Self has joined as Professor of Contemporary Thought. Brunel's Institute for the Environment won a Queen's Anniversary Prize for pioneering research revealing the link between chemicals in rivers and reproductive health.

Enrolments rose in 2013, but remain considerably lower than before £9,000 fees were introduced. Almost 40 per cent of the undergraduates are from working-class homes – a big increase on previous years and well ahead of the national average for Brunel's courses and entry qualifications. More than half come from the UK's ethnic minorities and there is also a large contingent of international students. The International Pathways and Language Centre was named as the top-performing British university language centre under the new British Council accreditation framework. A new international strategy will promote study opportunities abroad. Brunel featured in the top 40 in the *Times Higher Education*'s latest ranking of the world's leading universities under 50 years old, scoring particularly highly for its international outlook.

The students' union is in the top five in the country for satisfaction levels, and the residential stock has been increased: all new first years continue to be eligible for campus accommodation. A tradition of sporting excellence has seen several students compete in the London 2012 Olympic and Paralympic Games, and the level of facilities is such that Brunel hosted the South Korean Olympic and Canadian Paralympic teams. The university has won awards for its provision for disabled students, and for its placement and careers service.

Undergraduate Fees and Bursaries

- » Fees for UK/EU students 2015–16 £9000
- » Placement year £1,000
- » Fees for international students 2014–15 £14,250–£16,000
- » 300 bursaries with priority criteria of £1,000 each year.
- » 30 Academic Excellence scholarships of £2,000 a year for those with at least AAA at A level or equivalent.
- » 30 Local Borough scholarships, of £6,000 cash or fee waiver each year; 6 Alumni scholarships of £6,000 each year.
- » Other scholarships for care leavers, local students and in some subjects.

Students

Undergraduates:	**9,675**	**(365)**
Postgraduates:	**3,840**	**(1,435)**
Mature students:	**12.4%**	
International students:	**17%**	
Applications per place:	**6.9**	
From state-sector schools:	**92.6%**	
From working-class homes:	**39.4%**	
Satisfaction with students' union	**81%**	

For detailed information about sports facilities:
www.brunel.ac.uk/services/sport

Accommodation

Number of places and costs refer to 2014–15

University-provided places: 4,531

Percentage catered: 0%

Self-catered costs: £102.00 (standard) – £130.00 (en suite); £194.00 (studio flat) a week.

All new full-time first-year students (UG and PG) are eligible for on-campus accommodation.

International students: as above.

accom-uxb@brunel.ac.uk

www.brunel.ac.uk/life/accommodation

University of Buckingham

Buckingham is launching the UK's first private not-for-profit medical school, with the first students arriving in January 2015. The course will be 4.5 years long, modelled on Leicester University's MBChB programme, and costs £35,000 a year – in line with the overseas rate at other medical schools. The university has had a postgraduate medical school for six years, which attracts overseas medical graduates who find it difficult to secure junior doctor posts as a result of Government restrictions. The undergraduate school is a long-held ambition of the university and will provide clinical placements at Milton Keynes NHS Hospital Trusts and other local providers.

For many years Britain's only private university, Buckingham is still the only one in our main league table, sitting just inside the top 50. Buckingham had too few students to be classified in some measures for several years, but has seen dramatic growth in the last few years. The total number of students increased from 1,300 in 2010 to 2,000 in 2012, when applications grew by an unprecedented 200 per cent. Staffing levels dropped slightly, but are still among the best in the UK. The university has also boosted spending on student facilities, refurbishing the refectory, introducing Wi-Fi across the whole campus

and expanding the library and teaching space. Buckingham's students remain among the most satisfied in the National Student Survey and the graduate employment rate is also among the best in the country.

Even before the latest rise in fees elsewhere, Buckingham claimed to be no more expensive than other universities because its intensive two-year degrees cut maintenance costs and accelerate entry into employment. Total fees for UK undergraduates taking the two-year degree from January 2015 will be £25,647 for home and EU students and £35,097 for those from outside the EU. There is a range of scholarships for both home and international candidates.

The university, celebrating its 40th anniversary in 2016, has only around 2,000 full-time students. Small group tutorials, which have all but disappeared outside Oxbridge, are common: the average tutorial group contains about six students. Only its absence from the Research Assessment Exercise, which was restricted to state-funded institutions, prevented the university from finishing higher in our table. However, the university has a number of research groups and over 170 research students. Research income in 2011 was around £512,000.

A Conservative-backed experiment of the 1970s, Buckingham has long been an accepted part of the university system. Its

---

Hunter Street
Buckingham MK18 1EG

01280 814080
info@buckingham.ac.uk
www.buckingham.ac.uk
http://su.buckingham.ac.uk
Affiliation: none

The Times and Sunday Times **Rankings**
Overall Ranking: **48** (last year: 41)

Student satisfaction:	17	85.1%
Research quality:	n/a	
Entry standards:	=69	330
Student–staff ratio:	3	11.3
Services & facilities/student:	34	£1,894
Expected completion rate:	104	80.2%
Good honours:	123	43.5%
Graduate prospects:	30	75.3%

degrees carry full currency in the academic world and teaching standards are high. The university's culture of responsiveness to students was praised by the Quality Assurance Agency in its report on the university last year. The university has no party political ties. Its own statement on its independence declares that Buckingham was founded on the principles of classical liberalism, and teaches the ideals of free-thinking and liberal political thought. Professor Terence Kealey, a biochemist and libertarian commentator, has been Vice-Chancellor since April 2001. He has ambitions for Buckingham to "one day" challenge the cream of American higher education.

Students can begin courses in January, July or September. Most degree courses run for two 40-week years, minimising disruptive career breaks for mature students. Just over half of the students are from overseas, but the proportion from Britain is growing. They have the option of a three-year degree in the humanities and other schools are now following suit. Recent additions to the subjects on offer include MAs in human rights, archaeology and history of art by research. The BA in art history and heritage management offers the opportunity of a term at the British Institute in Florence. A new Foundation Department provides English language tuition for those with an IELTS score below 6.5. There are also international foundation programmes and a pre-master's for business for those whose first degree is not in a business-related subject.

Buckingham operates on two sites within walking distance of each other. The main campus includes the refectory, bar and fitness centre, with the Radcliffe Centre, which hosts internal and external events, nearby. The law school is within walking distance of the main campus. Two historic buildings have been refurbished at a cost of almost £2 million, and a new six-acre site has been acquired to make room for future expansion. Buckingham's campus has been judged to be the safest in the country. There is a university cinema, and the town of Buckingham is pretty, with a good selection of pubs and restaurants. Milton Keynes and Oxford are nearby.

Undergraduate Fees and Bursaries

Note that the course only lasts two years.

» Fees for UK/EU students for degree course starting in January 2015: £12,570, year 1; £13,077 year 2.

» Fees for international students for degree course starting in January 2015   £17,289, year 1; £17,808, year 2. Medicine   £35,000

» Household income below £42.6K, bursary of £1,100 a year.

» Academic scholarship of £2,500 for students (excluding medicine) with at least ABB or equivalent at A level; continued in other years based on academic performance.

» Four counties scholarship of £2,500 a year for students from Buckinghamshire, Bedfordshire, Northamptonshire and Oxfordshire.

Students

Undergraduates:	**1,305**	**(55)**
Postgraduates:	**675**	**(55)**
Mature students:	**19.1%**	
International students:	**52.4%**	
Applications per place:	**11.9**	
From state-sector schools:	**79.3%**	
From working-class homes:	**31.3%**	
Satisfaction with students' union	**66%**	

For detailed information about sports facilities:
www.buckingham.ac.uk/life/thingstodo/sport

Accommodation

Number of places and costs refer to 2014–15
University-provided places: 614
Percentage catered: 0%
Self-catered accommodation: £87–£178 a week (48 weeks).
All first-year students are guaranteed accommodation if they follow the application process.
International students: same as above.
accommodation@buckingham.ac.uk
www.buckingham.ac.uk/life/accommodation

Buckinghamshire New University

All universities are paying more attention to the student experience since the advent of £9,000 fees, but none has yet matched the package included in Buckinghamshire New University's "Big Deal". The programme, which was in place before the fees went up, entitles students to free entertainment, recreational activities, events and sport, and last year, the scheme provided 2,000 free sessions. It was extended in September 2014 through the "Big Deal on Course" to cover essential textbooks, equipment and materials, photocopying credits, and a contribution to the cost of field trips, up to a value of £1,000 over three years. There will also be means-tested bursaries to cover essential field trip costs above the standard package, a fund to assist with travel costs to attend job interviews, work placements and internships, and the university will pay for gown hire at graduation ceremonies. The new offers may help to improve student satisfaction ratings that are in the bottom five for all universities and have held the university back in *The Times and Sunday Times* league table. The university's own annual survey, carried out by independent academics, has been more positive, as have online reviews of its courses and lecturers,

but scores in the National Student Survey remain low.

Bucks now has some 9,000 students, three-quarters of them taking degree courses. More than a quarter of the undergraduates are over 25 years old and nearly 60 per cent are female. Applications grew in line with the national average in 2013, but there was a small drop in enrolments. It has continued to do well against the Government's benchmarks for widening participation in higher education: almost all the entrants are from state schools or colleges, and more than 40 per cent are from working-class homes. The projected dropout rate for those who entered in 2011 was significantly lower, at less than 12 per cent, than the national average for its subjects and entry qualifications.

Based in High Wycombe, the university has been carrying out a £200-million redevelopment plan which allows most students to be based at the main campus. The exceptions are those taking nursing, who have moved into a new building in Uxbridge, on the north-west edge of London. The prize-winning Gateway Building at High Wycombe has transformed the town-centre campus with improved teaching, social and administrative space. The complex includes a new sports hall, gym, treatment rooms and sports laboratory, open to the public as well as to students.

Queen Alexandra Road
High Wycombe
Buckinghamshire
HP11 2JZ

0800 0565 660 (enquiries)
advice@bucks.ac.uk
www.bucks.ac.uk
www.bucksstudent.com
Affiliations: GuildHE

***The Times and Sunday Times* Rankings**
Overall Ranking: **116** (last year: 113)

Student satisfaction:	=119	76.4%
Research quality:	=114	0.7%
Entry standards:	120	250
Student–staff ratio:	114	22.2
Services & facilities/student:	26	£2,051
Expected completion rate:	=83	82.9%
Good honours:	113	53.3%
Graduate prospects:	112	53.7%

At the same time, collaboration with two of the world's biggest IT companies is resulting in one of the most advanced student networks in UK higher education. Further improvements, which should be complete in September 2014, will include new student accommodation, changes to the exterior of the main building and additional space for the students' union. Two new accommodation blocks at the student village in High Wycombe will add 108 bedrooms. There will also be new laboratories and teaching rooms on the Uxbridge campus. In addition to the building projects, the university is planning further improvements to its online learning and IT capabilities.

The nursing provision is the largest in the London area and has growing links with the Imperial College London Healthcare Trust, including a joint appointment designed to promote innovation. The child nursing courses attract particularly good ratings. Only 26 staff were entered for the 2008 Research Assessment Exercise – half of them in art and design, which registered the only world-leading research. However, an official audit of academic standards was positive.

Sport is an important part of life at the new university, which partners the London Wasps rugby union team in a relationship which trades coaching for Bucks students for courses for Wasps players. But the university's main aim is to contribute to the social and economic life of the region, embracing workplace learning and close ties with local businesses. Employees of the bed company Dreams, which is based in High Wycombe, take a Foundation degree in retail management while at work, for example. The National School of Furniture works with local employers and further education colleges, offering qualifications from certificate level to PhD. Bucks has also won awards for its training of commercial pilots and courses for music industry management. Other Foundation degrees include animation and visual effects, protective security management, and sports coaching and performance, all run at partner colleges. Among the new courses introduced in 2014 was a degree in event and festival sustainability management, and a Foundation degree in kitchen design.

High Wycombe has a range of student pubs and clubs and is within easy reach of London.

Undergraduate Fees and Bursaries

» Fees for UK/EU students 2015–16   £9,000
» Franchised courses at partner colleges   £6,000–£9,000
» Fees for international students 2014–15   £9,500
» Support package to be announced. It will include support for social and academic engagement for all students and targeted support for priority groups.
» "Big Deal" package which encourages participation in a range of sporting, recreational and social activities.
» Check the university's website for the latest information.

Students		
Undergraduates:	**5,560**	**(2,640)**
Postgraduates:	**290**	**(720)**
Mature students:	**30.3%**	
International students:	**6.8%**	
Applications per place:	**4.4**	
From state-sector schools:	**98.4%**	
From working-class homes:	**40.6%**	
Satisfaction with students' union	**79%**	

For detailed information about sports facilities:
www.bucks.ac.uk/student_experience/sport

Accommodation

Number of places and costs refer to 2014–15
University-provided places: 924
Percentage catered: 0%
Self-catered costs: £99.98 (standard) – £166.50 (studio) a week (42 weeks).
First-year students applying before 1 June are guaranteed accommodation.
International students: priority allocation for first years.
accom@bucks.ac.uk;
http://bucks.ac.uk/home_eu_students/accommodation/

University of Cambridge

Cambridge is still top of *The Times and Sunday Times* league table, but it has to share that honour with Oxford this year, after the first dead heat since the inaugural edition more than 20 years ago. The light blues top half of the 66 subject tables and feature in the top five universities in the world in two of the three main rankings. Cambridge outperforms its ancient rival on research, student satisfaction and graduate prospects, but loses out on staffing levels, facilities spending and completion. It has the highest entry standards of any UK university, demanding at least A*AA at A level, although candidates may be made a lower offer if their school or personal circumstances are thought to disadvantage them. For most degrees, the top grade can come in any subject, but for some courses there will be additional tests, such as Cambridge's own Sixth Term Examination Papers in mathematics. With around five applicants for each place – fewer if you choose your subject carefully – the competition for places appears less intense than at the popular civic universities, but the real difference is that nine out of ten entrants have at least three A grades at A level. That competition shows no sign of easing since the university has not increased the size of its intake with the relaxation of recruitment restrictions by the Government.

Until 2001, Cambridge had enjoyed an unbroken run at the top of our table. The university produced the best results in the 2008 Research Assessment Exercise, when nearly a third of its research was considered world-leading and over 70 per cent was rated in the top two categories. John Gurdon, Emeritus Professor in Cell Biology, became the latest of 90 Nobel laureates when he won the prize for medicine in 2012. Research facilities are constantly upgraded. In 2012, for example, a new building opened to support integrated research activity in the humanities and social sciences. The following year, the Queen opened a new building for molecular biology which cost more than £200 million and houses 600 scientists, PhD students and research staff. Cambridge is involved in numerous national and international research networks. For example, it was chosen to host one of five Academic Health Science Centres to lead biomedical innovation.

More than 60 per cent of undergraduates now come from the state system, but the proportion of working-class undergraduates remains low, at less than 12 per cent. Summer schools, student visits and, in some colleges, sympathetic selection procedures are helping to attract more applications from comprehensive schools and further education colleges. Although Cambridge is charging the full £9,000 undergraduate fee, there are generous bursaries of up to

---

The Old Schools
Trinity Lane
Cambridge CB2 1TN

01223 333308 (admissions)
admissions@cam.ac.uk
www.cam.ac.uk
www.cusu.cam.ac.uk
Affiliation: Russell Group

The Times and Sunday Times **Rankings**
Overall Ranking: **=1** (last year: 1)

Student satisfaction:	**10**	85.6%
Research quality:	**1**	45.0%
Entry standards:	**1**	616
Student–staff ratio:	**=5**	11.6
Services & facilities/student:	**2**	£3,246
Expected completion rate:	**=1**	98.9%
Good honours:	**2**	88.6%
Graduate prospects:	**2**	88.7%

£3,500 a year, according to parental income. The application system has been simplified slightly, with candidates no longer required to complete an initial Cambridge form, as well as their UCAS form. However, they are sent the Supplementary Application Questionnaire, after they have submitted their UCAS form, covering the applicant's academic experience in more detail. The tripos system was a forerunner of the currently fashionable modular degree, allowing students to change subjects (within limits) midway through their courses. Students receive a classification for each of the two parts of their degree.

Choosing a college is an additional complication for those not familiar with Cambridge. Brief profiles of all the undergraduate colleges appear in Chapter 13. Making the right choice is crucial, both to maximise the chances of winning a place and to ensure an enjoyable three years if you are successful. Applicants can take pot luck with an open application if they prefer not to opt for a particular college. But, though the statistics show that this route is equally successful, only a minority takes it. Most teaching is now university-based, especially in the sciences, and a shift of emphasis towards the centre has been taking place more generally.

A £1-billion funding appeal to mark the university's 800th anniversary, in 2009, reached its target two years early, making Cambridge the first university outside the USA to raise such a sum. The money has gone into bursaries and scholarships, professorships and teaching posts, and new buildings for research, teaching and student accommodation. A £16-million sports centre opened in 2013, featuring a large sports hall and a strength and conditioning wing. In the longer term, the university now has planning permission for its first out-of-town site, which will cost £1 billion to develop and will include housing for staff, students and local people in its first phase. Cambridge is not for everyone, however bright. The amount of high-quality work to be crammed into eight-week terms can prove a strain, although the projected dropout rate of 1.1 per cent is the lowest at any university. Most students relish the experience and reap the rewards in their careers.

Undergraduate Fees and Bursaries

» Fees for UK/EU students 2015–16 £9,000
» Fees for international students 2014–15 £15,063–£22,923
   Medicine £36,459
   College fees £5,500–£6,500
» Household income below £25K, bursary of £3,500 a year (£5,650 for some mature students); household income £25K–£42.6K, bursary on a sliding scale of up to £3,500 a year.
» Many college scholarships and bursaries.
» Check the university's website for the latest information.

Students

Undergraduates:	11,900	(245)
Postgraduates:	6,365	(880)
Mature students:	4.9%	
International students:	18.8%	
Applications per place:	4.9	
From state-sector schools:	63%	
From working-class homes:	11.7%	
Satisfaction with students' union	37%	

For detailed information about sports facilities:
www.sport.cam.ac.uk

Accommodation

www.study.cam.ac.uk/undergraduate/life/accommodation.html
Also see chapter 13 for information about individual colleges.

Canterbury Christ Church University

Canterbury Christ Church has emerged apparently unscathed from a turbulent period in which one of the five campuses closed and the vice-chancellor left abruptly and without explanation. Applications and enrolments rose in 2013 and the demand for places is up again in 2014. The former Church of England college achieved university status in 2005, and there are now 20,000 students on campuses in four locations. It is the region's largest provider of courses for the public services, with teacher training courses that are rated "outstanding" by Ofsted, and strong programmes in health and social care, nursing and policing.

The Folkestone campus has closed, but the university has bases in Broadstairs, Tunbridge Wells and Chatham, as well as its headquarters in Canterbury. The purpose-built campus at Broadstairs offers a range of subjects from commercial music to digital media, photography, and child and youth studies. The Salomons Centre, just outside Tunbridge Wells, caters exclusively for postgraduate courses, while the newly expanded Medway site at Chatham is shared with Greenwich and Kent universities, offering education and health programmes at a variety of levels.

The majority of the students, however, are at the university's main campus at Canterbury, a World Heritage Site and one of the safest UK university cities. The Canterbury campus, which dates from 1962, is a few minutes' walk from the city centre, but the university has several buildings in other parts of the city. Augustine House, a £35-million library and student services centre, with specialist teaching and IT facilities, was joint winner of the Society of College, National and University Librarians' 2013 award for the best library design. The Sidney Cooper Gallery, in the heart of the city, hosts exhibitions and workshops from visiting artists as well as work by students before the best goes on to be exhibited in London galleries. St George's Centre opened in 2012, housing the students' union, residential accommodation, bar and coffee lounge within easy reach of the high street. Another 418 residential places are under construction close to the centre. The university has also renovated St Gregory's Centre for Music, a historic concert venue, and opened separate rehearsal, practice and performance space in a building named after Sir Peter Maxwell Davies, who is a visiting professor. It has also acquired the former Canterbury Prison site for future development. The Church of England link is underlined by the choice of the Archbishop of Canterbury as the university's Chancellor.

North Holmes Road
Canterbury CT1 1QU

01227 782900 (enquiries)
admissions@canterbury.ac.uk
www.canterbury.ac.uk
www.ccsu.co.uk
Affiliation: Cathedrals
  Group; million+

The Times and Sunday Times Rankings

Overall Ranking: **96** (last year: 90)

Student satisfaction:	81	80.9%
Research quality:	=102	1.7%
Entry standards:	114	277
Student–staff ratio:	82	18.9
Services & facilities/student:	107	£1,166
Expected completion rate:	92	82.1%
Good honours:	=61	66.7%
Graduate prospects:	86	59.9%

The subject mix, with an emphasis on health subjects and education, means that seven out of ten students are female. New courses for 2014 included a BSc in sports coaching science and the option of a year's work placement on business studies degrees. Some 97 per cent of the undergraduates are state-educated and well over a third come from working-class homes. The dropout rate has improved consistently and, at less than 11 per cent, is better than average for the university's courses and entry qualifications. Canterbury Christ Church was one of the new "teaching-led" universities, but was given the power to award research degrees in 2009. The university entered staff in seven areas in the 2008 Research Assessment Exercise. The best grades came in education and music, both of which had 10 per cent of their work assessed as world-leading.

Christ Church broke into the top 20 in the People and Planet Green League of universities' environmental performance in 2013, drawing praise for its work on sustainability and rigorous environmental auditing. All campuses are interconnected by a high-speed data network, providing access to online teaching and learning materials, the student web portal and email. The student support service – i-zone – can be accessed online or via staff at the i-zone desks. The Drill Hall Library at Medway provides 110,000 items, 400 computers and 280 study spaces, while the Augustine House Library has over 300,000 books, 250 computers, plus extensive wireless coverage throughout the building. The award-winning i-Borrow scheme has 200 laptops available for self-service loan within the building.

Social and sports facilities naturally vary between the campuses, although the students' union is present on all of them. The sports centre in Canterbury includes a large adaptable sports hall and a fitness suite, a sports and exercise studio and performance analysis rooms. The centre hosted the pre-Olympic training camp for the Puerto Rico team in 2012. The university also has facilities at Polo Farm Sports Club close to the city. There are 12 acres of playing fields about a mile from the main campus. Residential accommodation is available to all first years who meet certain conditions. The pressure is eased to some extent because more than 60 per cent of the students come from Kent, many of them among the 7,000 taking part-time courses.

Undergraduate Fees and Bursaries

- » Fees for UK/EU students 2015–16 — £9,000
- » Foundation degree at partner college — £8,000
- » Degree courses at partner colleges — £8,000–£9,000
- » Fees for international students 2014–15 — £9,710
- » Household income below £25K, 1,500 bursaries of £1,000 a year.
- » Sports and music scholarships available.
- » Check the university's website for the latest information.

Students

Undergraduates:	**10,460**	**(3,740)**
Postgraduates:	**1,140**	**(2,705)**
Mature students:	**25.7%**	
International students:	**6.6%**	
Applications per place:	**4.6**	
From state-sector schools:	**97.0%**	
From working-class homes:	**36.2%**	
Satisfaction with students' union	**63%**	

For detailed information about sports facilities:
www.canterbury.ac.uk/support/sport-recreation/

Accommodation

Number of places and costs refer to 2014–15
University-provided places: 1,616
Percentage catered: 0%
Self-catered costs: £99–£187 a week.
Accommodation guaranteed for first years if conditions are met.
International students: as above.
accommodation@canterbury.ac.uk
www.canterbury.ac.uk/study-here/accommodation/accommodation.aspx

Cardiff University

Cardiff is the perennial choice as *The Sunday Times* Best Welsh University. It is the Principality's only member of the Russell Group of research-led universities and its sole representative in the top 200 of the world rankings. It is also one of the few universities in the UK to boast two Nobel Laureates on its staff. Such obvious quality is bringing its rewards, with applications growing by 25 per cent in the last two years. Cardiff was able to increase the size of its undergraduate intake by 500 students in 2013, following similar growth in the previous year. It now has some 28,000 students, including 6,000 from outside the UK. Entry requirements have been rising and more than half of all applicants achieve at least AAB grades at A Level.

A third of Cardiff's students come from Wales, but it is the international dimension that has been the university's main focus recently. A new Global Opportunities Programme provides studying, working and volunteering options across the world to enhance the student experience. The university has also launched a Languages for All programme, giving all students the chance to learn a language alongside their chosen degree for free. Students were already offered the Cardiff Award to boost their employment prospects by recognising the skills acquired from extracurricular activities.

An audit by the Quality Assurance Agency complimented the university on its "powerful academic vision and well-developed and effectively articulated mission to achieve excellence in teaching and research". Student support services, including counselling facilities and the help offered to dyslexics, were among the features singled out for praise. Cardiff was the first Welsh university to be awarded the Frank Buttle Trust Quality Mark which recognises support for students who have been in care. Many full-time degrees share a common first year, and the modular system makes undergraduate study flexible thereafter. Recent additions include a range of journalism degrees, a BA in translation with a year abroad and a BSc or MESci in earth and environmental science. One undergraduate in six comes from an independent school and little more than one in five has a working-class background. The projected dropout rate of less than 4 per cent is comfortably the lowest in Wales. The 2008 Research Assessment Exercise rated almost 60 per cent of the submitted work in the top two categories, with 33 of the 34 subject areas containing some world-leading research. Journalism, media and cultural studies, English, city and regional planning, and business produced the best results. Cardiff takes more than half of the

---

Cardiff
Wales CF10 3XQ

029 2087 4455 (enquiries)
contact via website
www.cardiff.ac.uk
www.cardiffstudents.com
Affiliation: Russell Group

The Times and Sunday Times **Rankings**
Overall Ranking: **27** (last year: =33)

Student satisfaction:	=42	83.0%
Research quality:	=32	21.0%
Entry standards:	29	423
Student–staff ratio:	=15	13.0
Services & facilities/student:	71	£1,442
Expected completion rate:	9	95.6%
Good honours:	=22	78.0%
Graduate prospects:	9	81.7%

research funding awarded in Wales. It has enabled the university to establish three major new research institutes, offering radical new approaches to neurosciences and mental health, cancer stem cells and sustainable places.

The university occupies a significant part of the civic complex around Cathays Park in Cardiff. The five healthcare schools at the Heath Park campus share a 53-acre site with the University Hospital of Wales. The £18-million Cochrane Building provides teaching and learning facilities for all healthcare schools based on the Heath Park campus. The School of Dentistry has a new Dental Education Clinic offering students some of the UK's most modern training facilities. In recent years, there has been major investment in new buildings and equipment, including a £30-million development which will house highly advanced facilities for some of the university's scientific teams. A £3.3-million redevelopment of the students' union is ongoing, extending the nightclub, providing new outdoor social space and upgrading other facilities. A new student residence with 178 beds is close to completion at Talybont Gate, near three other residences, a sports centre and social centre. All rooms will be en-suite with modern fittings and large shared communal space. A £13.5-million learning and teaching centre for the Business School includes a 60-seat trading room and two large lecture theatres. The university has also bought a former railway site alongside the university to facilitate expansion over the next few years.

Library services continue to improve access to resources, increase the range of electronic resources, extend self-service provision and improve the environment for the study of rare collections. The IT working environment gives students online access to information about their studies and social life, from reading lists to social events. The university guarantees a residential place for those applying through the normal admissions cycle. The main residential site at Talybont boasts a "sports training village", and there is also a newly refurbished city-centre fitness suite and a sports ground. Cardiff is a popular student city, relatively inexpensive and with a good range of nightlife and cultural venues.

Undergraduate Fees and Bursaries

» Fees for UK/EU students 2015–16 £9,000
» Welsh Assembly non-means-tested grant to pay fees above £3,685 (2014–15) for Welsh students.
» Fees for international students 2014–15 £13,500–£18,000
  Medicine and dentistry £17,000–£29,800
» Household income up to £50K, bursary of £1,000 in year 1; reduced sums in following years.
» Scholarship of £1,500 (year 1) and £750 (years 2 and 3) to students achieving grades AAA at A-level or equivalent in selected subjects.
» Welsh medium and other subject scholarships available.

Students

Undergraduates:	**17,335**	**(3,685)**
Postgraduates:	**4,090**	**(3,430)**
Mature students:	**12%**	
International students:	**13.2%**	
Applications per place:	**5.6**	
From state-sector schools:	**83.9%**	
From working-class homes:	**21.9%**	
Satisfaction with students' union	**85%**	

For detailed information about sports facilities:
www.cardiff.ac.uk/sport

Accommodation

Number of places and costs refer to 2014–15
University-provided places: 5,353
Percentage catered: 5.2%
Catered costs: £99–£119 a week.
Self-catered costs: £82–£115 a week.
All first years (except Clearing students) are guaranteed accommodation if conditions are met.
Policy for international students: guaranteed accommodation if conditions are met.
www.cardiff.ac.uk/for/prospective/accommodation.html

Cardiff Metropolitan University

A report for the Welsh government cast doubt on the long-term viability of Cardiff Met as an independent university, but students seem not to share the concerns. Applications were up by almost 6 per cent in 2013, when the university increased the size of the undergraduate intake by more than 200. The university has a good record in the National Student Survey and does even better in the International Student Barometer. Ratings by overseas students from more than 140 countries placed Cardiff Met top in the UK for the learning experience, living experience, and for satisfaction with student support for a fifth year running. Cardiff Met has been awarded the Government's Charter Mark four times, the judges commenting particularly on the level of student satisfaction. Overseas partnerships also offer the university's programmes in Egypt, Korea, Morocco, Sri Lanka and Singapore. A new office in Beijing aims to develop joint research and exchange programmes in China.

The university had to threaten legal action to ensure that it did not become part of the new University of South Wales. It had already committed £50 million to improvements on its three campuses and is now continuing that programme. The £20-million Cardiff School of Management opened on the Llandaff campus in 2010, offering improved facilities for business, hospitality and tourism. A new campus centre, with a shop and catering facilities, has also been added, along with an Information Zone for student services. The Cyncoed campus already had a new student centre with a nightclub and all the normal catering and leisure facilities. The latest development will see Cardiff School of Art and Design brought together in a £10-million building on the Llandaff campus for the start of the 2014 academic year. The School was the star performer in the 2008 Research Assessment Exercise, when 70 per cent of its submission was rated either world-leading or internationally excellent. Sport also registered some world-leading research, and all six teacher training courses are rated as excellent by Estyn, the school inspectorate.

Cardiff Met is one of Britain's leading centres for university sport, with team performances that do justice to some excellent facilities. In recent years, the university has had British university champions in sports ranging from archery and gymnastics to squash, weightlifting and judo. More than 300 past or present students are internationals in 30 sports. Fifteen of them, including two gold medallists, took part in the London 2012

Llandaff Campus
Western Avenue
Cardiff CF5 2YB

029 2041 6070 (enquiries)
askadmissions@cardiffmet.ac.uk
www.cardiffmet.ac.uk
www.cardiffmetsu.co.uk
Affiliation: University
  Alliance

Edinburgh
Belfast
London
CARDIFF

***The Times and Sunday Times* Rankings**
Overall Ranking: **90** (last year: 87)

Student satisfaction:	**56**	82.5%
Research quality:	**=79**	3.3%
Entry standards:	**93**	304
Student–staff ratio:	**=97**	20.3
Services & facilities/student:	**80**	£1,392
Expected completion rate:	**66**	85.3%
Good honours:	**114**	52.9%
Graduate prospects:	**90**	58.7%

Olympic and Paralympic Games, where the university also provided three coaches and a physiologist. The £7-million National Indoor Athletics Centre is Cardiff Met's pride and joy, but other facilities are also of high quality. As well as participating in a thriving sports club scene, around 1,500 students pursue sport and dance related courses.

The university changed its name from the University of Wales Institute in 2011 to stress its location in the Principality's capital. Students from Wales account for two-thirds of the 8,000 undergraduates. Half of them are from Cardiff or the Vale of Glamorgan. Nearly 95 per cent of the UK undergraduates attended state schools and more than a third come from working-class homes. The dropout rate improved in the latest survey and, at 12 per cent, now matches the UK average for the university's subjects and entry grades. Entrance requirements are generally modest, but the menu of largely vocational courses means that many students come with qualifications other than A levels. Around a quarter are mature students and there are over 1,000 are international students. Postgraduates, make up nearly a quarter of the student population.

The three sites in Cardiff are all within three miles of the city centre. The Cyncoed campus, housing education and sport, is the main centre of activity, particularly for first years. As well as the new student centre,

the athletics centre is there, together with a multitude of outdoor facilities and also the upgraded Welsh Sports Centre for the Disabled. The IT suite has 250 computers available 24 hours a day. Howard Gardens is the home of fine art, while the Llandaff campus hosts design, engineering, food science and health courses. The student centre at Llandaff includes a dyslexia support unit among a number of advice and representation services, and a learning centre with more than 300 computers. The enterprising students' union owns a nightclub and bar in the city centre to add to the campus choices. During term-time, the Rider bus service links all the campuses with other parts of Cardiff. The halls of residence are a mile from the main campus on the Plas Gwyn Residential Campus, where there are enough hall places to accommodate most first years.

Undergraduate Fees and Bursaries

- » Fees for UK/EU students 2015–16   £9,000
- » Placement year   £1,800
- » Welsh Assembly non-means-tested grant to pay fees above £3,685 (2014–15) for Welsh students.
- » Fees for international students 2014–15   £9,700
  Podiatry   £11,400
- » For Welsh students from Community First areas, £1,050 package a year.
- » Sports and hospitality and tourism scholarships and bursaries for Cardiff residents.

Students		
Undergraduates:	7,845	(725)
Postgraduates:	2,585	(1,285)
Mature students:	25%	
International students:	14.2%	
Applications per place:	3.2	
From state-sector schools:	94.8%	
From working-class homes:	34.9%	
Satisfaction with students' union	67%	

For information about sports facilities: www3.cardiffmet.ac.uk/english/aboutus/facilities/sport/

Accommodation

Number of places and costs refer to 2014–15

University-provided places: 947

Percentage catered: 34%

Catered cost: £134–£147 a week (£90–£103 outwith term).

Self-catered costs: £96.50–£103.00 a week.

First-year students have no guarantee; terms and conditions apply.

International students: accommodation is reserved, subject to availability and if conditions are met.

accomm@cardiffmet.ac.uk

www3.cardiffmet.ac.uk/english/aboutus/facilities/accommodation

University of Central Lancashire (UCLan)

Central Lancashire has always been one of the most enterprising post-1992 universities. It already offers dentistry, pharmacy and astrophysics. Now medicine is being added to the list in 2015 with the enrolment of the first students on a five-year MBBS programme, which has been developed in line with General Medical Council guidelines with the expectation of full recognition in due course. The programme will be run in partnership with East Lancashire NHS Hospitals Trust, which will provide the majority of clinical placements. The students will be self-funding and predominantly international, paying £35,000 a year, in line with the overseas fees at other medical schools. The university also has a branch campus in Cyprus and was the UK's first post-1992 institution to appear in the QS World University Rankings.

UCLan is one of the largest universities in the country, with about 30,000 students, including part-timers. The university, which dominates the centre of Preston and also has a base in nearby Burnley, took an additional 800 undergraduates in 2013. It has invested over £100 million in new buildings and facilities, including the £13-million Sir Tom Finney Sports Centre and a £12.5-million building housing the university's forensic science, chemistry and fire courses. The main campus also boasts Europe's largest 3-D lecture theatre and a 24-hour-access library, as well as forensic crime scene houses, a motorsports workshop and child observation lab. The Dental School was one of the few to open in over a century, while the architecture degree was the first new course in the subject for a decade. The £5.3-million Allen Building includes some of Europe's most advanced facilities for students studying at the School of Medicine and Dentistry. Recent course additions include the BSc in airport security management – the first of its kind in the UK – and an MSc in counter terrorism.

The university's roots stretch back to 1828 and it has a strong reputation in some surprising fields. Astrophysics benefits from two observatories in Britain and a share in the Southern African Large Telescope, its academics working closely with NASA. The university is a partner in a nanotechnology research team in China and the nurse-led stroke research unit is the only one of its kind in the UK. Linguistics and journalism were classed as world-leading in the last Research Assessment Exercise and in total, 17 areas contained work considered world-leading or internationally excellent. The Undergraduate Research Internship Scheme enables students from all disciplines to work on research projects for up to ten

Preston

Lancashire PR1 2HE

01772 892400 (course enquiries)
cenquiries@uclan.ac.uk
www.uclan.ac.uk
www.uclansu.co.uk
Affiliation: million+

The Times and Sunday Times **Rankings**

Overall Ranking: **=77** (last year: 88)

Student satisfaction:	=66	82.1%
Research quality:	=76	3.7%
Entry standards:	62	337
Student–staff ratio:	=50	16.8
Services & facilities/student:	37	£1,836
Expected completion rate:	105	79.8%
Good honours:	106	57.5%
Graduate prospects:	89	59.3%

weeks. UCLan students formed the UK's first Undergraduate Research Society, which funds conference visits. An overall rating of teaching, research and facilities by QS gave the university four out of five stars.

UCLan has a strong focus on entrepreneurship and has established a range of business incubation facilities for its students and graduates. UCLan ranks in the top two nationally for the number of graduate start-ups and first for the number still trading after three years (about 70 per cent). The university works with a wide variety of industrial partners and many undergraduate programmes are directly linked to them. Travel bursaries are available for study or work experience abroad, and there is free tuition is a variety of languages, including Arabic, Chinese, Japanese and Russian. The Confucius Institute, on the Preston campus, supports the development of Chinese culture in the North West. More than 500 students have been helped to visit China.

Electives are used to broaden the curriculum; up to 11 per cent of students' time is spent on subjects outside their normal range. Four out of ten students come from working-class homes, and a high proportion are local people in their 20s or 30s. Almost a fifth of the UCLan's students are taught in colleges and UCLan has won official praise for the quality of its external programmes. Foundation-year courses are now available as access routes to all degrees. The Burnley campus gives local students the opportunity to take degree or Foundation degree courses without leaving home. In collaboration with Cisco Systems, the campus is the location for an advanced manufacturing facility incorporating robotics, computer vision, non-destructive testing and component assembly. UCLan is ranked among the top ten universities in the People and Planet Green League of environmental performance. It was the first university in the UK to install solar trackers.

The sports facilities were used as official training venues for the 2012 Olympics and the 2013 Rugby League World Cup. Compared with Manchester or Liverpool, the security risks and cost of living are both low. The students' union won the Best Campus Venue 2011 award from Live UK Music, and in 2012 was ranked in the top 25 per cent for its support, activities and academic representation.

Undergraduate Fees and Bursaries

» Fees for UK/EU students 2015–16	£9,000
» Foundation year	£3,900
» Burnley campus	£7,000 (Foundation degree £6,000)
» Placement year	£680
» Degree courses at partner colleges	£6,000–£9,000
» Fees for international students 2014–15	£10,950–£11,950
Medicine	£35,000
» Support package for students, including cash bursaries and provisions to support learning to be announced.	

Students

Undergraduates:	**17,590**	**(6,415)**
Postgraduates:	**1,510**	**(3,205)**
Mature students:	**29%**	
International students:	**8.8%**	
Applications per place:	**4.2**	
From state-sector schools:	**97.8%**	
From working-class homes:	**43%**	
Satisfaction with students' union	**73%**	

For detailed information about sports facilities:
www.uclansu.co.uk/teamuclan

Accommodation

Number of places and costs refer to 2014–15
University-provided places: around 2,200
Percentage catered: 0%
Self-catered costs: £79.03–£83.02 (standard) – £97.37–£99.47 (en suite) a week (42 weeks); £86.87–£107.80 (self-contained flats).
The Student Accommodation Service will assist all first years find suitable accommodation either in university owned/leased halls of residence, private sector registered halls or shared houses.
International students: as above.
www.uclan.ac.uk/accommodation/index.php

University of Chester

Chester, already among the largest of the new wave of universities established in the last ten years, has further expanded its footprint in the North West of England with a new campus near Ellesmere Port. The former Thornton Science Park has become the university's fifth campus and will focus on science, engineering and business engagement, welcoming its first students in 2014. The university already had a campus in Warrington, in addition to the three in Chester itself. There are now almost 18,000 students, including part-timers, and the university had been making progress in *The Times and Sunday Times* league table, before suffering a 15-place drop this year. A poor year for graduate employment was largely responsible. In a concerted effort to improve the student experience, Chester spent £600,000 refurbishing the refectory, around £3 million overhauling the university's learning resources centre and another £1 million on sports facilities. Applications were 12 per cent up in 2013 and the university was able to increase the size of its intake by 250 students.

The picturesque Roman city of Chester is one of those places that outsiders probably always expected to have its own university. William Gladstone was among the founders of the first Church of England teacher training college there in 1839. Although it took until 2005 for that college to achieve university status, it had been building up a solid reputation in a number of subjects beyond education. The main campus is only a short walk from the centre of Chester, a 32-acre site boasting manicured gardens and a number of new developments. A new students' union is just one of a stream of improvements. The latest addition is the £4.8-million North West Food Research Development Exchange Building to support food and drink businesses in the North West. A second campus in the city opened in 2007 as a base for the Faculty of Arts and Media, and a third site was added in 2010, following the purchase of the city's historic County Hall, which now houses the faculties of Health and Social Care and Education and Children's Services.

The Warrington campus, which has eight halls of residence, focuses on the creative industries and public services. It has seen the addition of high-quality production facilities and the university has also signed a partnership agreement with the BBC, which is intended to open up new employment opportunities and develop new talent following the transfer of parts of the corporation to Salford. The library has been tripled in size, and a business centre opened for students and local firms.

Approaching a fifth of the undergraduates are over 20 on entry and two-thirds are

---

Parkgate Road
Chester CH1 4BJ

01244 511000 (enquiries)
admissions@chester.ac.uk
www.chester.ac.uk
www.chestersu.com
Affiliation: Cathedrals Group

The Times and Sunday Times **Rankings**

Overall Ranking: **67** (last year: =52)

Student satisfaction:	29	83.8%
Research quality:	=110	1.0%
Entry standards:	=94	302
Student–staff ratio:	=53	16.9
Services & facilities/student:	63	£1,509
Expected completion rate:	91	82.2%
Good honours:	88	61.8%
Graduate prospects:	=62	65.8%

female. Nearly all are state-educated, and nearly 40 per cent have working-class roots. Progression agreements guarantee interviews to students at a number of local colleges, subject to certain conditions, but there is no reduction in entry requirements. The projected dropout rate has been improving and, at almost 14 per cent, now matches the national average for the university's courses and entry standards. There is also a limited range of Foundation degrees, mainly in health subjects. The Foundation degree in mortuary science was the first of its kind, as was one for guide dog trainers. Even the more traditional degrees have been designed to support the practical and vocational demands of the professions. Many include an extended period of work experience. Initial teacher training courses have been rated "outstanding" by Ofsted. Four of the ten subject areas entered for the last Research Assessment Exercise contained at least some world-leading work. History was the most successful, with nearly half of its submission placed in the top two categories.

A student contract of the type that is becoming universal in higher education sets out clear conditions on the offer of a place, as well as detailing the university's responsibilities. Students promise to "study diligently, and to attend promptly and participate appropriately at lectures, courses, classes, seminars, tutorials, work placements and other activities which form part of the programme". The university undertakes to deliver the student's programme, but leaves itself considerable leeway beyond that. There are extensive sports facilities at Warrington and especially on the main campus in Chester, where around £1 million has been spent on new tennis courts, a 100-metre sprint track and a floodlit 3G multi-use sports pitch. A new hall of residence on the main campus will house more than 200 students and another160 places have been added through the purchase of a former Travelodge, allowing most first-years to be offered university accommodation. Student union facilities form the basis of the social scene on all campuses, but the city of Chester also has a great deal to offer.

Undergraduate Fees and Bursaries

» Fees for UK/EU students 2015–16	£9,000
» Foundation degree	£7,650
» Foundation degree at partner colleges	£5,000–£7,650
» Fees for international students 2014–15	£10,700
» Household income below £25K, £1,000 cash, year 1; £500, years 2 and 3.	
» Students from targeted partner schools and colleges with household income of £25K–£42.6K, £1,000, year 1; £500 ,years 2 and 3.	
» Students with at least ABB or equivalent with household income below £42.6K, £1,000, year 1; £500, years 2 and 3.	
» Check the university's website for the latest information.	

Students

Undergraduates:	8,215	(2,560)
Postgraduates:	1,140	(2,435)
Mature students:	18.9%	
International students:	2.5%	
Applications per place:	7.6	
From state-sector schools:	97.6%	
From working-class homes:	39.5%	
Satisfaction with students' union	75%	

For detailed information about sports facilities:
www.chestersu.com/sports-societies

Accommodation

Number of places and costs refer to 2014–15
University-provided places: approx 1,442
Percentage catered: 38% (including semi-catered)
Catered costs: £82.95–£149.80 a week.
Self-catered costs: £78.75–£131.60 a week.
First years cannot be guaranteed accommodation.
International students: guaranteed accommodation if they apply by the advertised date.
www.chester.ac.uk/accommodation
accommodation@chester.ac.uk

University of Chichester

Chichester is aiming to be internationally recognised as a "beacon of good practice for high quality, student-centred higher education" by 2020. An overall satisfaction rate of 89 per cent in the 2014 National Student Survey suggests that many of its students think it already is. In most editions of the survey, Chichester has been among the leading modern universities. The smallest of the nine universities created in 2005, Chichester has recruited strongly since shedding its college title and is reinvesting the surplus this has produced in improved facilities. Applications were up by almost 6 per cent in 2013.

The university traces its history back to 1839, when the college that subsequently bore his name was founded in memory of William Otter, the education-minded Bishop of Chichester. It became a teacher training college for women, who still account for two-thirds of the places, and eventually merged with the nearby Bognor Regis College of Education. The Chichester campus – now the larger of two – continues to carry the Bishop Otter name, signifying a continuing link with the Church of England. The refurbishment of the chapel and landscaping of its surrounds was one of the main capital projects of 2013. Both campuses have seen improvements recently, carried out in the summer to minimise the inconvenience to students.

Developments in Bognor Regis that cost £13 million are now near to completion. The biggest project has been to transform the Dome into a business and research centre and creating a new learning resources centre. Since May 2012, Chichester has been implementing the second phase of its investment plan, which aims to bring facilities on the Bishop Otter campus up to the same standard as those in Bognor Regis. The learning resources centre has been overhauled to provide easier access to books, online resources, media and computer facilities, as well as adding a coffee shop. The old library on the Bognor Regis campus has been converted into a 150-seater lecture theatre and other teaching space. The former student support services building is being used as business incubator units for local firms. The Alexandra Theatre in Bognor is used as a base for the musical theatre programme and there are links, too, with the Chichester Festival Theatre. The Mathematics Centre, at Bognor, has an international reputation, working with over 30 countries as well as teaching the university's own students. It has become a focal point for curriculum development in Britain and elsewhere.

The university has two faculties, each of which operates on both sites. One covers business, teacher training and IT;

College Lane
Chichester
W. Sussex PO19 6PE

01243 816002 (admissions)
help@chi.ac.uk
www.chi.ac.uk
www.ucsu.org
Affiliation: Cathedrals
  Group; GuildHE

The Times and Sunday Times **Rankings**
Overall Ranking: **65** (last year: 68)

Student satisfaction:	19	84.5%
Research quality:	=102	1.7%
Entry standards:	90	306
Student–staff ratio:	=78	18.7
Services & facilities/student:	110	£1,125
Expected completion rate:	40	89.8%
Good honours:	77	63.7%
Graduate prospects:	95	58.1%

the other the arts, history, media, sport and social sciences. The portfolio of some 300 courses ranges from adventure education to humanistic counselling, fine art and the psychology of sport and exercise. The PE teacher training course is one of the largest in the country – recently training one in five PE teachers in England – and is highly rated by Ofsted. Sport was the only area in which the university registered any world-leading work in the 2008 Research Assessment Exercise, but history and drama, dance and performing arts also produced good results. About one in six of the 5,000 students are 21 or over on entry, but little more than a third come from working-class homes, which is well below average for the university's courses and entry grades. However, the opposite is true of the projected dropout rate, which is barely more than 6 per cent and half the benchmark figure. The university runs summer taster sessions and has a series of partnerships with schools in the Channel Islands and Sussex to encourage a broader intake. Courses are also run in collaboration with Isle of Wight College.

Both of the university's campuses are within ten minutes' walk of the sea and the residential places are roughly equally divided between them, enabling Chichester to guarantee accommodation to anyone making the university a firm choice before the January UCAS deadline. There is a university bus service linking the two and students' union bars at each. Sports facilities are good and the university was chosen to provide training facilities for competitors in athletics, boxing, road cycling and table tennis before the 2012 Olympic Games. Since then, a sports dome has been added to the existing tennis courts to provide an all-weather, multi-sport facility, and a new running track has been installed. The small cathedral city of Chichester is best known as a yachting venue and Bognor is said to have the longest stretch of coastline in the south where all types of water sports are available. Both offer a good supply of private housing and some student-oriented bars. Much of the surrounding countryside has been designated an area of outstanding natural beauty.

Undergraduate Fees and Bursaries

» Fees for UK/EU students 2015–16 £9,000
» Placement year £1,800
» Fees for international students 2014–15 £9,950–£11,350
» Household income below £42K, £1,000 cash bursary each year.
» Range of other scholarships and bursaries available.
» Check the university's website for the latest information.

Students

Undergraduates:	**4,175**	**(525)**
Postgraduates:	**360**	**(490)**
Mature students:	**13.5%**	
International students:	**2.8%**	
Applications per place:	**4.8**	
From state-sector schools:	**96.4%**	
From working-class homes:	**34%**	
Satisfaction with students' union	**70%**	

For detailed information about sports facilities:
www.chi.ac.uk/student-life/life-campus/sport

Accommodation

Number of places and costs refer to 2014–15
University-provided places: 751
Percentage catered: 58%
Catered costs: £119.98 (twin) – £158.27 (single, en suite) a week.
Self-catered costs: £96.18 (shared) – £128.59 (en suite) a week.
All catered and self-catered rooms available either 37 or 40 weeks.
First years applying by 15 January and then making Chichester first choice guaranteed accommodation.
International students: as above.
www.chi.ac.uk/student-life/accommodation

City University London

Time is running out for City to meet its targets of reaching the top 200 in the world rankings and the top 35 in *The Times and Sunday Times* league table by 2016. But other parts of the university's strategy are certainly bearing fruit: it enjoyed the biggest percentage rise in satisfaction scores in the 2013 National Student Survey, though it fell back a little in 2014. It is in the midst of an extensive programme of campus improvements. The Northampton Square campus has been rejuvenated and another £130 million of refurbishment and new developments are planned over the next five years. Both applications and enrolments grew in 2013, following falls the previous year, and City recruits international students from more than 160 countries to study on the borders of the financial district and a quarter of the academics are also from overseas.

Marketing itself as the "international university in the heart of London", City added the name of the capital to its title to make the most of its greatest asset. Once a college of advanced technology, the university now has roughly a quarter of its students taking business courses, another quarter health and community subjects, and the remaining half law, computing, mathematics, engineering, journalism and the arts. Another part of its strategy is to "rebalance" its undergraduate intake, focusing on the university's strengths in business and law at the expense of health subjects, and increasing its average entry qualifications at the same time. There is a range of scholarships worth up to £3,000 a year for UK and EU students who achieve exceptional grades at A level, International Baccalaureate or other qualifications. City has also been investing heavily in the recruitment of research-oriented academics.

There are over 17,000 students, more than a third of them postgraduates. City also remains among the most popular universities, with 7.3 applications for each undergraduate place. The university has also increased its part-time numbers, against the national trend, with many students taking short courses that do not lead to a formal qualification. City has a better record than most of its peer group for widening participation in higher education, with over 40 per cent of its undergraduates coming from working-class homes. The university has strong links with business and the professions, and reaps the benefits with consistently good graduate employment figures. Courses have a practical edge, and many of the staff hold professional, as well as academic, qualifications. Six interdisciplinary centres have been launched to increase collaborative teaching and research, as well as to build stronger links

---

Northampton Square
London EC1V 0HB

020 7040 5060
ugadmissions@city.ac.k
www.city.ac.uk
www.culsu.co.uk
Affiliation: none

between industry and academia.

The Cass Business School is one of City's great strengths, ranking among the top 50 business schools in the world. Based in the heart of the financial district, it has built up an impressive cadre of visiting practitioner lecturers who find it easy and convenient to visit. City has links with 50 European universities and many more further afield, and many students spend a year of their course abroad. The City Law School, which incorporated the Inns of Court School of Law in 2001, was the first in London to offer a "one-stop shop" for legal training, from undergraduate to professional courses. The School of Journalism, within the School of Arts, is highly regarded and the university has launched the UK's first graduate school of journalism in £12-million premises. There is a flourishing short course programme which ranges from sitcom writing to e-business. City also has a very high reputation in music, where it is associated with the Guildhall School of Music and Drama. Together with nursing and midwifery, music achieved the university's best results in the 2008 Research Assessment Exercise. Social work and social policy also produced good results.

Development is continuing at the university's Islington campus. The library has been renovated at a cost of £2.3 million, giving students more space, upgraded technology and better support. The Student Centre and Careers Centre have been refurbished and a new common room for students added. The School of Law has been upgraded and the School of Health Sciences has moved to the main campus with new facilities including a new biomedical and clinical skills centre. The Students' Union is popular and the Student Centre, which provides advice on a range of topics, is the only one in the UK to be recognised by The Institute of Customer Service. The Sports Centre's redevelopment will be complete by the end of 2014. Much-needed improvements will include a six-court sports hall, a 100-station fitness area, improved and expanded changing facilities and four multipurpose studios. The new CitySport facility will be open to local residents as well as students and staff.

Undergraduate Fees and Bursaries

- » Fees for UK/EU students 2015–16 — £9,000
- » Foundation year — £7,500–£9,000
- » Placement year — £1,800
- » Fees for international students 2014–15 — £12,000–£15,000
- » For English students with household income below £42.6K, annual bursaries of £800–£1,400.
- » Limited number of university accommodation bursaries of £2,000 each year.
- » Mature student with household income under £42.6K, £1,000 each year.
- » Lord Mayor of London Scholarship, from £1,000 a year for ABB at A Level or equivalent to £3,000 a year for at least A*AA
- » Other scholarships and bursaries available.

Students

Undergraduates:	**7,960**	**(1,470)**
Postgraduates:	**4,160**	**(2,930)**
Mature students:	**16%**	
International students:	**31.1%**	
Applications per place:	**7.3**	
From state-sector schools:	**90.8%**	
From working-class homes:	**41.0%**	
Satisfaction with students' union	**57%**	

For detailed information about sports facilities:
www.city.ac.uk/sport-and-leisure.

Accommodation

Number of places and costs refer to 2014–15

University-provided places: 1,331 through private providers

Percentage catered: 0%

Self-catered costs: £151–£306 a week.

Accommodation is guaranteed for first years if conditions are met. Residential restrictions apply.

International students: guaranteed if conditions are met.

accomm@city.ac.uk

www.city.ac.uk/study/undergraduate/accommodation

Coventry University

Applications to Coventry rose by 17 per cent in 2013, as the university became the leading post-1992 institution in our league table after shooting up more than 20 places and into the top 50. Much of the improvement was down to sharply increased satisfaction ratings. It was chosen as *The Times and Sunday Times* Modern University of the Year and increased the size of its undergraduate intake by 500 students. This year in our table it had the most satisfied students and enhanced its position as the top post-1992 university.

Coventry has been more innovative than many other universities since it became clear that higher fees would usher in much greater competition between universities. It was among the first provincial universities to offer courses in London and then took its rivals by surprise by opening its own university college in 2012. Its courses lead to Coventry degrees or diplomas, but fees in 2015 will be less than £7,000 a year because most campus facilities will not be available. Fees at the university will range from £8,331 to £9,000 for specialist subjects such as automotive engineering.

The university traces its origins back to 1843, and it is in the throes of a £150-million scheme to rejuvenate its 33-acre campus close to the city centre. Much of the ten-year programme involves student facilities such as the showcase turreted library, which cost £20 million. The latest development, the £55-million engineering and computing building, includes a dedicated ethical hacking lab, an ex-RAF Harrier Jump Jet and a wind-tunnel built by the Mercedes F1 team, all of which are used by undergraduates. The Hub contains the students' union, a music venue, plenty of informal study space, shops and restaurants. Other facilities have already been added, including more residential accommodation, an arts centre and a sports centre. The next addition will be a new Institute for Advanced Manufacturing and Engineering, developed in collaboration with Unipart. New undergraduate and postgraduate programmes in manufacturing engineering have been designed to provide students with an academic learning environment blended with access to real industry projects.

Coventry has adopted an innovative approach to computer-assisted learning, supported by an expanded computer network. The university was chosen to house national centres of excellence in teaching for e-learning in health and social care, as well as in maths, and transport and product design. There is a focus on employment, which is reflected in a predominantly vocational curriculum. The Add+vantage scheme is designed to help full-time undergraduates improve their employability while studying.

Priory Street
Coventry CV1 5FB

024 7615 2222 (admissions)
studentenquiries@coventry.ac.uk
www.coventry.ac.uk
www.cusu.org
Affiliation: University
  Alliance

The Times and Sunday Times Rankings

Overall Ranking: **42** (last year: 45)

Student satisfaction:	1	88.4%
Research quality:	=92	2.3%
Entry standards:	=85	313
Student–staff ratio:	34	15.3
Services & facilities/student:	88	£1,355
Expected completion rate:	=48	87.6%
Good honours:	65	66.1%
Graduate prospects:	43	71.2%

Its modules cover a wide range of skills and help students gain work-related knowledge and prepare for a career. The Institute for Applied Entrepreneurship (IAE) helps students and small firms to start up and growing a business.

Among the initiatives to improve the student experience has been the introduction of tangible rewards for excellent teaching and further development of electronic learning. The Centre for Academic Writing offers advice on essays and theses, with group sessions and one-to-one appointments, while the Maths Support Centre includes a statistics advisory service and specialist support service for students with dyslexia. The majority of students exercise their right to take "free-choice modules" that cover the full range of university provision, with IT skills and languages particularly popular.

Research grades improved in the 2008 assessments, when small amounts of world-leading work were recognised in seven of the sixteen areas the university submitted. Art and design and electrical and electronic engineering produced the best results. Design benefits from a £1.6-million digital modelling workshop. The university also has a Technology Park, housing start-ups and small knowledge-based businesses.

The civic-minded approach of the university has created many town–gown links. The university's main buildings open out from the ruins of the bombed cathedral, as university and public facilities mingle in the city. Student residences are within easy walking distance of the campus and city centre. The London campus, which opened in 2013, is business-oriented and mainly for international students. A degree in global business management includes a workplace project and a period of study abroad, while one-year top-up programmes give international students entry into the final year of a BA degree.

Over 40 per cent of the undergraduates have working-class backgrounds, and almost all attended state schools. For the second year in a row, the projected dropout rate had improved significantly in the latest survey. At only 8 per cent, it is much better than the national average for the university's courses and entry qualifications. Students in Coventry welcome the relatively low cost of living there, and the city is not short of student-oriented nightlife.

Undergraduate Fees and Bursaries

» Fees for UK/EU students 2015–16: £8,331–£9,000
» Foundation degree up to £6,000
» Courses provided by Coventry University College
£5,655–£6,695
» Fees for international students 2014–15
£10,950–£12,444 (Coventry); £10,375–£11,040 (London)
» Scholarship of £1,000 a year for students from low participation areas.
» Scholarships for sporting excellence and exceptional academic achievement.

Students

Undergraduates:	**16,545**	**(5,475)**
Postgraduates:	**3,055**	**(2,195)**
Mature students:	**19%**	
International students:	**17.7%**	
Applications per place:	**5.6**	
From state-sector schools:	**97.3%**	
From working-class homes:	**41.2%**	
Satisfaction with students' union	**81%**	

For detailed information about sports facilities:
www.coventry.ac.uk/life-on-campus/student-life/sport-coventry/

Accommodation

Number of places and costs refer to 2014–15
University-provided places: 2,457 (includes 385 beds on Nomination Agreements)
Percentage catered: 25%
Catered costs: £3,928–£4,906 (36 and 38 weeks).
Self-catered costs: £4,080–£5,720 (40–44 weeks).
First years are guaranteed housing provided conditions are met.
International students: as above.
accomm.ss@coventry.ac.uk;
www.coventry.ac.uk/study-at-coventry/student-support/

University for the Creative Arts (UCA)

The University for the Creative Arts (UCA) has jumped 25 places in this year's table to much the highest position it has occupied since becoming a university in 2008. With more than 5,000 students in total, UCA is sizeable by the standards of specialist institutions. It was the product of a merger between two well-established arts institutes straddling Kent and Surrey. Indeed, the first version of its title was the unwieldy University for the Creative Arts at Canterbury, Epsom, Farnham, Maidstone and Rochester, although the multiple locations have since been dropped. The constituent colleges all date back to Victorian times. UCA has moved out of its shared Maidstone campus. The location of each college is given in the map below: Canterbury (1), Epsom (2), Farnham (3) and Rochester (4).

The largest of the three Kent campuses, at Rochester, offers a full range of art and design, including fashion, photography and specialist design courses. The purpose-built campus is set on a hillside overlooking the city centre and River Medway. Halls of residence with 214 places are close to the campus, which has studio space, library and learning resource centre, and a gallery.

Students taking UCA's popular media courses, who will continue to use studios in Maidstone at the largest independent studio complex in the UK, also have access the facilities of the Rochester campus. Degrees in interactive media production and media business management are being added to the renamed existing degree in television production in 2015.

At Canterbury, the accent is on architecture, but there are also degrees in fine art, interior design and more general art and design. The modern site is close to the city centre and contains purpose-built studios, workshops and lecture theatres. The Canterbury School of Architecture is the only such school to remain within a specialist art and design institution, encouraging collaboration between student architects, designers and fine artists.

By far the largest enrolment is at Farnham, in Surrey, which was declared a Craft Town in 2013, with active support from the university. More than 2,000 students take courses in art, design, cinematics and communications there. A purpose-built student village in the centre of town has 350 rooms and there are two galleries, as well as teaching space and a library and learning centre. The campus includes research centres in animation, crafts and sustainable design. Courses range from pre-degree Foundation courses in art and design to degrees in film production, sports

---

UCA Canterbury
New Dover Road
Canterbury
Kent CT1 3AN

01252 892883 (enquiries)
enquiries@ucreative.ac.uk
www.ucreative.ac.uk
www.ucasu.com
Affiliation: GuildHE

The Times and Sunday Times Rankings
Overall Ranking: **74** (last year: 99)

Student satisfaction:	=112	77.7%
Research quality:	=63	5.0%
Entry standards:	=72	324
Student–staff ratio:	11	12.5
Services & facilities/student:	33	£1,901
Expected completion rate:	=71	84.7%
Good honours:	108	56.1%
Graduate prospects:	119	49.5%

journalism and three-dimensional design. A new suite of media and creative writing courses is starting in September 2014. Additional facilities have been provided for the growing Computer Games Arts degree course, which now has a dedicated studio room with specialist computers.

The second base in Surrey, at Epsom, specialises in fashion, graphics and new media, although it offers general art and design courses at further education level. Degrees include music journalism and fashion promotion and imaging. There is a modern library and learning resource centre for more than 1,200 students, a bar and café on campus and three halls of residence, the latest of which opened in 2010. A new £5.9-million teaching block includes learning and resource facilities, a 200-seat auditorium and a digital media centre. Photovoltaic cells on the roof and solar water heating will ensure that at least 20 per cent of the energy it uses is generated on site.

The university offers four-year degrees, incorporating a Foundation year, as well as the three-year format, and two-year Foundation degrees, which can be topped up to produce honours. UCA's courses are also taught in five partner colleges, including one in India. Dr Simon Ofield-Kerr, the Vice-Chancellor, is planning to increase the number of international students, while also maintaining the university's local roots. All the students will be "required" to develop international perspectives, understanding and ambitions so that they are able to practise across the world. However, results in the National Student Survey have been poor in all seven years of polling, as they have been for art and design in most universities.

Many staff are practitioners as well as academics, and the colleges have produced a string of famous graduates, such as Tracey Emin, Karen Millen and Zandra Rhodes, who has now become the university's Chancellor. There is also a strong research culture, although UCA had only limited success in the 2008 Research Assessment Exercise. Thirty per cent of the university's submission was considered world-leading or internationally excellent, but this left it well down the ranking for art and design.

Undergraduate Fees and Bursaries

» Fees for UK/EU students 2015–16 £9,000
» Foundation degree £9,000
» Fees for international students 2014–15 £11,030–£11,490
» Details of bursary scheme for those with household income below £25K to be announced.
» Range of other scholarships and bursaries available.
» Check the university's website for the latest information.

Students

Undergraduates:	**4,960**	**(90)**
Postgraduates:	**185**	**(105)**
Mature students:	**16.5%**	
International students:	**9.9%**	
Applications per place:	**3.7**	
From state-sector schools:	**98%**	
From working-class homes:	**36.4%**	
Satisfaction with students' union	**53%**	

For detailed information about sports facilities:
http://ucasu.com/clubs

Accommodation

Places and costs refer to 2014–15
University-provided places: 969
Percentage catered: 0%
Self catered costs: £64.06 (shared); £95.94–£141.02 (single); £116.62–£142.90 (en suite) a week.
Priority is given to disabled students (new and returning) and new full-time students by distance.
International students: guaranteed housing if application received by mid June.
www.ucreative.ac.uk/uca-accommodation

University of Cumbria

Cumbria has reopened one of the UK's most attractive campuses, in the Lake District setting of Ambleside, mainly as the base for the country's largest programme of outdoor education degrees. The former college site had been mothballed as a result of financial difficulties that have now been overcome. The transfer of courses from Newton Rigg, near Penrith, is part of a ten-year estates plan. Another element saw the university's London campus move to a new site on the doorstep of Canary Wharf in 2013. The Education Faculty has been helping schools and training teachers in East London for 15 years, long before the battle was won to establish a university in the far North West of England. Despite having only 10,500 students, Cumbria is one of the largest teacher training providers in England.

The university now operates on five sites in Cumbria itself, although the largest campus is in Lancaster. There are two campuses in Carlisle and one in Workington, as well as a university centre at Furness College, in Barrow. Nearly a third of first years are 21 or over, and only a quarter come from Cumbria itself. There are also partnerships with the four further education colleges in the county to provide higher education locally. The university is the only higher education institution based in the historically underprovided county. It was finally established in 2007, after a series of false starts, formed by the amalgamation of a former teacher training college and an arts institute, with the addition of two campuses acquired from the University of Central Lancashire.

While teacher education remains the largest recruiter of students, Cumbria has adopted a new business focus. The business school was re-launched in 2013 with an emphasis on programmes in areas of particular strength, such as small and medium-sized enterprises, ethics and leadership and sustainability. Business interaction centres in Carlisle and Ambleside support business development and student entrepreneurship. A number of institutes have been established in areas such as forestry, wildlife conservation, healthcare and international security.

The university's headquarters are in Carlisle, where there are about 3,500 students. The larger of the two main sites in the city is in a parkland setting close to the River Eden. The second campus, closer to the city centre, boasts a new Learning Gateway, an innovative multimedia learning resource centre, and a sports centre with a four-court sports hall and well-equipped fitness room. The former Cumbria Institute of the Arts can trace its history in Carlisle back to 1822, eventually becoming the only

---

Fusehill Street
Carlisle, Cumbria CA1 2HH

0845 606 1144 (enquiries)
enquirycentre@cumbria.ac.uk
www.cumbria.ac.uk
www.ucsu.me
Affiliations: Cathedrals
  Group, million+

The Times and Sunday Times **Rankings**		
Overall Ranking: **95** (last year: 95)		
Student satisfaction:	=59	82.3%
Research quality:	=117	0.3%
Entry standards:	106	288
Student–staff ratio:	101	20.8
Services & facilities/student:	118	£816
Expected completion rate:	69	84.9%
Good honours:	59	66.9%
Graduate prospects:	77	62.1%

specialist institute of the arts in the North West, and one of only a small number of such institutions in the country. The creative arts are one of the main areas for development in the university's planning. The Institute of Policing will also move to Carlisle as part of the reorganisation.

There are more than 4,500 students in Lancaster, at the former St Martin's College, which was founded by the Church of England in 1964. It is a ten-minute walk from Lancaster town centre. The centrepiece is the Gateway, a £9.2-million development which provides a range of student services. There is also a modern library and excellent sports facilities, including a £2.5-million sports complex, gymnastics centre and fitness centre. The Ambleside campus has been refurbished and new amenities provided in conjunction with the Lake District National Park Authority. Research has restarted there and the campus will host more business and enterprise activity, as well as some new courses. The Institute for Leadership and Sustainability (IFLAS), which is part of the business school, is developing a portfolio of activities that make the best use of its unique setting. One novel development has seen Cumbria become the first public university in the world to accept Bitcoin as payment for fees. The online currency is being accepted for the IFLAS's Certificate of Achievement in Sustainable Exchange,

which is being introduced at the London campus in 2014, and the Postgraduate Certificate in Sustainable Leadership, which is based in Ambleside.

Cumbria was bottom of the initial rankings from the 2008 Research Assessment Exercise, recording only a small amount of world-leading research in theology, divinity and religious studies. But the focus of the university has been on attracting more students from a region of low participation in higher education, as well as on serving the social and economic needs of the county. Almost all the students are from state schools and colleges and four in ten are from working-class homes. The proportion from areas without a tradition of higher education is also well above the national average for the university's subjects and entry grades. Student satisfaction rates increased sharply in 2013, helping Cumbria to a modest rise in *The Times and Sunday Times* league table, and rose again in 2014.

Undergraduate Fees and Bursaries

» Fees for UK/EU students 2015–16 £9,000
» Foundation degree £6,000–£9,000
» Fees for international students 2014–15 £10,500–£14,965
» For household income below £25K, up to 139 bursaries of £1,000 each year; up to 21 part-time bursaries of £500 each year.
» Up to 8 progression scholarships for students from partner colleges of £500 each year.
» Check the university's website for the latest information.

Students

Undergraduates:	**6,020**	**(1,905)**
Postgraduates:	**800**	**(870)**
Mature students:	**30.3%**	
International students:	**1.6%**	
Applications per place:	**4.1**	
From state-sector schools:	**97.9%**	
From working-class homes:	**39.8%**	
Satisfaction with students' union	**59%**	

For detailed information about sports facilities:
www.cumbria.ac.uk/StudentLife/Sport

Accommodation

Number of places and costs refer to 2014–15
University-provided places: 1,000
Percentage catered: 20%
Catered costs: £62.90–£86.00 a week (plus catering plan).
Self-catered costs: £62.90–£104.80 a week.
First year are guaranteed halls accommodation if Cumbria is first choice.
International students: guaranteed halls accommodation if conditions are met.
www.cumbria.ac.uk/StudentLife/Accommodation/Home.aspx

De Montfort University

De Montfort has achieved the biggest rise of any university in this year's table, jumping 32 places. Work has begun on striking new buildings for some of De Montfort's best-known schools: Fashion and Textiles, Arts, Design, and Architecture. The Fletcher Complex, which should be complete in 2016, will be the latest phase of a £90-million "campus transformation project" funded through one of the first investment bonds issued to a post-1992 university. The university has already spent more than £140 million concentrating all its activities on its Leicester headquarters, when once it stretched from Bedford to Lincoln via Milton Keynes. Some of the new developments will be ready before new entrants arrive in 2015 and a campus centre, including a new students' union, is scheduled for 2016. There will be better catering facilities and a "green lung" in the heart of the campus, replacing redundant buildings with more outdoor social space.

Other campus developments have included the diversion of part of the ring road to allow the university to open up the 15th-century Magazine Gateway building, now a focal point of a university quarter with public open spaces and new links to the city centre. The £35-million Hugh Aston Building caters for around 6,000 students, and includes a court room, law library, dedicated law clinic and bookshop, as well as more conventional teaching facilities. Elsewhere, the 24-hour library was remodelled with wireless networks and rooms equipped with audio visual and IT facilities, and new games development studios have been installed to enable students to see their work in 3-D. An £8-million leisure centre includes a 25-metre swimming pool and a eight-court sports hall.

De Montfort achieved one of the best performances any post-1992 university in the 2008 Research Assessment Exercise, when 43 per cent of its work was rated world-leading or internationally excellent. Much of the successful work took place in the Institute of Creative Technologies, which acts as a catalyst for research that defies the traditional boundaries of computer science, the digital arts and humanities, attracting interest the business world. Professor Bernard Stahl, the director of De Montfort's Centre for Computing and Social Responsibility, is a leading participant in the £1-billion EU project to simulate a human brain. The university has spent £3.7 million on creative technology studios, which feature video, audio and radio production suites, recording studios and laboratories with the latest broadcast and audio analysis technology. A Performance Arts Centre for Excellence allows the university to deliver innovative teaching for students of dance,

---

The Gateway
Leicester LE1 9BH

0116 250 6070 (enquiries)
contact via website
www.dmu.ac.uk
www.demontfortstudents.
  com
Affiliation: University
  Alliance

The Times and Sunday Times **Rankings**
Overall Ranking: **54** (last year: 86)

Student satisfaction:	=57	82.4%
Research quality:	59	6.0%
Entry standards:	=85	313
Student–staff ratio:	=67	18.1
Services & facilities/student:	57	£1,571
Expected completion rate:	=51	87.4%
Good honours:	64	66.5%
Graduate prospects:	50	69.1%

drama and music technology.

The professional accounting courses achieved "premier" status in a global accreditation scheme, and the university was awarded a national teaching centre for drama, dance and theatre studies. DMU Global, launched in 2013, offers the majority of students an international experience, using a network of overseas business partners and academic institutions to provide internships and field work. Strong links with local business and industry manifest themselves in courses such as the BSc in media production, run in conjunction with the BBC. There is also an agreement to work with Hewlett-Packard on innovative educational programmes to better connect academia and business, as well as to collaborate on research.

Four further education colleges across the East Midlands are associates, linked into De Montfort's network and offering its courses. The dropout rate has improved consistently: at less than 10 per cent, it is now significantly lower than the national average for the university's courses and entry grades. De Montfort went back to a three-term year, rather than semesters, partly because it believed the prospect of imminent assessment encouraged some students to give up at Christmas in their first year. The university has a proud record for widening access to higher education with almost 40 per cent of students coming from working-class homes. It was one of the first to set up an employment agency to help students find part-time work as well as find careers upon graduation. De Montfort also has a good reputation for the support it gives to disabled students. The award-winning Square Mile programme, launched in 2011, uses DMU's academic expertise and a network of student volunteers to offer potentially life-changing services in the Leicester community. Projects have included free support for primary and secondary schools in the city and a campaign to recruit people to the stem cell register.

Leicester has become a more vibrant location after £3 billion of regeneration. Rents in the private sector are low and the university has more than 2,300 rooms in halls within walking distance of lectures.

Undergraduate Fees and Bursaries

- » Fees for UK/EU students 2015–16 £9,000
- » Foundation degree £6,000
- » Degree courses at partner colleges £6,000–£7,950
- » Placement year / year abroad £650
- » Fees for international students 2014–15 £11,250–£11,750
- » Vice-Chancellor's Fund: academic scholarships of £1,000 a year and bursaries of £200 a year; bursaries of £1,000 a year for students on access courses.
- » Range of bursaries of £1,000 a year to help vulnerable groups of students.
- » Vice Chancellor's 2020 scholarship: 50% discount on fees for master's degrees for students graduating with 2:1 or higher undergraduate degree.

Students

Undergraduates:	**14,625**	**(2,125)**
Postgraduates:	**1,045**	**(2,520)**
Mature students:	**20.6%**	
International students:	**8.2%**	
Applications per place:	**4.7**	
From state-sector schools:	**97.0%**	
From working-class homes:	**37.4%**	
Satisfaction with students' union	**74%**	

For information about sports facilities:
www.demontfortstudents.com/getinvolved/sports/

Accommodation

Number of places and costs refer to 2014–15
University-provided places: around 2,356
Percentage catered: 0%
Self-catered costs: £83–£152 a week (38–43 weeks).
First years cannot be guaranteed accommodation.
International students: new students are guaranteed housing.
accommodation@dmu.ac.uk
www.dmu.ac.uk/study/undergraduate-study/accommodation/

University of Derby

Derby has set itself the target of becoming the pre-eminent university of its type by 2020. Its yardsticks are student satisfaction, employability, service to business and flexibility, delivered cost effectively. Although it is not high in our league table, it is doing well on most of these measures – particularly student satisfaction, where it it is just outside the top 30. Its engagement with business includes the opening in 2013 of the Institute for Innovation in Sustainable Engineering, which supports advanced manufacturing with 3-D printing and advanced testing, and other work with industrial partners such as Rolls Royce. A University Technical College will open in 2015, providing vocational education for 14- to 19-year-olds.

The new Institute for Learning Enhancement and Innovation works with academic staff to ensure that students receive a focused learning experience. The university's emphasis on "real world learning" is underlined by facilities that include a simulated hospital and working radiography suite; industry standard kitchens and a fine dining restaurant; computer games suites; a commercial spa and salon; a law court and sports science gym and a 58-acre Outdoor Leadership Centre. New courses include a degree in sports development, which builds on the university's partnership with Derby County Football Club. The degree is the first in the UK to use a field-based learning lab at a professional sports organisation.

A foundation programme allows students to begin work at a partner college before transferring to the university. Derby claims to award more work-based qualifications than any other UK university. Business and management is by far the university's biggest academic area, but work placements are encouraged in all relevant subjects. The accent on employability continues through the "Skillbuilder" career development programme, which covers a range of transferable skills to give graduates an edge in the employment market. Derby is at the forefront of development of a Higher Education Achievement Record that students can make available electronically to prospective employers. The university was quick to adopt new teaching methods, pioneering the use of interactive video for a national scheme. Distance learning is a growth area, either online or through Derby's nine regional centres. Prospective students can even sample a virtual open evening. The university won an award for the imaginative use of distance learning.

Campus developments are continuing, all part of a £75-million estates strategy that has created a University Quarter for the city of Derby. Beyond its home city, the

---

Kedleston Road
Derby DE22 1GB

01332 591167 (enquiries)
askadmissions@derby.ac.uk
www.derby.ac.uk
www.udsu.co.uk
Affiliation: none

The Times and Sunday Times **Rankings**
Overall Ranking: **81** (last year: =84)

Student satisfaction:	=31	83.5%
Research quality:	=110	1.0%
Entry standards:	=91	305
Student–staff ratio:	=50	16.8
Services & facilities/student:	=84	£1,370
Expected completion rate:	81	83.1%
Good honours:	94	60.2%
Graduate prospects:	=110	54.4%

university teaches nursing in Chesterfield and has a campus in Buxton that is based in the former Devonshire Royal Hospital and offers courses in spa, outdoor recreation and hospitality management, as well as further education programmes. The landmark building houses a training restaurant, a beauty salon and a health spa, as well as more conventional teaching facilities. The UK's only degree in ecotourism was launched there in 2013, while a Foundation degree in spa management will also be taught in London, at the London School of Beauty and Make-up. A new Sports Centre opened in Buxton in 2011.

The university has three main sites in Derby. An extended academic campus at Kedleston Road, two miles from the city centre, caters for most of the main subjects including business, computing, science, humanities, education and law. The students' union, multi-faith centre and main sports facilities are at the Kedleston Road site. It also houses the clinical skills facilities, which include a new purpose-built iDXA suite, opened in 2014. The Markeaton Street site hosts arts, design, engineering and technology courses, while courses in health and social care are based at Britannia Mill. At the Markeaton Street site, flexible spaces have been created for work or social activities. "Learning pods" fitted with the latest audio-visual technologies contain 100 seats where students can work in groups or simply listen to music. The sites are within ten minutes' walk of each other, as well as being linked by free shuttle buses and the UniBus service, which also connects with the train station and city centre. In another award-winning development, the university has also acquired the 550-seat Derby Theatre in the city to house theatre arts programmes as well as continuing as a producing theatre.

The university spent £30 million in five years to maintain its guarantee of accommodation for all first years and has improved student facilities. A new £10-million sports centre is due to open on the Kedleston Road in the first half of 2015. Almost 45 per cent of undergraduates are from working-class homes and 20 per cent are from areas of low participation in higher education – well above the national average for the courses and entry qualifications. The latest projected dropout rate saw another big improvement and, at 15 per cent, is close to the benchmark figure for the university.

Undergraduate Fees and Bursaries

» Fees for UK/EU students 2015–16   £8,500–£9,000
» Placement year   £1,000
» Fees for international students 2014–15   £10,445–£11,010
» Household income up to £25K, bursary of £1,000 a year; household income £25K–£36.6K, £600 a year.
» Bursary for students from Buxton and Leek Colleges.
» Range of other scholarships and bursaries available.
» Check the university's website for the latest information.

Students

Undergraduates:	**10,265**	**(3,330)**
Postgraduates:	**715**	**(1,980)**
Mature students:	**21.7%**	
International students:	**7.1%**	
Applications per place:	**5.5**	
From state-sector schools:	**97.8%**	
From working-class homes:	**44.2%**	
Satisfaction with students' union	**61%**	

For detailed information about sports facilities:
www.teamderby.com

Accommodation

Number of places and costs refer to 2014–15
University-provided places: 2,500
Percentage catered: 0%
Self-catered costs: £94.78 – £117.32.
First-year students are guaranteed accommodation if they apply before 31 July.
Policy for international students: as above.
studentliving-housingteam@derby.ac.uks
www.derby.ac.uk/student-accommodation

University of Dundee

Dundee was the top university in Scotland for the fifth year in succession and in the top five in the UK in *Times Higher Education* (THE) magazine's 2014 survey in terms of the student experience it provides. Its students gave it particularly high marks for good accommodation and students' union, cheap bars and amenities, and the quality of the social life. The university's ratings in the National Student Survey are also consistently good. Dundee is ranked in the top 200 in the world by both THE and QS, and had been seeing increased demand for places until 2013, when there were falls in both applications and enrolments. Scholarships and bursaries introduced in 2014 could save students from the rest of the UK up to £8,000 in their first year.

The university has completed a £200-million campus redevelopment designed by the leading architect, Sir Terry Farrell. Among the buildings added in recent years are those for clinical research, interdisciplinary research and applied computing. There have been extensions to the library and the sports centre, while almost £40 million was spent on wireless-networked student residences. The IT facilities include a superfast broadband network and are among the best in the UK, allowing the latest technologies to be used to enhance teaching. The university doubled in size over two decades and there are now more than 16,000 students, including a healthy number from overseas. Dundee has been looking outwards to achieve the "critical mass" which experts regard as essential to break into the higher education elite, with the acquisition of education, nursing and art colleges, which have greatly increased its scope. But it resisted ministerial encouragement to amalgamate with Abertay University in 2012.

The university is best known for its work in the life sciences and medicine, where research into cancer and diabetes is recognised as world-leading. Biochemistry is the flagship department, housed in a complex that includes the £13-million Wellcome Trust Building and the Sir James Black Centre, which cost £21 million. Its academics were the first in Britain to be invited to take part in Japan's Human Frontier science programme and are now the most-quoted researchers in their field. Set in 20 acres of parkland, the medical school is the one of the few components of the university outside the compact city-centre campus – some of the nursing and midwifery students are 35 miles away in Kirkcaldy. More than half the work submitted for the 2008 Research Assessment Exercise was rated world-leading or internationally excellent. Dundee recorded the best results in Scotland for

---

Nethergate
Dundee DD1 4HN

01382 383838 (enquiries)
contact via website
www.dundee.ac.uk
www.dusa.co.uk
Affiliation: none

The Times and Sunday Times **Rankings**
Overall Ranking: **45** (last year: 49)

Student satisfaction:	18	84.6%
Research quality:	47	15.7%
Entry standards:	34	409
Student–staff ratio:	=26	14.9
Services & facilities/student:	76	£1,422
Expected completion rate:	=75	84.2%
Good honours:	40	71.7%
Graduate prospects:	45	70.7%

art and design, civil engineering, biological and laboratory-based clinical sciences. The university leads one of four "knowledge exchange hubs for the creative economy", tasked with bringing academics together with business and charities, and raising public awareness of the creative industries. The highly rated design courses are taught at the Duncan of Jordanstone College of Art. The university is a key participant in the Dundee-based V&A project to improve design in Scotland.

Vocational degrees predominate, helping to produce consistently strong graduate employment. The university claims to send more graduates into the professions than any other institution in Scotland, and only Oxbridge graduates came out ahead of Dundee's in a national survey of starting salaries. Most degrees include a career planning module and an internship option, and students are now provided with their own personal development website. The Enterprise Gym gives students the chance to improve their self-reliance and employability, and exercise their business creativity through business enterprise skills development training. Students can take the Scottish Internship Graduate Certificate, an eight-month programme combining a six-month internship with career management learning. There is a global equivalent, lasting seven months and with an internship in India or China.

Two-thirds of Dundee's students are from Scotland and nearly one in ten from Northern Ireland. More than one in five come from areas with little tradition of higher education, although less than a quarter are from working-class homes. Applicants have access to MyDundee, an online portal giving further information during the application process and to prepare them for the academic year. The city is profiting from regeneration programmes and enjoys a cost of living that is among the lowest at any UK university city. Dundee is experimenting with a range of three-year degree programmes for qualified candidates, bringing costs down further. Despite spectacular mountain and coastal scenery, social life tends to be concentrated on one of Scotland's most active students' unions.

Undergraduate Fees and Bursaries

» Fees for Scottish and EU students 2014–15   No fee
» Fees for Non-Scottish UK (RUK) students 2013–14   £9,000 a year, capped at £27,000 for most 3- and 4-year courses.
» Fees for international students 2014–15   £10,700–£15,500
   Medicine and dentistry   £18,600–£31,500
» Widening Access bursaries for Scottish students up to £3,000 in year 1. Subject scholarships available.
» For RUK students, bursary of £3,000 a year if household income below £20K, and £1,000 a year if household income £20K–£42K; RUK academic scholarship of £3,000 a year for those with at least ABB at A level or equivalent (excluding medicine and dentistry students); Discover Dundee scholarship of £2,000 in year 1 to all RUK students.

Students

Undergraduates:	9,090	(1,460)
Postgraduates:	1,735	(3,425)
Mature students:	23.3%	
International students:	13.3%	
Applications per place:	8.2	
From state-sector schools:	86.7%	
From working-class homes:	24.0%	
Satisfaction with students' union	86%	

For detailed information about sports facilities:
www.dundee.ac.uk/ise

Accommodation

Number of places and costs refer to 2014–15
University-provided places: 1,587
Percentage catered: 0%
Self-catered costs: £112.21–£132.51 a week.
First-year students are guaranteed accommodation if conditions are met. No residential restrictions.
International students are guaranteed accommodation if conditions are met.
residences@dundee.ac.uk
www.dundee.ac.uk/accommodation

Durham University

Durham seized the opportunity to recruit unlimited numbers of highly qualified candidates to increase the size of its undergraduate intake for the second year in a row, despite a marginal decline in applications in 2013. The university had enjoyed sharply increased demand for places the previous year after it had joined the Russell Group of leading research universities. Entrance requirements were already among the highest in Britain – and the projected dropout rate of little more than 3 per cent among the lowest. Durham slipped one place to sixth in our league table last year, but has been moving up the world rankings, finishing in the top 100 in both the *Times Higher Education* and QS world rankings in 2013.

Long established as a leading alternative to Oxford and Cambridge, Durham has a collegiate structure and picturesque setting that attracts a largely middle-class student body. The university has been attracting more applicants from non-traditional backgrounds, partly through a scheme that targets able pupils from schools in County Durham and Teesside where progression to higher education is low. But still more than a third of undergraduates come from independent schools. In addition to the normal open days, all those who receive an offer are invited to a special open day to see if Durham is the university for them. Since around 80 per cent come from outside the northeast of England, most are seeing the small cathedral city for the first time.

Undergraduates apply to one of 15 colleges, all of which are mixed. Colleges range in size from 300 to 1,300 students and are the focal point of social life, although all teaching is done in central academic departments. There are significant differences in atmosphere and student profile, ranging from the historic University College, in Durham Castle, to modern buildings on the city's outskirts and on Queen's Campus, 23 miles away at Stockton-on-Tees. Investment continues on the Mountjoy Site for the sciences, with improved student facilities and an extension of the Bill Bryson Library (named after Durham's former Chancellor). The new law school has opened and the £16.6-million extension of the Business School is now complete. But the main development has been the Palatine Centre, the culmination of a £50-million programme to create a student services hub at the heart of the university.

As the third-oldest university in England, Durham is generally quite traditional. Wherever possible, teaching takes place in small groups and most assessment is by written examination. However, the establishment of Queen's Campus in Stockton broke the mould. Initially a joint

---

The Palatine Centre
Stockton Road
Durham DH1 3LE

0191 334 6128 (admissions)
admissions@dur.ac.uk
www.dur.ac.uk
www.dsu.org.uk
Affiliation: Russell Group

The Times and Sunday Times **Rankings**
Overall Ranking: **6** (last year: 6)

Student satisfaction:	=13	85.3%
Research quality:	=7	29.7%
Entry standards:	5	525
Student–staff ratio:	=40	15.6
Services & facilities/student:	5	£2,544
Expected completion rate:	7	95.8%
Good honours:	6	84.8%
Graduate prospects:	16	79.5%

venture with Teesside University, Stockton is now home to a wide range of courses including applied psychology, business and business finance, pharmacy and primary education. The campus has also seen the fulfilment of Durham's long-held ambition to restore the medical education it lost when Newcastle University went its own way in 1963. An innovative joint project allows students to do the first two years of their training at Stockton, concentrating on community medicine, before transferring to Newcastle to complete their degree.

Significant investment has been made to improve social facilities for the 2,000 students in Stockton, including the opening of a £5.5-million sports centre, relocating some of the university's elite sports activities from Durham as part of a strategy to increase integration between the two sites. The university's aim is for the campus to be equal in academic status to Durham City, focusing on interdisciplinary research and covering the full range of research, taught postgraduate and undergraduate study.

More than 60 per cent of the work submitted for the 2008 Research Assessment Exercise was rated world-leading or internationally excellent. Applied maths, archaeology and theology achieved among the best results in the UK. Music, English and geography and environmental science also did well. In the 2013 QS subject rankings, geography was placed fourth in the world, while the space science researchers are rated in the top four for global influence by Thomson-Reuters.

The university dominates the city of Durham to an extent which sometimes causes resentment, but adds considerably to the local economy. For those looking for nightlife, or just a change of scene, Newcastle is a short train journey away. Sports facilities are excellent at both Durham and Stockton – and Durham is among the premier universities in national competitions. The university hosts centres of excellence in cricket, rowing and fencing, and offers a range of sports scholarships. Nine out of ten students take part in sport on a regular basis, and Durham's College Sport programme is the largest intramural competition in the UK. Some 380 teams compete in 15 sports every week.

Undergraduate Fees and Bursaries

» Fees for UK/EU students 2015–16 £9,000
» Fees for international students 2014–15 £14,000–£17,900
» Household income below £25K, £2,000 each year for college living expenses or as cash if living out.
» Students from the Supported Progression Compact Scheme, bursary of £5,500 a year (in year 1, as an accommodation subsidy).
» Academic, music, art and sports scholarships based on circumstances or by competition, up to £2,000. Scholarships for students from Co. Durham and Newcastle up to £10,000 a year.

Students

Undergraduates:	**11,835**	**(250)**
Postgraduates:	**3,155**	**(1,560)**
Mature students:	**5.7%**	
International students:	**14.8%**	
Applications per place:	**6.2**	
From state-sector schools:	**63.4%**	
From working-class homes:	**12.5%**	
Satisfaction with students' union	**44%**	

For detailed information about sports facilities:
www.teamdurham.com

Accommodation

Number of places and costs refer to 2014–15
University-provided places: 5,398
Percentage catered: 50%
Catered costs: £156.10–£210.37 a week (28–39 weeks); 29 weeks catered.
Self-catered costs: £108.56–£127.30 a week (38 or 39 weeks).
All full-time students become members of one of the university's colleges or societies and are allocated housing if they want it.
International students: first years are guaranteed housing.
www.dur.ac.uk/undergraduate/accommodation/

University of East Anglia

East Anglia (UEA) began the growing trend for provincial universities to open campuses in London, but it is closing the base in the City that it shared with a private company to concentrate on its activities in Norwich. The campus was mainly for overseas students, and the university is not abandoning its international ambitions – it has opened a new office in Kuala Lumpur. The decision was part of a move to "streamline the university's course offering". Applications fell by 13 per cent for the second year in a row in 2013, and enrolments also declined despite an increase in the number of international students.

Nevertheless, UEA has been doing well in *The Times and Sunday Times* league table, leaping more than 20 places in 2013 to enter the top 20, and following up with another rise of three places this year. UEA always does well in the National Student Survey and was fifth in 2014. The 15,000 students appear to like the scale of this relatively small campus university, as well as the quality of its courses. They can bring any inquiries to four learning and teaching "hubs", one for postgraduates, another for nursing and two for undergraduates in the other 25 schools.

The university has been engaged in an ambitious building and refurbishment programme on the 320-acre site on the outskirts of Norwich. Recent projects include the refurbishment of the Law School's Earlham Hall complex, the addition of more student accommodation and common space facilities, and a Gymnastics Centre in UEA's community Sportspark. In recent years, it has also provided a new health centre, and extended and refurbished the central library, catering facilities and students' union. An Enterprise Centre to develop students' entrepreneurial skills is due to open in 2015, along with a new Medical Research Building for the Medical School. The new Centrum building on the Norwich Research Park will create and support new companies and graduate jobs. The new developments continue UEA's longstanding commitment to sustainability, which is reflected in a top-30 position in the People and Planet Green League of environmental performance.

UEA celebrated its 50th anniversary in 2013, still offering some of the highly regarded broad subject combinations that it pioneered in its early days. The university is ranked among the top 200 in the world by *Times Higher Education* magazine. Environmental sciences is the flagship school – another international ranking placed UEA in the top 30 in the world for the impact of its research in this field. The Climatic Research Unit and the Government-funded Tyndall Centre for

---

Norwich Research Park
Norwich NR4 7TJ

01603 591515 (admissions office)
admissions@uea.ac.uk
www.uea.ac.uk
www.ueastudent.com
Affiliation: none

The Times and Sunday Times **Rankings**
Overall Ranking: **14** (last year: 17)

Student satisfaction:	5	86.5%
Research quality:	=32	21.0%
Entry standards:	=25	431
Student–staff ratio:	=15	13.0
Services & facilities/student:	16	£2,229
Expected completion rate:	=27	92.2%
Good honours:	34	74.3%
Graduate prospects:	=47	70.3%

Climate Change Research, which has a hub in Shanghai, are among the leaders in the investigation of climate change.

History of art, film and American studies were the stars in the 2008 Research Assessment Exercise, when half of their research was considered world-leading. Art history has the benefit of the Sainsbury Centre for the Visual Arts, perhaps the greatest resource of its type on any British campus. The refurbished and extended centre houses a priceless collection of modern and tribal art in a building designed by Norman Foster. Creative writing is another of UEA's best-known features and the recipient of a Diamond Jubilee Queen's Anniversary Prize. Health studies have been among UEA's fastest-developing areas. The university was awarded one of the first new medical schools for 20 years, and has since added pharmacy and speech and language therapy degree courses.

Nearly nine out of ten undergraduates come from state schools or colleges, and a quarter have a working-class background. Most have the opportunity of work experience as part of their course. An academic adviser guides all students on their options under the modular course system and monitors their progress through to graduation. The university has sharpened its focus on employability with a strategy that promotes the development of the academic and wider skills that employers demand through the curriculum. In addition, a Graduate Intern Programme enables recent graduates to work full- or part-time for between four and twelve weeks at a business in the eastern region.

UEA opened University Campus Suffolk in 2007, in partnership with Essex University, with a main site in Ipswich and smaller bases in Bury St Edmunds, Great Yarmouth, Lowestoft and Otley. Dropout rates have improved enormously in recent years. The latest projected figure of 6 per cent was better than the national average for the university's subjects and entry standards. The university is situated in parkland, with easy access to Norwich, voted one of the best small cities in the world. The Sportspark is impressive, and the university was chosen as the base for the English Institute of Sport in the East.

Undergraduate Fees and Bursaries

» Fees for UK/EU students 2015–16   £9,000
» Placement year/ year overseas   £1,350
» Courses at partner colleges   £6,900–£8,500
» Fees for international students 2014–15   £12,900–£15,900
   Medicine   £27,500
» Household income below £16K, £1,800 a year as fee waiver, accommodation discount or cash; household income £16K–£20K, £1,000.
» Entry scholarships, £1,500 cash for students with at least AAA or equivalent.
» Subject scholarships and annual Excellence Awards (£1,000) also available.

Students

Undergraduates:	11,335	(1,020)
Postgraduates:	3,105	(1,755)
Mature students:	16.7%	
International students:	18.4%	
Applications per place:	5.4	
From state-sector schools:	89.6%	
From working-class homes:	25.4%	
Satisfaction with students' union	77%	

For detailed information about sports facilities:
http://sportspark.co.uk

Accommodation

Number of places and costs refer to 2014–15
University-provided places: 3,842
Percentage catered: 0%
Self-catered costs: £2,620.10–£8,995.00 (38 weeks)
First years are guaranteed accommodation if conditions are met. Distance restrictions.
International students (non EU) cannot be guaranteed housing.
accom@uea.ac.uk
www.uea.ac.uk/accommodation

University of East London

East London (UEL) opened its new campus in Stratford – a joint venture with Birkbeck, University of London – in 2013, and stemmed what had been a serious decline in applications and enrolments since the introduction of £9,000 fees. The £33-million University Square development houses a selection of departments from UEL and Birkbeck and incorporates a range of flexible teaching and administrative spaces, alongside teaching accommodation for subjects including law, performing arts, dance, music and information technology that are offered as daytime or evening courses. The opening of the new campus saw applications stabilise, although there was another small decline in enrolments on full-time courses. As one campus opened, another closed: an ill-fated and costly venture in Cyprus lasted only six months.

UEL remains close to the bottom of our league table with scores for graduate prospects and entry standards that are among the lowest in the UK. But student satisfaction rates have been improving, albeit from a low base, and the completion rate is now significantly better than the national average for UEL's courses and entry qualifications. The student charter urges undergraduates to adopt the "35-hour attitude", which means studying for at least 35 hours a week, making good use of the Learning Resources Centre and handing work in on time.

The university is building on the legacy of the London 2012 Olympics, which took place on its doorstep. Indeed, it hosted the United States team at its new £21-million sports and academic centre at the Docklands Campus, called the Sports Dock. The campus, which opened in 2000, was the first such venture in London for 50 years and gave the university a new focal point, with its modern version of traditional university features of cloisters and squares. The university spent more than £190 million on the campus in the shadow of Canary Wharf, where student residences and recreational facilities sit side by side with academic buildings in a prize-winning waterside development. The business school and Knowledge Dock, a support centre for local companies, are also there and a £40-million student village by the Royal Albert Dock added 800 more beds.

The focus of new developments has now shifted to nearby Stratford, the original headquarters in UEL's days as a pioneering polytechnic. The Great Hall in University House boasts a high-tech, 230-seat fully retractable lecture theatre, while the health and bioscience laboratories have been refurbished. The Cass School of Education has now opened and law is next on the development agenda. In addition

Stratford Campus,
Water Lane
London E15 4LZ
Docklands Campus
University Way
London E16 2RD
020 8223 3333 (admissions)
study@uel.ac.uk
www.uel.ac.uk
www.uelunion.org
Affiliation: million+

The Times and Sunday Times Rankings
Overall Ranking: **119** (last year: 120)

Student satisfaction:	=78	81.1%
Research quality:	=73	4.0%
Entry standards:	113	278
Student–staff ratio:	121	26.3
Services & facilities/student:	69	£1,451
Expected completion rate:	=122	67.4%
Good honours:	111	54.2%
Graduate prospects:	=117	50.5%

to University Square, a new £14.7-million library opened in Stratford in 2013, housing extensive digital resources and a 24-hour café.

Extending access to higher education is UEL's top priority. Barely more than half of first years arrive with A levels and very nearly half are 21 or older on entry – many choosing to start courses in February rather than in the autumn. More than half of the undergraduates come from working-class homes, many from the area's large ethnic minority populations. A successful mentoring scheme for black and Asian students has become a model for other institutions, while a guidance unit advises local people considering returning to education. The Noon Centre for Equality and Diversity in Business, which opened in 2013 at UEL's Royal Docks Business School, gives extra help to its black, Asian, and minority ethnic students to prepare for a successful career in business. UEL is also strong on provision for disabled students and houses the Rix Centre for Innovation and Learning Disability.

Most degrees are vocational and almost 1,000 businesses are involved in mentoring programmes and/or a work-based learning initiative which offers accredited placements. All but one of the nine subject areas in which UEL entered the 2008 Research Assessment Exercise contained at least some world-leading research. Communication, culture and media studies, produced particularly good results, while art and design and sociology also did well. Centres of excellence include an Islamic Banking and Finance Centre, launched in 2011 and partly funded by one of Saudi Arabia's biggest banks, which has become a hub for international scholars who are looking to conduct research in this field. The Centre for Clinical Education is London's only provider of clinical facilities and training in podiatry.

University housing is not plentiful, although there are now 1,200 bed spaces and the rents are good value for London. The social mix means that UEL has not been the place to look for the archetypal partying student lifestyle, although the Docklands campus has changed this to some extent and Stratford has been transformed since the Olympics. Sports facilities and new students' union premises have been added at both Stratford and Docklands. Three UEL sports scholars were selected to compete in track events at the 2014 Commonwealth Games.

Undergraduate Fees and Bursaries

» Fees for UK/EU students 2015–16 £9,000
» Placement year/overseas year £800
» Fees for international students 2014–15 £10,400
» Household income below £25K, bursary of £250 a year; household income £25K–£30K, £200 a year.
» Sports scholarships, free textbook offer and enhanced study skills support.

Students

Undergraduates:	**12,725**	**(2,300)**
Postgraduates:	**2,345**	**(2,220)**
Mature students:	**47%**	
International students:	**11.4%**	
Applications per place:	**4.4**	
From state-sector schools:	**98.1%**	
From working-class homes:	**51.9%**	
Satisfaction with students' union	**65%**	

For detailed information about sports facilities:
www.uel.ac.uk/sport

Accommodation

Number of places and costs refer to 2014–15
University provided places: 1,200
Percentage catered: 0%
Self-catered costs £121.84 (en-suite single) – £160.53 (studio flat) a week (39 weeks).
First years are guaranteed accommodation if conditions are met; priority given to disabled students and those living furthest away.
International students: same as above
www.uel.ac.uk/residential
dlres@uel.ac.uk

Edge Hill University

Edge Hill opened its £17-million flagship building, Creative Edge, in 2014. It houses industry-standard equipment and resources for students on media, film, animation, advertising and computing degrees.

The complex is also home to the newly established Institute for Creative Enterprise, which acts as an interface between academic research and the creative industries. A partnership with the Liverpool-based internet broadcaster Bay TV, which now broadcasts regularly from Creative Edge, gives students the opportunity to work on live TV and secure work placements without leaving the campus. The Label Recordings, Edge Hill's own record label, also gives students the chance to work in an industry setting on everything from talent spotting and recording, to creating music videos, and PR and marketing campaigns.

More than £180 million has been spent on the 160-acre campus over the past decade, and there are plans for significant expansion following the purchase of land adjoining the existing site. The spacious £13.5-million Student Hub building houses the students' union and also contains open access computers, dining and shopping facilities, and social space. The university has invested £41 million in facilities in the last year alone. They include a new Biosciences building, upgraded accommodation for Geosciences, plus a further 273 student bed spaces. There are now some 1,750 residential places on campus. Work also began on a £25-million sports complex for students and the local community. New 3G pitches and a competition-standard athletics track are already in use, with a new sports centre, including 25-metre swimming pool, 100-station fitness centre and 8-court sports hall, scheduled for completion later in the year. The new facilities have enabled Edge Hill to introduce a range of new undergraduate degree programmes including human biology, ecology, motion graphics, games programming, and networking, security and forensics. Other new degrees include counselling and psychotherapy and psychosocial analysis of offending behaviour.

Edge Hill has moved up nearly 30 places in five years in our league table and slipped only marginally this year. The university had promised to use most of the income from £9,000 undergraduate fees to continue enhancing its students' learning experience after losing 95 per cent of its teaching grant in the switch to the new fees regime. Based at Ormskirk, Edge Hill had been one of the fastest growing universities in the UK before the fees went up, as well as one of the newest. It has more than doubled its complement of students since the millennium to reach over 22,000, with nearly

St Helens Road
Ormskirk
Lancashire L39 4QP

01695 575171 (enquiries)
study@edgehill.ac.uk
www.edgehill.ac.uk
www.edgehillsu.org.uk
Affiliation: none

The Times and Sunday Times Rankings
Overall Ranking: **72** (last year: 69)

Student satisfaction:	=26	83.9%
Research quality:	=114	0.7%
Entry standards:	89	308
Student–staff ratio:	=50	16.8
Services & facilities/student:	54	£1,614
Expected completion rate:	67	85.2%
Good honours:	=98	59.3%
Graduate prospects:	93	58.3%

10,000 of them on full-time undergraduate courses. Large numbers are enrolled on part-time postgraduate courses for the professions. From 2014, all undergraduates on arts and science programmes have the opportunity to undertake a sandwich year in industry or a year studying abroad to enhance their learning and boost their employability.

Although university status arrived only in 2005, Edge Hill moved to its landscaped campus in the 1930s and has been training teachers since the 19th century. It has long since expanded into other subjects, but remains the largest provider of secondary teacher training and courses for classroom assistants. It also won the lion's share of funding to deliver further training for qualified secondary school teachers. In 2011, the Faculty of Education achieved an unprecedented "outstanding" grade in all 33 possible graded areas of its Ofsted inspection across all three phases of its teacher-training provision. The SOLSTICE (Supported Online Learning for Students using Technology for Information and Communication in their Education) e-learning centre is recognised officially as a national centre of excellence in teaching and learning. It has a particular focus on learning in the workplace, but is involved with curriculum development and delivery in all three of the university's faculties. Three-quarters of all graduates leave with professional accreditation. All students have a personal tutor, as well as access to counsellors and financial advice.

Beyond Ormskirk, there are seven satellite campuses in Liverpool, Manchester and other parts of the North West to facilitate local learning. In addition, a range of further education colleges in the region teach the university's Foundation degrees. Edge Hill has one of the highest proportions of state-educated students in England – 98 per cent – and 42 per cent of undergraduates have a working-class background. The projected dropout rate of 11 per cent is also better than the university's benchmark. An award-winning student finance support package rewards achievement, as well as encouraging students to complete their studies, rather than simply offering incentives for enrolling, and bursaries and scholarships have been extended.

Undergraduate Fees and Bursaries

» Fees for UK/EU students 2015–16   £9,000
» Foundation degree   £6,000
» Placement year / overseas year   £1,000
» Fees for international students 2014–15   £10,950
» Household income below £25K, bursary of £1,000 in year 1.
» Scholarship of £1,000 for those with at least 320 UCAS points.
» Access scholarship of £1,000, year 1; £500, years 2 and 3, particularly for mature students.
» Competitive entrance scholarship of £1,000, year 1, £500, years 2 and 3, not linked to subject choice, in sport, performing arts, creative arts and volunteering.

Students

Undergraduates:	**9,815**	**(3,175)**
Postgraduates:	**835**	**(4,710)**
Mature students:	**23.1%**	
International students:	**1.1%**	
Applications per place:	**5.4**	
From state-sector schools:	**98%**	
From working-class homes:	**42.2%**	
Satisfaction with students' union	**72%**	

For detailed information about sports facilities:
www.edgehill.ac.uk/edgehillsport

Accommodation

Number of places and costs refer to 2014–15
University provided places: 1,700
Percentage catered: 17.6%
Catered costs: £99 a week (40 weeks).
Self-catered costs: £63 – £109 a week (40 weeks).
First years cannot be guaranteed housing. Residential restrictions apply.
Students designated overseas for fees are guaranteed accommodation if conditions are met.
www.edgehill.ac.uk/undergraduate/accommodation

University of Edinburgh

Edinburgh became the latest UK university to boast a Nobel Laureate on its staff when Professor Peter Higgs was awarded the 2013 physics prize for predicting the existence of the so-called "God particle". The new Higgs Centre for Theoretical Physics will offer masters programmes and enable students to take up PhDs in relevant areas. His success will boost Edinburgh's performance in at least one of the international rankings that currently give the most positive view of the university: it is rated among the top 20 in the world by QS. Unusually poor student satisfaction ratings contributed to it remaining outside the top 20 in *The Times and Sunday Times* league table this year. The university is trying to address undergraduates' concerns with a new personal tutor system and a peer support scheme, and other developments designed to improve the student experience.

The university retains a special status north of the border, where it is regarded as the nearest thing to Oxbridge. It is one of the two most expensive universities in the UK for undergraduates from outside Scotland, who pay £9,000 for the full four years of their degree. However, that has not prevented Edinburgh attracting more applications in each of the last two years. The fact that more than a quarter of its undergraduates come from outside the UK testifies to its worldwide reputation. Edinburgh is the largest university in Scotland. Its buildings are spread around the city, but most border the historic Old Town. These include the university's main library, which has been redeveloped at a cost of £60 million. The science and engineering campus is two miles to the south. The university got even larger in 2011, when it merged with Edinburgh College of Art, extending the opportunity for students and staff to collaborate across disciplines.

Competition for places remains intense: more than nine applications for each place in 2013. Edinburgh has been trying to widen its intake, with a range of bursaries, some worth up to £7,000 a year to English, Welsh or Northern Irish students. Other measures include an eight-week summer school for local teenagers and support for students in the transition to higher education. The university has always attracted a high proportion of middle-class candidates – many from England – and is a favourite in independent schools, whose students take about three places in ten. Selection guidelines aim to look beyond grades to consider candidates' potential, giving particular weight to references and personal statements.

A fundraising campaign has contributed to a new informatics building, as well as to the development of a "BioQuarter", a

---

Old College
South Bridge
Edinburgh EH8 9YL

0131 650 4360 (admissions)
contact via website
www.ed.ac.uk
www.eusa.ed.ac.uk
Affiliation: Russell Group

The Times and Sunday Times **Rankings**
Overall Ranking: **=22** (last year: 22)

Student satisfaction:	115	77.4%
Research quality:	6	32.7%
Entry standards:	=9	489
Student–staff ratio:	18	13.8
Services & facilities/student:	17	£2,188
Expected completion rate:	=37	90.4%
Good honours:	9	83.7%
Graduate prospects:	=21	78.1%

ground-breaking collaboration between the university and a number of public bodies that is intended to consolidate Scotland's reputation as a world leader in biomedical science. In 2010, the author J.K. Rowling gave £10 million to the university to set up a new clinic which conducts research into neurodegenerative diseases. A new library opened this year on the Science and Engineering campus, named after Noreen and Kenneth Murray, the Edinburgh-based husband and wife team who developed the Hepatitis B vaccine. The Business School has relocated to the main campus and a new research centre has been established for the study of Islamic civilisation and issues relating to Islam in Britain. Elsewhere, £90 million has been spent on the redevelopment of the Easter Bush site, where a veterinary school building, a research building for the recently incorporated Roslin Institute and a cancer centre opened in 2011.

Almost two-thirds of the work submitted for the last Research Assessment Exercise was rated as world-leading or internationally excellent, the highest proportion in Scotland. The university's entry was among the largest in the UK and produced strong results. The College of Medicine and Veterinary Medicine was the star performer, with all of the work in hospital-based clinical subjects rated at the international level and 40 per cent at the

highest grade. Informatics, linguistics and English literature also produced outstanding results.

New undergraduates generally take three subjects in both their first and second years. Every student has a personal tutor to help them narrow down the selection of a final degree and give personal advice when necessary.

The university's Centre for Sport and Exercise was extended in 2010, adding to the already impressive sports facilities. Considerable sums have also been spent making the university more accessible to disabled students. The students' union operates on several sites and there is a regular bus link between the science areas and the main university around George Square. The city is a treasure-trove of cultural and recreational opportunities, and most students thrive on Edinburgh life.

Undergraduate Fees and Bursaries

» Fees for Scottish and EU students 2014–15   No fee
» Fees for Non-Scottish UK (RUK) students 2014–15:   £9,000 a year, for up to 4 years (total £36,000)
» Fees for international students 2014–15   £15,250–£20,050
   Medicine: £23,450–£45,400   Veterinary studies: £28,450
» Accommodation bursaries of £500–£2,000 a year for Scottish students in receipt of SAAS bursaries.
» Edinburgh RUK Bursary taken as fee waiver or cash: household income below £16K, £7,000 a year (£3,685 for Welsh students), and then a sliding scale to £42.6K, £5,700–£500 (£3,685–£500 for Welsh students).

Students

Undergraduates:	18,390	(735)
Postgraduates:	6,605	(1,960)
Mature students:	9%	
International students:	25.2%	
Applications per place:	9.2	
From state-sector schools:	67.3%	
From working-class homes:	16.6%	
Satisfaction with students' union	58%	

For detailed information about sports facilities:
www.sport.ed.ac.uk

Accommodation

Number of places and costs refer to 2014–15
University-provided places: about 6,300
Percentage catered: 18.1%
Catered costs: £118.16–£200.62 a week
Self-catered costs: £57.82–£154.00
First years are guaranteed an offer of accommodation providing they fulfil requirements. Residential restrictions apply.
International students: accommodation guaranteed if conditions are met.
accom.allocations@ed.ac.uk; www.accom.ed.ac.uk

Edinburgh Napier University

Once Scotland's first and largest polytechnic, the Edinburgh Napier is named after John Napier, the inventor of logarithms. It has been celebrating its 50th anniversary as one of the largest universities in Scotland with 17,500 students at all levels, including more than 4,000 international students from 109 countries. Another 4,000 take courses delivered with partners in China, Hong Kong, India and Singapore. It has invested more than £100 million in its Edinburgh campuses, the most recent development being a new student residence in the city centre. At Sighthill, the Faculty of Health, Life and Social Sciences has been brought together on one site for the first time. The student-focused campus includes a 5-storey learning resource centre, 25 specialised teaching rooms including clinical skills laboratories, an environmental chamber and biomechanics laboratory, a crime scene scenario room, three IT-enabled lecture theatres and seminar rooms, as well as integrated sports facilities. The Faculty of Engineering, Computing and Creative Industries has been brought together on the Merchiston campus, where there is a new student hub and reception area, as well as fully soundproofed music studios. The Napier Students' Association will also be based on the campus for the first time, and

the library has been refurbished and is now open 24 hours a day.

The 500-seat computing centre at Merchiston is open all hours and students have access to online lecture notes and study aids via Moodle, the university's Virtual Learning Environment. The web-based system supports learning, teaching and assessment via the student portal and is accessible from smart phones and tablet computers. The university has plans for continued development of study spaces to access technology-based learning. There are fully networked libraries on each campus and a multimedia language laboratory and adaptive learning centre for students with special needs. The Craiglockhart campus houses the business school. It features a glass atrium with a cyber café and two spherical lecture theatres. The Craiglockhart studio has been refurbished and is the venue for an assortment of fitness classes. The Screen Academy Scotland, run in partnership with Edinburgh College of Art, reflects the university's strong reputation in film education. There are several smaller sites, ranging from a converted church to a former school, as well as outposts in Melrose and Livingston.

For two successive years, the university enjoyed among the biggest increases in applications in the UK, defying the national trend. Although partly fuelled by changes in art and design and nursing qualifications,

---

Craiglockhart Campus
Edinburgh EH14 1DJ

08455 203050 (admissions)
ugadmissions@napier.ac.uk
www.napier.ac.uk
http://napierstudents.com
Affiliation: million+

The Times and Sunday Times Rankings

Overall Ranking: **97** (last year: 100)

Student satisfaction:	72	81.6%
Research quality:	=84	3.0%
Entry standards:	50	348
Student–staff ratio:	=110	21.6
Services & facilities/student:	114	£1,019
Expected completion rate:	116	75.1%
Good honours:	=57	67.3%
Graduate prospects:	80	61.2%

the demand for places reflected the university's growing popularity. However, enrolments dropped by around 10 per cent in 2012 and 2013 and the university dropped sharply in *The Times and Sunday Times* league table. It lost ground to its rivals on student satisfaction, completion and spending on facilities. The modular system allows movement between courses at all levels, and the option of starting courses in February, rather than September. A model to other universities trying to reduce non-completion rates, Edinburgh Napier uses its students to mentor newcomers, runs bridging programmes and offers pre-term introductions to staff and information on facilities, as well as running summer top-up courses and teaching employability skills and personal development. The latest projected dropout rate of 12 per cent represents continued improvement on previous years and almost matches the UK average for the subjects on offer.

Agreements with a number of partner universities and colleges enable students to complete their qualifications as under-graduates or postgraduates overseas. A dual degree with the State University of New York (SUNY) allows students to complete a degree from Edinburgh Napier and SUNY in four years, for example. Closer to home, some 2,000 "college articulation routes" enable students to use their college qualifications to gain direct entry into

year two or three of a university degree. Widening participation is high on the university's list of priorities, and more than 30 per cent of undergraduate places go to students from working-class homes.

Many courses include a work placement, and a close relationship with industry has traditionally produced good employment prospects. The university's students and graduates are set to benefit from a new £1.8-million initiative designed to ensure that this continues. The Stand Out project aims to improve graduate employment levels, partly by increasing the uptake of opportunities to study abroad as well as by improving links with small- and medium-sized enterprises. Another employability programme, Confident Futures, is said to be unique in higher education. Workshops are designed to improve students' confidence and help them to develop skills, attributes and attitudes that will enhance their chances of being successful while at university, and in their careers.

Undergraduate Fees and Bursaries

» Fees for Scottish and EU students 2014–15   No fee
» Fees for Non-Scottish UK (RUK) students 2014–15:   £6,630 a year, for up to 4 years (total £26,520).
» Fees for international students 2014–15   £10,690–£12,410
» For RUK students, household income below £25K, £2,000 a year; household income £25K–£42.6K, £1,000 a year. RUK merit award of £1,000 a year for students with at least BBB at A level or equivalent.

Students

Undergraduates:	**9,210**	**(1,510)**
Postgraduates:	**995**	**(1,140)**
Mature students:	**42.9%**	
International students:	**18.8%**	
Applications per place:	**7.3**	
From state-sector schools:	**94.7%**	
From working-class homes:	**31.3%**	
Satisfaction with students' union	**55%**	

For detailed information about sports facilities:
www.napier.ac.uk/engage/

Accommodation

Number of places and costs refer to 2014–15
University-provided places: 1,298
Percentage catered: 0%
Self-catered costs: £103 (standard) – £122 (en suite) (38 and 50 weeks).
First years and direct entrant undergraduates are guaranteed a place if requirements are met. Residential restrictions apply.
International students: as above.
www.napier.ac.uk/study/edinburgh/accommodation/

University of Essex

Essex has set itself ambitious targets to be "firmly established" in the top 25 UK universities in five years' time, while also increasing its student numbers by 50 per cent. By 2019, too, every subject should be in the top 20 per cent of its discipline. The university sees these ambitions as chiming with those of its founders, who wanted Essex to be "freer, more daring, more experimental". The social sciences already meet those standards comfortably and the university achieves excellent student satisfaction scores across the board. The university went up seven places in our table this year and has only seven more to go to meet its principal target.

Essex, which has been celebrating its 50th anniversary in 2014, is ranked by *Times Higher Education* magazine in the top 100 in the world for social sciences and in the top 200 overall. The university received the only Regius professorship in Political Science in the awards to mark the Queen's Diamond Jubilee and achieved the best results in the last Research Assessment Exercise for both politics and sociology. It was also in the top three for accounting and finance, history and economics. Essex featured in the top ten in more than half of the 14 areas in which it was assessed, demonstrating quality well beyond its traditional strengths in the social sciences. It has been building up its science departments, and is strong in biological sciences and computing.

The main campus, two miles from Colchester, is set in 200 acres of parkland. The university has been carrying out major refurbishments to its 1960s buildings, at the same time as expanding student facilities. The Albert Sloman Library is being expanded by 30 per cent and a new Student Centre will open in 2015, providing a one-stop hub for student services. The new developments are costing more than £200 million and include a £1.4-million gym, renovation of the students' union bar, a café with adjoining learning space and an innovative shared IT workspace. Wivenhoe House, the original centrepiece of the campus, has been converted into a thriving four-star hotel run by and home to the Edge Hotel School. Essex Business School will open a new £21-million building during 2014 with the same low-carbon features that have taken the university to the top three in the national Carbon Reduction Commitment rankings. The next change will be the completion of the Knowledge Gateway development, which will provide space for research and business, as well as residential accommodation for 1,300 students.

The incorporation of the East 15 Acting School, in Loughton, as a department of the university was the university's first venture beyond Colchester. There has since been

---

Wivenhoe Park
Colchester
Essex CO4 3SQ

01206 873666 (enquiries)
admit@essex.ac.uk
www.essex.ac.uk
www.essexstudent.com
Affiliation: none

The Times and Sunday Times **Rankings**
Overall Ranking: **32** (last year: 39)

Student satisfaction:	=8	85.7%
Research quality:	=27	22.7%
Entry standards:	=53	343
Student–staff ratio:	43	16.1
Services & facilities/student:	8	£2,401
Expected completion rate:	58	86.6%
Good honours:	70	64.7%
Graduate prospects:	65	65.2%

heavy investment in a third site in Southend – a modern multi-faculty campus offering courses in business, health and the arts. Situated in the town centre, the Southend Campus has been based around the Gateway Building and Clifftown Studios, a former church that is now the university's theatre. There is an accommodation complex which also houses a gym and fitness studio. The Forum was added in 2013, a £27-million project comprising a public and academic library, learning facilities, café and gallery. Another regional project has seen Essex collaborate with the University of East Anglia on University Campus Suffolk, which offers courses in Ipswich and at smaller centres across the county. Essex degrees are also taught at Writtle College, near Chelmsford, the Colchester Institute and South East Essex College, in Southend.

The university now has almost 12,000 undergraduates. The student population is unusually diverse for a pre-1992 university, with high proportions of mature and overseas students. A third of undergraduates are from working-class homes and 96 per cent went to state schools or colleges. The Employability and Careers Centre has seen major investment over recent years. The award-winning Frontrunners scheme, established by the university and students' union, arranges on-campus, paid work experience for students. Many courses offer work placement opportunities. Essex Abroad supports students studying, working or volunteering abroad, while the new Languages for All scheme offers all students language tuition at no extra cost. The university does not charge a fee for a full year abroad, and many courses also include work placement opportunities where students are based.

Social and sporting facilities are good, with an active students' union and some 40 acres of land on the Colchester campus devoted to sports facilities. All new first years are guaranteed a residential place in university accommodation, which has been voted some of the best in the UK. Some ground-floor flats have been adapted for disabled students. A £23-million new development opened on the main campus in 2013 with 648 student bedrooms in flats and town houses. All the campuses are within easy access of London.

Undergraduate Fees and Bursaries

» Fees for UK/EU students 2015–16 £9,000
» Placement year/ overseas year no fee
» Fees for international students for 2014–15 £11,950–£13,950
» Household income below £25K, bursary of £1,000 in years 1 and 2, £500, year 3.
» Academic scholarship of £2,000 in year 1 for students with a score of 34 or above in the International Baccalaureate.
» Range of other scholarships and bursaries available.
» Check the university's website for the latest information.

Students

Undergraduates:	9,755	(1,670)
Postgraduates:	2,325	(915)
Mature students:	13.6%	
International students:	27.5%	
Applications per place:	5.8	
From state-sector schools:	95.7%	
From working-class homes:	33.3%	
Satisfaction with students' union	75%	

For detailed information about sports facilities:
www.essex.ac.uk/sport

Accommodation

Number of places and costs refer to 2014–15
University-provided places: 4,266
Percentage catered: 0%
Self-catered costs: Colchester: £73.15 (South Towers) – £133.14 (Meadows en suite) a week; Southend: £128.59 (en suite) – £158.62 (studio flat).
New first years are guaranteed accommodation if conditions met.
International students: new students are guaranteed accommodation if conditions are met.
accom@essex.ac.uk ; www.essex.ac.uk/accommodation

University of Exeter

Exeter reaped the rewards from joining the Russell Group and becoming *The Sunday Times* University of the Year in 2012, enjoying huge growth in applications – 29 per cent – and increasing the size of the undergraduate intake by a quarter, or more than 1,000 students. Consistently high levels of student satisfaction, combined with good research grades, are making the university a fixture in the top 10 of our league table. It has been introducing a raft of new degrees, such as the undergraduate Masters courses in international politics and Arabic and Islamic studies, and will add a BSc in criminology and five new pathways in the Medical Sciences programme in 2015.

The main Streatham Campus, close to the centre of Exeter, is one of the most attractive settings of any university, and has benefited from £380 million of investment. This has included £130 million for student residences, substantial investment in the Business School, a new Mood Disorders Centre and new facilities for biosciences and the Law School. The jewel in the crown of the new developments is the Forum, a £50-million development which creates a central hub and features an extended library, new student services centre, technology-rich learning spaces, a new auditorium and additional social and retail facilities. An £8.1-million investment in the sports facilities, featuring a well-equipped new fitness centre, is due to be completed by September 2014. Another £50-million facility, the Living Systems Building, will follow in 2016, housing interdisciplinary research on food security, health and a sustainable environment.

Elsewhere in Exeter, the medical school is being extended on the St Luke's Campus, with new teaching and research facilities scheduled to open in September 2015. A £27.5-million health education and research centre has already opened at the Royal Devon and Exeter Hospital. The school grew out of the former Peninsular College of Medicine and Dentistry, which was established in association with Plymouth University in 2006. The partners have gone their separate ways, with Plymouth taking dentistry and Exeter offering a BSc in medical sciences in addition to the established Bachelor of Medicine, Bachelor of Surgery (BMBS). The new pathways, in genetics and genomics, neuroscience, pharmacology, environment and public health, and health research, will include the option of a competitive entry Professional Training Year. The highly rated department of sport and health sciences and the graduate school of education are also located at St Luke's, which is a mile away from the main campus.

The university's other base is the

Northcote House
The Queen's Drive
Exeter, Devon EX4 4QJ

0300 555 6060 (UK admissions)
44 1392 723044 (non-UK admissions)
ug-ad@exeter.ac.uk
www.exeter.ac.uk
www.exeterguild.org
www.fxu.org.uk
Affiliation: Russell Group

The Times and Sunday Times Rankings

Overall Ranking: **7** (last year: 8)

Student satisfaction:	6	86.4%
Research quality:	=13	28.0%
Entry standards:	15	459
Student–staff ratio:	=48	16.6
Services & facilities/student:	12	£2,356
Expected completion rate:	5	96.5%
Good honours:	7	84.6%
Graduate prospects:	15	79.6%

£100-million Penryn Campus in Cornwall, which has helped boost applications in recent years. Shared with Falmouth University, the campus offers Exeter degrees in biosciences, geography, geology, clean energy, English, history, politics and mining engineering. A £30-million Environment and Sustainability Institute has opened on the campus and a new £5.5-million facility will enable the Business School to expand into Cornwall in 2015. This new building will also provide space for marine research and the growing Centre for Ecology and Conservation. The 2008 Research Assessment Exercise saw Exeter move up the pecking order of research universities, with most of its work judged to be world-leading or internationally excellent despite a much larger submission (involving 95 per cent of academics) than most of its peers. English, classics, archaeology, and accounting and finance did particularly well.

Almost a third of Exeter's under-graduates come from independent schools – a much higher proportion than the national average for the university's subjects and entry qualifications, although this figure has been coming down gradually. The university used to focus its attempts to broaden the intake mainly on the rural South West, but is now targeting schools and colleges further afield. The share of places taken by students from working-class homes is among the lowest in the UK, at less than 16 per cent. However, the dropout rate of 3 per cent is also among the lowest. Exeter's longstanding international focus is exemplified by a large range of four-year programmes "with international study" and by its partner universities in over 40 countries. All students are offered tuition in foreign languages and even some three-year degrees include the option of a year abroad. Career management skills are built in and students have a wide range of work experience opportunities. The Career Zone has been expanded to increase career support and internships and graduate employment rates have been improving. The university's Exeter Award provides official recognition of all the extracurricular activities that students undertake.

Over £20 million has been invested in first-class sports facilities in the last few years. Exeter, for example, is one of only nine UK universities to have indoor tennis facilities to national competition standards. There is no shortage of student-oriented bars and clubs in the city.

Undergraduate Fees and Bursaries

» Fees for UK/EU students 2015–16 £9,000
» Fees for international students 2014–15 £15,000–£17,500
  Medicine £17,500–£29,500
» Household income below £16K, bursary of £2,000, year 1, £1,500 year 2 onwards; household income 16K–£25K, £1,000 bursary each year.
» Sports and music scholarships.

Students		
Undergraduates:	**14,080**	**(155)**
Postgraduates:	**3,475**	**(1,155)**
Mature students:	**6.9%**	
International students:	**22.9%**	
Applications per place:	**6.1**	
From state-sector schools:	**69.1%**	
From working-class homes:	**15.8%**	
Satisfaction with students' union	**77%**	

For detailed information about sports facilities:
http://sport.exeter.ac.uk

Accommodation
Number of places and costs refer to 2014–15
University-provided places: 5,242
Percentage catered: 22%
Catered costs: £148.26–£218.40 a week (32 weeks).
Self-catered costs: £81.41–£147.21 a week (40, 42, 44 or 51 weeks).
Unaccompanied first years are guaranteed accommodation provided conditions are met.
International students: as above.
sid@exeter.ac.uk; www.exeter.ac.uk/accommodation

University of Falmouth

Falmouth made its debut in *The Times and Sunday Times* last year, comfortably in the middle third. It has now jumped 26 places with outstanding employment scores to become one of the leading modern universities in our table. Falmouth almost doubled in size in the five years before being awarded full university status in 2012. There are now 4,700 students taking a range of subjects including architecture, digital media and creative writing, as well as the art and craft courses that were its exclusive territory for almost a century. The university still regards itself as a specialist institution, but degrees now include acting, business entrepreneurship and marketing, among many others.

Founded in 1902 as Falmouth School of Art, the institution merged with Dartington College of Arts, in south Devon, in 2008, thereby adding a variety of performance-related courses to its portfolio. The former Dartington courses have relocated to a purpose-built Performance Centre at Penryn. Falmouth has also collaborated with the University of Exeter since 2002, sharing the Penryn campus. There is a unique £10-million joint students' union, FXU, which serves all Falmouth students and those attending Exeter's Cornish outpost. The Exchange, which contains teaching and library space as well as study areas, opened in 2012 on the Penryn campus, where there has been a major extension to the library and the establishment of an Academy for Innovation and Research, which has a particular focus on the digital economy and sustainable design, and includes an open-access digital manufacturing laboratory. More than 70 per cent of the staff submitted work to the 2008 Research Assessment Exercise in music, theatre, choreography, visual performance and performance writing. The research programme covers areas such as smart technologies, future transport solutions, pervasive media, eco-town developments and Britain's ageing population, as well as art.

The original Falmouth campus, near the town centre, boasts subtropical gardens and an outdoor sculpture canopy, as well as studios, library and catering facilities. Most courses demand between 260 and 300 UCAS tariff points, but portfolios or auditions are as important as A levels on many courses. A few degrees hold out the possibility of unconditional offers for promising applicants. About 60 per cent of the undergraduates are female, and 95 per cent were state educated, with almost 30 per cent coming from working-class homes. The university has an internal teaching qualification for staff to ensure high standards in teaching, learning and assessment.

Woodlane
Falmouth, Cornwall TR11 4RH

01326 213 730 (admissions)
admissions@falmouth.ac.uk
www.falmouth.ac.uk
www.fxu.org.uk
Affiliation: GuildHE

The Times and Sunday Times Rankings
Overall Ranking: **51** (last year: =77)

Student satisfaction:	=78	81.1%
Research quality:	=94	2.0%
Entry standards:	=82	316
Student–staff ratio:	=116	23.0
Services & facilities/student:	35	£1,877
Expected completion rate:	44	88.6%
Good honours:	48	70.4%
Graduate prospects:	44	70.9%

Most of the degrees are single honours. The university has introduced new "externally facing" courses, including programmes that enable students to set up a business while studying. The unique BA in business entrepreneurship, introduced in 2014, uses the successful Team Academy model for teaching – prioritising practical experience and mentoring. There is also new provision in the growing creative industries sectors, with courses in creative computing, gaming, social media, creative leadership, business and management. "Alacrity Falmouth", launched in May 2014, is a graduate entrepreneurship programme with a focus on digital games, including a new degree in the subject, which will benefit from the university's recent European Research Area Chair in digital games technology. There will also be a focus on the "learning and leisure" market, making use of Cornwall's tourist attractions, businesses and landmarks.

There has already been considerable expansion in media teaching and research, with an extended Media Centre on the Penryn Campus, which also houses the Photographic Centre. Falmouth has been awarded Skillset Academy status for its media courses. The animation and visual effects department has become part of the Cross Channel Film Lab, a project that aims to develop an innovative visual effects for use in low-budget feature film production, working on films alongside experts from the within the industry. Partners include BBC Films, Film 4 and Arte France, and the university benefits from new computers, a 3-D printer and stereoscopic projector, all of which will be available for student use.

The university offers each new arrival a student mentor for a year to help support them during their transition to university life. Student residences are shared with the University of Exeter. Glasney Student Village, on the Penryn Campus, opened in 2004 and expanded in 2012 and there are also residential places in Falmouth, so the university can guarantee all full-time first years accommodation as long as they apply by the published deadline. The Sports Centre has a gymnasium, exercise studio and multi-use games area. As befits the seaside location, there are many water sports activities. Students make full use of Cornwall's coastline and rugged moors, but there are good transport links to London and Europe. Plenty of tourist-related work is available and lively nightlife during the holiday season.

Undergraduate Fees and Bursaries

» Fees for UK/EU students 2015–16 £9,000
» Fees for international students 2014–15 £11,500
» Support to be given to students from households with low incomes. Details not available in August 2014.
» Range of scholarships and bursaries by subject, for travel and for care leavers and disabled students.

Students

Undergraduates:	**3,670**	**(5)**
Postgraduates:	**155**	**(165)**
Mature students:	**14.5%**	
International students:	**4.9%**	
Applications per place:	**3.5**	
From state-sector schools:	**94.7%**	
From working-class homes:	**28.5%**	
Satisfaction with students' union	**75%**	

For detailed information about sports facilities:
www.fxplus.ac.uk/enjoy/sports-recreation

Accommodation

Places and costs refer to 2014–15
University-provided places: approx. 1,300
Percentage catered: 0%
Self-catered costs: £73.92 (shared en suite) – £126.35 (single en suite) for 41 weeks.
First year full-time students are guaranteed housing if conditions are met.
International students: non EU students, as above
accommodation@fxplus.ac.uk;
www.falmouth.ac.uk/accommodation

University of Glasgow

Glasgow has bought 15 acres of land around the city's Western Infirmary, which closes in 2015, to reshape the university in a way that it describes as the third major staging point in its 560-year history. Consultation is still under way on how the site will be used, but £80 million has been set aside for new buildings and another £55 million for refurbishments. The moves will allow Glasgow to expand. Applications were 12.5 per cent up in 2013, enabling the university to take an extra 600 undergraduates. Its latest strategy talks of extending the university's global reach to become a truly international university with a multicultural community of students and staff. It is already on the verge of the top 50 in the QS World University Rankings and has been playing a full part in Glasgow's Commonwealth Games, adding a cultural dimension. The university's Commonwealth Scholarship scheme celebrates the Games by offering awards for students from developing countries.

With almost two-thirds of the students coming from Scotland – many from Glasgow and the surrounding area – the university benefits more than some of its rivals from the policy of free tuition for Scottish students. However, nearly 15 per cent of undergraduates are from outside the UK. They seem to enjoy the experience, having voted Glasgow fourth in the UK and top among Russell Group universities in i–graduate's independent International Student Barometer. The university opened its first overseas branch in 2011, as part of an agreement with the Singapore Institute of Technology (SIT) to deliver joint engineering and mechatronics degree programmes. Students will complete three years at one of SIT's partner polytechnics before finishing their studies at the University of Glasgow Singapore. The Centre for International Development, which was the first of its kind in Scotland and the largest in the UK, has helped to secure more than £20 million of research income.

Glasgow enjoys the rare distinction of having been established by Papal Bull, and began its existence in the chapterhouse of Glasgow Cathedral in 1451. Since 1871 it has been based on the Gilmorehill campus in the city's fashionable West End, with its 104 listed buildings. The Veterinary School and outdoor sports facilities are located at Garscube, four miles away, and there is also a campus at Dumfries, which is taking liberal arts and teacher education degrees to southwest Scotland. The university has spent £7.5 million in five years improving teaching and learning facilities and plans to spend a further £3.5 million by 2017. In addition, more than £13 million has been committed to an extension of sporting and social

University Avenue
Glasgow G12 8QQ

0141 330 2000 (switchboard)
student.recruitment@
  glasgow.ac.uk
www.gla.ac.uk
www.guu.co.uk
www.qmunion.org.uk
Affiliation: Russell Group

***The Times and Sunday Times* Rankings**
Overall Ranking: **26** (last year: 25)

Student satisfaction:	=26	83.9%
Research quality:	20	24.3%
Entry standards:	11	487
Student–staff ratio:	=31	15.2
Services & facilities/student:	21	£2,131
Expected completion rate:	=51	87.4%
Good honours:	32	74.5%
Graduate prospects:	14	79.9%

facilities, which will be complete by 2015.

Glasgow is no stranger to innovation: it was the first university in Britain to have a school of engineering, and the first in Scotland to have a computer. It has now appointed Scotland's first Gaelic language officer and the country's first chair of Gaelic. More than half of the work submitted for the last Research Assessment Exercise was considered world-leading or internationally excellent, and the university finished in the UK's top ten in 18 subject areas. The Boyd Orr Centre for Population and Ecosystem Health was awarded a Queens Anniversary Prize in 2014. The latest development, opening in 2015, is the £20-million Stratified Medicine Scotland Innovation Centre (SMS-IC) at the new South Glasgow Hospitals Campus, which involves a consortium of universities, NHS Scotland and industry partners.

Almost half of the university's applications are for arts or sciences degrees, rather than specific subjects, reflecting the popularity of a flexible system that allows students to delay choosing a specialism until the end of their second year. The university operates a number of access initiatives, including the Top Up programme, which has been working with schools in the West of Scotland since 1999, and the Talent Scholarships, which are worth £1,000 a year to 60 academically able entrants who could face financial difficulties in taking up a

place at Glasgow. Nevertheless, little more than 20 per cent of the undergraduates are from working-class homes. The Club 21 programme provides students with paid work experience placements in the UK and overseas. It involves more than 100 employers from Santander to T-Mobile, some of whom sponsor undergraduates at £1,000 a year.

Most students like the combination of campus and city life, with the added bonus that Glasgow has been rated among the most cost-effective cities in which to study. Undergraduates have the choice of two students' unions, plus a sports union supporting more than 40 clubs and activities. New student union facilities, including a nightclub and four café-bars will be ready during 2015.

Undergraduate Fees and Bursaries

» Fees for Scottish and EU students 2014–15   No fee
» Fees for Non-Scottish UK (RUK) students 2014–15   £6,750 a year (total £27,000); medicine, dentistry, veterinary medicine £9,000 (total £36,000).
» Fees for international students 2014–15   £13,750–£17,250 Medicine, dentistry and veterinary medicine   £17,250–£31,250
» Talent Scholarships of £1,000 a year for Scottish students facing financial difficulties in taking up a place.
» For RUK students, Welcome bursary of £1,000 in year 1. Tuition fee waiver of £2,000 a year when household income below £20K, £1,000 (£20K–£30K), £500 (£30K–42.6K). Scholarship of £1,000 a year for students with at least AAB at A Level or equivalent and household income below £42.6K.

Students

Undergraduates:	**16,375**	**(3,635)**
Postgraduates:	**4,900**	**(1,725)**
Mature students:	**15.5%**	
International students:	**14.3%**	
Applications per place:	**6.6**	
From state-sector schools:	**86.3%**	
From working-class homes:	**22.3%**	
Satisfaction with students' union	**75%**	

For detailed information about sports facilities:
www.gla.ac.uk/services/sport

Accommodation
Number of places and costs refer to 2014–15

University-provided places: 3,457
Percentage catered: 7%
Catered costs: £152.32–£168.49 a week.
Self-catered costs: £85.40 (twin) – £139.30 (large en suite) a week.
First years are guaranteed accommodation if conditions are met. Deadline applies.
International students: first years are guaranteed accommodation if conditions are met. 10% of returners are also housed.
www.gla.ac.uk/undergraduate/accommodation/

Glasgow Caledonian University

Not content with having been the first Scottish university to open a campus in London, Glasgow Caledonian went one better in April 2014 by becoming the first in the UK to open in New York. The new outpost will offer executive education programmes and masterclasses in areas of strength, including the business of fashion, luxury brand management, finance and risk management. GCU London also offers fashion business education in luxury brand marketing and management, luxury retail management and international fashion marketing at its British School of Fashion. The university's international flavour was already well established through the co-founding of the Grameen Caledonian College of Nursing in Bangladesh, an affiliation with an engineering college in Oman and partnerships in China, India, USA and South America. The Chancellor is the Nobel Laureate and anti-poverty campaigner Professor Muhammad Yunus.

Work began in 2014 on the £30-million Heart of the Campus development which will transform the Glasgow campus. There is to be a striking new glass reception area and atrium, a 500-seat teaching and conference facility, and a new eating mall.

Two of the main buildings will be renovated and better connected to the award-winning Saltire Centre. The university has already spent more than £70 million transforming its facilities into a single campus that does justice to a thriving institution of 17,000 students. Development of the £1.2-million Doble Innovation Centre for On-line Systems is under way, which will create new research and student placement opportunities in the engineering sector. The campus includes the only INTO centre in Scotland, running preparatory courses for international students. The health building brings together teaching and research facilities, including a virtual hospital. Other learning resources include multimedia studios, a Fashion Factory and an eye clinic equipped with latest technologies for teaching and research. Student facilities include the Arc sports centre, 24-hour computer labs, an employability centre and a dedicated Students' Association building.

Almost two-thirds of the undergraduate programmes are accredited by professional bodies and more than half include work placement opportunities. The university is one of the largest providers of health-related graduates to the NHS in Scotland, covering a wide range of professions. As the only Scottish university delivering optometry degrees, it trains 90 per cent of the country's eye care specialists. GCU has also launched its new Scottish Ambulance

---

Cowcaddens Road
Glasgow G4 0BA

0141 331 8630 (enquiries)
studentenquiries@gcu.ac.uk
www.gcu.ac.uk
www.gcustudents.co.uk
Affiliation: University Alliance

The Times and Sunday Times Rankings
Overall Ranking: **84** (last year: 81)

Student satisfaction:	=98	79.2%
Research quality:	=84	3.0%
Entry standards:	46	370
Student–staff ratio:	=102	20.9
Services & facilities/student:	56	£1,588
Expected completion rate:	99	80.9%
Good honours:	55	68.5%
Graduate prospects:	=53	67.9%

Academy, the only education establishment in the UK to be formally endorsed by the College of Paramedics and certified by the Health Professions Council. The School of Engineering and Built Environment teaches three quarters of Scotland's part-time construction students. Glasgow School for Business and Society boasts more undergraduates than any other business school in Scotland. The university pioneered subjects such as entrepreneurial studies and risk management and offers highly specialist degrees, such as tourism management, fashion marketing, leisure management and consumer protection. Half of the 14 subject areas in which the university entered the 2008 Research Assessment Exercise contained at least some world-leading work, with 30 per cent of all researchers judged to have produced world-leading or internationally excellent work. Health subjects registered the best results, and were particularly good in rehabilitative health sciences, which covers long-term health conditions such as arthritis and strokes.

Widening participation in higher education has always been one of the university's main aims. The Caledonian Club works with children as young as three years old and their families in Glasgow and London. More than a third of the undergraduates are from working-class homes and about three-quarters are the first in their family to attend university. The Advanced Higher Hub, opened in 2013, offers students in their final year at schools across Glasgow specialist teaching, access to GCU's facilities and preparation for university life. The university has introduced a series of measures – such as better academic, social and financial support – for those at risk of dropping out. The projected dropout rate of 10.5 per cent in the most recent survey is better than the UK average for GCU's courses and entry qualifications.

The university has enjoyed a run of good results in the International Barometer survey for overseas students, ranking second in the UK for international student satisfaction and top in Scotland for student support, accommodation costs and visa advice. Undergraduates are encouraged to participate in international exchanges and study abroad. Glasgow is a lively city with a large student population, where the cost of living is reasonable.

Undergraduate Fees and Bursaries

» Fees for Scottish and EU students 2014–15 — No fee
» Fees for Non-Scottish UK (RUK) students 2014–15 — £7,000 a year, capped at £25,000 for 4 year courses.
» Fees for international students 2014–15 — £10,200–£14,500
» For RUK students, household income below £25K, £2,000 a year fee waiver to total of £6,000. £1,000 a year fee waiver to total of £3,000 for students with at least ABB at A Level or equivalent. Principal's Common Good Scholarship: 5 awards of full fee waiver for first-generation, talented students from low income households.

Students		
Undergraduates:	10,855	(2,530)
Postgraduates:	1,450	(1,090)
Mature students:	34%	
International students:	6.7%	
Applications per place:	5.9	
From state-sector schools:	96.6%	
From working-class homes:	34.2%	
Satisfaction with students' union	70%	

For detailed information about sports facilities:
www.gcal.ac.uk/arc/

Accommodation
Number of places and costs refer to 2014–15
University-provided places: 660
Percentage catered: 0%
Self-catered costs: £96.39 (standard) or £109.24 (en suite) a week (39 weeks).
Students under 19 living outside the Glasgow area have priority for accommodation.
International students: new non-EU students guaranteed housing.
accommodation@gcu.ac.uk
www.gcu.ac.uk/study/undergraduate/accommodation

University of Gloucestershire

Gloucestershire claims to offer undergraduates more time with academics than almost any other UK university. In most subjects, students are said to spend at least a quarter of their time in lectures, seminars or other supervised activities. With 10,000 students on three campuses, the university sells itself to applicants as a "close-knit, supportive community of staff and students" with relatively small teaching groups. An emphasis on teaching is reflected in the fact that 14 of the staff have been recognised as National Teaching Fellows by the Higher Education Academy.

Gloucestershire was the first university for more than a century to have formal links with the Church of England when it achieved full university status in 2001. Originally a teacher training college founded in 1847, the university's primary training courses are still rated as outstanding by Ofsted. Other strengths are in sport, media, and art and design. There is a good range of work placements for students, which are undertaken by a third of all undergraduates. The Degreeplus initiative combines internships with additional training to improve students' chances of getting a good job after graduating. There are dedicated "helpzones" on each campus providing advice on academic or personal issues.

The university is investing £4 million on new teaching accommodation after a campus reorganisation. A new media hub, with studio areas for fine art, photography and specialist design, has been the main addition. Park Campus is on the attractive site of the former College of St Mary, a mile from the centre of Cheltenham, and is the main base for the Faculty of Business, Education and Professional Studies. Art and design, and the Institute of Education and Public Services, are closer to the town centre, at Francis Close Hall. The Oxstalls campus, in Gloucester, was purpose-built a year after university status arrived and caters for sport and exercise sciences, leisure, tourism, hospitality and event management. Oxstalls also houses the Countryside and Community Research Institute, the largest rural research centre in the UK. The three campuses are only seven miles apart, so students are not as isolated as they are in some split-site institutions.

Gloucestershire has a longstanding focus on green issues, and finished in the top three in the People and Planet Green League of universities' environmental performance in 2013. There are allotments for students, diplomas in environmentalism and an International Research Institute in Sustainability that brings together

---

The Park Campus
The Park
Cheltenham GL50 2RH

01242 714501 (admissions)
admissions@glos.ac.uk
www.glos.ac.uk
www.yourstudentsunion
.com
Affiliations: Cathedrals
Group

The Times and Sunday Times **Rankings**
Overall Ranking: **83** (last year: =91)

Student satisfaction:	=82	80.6%
Research quality:	=94	2.0%
Entry standards:	103	295
Student–staff ratio:	=118	23.6
Services & facilities/student:	64	£1,499
Expected completion rate:	=48	87.6%
Good honours:	52	69.9%
Graduate prospects:	=96	58.0%

researchers from around the world, undertaking work for agencies such as UNESCO. The university also plays an active role promoting economic, cultural and social wellbeing in its county. It is launching a Gloucestershire Growth Hub, in association with the Local Enterprise Partnership, to help local businesses and give students more opportunities to work on "real life" business projects. The main research strengths are in the environment, humanities and sports sciences. Some world-leading research was found in five of the 12 areas in which the university submitted work in the 2008 Research Assessment Exercise, but less than 20 per cent of all work reached the top two categories.

The university's intake is diverse, with nearly 96 per cent of undergraduates from state schools and more than a third from working-class homes. About a third are recruited from Gloucestershire, and around a quarter from elsewhere in the South West of England. There is also a new joint venture with INTO providing preparatory programmes for international students. The projected dropout rate has improved dramatically over recent years, and the latest projection of less than 7 per cent is well below the national average for the university's subjects and entry qualifications. In addition to its conventional degrees, the university is offering 15 two-year "fast track" degrees, in subjects ranging from biology to events management and law. New courses for 2015 will include fashion design and sports journalism.

The university has a strong sporting tradition, with links to around 30 sports governing and coaching bodies. Gloucestershire is the only university to have a professional rugby league team. It hosted the Malawi Olympics team for the London 2012 games, and the facilities include a sports hall, gym and tennis courts. All first-year applicants in 2015 will be guaranteed accommodation in university halls or university managed accommodation if they accept us as their first choice and apply by the required deadline.

Undergraduate Fees and Bursaries

» Fees for UK/EU students 2015–16   £9,000
» Foundation degrees and courses at partner colleges
                                           £6,000–£7,500
» Placement year   £1,000
» Fees for international students 2014–15   £10,500
» Students from Compact schools and Strategic Alliance partners with at least ABB at A level or equivalent, £1,000 scholarship; other students from these institutions, £500.
» Care leaver's package includes 50% fee waiver and up to £4,500 a year for living and studying costs.
» Enhanced hardship fund, awarded after individual application.

Students

Undergraduates:	**6,175**	**(690)**
Postgraduates:	**610**	**(930)**
Mature students:	**18.3%**	
International students:	**4.4%**	
Applications per place:	**4.4**	
From state-sector schools:	**95.8%**	
From working-class homes:	**34.2%**	
Satisfaction with students' union	**66%**	

For detailed information about sports facilities:
www.glos.ac.uk/living/sport

Accommodation

Number of places and costs refer to 2014–15
University-provided places: about 1,378
Percentage catered: 0%
Self-catered costs: £95–£145 a week (40 weeks).
First-year undergraduates have priority for halls.
International students: first-year undergraduates are guaranteed housing if conditions are met.
accommodation@glos.ac.uk
www.glos.ac.uk/living/Pages/accommodation.aspx

Glyndŵr University

Glyndŵr has enjoyed a big increase in applications in 2014, after three years of decline which left little more than two applicants for each place in the previous year. That did not prevent the Wrexham-based university from registering one of the biggest percentage increases in enrolments in the UK in 2013 – more than 30 per cent. Glyndŵr subsequently suffered a serious setback when its license to admit students from outside the EU was suspended over allegations that some had been recruited with fake language qualifications. Although the decision may yet be reversed, the suspension covered the main recruiting period for 2014. Glyndŵr has made further progress on its international strategy even during the suspension with agreements to open an engineering campus in Malaysia and bring more Malaysian students to Wales, as well as to collaborate on research. The university already has a campus in London offering mainly business courses in partnership with the London School of Management and Science.

The former North East Wales Institute of Higher Education took the name of the 15th-century Welsh prince Owain Glyndŵr (who championed the establishment of universities throughout Wales) when it was awarded university status in 2008. The university has two campuses in Wrexham and one at Northop, in Flintshire, on the site of the former Welsh College of Horticulture. The Flintshire campus is the first university presence in the county, and £1.7 million has been invested to make it a centre of excellence for land- and animal-based studies. Glyndŵr has 8,800 students, but fewer than half are full-time undergraduates. Over half are 21 or more on entry. The two campuses in Wrexham are within five minutes' walk of each other. The university's art school is based at the Regent Street campus, nearer the town centre.

In 2011, Glyndŵr became the only university to own an international football stadium – the oldest in the world – when it bought the Racecourse Ground to safeguard the future of Wrexham FC and provide more facilities for its students. The new Glyndŵr Wrexham Football Academy, a partnership between the university and the club, allows professional footballers to take degrees without interrupting their careers – the only initiative of its kind in the UK. The university already had a partnership with the club, whose land, next door to the university's Plas Coch site, hosts the 200-bed student village. Part of the Plas Coch Hostel was transformed in 2013 into a library featuring more than 13,000 books collected by a New York scholar. The campus also contains a modern sports centre with two floodlit artificial pitches, including

---

Mold Road
Wrexham
N. Wales LL11 2AW

01978 293439 (enquiries)
enquiries@glyndwr.ac.uk
www.glyndwr.ac.uk
www.studentsguild.
    glyndwr.ac.uk
Affiliation: none

The Times and Sunday Times Rankings
Overall Ranking: **113** (last year: 109)

Student satisfaction:	**118**	76.9%
Research quality:	**=108**	1.3%
Entry standards:	**105**	289
Student–staff ratio:	**95**	20.1
Services & facilities/student:	**38**	£1,815
Expected completion rate:	**110**	78.0%
Good honours:	**112**	53.5%
Graduate prospects:	**70**	63.7%

an international standard hockey pitch, a human performance laboratory and indoor facilities that include a sports hall with a 1,000 square-metre sprung floor.

The university has embarked on a series of academic developments, including two-year fast-track degrees and the four-year MEng. The £2-million Centre for the Child, Family and Society, based on a Scandinavian concept, allows those working in the field of child development to hone their skills in both an academic and practical manner. The Advanced Composite Training and Development Centre, at Broughton, is a partnership with Airbus, which has a large plant nearby. Research carried out there will help to improve the efficiency of aircraft and feed into the university's undergraduate engineering courses, which are also developed in association with Airbus. The Centre for the Creative Industries has up-to-date TV, radio and online production studios, which are the regional home of BBC Cymru Wales as well as playing a key role in the university's television degree. At St Asaph the university has a centre for the research and development of cutting-edge opto-electronics technology and the headquarters of its commercial arm, Glyndŵr Innovations, which was named among the top businesses in Wales for growth. The university entered only 27 academics for the last Research Assessment Exercise, but almost a quarter of their work was judged to be world-leading or internationally excellent.

Nearly all the undergraduates are state-educated, 46 per cent of them coming from working-class homes – far more than average for the university's subjects and entry grades. Glyndŵr also has the largest proportion of disabled students in Wales and was nominated for an award for its provision for them. There is a dedicated centre for students with disabilities that assesses students' needs before they embark on a course.

Two-thirds of the students are local, many living at home, which inevitably affects the social scene, but eases the pressure on residential accommodation. Wrexham is not without nightlife, and there has been a £90,000 upgrade of the students' union, where the Centenary Club has become a popular venue. Both Manchester and Liverpool are within easy reach.

Undergraduate Fees and Bursaries
» Fees for UK/EU students 2014–15   £7,400–£8,450
» Foundation degree   £5,400
» Welsh Assembly non-means-tested grant to pay fees above £3,685 (2014–15) for Welsh students.
» Fees for international students 2014–15   £8,950–£9,450 (includes accommodation for year 1)
» £1,000 cash in year 1 for students on a selection of courses.
» Care Leaver's scholarship of £1,000 a year and other scholarships available.
» Check the university's website for the latest information.

Students
Undergraduates:	3,915	(3,220)
Postgraduates:	805	(580)
Mature students:	54.9%	
International students:	40.7%	
Applications per place:	2.3	
From state-sector schools:	99.1%	
From working-class homes:	45.9%	
Satisfaction with students' union	66%	

For detailed information about sports facilities: www.sport.glyndwr.ac.uk

Accommodation
Number of places and costs refer to 2014–15
University-provided places: 615
Percentage catered: 0%
Self-catered costs: £80 (single) – £108 (en suite) a week (37–40 weeks).
First-year full-time undergraduates are given priority in accordance with the university's allocation policy.
International students: guaranteed housing if conditions are met.
www.glyndwr.ac.uk/en/Accommodation/
accommodation@glyndwr.ac.uk

Goldsmiths, University of London

Goldsmiths is expecting to increase the number of undergraduates it admits this year by more than a third compared with 2012, when the fees went up to £9,000. The college has a stellar reputation in the arts, but the expansion has been made possible by the introduction of a range of new degrees including management and entrepreneurship, politics, philosophy and economics (PPE), and clinical psychology. Applications are back to the record levels seen in 2011 and more are making Goldsmiths their first choice. Recent rankings have placed Goldsmiths in the world's top 100 and the UK's top 10 for art and design, but the portfolio of courses spans the humanities, social sciences, cultural studies, computing, and entrepreneurial business and management. New degrees include a BA in anthropology and visual practice, which looks at the subject alongside training in photography, video-making and editing.

Alumni such as Damien Hirst and Antony Gormley are at the top of their fields. In the last year alone, director Steve McQueen won the Best Picture Oscar for *12 Years A Slave*, James Blake won the Mercury Prize for his album *Overgrown*, and Laure Prouvost was named winner of the Turner Prize, making her the seventh former Goldsmiths student to receive the award. The £10,000 Goldsmiths Prize, launched in 2013, has cemented Goldsmiths' position in the field of creative writing – the subject is offered at both undergraduate and postgraduate level, and former students have won awards including *The Sunday Times* Young Writer of the Year Award and the Dylan Thomas Award, while two MA creative and life writing graduates were named in *Granta*'s 2013 Best of Young British Novelists list. More than half of the work submitted for the last Research Assessment Exercise was considered world-leading or internationally excellent. Indeed, it was among the top ten universities for the proportion of work (22 per cent) placed in the highest category. Current projects include the UN-funded research into forensic architecture in places of conflict and a variety of studies into autism.

Goldsmiths is based on a single site campus that has a mixture of traditional and modern buildings, including a New Academic Building containing purpose-built media facilities (including radio and TV studios), the Ben Pimlott Building (with state-of-the-art research facilities and studio space for art students), and the flagship Richard Hoggart Building has been refurbished and re-landscaped to create a space for outdoor arts and events. This refurbishment is part of a £6-million programme of investment in the campus

New Cross
London SE14 6NW

020 7919 7766 (enquiries)
course-info@gold.ac.uk
www.gold.ac.uk
www.goldsmithssu.org
Affiliation: none

The Times and Sunday Times **Rankings**
Overall Ranking: **55** (last year: 48)

Student satisfaction:	=98	79.2%
Research quality:	=18	24.7%
Entry standards:	51	346
Student–staff ratio:	=53	16.9
Services & facilities/student:	112	£1,052
Expected completion rate:	86	82.6%
Good honours:	28	76.7%
Graduate prospects:	106	55.7%

that also includes a new recording studio – giving music students the chance to record in a professional setting – and a new Fairtrade coffee shop and social learning space in the Library building. Developments currently underway include creating an art gallery on campus, and transforming a 19th-century church into a space that will be used for teaching, exhibitions, performances and studios.

Determinedly integrated into its southeast London locality, the campus has a cosmopolitan atmosphere. Around a third of new undergraduates are 21 or over on entry with a strong representation from the area's ethnic minorities, and there is a growing cohort of international students. Nearly a third of students are from working-class backgrounds, but only 6 per cent are from areas of low participation in higher education.

There are integrated work placements on many of their degrees, and Goldsmiths places great emphasis on equipping students with creative thinking skills and has introduced workshops to help students develop entrepreneurial skills. Personal development opportunities include the Gold Award, encouraging students to develop the skills and experience that employers are looking for.

Student politics is alive and well at Goldsmiths, and there is a thriving music scene, featuring a varied events programme includes music recitals, exhibitions, public lectures and readings. The union has a strong tradition in volunteering and an award-winning newspaper/magazine, and in recent years it has been the winner of several Sound Impact Awards, in recognition of work on ethical and environmental issues.

There are around 1,200 rooms available in halls of residence, 900 of them in Goldsmiths halls within a 2-minute walk of the campus. Those further away are managed by a private provider. Priority for places is given to international students and new undergraduates from outside London. There is a well-equipped and affordable gym on campus, but the sports pitches are 30 minutes away.

Undergraduate Fees and Bursaries

» Fees for UK/EU students 2015–16 £9,000
» Fees for international students 2014–15 £12,100–£16,700
» Ten £9,000 a year awards for best students from Lewisham and five £4,500 per year awards for students from other local boroughs.
» Range of scholarships and bursaries for local students, mature students, care leavers, disabled students, refugees, computer, music and education students.
» Check the university's website for the latest information.

Students

Undergraduates:	**4,670**	**(210)**
Postgraduates:	**2,135**	**(1,065)**
Mature students:	**28.2%**	
International students:	**18.7%**	
Applications per place:	**5.3**	
From state-sector schools:	**88.8%**	
From working-class homes:	**32%**	
Satisfaction with students' union	**61%**	

For detailed information about sports facilities: www.gold.ac.uk/sports/

Accommodation

Number of places and costs refer to 2014–15

University-provided places: 1,239 (on- and off-campus halls of residence managed by Goldsmiths or private providers).

Percentage catered: 0%

Self-catered costs: £102–£199 a week (includes heating and lighting costs).

Priority is given to new full-time students if conditions are met; distance restrictions apply.

International students will be given priority. www.goldsmiths.ac.uk/accommodation

University of Greenwich

Greenwich's new Stockwell Street development opened in September 2014 as the centrepiece of a £150-million investment programme. The university's own specialists in architecture have contributed to a building that includes 14 landscaped roof terraces, dedicated to research and teaching. Students will also benefit from a large architecture studio, a model-making workshop, TV and sound studios. Students from across the campus will use the building's library – which is double the size of the current one, with 370 study spaces – as well as its lecture theatres, seminar rooms and other facilities. The high-quality digital TV and sound studios will be a major fillip to the university's work in digital media and creative design. The investment programme includes a new hall of residence nearby, also opening in 2014, which will provide 358 en-suite rooms for students, as well as a café and gym for residents.

The university already had what it regards (fairly) as "one of the grandest university settings in the world". The former Royal Naval College buildings designed by Sir Christopher Wren provide a campus worthy of a name which conjures up images of history and science in equal measure. The main campus is now part of a World Heritage Site. Wren's baroque masterpiece is being used, with the former Dreadnought Hospital, to teach over half the university's students. There is also a prize-winning Medway campus, centred on the former Chatham naval base, which has been developed in partnership with Kent and Canterbury Christ Church universities. Greenwich put £20 million into the campus, which houses the schools of pharmacy, science and engineering, the Natural Resources Institute, nursing and some business courses. A joint learning resources centre serves the Chatham Maritime campus and the University of Kent's neighbouring premises. The campus has exceeded its original target of 6,000 students, and now has improved teaching facilities and expanded student services.

Other schools are situated at Avery Hill, a Victorian mansion on the outskirts of southeast London, which boasts a £14-million sports and teaching centre with a café, sports hall and 220-seat lecture theatre. There are also laboratories for health courses that replicate NHS wards. The campus contains a student village of 1,300 rooms, alongside teaching accommodation for the social sciences. The large education faculty is one of the few to offer both primary and secondary teacher training courses. Greenwich is also the only university in the country to have an on-campus strategic relationship with a recruitment firm. It has invested more than

---

Old Royal Naval College
Park Row
Greenwich
London SE10 9LS

020 8331 9000 (course enquiries)
courseinfo@greenwich.ac.uk
www.gre.ac.uk
www.suug.co.uk
Affiliation: University
Alliance

The Times and Sunday Times **Rankings**
Overall Ranking: **98** (last year: 101)

Student satisfaction:	=59	82.3%
Research quality:	=84	3.0%
Entry standards:	87	312
Student–staff ratio:	=108	21.5
Services & facilities/student:	79	£1,403
Expected completion rate:	93	82.0%
Good honours:	=80	63.3%
Graduate prospects:	=121	49.0%

£1 million in the service, launched in 2013, which aims to place final-year students or recent graduates in full-time, graduate-level jobs that are suited to their skills, as well as finding them high-quality internships and other opportunities along the way. The consultants also provide one-to-one mentoring and advice and coaching sessions such as CV workshops.

Greenwich has set itself some challenging targets: among them are to reach the top 50 in the UK and the top ten in London within five years. The undergraduate intake was up by 800 in 2013, compensating for an even larger fall when the fees went up in the previous year. The university achieved good results in the last Research Assessment Exercise, which showed a quarter of the work reaching world-leading or internationally excellent levels. A fifth of the university's income is from research and consultancy – the largest proportion at any former polytechnic – and it is planned that the total should reach £21 million. Greenwich is undertaking an ambitious programme of investment in research by increasing the proportion of research-active staff to 75 per cent. More than one in five of its students is a postgraduate. Thirteen associated colleges in Kent and London teach the university's courses, while strong links with institutions in Europe and further afield provide a steady flow of overseas students, as well

as exchange opportunities for those at Greenwich. The 5,000 students from outside the European Union put the university among the top six international recruiters. The university attracts more students than any other UK institution from India and large numbers from Bangladesh, Ghana, Sri Lanka, Mauritius and Nigeria.

A commitment to extending access is reflected in a high proportion of mature students. More than half of the undergraduates come from working-class homes – the biggest proportion in the UK. Greenwich is in the top six in the People and Planet Green League of universities' environmental performance: the new hall of residence will be powered by biomass and has green roofs on each of its three blocks, along with other sustainable features.

Undergraduate Fees and Bursaries

» Fees for UK/EU students 2015–16	£9,000
» Partner colleges degree	£8,400–£9,000
» Foundation degree	£6,000
» Placement year	£1,000
» Fees for international students 2014–15	£10,350

» Greenwich Scholarship Programme (GSP) for those with household income below £25K, £1,000 fee waiver, £200 voucher and £800 in-kind support in year 1; conditions apply.

» Access Scholarship for students with household income below £25K and not receiving a GSP award, £500 for university services in year 1.

» For all other Home/EU students, £200 university services in year 1.

Students

Undergraduates:	14,405	(4,215)
Postgraduates:	2,500	(2,800)
Mature students:	33.8%	
International students:	13%	
Applications per place:	6.5	
From state-sector schools:	97.9%	
From working-class homes:	54.4%	
Satisfaction with students' union	62%	

For detailed information about sports facilities:
www2.gre.ac.uk/about/campus/facilities/sport

Accommodation

Number of places and costs refer to 2014–15
University-provided places: 2,500
Percentage catered: 0%
Self-catered costs: £107.38–£232.47 a week.
First years are guaranteed a place. Conditions apply.
International students: new students get priority.
ah.accommodation@gre.ac.uk (Avery Hill Campus)
gr.accommodation@gre.ac.uk (Greenwich Campus)
me.accommodation@gre.ac.uk (Medway Campus)
www2.gre.ac.uk/study/accommodation

Harper Adams University

Harper Adams, one of two specialist agricultural institutions given full university status in 2012, has more than 4,000 students, but less than half are on campus at any one time. The rest are on placement years or accredited part-time programmes in industry. The new university made its debut in *The Times and Sunday Times* league table close to the mid-way point and has made further progress this year. It benefits from its customary high scores for student satisfaction and graduate prospects. Harper Adams has been close to the top in the National Student Survey in every year that it has been published, its students praising the personal attention they receive. Based in a single campus in the Shropshire countryside, the university offers degrees in business, veterinary nursing and physiotherapy, land and property management, engineering and food studies, as well as agriculture. There is also a range of Foundation degrees that can be converted into honours. New degrees in wildlife, conservation and resource management were added in 2013.

The university has been upgrading the teaching and research facilities, and also investing in new academic appointments. A new teaching block opened in May 2014, adding a 250-seat lecture theatre, IT classrooms, accessible computers and seminar rooms. The Agricultural Engineering Innovation Centre also opened in 2014 and a Veterinary Services Centre will follow later in the year to cope with rising demand for courses in veterinary nursing, clinical animal behaviour and veterinary physiotherapy. The Faccenda Centre, opened in 2011, is located at the heart of the campus and acts as a hub for students with the Students' Union, Careers Service and café under one roof. The building also contains social space with open access computers to allow students to work and socialise in the same space.

The Main Building, which dates from the opening of the institution in 1901, was once the centre of all campus activities with bedrooms, teaching rooms and even a shooting gallery. The Bamford Library is one of the largest specialist land-based collections in the UK, 41,000 books and 3,000 journals. Open access computing areas are open 24 hours. But the new university's most prized feature is its 640-hectare commercial farm, which has been undergoing a multimillion pound development, including expanded dairy, pig and poultry units and a new food research centre. At the heart of the University Farm, Ancellor Yard is a redevelopment of the original farm courtyard, the former home of Thomas Harper Adams after whom the university is named. It houses the Frank Parkinson Farm Education Centre and

---

Newport
Shropshire TF10 8NB

01952 815000 (admissions)
admissions@harper-adams.ac.uk
www.harper-adams.ac.uk
www.harpersu.com
Affiliation: GuildHE

The Times and Sunday Times **Rankings**

Overall Ranking: **63** (last year: =64)

Student satisfaction:	=13	85.3%
Research quality:	=94	2.0%
Entry standards:	56	342
Student–staff ratio:	=88	19.8
Services & facilities/student:	104	£1,183
Expected completion rate:	45	88.3%
Good honours:	115	52.8%
Graduate prospects:	=57	67.0%

the Frontier Crops Centre. The £2-million dairy unit serves 400 cows and there is a £3-million anaerobic digestion plant that provides 75 per cent of the electricity used by the university, as well as organic fertiliser for the estate.

Not surprisingly, given its agricultural specialisms, the university is one of a shrinking band where male students marginally outnumber female. Nearly one undergraduate in five went to an independent school, but still nearly half have a working-class background. Almost every course includes work placements, provided by a network of 500 regular placement employers, some of whom also endow student scholarships. The projected dropout rate of less than 7 per cent is much better than the national average for the university's courses and entry qualifications.

Only 19 staff members were entered for the 2008 Research Assessment Exercise, when 25 per cent of the work was judged to be internationally excellent. Since then, Harper Adams has become new centre of excellence for entomology teaching and research in the UK and has launched the Soil and Water Management Centre, an industry-led initiative to help UK farming make the most of its two most precious assets. It has also established the Centre for Integrated Pest Management, a multidisciplinary team addressing UK and global issues in agricultural, forestry and horticultural crop production. New appointments have also boosted research excellence in precision livestock and arable farming, food studies, plant pathology, animal science and crop physiology.

There should be more than 800 residential places on campus in 2015 in 11 halls of residence. First years take priority in the allocation of places. A shuttle bus runs three times a day for students living in nearby Newport to get to campus and there is free parking for students. Sports facilities include a gymnasium, heated outdoor swimming pool, rugby, cricket, football and hockey pitches, tennis courts and an all-weather sports pitch. There is a dance/fitness studio and even a 4x4 club.

Undergraduate Fees and Bursaries

» Fees for UK/EU students for 2015–16	£9,000
» Placement year	£1,000
» Fees for international students 2014–15	£10,000

» £1,000 Access to the Professions Bursary, for disadvantaged students and targeted at engineering, food and land management courses, under review in August 2014.
» Range of scholarships and sponsorships available.
» Check the university's website for the latest information.

Students

Undergraduates:	**2,195**	**(2,555)**
Postgraduates:	**65**	**(350)**
Mature students:	**5%**	
International students:	**3.5%**	
Applications per place:	**4**	
From state-sector schools:	**81.0%**	
From working-class homes:	**46.3%**	
Satisfaction with students' union	**78%**	

For detailed information about sports facilities:
www.harper-adams.ac.uk/facilities/sports.cfm

Accommodation

Places and costs refer to 2014–15
University-provided places: 700
Percentage catered: 60%
Catered costs: £95.33 – £158.33 a week (36 weeks).
Self-catered costs: £63.21 – £114.28 a week (36 or 42 weeks).
Priority is given to new full-time students on a first come first served basis. Provision for students with disabilities.
International students: entitled to housing for first year of study.
www.harper-adams.ac.uk/accommodation/

Heriot-Watt University

Heriot-Watt has a striking new campus in Malaysia to add to those in Dubai, Orkney, Galashiels and its original base on the outskirts of Edinburgh. The university is Scotland's most international institution, responsible for almost half of all Scottish degrees awarded to students studying overseas. International students also fill around a third of the places on the Edinburgh campus – one of the biggest proportions in the UK. Heriot-Watt won an award from the Scottish Council of Development and Industry, partly for its support for international students. In addition to the 11,000 students based in Scotland, the university delivers degree programmes to over 18,500 students in 150 countries. As well as offering opportunities for independent learners to study in their own country, Heriot-Watt has 50 partner universities and colleges in over 35 countries. In the UK, however, it is known above all for a consistently good graduate employment record.

The university's strengths lie in the physical sciences, mathematics, business and management, engineering and the built environment. Concentration on these areas is fitting for a university which commemorates James Watt, the pioneer of steam power, and George Heriot, financier to King James VI. The university has fostered interdisciplinary teaching and research, with a battery of employment-related degrees.

More than half of the UK-based students are from Scotland and just under 20 per cent from other parts of Britain. Almost nine out of ten are from state schools and colleges, while a quarter come from working-class homes. The demand for places has been rising: applications were up by 11 per cent in 2013, enabling the university to increase the size of the undergraduate intake and compensate for a drop in the previous year.

The main campus, in an attractive parkland setting in the Edinburgh suburb of Riccarton, still has a modern feel more than 40 years after it opened, and a £34-million project has seen the opening of new residences at both Heriot-Watt's Edinburgh and Scottish Borders campuses. The main campus is to be the location for the purpose-built National Performance Centre for Sport (NPCS), a joint venture with the City of Edinburgh Council. The £30-million facility will feature a Hampden replica pitch, outdoor synthetic and grass pitches for football and rugby, a nine-court sports hall, a 3G indoor pitch and a fitness suite, as well as world-class facilities for sports science and medicine.

The Scottish Borders Campus in Galashiels, 35 miles south of Edinburgh, specialises in textiles, fashion and design.

Edinburgh Campus
Edinburgh EH14 4AS

0131 449 5111
enquiries@hw.ac.uk
www.hw.ac.uk
www.hwunion.com
Affiliation: none

The Times and Sunday Times **Rankings**
Overall Ranking: **41** (last year: 38)

Student satisfaction:	=48	82.9%
Research quality:	41	18.0%
Entry standards:	=27	424
Student–staff ratio:	46	16.4
Services & facilities/student:	=47	£1,736
Expected completion rate:	89	82.4%
Good honours:	47	70.5%
Graduate prospects:	38	73.2%

Heriot-Watt and Borders College have signed a partnership agreement for a long-term collaboration to deliver higher and further education in the historically under-provided region, both institutions now sharing new campus facilities costing £12 million. The campus at Stromness, in Orkney, is for postgraduates and specialises in renewable energy. Students in Dubai take business, engineering, science and technology, or textiles and design courses. Numbers in the Gulf state have risen to almost 3,700 and continue to grow towards 6,000, as the university invests £35 million in the campus. The new Malaysian campus is now accepting students and is scheduled to open in the autumn, with space for up to 4,000 students to take a range of degree programmes in science, engineering, business, mathematics and design.

More than half of the work submitted for the last Research Assessment Exercise was rated world-leading or internationally excellent. Mathematics produced the best results, but there were good grades, too, in petroleum engineering, physics, general engineering, the built environment, and art and design. An estimated £14 million will be needed to provide extra room for growing numbers of research-active staff and a separate project will create a new facility for the geosciences, marine sciences and related engineering disciplines that will also house the British Geological Survey.

The students' union was named Scottish Student Union of the Year by NUS Scotland. The 12 halls of residence are conveniently placed and house some 1,800 students. Built on the grounds of a country house, the landscaped campus boasts a loch and a sunken garden. Regular bus services link the campus to the city centre and its wide range of nightlife and cultural events. The university has a programme of sports scholarships, and representative teams do well. Music also thrives: there is a professional Director of Music and a number of music scholarships, as well as a varied programme of musical events.

Undergraduate Fees and Bursaries

» Fees for Scottish and EU students 2014–15   No fee
» Fees for Non-Scottish UK (RUK) students for 2014–15   £9,000
» Fees for international students 2014–15   £12,280–£15,490
» Range of scholarships and bursaries for Scottish students.
» For all RUK students entering at year 1, £2,250 fee waiver a year plus £1,500 bursary in year 1; full fee waiver for placement year. From year 2, and for students entering at year 2, with household income below £25K, £3,000 bursary a year; household income £25K–£42.6K, £2,000 a year.
» RUK academic scholarship of £1,000 a year for students who achieve specified grades at A Level, or equivalent.
» Other bursaries and scholarships available.
» Check the university's website for the latest information.

Students

Undergraduates:	6,175	(655)
Postgraduates:	2,080	(2,155)
Mature students:	17%	
International students:	32.3%	
Applications per place:	6.2	
From state-sector schools:	89.3%	
From working-class homes:	25.3%	
Satisfaction with students' union	63%	

For detailed information about sports facilities:
www.hw.ac.uk/sports/sports-union.htm

Accommodation

Number of places and costs refer to 2014–15
University places provided: 1,867
Percentage catered: 0%
Self-catered costs: £84.00 (standard) – £159.04 (en suite) a week.
All new first years are guaranteed accommodation provided conditions are met and applications in place by noon on 21 August.
International students: as above.
halls@hw.ac.uk
www.hw.ac.uk/student-life/campus-life.htm

University of Hertfordshire

Hertfordshire has begun to climb back up *The Times and Sunday Times* league table after a surprise drop of almost 30 places last year, due mainly to a decline in student satisfaction. A small decline in applications has been reversed in 2014; enrolments had already started to grow again after a big drop in 2012. Hertfordshire describes itself as "the UK's leading business-facing university" and may have coined the term, which is now used by a growing number of institutions. It plays an important role in the regional economy and even runs the local bus service, as well as offering work placements on many courses.

The university has a purpose-built £120-million campus, close to the original Hatfield headquarters, which boasts some outstanding facilities. The de Havilland campus, named after the aircraft manufacturer which once occupied the site, houses business, education, law and the humanities. It has a 24-hour learning resources centre, £15-million sports complex and 1,600 networked, en-suite residential places. The new Law School includes a fully functioning court room with a public gallery, mediation centre, law clinic, café and teaching rooms. The two sites are linked by cycleways, footpaths and university-owned shuttle buses. One of the biggest developments is a £38-million entertainment venue on the College Lane campus. The Forum has three entertainment spaces, a restaurant, a café and multiple bars, attracting young people from all over the county, as well as the university's students. A new learning and student zone, housing all student services, will open alongside it in 2014. A new science building will follow in 2015.

Health subjects account for the largest share of places. An innovative degree in paramedic science was Britain's first, its students using the UK's largest medical simulation centre to learn how to treat patients in emergency situations. The opening of a School of Pharmacy and a postgraduate medical school strengthened its position in the health sector. The university is also working with the NHS Trusts in the East of England as a preferred provider for a BSc healthcare science degree. Increased research activity resulted in the establishment of the Health and Human Sciences Institute. The creative arts have also been growing, particularly the multimedia courses. The School of the Creative Arts occupies a £10-million media centre on the College Lane campus, with the latest technology for the teaching of music, animation, film, television and multimedia. It includes one of the largest art galleries in the eastern region. *3DWorld* magazine rated Hertfordshire as one of the top 20

College Lane

Hatfield

Hertfordshire AL10 9AB

01707 284800 (admissions)
ask@herts.ac.uk
www.herts.ac.uk
www.hertfordshire.su
Affiliation: University
   Alliance

The Times and Sunday Times **Rankings**

Overall Ranking: **79** (last year: =96)

Student satisfaction:	=108	78.3%
Research quality:	=79	3.3%
Entry standards:	52	344
Student–staff ratio:	=70	18.3
Services & facilities/student:	=47	£1,736
Expected completion rate:	=79	83.3%
Good honours:	60	66.8%
Graduate prospects:	51	68.5%

universities in the world to study animation. A 460-seat auditorium on the de Havilland campus enhances the cultural programme. An Automotive Centre has upgraded the teaching facilities for that branch of engineering, as well as boosting interaction with industry – every British Formula One team has at least one Hertfordshire graduate.

The student intake is more diverse than might be expected, given the location and subject mix: more than four in ten come from working-class homes and 98 per cent are state-educated. The projected dropout rate has improved, and is now less than 14 per cent, only marginally more than the national average for the university's subject mix and entry grades. The Careers and Placements Service offers students support for two years after they graduate as well as during their time at university. The Enterprise Team helps to turn business or social enterprise ideas into successful ventures.

Hertfordshire produced some of the best results of any post-1992 university in the 2008 Research Assessment Exercise, when nearly half of its submission was judged to be world-leading or internationally excellent. History, nursing and midwifery, engineering and computing collected the highest grades, but the Centre for Astrophysics Research also did well. The university claims that 10 per cent of all known planets were discovered by Hertfordshire's astronomers.

The award-winning learning and resource centre at College Lane is among Britain's biggest. It and the learning resource centre on the de Havilland campus are open 24 hours a day and seven days a week, providing 3,000 study places, 1,200 computer workstations and Wi-Fi for laptop users; plus 30,000 academic journals and over 800,000 volumes (which include 300,000 e-books). The StudyNet information system has been a leader in its field, giving all staff and students their own storage space. Students can use it for study, revision or communication, as well as to access university information. About 3,200 students live on campus. The £15-million Hertfordshire Sports Village includes a 110-station health and fitness centre, a 25-metre pool and a large, multipurpose sports hall. Principally for student use, it is also open to local residents.

Undergraduate Fees and Bursaries

» Fees for UK/EU students 2015–16   £9,000
» Foundation degrees at partner colleges   £5,500
» Fees for international students 2014–15   £10,100
» Fee waivers for placement year and year abroad.
» Enhanced schemes for student retention and employability.
» Range of other scholarships and bursaries available.
» Check the university's website for the latest information.

Students

Undergraduates:	**16,550**	**(3,460)**
Postgraduates:	**2,200**	**(2,925)**
Mature students:	**19.5%**	
International students:	**15.4%**	
Applications per place:	**6.1**	
From state-sector schools:	**97.7%**	
From working-class homes:	**41.2%**	
Satisfaction with students' union	**71%**	

For detailed information about sports facilities:
www.uhsport.co.uk

Accommodation

Number of places and costs refer to 2014–15
University-provided places: 3,215
Percentage catered: 0%
Self-catered costs: £72.66 (twin); £128–£138 (single en suite); £160 (studio) a week.
First years are not guaranteed accommodation, which is allocated on a first come, first served basis.
International students: as above.
accommodation@herts.ac.uk
www.herts.ac.uk/university-life/accommodation

University of the Highlands and Islands

The University of the Highlands and Islands (UHI) has taken a while to establish itself – it had to wait 20 years for university status – but an unprecedented surge in applications in 2013 suggests that its time has come. The 38 per cent increase was one of the biggest in the UK and enabled the university to take an additional 250 students. UHI's priority is to give people living in the region local access to learning and research relevant to their needs and to those of local employers. The students are predominantly mature and part-time, drawn largely from the Highlands and Islands, but UHI has begun to recruit more young entrants, as well as attracting greater numbers from the rest of Scotland, other parts of the UK and overseas. Students take a broad range of qualifications, from higher national certificates and diplomas and degrees to professional development awards. Teaching is increasingly through "blended" learning, combining online and face-to-face teaching, with small class sizes and extensive use of video conferencing. UHI is widely acknowledged as a major asset to the regional economy, helping to create and sustain businesses, as well as championing local culture and the environment.

A federation of 13 colleges and research institutions spread across hundreds of miles in the Highlands and Islands of Scotland, UHI is unlike any other in the UK. As such, it fits uneasily into our league table – it proved impossible to calculate a meaningful staff/student ratio last year, for example, from the unique mix of part-time and full-time staff and students. UHI's colleges spread from Dunoon in the southwest to the village of Scalloway, the ancient capital of the Shetland Islands, in the north. But that does not begin to do justice to the university's network of campuses. Argyll College, for example, has 13 sites on the mainland and on islands such as Arran, Islay and Mull. UHI courses are also taught at more than 50 learning centres located throughout the Highlands and Islands, Moray and Perthshire. Some colleges are relatively large and located in the urban centres of the region such as Perth, Elgin and Inverness. Others are smaller institutions, including some whose primary focus is research. The university insists, however, that all have a student-centred culture and an individual approach.

Several of the colleges are in spectacular locations. Lews Castle College UHI, in Stornoway in the Outer Hebrides, for example, is set in 600 acres of parkland. It claims "possibly the UK's most attractive location to study art" for its harbour-side Lochmaddy campus in North Uist. Sabhal

---

126 Ness Walk
Inverness IV3 5QS

01463 279 000 (general enquiries)
contact via website
www.uhi.ac.uk
www.uhisa.org.uk
Affiliation: none

The Times and Sunday Times **Rankings**
Overall Ranking: **121** (last year: 116)

Student satisfaction:	=102	78.9%
Research quality:	=94	2.0%
Entry standards:	=101	298
Student–staff ratio:	n/a	
Services & facilities/student:	122	£545
Expected completion rate:	=122	67.4%
Good honours:	=45	70.6%
Graduate prospects:	120	49.1%

Mòr Ostaig UHI is the only Gaelic-medium college in the world, set in breath-taking scenery on the Isle of Skye, while the Highland Theological College UHI is in Dingwall. West Highland College UHI does not even have a central campus, although its degree in adventure tourism management, is taught in Fort William, close to Ben Nevis. North Highland College UHI has opened a new equestrian centre in Caithness, six miles from the main campus in Thurso, with international-sized outdoor and indoor arenas.

A report to the Highland Regional Council recommended the establishment of UHI in 1990 and envisaged that the process might take four years. The region had already waited a lot longer than that for a university: Perth was first identified as a suitable location for a university in 1425. UHI's development has come in stages since its establishment was formally recommended in 1992. As the UHI Millennium Institute, it became a higher education institute in 2001 and received degree-awarding powers in 2008. University status finally came in February 2011. There are now 7,500 students taking more than 100 undergraduate courses at 70 learning centres across the region. Many courses are available entirely online. Degree courses intended to lead to careers in renewable engineering, tourism and hospitality, health care, and children's services were among the options for 2014. UHI was the first higher education institution to publish a Gaelic language plan, promising students more opportunities to learn Gaelic, improve existing skills, or study for qualifications entirely through the language. There is now a growing community of students with Gaelic skills throughout the UHI network and there are plans to extend the course portfolio.

Environmental science produced the best results and made by far the largest submission in the 2008 Research Assessment Exercise, but there was some world-leading research in Celtic studies and archaeology. There are a dozen research centres specialising in everything from agronomy and marine science to Nordic studies, diabetes and rural childhood.

Undergraduate Fees and Bursaries

» Fees for Scottish and EU students 2014–15   No fee
» Fees for Non-Scottish UK (RUK) students for 2014–15 £7,740–£9,000, capped at a maximum of £23,200–£27,000 for 4 year courses.
» Fees for international students 2014–15   £8,700–£10,320 Online courses   £4,860–£5,760
» For RUK students , household income below £20K, £1,590 bursary; £20K–£22.5K, £1,060 bursary; £22.5–£25K, £530 bursary, all for three years.
» Other bursaries and special funds are available.
» Check the university's website for the latest information.

Students

Undergraduates:	**4,160**	**(2,825)**
Postgraduates:	**65**	**(375)**
Mature students:	**51.8%**	
International students:	**3.6%**	
Applications per place:	**n/a**	
From state-sector schools:	**97.2%**	
From working-class homes:	**40.8%**	
Satisfaction with students' union	**45%**	

For detailed information about sports facilities: Sports provision for each campus is through local community facilities.

Accommodation

On-site halls of residence are available at four of the partner colleges. The other colleges provide lists of local lodgings or private rented accommodation. Some international students prefer to stay with host families.

Perth College UHI: pc.enquiries@perth.uhi.ac.uk
Sabhal Mòr Ostaig UHI: trusadh@smo.uhi.ac.uk
Lews Castle College UHI: enquiries@lews.uhi.ac.uk
www.uhi.ac.uk/en/students/student-life/life-near-you

University of Huddersfield

Huddersfield is *Times Higher Education* magazine's university of the year, in recognition of its contribution to its town and its region, as well for consistently good records for student satisfaction and graduate employment. The judges were particularly impressed by the university's Graduate Opportunities Programme, which provides careers advice and guidance to all unemployed graduates – whatever their former university – who live in the areas of Calderdale and Kirklees. It had also been one of the dwindling band of universities persevering with fees of less than £9,000, but it will be charging the maximum in 2015–16. Those on placement years will pay only £750. A third of the students take sandwich courses – one of the highest proportions in the UK – while all of them do some work experience during their studies. The university's links with employers helped it to become Entrepreneurial University of the Year for 2012, an award which also recognised the way in which degree courses embed entrepreneurship into the curriculum and in particular the university's BA in enterprise development. Seven out of ten students receive a professional qualification alongside their degree.

The university lives up to its mission to widen participation in higher education. Over 46 per cent of full-time undergraduates are from working-class homes – far more than the national average for the university's courses and entry qualifications – and the numbers coming from areas without a tradition of higher education are among the highest in the country. The university has opened satellite centres in Barnsley and Oldham to widen participation further. The dropout rate has improved, and the latest projection of 13 per cent matches the national benchmark.

Imaginative conversions and new buildings have brought the university together on one town-centre campus. The university capitalised on Huddersfield's industrial past to ease the strain on facilities that were struggling to cope with growing student numbers. Canalside, a refurbished mill complex, provided extra space for mathematics and computing, and education occupies another mill site. The university has created "pocket parks" and a landscaped area along the reopened Narrow Canal to provide additional green space. It spent £4 million on a new students' union, allowing drama courses to take over the existing union complex. The union building includes alcohol-free social areas to encourage participation by those overseas students and ethnic minorities who would otherwise avoid the facilities. Recent developments include a striking creative arts building, which cost around £16 million, and a similar

---

Queensgate
Huddersfield
West Yorkshire HD1 3DH

0870 901 5555 (prospectus)
prospectus@hud.ac.uk
www.hud.ac.uk
www.huddersfield.su
Affiliation: University
   Alliance

The Times and Sunday Times Rankings

Overall Ranking: **=77** (last year: 66)

Student satisfaction:	=59	82.3%
Research quality:	=94	2.0%
Entry standards:	65	334
Student–staff ratio:	=70	18.3
Services & facilities/student:	94	£1,288
Expected completion rate:	95	81.6%
Good honours:	95	60.0%
Graduate prospects:	49	69.5%

sum was spent on a new business school. A £22.5-million Learning and Leisure Centre opened in 2014, bringing together library, computing, sport, leisure, eating, social and meeting facilities. The centre is part of a £58-million investment in teaching and research facilities.

The 19th-century Ramsden Building, the historical heart of the university, has been refurbished and there are ultra-modern facilities behind its carefully preserved exterior. A tradition of vocational education dates back to 1841, and the university has a long-established reputation in areas such as textile design and engineering. The university was awarded an £8-million Centre for Innovative Manufacturing in Advanced Metrology by the Engineering and Physical Sciences Research Council. Other strengths include music and social work, as well as teacher training, for which Huddersfield was awarded a national centre of excellence. Fourteen academics have been selected as National Teaching Fellows, the largest total in the UK.

Most of the areas in which Huddersfield entered the 2008 Research Assessment Exercise contained at least some world-leading work. A third of the university's submission was placed in the top two categories, with music producing by far the best results and social work also doing well. The university has sealed partnerships recently with the National Physical Laboratory, the Food and Environment Research Agency and the Royal Armouries in developments that it expects to benefit undergraduates as well as researchers. The most popular courses are in human and health sciences. Many arts and social science courses have a vocational slant, for example, politics features a six-week placement, which often takes students to the House of Commons. The university's Chancellor, the actor Sir Patrick Stewart, teaches drama in his capacity as professor of performing arts, as well as undertaking other duties.

Most residential accommodation is now concentrated in the Storthes Hall Park student village, but additional housing is available at Ashenhurst, just over a mile from the campus. Town–gown relations are good, although students tend to base their social life around the students' union. There is easy public transport access to Leeds and Manchester.

Undergraduate Fees and Bursaries

» Fees for UK/EU students 2015–16   £9,000
» Placement year   £750
» Fees for international students 2014–15   £12,000–£13,000
» 1,000 bursaries of £1,000 in year 1 to students with household income below £25K and either a minimum of 280 UCAS points or joining Foundation programmes in Science and Engineering.
» Enhanced retention and career development programme.

Students

Undergraduates:	**13,600**	**(2,910)**
Postgraduates:	**1,730**	**(2,195)**
Mature students:	**25.5%**	
International students:	**11.3%**	
Applications per place:	**4.7**	
From state-sector schools:	**98.3%**	
From working-class homes:	**46.5%**	
Satisfaction with students' union	**68%**	

For detailed information about sports facilities:
www.hud.ac.uk/sport-fitness-health/

Accommodation

Number of places and costs refer to 2014–15
University-provided places: 1,666 in privately owned halls
Percentage catered: 0%
Self-catered costs: £77–£111 a week.
First years are housed on a first come, first served basis provided conditions are met.
International students: as above.
mail@digstudent.co.uk
www.hud.ac.uk/undergraduate/accommodation/

University of Hull

Hull is closing entry to courses on its Scarborough campus in 2015 and transferring them to its home city. The former teacher training college became part of the university in 2000 and has about 1,500 students taking degrees in education, business, digital media, environmental science and marine biology. The university blames increased competition and believes that concentrating its activities on Hull will produce economies of scale and enable teaching to be better aligned with research. Hull dropped into the bottom half of our league table last year for the first time, after falls in student satisfaction and graduate employment. But it succeeded in arresting sharp falls in applications and enrolments that followed the introduction of £9,000 fees.

The university has been focusing on improvements to the student experience. The Brynmor Jones Library, redeveloped at a cost of £27.4 million, has a striking new atrium and revamped exterior that will be the centrepiece of the campus. Another £2 million has been spent remodelling University House, which houses student services and a refurbished students' union. The £2.5 million refurbishment of The Lawns, at Cottingham, where seven hall of residence house 1,000 students, will bring improved student dining and social spaces as well as a gym and lecture facilities. There has also been a focus on employability, which includes the option of a 20-credit module on career management skills. The careers service approaches undergraduates early in their time at Hull and sets up meetings with potential employers on campus.

The university and the city have always commanded loyalty among students, who appreciate the modest cost of living and ready availability of accommodation, as well as the quality of courses. The council is spending £25 million to transform the city centre to celebrate its award as the City of Culture for 2017. There are now around 20,000 students on the main campus, in Scarborough and at the adjoining West Campus, which contains the Business School, a new Enterprise Centre to support local firms and the medical school, which is run jointly with the University of York.

The original 94-acre main campus, less than three miles from the centre of Hull, has seen considerable development, with new buildings for languages and chemistry, a Graduate Research Institute and a state-of-the-art sport, health and exercise science laboratory. The latest addition is a new building for the biomedical research centre. The Wilberforce Building for law, politics and international studies has been refurbished.

There are 2,000 courses to choose from. A longstanding focus on Europe shows

---

Cottingham Road
Hull HU6 7RX

01482 466100 (admissions)
admissions@hull.ac.uk
www.hull.ac.uk
www.hyms.ac.uk
www.hullstudent.com
Affiliation: none

The Times and Sunday Times **Rankings**
Overall Ranking **58** (last year: 63)

Student satisfaction:	=42	83.0%
Research quality:	=52	11.0%
Entry standards:	66	333
Student–staff ratio:	=63	17.8
Services & facilities/student:	67	£1,472
Expected completion rate:	=64	85.4%
Good honours:	=61	66.7%
Graduate prospects:	73	63.5%

in the wide range of languages available at degree level, with the purpose-built Language Institute heavily used by all the students. Strength in politics – confirmed by one of three top research grades – is reflected in a steady flow of graduates into the House of Commons. The Westminster Hull Internship Programme (WHIP) offers a year-long placement and month-long internships for British politics and legislative studies students. The Legal Advice Centre, staffed by law students, provides guidance and advice to the public. The university offers 400 adult education modules, as well as 2,000 courses for its full-time students.

Hull had the lowest proportion of world-leading research among England's older universities in the 2008 Research Assessment Exercise. Health subjects, geography and environmental science, and drama, dance and performance achieved the best grades. The new biomedical research building, funded partly through a gift from a local businessman, will focus on cancer and cardiovascular and metabolic diseases – both areas in which the university has an international reputation. By bringing together both academics and health professionals, it aims to quickly translate research into tangible benefits for patients. An Institute for Learning encourages academics to put research findings into practice, developing training courses and developing the university's interest in lifelong learning.

More than 90 per cent of Hull's undergraduates are state-educated, while three in ten are from working-class homes. Nearly one undergraduate in five is from an area with little tradition of participation in higher education, far higher than the national average for the university's courses and entry qualifications. The projected dropout rate of 10 per cent is also better than the university's benchmark. The popular and active students' union is one of only eight six in 2014 to achieve the top grade at the Best Bar None Awards. New football pitches have been added recently on campus and the Sports and Fitness Centre has been attracting praise. There is a rolling programme of refurbishment of the halls of residence.

Undergraduate Fees and Bursaries

» Fees for UK/EU students 2015–16 £9,000
» Foundation degree £7,000
» Fees for international students 2014–15 £12,000–£14,400
   Medicine £25,420
» University of Hull Scholarship for those with at least AAB at A Level or equivalent and household income below £42.6K, £2,100 cash a year.
» If not eligible for this scholarship and household income below £25K, bursary of £2,100 cash in year 1.
» HYMS has its own bursary scheme (£2,400 a year accommodation bursary for 5 years when household income below £25K).

Students

Undergraduates:	**12,280**	**(2,975)**
Postgraduates:	**2,295**	**(1,330)**
Mature students:	**30.1%**	
International students:	**12.2%**	
Applications per place:	**3.9**	
From state-sector schools:	**92.0%**	
From working-class homes:	**33.0%**	
Satisfaction with students' union	**80%**	

For detailed information about sports facilities:
www2.hull.ac.uk/student/sportscentre1.aspx

Accommodation

Number of places and costs refer to 2014–15
University-provided places: 2,601; 150 (leased/associated stock)
Percentage catered: 49%
Catered costs: £88.69–£150.00 (34–37 weeks).
Self-catered costs: £69.16–£114.03 (37–50 weeks).
Unaccompanied first years are guaranteed accommodation if conditions are met.
International students: as above.
rooms@hull.ac.uk
www2.hull.ac.uk/student/accommodation-new.aspx

Imperial College of Science, Technology and Medicine

One of the biggest-ever donations to a UK university is helping Imperial to turn a 25-acre site near the former BBC Television Centre in West London into the country's most exciting new campus. Michael Uren, an industrialist and Imperial graduate, has given £40 million to build a biomedical engineering centre at the heart of the Imperial West campus. The full development will cost a total of £3 billion and will also feature a Research and Translation Hub, bringing together the academic and business communities. Imperial now has nine campuses in London and one in Singapore, due mainly to the expansion of its activities in medicine in the 1990s. But undergraduates in most other subjects will continue to be based at the South Kensington campus where Imperial has made its name as one of the world's leading universities of science, engineering and medicine. Never out of the top five in our league table, Imperial also features in the top ten of both the QS and *Times Higher Education* world rankings.

Entrance requirements are high. Even in subjects that struggle for candidates elsewhere, entrants average better than A*AA at A level and there are almost seven applications per place. More than a third of the undergraduates are from independent schools – one of the highest proportions at any university and considerably more than the national average for Imperial's courses and entry qualifications. About a third of the undergraduates are female – a proportion that has risen steadily over recent years – and roughly the same proportion of total student population are from outside the EU. The projected dropout rate of less than 3 per cent is among the lowest in the UK. The 2,200 academics and researchers include 73 Fellows of the Royal Society, 77 Fellows of the Royal Academy of Engineering and 81 Fellows of the Academy of Medical Sciences. Imperial's submission for the 2008 Research Assessment Exercise contained a higher proportion of world-leading or internationally excellent work (73 per cent) than any other university's submission.

The Faculty of Medicine is one of Europe's largest in terms of its staff and student numbers, as well as its research income. There are teaching bases attached to a number of hospitals in central and west London, while the UK's first Academic Health Science Centre (AHSC), run in partnership with Imperial College Healthcare NHS Trust, aims to translate research advances into patient care. The centre is one of only five in the country, denoting international excellence in biomedical research, education and

---

South Kensington Campus
London SW7 2AZ

020 7589 5111 (switchboard)
contact via website
www.imperial.ac.uk
www.imperialcollege
union.org
Affiliation: Russell Group

The Times and Sunday Times Rankings
Overall Ranking: **4** (last year: 5)

Student satisfaction:	=31	83.5%
Research quality:	=4	33.0%
Entry standards:	3	576
Student–staff ratio:	7	11.7
Services & facilities/student:	3	£2,833
Expected completion rate:	3	97.1%
Good honours:	5	85.9%
Graduate prospects:	1	89.9%

patient care. In its first overseas venture, Imperial has also opened a new medical school jointly with Nanyang Technological University, in Singapore.

Engineering degrees last four years and lead to an MEng. Imperial is unique in the UK for providing teaching and research in the full range of engineering disciplines. The growing business school is Imperial's main venture beyond the world of science and technology. It is highly rated and is accredited by the three largest and most influential business school accreditation associations worldwide. There is also an environmental research campus at Silwood Park, 25 miles west of London.

The Imperial Horizons programme, designed to give students an edge in their future career, provides opportunities to debate global challenges such as climate change, drawing on expertise from across the university. Many degrees offer a work placement or year abroad, and students are actively encouraged to seek summer internships. The Undergraduate Research Opportunities Programme offers "hands-on" research experience. It is especially popular in the summer vacation, when students can be paid bursaries and international undergraduates can participate without needing a work permit. Imperial's graduates have the highest average starting salaries in the UK.

Imperial celebrated its centenary in 2007

having left the University of London for greater autonomy and to take advantage of its global reputation. It has been redeveloping and expanding facilities on its main campus close to the South Kensington museums. A new sports centre, a second residential complex and refurbishments to the central library were followed by improvements to the students' union bar and nightclub. Further improvements to the library are being phased in over several years to minimise disruption. The latest campus development saw the launch in April 2014 of a Data Science Institute: a new hub for education, research and the application of big data technology.

The students' union claims to have the largest selection of clubs and societies in the country. Outdoor sports facilities are remote, but the new and well-equipped sports centre at the South Kensington campus offers students free gym and swimming facilities.

Undergraduate Fees and Bursaries

» Fees for UK/EU students 2015–16	£9,000
» Placement year	£900–£1,800
» Year overseas	£900–£1,350
» Fees for international students 2014–15	£22,950–£26,000
Medicine	£35,000
» Sliding scale of annual support: household income below £25K, £6,000 cash; £25K–£32K, £4,600 cash; £33K–42K, £1,200 cash.	
» Range of subject scholarships and Rector's Scholarships.	

Students

Undergraduates:	8,810	(0)
Postgraduates:	5,625	(1,570)
Mature students:	4.2%	
International students:	38.4%	
Applications per place:	6.3	
From state-sector schools:	64.7%	
From working-class homes:	18.4%	
Satisfaction with students' union	75%	

For detailed information about sports facilities:
www3.imperial.ac.uk/sports

Accommodation

Number of places and costs refer to 2014–15

University-provided places: 2,565

Percentage catered: 0%

Self-catered costs: £58–£253 a week.

First-year undergraduates are guaranteed accommodation if application received by 25 July.

International students: as above.

accommodation@imperial.ac.uk

www3.imperial.ac.uk/accommodation

Keele University

Keele has gone further than most universities to help its graduates in the employment market by formally recognising their achievements both in and out of the classroom. The distinctive Keele Curriculum, introduced as the university celebrated its 50th anniversary in 2012, covers voluntary and sporting activities as well as the academic core. It is the only one in the UK that can lead to accreditation by the Institute of Leadership and Management. The student charter identifies ten "graduate attributes" that include independent thinking, synthesising information, creative problem solving, communicating clearly, and appreciating the social, environmental and global implications of all studies and activities. The university has been at the forefront of moves to record in more detail what graduates have achieved through a Higher Education Annual Report.

Keele remains small by modern standards, with little more than 10,000 students at all levels. They share the largest campus in the country – 600 acres of parkland near Stoke – and consistently demonstrate high levels of satisfaction with their experience. Keele is seldom far from the top ten universities in the National Student Survey and shared second place this year, scoring heavily on the measures of teaching quality. There are plans for limited growth, especially at postgraduate level. This has already started, and almost a quarter of the students now take higher degrees.

More than £115 million has been spent on the campus since the turn of the century. The latest phase has transformed the heart of the campus, reconfiguring the Union Square plaza and providing a social hub for both informal and formal events. A third of all undergraduates, as well as many postgraduates and even some staff, live on a campus which includes an arboretum and has won a clutch of environmental awards. The university's commitment to green issues was underlined with the installation of environmental campaigner Jonathan Porritt as Chancellor in 2012. Keele topped the Environment Agency's inaugural energy efficiency ranking and its new Sustainability Hub brings together a wide range of organisations and experts in the field. There is a degree in environment and sustainability and all undergraduates can take a module in sustainability or environmental studies.

The academic year divided into two 15-week semesters, with breaks at Christmas and Easter. Nearly all undergraduates have the option of spending a semester abroad at one of the university's 50 partner universities. Nine out of ten undergraduates are state educated and approaching 30 per cent come from working-class homes. The university has been trying to broaden its

---

Keele

Staffordshire ST5 5BG

01782 734005 (admissions)
admissions.ukeu@keele.ac.uk
www.keele.ac.uk
www.keelesu.com
Affiliation: none

The Times and Sunday Times **Rankings**

Overall Ranking: **40** (last year: 44)

Student satisfaction:	=2	87.1%
Research quality:	51	12.7%
Entry standards:	=40	384
Student–staff ratio:	=31	15.2
Services & facilities/student:	109	£1,131
Expected completion rate:	=41	89.2%
Good honours:	56	67.5%
Graduate prospects:	41	72.3%

intake further by offering special projects and masterclasses in local schools and hosting a summer school. The projected dropout rate of less than 7 per cent is below the national average for the university's subjects and entry qualifications.

Health subjects have been the main focus of development in recent years. First degrees in physiotherapy and nursing and midwifery were added to the well-established postgraduate medical school. Keele also offers a five-year undergraduate medical course. Some 130 students each year are taught in new facilities on the Keele campus, at the University Hospital of North Staffordshire NHS Trust, three miles away, and at the Associate Teaching Hospital at the Shrewsbury and Telford Hospitals NHS Trust in Shropshire. Students take the new Keele undergraduate degree programme, which was approved by the GMC in 2011. Facilities for pharmacy and the natural sciences have also been improved. The latest development is a £2.8-million extension of the Anatomy Skills Facility, which will allow the School of Medicine to attract surgeons from across the UK. The extension will not only improve facilities for students, but will also offer senior surgeons the chance to improve their skills in the most up-to-date teaching environment.

An increased emphasis on research brought some success in the last Research Assessment Exercise. Almost half of the work submitted was judged to be world-leading or internationally excellent, but Keele was still towards the bottom of the traditional universities on this measure. The university is within an hour's drive of Manchester and Birmingham. Crime statistics suggest that Keele is the safest university campus in the West Midlands. For those who live off campus, the cost of living in the Potteries and the surrounding area is relatively low. The highly rated students' union, which has undergone a £2.7-million renovation, offers entertainment on campus every night of the week. The sports facilities have benefited from a new all-weather pitch, and the leisure centre has a refurbished fitness suite. A new £2.9-million nursery caters for more than 100 children from three months to school age.

Undergraduate Fees and Bursaries

» Fees for UK/EU students 2015–16 £9,000
» Placement year £500
» Year abroad £1,350
» Fees for international students 2014–15 £12,000–£14,500
  Medicine £24,100
» English students with household income below £25K, bursary of £1,000 a year.
» Study abroad bursary of £1,000 for those with household income below £25K.
» Scholarships for those with excellent pre-entry qualifications of up to £2,000 a year.
» Check the university's website for the latest information.

Students

Undergraduates:	7,135	(515)
Postgraduates:	995	(1,590)
Mature students:	13.2%	
International students:	15.2%	
Applications per place:	8.9	
From state-sector schools:	92.1%	
From working-class homes:	29%	
Satisfaction with students' union	83%	

For detailed information about sports facilities:
www.keele.ac.uk/sport

Accommodation

Number of places and costs refer to 2014–15
University-provided places: 3,200
Percentage catered: 5%
Catered costs: £125.76–£156.11 a week (37 weeks).
Self-catered costs: £78.54–£171.81 a week (34–51 weeks).
First years are guaranteed accommodation on campus if Keele is first or firm choice university.
International students: guaranteed accommodation for the duration of their course. Deadlines apply.
www.keele.ac.uk/studyatkeele/accommodation

University of Kent

Kent will open its first new college for undergraduates in 45 years before its 2015 intake arrives. Turing College will have 800 study bedrooms and a hub building with social and study areas, catering facilities and a launderette. The development will not only maintain the university's position as one of the best-provided in terms of accommodation – with nearly 6,000 places in Canterbury alone for 15,000 full-time students there – but also give it scope to expand. In 2014 Kent offered scholarships of £2,000 a year (renewable annually) to candidates who achieved at least three As at A level, or the equivalent, to remain competitive at the top level in today's more competitive higher education market. Applications rose by more than 7 per cent in 2013 and a similar increase in enrolments. Every student is attached to college, although they do not select it themselves. The colleges act as the focus of social life – especially in the first year – and include academic as well as residential facilities.

Capitalising on its location, Kent has become probably the UK's most active in Europe, both in terms of its participation in EU programmes and in its continental ventures. Styling itself "the UK's European university", Kent now has postgraduate sites in Brussels, Paris, Athens and Rome, as well as giving many undergraduates the option of a year abroad. There are partnerships with over 100 European universities. and 25 per cent of all students are from outside the UK. The university has been broadening its horizons at home as well, with access courses throughout the county and a Medway campus, at the old Chatham naval base, that is shared with Greenwich and Canterbury Christ Church universities and Mid-Kent College. The School of Pharmacy, is the main feature of a £50-million development which now has more than 2,000 students from the university. The university has another base in Tonbridge serving 3,000 part-time students, who are mainly taught in associate colleges.

Kent's original low-rise campus is set in 300 acres of tidy parkland overlooking Canterbury. Recent developments include the prize-winning Colyer-Fergusson Music Building, which cost £8 million and boasts flexible performance space with outstanding, adjustable acoustics and retractable seating for up to 500. Kent School of Architecture's new Crit Building contains one of the most advanced learning environments of its type in the UK. Among several other major projects is an ongoing redevelopment of the library and a student media centre opened in 2014. The student centre has a nightclub large enough to attract big-name bands, as well as a theatre, cinema and bars. On the Medway campus, a new School of

---

The Registry
Canterbury
Kent CT2 7NZ

01227 827272 (admissions)
information@kent.ac.uk
www.kent.ac.uk
www.kentunion.co.uk
Affiliation: none

The Times and Sunday Times **Rankings**
Overall Ranking: **30** (last year: =33)

Student satisfaction:	23	84.1%
Research quality:	=42	17.0%
Entry standards:	45	372
Student–staff ratio:	17	13.6
Services & facilities/student:	82	£1,376
Expected completion rate:	=31	91.4%
Good honours:	31	74.7%
Graduate prospects:	31	75.2%

Arts opened in 2012, with flexible work spaces for painting, sculpture, printmaking, film, photography, music and performance projects. There is also a £1-million sculpture workshop and recording studios, as well as more than 1,000 residential places nearby.

The university has a good record in the National Student Survey and tries to safeguard teaching standards by encouraging all academics to take a Postgraduate Certificate in Higher Education. Kent academics have been awarded National Teaching Fellowships in five of the last six years. The student population is more diverse than many in the south of England: over nine out of ten undergraduates are from state schools and nearly 30 per cent come from working-class homes. Entry grades for full-time degrees have been rising in most subjects. Offers are pitched according to the UCAS points tariff, although those taking A levels are expected to pass at least three subjects (one of which may be general studies). Graduates of all disciplines fare well in the employment market – the university regularly features among the top 20 for graduate starting salaries.

Kent was much more successful in the 2008 research assessments than in previous exercises, with more than half of its submission placed in the top two categories. The university has been building up its science departments, among which computing is particularly well regarded, but still a majority of the students take arts or social science subjects.

Campus security is good, although some complain that Canterbury itself is expensive and limited socially. Residential accommodation was upgraded and extended with the £25-million redevelopment of Keynes College and completion of the Park Wood student village. Sports facilities have improved considerably following an investment of £4.8 million in a fitness suite includes an extensive range of free weights, as well as four Olympic power-lifting platforms. A multipurpose fitness and dance studio has also been built, and a new indoor tennis centre has been added alongside the sports centre.

Undergraduate Fees and Bursaries

- » Fees for UK/EU students 2015–16   £9,000
- » Partner colleges   £6,000–£9,000
- » Placement year / year abroad   £1,350
- » Fees for international students 2014–15   £12,450–£14,860
- » Household income below £42.6K and meeting various conditions with priority to those from areas of low participation in higher education, a bursary of £2,000 a year.
- » Subject scholarships and partner school and college scholarships.
- » Check the university's website for the latest information.

Students

Undergraduates:	**14,735**	**(1,035)**
Postgraduates:	**2,385**	**(1,655)**
Mature students:	**12.8%**	
International students:	**19.6%**	
Applications per place:	**5.4**	
From state-sector schools:	**91.8%**	
From working-class homes:	**28.9%**	
Satisfaction with students' union	**71%**	

For detailed information about sports facilities:
www.kent.ac.uk/sports

Accommodation

Number of places and costs refer to 2014–15
University-provided places: 5,143
Percentage catered: 14%
Catered costs: £103–£117 a week.
Self-catered costs: £102–£152 a week.
First years are guaranteed accommodation provided applications received before 31 July.
International students: as above.
hospitality-enquiry@kent.ac.uk;
www.kent.ac.uk/accommodation

King's College London

King's is one of the Russell Group institutions to take advantage of the relaxation of recruitment restrictions to take more undergraduates: the intake has grown by 13 per cent – more than 500 students – in two years. With applications up by 7 per cent in 2013, there is scope to continue, although there are hotly contested plans to cut the staff by up to 120 academics, mainly in the large schools of medicine and biosciences. King's was once known primarily for science, but now has a distinguished reputation across nine schools including humanities, law and social sciences, which includes war studies. The college's research strength has secured a place in the top 20 of the QS World University Rankings, although declining student satisfaction saw it drop seven places in our league table in two years..

One of the oldest and largest of the University of London's colleges, King's has played a part in many of the advances that shape modern life, including the discovery of DNA and the development of radar. Twelve alumni or academics have won Nobel Prizes, including Archbishop Desmond Tutu for his work to end apartheid and Maurice Wilkins for his contribution to identifying the structure of DNA. A £500-million fundraising campaign is focused on some of today's most pressing challenges in five priority areas, including neuroscience and mental health, cancer and global power. In the 2008 Research Assessment Exercise, 60 per cent of the college's submission was judged to be world-leading or internationally excellent. It is Europe's largest centre for the education of doctors, dentists and other healthcare professionals, and home to six Medical Research Council centres. King's Health Partners Academic Health Sciences Centre represents a pioneering collaboration between the college and three NHS foundation trusts.

King's describes itself as "the most central university in London" because four of its five campuses are within a single square mile around the banks of the Thames. The fifth is not far away at Denmark Hill in south London. The original Strand site and the Waterloo campus, which includes the largest university building in London, house most of the non-medical departments. Nursing and midwifery and some biomedical subjects are also based at Waterloo, while medicine and dentistry are mainly at Guy's Hospital, near London Bridge, and in the St Thomas' Hospital campus, across the river from the Houses of Parliament. The Denmark Hill campus houses the Institute of Psychiatry, as well as more medicine and dentistry. The Maurice Wohl Institute, which is due to open by the end of 2014, is set to be one of

---

Strand
London WC2R 2LS

020 7848 7000 (enquiries)
contact via website
www.kcl.ac.uk
www.kclsu.org
Affiliation: Russell Group

The Times and Sunday Times **Rankings**
Overall Ranking: **29** (last year: 27)

Student satisfaction:	**106**	78.7%
Research quality:	**=23**	23.3%
Entry standards:	**=13**	470
Student–staff ratio:	**4**	11.4
Services & facilities/student:	**23**	£2,090
Expected completion rate:	**=23**	92.5%
Good honours:	**=11**	81.1%
Graduate prospects:	**12**	80.1%

Europe's leading centres of interdisciplinary neuroscience research. Libraries on all the main campuses have been upgraded recently – part of a £60-million programme of improvements to student facilities. Further investment of £140 million is planned over the next few years. The expansion of the Strand Campus into the East Wing of Somerset House in 2012 provided impressive new premises for the 175-year-old School of Law. A £12-million science gallery will open on the Guy's campus in 2015, focused on 15–25 year-olds.

About one student in five is from outside the European Union, many of them among the 6,500 full-time postgraduates. An institutional audit by the Quality Assurance Agency gave King's the highest mark, stressing the excellence of the student support services.

Graduates enjoy among the best employment rates in the UK and typically also earn some of the highest starting salaries. The college's location means King's students are in an enviable position for accessing opportunities for work experience. A new Internships Office is working with King's Careers Service to support development in this area.

Almost three undergraduates in ten come from independent schools, in spite of the college's efforts to widen its intake. King's launched a new Enhanced Support Dentistry Programme to attract talented school-leavers from lower performing schools, along the lines of its celebrated Access to Medicine course.

The active students' union, which runs bars, cafés and a nightclub, puts on an extensive programme of events. The college is well provided with accommodation in a variety of residences, in busy central locations as well as in quieter, residential areas. There are privately operated residences and others run by the University of London, as well as more than 2,500 places in university-owned provision. Some of the outdoor sports facilities are a long train ride from the college, but there are facilities for all the main sports, as well as rifle ranges, two gyms and a swimming pool.

Undergraduate Fees and Bursaries

» Fees for UK/EU students 2015–16   £9,000
» Year abroad   £1,350
» Fees for international students 2014–15   £15,200–£19,570
  Medicine and dentistry   £19,570–£36,050
» King's Living Bursary of £1,500 (household income below £25K) or £1,000 (£25K–£42.6K), payable for all years.
» Bursaries and merit scholarships, including 50 Access to Professions scholarships of £3,000 for years 1–3 for certain courses in medicine and dentistry; Dickson Poon law scholarships: 25 of £9,000 a year and 50 of £6,000 a year.
» Enhanced student hardship fund.
» Check the university's website for the latest information.

Students

Undergraduates:	**13,005**	**(3,535)**
Postgraduates:	**6,490**	**(4,260)**
Mature students:	**14.9%**	
International students:	**22.9%**	
Applications per place:	**8.1**	
From state-sector schools:	**70.9%**	
From working-class homes:	**24.2%**	
Satisfaction with students' union	**67%**	

For detailed information about sports facilities:
www.kcl.ac.uk/campuslife/sport

Accommodation

Number of places and costs refer to 2014–15
University-provided places: 2,568, 1,480 nominated; 473 inter-collegiate.
Percentage catered: 0% overall; 100% intercollegiate.
Catered costs: £136.50 (small single) – £453.25 (flat) a week.
Self-catered costs: £119.00–£206.50 (40 weeks).
New full-time undergraduate students are guaranteed the offer of one year in accommodation if specific conditions are met.
International students: priority for new students.
www.kcl.ac.uk/campuslife/accom

Kingston University

For the last five years in a row, Kingston has helped its graduates launch more companies than any other university – an increasingly important service at a time when self-employment is becoming a career choice for growing numbers of those completing a degree. The university assisted with 270 start-ups in 2012–13, an increase of more than a third on the previous year, and was praised by Business Secretary Vince Cable as a result. It established an Enterprise Department more than a decade ago, giving advice to would-be entrepreneurs in any subject, offering them expert mentors and the possibility of financial support with start-up companies. The scheme epitomises the career focus that runs through all Kingston's courses. The university has the third largest engineering faculty in London, for example, with its own Learjet and a flight simulator to support its highly regarded aeronautical engineering courses.

The university markets itself as in "lively, leafy London", making a virtue of its suburban, riverside location southwest of central London as well as its proximity to the bright lights. Two of its four campuses are close to Kingston town centre; another, two miles away, is at Kingston Hill; the fourth is in Roehampton Vale, where a site once used as an aerospace factory now contains a new technology block. Kingston has opened three impressive new buildings as part of a £123-million programme to revitalise its entire estate. The centrepiece will be £55-million building on the Penrhyn Road campus, which will become the main reception point for all four campuses by 2017. The university has already spent £20 million on the John Galsworthy Building on the campus, which incorporates lecture theatres, flexible teaching space and information technology suites as well as a "Knowledge Centre" for students to do coursework. The Business School acquired a new £26-million home in 2012, complete with atrium, modern teaching rooms and break-out spaces. A new learning resources centre is part of an £11-million improvement programme at the University's Knights Park campus, which includes the refurbishment of studio space, an upgraded reception and gallery area and external landscaping. There have been extensive upgrades of the library facilities on each campus, bringing together library, computing and multimedia facilities to encourage interactive and group learning. There are bookable study rooms with multimedia facilities and specially equipped spaces dedicated to meeting the needs of disabled users. The main centres are open 24 hours a day during term-time weekdays and a high-tech self-issue system makes borrowing much quicker and easier.

Approaching a third of the university's

River House
53–57 High Street
Kingston upon Thames
Surrey KT1 1LQ

0844 855 2177 (enquiries)
aps@kingston.ac.uk
www.kingston.ac.uk
www.kusu.co.uk
Affiliation: University
    Alliance

The Times and Sunday Times Rankings
Overall Ranking: **117** (last year: 111)

Student satisfaction:	121	75.7%
Research quality:	=79	3.3%
Entry standards:	=101	298
Student–staff ratio:	86	19.4
Services & facilities/student:	81	£1,378
Expected completion rate:	107	79.6%
Good honours:	100	59.0%
Graduate prospects:	=110	54.4%

submission to the 2008 Research Assessment Exercise was rated world-leading or internationally excellent. The star performance was in history of art, architecture and design, where half of the submission was at least internationally excellent.

The Faculty of Health and Social Care Sciences (run jointly with St George's, University of London) now has more than 4,000 students and has won two major NHS London contracts, which will increase numbers in nursing and physiotherapy. Radiotherapists hone their clinical skills in a simulated cancer treatment room, while the Centre for Paramedic Science serves as a hub for course delivery and research projects. There is a link with the Royal Marsden School of Cancer Nursing and Rehabilitation, enabling students to spend up to half of their course on clinical placements working in hospital, primary care and community settings. Kingston is to head the largest project in a new Government-funded programme to boost postgraduate study. Its aim is to encourage students who might not normally become postgraduates to continue on to Master's courses in science, technology, engineering and mathematics and then track how they progress.

Kingston has one of the most ethnically mixed student populations of any UK university, and many undergraduates are also the first in their family to experience higher education. More than a quarter of Kingston's places go to mature students and 42 per cent to those from working-class families. Most students like the university's location, although they complain about the high cost of living. A "one-stop shop" deals with student issues ranging from careers and accommodation to complaints and financial advice. There is also a new unit, thought to be unique in the UK, offering free mediation of disputes involving local people. Each session is conducted by a student, but supervised by staff from the university law school who are accredited mediators. More than £20 million has been spent on halls of residence and Kingston's sports facilities have improved. A £2.65-million sports pavilion, designed to suit both able-bodied and disabled users, and an upgraded sports ground opened in 2010.

Undergraduate Fees and Bursaries

- » Fees for UK/EU students 2015–16   £9,000
- » Foundation degree   £4,700–£6,800
- » Fees for international students 2014–15   £11,000–£13,300
- » Household income below £25K, 420 bursaries of £2,000 in year 1.
- » Progression awards (£500–£1,500) in years 2 and 3 with conditions.
- » Assistance from Study Support and Retention Fund.
- » Range of other scholarships and bursaries available.
- » Check the university's website for the latest information.

Students

Undergraduates:	**17,175**	**(1,980)**
Postgraduates:	**2,370**	**(2,570)**
Mature students:	**27.9%**	
International students:	**13.5%**	
Applications per place:	**6.4**	
From state-sector schools:	**95.7%**	
From working-class homes:	**41.8%**	
Satisfaction with students' union	**62%**	

For detailed information about sports facilities: www.kingston.ac.uk/sport.

Accommodation

Number of places and costs refer to 2014–15

University-provided places: 2,365; private hall: 214

Percentage catered: 0%

Self-catered costs: £107.50–£137.00 a week (university provided; 40 weeks); £186.00 and £266.00 (private hall; 50 weeks).

Offers accommodation to many first-years who make Kingston their firm choice.

International students: offered places if conditions met, subject to availability.

www.kingston.ac.uk/accommodation

Lancaster University

Lancaster has opened the only UK university campus in Africa as a further demonstration of its determination to be a global university. The new venture in Ghana follows partnerships with universities in India, Pakistan, Malaysia and China that mean the current total of 2,000 students taking Lancaster degrees abroad will soon rise considerably and may even outnumber those in the UK. Hundreds of Lancaster students also spend part of their courses in America, Asia, Australia or Europe. The university is celebrating its 50th anniversary on the verge of the top ten in *The Times and Sunday Times* league table and comfortably the highest-placed university in the northwest of England. Its student satisfaction rates are consistently high, but its greatest strength is in research, with more than 60 per cent of its submission to the last Research Assessment Exercise rated as world-leading or internationally excellent.

Lancaster is more successful than most research universities in widening participation among under-represented groups. Nine out of ten undergraduates are state educated and a quarter come from the four lowest socio-economic classes. Outreach activity includes summer schools for 600 sixth-formers and college students, masterclasses for 2,000 and mentoring

for 250 students. The projected dropout rate of 6 per cent matches the national average for the subjects on offer. There was a surprisingly large fall in applications, of more than 8 per cent, in 2013, but the Lancaster was still able to increase enrolments.

The university has completed a £500-million makeover for its campus, with much of the money going on eco-friendly student residences. Lancaster has held the title of Best University Halls since 2010 in the National Student Housing Survey, and is one of only three UK universities to be awarded an International Accommodation Quality Mark based on more than 90 per cent positive feedback from international students. A new 24-hour student learning space at the centre of the campus provides flexible learning environments and social space with up-to-date technology. Infolab 21, the £15-million centre of excellence in information communication technology, acts as a technology transfer and incubation facility and houses a training facility for high-tech businesses. Other recent developments include a leadership centre for the highly rated Management School and the establishment of a Confucius Institute as a hub for Chinese language teaching and culture. Lancaster has also invested heavily in new facilities for engineering, which has doubled its undergraduate numbers in the last five

---

Bailrigg

Lancaster LA1 4YW

01524 592028 (admissions)
ugadmissions@lancaster.ac.uk
www.lancaster.ac.uk
www.lusu.co.uk
Affiliation: none

The Times and Sunday Times **Rankings**		
Overall Ranking: **12** (last year: =12)		
Student satisfaction:	22	84.2%
Research quality:	12	28.3%
Entry standards:	16	448
Student–staff ratio:	=26	14.9
Services & facilities/student:	43	£1,752
Expected completion rate:	=16	93.9%
Good honours:	25	77.6%
Graduate prospects:	23	78.0%

years. A £10-million building for the Lancaster Institute for the Contemporary Arts has brought together art, design and theatre studies with the university's public art gallery, concerts and theatre.

Lancaster is another of the campus universities which has always championed a flexible degree structure. Most undergraduates can broaden their first-year studies by taking a second or third subject. The final choice of degree comes only at the end of that year. Combined degree programmes, with 200 courses to choose from, are especially popular. The degree portfolio now includes medicine, with Lancaster now awarding its own degrees in the subject, having previously collaborated with the University of Liverpool. The university has established a new Department of Chemistry, which offers an undergraduate degree in the subject, while another partnership with Liverpool has seen the opening of the £9.8-million Centre for Global Eco-Innovation. Other recent developments have included a research centre specialising in bipolar disorder and a new Centre for Organisational Health and Wellbeing. Lancaster is well known for research into ageing, cyber security and energy. In an unusual move, the university has also acquired the London-based think tank, the Work Foundation.

Students join one of eight residential colleges on campus, which become the centre of most students' social life. Most house between 800 and 900 students in self-catering accommodation and each has its own bar and social facilities. Cartmel and Lonsdale colleges have transferred to the New Alexandra Park area of the campus with enhanced social facilities. The pioneering 800-room Eco Residence, which opened in 2008, has won an environmental award. Lancaster itself is a ten-minute bus ride away. Both the campus and city have been rated among the safest in the UK. The university hosts a thriving live arts scene for the campus, the city and the region, with professional theatre, dance, exhibitions and concerts. Sports facilities are good and conveniently placed, with £20-millon sports centre on campus, while for the outdoor life, the Lake District is within easy reach. Road and rail communications are good, but Lancaster is inevitably more limited for off-campus nightlife.

Undergraduate Fees and Bursaries

» Fees for UK/EU students 2015–16 £9,000
» Fees for international students 2014–15 £13,270–£16,640
   Medicine £22,500
» Household income below £42.6K, £1,000 a year cash bursary.
» Scholarship of £2,000 in year 1 for those with A*A*A at A Level or equivalent.
» Scholarship of £1,000 a year for those with A*AA at A Level or equivalent and with household income below £42.6K.
» Range of other scholarships and bursaries available.
» Check the university's website for the latest information.

Students

Undergraduates:	**8,970**	**(185)**
Postgraduates:	**2,200**	**(1,380)**
Mature students:	**4.5%**	
International students:	**25.1%**	
Applications per place:	**5.4**	
From state-sector schools:	**90.9%**	
From working-class homes:	**25.3%**	
Satisfaction with students' union	**72%**	

For detailed information about sports facilities:
http://sportscentre.lancs.ac.uk

Accommodation

Number of places and costs refer to 2014–15
University-provided places: 6,600 (plus about 900 places in university-managed houses)
Percentage catered: 5%
Catered costs: £126.21 (standard) – £162.96 (en suite) a week.
Self-catered costs: £86.10 (standard) – £146.65 (studio) a week.
All first years are normally accommodated; no formal guarantee for Insurance, Clearing and late applicants.
International students: as above.
www.lancaster.ac.uk/sbs/accommodation/

University of Leeds

Leeds has reached its highest-ever position in our league table this year, a rise of 12 places taking it into the top 20. The university is making significant changes to its undergraduate curriculum, encouraging students to take courses outside their immediate subject and introducing a compulsory research project in the final year. The project is intended to be seen by students as the "pinnacle of their academic achievement" and will normally be worth at least 40 credits to recognise its importance in a new curriculum that will be distinctive to Leeds. Even before the changes, the university was commended by the Quality Assurance Agency for its enhancement of the student learning experience. Students already have access to academic and careers advice, as well as help to identify work placements and volunteering opportunities, through the LeedsforLife service, which they can continue using for five years after graduation. The university has devoted one of the largest amounts of any institution to student support, and will continue to do so in 2015, when up to a third of UK and EU undergraduates are expected to benefit.

A member of the Russell Group of research-led universities, Leeds occupies a 98-acre site within walking distance of the city centre. By 2015–16 it will have spent £157 million on new buildings and refurbishment to enhance the student experience and improve research facilities. A new undergraduate library is due to open in September 2015. Recent developments have included a new £4.4-million home for the Institute of Communications Studies with 41 edit suites, TV and radio studios, newsroom and 60-seat cinema; a £12.5-million Energy Research building that contains a suite of advanced laboratories; and a £9.5-million refurbishment of the Leeds Dental Institute. The already large students' union, famous for its long bar and big-name rock concerts, has been extended to provide better services and more space for students to socialise. The union is the only one in the country to have won two gold standard awards in the Students' Union Evaluation Initiative. The award-winning Careers Centre hosts some of the world's biggest employers at the university, as well as advising those who choose to set up on their own.

The university is truly cosmopolitan, with 5,000 international students from 145 countries among a total of more than 30,000. New enrolments were 400 up in 2013. Leeds has one of the largest Study Abroad programmes in the country, with nearly 200 options ranging from Spain to Singapore. It is part of the Worldwide Universities Network, which brings together 18 research-led universities to collaborate

---

Leeds
West Yorkshire LS2 9JT

0113 343 2336 (enquiries)
study@leeds.ac.uk
www.leeds.ac.uk
www.leedsuniversityunion.
  org.uk
Affiliation: Russell Group

The Times and Sunday Times Rankings

Overall Ranking: **17** (last year: =29)

Student satisfaction:	21	84.3%
Research quality:	=27	22.7%
Entry standards:	24	434
Student–staff ratio:	=24	14.7
Services & facilities/student:	24	£2,068
Expected completion rate:	12	94.4%
Good honours:	=13	81.0%
Graduate prospects:	33	74.8%

on research and postgraduate programmes. Leeds features among the top 100 in the QS World University Rankings, and in the top 50 for English, education, communication, geography and earth sciences. More than 60 per cent of the university's submission was rated as world-leading or internationally excellent in the last Research Assessment Exercise. Electrical and electronic engineering produced the best results in the country, with social work and social policy, English, Italian, geography and nursing also highly rated. But teaching is not neglected: Leeds has been awarded more National Teaching Fellowships than any other university in England. Leeds does better than many big city universities in the National Student Survey and is the top Russell Group university overall in the International Student Barometer, which gathers the views of students from outside the EU on various aspects of their experience. Almost a quarter of the undergraduates attended independent schools and only a fifth come from working-class homes – both missing the university's benchmark for widening participation in higher education.

The rise of Leeds as a shopping and clubbing centre has added to the attractions of a university which has long been one of the giants of the higher education system. An unusually wide range of degree subjects gives applicants more than 560

undergraduate programmes. Town–gown relations are generally good. There were tensions in Headingley, the main student area, but in recent years there has been an increase in students living in purpose-built student accommodation close to campus and the city centre. The wider local community benefits from 2,000 student volunteers and a partnership initiative introduced in 2011 sets out students' rights and responsibilities. Leeds guarantees accommodation for all first-year undergraduates, international and exchange students and students with disabilities. Sports and social facilities are first rate, and Leeds teams regularly excel in competition. The university hosts one of six centres of cricketing excellence. It has more playing field space than any other, while The Edge sports centre includes a 25-metre swimming pool and a huge fitness suite.

Undergraduate Fees and Bursaries

» Fees for UK/EU students 2015–16 £9,000
» Placement year / year abroad £1,350
» Fees for international students 2014–15 £12,900–£16,500
  Medicine and dentistry £18,450–£30,700
» Household income below £25K, £3,000 cash, accommodation contribution or fee waiver, Foundation year (year 0), £2,500 all other years; household income £25K–£30K, £1,500 all years; household income £30K–£36K, £1,000 all years; £36K–£42.6K, £500 all years.
» Foundation year fee waiver of £3,000 (household income below £25K) and £1,500 (household income £25K–£42.6K).
» A range of scholarships and bursaries are available.

Students

Undergraduates:	22,425	(865)
Postgraduates:	4,370	(2,720)
Mature students:	9.8%	
International students:	10.5%	
Applications per place:	7.1	
From state-sector schools:	76.2%	
From working-class homes:	20.2%	
Satisfaction with students' union	91%	

For detailed information about sports facilities:
http://sport.leeds.ac.uk

Accommodation

Number of places and costs refer to 2014–15
University-provided places: 7,900
Percentage catered: 23%
Catered costs £138–£186 a week (39 weeks).
Self-catered costs: £78–£158 a week (41–51 weeks).
Single first years are guaranteed a place if conditions are met.
International students: guaranteed to full free-paying undergraduates if conditions are met.
accom@leeds.ac.uk
www.accommodation.leeds.ac.uk

Leeds Metropolitan University

Leeds Metropolitan becomes Leeds Beckett University in September 2014, having decided that it had "outgrown" its former name. The undergraduate intake has fluctuated since the introduction of higher fees. The university took an additional 1,100 undergraduates in 2013, in spite of a big fall in applications, but had seen enrolments drop by a quarter in the previous year. The change of name – taken from the campus at Beckett Park – was controversial among students and alumni, but is intended to usher in a more stable era.

The university has achieved Customer Service Excellence accreditation for the entire university, one of only two in the UK to do so. It also holds the Gold Investors in People standard, and is the only university to achieve both of these independent standards. Students are included on the committees that design and manage courses.

Little more than half of all undergraduates are taking conventional full-time degrees, such is the popularity of sandwich and part-time courses. It is intended that all Leeds Beckett students should leave the university with three graduate attributes: to be enterprising, digitally literate and have a global outlook. All undergraduate courses have been redesigned with these qualities in mind and all include at least two weeks work-related learning a year. The university has a longstanding reputation for widening participation in higher education: well over 90 per cent of undergraduates are state-educated and more than a third come from working-class homes. A quarter of the students come from the Yorkshire and Humberside region, and around one in five is 21 or over on entry. The university runs a wide range of summer schools, which benefit more than 24,000 young people a year. A Regional University Network of further education colleges, which stretches as far as Belfast and Glasgow, enables students to take Leeds Beckett courses locally. However, the university's projected drop-out rate of more than 18 per cent is significantly higher than the national average for its courses and entry qualifications.

There are two bases in Leeds: the City Campus, in the heart of the city centre, and the Headingley Campus, three miles away in 100 acres of park and woodland at Beckett Park. The latter boasts outstanding sports facilities, including a new sports arena and multi-use sports pitches, which opened in 2012. The sports centre offers a variety of options for performance and participation sport, alongside the £2-million Carnegie Regional Tennis Centre and teaching accommodation for education, informatics,

---

City Campus
Leeds
West Yorkshire LS1 3HE

0113 812 3113 (enquiries)
admissions.enquiries@
  leedsmet.ac.uk
www.leedsmet.ac.uk
www.leedsbeckettsu.co.uk
Affiliation: million+

law and business. Over 7,000 students take part in some form of sporting activity, and there is a range of sports scholarships. The Athletic Union hosts 32 clubs and university teams – especially those for women – are among the most successful in national competition. An annual pass for both the Headingley and City campus facilities cost £125 in 2014. In the first developments of its kind, a new stand was built at the Headingley rugby ground, with classrooms, coaching facilities and social space for use by the university and the two professional clubs, and a new pavilion at the adjacent Test and County Cricket ground has similar multi-use facilities.

The City Campus has seen a £100-million transformation over the past six years, with the opening of the award winning Rose Bowl and Broadcasting Place. The futuristic lecture theatre complex next to Leeds Civic Hall now houses the business school, while Broadcasting Place is home to the Faculty of Arts and Society. The former BBC building next door has reopened as Old Broadcasting House and hosts the Enterprise Office, which helps identify opportunities to generate commercial income and support bids for funding and contracts. A growing emphasis on educational technology is enhanced by 24-hour libraries, which have achieved the Customer Service Excellence standard for ten years in a row. They contain more than 800 computers and over 2,000 study spaces.

Relatively few academics were entered for the 2008 Research Assessment Exercise, but nearly a third of their work was judged to be world-leading or internationally excellent. Communication, cultural and media studies, sport, and library and information management produced the best results. Leeds Beckett's reputation is mainly for applied research: three interdisciplinary research institutes focus on health, sport and sustainability, and there are ten centres in more specialist fields such as retail excellence, active lifestyles and diversity and equity.

The university is benefiting from the city's growing reputation for nightlife, but it is making its own contribution with a famously lively entertainments scene. With 4,500 bed spaces, those who accept places before Clearing are guaranteed university accommodation.

Undergraduate Fees and Bursaries

» Fees for UK/EU students 2015–16 £9,000
» Placement year no fee
» Fees for international students 2014–15 £9,500
» Support to be in form of high achiever scholarships, associated schools and colleges bursaries and enhanced student hardship fund. Details not available in August 2014.
» Range of other scholarships and bursaries available.
» Check the university's website for the latest information.

Students

Undergraduates:	**17,800**	**(4,360)**
Postgraduates:	**1,325**	**(2,325)**
Mature students:	**19.5%**	
International students:	**4.9%**	
Applications per place:	**4.3**	
From state-sector schools:	**94%**	
From working-class homes:	**35.0%**	
Satisfaction with students' union	**65%**	

For detailed information about sports facilities:
www.leedsmet.ac.uk/sport

Accommodation

Number of places and costs refer to 2014–15
University-provided places: 4,500
Percentage catered: 0%
Self-catered costs: £85–£165 a week (40–45 weeks).
First years with Conditional Firm or Unconditional Firm offers guaranteed accommodation.
International students: guaranteed accommodation if conditions are met.
accommodation@leedsmet.ac.uk
www.leedsmet.ac.uk/accommodation

Leeds Trinity University

Leeds Trinity enjoyed the biggest increase in applications – 65 per cent – of any university in 2013, following the award of full university status. It took an additional 150 undergraduates, many of them on the 18 new courses it had launched as other institutions were scaling back their options. The new offerings included accelerated two-year degrees in education and sport, and tourism and leisure management. Like all the university's degrees, they include full-time professional work placements.

Leeds Trinity is one of two new UK universities that are Catholic foundations. It "promotes dialogue and teaching of the Catholic Church", but is not controlled by the Church and welcomes students of all faiths and none. The university grew out of two Catholic teacher training colleges established in the 1960s, which merged in 1980. Education is still the biggest subject, but there are also departments of media, film and culture; journalism; business, management and marketing; psychology; and sport, health and nutrition.

Leeds Trinity's campus is 20 minutes north-west of Leeds city centre, in Horsforth. Millions of pounds have been spent in recent years to transform it into a modern campus village. The latest big development was the upgrading of the Media Centre, which is now fully digital for video and audio operations, and students are able to shoot in HD following the purchase of broadcast-quality portable cameras. A new range of computers and studio cameras have been installed to meet the demands of journalism and media production courses. The Centre for Journalism has developed two additional multimedia newsrooms with easy access to studios, equipment and edit suites. Postgraduate journalism students also spend time in the newsroom of Yorkshire's biggest regional newspaper.

The university's Digital Campus project will see the investment of £1.2 million over three years to provide a seamless, resilient and flexible ICT environment. The new technology will also reduce the university's carbon footprint by using lower wattage computers that have much longer lifespan than the current PCs. Users will be able to access the system from off campus with no loss of functionality. The launch of a self-service system for borrowers at the library has already doubled usage figures. The Students' Union was re-launched in 2013, when it relocated to the main campus building and restructured itself to have a greater focus on academic representation and meeting the needs of a diverse range of students. Extra social space for students and staff has been developed at the same time. The student bar and venue has been revamped and given a new location. The

---

Brownberrie Lane
Horsforth, Leeds LS18 5HD

0113 283 7150 (enquiries)
enquiries@leedstrinity.ac.uk
www.leedstrinity.ac.uk
www.ltsu.co.uk
Affiliation: GuildHE,
   Cathedrals Group

The Times and Sunday Times **Rankings**
Overall Ranking: **=91** (last year: 104)

Student satisfaction:	**=34**	83.4%
Research quality:	**=102**	1.7%
Entry standards:	**=109**	280
Student–staff ratio:	**=118**	23.6
Services & facilities/student:	**100**	£1,236
Expected completion rate:	**70**	84.8%
Good honours:	**109**	56.0%
Graduate prospects:	**=62**	65.8%

old Union building has been transformed into a modern teaching and learning block, creating two new lecture theatres with capacity for 100 in tiered seating, and five large classrooms with capacity of 40. A new Student Achievement Team offers one-to-one tutorials, group tutorials and seminars and workshops to promote academic skills.

There have also been significant educational developments. The launch of the Centre for Children, Young People and Families, for example, was a response to the reorganisation of those services in central and local government, offering learning opportunities through external partners. The new university's stated aim is to be an "autonomous teaching-led research-informed institution providing higher education characterised by vocational excellence". Results in the last Research Assessment Exercise were modest, but the university has a strong research tradition in certain areas. The flagship research centre, the Leeds Centre for Victorian Studies, celebrated its 20th anniversary in 2014.

Nearly two-thirds of the students are female and over three-quarters are school or college leavers, rather than mature students. Almost 60 per cent are the first in their family to attend university. Leeds Trinity exceeds all its national benchmarks for widening participation in higher education: more than 40 per cent of undergraduates come from working-class homes, while nearly a quarter are from areas with little tradition of sending students to university – one of the highest proportions in the country. The projected dropout rate has improved considerably and is now lower than the national average for Leeds Trinity's courses and entry qualifications. There are still little more than 3,000 students, despite recent growth. The new university was displaying high levels of student satisfaction well before its new status was conferred, and it recorded a further increase in 2014.

Leeds Trinity provides 575 residential places, most of which are reserved for first-year students. They include the £6-million All Saints Court development, which has almost 200 en-suite bedrooms. Sports facilities are good and include a new 3G pitch. The city is one of the most popular with students, although the campus is not central.

Undergraduate Fees and Bursaries

- » Fees for UK/EU students 2015–16 £9,000
- » Foundation degree £5,000
- » Fees for international students 2014–15 £9,500–£11,000
- » Household income below £25K, a bursary of £1,000 paid in year 2 only.
- » Enhanced hardship fund.
- » Range of other scholarships and bursaries available.
- » Check the university's website for the latest information.

Students

Undergraduates:	**2,575**	**(85)**
Postgraduates:	**180**	**(425)**
Mature students:	**13.2%**	
International students:	**1.9%**	
Applications per place:	**6.7**	
From state-sector schools:	**97.9%**	
From working-class homes:	**43.9%**	
Satisfaction with students' union	**63%**	

For detailed information about sports facilities:
www.leedstrinity.ac.uk/services/trinitysport/

Accommodation

Places and costs refer to 2014–15
University-provided places: 575
Percentage catered: 35%
Catered costs: £107–£115 a week (41 weeks).
Self-catered costs: £88–£113 a week (41 weeks).
Priority is given to first-year students.
International students: same as above.
accommodation@leedstrinity.ac.uk
www.leedstrinity.ac.uk/services/accommodation

University of Leicester

Leicester was founded as a memorial to the fallen of the First World War and it is playing a full part in the commemoration of the war's centenary. But it is a connection with a much earlier period that continues to thrust the university into the headlines. The discovery by its archaeologists of the body of Richard III buried under a car park in the city has raised the profile of the university like never before. Both applications and enrolments rose in 2013, as Leicester won a string of awards. Archaeology is one of a number of subjects in which the university excels and which have been keeping it in the top 20 in our league table. It is in the top 15 for staffing levels and in the top ten for spending on student facilities. The university has been trialling the use of social media to improve feedback in an attempt to increase the satisfaction levels recorded in the National Student Survey even more.

Leicester has shown the scale of its ambitions with a £1-billion development plan. The Queen opened the £32-million library in 2008, and another £16 million has been spent more recently on an award-winning students' union. A new £42-million Centre for Medicine will open in 2015, housing Social Care Education, Health Sciences and Psychology, as well as the Medical School. This major investment follows the opening of a £12.5-million cardiovascular research centre. Clinical medicine is taught at the city's three hospitals, but all other teaching and much of the residential accommodation is concentrated in a leafy suburb a mile from the city centre. The £32-million library has doubled the available space and brought the total number of workspaces to 1,500.

Little more than 10,000 full-time undergraduates are based on the main campus, but substantial postgraduate and distance learning programmes bring Leicester close to the size of other big city universities. The undergraduate population is the most socially diverse of any university in our top 20. Nearly nine out of ten undergraduates come from state schools and more than a quarter are from working-class homes. The university has recently introduced a number of employability initiatives, including a new undergraduate internship programme which promises to make up to 500 paid internships available each year. The refurbished students' union has won numerous design awards and was named as the NUS students' union of the year in 2013. It is the only union in the country to contain an O_2 Academy, which has hosted gigs from the likes of Kasabian and Noah and the Whale.

Leicester entered a much larger proportion of its academics than many of its peers in the 2008 Research Assessment

---

University Road
Leicester LE1 7RH

0116 252 5281 (admissions)
admissions@le.ac.uk
www.le.ac.uk
http://leicesterunion.com
Affiliation: none

The Times and Sunday Times Rankings

Overall Ranking: **20** (last year: 14)

Student satisfaction:	**39**	83.2%
Research quality:	**=38**	20.0%
Entry standards:	**37**	401
Student–staff ratio:	**14**	12.9
Services & facilities/student:	**9**	£2,384
Expected completion rate:	**22**	93.1%
Good honours:	**=18**	79.0%
Graduate prospects:	**36**	73.9%

Exercise, thereby depressing its scores but producing a big increase in research funding. The star performers were the nine entrants in museum studies, who produced the highest proportion of world-leading research in any subject at any UK university. The university also has a long-established reputation in space science, with Europe's largest university-based space research facility, including the £52-million National Space Centre. The genetics department, where DNA genetic fingerprinting was discovered, has helped make Leicester's academics among the most cited in Britain. The university believes in blending teaching and research: it was the only institution to see three of its academics awarded National Teaching Fellowships in 2014, adding to an already impressive total.

Extensive residential accommodation includes a £21-million 600-bed en-suite development. The university has over 4,000 student bed spaces so first years are guaranteed a residential place. New facilities at Oadby Student Village being added over the summer of 2014 include group study areas, social spaces, cinema room and a refurbished bar. Many second- and third-year students also live in hall, although the majority choose to live in the reasonably priced private accommodation available nearby. The main sports facilities are conveniently located: in 2014–15, students will pay as little as £115 a year to use them.

As a city, Leicester is not one of the most fashionable student destinations, but its ethnic diversity makes for a rich cultural experience and in term time 12 per cent of the population are students. It is big enough to provide all the normal sports and entertainment opportunities, but also offers events such as the biggest Diwali celebrations outside India. The Demos Bohemian index rated Leicester the second most creative city in Britain behind London, and Birmingham is also easily accessible via public transport.

Undergraduate Fees and Bursaries

» Fees for UK/EU students 2015–16	£9,000
» Placement year	£1,000
» Fees for international students 2014–15	£13,395–£16,525
Medicine	£16,525–£33,655

» Household income below £25K or completed approved Compact Scheme, a bursary of £1,000 a year.
» Academic scholarship of £1,000 fee waiver for those with specified A level (or equivalent) grades.
» Enhanced student hardship fund.
» Range of other scholarships and bursaries available.
» Check the university's website for the latest information.

Students

Undergraduates:	9,965	(920)
Postgraduates:	3,660	(2,615)
Mature students:	15.1%	
International students:	20.7%	
Applications per place:	6.3	
From state-sector schools:	89.5%	
From working-class homes:	26.2%	
Satisfaction with students' union	76%	

For detailed information about sports facilities:
www.le.ac.uk/sports

Accommodation

Number of places and costs refer to 2014–15
University-provided places: 4,313
Percentage catered: 26%
Catered costs: £127.40–£227.50 a week (30 weeks).
Self-catered costs: £79.10–£179.20 (39-42 weeks).
First-year students are guaranteed accommodation if conditions are met.
International students: as above.
www2.le.ac.uk/offices/accommodation

University of Lincoln

Lincoln enjoyed a huge (24 per cent) rise in applications in 2013 after two years in which the university went up more than any other in our league table. It settled for a much more modest increase in enrolments but, since it is now among the top ten post-1992 universities and close to the top 50 overall, the demand for places is likely to remain high. The impressive purpose-built campus alongside a marina in the city centre that opened in 1996 is a major attraction: Lincoln markets itself as "the modern university in a historic setting". The university had been based in Hull until the early 1990s and had a double location for a time, but has now moved out of Humberside completely. In most respects, it has never looked back since moving to its Brayford Pool campus, where £150 million has been invested in top-class facilities. Lincoln has been able to attract high-quality academics and raise its admission requirements while also growing in size.

The most recent addition to the campus is the £11-million Art and Design Building, which opened in 2013. The £7-million Engineering Hub, built in collaboration with Siemens and emda, was the UK's first purpose-built engineering school in 25 years and won the Lord Stafford Award for Open Collaboration. The university has planning permission for considerable further development over the next ten years. It is now working with the Lincolnshire Co-operative on a £14-million Science and Innovation Park on an 11-acre site alongside the main campus. As well as housing local firms, it will be the base for the university's new Schools of Pharmacy and Chemistry, as well as for students from the School of Life Sciences.

New science laboratories, sports facilities, a school of architecture, a library in a converted warehouse and a students' union and entertainment venue in a former railway engine shed were previous developments. A £6-million performing arts centre contains a 450-seat theatre and three large studio spaces, while the Human Performance Centre is a regional facility for excellence in sport, coaching and exercise science. In addition, the Lincoln Business School has its own building and there is a thriving business incubation unit. A one-stop-shop provides students with careers advice, enhances their CVs, helps them to gain work experience and find jobs, as well as supporting graduates who are setting up their own businesses. The university expanded its graduate internship scheme and launched a new summer placement programme in 2011.

Lincoln initially concentrated on social sciences, but the university now has a much wider range of courses. The School of Architecture, for example, has over 400

Brayford Pool
Lincoln LN6 7TS

01522 886644 (enquiries)
contact via website
www.lincoln.ac.uk
http://lincolnsu.com
Affiliation: University
   Alliance

The Times and Sunday Times Rankings
Overall Ranking: **60** (last year: =57)

Student satisfaction:	=48	82.9%
Research quality:	=63	5.0%
Entry standards:	61	338
Student–staff ratio:	=75	18.6
Services & facilities/student:	70	£1,450
Expected completion rate:	=48	87.6%
Good honours:	105	57.9%
Graduate prospects:	=55	67.6%

students. Science provision has expanded considerably, with pharmacy, chemistry and zoology recent additions. New courses in mathematics and physics are also on the way. Animal behaviour and welfare courses are at the Riseholme Campus, a 1,000-acre site ten minutes outside Lincoln. Riseholme was chosen as one of the training centres for equine events ahead of the 2012 Olympic Games.

The university entered more of its academics for the last Research Assessment Exercise than many institutions in its peer group and still improved on previous grades, achieving a sizeable increase in research income as a result. Lincoln has also had successes in applied research and knowledge transfer, notably with the National Centre for Food Manufacturing, based in Holbeach, which specialises in the production of chilled foods.

Lincoln heads up the innovative Student as Producer project, funded by the Higher Education Academy to investigate and promote student involvement in research right from the start of their studies. The university is committed to research-engaged teaching across its curriculum, and encourages undergraduates to work with postgraduates and academic staff on research projects. Some degrees can be taken as work-based programmes, with credit awarded for relevant aspects of the jobs. Lincoln was the first university to win a Charter Mark for exceptional service. In its most recent Quality Assurance Agency review, the university was commended for the innovative ways in which it gives its students a voice.

More than a third of the undergraduates come from working-class homes and the improved dropout rate of less than 10 per cent is below the average for the subjects on offer, given the entry standards. The city is adapting to its student population with new bars and clubs, although the social scene there is not the prime draw for students. The campus now has more than 1,200 beds, while private developments close to the university now provide well over 3,500 further residential places.

Undergraduate Fees and Bursaries

» Fees for UK/EU students 2015–16   £9,000
» Placement year / year abroad   no fee
» Fees for international students 2014–15   £11,798–£13,648
» Household income below £25K, bursary of £700 a year; household income £25K–£40K, £450 a year.
» Scholarships and bursaries for local students, sports, engineering and care leavers.
» Enhanced student hardship fund..
» Check the university's website for the latest information.

Students

Undergraduates:	**8,870**	**(1,825)**
Postgraduates:	**825**	**(1,200)**
Mature students:	**11.8%**	
International students:	**5.2%**	
Applications per place:	**5**	
From state-sector schools:	**97.4%**	
From working-class homes:	**37.5%**	
Satisfaction with students' union	**74%**	

For detailed information about sports facilities:
www.lincoln.ac.uk/home/campuslife/sportatlincoln

Accommodation

Number of places and costs refer to 2014–15
University-provided places: 1,200
Percentage catered: 0%
Self-catered costs: £90–£130 a week.
First years guaranteed accommodation if they confirm Lincoln as their first choice by 30 June 2015.
International students are given detailed information and assistance.
accommodation@lincoln.ac.uk
www.lincoln.ac.uk/home/accommodation/

University of Liverpool

Liverpool compensated to some extent for a big fall in new enrolments when £9,000 fees were introduced by taking an additional 450 undergraduates in 2013. The demand for places had been growing and appears to be doing so again now. The university is investing £600 million in its campus, as well as extending its reach beyond its home city. There is a joint venture in China, which will have 10,000 students by 2015, and it has added a postgraduate site in the City of London for professional courses. The 10-year development plan for the main campus has already provided new and upgraded teaching and research facilities, as well as improved leisure facilities and more student accommodation. New teaching laboratories for the sciences are said to be Europe's most advanced. The university is also spending £70 million on interdisciplinary research facilities for the health and life sciences that will bring together more than 600 scientists to focus on the major health challenges of the 21st century. The management school has been extended and the Guild of Students building refurbished. Other new developments include major improvements in student social space and a £4-million investment in sports facilities.

A major beneficiary of recent investment has been the university's library, which offers 24-hour access following a £17-million redevelopment. More than half of the work submitted for the last Research Assessment Exercise was judged to be world-leading or internationally excellent. The university focuses on interdisciplinary research wherever possible.

The university is committing nearly 30 per cent of its additional fee income to support for students from lower-income backgrounds and enhanced measures to prevent students from dropping out. More than a quarter of new undergraduates qualify for a support package totalling £2,000 a year for the duration of their course. The 5 per cent projected dropout rate is significantly better than average for Liverpool's subjects and entry grades. The proportion of undergraduates from working-class homes is among the highest in the Russell Group of leading research-based universities, although still slightly less than the national average for the courses and entry qualifications.

Liverpool's Chinese initiative began in 2006 with the opening of a new university in the historic city of Suzhou in partnership with Xi'an Jiaotong University. Chinese students can complete the latter part of their studies in Liverpool, while Liverpool-based students are offered work experience at Suzhou Industrial Park, which is home to 84 "Fortune 500" companies. Students

---

Liverpool L69 3BX

0151 794 5927 (enquiries)
contact via website
www.liv.ac.uk
www.liverpoolguild.org
Affiliation: Russell Group

The Times and Sunday Times Rankings
Overall Ranking: **36** (last year: 36)

Student satisfaction:	=91	79.8%
Research quality:	=38	20.0%
Entry standards:	32	414
Student–staff ratio:	12	12.7
Services & facilities/student:	20	£2,134
Expected completion rate:	=23	92.5%
Good honours:	27	76.8%
Graduate prospects:	39	72.7%

in electrical engineering and electronics, computer science and maths have the opportunity to spend a year studying in China. All staff and students across the university can take a course in Mandarin for £10. Liverpool is involved in further collaborations with universities in Chile, Mexico and Spain that will allow students to complete part of their degree at one or more of these institutions via a range of options such as projects or placements. The university intends not only to increase the number of students who study abroad, but also to expand the availability of courses for those who may not be able to travel. It is already the largest provider of online postgraduate courses in Europe, with some 10,000 students taking Liverpool degrees all around the world.

On the main campus, in Liverpool, the university has one of Europe's largest facilities for training dentists. There has also been substantial investment in new educational technology. But by far the biggest spending programme, totalling some £250 million, is devoted to student accommodation. A 710-bedroom development, featuring shops and a restaurant, opened on the city-centre campus in 2012. The university's off-campus accommodation is being refurbished and another 1,500 study bedrooms will open on the main campus in time for the 2014 intake. New residences will also be built at the Greenbank site, at suburban Mossley Hill, to provide a self-contained student village.

The Guild of Students is the centre of campus social activity. The university's indoor and outdoor sports facilities have been refurbished at a cost of £4.5-million and a new gym has opened at the Greenbank Halls site. A new 25-metre swimming pool is open to the public as well as students. The university has one of the largest careers resources centres in the UK and has introduced an innovative programme of "boot camps" giving new graduates opportunities for networking with employers while developing a range of employability skills. More than £2 million is being invested in student and graduate internships, most of them paid and lasting for substantial periods.

Undergraduate Fees and Bursaries

» Fees for UK/EU students 2015–16	£9,000
» Foundation year at partner colleges	£5,000
» Placement year	£1,800
» Year abroad	£1,350
» Fees for international students 2015–16	£13,400–£16,800
(fixed for length of course)	
Medicine, dentistry and veterinary medicine	£29,950
» Household income below £25K, a bursary of £2,000 a year; household income £25K–£42.6K, £1,000 a year.	
» Other scholarships and bursaries are available.	
» Check the university's website for the latest information.	

Students

Undergraduates:	**15,775**	**(445)**
Postgraduates:	**3,025**	**(1,630)**
Mature students:	**11.6%**	
International students:	**21%**	
Applications per place:	**8.3**	
From state-sector schools:	**87.3%**	
From working-class homes:	**24.4%**	
Satisfaction with students' union	**48%**	

For detailed information about sports facilities:
www.liv.ac.uk/sports

Accommodation

Number of places and costs refer to 2014–15
University-provided places: 4,055
Percentage catered: 53%
Catered costs: £131.25–£192.85 a week.
Self-catered costs: £115.85–£148.75 a week.
First-year students are guaranteed accommodation if Liverpool is their first choice and requirements are met.
International students: as above and must apply by 31 July.
accommodation@liverpool.ac.uk
www.liv.ac.uk/accommodation

Liverpool Hope University

Liverpool Hope continues to opt out of league tables after finishing at the bottom of the table on its only appearance in *The Times Good University Guide*. The university believes that the criteria used in league tables are biased in favour of wealthier institutions with a longer history, although it insists that its objections "can't be summed up in one sentence". Hope had enjoyed big increases in applications before a substantial drop when the fees went up to £8,250 in 2012. This was followed by further declines in both applications and enrolments in the following year. Home and EU undergraduates will pay £9,000 in 2015–16. For students from low-income families, there will be scholarships for academic achievement and for national level involvement in sport, music, dance and drama.

Hope is a unique ecumenical institution formed from the merger of two Catholic and one Church of England teacher training colleges in 1980. A university since 2005, it describes itself as "teaching led, research informed and mission focused" and includes "taking faith seriously" among its five key values. The university opened its own joint Church of England and Roman Catholic academy in September 2011, replacing two comprehensive schools. There are also partnerships with the Royal Liverpool Philharmonic Orchestra, Liverpool Tate and the National Museums Liverpool to develop cultural programmes and new curricular areas such as art history and curating. The university made Frank Cottrell Boyce, a scriptwriter for the opening ceremony in the 2012 Olympics, the first Professor of Reading in the UK.

Most students opt for combined subject degrees, choosing after the first year whether to give them equal weight or to go for a major/minor arrangement. Hope is moving away from modular degrees to an "integrated undergraduate curriculum" in order to give students a more rounded view of their subject. The university has increased its national recruitment profile, with nearly 60 per cent of students now coming from beyond Merseyside. Hope undergraduates can register for the Service and Leadership Award, which is credit-rated and runs alongside their degree work. Students can volunteer locally, within the region or internationally as part of Global Hope, the university's award winning overseas charity.

Nearly 20 per cent of the undergraduates are over 20 on entry and female students outnumber their male counterparts by more than two to one. Hope comfortably exceeds all the official benchmarks for widening participation in higher education. Almost all the undergraduates are state educated, over 40 per cent are from working-class families

Hope Park
Liverpool L16 9JD

0151 291 3111 (enquiries)
enquiry@hope.ac.uk
www.hope.ac.uk
www.hopesu.com
Affiliation: Cathedrals
 Group

The Times and Sunday Times Rankings

Liverpool Hope blocked the release of data from the Higher Education Statistics Agency and so we cannot give any ranking information.

and more than one in five is from an area with little tradition of higher education – one of the highest proportions in England. The Network of Hope brings university courses to sixth-form colleges across the northwest of England, in areas where there is limited higher education. The projected dropout rate has improved and remains below average for the university's courses and entry qualifications.

The university is concentrated on two sites in Liverpool, and there is a residential outdoor education centre in Snowdonia, North Wales. The main campus – Hope Park – is three miles from the city centre in the suburb of Childwall, while the creative and performing arts are based at the more central Creative campus in Everton, where a performance centre houses one of only three Steinway Schools in England, as well as practice rooms, recording spaces and a theatre. The £5-million main library, on the Hope campus, has 270,000 items and 700 study spaces, with electronic access from other sites. More than a quarter of the academics were entered for the 2008 Research Assessment Exercise – a higher proportion than at most comparable institutions – when theology was the top scorer. There is a research partnership with Sun Yat-Sen University, in China, and study abroad opportunities in Europe, North America and Asia.

Recent campus developments have included a Centre for Education and Enterprise, which supports local business and hosts the Faculty of Education. More than £1 million has been spent on a new food court and a library and reading room on the Creative campus, with a Renaissance-style garden which includes an outdoor performance area. "Our Place", which opened in 2012, includes student dining and social facilities, as well as a new auditorium where comedy nights and live music events are held. The university has its own radio station. Sports facilities have been improving and there is a range of residential accommodation, some of it provided by a private firm. Places are guaranteed for first years who apply before Clearing.

Undergraduate Fees and Bursaries

» Fees for UK/EU students 2015–16   £9,000
» Fees for international students 2014–15   £10,800
» Enhanced student hardship fund.
» Range of other scholarships and bursaries available.
» Check the university's website for the latest information.

Students

Undergraduates:	**4,480**	**(395)**
Postgraduates:	**725**	**(940)**
From state-sector schools:	**99.1%**	
From working-class homes:	**42.5%**	
Satisfaction with students' union	**54%**	

For detailed information about sports facilities:
www.hope.ac.uk/hopeparksports

Accommodation

Number of places and costs refer to 2014–15
University-provided places: 1,111
Percentage catered: 0% (catering packages an optional extra)
Self-catered costs: £80–£87 (shared); £100–£123 (en suite) a week.
First years are guaranteed accommodation if Liverpool Hope is their first choice and they apply before Clearing.
International students: rooms are available at specific locations, depending on course
accommodation@hope.ac.uk
www.hope.ac.uk/lifeathope/residentiallife

Liverpool John Moores University (LJMU)

Liverpool John Moores attracted a record number of new undergraduates in 2013, taking it back to the levels of enrolment it enjoyed before the fees went up to £9,000 and prompted a sharp decline. The biggest draw for prospective students is the prizewinning World of Work (WoW) initiative, which ensures that every degree includes opportunities for work-related learning both on and off campus and encourages all undergraduates to become expert in eight transferable skills, applicable to a wide range of careers. The programme has been shaped and steered by leading companies and business organisations. More than 150 local employers have been trained as WoW skills verifiers, working with LJMU to deliver graduate-entry-level interviews. The Centre for Entrepreneurship supports students and graduates who want to start up in business, become self-employed or work freelance, as well as working closely with programme teams to provide enterprise education through the curriculum.

Naming itself after a football pools millionaire set a pattern of innovation for LJMU. Early examples included the original student charter and the first degrees in sports science and criminal justice, as well as the first distance learning degree in astronomy. It has invested £180 million over the last ten years to transform its three campuses. Developments include the award-winning John Lennon Art and Design Building and the £25.5-million life sciences building, opened by Liverpool footballer and LJMU honorary fellow Steven Gerrard, where the world-class facilities include an indoor 70-metre running track and labs for testing cardiovascular ability, motor skills and biomechanics functions. A new £37.6-million Redmonds Building now houses Liverpool Screen School, the Faculty of Business and Law, and industry-standard TV and radio studios. There is a learning resource centre on each of the three campuses, two of which are open 24 hours a day, seven days a week during semesters. The university's virtual learning environment, Blackboard, enables students to access most teaching materials and a range of other support features online.

Mainly concentrated in an area between Liverpool's two cathedrals, the university now has 22,500 students in the city and another 4,500 taking LJMU courses overseas. Arts, technology and science courses occupy separate sites within easy reach of the city centre, with the IM Marsh campus three miles away for education and community studies. Nearly half of the students are drawn from the Merseyside area. A growing research reputation is a

Roscoe Court
4 Rodney Street
Liverpool L1 2TZ

0151 231 5090 (course enquiries)
courses@ljmu.ac.uk (enquiries)
www.ljmu.ac.uk
www.liverpoolsu.com
Affiliation: University Alliance

The Times and Sunday Times Rankings

Overall Ranking: **71** (last year: 83)

Student satisfaction:	=51	82.8%
Research quality:	=76	3.7%
Entry standards:	=63	336
Student–staff ratio:	87	19.7
Services & facilities/student:	93	£1,308
Expected completion rate:	74	84.4%
Good honours:	=45	70.6%
Graduate prospects:	79	61.5%

source of particular pride. A third of the research assessed in 2008 was rated as world-leading or internationally excellent. LJMU was among the top four of post-92 universities for electrical and electronic engineering, general engineering, sports-related studies, architecture and built environment, anthropology, physics, biological sciences, and computer sciences and informatics. A £1.6-million maritime centre features the UK's most advanced 360-degree ship-handling simulator and there is a sophisticated robotic telescope in La Palma, in the Canaries for the astronomers.

The university's efforts to extend access to higher education are successful: almost all the undergraduates are state-educated and 42 per cent – a big increase on last year – are from working-class homes. Among the scholarships and bursaries introduced to offset the impact of higher fees are the John Lennon Imagine Awards, match-funded through a gift of £260,000 from Yoko Ono, which help students who have either been in local authority care or who are estranged from their parents. LJMU is also the highest ranking university in the Stonewall index of Britain's best employers for lesbian, gay and bisexual staff. The university has a wide range of disability support services and continues to improve its dropout rate, which is now better than the national average for the university's courses and entry grades. An assessment room is available for students with disabilities and requiring additional support to test out a range of furniture, equipment and technologies based on their own specific needs.

Student facilities have been improving. The university has partnerships with a range of private accommodation providers so that all new students are guaranteed accommodation if they require it. Liverpool is now ranked in the ten best cities in the world to visit by Rough Guides and is also one of the most affordable student cities in the UK. Links with a range of cultural organisations give students free access to art exhibitions and orchestral performances, and discounted theatre tickets. They also have free off-peak access to 12 Lifestyles Fitness Centres across the city. Sports facilities include an Olympic-sized swimming pool, two golf courses, fitness suites and weights rooms and all-weather football pitches.

Undergraduate Fees and Bursaries

» Fees for UK/EU students 2015–16   £9,000
» STEM Foundation year   £6,000
» Placement year   £975
» Fees for international students 2014–15   £11,000–£12,000
» Household income below £25K, a bursary of £500 a year (excluding Foundation year).
» Further academic, sports and care leaver's awards including six Vice Chancellor's Scholarships of £10,000 a year.
» Enhanced student hardship fund.

Students

Undergraduates:	**16,710**	**(2,390)**
Postgraduates:	**1,375**	**(2,110)**
Mature students:	**18.6%**	
International students:	**7.7%**	
Applications per place:	**5.2**	
From state-sector schools:	**97.7%**	
From working-class homes:	**42.0%**	
Satisfaction with students' union	**58%**	

For detailed information about sports facilities:
www.ljmu.ac.uk/sport

Accommodation

Number of places and costs refer to 2014–15
University-provided places: 3,800 plus 15,000 through Liverpool Student Homes.
Percentage catered: 0%
Self-catered costs: £86–£127 a week.
All new students are guaranteed a place in university approved housing, even if applying through Clearing.
International students: as above.
accommodation@ljmu.ac.uk
www.ljmu.ac.uk/accommodation

University of London

The federal university is by far Britain's biggest conventional higher education institution, with more than 120,000 students. The majority study at colleges in the capital, but such is the global prestige of the university's degrees that over 50,000 students in 180 different countries take University of London International Programmes.

The university, which celebrated its 175th anniversary in 2011, consists of 18 self-governing colleges, the Institute in Paris and the School of Advanced Study, which comprises ten specialist institutes for research and postgraduate education (details at **www. sas.ac.uk**). The members include some of the most famous names in UK higher education, although Imperial College left in 2007. The university's students have access to joint residential accommodation, sporting facilities and the University of London Union, but most identify with their college.

Other prestigious colleges have considered following Imperial in going their own way and applied for their own degree-awarding powers to hold in reserve, but they remain bound together by the London degree. Reforms to the university's governance have given the colleges more autonomy and look to have staved off further departures for now.

The following colleges – some of which have dropped the word from their title to underline their university status – have separate entries in this chapter. Each also appears in the main university league table, with the exception of Birkbeck, whose overwhelmingly part-time provision does not lend itself to a full comparison on the measures used in our *Guide*.

» Birkbeck College
» Goldsmiths, University of London
» King's College London
» London School of Economics and Political Science
» Queen Mary, University of London
» Royal Holloway
» SOAS London
» University College London

Many of London's teaching hospitals have now merged with colleges of the university:

» King's College London now incorporates Guys and St Thomas's.
» Queen Mary now incorporates St Bartholomew's and the Royal London School of Medicine and Dentistry.
» University College London now incorporates the Royal Free Hospital Medical School and the Eastman Dental Hospital.

The School of Slavonic and Eastern European Studies and the School of Pharmacy are both now part of University College London. The Institute of Education is discussing merging with UCL by the end of 2014.

Senate House
Malet Street
London WC1E 7HU

020 7862 8360
contact via website
www.london.ac.uk
www.ulu.co.uk

Enquiries: to individual colleges, institutes or schools.

Nine colleges (and the Institute in Paris) do not have separate entries in the *Guide*. These are listed below, with postal, telephone and electronic contacts.

Courtauld Institute of Art

Somerset House, Strand
London WC2R 0RN
020 7848 2645 (admissions)
ugadmissions@courtauld.ac.uk
www.courtauld.ac.uk
155 undergraduates. History of art degree.
Undergraduate fee £9,000.

Heythrop College

Kensington Square, London W8 5HN
020 7795 6600 (switchboard)
admissions@heythrop.ac.uk
www.heythrop.ac.uk
505 undergraduates. Degrees in theology and philosophy.
Undergraduate fees £9,000.

Institute of Education

20 Bedford Way, London WC1H 0AL
020 7612 6000 (switchboard)
info@ioe.ac.uk
www. ioe.ac.uk
Mainly postgraduate education courses;
270 undergraduates.
Undergraduate fees £7,200–£9,000.

London Business School

Regent's Park, London NW1 4SA
020 7000 7000 (switchboard)
webenquiries@london.edu
www.london.edu
Postgraduate MBA and other courses.

London School of Hygiene and Tropical Medicine

Keppel Street, London WC1E 7HT
020 7299 4646 (admission enquiries)
registry@lshtm.ac.uk
www.lshtm.ac.uk
Postgraduate medical courses.

Royal Academy of Music

Marylebone Road, London NW1 5HT
020 7873 7393 (registry)
registry@ram.ac.uk
www.ram.ac.uk
325 undergraduates. Degrees in music.
Undergraduate fees £9,000.

Royal Central School of Speech and Drama

Eton Avenue , London NW3 3HY
020 7722 8183 (undergraduate admissions)
enquiries@cssd.ac.uk
www.cssd.ac.uk
660 undergraduates. Acting and theatre practice.
Undergraduate fees £9,000.

Royal Veterinary College

Royal College Street, London NW1 0TU
020 7468 5147 (undergraduate admissions)
enquiries@rvc.ac.uk
www. rvc.ac.uk
1,605 undergraduates. Degrees in veterinary medicine.
Undergraduate fees £9,000.

St George's, University of London

Cranmer Terrace, London SW17 0RE
020 8725 2333 (admissions)
contact via website
www.sgul.ac.uk
4,515 undergraduates. Degrees in medicine.
Undergraduate fees £9,000;
Foundation degree £9,000.

University of London Institute in Paris

9–11 rue de Constantine
75340 Paris Cedex 07, France
(+33) 1 44 11 73 83
french@ulip.lon.ac.uk
www.ulip.lon.ac.uk
Degrees offered in conjunction with Queen Mary and Royal Holloway colleges.

London Metropolitan University

London Met has survived a tumultuous period during which it was stripped of the right to recruit international students and its intake of new undergraduates dropped by more than 40 per cent. Applications continued to fall in 2013, but the university was able to take an additional 200 undergraduates and produce a surplus of £2 million. It had already reduced the number of courses from more than 550 to fewer than 200 to address previous financial difficulties. All degree courses will cost UK and EU students £9,000 in 2015–16, but much lower fees for Foundation degrees taught at partner colleges will bring the average down to £8,112. In contrast to many other universities, London Met is increasing the size of its bursaries for students from poor backgrounds in 2015. The university has always catered particularly for groups who are under-represented at traditional universities. More than a third of the students are Afro-Caribbean, and the proportion of mature students is among the highest in England. More than half of the UK undergraduates come from working-class homes, far above the average for the courses and entry qualifications.

London Met was the product of the merger of London Guildhall and North London universities in 2002. The university's sites are centred on the City of London and the capital's Holloway Road, where there is a Graduate Centre designed by Daniel Libeskind. The university has strong business links, especially in London's "Tech City", where the university has a business accelerator which attracted a visit from Australia's Communications Minister. London Met was the first university in the UK to implement IBM Academic Skills Cloud to enhance the development of workplace skills. Its graduates had the highest average starting salaries in the country in 2013. The university's roots go back to 1848, with the Metropolitan Evening Classes for Working Men, and there is still a strong part-time programme. The Business School is one of Europe's largest, with almost 10,000 students.

Undergraduates take year-long modules consisting of 30 weeks of timetabled teaching. Over a year, students will typically study four modules worth 30 credits each and receive a minimum of 60 teaching hours per module. The university is in the top ten for the amount of supervised teaching time and expects first-year students to have 12 hours of teaching a week, giving the maximum possible opportunity for development and guidance. Student support services, from admission to careers

---

166–220 Holloway Road
London N7 8DB

020 7133 4200 (enquiries)
admissions@londonmet.ac.uk
www.londonmet.ac.uk
www.londonmetsu.org.uk
Affiliation: million+

advice, have been remodelled and there is a particular emphasis on academic and pastoral counselling on entry and at other key points of courses. However, the projected dropout rate of 28 per cent is now the highest in England by some distance. The university administration promised a "renewed focus on student satisfaction and the quality of student learning" following a succession of low scores in the National Student Survey.

There has been increased investment in the campus, with more study zones and a £13.5-million refurbishment programme, which has seen major improvements to the Faculty of Business and Law building at Moorgate and in The Cass Faculty of Art and Design, at Aldgate. A newsroom for journalism students opened in 2012 and the refurbished library on the Holloway Road site has more computers, informal learning spaces, technobooths and teaching rooms, as well as a café. The £30-million Science Centre features a "superlab" with 280 workstations, specialist laboratories for tissue culture research and microbiology, and a nuclear-magnetic resonance room. The biomedical sciences degree leads on to an MD course from the University of Health Studies in Antigua. The six-year programme is based in London and graduates will complete the United States Medical Licensing Examination, enabling them to practise in America.

London Met entered more academics than most former polytechnics in the 2008 Research Assessment Exercise, when almost a quarter of its work was placed in the top two categories. About half of the 21 subject areas contained some world-leading research.

There is a new headquarters for the students' union on the Aldgate site to add to the well-used building on Holloway Road. The university has also been working hard to reduce its carbon footprint and is among the top five universities on this measure. Residential accommodation is limited, but many of London Met's students live at home. There are nine fitness centres, as well as other sports facilities. The competitive teams are successful and the social scene is lively, particularly in north London.

Undergraduate Fees and Bursaries

» Fees for UK/EU students 2015–16	£9,000
» Foundation degree at partner colleges	£5,860
» Fees for international students 2014–15	£10,000
» Household income below £25K, a bursary of £1,000 a year.	
» Progression bursary of £1,000 for students on Extended degree / year 0 courses who progress to year 1.	
» Range of other scholarships and bursaries available.	
» Check the university's website for the latest information.	

Students

Undergraduates:	**12,355**	**(1,935)**
Postgraduates:	**1,920**	**(1,895)**
Mature students:	**55.1%**	
International students:	**14.3%**	
Applications per place:	**4.3**	
From state-sector schools:	**97.2%**	
From working-class homes:	**51.2%**	
Satisfaction with students' union	**51%**	

For detailed information about sports facilities:
www.londonmet.ac.uk/services/sport-and-recreation/

Accommodation

Number of places and costs refer to 2014–15

University-provided places: Students have access to housing in a wide range of halls of residences provided by specialist student accommodation providers.

Percentage catered: 0%

Self-catered costs: approximately £130–£411 a week.

The university cannot guarantee a place in halls.

International students: as above.

www.londonmet.ac.uk/services/studentservices/advice-and-well-being/accommodation/

London School of Economics and Political Science (LSE)

Always among the leading universities in the world for the social sciences, the LSE has been hemmed in by its cramped estate around London's Aldwych. It once considered moving to Canary Wharf or across the river to County Hall, but now the school is developing its original site. It opened its first new building for more than 40 years, the Saw Swee Hock Student Centre (SAW), in January 2014. SAW, which is the Royal Institute of British Architects' London Building of the Year, houses the students' union, as well as the careers and accommodation services and a multi-faith prayer centre. Now the school is spending £90 million on Global Centre for Social Sciences, which will involve the redevelopment of a number of existing buildings. It had already improved and extended the teaching space considerably in 2008 and added converted Government buildings near the campus in 2013.

The LSE, which is seldom out of the top three in our league table, had 12 applicants to the place in 2013 – more than any other university in the UK. It is expanding the number of undergraduate places over a four-year period, but will remain highly selective. Areas of study range more broadly than the School's name suggests: the 250 undergraduate courses range as far as law, management, mathematics and environmental policy. Two new degrees are introduced in 2015: a four-year BSc in philosophy, politics and economics (PPE) and a three-year BSc in politics and international relations. Only Cambridge recorded higher average scores than the LSE in the last Research Assessment Exercise, which saw almost 70 per cent of the school's submission rated world-leading or internationally excellent. Ninety-five per cent of the economics submission, 80 per cent in social policy and 75 per cent in law reached the top two categories.

The school has a long history of political involvement, from its foundation by Beatrice and Sidney Webb, pioneers of the Fabian movement, to the 31 alumni who are MPs and 42 current members of the House of Lords. The tradition lives on, not only among the academics, but in a students' union which claims to be the only one in Britain to hold weekly general meetings at which every student may attend and vote. The campus has a cosmopolitan feel that derives from the highest proportion of overseas students at any publicly funded university. More than 30 past or present heads of state have either been students at, or taught at, the university, as have 16 Nobel prizewinners in economics, literature and peace – including George Bernard Shaw,

Houghton Street
London WC2A 2AE

020 7955 7125 (admissions)
contact via website
www.lse.ac.uk
www.lsesu.com
Affiliation: Russell Group

Edinburgh
Belfast
Cardiff
LONDON

The Times and Sunday Times **Rankings**
Overall Ranking: **5** (last year: 3)

Student satisfaction:	=108	78.3%
Research quality:	3	38.7%
Entry standards:	4	537
Student–staff ratio:	=8	11.8
Services & facilities/student:	10	£2,381
Expected completion rate:	6	96.3%
Good honours:	17	79.3%
Graduate prospects:	5	83.4%

Bertrand Russell, Friedrich von Hayek and Amartya Sen. The latest of them was Professor Christopher Pissarides, who shared the prize for economics in 2010.

Its international character not only gives the LSE global prestige but also an unusual degree of financial independence: only a small proportion of its funding comes from Government sources. Almost 30 per cent of the British undergraduates are from independent schools, almost ten percentage points more than the national average for the LSE's subjects and entry qualifications. Substantial efforts are being made to attract a broader intake: the school is spending half of its additional fee income on student support and other activities to widen participation – a bigger proportion than any other university. The LSE is one of 12 universities selected to deliver the Sutton Trust's Pathways to Law programme, giving state school students from non-privileged backgrounds the opportunity to sample a specialised legal programme before choosing a degree. The LSE's projected dropout rate of less than 4 per cent is among the lowest at any university.

The 2001 Norman Foster-designed redevelopment of the Lionel Robbins Building houses a much-improved library. The move was a welcome one since the number of books borrowed by LSE students is more than four times the national average, according to one survey.

Routes between most of the buildings have been pedestrianised, in keeping with a commitment to green issues that has seen the School in the top echelons of the People and Planet Green League of universities' environmental performance for five years in a row.

Partying is not the prime attraction of the LSE for most applicants, who tend to be serious about their subject, but London's top nightspots are on the doorstep for those who can afford them. The 3,700 residential places for 9,500 full-time students offer a good chance of avoiding central London's notoriously high private sector rents; there are spaces in hall for all first year undergraduates who want them.

Undergraduate Fees and Bursaries

» Fees for UK/EU students 2015–16 £9,000
» Year abroad £1,350
» Fees for international students 2014–15 £16,392
» For UK students, annual bursary of £4,000 for those with household income below £18K decreasing in 5 bands to £750 for household income £40K–£42.6K.
» Range of specific scholarships available.
» 2 awards for asylum seekers of £9,000 fee waiver and up to £11,000 bursary for each year.
» Check the university's website for the latest information.

Students			Accommodation
Undergraduates:	**3,900**	**(70)**	Number of places and costs refer to 2014–15
Postgraduates:	**5,390**	**(585)**	University-provided places: 3,740
Mature students:	**3.2%**		Percentage catered: about 38%
International students:	**44.5%**		Catered costs: £100.80–£220.85 a week (31 or 40 weeks).
Applications per place:	**12.1**		Self-catered costs: £91.70–£488.95 a week (40 or 50 weeks).
From state-sector schools:	**70.9%**		First-year undergraduates are guaranteed an offer of
From working-class homes:	**20%**		accommodation.
Satisfaction with students' union	**58%**		Policy for international students: same as above.
For detailed information about sports facilities:			accommodation@lse.ac.uk
www.lsesu.com/activities/ausports/			www.lse.ac.uk/lifeAtLSE/accommodation/home.aspx

London South Bank University

London South Bank (LSBU) hopes to benefit from the £3-billion regeneration of the Elephant and Castle area on its doorstep. But the new Vice-Chancellor, Professor David Phoenix, is not waiting for that to make changes that he hopes will make the university more attractive to students and more successful with business and industry. New undergraduate enrolments have dropped for three years in succession, although applications were up in 2013. The first step has been to turn the four faculties into seven academic schools to create their own brands and become more active. He also wants more students to spend part of their course in industry and he plans to create more of a campus feel by knitting together the university's various buildings with more green spaces. LSBU has already invested over £50 million in modern teaching facilities and developments costing another £38 million are planned. The latest major project upgraded the university's digital facilities at a cost of £14 million.

Students are attracted by the carefully tailored programme of vocational courses that regularly produce the best-paid graduates of any post-1992 university. But about half of them are 21 or over on entry,

the group that has seen the biggest drop in applications nationally. Three-quarters of the students are from the capital and more than half are drawn from ethnic minorities. Of about 15,000 undergraduates, a third study part-time and many are on sandwich courses. Fewer than half enter with traditional academic qualifications. The diversity of the intake is encouraged by initiatives such as the summer school for local people to upgrade their qualifications. The courses, some catering for mature students and others for younger age-groups, start at the end of June and are limited to 15 hours a week so as not to affect students' benefit entitlement. South Bank has always given a high priority to widening participation in higher education and takes far more students from the lowest socio-economic groups than other universities with similar courses and entry qualifications.

Diploma and degree courses run in parallel so that students can move up or down if they are better suited to another level of study. However, the projected dropout rate is among the highest in the country and the university struggles in the National Student Survey. LSBU is targeting much of its fee income on measures to ensure that more students complete their courses in the expected time. Fees for full-time degree courses are £9,000 a year, but Foundation degrees are available at a number of partner colleges in and around

---

103 Borough Road
London SE1 0AA

0800 923 8888 (course enquiries)
course.enquiry@lsbu.ac.uk
www.lsbu.ac.uk
www.lsbsu.org
Affiliation: none

The Times and Sunday Times Rankings

Overall Ranking: **122** (last year: 118)

Student satisfaction:	=112	77.7%
Research quality:	=89	2.7%
Entry standards:	122	233
Student–staff ratio:	120	24.2
Services & facilities/student:	98	£1,250
Expected completion rate:	118	72.4%
Good honours:	97	59.7%
Graduate prospects:	=121	49.0%

London for a fee of £6,120. LSBU degrees are also taught at a network of overseas colleges that stretches from China to the Caribbean.

The main campus is in Southwark, not far from the South Bank arts complex. It includes the Centre for Efficient and Renewable Energy in Buildings, a unique teaching, research and demonstration resource for low-carbon technologies, and the UK's first inner-city green technology research centre. The Clarence Centre for Enterprise and Innovation supports start-up businesses – LBSU is one of the top universities for "knowledge transfer partnerships" with outside organisations. Specialist facilities such as the Centre for Explosion and Fire Research lead the way. Although the university entered only 87 academics for the 2008 Research Assessment Exercise, their average grades were among the best of the new universities. More than 40 per cent of the submission was rated as world-leading or internationally excellent.

Some health students are based on the other side of London, in hospitals in Romford and Leytonstone, where there is a smaller satellite campus in Havering to supplement that in Southwark. The university now trains 40 per cent of London's nurses and has well-regarded courses in occupational therapy and radiography. Psychology degrees were revamped for

2012–13, making the university one of the first to adopt industry recommendations for an integrated curriculum that provides a deeper knowledge of the subject.

A new student centre opened in 2012, bringing the students' union and many support services together to make them more convenient and accessible. A new hall has been added to the residential places within ten minutes' walk of the main campus, but first years cannot yet be guaranteed housing. The university's new-look sports centre opened in July 2014 after a million-pound makeover, with a multipurpose sports hall, therapy services and facilities that include a 40-station fitness suite and a sports injury clinic. Southwark Council contributed £300,000 to improve the facilities and guarantee public access. The university provides a comprehensive sports scholarship scheme.

Undergraduate Fees and Bursaries

» Fees for UK/EU students 2015–16 £9,000
» Foundation degree £6,120
» Fees for international students 2014–15 £10,500
» Up to 300 scholarships of £2,000 in year 1, based on need. See website for criteria. Progression bursary of £1,000 for those in receipt of these scholarships who are successful at July 2016 examinations.
» Progression bursary of £500 for all others who are successful at July 2016 examinations.
» Students with at least ABB at A level or equivalent a scholarship of £1,000 a year.

Students

Undergraduates:	10,325	(4,775)
Postgraduates:	1,885	(2,810)
Mature students:	50.1%	
International students:	5.8%	
Applications per place:	6.2	
From state-sector schools:	97.8%	
From working-class homes:	47.5%	
Satisfaction with students' union	59%	

For detailed information about sports facilities:
www1.lsbu.ac.uk/sports

Accommodation

Number of places and costs refer to 2014–15
University-provided places: 1,400
Percentage catered: 0%
Self-catered costs: £111–£114.25 (standard) – £136.70 (en suite) a week.
First-year UK students are not guaranteed accommodation, but high priority is given to those living outside Greater London.
International students: first years are guaranteed accommodation if conditions are met.
www.lsbu.ac.uk/student-life/accommodation

Loughborough University

Loughborough's illustrious sporting pedigree makes the Queen Elizabeth Olympic Park the ideal location for Loughborough's new London campus, opening in 2015. Ninety athletes with Loughborough connections competed at the 2012 Olympic and Paralympic Games, winning a total of 13 medals. The university is moving into the Olympic press and broadcast centres, initially to run postgraduate and executive courses. Lord Coe, who chaired the organising committee for the Games and is himself a double gold medallist, is a Loughborough alumnus and now a Pro Chancellor of the university. The tradition continued at this summer's Commonwealth Games, when 120 Loughborough-connected athletes represented eight different countries in nine sports. However, there is much more to Loughborough than sport: it has risen eight places to 13th in our table this year and increased its intake of new undergraduates by more than 20 per cent in 2013.

The university consistently registers among the best scores in the National Student Survey and ranks first in the UK in the International Student Barometer, which reflects the views of overseas students. At least nine out of ten were satisfied and would recommend the university to others. The Office for Standards in Education also rates Loughborough in its top category for teacher training in physical education, design and science. Loughborough is a leader in art and design and remains a major centre of engineering, with more than 2,800 students in a £20-million integrated engineering complex. Civil, aeronautical and automotive engineering are particularly strong. Loughborough is also taking the lead in a £5-million project to boost research, training and industry partnerships in solar energy.

The original 216-acre campus has benefited from a sustained development programme which included a large student union extension and a new business school, as well as the gradual refurbishment of residential accommodation. The first phase of a £68-million on-campus accommodation development has more than 5,000 rooms, with another 1,300 bedrooms to come in four new halls. Arts facilities are improving with the upgrading of the Cope Auditorium to serve the campus and local community. An £8-million building for Health, Exercise and Biosciences opened in 2010 and a new Design Centre, the first project in a wider masterplan for the East Park area of the campus, opened its doors in October 2011. The purchase of the adjacent Holywell Park site increased the size of the campus by 75 per cent, offering new scope for research and collaboration with industry. The Science and Enterprise Park includes the £59-million BAE-sponsored Systems Engineering Innovation Centre.

Loughborough
Leicestershire LE11 3TU

01509 223522 (admissions)
admissions@lboro.ac.uk
www.lboro.ac.uk
www.lufbra.net
Affiliation: none

The Times and Sunday Times **Rankings**
Overall Ranking: **13** (last year: 21)

Student satisfaction:	=8	85.7%
Research quality:	=18	24.7%
Entry standards:	35	406
Student–staff ratio:	=40	15.6
Services & facilities/student:	32	£1,956
Expected completion rate:	19	93.5%
Good honours:	=22	78.0%
Graduate prospects:	13	80.0%

Close relationships with industry have helped to amass a record haul of seven Queen's Anniversary Prizes.

Most subjects are available either as three-year full-time or longer sandwich degrees, which include a year in industry. This has helped to give graduates a strong employment record, as well a dropout rate of less than 5 per cent, which is particularly low for the subjects Loughborough offers. The university is a leader in the use of computer-assisted assessment, offering students the chance to gauge their own progress online. However, Loughborough misses all its access benchmarks: fewer than a quarter of the undergraduates are from working-class homes and less than 6 per cent are from areas of low participation in higher education. The university will spend more than £4 million in scholarships and bursaries and larger sums on outreach activities in 2015–16.

The sports facilities are among the best in the country – and still improving. Loughborough was chosen as the official preparation camp headquarters for Team GB prior to the London 2012 Olympics. It has since been named as the official Innovation Partner of the International Hockey Federation and will be one of two national centres for British swimming as it prepares for the Rio 2016 and Tokyo 2020 Olympic Games. The university will also host a £10-million National Sport and Exercise Medicine Centre of Excellence, one of three in the UK. A new £5.6-million health and fitness centre will open in October. The campus boasts a 50-metre swimming pool, national academies for cricket and tennis, a gymnastics centre and a high-performance training centre for athletics. The university also boasts the UK's only centre for disability sport and has spent £15 million on its Sports Technology Institute. The programme of sports scholarships is the largest at any university. Social activity is concentrated on a students' union which is among the most popular in the country with its members. The relatively small town of Loughborough, a mile away, is never going to be a clubber's paradise, but both Leicester and Nottingham are within easy reach.

Undergraduate Fees and Bursaries

» Fees for UK/EU students 2015–16 £9,000
» Placement year / year abroad £840 (taken in 2015–16)
£880 (taken in 2016–17)
» Fees for international students 2014–15 £13,750–£17,300
» For UK (excluding Welsh) students, household income below £18K, a bursary of £2,000, years 1–3; fee waiver for placement year; £2,000 bursary and £5,000 fee waiver, year 4 Integrated Masters;
£18K–£22K, £2,000, years 1–3; £2,000 and £4,000 fee waiver, year 4;
£22K–£25K, £1,000, years 1–3; £1,000 and £3,000 fee waiver, year 4;
enhanced terms for mature students.
» Scholarships for high achievers from low HE participation areas.
» Range of sports and subject scholarships.

Students

Undergraduates:	11,090	(385)
Postgraduates:	2,305	(1,685)
Mature students:	3.2%	
International students:	10.9%	
Applications per place:	5.3	
From state-sector schools:	82.1%	
From working-class homes:	22.9%	
Satisfaction with students' union	89%	

For detailed information about sports facilities:
http://loughboroughsport.com

Accommodation

Number of places and costs refer to 2014–15

University-provided places: 5,550

Percentage catered: 43%

Catered costs: £124 – £167 a week (39-week contract).

Self-catered costs: £83 – £140 a week (39-week contract).

Undergraduate first-year first-choice students are guaranteed accommodation if they apply prior to 1 August.

International students: guaranteed housing in same residence for two years.

www.lboro.ac.uk/services/campus-living/accommodation/

University of Manchester

The University of Manchester has embarked on a £1-billion, ten-year plan to create a world-class campus. By 2022, there will be a single campus with new student facilities and buildings for teaching and research, as well as major improvements to the public realm. The first phase is now underway and will include a new Manchester Engineering Campus Development, new centres for the School of Law and Manchester Business School, a major refurbishment of the university library, and a bigger and better students' union. The university is also spending several million pounds to bring benefits to the local area, capitalising on improvements due to be made to Oxford Road. The first projects, due to complete in the next 12 months, will see the opening of the Manchester Cancer Research Centre and the National Graphene Institute, as well as the refurbishment of the Whitworth Art Gallery. The overriding aims are to improve the student experience and reduce carbon emissions.

The university has moved back into the top 30 in our league table and its international ranking is almost as high. With global league tables focusing mainly on research and the domestic variety designed with undergraduates in mind, the contrast suggests that research rather than teaching is Manchester's strength. But outstanding teaching is one of the three goals in the university's strategy to be among the top 25 in the world by 2020. It already seen an improvement in previously disappointing student satisfaction ratings and has set aside £20 million to attract top academics. The new recruits will join three Nobel prizewinners on the staff. Professors Andre Geim and Professor Konstantin Novoselov brought the all-time complement of laureates to 25 when they took the physics prize in 2010. Sir John Sulston, who chairs the Institute of Science, Ethics and Innovation, won the prize for physiology and medicine in 2002.

The 2004 merger with the neighbouring University of Manchester Institute of Science and Technology (UMIST) created the biggest conventional university in the UK outside the federal University of London. One result was the largest engineering school in the UK, with a £20-million budget and 1,200 students. A £400-million building and refurbishment programme, the largest ever in UK higher education, came as part of the package. The £24-million "Learning Commons" building opened in 2012, the first phase providing more than 1,000 flexible learning spaces, high-quality IT facilities, and a hub for student-centred activities and learning support services. Close to the university's iconic Jodrell Bank telescope, in Cheshire,

---

Oxford Road
Manchester M13 9PL

0161 275 2077 (admissions)
ug-admissions@manchester.ac.uk
www.manchester.ac.uk
http://manchesterstudents
  union.com
Affiliation: Russell Group

The Times and Sunday Times **Rankings**
Overall Ranking: **28** (last year: 26)

Student satisfaction:	=68	81.9%
Research quality:	11	28.7%
Entry standards:	19	443
Student–staff ratio:	=19	13.9
Services & facilities/student:	50	£1,734
Expected completion rate:	=20	93.2%
Good honours:	36	73.8%
Graduate prospects:	29	75.7%

Manchester will host the control centre for what will be the world's largest radio telescope. Manchester was among the top ten universities in the 2008 Research Assessment Exercise, with almost two-thirds of its submission considered world-leading or internationally excellent.

Manchester again attracted more applications than any university in the UK in 2013, taking an additional 750 undergraduates compared with the previous year. The university has been trying to broaden its intake, with a particular focus on increasing recruitment from the city and its surrounding area. It is now close to the national average for its courses and entry qualifications for the recruitment of state-educated students or those from working class homes. The Manchester Leadership Programme and the University College for Interdisciplinary Learning encourage students to think beyond academia and towards their impact as citizens.

Surveys of employers frequently place Manchester among their favourite recruiting grounds, helping to produce an unrivalled network of industrial sponsorship. Employers have also rated Manchester's careers service the best at any university.

The first phase of a new chemical engineering facility, with a sophisticated industrial pilot plant as well as teaching laboratories, opened in 2011. The £39-million research centre dedicated to biomedical science is one of the largest in Europe. A £60-million development is creating a new hotel, conference venue and executive education centre for Manchester Business School. The business school is among the strengths of the merged institution, as is the medical school, which was rewarded for impressive teaching ratings with extra places. A new teaching block helps to cater for 2,000 undergraduates following a problem-based curriculum.

Manchester's famed youth culture and the university's position at the heart of a huge student precinct help to ensure keen competition for places – and hence high entry standards – in most subjects. There are first-rate sports facilities and the university's teams frequently rank near the top of the BUCS league. The city's reputation for violent crime has subsided, but the students' union runs late-night minibuses, self-defence classes and regular safety campaigns.

Undergraduate Fees and Bursaries

» Fees for UK/EU students 2015–16 £9,000
» Fees for international students 2014–15 £14,000–£18,000
   Medicine £18,000–£33,000
» Household income below £17K, £3,000 cash a year; £17K–£25K, £2,000 a year; £25K–£42.6K, £1,000 a year.
» Foundation year bursary of £5,000–£2,000 for household income up to £35K.
» Bursaries up to £3,000 for year abroad or placement year.
» Manchester Access Programme scholarships of £1,000 a year.

Students

Undergraduates:	26,200	(880)
Postgraduates:	7,575	(3,775)
Mature students:	11.2%	
International students:	23%	
Applications per place:	6.5	
From state-sector schools:	81.4%	
From working-class homes:	25.3%	
Satisfaction with students' union	72%	

For detailed information about sports facilities:
www.sport.manchester.ac.uk

Accommodation

Number of places and costs refer to 2014–15
University-owned/managed places: 7,642
Percentage catered: approx 29%
Catered costs: £90 – £171 a week (40 weeks).
Self-catered costs: £90 – £135 a week (40 weeks).
First years are guaranteed housing provided conditions are met.
International non-EU students are guaranteed accommodation for the duration of their stay if conditions met.
accommodation@manchester.ac.uk
www.accommodation.manchester.ac.uk

Manchester Metropolitan University

Manchester Met (MMU) registered the biggest increase in enrolments of any university in 2013, an extra 1,400 undergraduates, more than compensating for a big drop when higher fees were introduced. The rise made the university the biggest recruiter in the UK, with more than 9,000 undergraduates beginning courses. More than a sixth of the students are 21 or over on entry, the group which has seen the biggest decline in the new fees regime. There is a longstanding commitment to extending access to higher education: just over 40 per cent of the undergraduates come from working-class homes, many from areas of low participation in higher education. The projected dropout rate has improved considerably and is now close to the national average for the university's subjects and entry qualifications.

With some 36,000 students including part-timers, MMU is one of the largest universities in Britain. More than 1,000 courses are offered in over 70 subjects. But the giant institution boasts quality as well as quantity: academics are encouraged to take a three-year MA in teaching and more than a third of the work entered for the 2008 Research Assessment Exercise was rated as world-leading or internationally excellent. Education, English, and art and design produced the best results. The Poet Laureate, Professor Carol Ann Duffy, is Creative Director of the Writing School in the English department. The university is also proud of its record on green issues, finishing top of the People and Planet Green League of environmental performance in 2013.

The university has more professionally accredited courses than any other university and many courses involve work placements. Education courses have fared well in the Teaching Agency's performance indicators, especially for primary training. The university trains more teachers than any other and has launched a Centre for Urban Education to develop its expertise further.

Some 800 trainees and other students taking contemporary arts and sports science are based at Crewe, 40 miles south of Manchester and now rebranded as MMU Cheshire. A former campus at Alsager has been closed and courses moved to the Crewe campus in an area now known as the University Quadrant. Some arts subjects moved there with the opening of a £6-million drama, music and dance centre, and there is a £30-million student village. The £10-million Sport Science Centre opened in 2010 and the Business School followed in 2012. Exercise and sport science students were the final group to make the

---

All Saints Building
All Saints
Manchester M15 6BH

0161 247 6969 (general enquiries)
contact via website
www.mmu.ac.uk
www.theunionmu.org
Affiliation: University
 Alliance

The Times and Sunday Times **Rankings**
Overall Ranking: **89** (last year: 89)

Student satisfaction:	=95	79.3%
Research quality:	=70	4.3%
Entry standards:	=53	343
Student–staff ratio:	69	18.2
Services & facilities/student:	102	£1,206
Expected completion rate:	82	83.0%
Good honours:	=66	65.8%
Graduate prospects:	=83	60.2%

move to Crewe.

The five sites in Manchester have now been reduced to two linked campuses as part of a £350-million development programme, much of which has been devoted to learning resources rather than buildings. The prize-winning EQAL programme recast undergraduate courses in line with student feedback and integrated them with the Moodle virtual learning environment. The Faculties of Education and Health, Psychology and Social Care are now based on a £120-million "Campus for the Professions" in the city centre. The Birley Fields campus is one of the most environmentally sustainable in the UK, uniting the remaining provision for teachers with that for nurses, health and youth workers. The new site is close to the existing All Saints campus, on the university's border with Hulme and Moss Side. New science and engineering buildings at All Saints cost £42 million, while an impressive new £75-million business school headquarters next to the Mancunian Way opened in 2012. A new School of Art opened in 2013.

Overseas links have expanded rapidly in recent years, with MMU offering exchange opportunities in Europe and further afield, as well as establishing teaching bases abroad. There are new partnerships in China and additional locations for exchanges through the EU's Erasmus programme. However, more than half of the students come from the Manchester area, easing the pressure on accommodation in a city of nearly 70,000 students. The university plays an important role in the region's economy, not least because 70 per cent of graduates stay and work in the North West. MMU is currently employing 50 of its own graduates on paid internships for up to 12 months.

All first years who request accommodation can be housed, with priority for university-owned halls going to the disabled and those who live furthest from Manchester. The university's sports facilities are good and the city's attractions do no harm to recruitment levels, but much depends on where the course is based; students at Crewe can feel isolated. Some potential applicants are daunted by the sheer size of the university, but individual courses and sites usually provide a social circle.

Undergraduate Fees and Bursaries

» Fees for UK/EU students 2015–16	£9,000
» Foundation year	£6,000
» Placement year / year abroad	£680
» Fees for international students 2014–15	£10,250–£11,000
Architecture	£18,000
» For all UK students with household income below £25K, £1,000 a year as university services or accommodation discount.	
» Other scholarships and bursaries available.	
» Check the university's website for the latest information.	

Students

Undergraduates:	**24,210**	**(2,345)**
Postgraduates:	**2,320**	**(3,590)**
Mature students:	**17%**	
International students:	**6%**	
Applications per place:	**5.7**	
From state-sector schools:	**96.1%**	
From working-class homes:	**40.8%**	
Satisfaction with students' union	**59%**	

For detailed information about sports facilities:
www2.mmu.ac.uk/sport

Accommodation

Number of places and costs refer to 2014–15
University provided places: 4,493
Percentage catered: 0%
Self-catered costs: Manchester: £89 – £125; Cheshire: £77 – £87 a week.
All new full-time students will be housed if applications are received by 15 August and requirements are met.
International students: as above.
accommodation@mmu.ac.uk
www.mmu.ac.uk/accommodation

Middlesex University

Middlesex has completed a long-running reorganisation programme, which has reduced the seven campuses which used to straggle around north London to one impressive base at Hendon. The university has invested more than £200 million bringing about the transformation and attracting 150 new academics. The last phase of the programme saw nursing and the other health subjects move to Hendon, where The Grove, the £80-million centre for art, design and media, has won a string of accolades. It includes Sony-designed, equipped and built TV studios and newsroom, and flexible performance and exhibition spaces centred around an atrium. Earlier developments Hendon saw the construction of a new library and the roofing over of the main quadrangle to provide social space. This was followed by a new building for science subjects and the opening of the Forum for student services and leisure facilities. The campus even boasts one of the country's few Real Tennis courts. ICT facilities have been updated with wireless access throughout the campus. The university reports higher spending on student facilities than any institution outside the top five in the table – £1,000 per student more than many of its peers – which has helped it to a rise of 19 places in this year's table.

While the university has been concentrating its activities in London, it has been spreading its wings abroad. Having opened campuses in Mauritius and Dubai, it added another in Malta in 2013 after six years of offering business and computing degrees through one of the island's colleges. Middlesex is the first overseas university on the island, where it expects to attract students from North Africa and the Middle East, as well as from Malta itself. More than 10,000 students now take the university's degrees outside the UK, while almost a fifth of the undergraduates studying in London also come from other countries. They include more than 1,000 from other parts of the EU, the legacy of a longstanding commitment to Europe.

There was a 9 per cent decline in applications in 2013, but the university compensated to some extent for a big drop in enrolments when £9,000 fees were introduced by taking an additional 300 undergraduates. A new pattern of courses that accompanied the university's physical reorganisation was proving popular before the fees went up. Middlesex also rationalised its schools to focus on its strengths in business, computing and the arts, registering particular successes with work-based courses, which drew praise from quality assessors. The highly flexible course system allows students to start some courses in January if they prefer not to wait

The Burroughs
London NW4 4BT

020 8411 5555 (enquiries)
contact via website
www.mdx.ac.uk
www.mdxsu.com
Affiliation: million+

The Times and Sunday Times **Rankings**
Overall Ranking: **75** (last year: 94)

Student satisfaction:	**71**	81.7%
Research quality:	**=63**	5.0%
Entry standards:	**=107**	287
Student–staff ratio:	**=99**	20.5
Services & facilities/student:	**4**	£2,595
Expected completion rate:	**114**	76.5%
Good honours:	**=98**	59.3%
Graduate prospects:	**=102**	56.8%

until autumn, and offers the option of an extra five-week session in the summer to try out new subjects or add to their credits. The introduction of year-long modules had the benefit of instilling a deeper level of learning, allowing students to get to grips with a subject before assessment. Nine out of ten students take vocational courses. Media students, for example, benefit from a Skillset Academy. The business school is the biggest subject area, but almost half of the undergraduates are on multidisciplinary programmes.

Almost a third of the full-time undergraduates are 21 or more on entry and nearly nine out of ten of those from the UK come from the London area. The university has a longstanding focus on Europe and has almost 1,000 undergraduates from other EU countries. Across all campuses, more than a quarter of Middlesex's students are from outside the UK. Almost all of the British students are from state schools, more than half of them from working-class homes. Having increased its spending on bursaries in 2014, Middlesex will be one of seven universities not offering any in 2015, believing that outreach activities are a more effective means of broadening the intake. The projected dropout rate has improved considerably in recent years and, at less than 17 per cent, is close to the national average for the university's subjects and entry qualifications. But, like other institutions in London, Middlesex has struggled in the National Student Survey with scores that have held it back in *The Times and Sunday Times* league table.

There are almost 950 residential places, with more to come in the next few years. Priority in their allocation is given to international students and other first years who live outside London. Sports facilities have been improving and now include a well-equipped "fitness pod" at Hendon with a gym and multipurpose outdoor courts. The West End and London's other attractions are only a tube ride away.

Undergraduate Fees and Bursaries
» Fees for UK/EU students 2015–16 £9,000
» Fees for international students 2014–15 £10,700
» Support to be targeted at widening participation in higher education. Details not available in August 2014.
» Academic, sports and other scholarships available..
» Check the university's website for the latest information.

Students
Undergraduates:	14,400	(2,350)
Postgraduates:	2,205	(2,175)
Mature students:	29.6%	
International students:	20.4%	
Applications per place:	6.3	
From state-sector schools:	98.6%	
From working-class homes:	50.6%	
Satisfaction with students' union	65%	

For detailed information about sports facilities:
www.mdx.ac.uk/life-at-middlesex/sport

Accommodation
Number of places and costs refer to 2014–15
University-provided places: 940
Percentage catered: 0%
Self-catered costs: £121–£139 a week (40 weeks).
Full-year students have priority; residential restrictions apply.
International students are guaranteed a room provided they apply by the deadline.
accomm@mdx.ac.uk
www.mdx.ac.uk/life-at-middlesex/accommodation

Newcastle University

Newcastle is a city-centre university in a way that few of its counterparts in the Russell Group of leading research-focused universities can claim to be. Its main campus opens on to the busy Haymarket area, while the new Science Central site, which it operates in partnership with the city council, represents one of the UK's biggest inner-city regeneration projects. It will be a testbed for research into urban sustainability and digital technology. A third campus, on the site of the former Newcastle General Hospital, focuses on research into ageing and is another element of the university's lead role in turning Newcastle into one of the six officially designated science cities. The university will be spending £100 million in the next three years on student facilities and information technology. The Digital Campus scheme has already produced mobile apps used by almost 20,000 students and staff each week and a lecture recording service that amassed almost 16,000 recordings in its first year.

The university is aiming to raise its profile as a "world-class civic university", combining local engagement with growing international activity. Newcastle was the first UK university to open an overseas medical school: the first cohort in Johor, Malaysia, graduated in 2014. The university already had a joint venture with Singapore Institute of Technology, offering seven academic programmes in a range of engineering disciplines and food sciences in the island state. There are also strategic partnerships with institutions in Australia, China, Brazil, Angola and Indonesia. At Newcastle a designated teaching and accommodation complex to prepare international students for undergraduate and graduate courses opened in 2012.

The university's origins can be traced back to a school of medicine and surgery established in Newcastle in 1834, which later became part of Durham University before going its own way again in 1963. The Medical School now has a partnership with Durham, with about a third of trainees spending their first two years at Durham's Stockton campus. The university has seen two years of growing enrolments since the introduction of £9,000 fees, taking an additional 600 undergraduates in 2013. Newcastle is popular with students from independent schools, who took 30 per cent of the places in 2012. The university expects this figure to drop substantially when the statistics for 2013 are published and has longstanding programmes aimed at attracting more students from non-traditional backgrounds. It leads the Realising Opportunities Scheme, which brings together a number of leading universities to promote fair access to higher

---

King's Gate
Newcastle upon Tyne
NE1 7RU

0191 208 6000 (enquiries)
contact via website
www.ncl.ac.uk
www.nusu.co.uk
Affiliation: Russell Group

The Times and Sunday Times **Rankings**
Overall Ranking: **=22** (last year: =18)

Student satisfaction:	=13	85.3%
Research quality:	=30	21.7%
Entry standards:	23	438
Student–staff ratio:	=31	15.2
Services & facilities/student:	41	£1,762
Expected completion rate:	=13	94.2%
Good honours:	26	76.9%
Graduate prospects:	19	78.8%

education and social mobility.

Recent developments on the 50-acre main campus include the glass-fronted King's Gate building for student services, which created a new "front door" to the university. New buildings have opened for music and medical sciences, science and engineering laboratories have been upgraded, and disabled access improved. A major refurbishment of the library included the provision of more social learning spaces and improved facilities for researchers. The library, which is open 24 hours a day, seven days a week during term time, is the only one in the UK to have been awarded five Charter Marks in a row for excellent customer service. The library provides extra help with academic writing styles and maths, and there is a separate centre offering free tuition in 50 languages.

Newcastle has a number of unusual features for a traditional university, such as a fine art degree with intense competition for places, and a longstanding reputation for agriculture, which benefits from two farms in Northumberland. The award-winning NCL+ initiative encourages all students to develop employability skills through extra-curricular activities. On many courses, a career development module gives credit for work experience, volunteering or part-time employment. The university is in the top 20 for graduate prospects and is one of those most targeted by leading graduate employers. It also registers high levels of satisfaction both in the National Student Survey and in the International Student Barometer, which focuses on overseas students alone. There are particular research strengths in liver disease, ageing, civil engineering and geography.

The university was in the top three for social life in *Times Higher Education* magazine's latest student experience survey and Newcastle has been a frequent winner of the "best student city" title. The students' union has been refurbished and a Student Forum created alongside it as a central outdoor social space. The campus also hosts an independent theatre, museum and art gallery. The already extensive stock of accommodation is being extended in 2014 and rents elsewhere are reasonable. Sport is a particular strength: a £5.5-million sports centre supplements two older venues, which have been extensively refurbished.

Undergraduate Fees and Bursaries

» Fees for UK/EU students 2015–16 £9,000
» Fees for international students 2014–15 £12,075–£15,490
  Medicine and dentistry £15,490–£28,670
» Household income below £25K, bursary of £2,000 a year; household income £25K–£35K, £1,000 a year.
» Access scholarships, with conditions, of £500 a year.
» 20 Promise Scholarships of £4,500 fee waiver, £4,500 cash each year for high-achieving students with household income up to £15K. Other widening participation and subject scholarships available.
» Check the university's website for the latest information.

Students

Undergraduates:	**15,465**	**(50)**
Postgraduates:	**4,145**	**(1,530)**
Mature students:	**8%**	
International students:	**18.4%**	
Applications per place:	**6.1**	
From state-sector schools:	**70%**	
From working-class homes:	**19.2%**	
Satisfaction with students' union	**82%**	

For detailed information about sports facilities:
www.ncl.ac.uk/sport

Accommodation

Number of places and costs refer to 2014–15
University-provided places: 4,427
Percentage catered: 17%
Catered costs: £127.89 a week.
Self-catered costs: £78.89–£139.50 a week.
All single undergraduates are guaranteed a room in university-managed accommodation provided requirements are met. Local restrictions apply.
International students: as above.
www.ncl.ac.uk/enquiries/ ; www.ncl.ac.uk/accommodation/

Newman University

Newman increased its undergraduate intake by almost 25 per cent in 2013, following the award of full university status. The increase was among the five biggest at any university and more than made up for a decline when higher fees were introduced. But the university has dropped more than 30 places in its second year in the *Guide*, largely because of a decline in student satisfaction.

The institution is one of three Catholic foundations among the latest crop of institutions to be upgraded. It takes its name from John Henry Newman, the author of *The Idea of the University* and a Catholic cardinal in the 19th century. His vision of a community of scholars guides the university, which was established in 1968 as a teacher training college, but now has a wider portfolio of degrees, mainly in the social sciences and humanities. The influence of John Henry Newman is evident in the small class sizes and interactive teaching style adopted by the university. The university stresses its Catholic affiliation, but also its commitment to be inclusive in its recruitment and subsequent activities. It says it is proud to welcome staff and students of all religions and backgrounds, adding that, "In line with Newman's view of a university we focus on a formative education, developing the whole student into independent thinkers who have the ability to question, evaluate and develop creative solutions to problems rather than just retain knowledge about their subject."

Based in Bartley Green, eight miles southwest of Birmingham city centre, the campus is in a quiet residential area with views over the Bartley Reservoir and the Worcestershire countryside beyond. The modern buildings are arranged around a series of inner quadrangles of lawns and trees. A £20-million development programme is now complete and includes an impressive new library and entrance building. The project has also added more lecture theatres, a research centre and a state-of-the-art sport performance suite. Community sports facilities have also been refurbished.

Newman received one of eight national awards to bring about change in the strategic approach to technology in learning and teaching. The university's successful bid involves students producing their own online resources while learning about their subject, and consequently also improving their digital literacy, as well as their graduate employment prospects. The project started in 2013 and is part of a larger initiative called "Newman in the Digital Age", which aims to improve students' digital literacy.

All full-time degrees include work placements, with students working with a wide range of employers including

---

Genners Lane
Bartley Green
Birmingham B32 3NT

0121 476 1181 (admissions)
admissions@newman.ac.uk
www.newman.ac.uk
www.newmansu.org
Affiliation: GuildHE,
   Cathedrals Group

The Times and Sunday Times **Rankings**
Overall Ranking: **104** (last year: =73)

Student satisfaction:	**=40**	83.1%
Research quality:	**=117**	0.3%
Entry standards:	**=94**	302
Student–staff ratio:	**=67**	18.1
Services & facilities/student:	**=84**	£1,370
Expected completion rate:	**113**	77.2%
Good honours:	**116**	52.7%
Graduate prospects:	**100**	57.2%

Aston Villa Football Club, Capital FM and Warwick Castle. There are also opportunities to gain work experience abroad and undergraduates can opt to study at a partner university in Europe or further afield to broaden their horizons and boost their CVs. The degree options include one of the first business studies programmes to have an emphasis on business ethics, early childhood education and care, sports coaching science and combined honours in maths or chemistry in association with Aston University. There is also a range of part-time courses and Foundation degrees, most of which are taught at Newman, rather than partner colleges. Many of the courses are recognised by professional bodies such as the Chartered Management Institute and British Psychological Society.

Newman has done well over a number of years in the National Student Survey, scoring particularly highly on personal development. Three-quarters of the undergraduates are female, almost all of them state-educated. More than half come from working-class homes – only three universities in England have a higher proportion – while more than 20 per cent come from an area of low participation in higher education, also in the top six in the country. Psychology, education, sport and the early years are the university's main research areas. Fewer than a dozen academics were entered for the last Research Assessment Exercise (RAE), when a quarter of the submission in education was considered "internationally excellent". A specialist research centre for Children, Young People and Families will form the backbone of a much larger entry in this year's successor to the RAE.

Halls of residence provide single study-bedrooms for 217 students, close to the teaching areas and library. First-year students are given priority in their allocation, but those coming through Clearing may have to live off campus. The newly refurbished fitness suite and performance room have improved sports facilities that already included an artificial sports pitch, sports hall, gymnasium and squash courts. Birmingham city centre, with its abundance of cultural venues and student-oriented nightlife, is about 20 minutes away.

Undergraduate Fees and Bursaries

» Fees for UK/EU students 2015–16 £9,000
» Foundation degree £9,000
» Fees for international students 2014–15 £9,700
» Academic achievement and progression scholarships from £2,000 to £10,000 over three years, subject to conditions..
» Other scholarships and bursaries available.
» Check the university's website for the latest information.

Students

Undergraduates:	1,690	(675)
Postgraduates:	300	(160)
Mature students:	25.1%	
International students:	0.8%	
Applications per place:	4.2	
From state-sector schools:	98.9%	
From working-class homes:	52.1%	
Satisfaction with students' union	63%	

For detailed information about sports facilities:
www.newman.ac.uk/sport

Accommodation

Places and costs refer to 2014–15
University-provided places: 217
Percentage catered: 0%
Self-catered costs: around £3,222 – £4,286 for academic year.
Priority, but no guarantee, is given to new first-year students.
International students: guaranteed housing.
www.newman.ac.uk/accommodation/500

University of Northampton

Northampton shot up 40 places in our league table last year – the biggest rise by any university – and consolidated its position this year. Every student has the opportunity to work in a social enterprise as part of their course to develop new entrepreneurial skills that make them more employable. This may involve a work placement, volunteering or building sustainable social and economic partnerships which would, in turn, be supported by the university. The Ashoka global network of social entrepreneurs named Northampton as the first "Changemaker Campus" in the UK in 2013, and the university aims to be number one in the UK for social enterprise by next year. Podiatry, occupational therapy and events management degree programmes are already developing new social enterprises, allowing students to earn money while they work and learn.

Although it was awarded university status only in 2005, Northampton can trace its history back to the 13th century. Henry III dissolved the original institution, allegedly because his bishops thought it posed a threat to Oxford. The modern university originated in an amalgamation of the town's colleges of education, nursing, technology and art. It has a particular focus on training for public services in the region, with students combining their studies with work placements in the community. The police and criminal justice studies Foundation degree, for example, is delivered for Northamptonshire Police Authority and has been designed to prepare students for a career in policing or the criminal justice system.

The university's league table successes are yet to lead to big increases in applications and enrolments – both were up by a modest amount in 2013. Overall student numbers have topped 14,000, more than 1,000 of them coming from outside the EU. Business is the university's most popular area, but teacher training and health subjects are not far behind – the university is the region's largest provider of teachers and healthcare professionals. Northampton takes its mission to widen participation in higher education seriously: almost all the undergraduates attended state schools or colleges and more than a third come from working class homes. At just over 12 per cent, the projected dropout rate is lower than the national average for the university's courses and entry qualifications. The university was close to the bottom of the ranking for the 2008 Research Assessment Exercise, although there was some world-leading research in four of the ten subject areas. There are now 11 research centres, focusing on everything

---

Park Campus
Boughton Green Road
Northampton NN2 7AL

0800 358 2232 (courses freephone)
study@northampton.ac.uk
www.northampton.ac.uk
www.northamptonunion.com
Affiliation: none

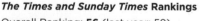

The Times and Sunday Times Rankings
Overall Ranking: 56 (last year: 59)

Student satisfaction:	=13	85.3%
Research quality:	=108	1.3%
Entry standards:	=109	280
Student–staff ratio:	=88	19.8
Services & facilities/student:	7	£2,439
Expected completion rate:	77	84.1%
Good honours:	=91	61.1%
Graduate prospects:	=83	60.2%

from contemporary fiction to anomalous psychological processes and transitional economics in China.

Northampton is in the throes of gaining planning permission for a new Waterside Campus on the banks of the River Nene, which would be close to the new planned halls of residence and within an enterprise zone. If planning permission is granted, the campus would open sometime between 2018 and 2020.

Of the two existing sites, Park Campus is on the edge of Northampton, while the smaller Avenue Campus occupies a more central position. They are linked by a regular and free weekday bus service and "Boris bike" hubs will be installed from September 2015. Park Campus is set in 80 acres of open green parkland, with accommodation, a sports hall, students' union centre and nightclub. Two of the main buildings have been refurbished and expanded as part of an £80-million programme of improvements. The Business School, which benefited from a £1.7-million extension in 2011, is also on the campus.

Avenue Campus, the centre for art, design, science and technology, and the performing arts, hosts frequent theatre performances and exhibitions in its own art gallery. A £13-million investment saw the conversion of an adjacent Grade II listed former school into a technology and research centre with NVision and a 3-D immersive technology and visualisation facility. Another university-backed development is the iCon building in Daventry, which provides a base for a range of innovative, green businesses. The university also sponsors a University Technical College on the nearby Silverstone motor racing circuit.

There are more than 2,100 residential places, including a choice of mixed and single-sex halls. The latest development added 475 rooms in the centre of Northampton in 2013. Sports enthusiasts are well catered for, with rugby union, football, first-class cricket and Silverstone on the doorstep. The university has added a £100,000 gym to its sports facilities, which include a sports hall and outdoor pitches on the Park Campus. The town has a number of student-oriented bars, but the two campuses' union bars remain the hub of the social scene. Both London and Birmingham are about an hour away by train.

Undergraduate Fees and Bursaries

» Fees for UK/EU students 2015–16   £9,000
» Placement year   £825
» Foundation degree   £7,700
» Fees for international students 2014–15   £10,500–£11,500
     £11,500 (2-year fast-track)
» Household income below £25K, a bursary of £500 a year.
» Enhanced access and retention support.
» Other scholarships and bursaries available.
» Check the university's website for the latest information.

Students

Undergraduates:	**9,085**	**(2,505)**
Postgraduates:	**765**	**(1,685)**
Mature students:	**28%**	
International students:	**8.7%**	
Applications per place:	**5.4**	
From state-sector schools:	**98.2%**	
From working-class homes:	**38.0%**	
Satisfaction with students' union	**70%**	

For information about sports facilities:
www.northamptonunion.com/sports

Accommodation

Number of places and costs refer to 2014–15
University-provided places: 2,156
Percentage catered: 0%
Self-catered costs: £60 (small twin) – £123 (en-suite single) a week (42-week contract).
New first years have priority, on first come, first served basis, provided requirements are met.
International students: As above.
accommodation@northampton.ac.uk
www.northampton.ac.uk/study/student-life/accommodation

Northumbria University

Northumbria is the biggest university in the North East of England, with close to 30,000 students, and it is still growing. Undergraduate applications and enrolments reached record levels in 2013, when the intake increased by more than 10 per cent. It has ambitious designs on a place among the top 30 universities and considers itself a "new type of excellent university". Northumbria has invested £160 million in its impressive city centre campus and is opening another in the City of London in September 2014, with an initial focus on business courses. At the same time, it has doubled the number of academics entered for the new Research Excellence Framework compared with its complement in the 2008 assessments. The university has an £18-million staffing plan, which has increased the number of academics and its research capability.

Around 60 per cent of students are from the North East, but numbers drawn from other parts of the UK have been rising year on year. There are more than 3,000 international students on campus and over 5,500 students taking Northumbria courses overseas. More than a third of the undergraduates are from the four lowest socio-economic classes, but the university has managed to bring the projected dropout rate below 10 per cent – lower than the national average for its courses and entry grades. While other universities are cutting back on their bursaries for 2015, Northumbria will continue to offer financial support worth up to £3,000 to applicants from the poorest homes. Only two universities will spend more on bursaries and scholarships. Free one-day taster courses run throughout the year to give prospective students an idea of what university life would be like.

Most subjects are based on the main campus, with health, education and community programmes located at the Coach Lane campus less than two miles away, where £18 million has been spent upgrading facilities and nearly £2 million more will be invested this year. The award-winning City Campus East development is linked to the original main campus by an iconic footbridge spanning Newcastle's central motorway. A recent expansion of the University Library has added 100 IT spaces, more social learning and informal space, a zone fitted with Smart boards and a dedicated Language Zone. Coach Lane also has a learning resources centre, as well as new sports facilities and a clinical skills centre, where students can learn in simulated hospital environments. Northumbria's pre-registration nursing programmes were the first in the country to receive accreditation from the Royal

---

Ellison Terrace
Newcastle upon Tyne
NE1 8ST

0191 243 7420 (admissions)
er.admissions@northumbria.ac.uk
www.northumbria.ac.uk
http://mynsu.northumbria.
  ac.uk
Affiliation: University
  Alliance

The Times and Sunday Times **Rankings**
Overall Ranking: **66** (last year: 62)

Student satisfaction:	=75	81.3%
Research quality:	=89	2.7%
Entry standards:	48	365
Student–staff ratio:	=63	17.8
Services & facilities/student:	65	£1,486
Expected completion rate:	47	87.8%
Good honours:	76	63.8%
Graduate prospects:	78	61.8%

College of Nursing.

More than 550 employers sponsor undergraduate programmes and accreditation comes from almost 60 professional bodies. This is one of the highest rates in the UK, enabling a high proportion of students to leave with professionally certified qualifications. Only three universities had established more start-up companies in a 2013 review of universities' contribution to economic growth. Teacher education is a strength – Northumbria has been rated as outstanding by Ofsted for 12 years in a row – and its post-registration nursing provision has been voted the best in Britain for three successive years. The Student Law Office, which offers legal advice under professional supervision as part of a degree, won a Queen's Anniversary Prize in 2013.

Also in 2013, Northumbria was rated as one of the leading universities for sport and broke into the top ten of the British Universities and Colleges Sport (BUCS) league table for the first time. An investment of over £40 million has been made in facilities and staff over recent years. A £30-million sports centre includes a swimming pool with an adjustable floor, multiple laboratories and a climbing wall, and there is a 3,000-seater indoor arena for professional sport and other events. There is also a generous Sport Scholarship scheme that supports talented student athletes financially throughout their degree programme.

Most first years are offered places in university accommodation. Two large residential developments with en-suite rooms opened in 2011, and almost 1,000 new bedrooms became available in September 2014 with the opening of new student accommodation in nearby Gateshead as a core element of the regeneration of the town centre. Designed with students in mind, the development is based in the heart of a thriving town centre filled with shops, restaurants and cultural attractions. It boasts landscaped walkways, fitness facilities and a multi-use games area as well as offering stunning views across the Tyneside skyline. There is a plentiful supply of privately rented flats and houses in Newcastle, a location that frequently wins awards as the best student city in the UK.

Undergraduate Fees and Bursaries

» Fees for UK/EU students 2015–16 £9,000
» Placement year £1,000
» Fees for international students 2014–15 £11,200–£13,200
» Household income below £16K, a bursary of £3,000 a year; £16K–£25K, £1,000 a year.
» Academic scholarships for entrants with over 400 UCAS points, £4,000; 360–399 UCAS points, £3,000; 320–359 UCAS points, £2,000.
» Progression scholarships for those with grades of 70% or above, £1,000; 60%–69.9%, £500.
» Sports scholarships and other awards.

Students

Undergraduates:	**18,910**	**(4,285)**
Postgraduates:	**2,315**	**(2,305)**
Mature students:	**16.9%**	
International students:	**9.3%**	
Applications per place:	**4.5**	
From state-sector schools:	**92.4%**	
From working-class homes:	**33.6%**	
Satisfaction with students' union	**74%**	

For detailed information about sports facilities:
www.nusportcentral.com

Accommodation

Number of places and costs refer to 2014–15
University-provided places: 5,270
Percentage catered: 5%
Catered costs: £130.90 a week.
Self-catered costs: £88.90 (single) – £113.50 (en suite); £170.10 (studio) a week.
First years who need accommodation can be offered rooms.
International students: first years are guaranteed accommodation if requirements met.
www.northumbria.ac.uk/study-at-northumbria/accommodation/

Norwich University of the Arts (NUA)

NUA does not appear in *The Times and Sunday Times* league table, despite being awarded full university status in 2012, because it does not offer the broad range of subjects needed for meaningful comparisons to be made with less specialist institutions. However, it has a powerful reputation in its field and may acquire the necessary breadth if it carries out its plan to double in size over the next few years. The process will be gradual so as not to place too much strain on the specialist facilities that its students value highly, but developments such as the opening of a new building for the School of Architecture in 2015 will allow for a larger intake. The school will move to the Grade II-listed Boardman House, in the city centre, purchased as the first stage of a £10-million development plan. The university should have no trouble recruiting more students: applications rose by 15 per cent in 2013 and there would have been similar growth in enrolments, had it not been for recruitment restrictions that will soon be lifted.

Unlike the other arts universities, NUA makes a virtue of focusing entirely on the arts, design and media, rather than venturing into business or the humanities and social sciences. There are only 12 BA degrees and fewer than 2,000 students, 57 per cent of whom are female. More than a third of the undergraduates come from working-class homes. Norwich produces higher levels of overall satisfaction than the other specialist arts universities in the National Student Survey, improving considerably in recent years and featuring among the top 50 of all universities in 2013. Its projected dropout rate of 7 per cent, is little more than half the national average for its courses and entry qualifications.

NUA traces its history back to 1845, when the Norwich School of Design was established by the artists and followers of the Norwich School of Painters, the only provincial British group with an international reputation for landscape painting. Former tutors include Lucian Freud, Michael Andrews and Lesley Davenport.

The campus is concentrated on the pedestrianised centre of Norwich, from the 13th-century Garth, which is now the photography centre, to the Monastery Media Lab and St Georges, where the traditional high ceilings and huge windows make it an ideal setting for Fine Art. The university's public art gallery enables students to showcase their work and gain experience curating and organising exhibitions, while the library houses the largest specialist art, design and media collection in the eastern region.

Francis House
3-7 Redwell Street
Norwich NR2 4SN

01603 610561 (enquiries)
info@nua.ac.uk
www.nua.ac.uk
www.nua.ac.uk/study/
    support/studentunion
Affiliation: none

The Times Rankings

Norwich University of the Arts does not appear in the league table this year because its courses do not cover the broad range of subjects needed for meaningful comparisons to be made with less specialist institutions.

NUA has invested significantly in hardware and software that is professionally relevant and suitable for its diverse range of academic requirements. IT resources can be accessed in the workshops, library, computer-teaching rooms, seminar rooms, and at numerous terminals available throughout the campus. NUA has its own art materials shop, open daily, which sells basic and specialist art supplies at discounted prices. Individual studio space is provided for all full-time students in the faculties of art and design, while students in the media faculty have access to digital media workstations. Workshops for everything from digital video editing to laser cutting provide specialised resources and are staffed by experienced professionals, including graduates and practising artists.

Applications in art and design are judged primarily on the quality of students' portfolios, but minimum entry requirements for every course are published on the university's website. Most courses include units of self-managed learning and exploration that allow students to concentrate on areas of particular interest. Agreements with tutors focus on personal study and help students negotiate individual pathways through their courses. More than a third of the work submitted to the last Research Assessment Exercise was judged to be world-leading or internationally excellent.

There are only 165 places in the three housing complexes managed by the university. Almost half of them are in the one university-owned block of four and 12-bedroomed units, while the two privately owned sites also group students together in self-catering houses. Priority for residential places is given to international students and first years living furthest away from the university. NUA does not have its own sports facilities, but its students have access to the University of East Anglia's Sportspark, which boasts some of the best facilities in the higher education system, including an Olympic-sized swimming pool. The campus is located in Norwich's cultural quarter, a ten-minute walk from the railway station. The city is attractive and popular with students, as well as being safer than most university centres.

Undergraduate Fees and Bursaries

» Fees for UK/EU students 2015–16 £9,000
» Foundation year £5,000
» Fees for international students 2014–15 £12,000
» Bursary scheme to encourage wider participation in Higher Education. Details had not been announced in August 2014.
» Other scholarships and bursaries available.
» Check the university's website for the latest information.

Students

Undergraduates:	**1,680**	(0)
Postgraduates:	15	(55)
Mature students:	14.3%	
International students:	4%	
Applications per place:	3.7	
From state-sector schools:	97%	
From working-class homes:	40.3%	
Satisfaction with students' union	58%	

For detailed information about sports facilities:
www.nua.ac.uk/norwich/sport

Accommodation

Number of places and costs refer to 2014–15
University-provided places: 165
Percentage catered: 0%
Self-catered costs: £98–£136 a week (46 weeks)
First years cannot be guaranteed housing. Distance restrictions apply.
International students: as above
accommodation@nua.ac.uk
www.nua.ac.uk/study/accommodation

University of Nottingham

Nottingham is the university most targeted by recruiters from *The Times* Top 100 graduate employers. The university generally does well in High Fliers' Graduate Market survey – it was second in 2013 – but this is the first year in which it has been the employers' favourite. Nottingham is popular, too, with degree applicants: only the two large Manchester universities drew more applications in 2013. It is seen as a prime alternative to Oxbridge, and attracts more than seven applicants for each of the 7,000 undergraduate places it fills each year. A member of the Russell Group, Nottingham is in the top 75 in the QS World University Rankings. It has campuses in China and Malaysia, as well as its home city, making it the nearest Britain has to a truly global university. Nottingham, in fact, now has two bases in China, the only UK university to do so.

The university has shown its strength in research with two Nobel prizes since the millennium for work carried out at Nottingham. Professor Sir Peter Mansfield, who won the medicine prize for research leading to the development of the MRI scanner, has spent almost his entire academic career there. The university further underlined its status by winning a grant from GlaxoSmithKline to establish a £20-million Carbon Neutral Laboratory for Sustainable Chemistry. While under construction, the building was destroyed by fire in September 2014. It will be rebuilt. Almost 60 per cent of a big submission to the last Research Assessment Exercise was judged to be world-leading or internationally excellent.

The original University Park campus has won 11 consecutive Green Flag awards for its 330 acres of parkland and was named as the most sustainable campus in the world by the UI Greenmetric in 2013. A £50-million building programme includes the extension and refurbishment of the specialist library for engineering and science, which will double in size. A mile away is the 30-acre Jubilee campus, which was also awarded a Green Flag this year. It houses the schools of management and finance, computer science and education, as well as 750 residential places. New sports facilities, research laboratories, teaching space and student accommodation have all been added in recent years. The newly reorganised Medical School is also close to University Park, with a £4.5-million outpost for nursing at Derby Hospital. The biosciences and the veterinary school are at Sutton Bonington, 12 miles south of the city in a rural setting. The latest development there is a new £9-million Amenities Building, which will include a 500-seat dining hall, student common rooms and staff lounge, as well as

---

University Park
Nottingham NG7 2RD

0115 951 5559 (enquiries)
undergraduate-enquiries@
   nottingham.ac.uk
www.nottingham.ac.uk
www.su.nottingham.ac.uk
Affiliation: Russell Group

The Times and Sunday Times Rankings

Overall Ranking: **=22** (last year: 23)

Student satisfaction:	=64	82.2%
Research quality:	=21	24.0%
Entry standards:	20	442
Student–staff ratio:	=21	14.1
Services & facilities/student:	31	£1,961
Expected completion rate:	15	94.0%
Good honours:	=22	78.0%
Graduate prospects:	17	79.2%

a graduate centre, faith room and Student Guild service.

Nottingham has longstanding links with the Far East, which provides the majority of its 8,000 overseas students in the UK. The branch campuses outside Kuala Lumpur, in Malaysia, and at Ningbo, in China, now host another 8,000 students. The purpose-built campuses have echoes of Nottingham's distinctive clock tower. All students have the opportunity to move between the three countries. The latest venture is collaboration with the East China University of Science and Technology, where the Shanghai Nottingham Advanced Academy will be based. It will deliver joint courses that include periods of study in Nottingham UK, with teaching and research at undergraduate, postgraduate and doctoral levels.

The university has succeeded in broadening its UK intake, but still has more independent school students and fewer from working-class homes than the national average for the subjects it offers. Summer schools and master classes provide support for teenagers from backgrounds without a history of progressing to selective universities and the university has joined the Sutton Trust's Pathways to Law access programme. Once in, students tend to stay the course – the dropout rate of less than 5 per cent is among the best in the country. The Nottingham Advantage Award offers extra-curricular modules, as well as providing scores of internships for graduates, who enjoy lifetime access to the careers service, which has teams in each faculty. The university featured in the top 50 of a global employability survey published in 2013.

The two main campuses in Nottingham are within three miles of the city centre, which has a good selection of student-friendly clubs. However, halls of residence and the students' union tend to be the centre of social life for students, especially in the first year. New bars, café facilities and a nightclub were included in a £1-million makeover of student facilities. Sports provision is excellent. Almost £5 million is being spent on two new sports pavilions and the university's playing fields adjoin the main campus.

Undergraduate Fees and Bursaries

- » Fees for UK/EU students 2015–16 — £9,000
- » Placement year — £1,350
- » Fees for international students 2014–15 — £13,470–£17,340
  Medicine — £18,700–£31,750
  Veterinary medicine — £17,340–£25,690
- » Household income below £15K, a bursary of £3,000 a year; then sliding scale to £42.6K, £2,000–£750 a year. Additional £1,000 a year if certain conditions met.
- » Range of subject scholarships available.
- » Check the university's website for the latest information.

Students

Undergraduates:	**23,445**	**(1,690)**
Postgraduates:	**7,665**	**(2,740)**
Mature students:	**9.8%**	
International students:	**17.2%**	
Applications per place:	**7.3**	
From state-sector schools:	**75.8%**	
From working-class homes:	**19.1%**	
Satisfaction with students' union	**72%**	

For detailed information about sports facilities:
www.nottingham.ac.uk/sport

Accommodation

Number of places and costs refer to 2014–15
University-provided places: 7,500
Percentage catered: 33.3%
Catered costs: £100–£207.94 a week (31–51 weeks).
Self-catered costs: £92–£132.72 a week (44 or 51 weeks).
First years are guaranteed accommodation if conditions are met.
International undergraduates: as above.
accommodation@nottingham.ac.uk
www.nottingham.ac.uk/accommodation/accommodation.aspx

Nottingham Trent University

Nottingham Trent (NTU) saw one of the biggest increases in enrolments of any UK university in 2013, taking 700 more undergraduates than it did in the previous year in spite of a decline in applications. The influx took the university back to levels of recruitment it enjoyed before £9,000 fees were introduced. The new students will join a university that is increasing its international dimension: more than 7,000 students take NTU degrees in partner colleges overseas and the university is aiming to offer all its students an "international learning experience". This may involve a study or work placement abroad, learning a foreign language or studying another culture or country. The 27,000 students in Nottingham already include about 1,000 from outside the EU.

The university has spent £350 million in ten years recruiting new staff and upgrading its three campuses, the latest tranche going on a new students' union building, which opened on the main City site in 2014. The development includes sports facilities and over 500 student bedrooms, as well as bars and other social space. Other projects, which included the regeneration of two Grade II-listed buildings in the city centre, have added new lecture theatres, restaurants, student services areas and laboratories. The Boots Library and the art and design facilities on the City site have been upgraded, while the Clifton Campus, five miles away, has a new "superlab" for 200 science students. At the same time, £20 million has been spent on a new animal unit and veterinary nursing centre at the Brackenhurst campus, 14 miles outside Nottingham, where an eco-friendly library opened in 2013.

A third of the undergraduates come from working-class homes and over 93 per cent attended state schools or colleges. The projected dropout rate has improved and, at less than 10 per cent, is now lower than the national average for the university's courses and entry grades.

Best known for fashion and other creative arts, the university also boasts one of the UK's biggest law schools, offering legal practice courses for both solicitors and barristers, as well as degrees. A three-year LLB(Hons) Law and Legal Practice course integrates an LLB law degree with the solicitors' Legal Practice Course. Other recent academic developments include a number of sponsored degrees offered by the business school, where the students work full-time for a company whilst studying for their degree. Students have their fees paid by the sponsoring company and also receive a salary. A new management and finance degree gives students a degree and CIMA qualification in four years instead of the

---

Burton Street
Nottingham NG1 4BU

0115 848 4200 (admissions)
contact via website
www.ntu.ac.uk
www.trentstudents.org
Affiliation: University
  Alliance

The Times and Sunday Times Rankings

Overall Ranking: **52** (last year: 61)

Student satisfaction:	=40	83.1%
Research quality:	=70	4.3%
Entry standards:	=77	320
Student–staff ratio:	58	17.2
Services & facilities/student:	58	£1,568
Expected completion rate:	57	86.9%
Good honours:	63	66.6%
Graduate prospects:	=71	63.6%

usual seven, also with fees and salary paid by a company.

An extensive research programme attracted an £8-million donation – thought to be the largest to a post-1992 university – to advance the university's work in cancer diagnosis and therapy. Researchers at the purpose-built facility on the Clifton Campus work with leading cancer research institutions in the USA, Europe and Asia. The university held its own in the last Research Assessment Exercise, although it entered fewer academics than some of the other leading new universities. More than a third of its submission was rated world-leading or internationally excellent.

Art and design, architecture, law, business and the social sciences are taught on the main campus, while science and technology, education, and the humanities are based at Clifton, which has seen the addition of six new blocks of high-quality student accommodation that will form part of a student village. The Brackenhurst Campus is devoted to animal, rural and environmental studies. It includes one of the region's best-equipped equestrian centres, with a purpose-built indoor riding area. There are 340 residential places there and a renewal of the teaching facilities took place in 2006. With private providers adding to the university's residential stock of around 4,800 beds, all first years and international students can be housed.

NTU has a strong sporting reputation and always fares well in the BUCS leagues. The new Lee Westwood Sports Centre, opened by the golfer himself, is on the Clifton Campus and boasts an array of top facilities, including sports halls, studios, fitness suites and a nutrition training centre. NTU alumni include England rugby player Nick Easter and Great Britain hockey players Crista Cullen, Alistair Wilson and Adam Dixon, who was one of three current or former NTU students participating at the 2014 Commonwealth Games. Social life varies between campuses, but all have access to the city's lively cultural and clubbing scene. A bus service links the main campuses and the city's new tram system serves the university.

Undergraduate Fees and Bursaries

» Fees for UK/EU students 2015–16   £9,000
» Foundation degree   £6,750
» Placement year / year abroad   £900
» Fees for international students 2014–15   £11,500–£12,000
» Household income below £30K, a bursary of £1,000 a year.
» Additional bursaries for students from particular backgrounds or circumstances.
» Check the university's website for the latest information.

Students

Undergraduates:	**20,020**	**(1,720)**
Postgraduates:	**2,480**	**(2,650)**
Mature students:	**11.5%**	
International students:	**6.1%**	
Applications per place:	**5.1**	
From state-sector schools:	**93.1%**	
From working-class homes:	**32.3%**	
Satisfaction with students' union	**81%**	

For detailed information about sports facilities:
www.ntu.ac.uk/sport

Accommodation

Number of places and costs refer to 2014–15
University-provided places: 4,800
Percentage catered: 0%
Self-catered costs: £80.71–£147.98 (44–51 weeks).
First years and new students are guaranteed accommodation if conditions are met.
International students: guaranteed accommodation if conditions are met.
accommodation@ntu.ac.uk
www.ntu.ac.uk/study_with_us/accommodation/index.html

The Open University (OU)

The Open University (OU) is about to lose one of the most successful Vice-Chancellors in its 45-year history, as Professor Martin Bean returns to his native Australia. He leaves behind one of the world's largest and most highly regarded distance learning universities, having established the platform for the UK's first venture into massive open online courses (MOOCs). The university is hosting FutureLearn, a consortium of leading universities and cultural organisations such as the British Museum and the British Council, offering free higher education courses of varying lengths, also free of charge. Current courses cover everything from cardiovascular disease to the Scottish referendum. MOOCs have taken off in the United States, where universities like Stanford and Harvard have invested heavily in the concept. Some see them as a threat to traditional university education, but the OU expects the new courses to complement its 408 undergraduate modules and other higher education courses.

The OU does not appear in *The Times and Sunday Times* league table because the absence of on-campus undergraduates makes the OU unsuitable for comparison with other universities on some of the measures used. But it has been the model for open and distance learning institutions around the world. It offers curriculum resources free via its OpenLearn website and recently became the first UK university to extend free learning to the social media site Bibblio, another platform to view and share multimedia materials. With more than 200,000 students across all types of courses, it is more than twice the size of any in the UK. That has not prevented it ranking at or very near the top of the National Student Survey every year since 2005. Undergraduate fees were £5,264 for the equivalent of full-time study (120 credits) in 2014 – the cheapest at any university. The OU provides financial support for those from poor backgrounds through its Access to Success programme. The average age of new undergraduates has come down to 29, as the demand from school leavers has grown. Three in ten are under 25 years old and three-quarters work either full or part-time while studying. Over 60 per cent of undergraduates are female and most live in the UK, but there are now 13,000 students outside the country. The OU offers special support for disabled students and currently has around 20,000 students with disabilities.

The university's headquarters are at Milton Keynes, Buckinghamshire, but it has 350 study centres and regional centres in each of its 13 regions around the UK, as well as offices and exam centres in other countries. The open access principle that

Walton Hall
Milton Keynes MK7 6AA

0845 300 6090 (enquiries)
contact via website
www.open.ac.uk
www.open.ac.uk/ousa
Affiliation: University
    Alliance

The Times and Sunday Times **Rankings**
The available data do not match the data used to rank the other full-time universities, so the Open University could not be included in the league table this year.

was a cornerstone of its foundation remains in place: no formal qualifications are required to study on most undergraduate programmes. Almost 6,400 part-time associate lecturers (tutors) guide students through degrees. The OU's "Supported Open Learning" system allows students to work where they choose – at home, in the workplace or at a library or study centre. They can study full-time or part-time, at a pace to suit their circumstances. They have contact with fellow students at tutorials, day schools or through online conferencing and electronic forums, social networks and informal study groups. An increasing amount of material is delivered online, and can be accessed on mobile devices as well as computers.

Gone are the late-night BBC television programmes that were the mainstay of teaching until 2006. The OU now produces mainstream television and radio programming aimed at bringing learning to a wider audience. The university also leads the universities placing material on the iTunes U site and was one of the first in the world to make e-books available there. The 1,100 full-time academics have a proud research record: more than half of the work submitted for the last Research Assessment Exercise was regarded as world-leading or internationally excellent. The OU employs more than 500 people engaged in research and there are over 1,300 research students.

The university covers all the main academic disciplines, and its business school produces more MBAs than the rest of the UK's business schools put together, as well as offering Honours and Foundation degrees. In addition to degrees in a named subject, the OU also awards "Open" Bachelor degrees, where the syllabus is designed by the students combining a number of modules. The OU has strong links to business and industry, and offers a range of professional and vocational qualifications. Assessment is by both continual assessment and examination or, for some modules, a major assignment. Except in fast-moving areas such as computing, there is no limit on the time taken to complete a degree.

Undergraduate Fees and Bursaries

» Fees vary depending upon the type of course, on where you live and the number of credits you plan to study. In 2014–15, in England a course of 120 credits of study (a year's full-time study) is £5,264, which can be covered by a tuition fee loan. In Scotland, Wales and Northern Ireland, a course of 120 credits is £1,550–£2,885, and there may be government assistance in paying the fee.
» For international students, a course of 120 credits is £5,264.
» The costs of all courses are given in the course descriptions: **www.open.ac.uk/courses**
» Various forms of financial help are available. Details are given at: **www.open.ac.uk/courses/fees-and-funding**

Students

Undergraduates:	**5**	**(156,970)**
Postgraduates:	**290**	**(10,945)**
Satisfaction with students' union	**64%**	

Accommodation

As the courses provided are part time, the university does not provide accommodation.

University of Oxford

Oxford is back at the top of our league table after a single year's absence, but this time it has to share the leadership with Cambridge. There has never been much to separate the two, but this is the first dead heat since the inaugural edition of the *Guide*. Both are head and shoulders above the other institutions in the table and in the view of most experts. Oxford's recovery is due largely to improved graduate destinations, and it outscores Cambridge on staffing, degree classifications and spending on student facilities, but it tops only seven subject tables to Cambridge's 33. Oxford is the oldest and probably the most famous university in the English-speaking world. It is also among the top six universities in the world, according to the QS and *Times Higher Education* world rankings.

The university continues to lobby for undergraduate fees to rise beyond £9,000, but this will remain the maximum for entrants in 2015 – and probably for some time thereafter. The university claims the true cost of its world-famous tuition is at least £16,000 and it also continues to offer the most generous financial support in UK higher education for students from poor backgrounds. A £75-million donation helps to provide bursaries and fee waivers worth up to £7,500 a year for those whose family income is less than £16,000. However, Oxford also admits the lowest proportion of undergraduates from the bottom four socio-economic groups: less than one in ten. There have been numerous initiatives to broaden the intake, including summer schools, recruitment fairs and student visits to comprehensive schools. Still more than 40 per cent of the applicants are from independent schools, however, and there are fewer than six applicants to each place overall – a much more favourable ratio than at some other leading universities – but 99 per cent of successful candidates achieve at least three As at A level, or their equivalent. Some subjects now demand two A* grades and another A at A level.

Applications were down slightly in 2013, but the long-term trend is upwards and the university never ceases to remind sixth-formers that Oxford is open to all who can meet the exacting entrance requirements. Enrolments from outside the EU have risen slightly over the last five years, but there are still approaching 3,000 places for home and European students. Applications must be made by mid October – a month earlier if you wish to be interviewed overseas – and it is not possible to apply to both Oxford and Cambridge. There are written tests for some subjects and you may be asked to submit samples of work. Selection is in the hands of the 30 undergraduate colleges, which vary considerably in their approach

University Offices
Wellington Square
Oxford OX1 2JD

01865 288000 (admissions)
contact via website
www.ox.ac.uk
www.ousu.org
Affiliation: Russell Group

The Times and Sunday Times **Rankings**
Overall Ranking: **=1** (last year: 2)

Student satisfaction:	=11	85.4%
Research quality:	2	44.3%
Entry standards:	2	580
Student–staff ratio:	2	11.0
Services & facilities/student:	1	£3,506
Expected completion rate:	=1	98.9%
Good honours:	1	91.5%
Graduate prospects:	6	82.6%

to this issue and others. Sound advice on academic strengths and social factors is essential for applicants to give themselves the best chance of winning a place and finding a setting in which they can thrive. A minority of candidates opt to go straight into the admissions pool without expressing a preference for a particular college. The choice is particularly important for arts and social science students, whose world-famous individual or small group tuition is based in college. Science and technology are taught mainly in central facilities. All subjects operate on eight-week terms and assess students entirely on final examinations – a system some find too pressurised. Nevertheless, Oxford remains one of the top universities for student satisfaction.

The development of a new campus on the site of the Radcliffe Infirmary represents the first fruit of the Oxford Thinking fundraising campaign, which passed its £1.25-billion target in 2012 and has now been extended to £3 billion. Oxford's biggest capital development for more than a century will provide more student accommodation for neighbouring Somerville College, a new Mathematical Institute building and a new building for the humanities. In the Science Area, existing buildings will be refurbished and modernised. Among the many recent projects was the opening of a new building at the Botnar Research Centre for research on arthritis, osteoporosis and other bone and joint diseases. Professor Andrew Hamilton, the Vice-Chancellor, has identified the digital infrastructure as the next big area of investment.

There was never much doubt about the strength of Oxford's research, but the 2008 Research Assessment Exercise found more than 70 per cent of it to be world-leading or internationally excellent. Oxford entered more academics for assessment than any other university – twice as many as some research-based universities of similar size. There were good results in all areas. Oxford also attracts the largest amount of research income among UK universities.

Undergraduate Fees and Bursaries

» Fees for UK/EU students 2015–16 £9,000
» Year abroad £1,350
» Fees for international students 2014–15 £14,415–£21,220
  Medicine £16,545–£29,225
  College fees £6,725 (£2,765 for clinical medicine years)
» UK/EU students with household income up to £16K, a bursary of £4,500 a year; £16K–£42.6K, bursary on sliding scale £3,500–£500 a year.
» In addition Moritz–Heyman scholarships for students with household income below £16K and other conditions, £3,000 a year fee waiver.
» Wide range of departmental and College awards.
» Check the university's website for the latest information.

Students

Undergraduates:	**11,525**	**(5,225)**
Postgraduates:	**7,305**	**(1,620)**
Mature students:	**3.2%**	
International students:	**12.2%**	
Applications per place:	**5.5**	
From state-sector schools:	**57.4%**	
From working-class homes:	**9.6%**	
Satisfaction with students' union	**31%**	

For detailed information about sports facilities:
www.sport.ox.ac.uk

Accommodation

www.ox.ac.uk/students/life/accommodation
Also see chapter 13 for information about individual colleges.

Oxford Brookes University

Oxford Brookes is the first UK university to introduce the Grade Point Average (GPA) system to give its students a more accurate assessment of their work than the traditional British honours degree classification. Students will still be classified as well, but all their marks from the first year onwards now count towards their GPA, which has strong recognition internationally. The change follows a tradition of innovation at Brookes that dates back to its time as a polytechnic, when it pioneered the modular degree system that has swept British higher education. After more than 20 years' experience, the university has now trimmed the 2,000 modules it once offered, but undergraduates can pair subjects as diverse as history and biology. Each subject has compulsory modules in the first year and a list of others that are acceptable later. Students are encouraged to take advantage of a range of placement and exchange opportunities and to take subjects outside their main area of study. Another innovative feature is a global partnership with the Association of Chartered Certified Accountants, which means that Brookes has far more students than any other UK university – over 200,000 – taking its qualifications in other countries.

The university is always among the highest-placed in our league table of those established since 1992. Brookes is particularly popular with independent schools, which provide just over a quarter of the undergraduates – by far the highest proportion among the new universities and twice the national average for the university's subjects and entry grades. However, the proportion from working-class homes, at 45 per cent, is also considerably ahead of the official benchmark. Brookes has been trying to attract more students from state schools and has targeted areas in Oxfordshire and the wider region, as well as offering a range of bursaries for those from low-income families. The university's location is an advantage in student recruitment, but the quality of provision is the real draw. Ofsted rates the primary teacher training as outstanding and the university's departments feature near the top of *The Times and Sunday Times* rankings for several subjects.

Brookes is celebrating the 150th anniversary of the original institution, the Oxford School of Art, but its main campus at Headington is almost unrecognisable even from four years ago. The £132-million John Henry Brookes Building opened in February 2014 and has been rated among the top 15 new buildings in the UK. It brings together the library and teaching space with the students' union and support services. Wheatley Campus, seven miles from the city centre is the base for business

---

Headington Campus
Gypsy Lane
Oxford OX3 0BP

01865 484848 (enquiries)
query@brookes.ac.uk
www.brookes.ac.uk
www.brookesunion.org.uk
Affiliation: University
    Alliance

The Times and Sunday Times **Rankings**
Overall Ranking: **49** (last year: 50)

Student satisfaction:	=36	83.3%
Research quality:	60	5.7%
Entry standards:	47	369
Student–staff ratio:	=53	16.9
Services & facilities/student:	=77	£1,416
Expected completion rate:	43	89.1%
Good honours:	=53	69.6%
Graduate prospects:	=53	67.9%

engineering and technology students. A new engineering building supports the university's status as a Government-designated regional centre for motorsport and high performance engineering: graduates now work in all F1 teams. The Harcourt Hill campus, at Botley, is the home of the School of Education. There is also a small site in Swindon, which focuses mainly on nursing and has its own osteopathic training clinic. Brookes sponsors a university technical college for 14–19 year-olds in the town.

The undergraduate intake grew by almost 1,000 students in 2013, reaching record levels. The demand for places had fallen a little, but there were still about six applications for every place. The university has an integrated e-learning network, which is designed to give students greater flexibility over when, where and how they learn. There is a personal information portal for tasks such as choosing study modules and checking grades. Grades in the last Research Assessment Exercise showed improvement, with more than a third of the work judged to be world-leading or internationally excellent.

Oxford Brookes was one of 11 UK universities to win a Green Flag award in 2014 and the only one to be given three, one for each campus. It also featured in the top ten in the People and Planet Green league of 2013, the sixth successive year that has featured in the top category of the environmental assessments.

A 25-metre swimming pool and 9-hole golf course have been added to the already impressive sports facilities. Brookes is home to the top university squad for young rowers aiming to get into Team GB and hoping to match the successes of previous alumni who won medals at three consecutive Olympic games. A new £600,000 boathouse opened in 2013. Their cricketers combine with Oxford University to take on county teams. The students' union runs one of the biggest entertainment venues in Oxford, a city that can be expensive, but which offers enough to satisfy most students.

Undergraduate Fees and Bursaries

» Fees for UK/EU students 2015–16	£9,000
» Foundation degree at partner colleges	£6,000
» Bachelor degree at partner colleges	£7,000
» Placement year / year abroad	£1,350
» Fees for international students 2014–15	£11,900–£13,670
» Household income below £10K: a bursary of £2,000 in year 1, £3,000 in years 2 and 3; £10K–£15K, £1,500 in year 1, £2,500 in years 2 and 3; £15K–£25K, £1,000 in year 1, £1,750 in years 2 and 3.	
» Community scholarships of £1,000 in year 1 for local students.	
» Check the university's website for the latest information.	

Students		
Undergraduates:	11,295	(2,330)
Postgraduates:	1,775	(2,465)
Mature students:	20.4%	
International students:	15.5%	
Applications per place:	5.8	
From state-sector schools:	73.6%	
From working-class homes:	44.9%	
Satisfaction with students' union	36%	

For detailed information about sports facilities:
www.brookes.ac.uk/brookes-sport

Accommodation

Number of places and costs refer to 2014–15
University-provided places: 4,600
Percentage catered: 3%
Catered cost: £143.26 a week (38 weeks).
Self-catered cost: £102.41–£188.19 (from 38 weeks).
All accommodation is allocated to first year who select Oxford Brookes as Firm choice through UCAS and meet all deadlines for application.
International students: as above.
www.brookes.ac.uk/students/accommodation

Plymouth University

Plymouth featured in the top 50 of *Times Higher Education* magazine's ranking of the leading universities in the world that are under 50 years old. But within a few weeks, Professor Wendy Purcell, the Vice-Chancellor, had been "placed on leave" pending a review without explanation from the university. The action inevitably prompted speculation about the university's finances and distracted attention from a series of developments that had raised its profile. Chief among them was to have become the only post-1992 university with its own medical school when it ended its partnership with Exeter University in the management of the former Peninsula College of Medicine and Dentistry. The new school is small, with an annual entry of only 75 students taking medicine, but Plymouth has kept all 50 of Peninsula's places in dentistry. As part of the plans, Plymouth has invested £25 million to further medical and health research in the South West. The university is the largest provider of nursing, midwifery and health professional education and training in the region.

Plymouth is one of the largest universities in the UK, with around 30,000 students, and is aiming to be the country's top "enterprise university". It was awarded a Queen's Anniversary Prize for Higher and Further Education in 2012 and was the first university to be awarded Regional Growth Fund money to promote economic development. The university has one of the country's top 10 business incubation facilities – part of its managed portfolio of £100-million worth of incubation and innovation assets. In 2013, it became the first university in the world to be awarded the Social Enterprise Mark, the only independent accreditation of social enterprise.

Over £200 million has been spent on the main city campus. The library has been extended and upgraded and the students' union refurbished. There have been new buildings for the Faculty of Health and the Faculty of Education and Society, as well as a £35-million arts complex. More recently, Plymouth has opened a £1-million Immersive Vision Theatre, thought to be the first of its kind at a UK university, which gives the feeling of being "in", rather than just observing, different types of image. In 2012, the university added the £19-million Marine Building, which contains the country's most advanced wave tanks, a navigation centre with ship simulator, and business incubation space for companies in the marine renewables sector. A £7-million centre for performing arts opens in September. The university's commitment to sustainability has also been recognised through two successive rankings as the

---

Drake Circus
Plymouth
Devon PL4 8AA
01752 585858 (enquiries)
contact via website
www.plymouth.ac.uk
www.upsu.com
Affiliation: University
  Alliance

The Times and Sunday Times Rankings
Overall Ranking: **80** (last year: =73)

Student satisfaction:	70	81.8%
Research quality:	58	6.7%
Entry standards:	=82	316
Student–staff ratio:	=44	16.2
Services & facilities/student:	95	£1,285
Expected completion rate:	73	84.6%
Good honours:	84	63.0%
Graduate prospects:	98	57.9%

second greenest university in the People and Planet league.

Plymouth is a partner in the Combined Universities in Cornwall, which is boosting further and higher education in the county. Plymouth has established a unique relationship with its 18 partner colleges, which have become a faculty of the university, sharing £3.5 million in capital investment. They spread from Cornwall to Somerset, taking in Jersey, and have 10,000 students taking university courses. The intake reflects Plymouth's position as the working-class hub of the South West, with almost 95 per cent of students state-educated and nearly a third from the poorest social classes. The projected dropout rate of less than 11 per cent is below average for the courses and entry grades. Some 12,000 students undertake work-based learning or placements with employability skills embedded throughout the curriculum from day one, while the new Plymouth Award recognises extra-curricular achievements.

Plymouth was awarded national teaching centres in health and social care, experiential learning in environmental and natural sciences, institutional partnerships, and education for sustainable development – all of which have now been brought into the university's core activities. No university has exceeded the 16 National Teaching Fellowships won by its academics.

Plymouth entered by far the largest number of academics of any post-1992 university in the latest research assessments – twice the proportion entered by some of its peer group. More than a third of the submission was rated world-leading or internationally excellent.

A 1,300-bed student village costing £15 million, has greatly improved the university's residential stock. Upgraded facilities for water sports and an £850,000 fitness centre have added to the sports facilities, while a range of sports scholarships and bursaries support high-fliers. The university has a partnership with Plymouth Albion Rugby Club to promote and support sport in the city and it invested £2.5 million in the new £45-million Plymouth Life Centre. There are exclusive sessions for students at the international-standard swimming and fitness facility. Plymouth is the only university in the UK to have its own diving and water sports centre.

Undergraduate Fees and Bursaries

» Fees for UK/EU students 2015–16	£9,000
» Foundation degree at partner colleges	£7,200–£7,500
» Placement year	£900
» Fees for international students 2014–15	£11,500
Medicine	£17,500–£32,000
» Details of bursaries and scholarships in 2015–16 were not available in August 2014. Consult university website for details.	
» Care leaver and sports bursaries.	

Students

Undergraduates:	20,540	(4,130)
Postgraduates:	1,645	(2,310)
Mature students:	22%	
International students:	7.7%	
Applications per place:	4.4	
From state-sector schools:	93.1%	
From working-class homes:	30.5%	
Satisfaction with students' union	82%	

For detailed information about sports facilities:
www1.plymouth.ac.uk/getactive/

Accommodation

Number of places and costs refer to 2014–15
University-provided places: 3,000
Percentage catered: 0%
Self-catered costs: £91–£151 a week (40–51 weeks).
First years are not guaranteed university provided accommodation.
International students: overseas students have priority for allocation.
accommodation@plymouth.ac.uk
www5.plymouth.ac.uk/student-life/accommodation

University of Portsmouth

Portsmouth is one of the few universities to release details of its applications for courses starting in 2014. It has seen an increase roughly four times the national average, more than doubling the 5 per cent growth it enjoyed in 2013. The university is among the leading post-1992 institutions in our league table, benefiting particularly from strong student satisfaction ratings. It has one of the largest language departments in the country, teaching six languages to degree level and offering free language courses to all students. About 1,000 Portsmouth students go abroad for part of their course, and at least as many come from the continent. The university also has a growing reputation in health subjects. The £9-million Dental Academy trains student dentists in their final year at King's College London in a team-based setting with dental therapists and hygienists. More than 600 radiographers, paramedics, medical technologists, pharmacists, clinicians and social workers graduate each year. Specialist research centres include the UK's first Brain Tumour Research Centre of Excellence, as well the Institute of Biomedical and Biomolecular Sciences and the Institute of Cosmology and Gravitation.

Teaching in all subjects is concentrated on the Guildhall campus in the centre of Portsmouth, with most residential accommodation nearby. The campus has undergone extensive redevelopment. A new £14-million wing on the Eldon building opened in 2014 created an additional 3,000 square metres of space and provided the Faculty of Creative and Cultural Industries with new purpose-built facilities. These include a 200-seat screening room and lecture theatre, exhibition space and seminar rooms, as well as fashion, textiles, architecture and interior design studios, a new café designed by the architecture students, and learning space. Students in the faculty will also benefit from a partnership with the New Theatre Royal, which will allow them to use the facilities in an £8-million building that will adjoin the original theatre. Refurbishment of the university library, costing £4 million, will be complete in time for the start of the 2014–15 academic year, with improved social learning space and IT provision. Another refurbishment project will create new accommodation for the School of Engineering and Surveying, the Business School and Information Services, also for use in Autumn 2014.

Employability skills and training are embedded throughout 450 different degree programmes. A significant number are accredited by professional bodies and, wherever possible, students are given opportunities for hands-on practice in

---

University House
Winston Churchill Avenue
Portsmouth
Hampshire PO1 2UP

023 9284 8484
info.centre@port.ac.uk
www.port.ac.uk
www.upsu.net
Affiliation: University
    Alliance

The Times and Sunday Times Rankings
Overall Ranking: **57** (last year: 55)

Student satisfaction:	=42	83.0%
Research quality:	=61	5.3%
Entry standards:	84	314
Student–staff ratio:	=75	18.6
Services & facilities/student:	74	£1,431
Expected completion rate:	46	88.1%
Good honours:	41	71.2%
Graduate prospects:	60	66.3%

Edinburgh
Belfast
Cardiff   London
PORTSMOUTH

their chosen career. Up-to-date learning facilities, such as a mock courtroom, pharmacy, journalism newsroom, forensic suite and the Dental Academy provide real-life professional skills. Forty per cent of the work submitted for the last Research Assessment Exercise was considered world-leading or internationally excellent. The university is an official centre of teaching and research about the EU.

Portsmouth has a larger working-class population than most cities in the south of England. One third of undergraduates come from the four lowest socio-economic groups, although this is just below the national average for the university's subjects and entry qualifications. Much of the extra income from £9,000 fees is being spent on initiatives to broaden the intake, such as the award-winning membership club that introduces teenagers to higher education through workshops, holiday courses and access to university facilities. Unlike many other universities, Portsmouth is also maintaining its spending on bursaries for students from poor homes, having found that most of the recipients would have struggled to stay on their courses without financial support. A threshold of £25,000 family income to qualify for full bursaries is more generous than in most such schemes, and there are extra awards for modern languages – one of the university's strengths and an area of national decline.

The projected dropout rate has improved considerably in recent years and, at less than 10 per cent, is now significantly lower than the university's benchmark.

A £6.5-million student centre caters for the multicultural population of the university with alcohol-free areas and an international students' bar. Modernised sport, exercise and fitness facilities include gyms, dance studios and a sports hall. Many students live in Southsea, which has a vibrant social scene and quirky shops. Portsmouth has seen considerable regeneration, notably through the retail and entertainment complex at Gunwharf, with its 170-metre Spinnaker Tower. The cost of living is not as high as at many southern universities, and the sea is close at hand. University-allocated accommodation is offered to around two-thirds of new first years who apply, and assistance is offered to those seeking accommodation in the private rented sector, including house-hunting events, online resources and regular drop-in advice sessions.

Undergraduate Fees and Bursaries

- » Fees for UK/EU students 2015–16 £9,000
- » Courses at partner colleges £6,000
- » Fees for international students 2014–15 £11,000–£12,500
- » English students (excluding those at partner colleges) with household income below £25K, a bursary of £1,500 in year 1, £1,000 all other years; £25K–£32K, £500 a year.
- » Check the university's website for the latest information.

Students

Undergraduates:	**17,015**	**(1,965)**
Postgraduates:	**1,705**	**(2,005)**
Mature students:	**14%**	
International students:	**14.6%**	
Applications per place:	**5.7**	
From state-sector schools:	**95%**	
From working-class homes:	**33.6%**	
Satisfaction with students' union	**79%**	

For detailed information about sports facilities:
www.port.ac.uk/students/sport-and-recreation

Accommodation

Number of places and costs refer to 2014–15
University-provided places: around 3,000
Percentage catered: 25%
Catered costs: £98–£126 a week (37 weeks).
Self-catered costs: £81–£128 a week (37 weeks).
Majority of first years offered university accommodation.
International, Channel Islands and Isle of Man students guaranteed university accommodation subject to terms and conditions.
student.housing@port.ac.uk
www.port.ac.uk/why-portsmouth/accommodation/

Queen Margaret University

Queen Margaret (QMU) moved into an impressive, modern campus designed in consultation with the students in the seaside town of Musselburgh, to the southeast of Edinburgh, when it was awarded university status in 2007. It has proved a big attraction for applicants and now its facilities are being made available to college students who may be unsure whether to commit to a degree. The innovative Associate Student Scheme was launched with Edinburgh College, where students have signed up for an Associate BA in events management or international tourism and hospitality management. It has now been extended to Newbattle Abbey College, in Dalkeith, for degrees in psychology and sociology. Students are taught in college for the first two years of their course, making regular visits to the campus, where some even choose to live, before transferring to QMU. Other institutional partnerships have seen the university open the first UK branch campus in Singapore, a joint venture with the East Asia Institute of Management, which already taught Queen Margaret degree courses. The university also has international programmes in Nepal, Egypt, Saudi Arabia, Greece and Switzerland.

Named after Saint Margaret, the 11th-century Queen of Scotland, the institution dates back to 1875 and was originally a school of cookery for women. True to its roots, the university is investing heavily in research and knowledge exchange facilities in the area of food, launching the Scottish Centre for Food Development and Innovation in 2014. It also has a partnership with the Edinburgh New Town Cookery School, run by a former graduate of QMU, to hone the practical skills of students on the international hospitality management degree.

There are now more than 6,000 students, three-quarters of them female, divided between two schools: Arts, Social Sciences and Management, and Health Sciences. The university has established three flagship areas as a focus for future investment and development: health and rehabilitation, sustainable business, and culture and creativity. It promises "inter-professional" teaching and research to encourage the professions to work better together.

Health is an area of particular strength: QMU has the broadest range of allied health courses in Scotland, from dietetics, podiatry and audiology, to art therapy, music therapy and health psychology. The university has an international reputation for its work in speech sciences, and launched a Clinical Audiology, Speech and Language Research Centre in 2011. Courses in international health attract students from all over the world. The interdisciplinary

Queen Margaret University Drive
Musselburgh EH21 6UU

0131 474 0000 (enquiries)
contact via website
www.qmu.ac.uk
www.qmusu.org.uk
Affiliation: none

drama and performance degree draws together the university's recognised strengths in acting, screen work, community theatre, contemporary performance and playwriting to reflect the current needs of a changing profession. QMU also offers a degree in costume design and construction. All has not been plain sailing for the new university, however. Only one university had a lower average score in the last Research Assessment Exercise, and QMU experienced financial problems in its early years, which it has since overcome.

The university has a good record for graduate employment, which it attributes to a strong relationship between teaching and research, and up-to-date course design that is relevant to the world of work. Specialist laboratories and clinics are well equipped. The nursing simulation lab, for example, is set out exactly like a hospital ward, helping to instil students with the confidence to move on easily to a work placement or career in the NHS or private practice. There are also well-equipped rooms for podiatry, radiography, occupational therapy, physiotherapy and art therapy. An impressive learning resource centre, parts of which are open 24 hours a day, offers a variety of study spaces. There are a number of sponsored awards, including five worth £1,000 each from Ryder Cup Europe to fund tourism, hospitality and event students.

The campus, which has won a string of awards, is one of the most environmentally sustainable in the UK, exceeding current standards. The university has made sustainability a top priority, in the curriculum as well as in the way it operates, and ties with Edinburgh Napier for top place in Scotland in the People and Planet league of environmental performance. The campus is located next to Musselburgh train station, from where Edinburgh city centre is only a six-minute journey. There is also a frequent bus service from the campus to the city centre. There are 800 residential places on the campus, about 300 of them larger, premier rooms with double beds and more space. Other features include a students' union building, indoor and outdoor sports facilities, a variety of catering outlets and landscaped gardens with a range of environmental features.

Undergraduate Fees and Bursaries

» Fees for Scottish and EU students 2014–15   No fee
» Fees for Non-Scottish UK (RUK) students 2014–15   £6,750
» Fees for international students 2014–15   £10,170–£12,090
» For RUK students, annual bursaries: household income up to £20K, £2,000 cash; sliding scale to £42.6K, £1,500–£500.
» Range of other scholarships and bursaries available.
» Check the university's website for the latest information.

Students

Undergraduates:	**2,905**	**(525)**
Postgraduates:	**525**	**(1,380)**
Mature students:	**26.2%**	
International students:	**18.5%**	
Applications per place:	**6.8**	
From state-sector schools:	**94.5%**	
From working-class homes:	**30.3%**	
Satisfaction with students' union	**45%**	

For detailed information about sports facilities: www.qmu.ac.uk/sports

Accommodation

Number of places and costs refer to 2014–15
University-provided places: 800
Percentage catered: 0%
Self-catered costs: £99–£116 a week (40 or 50 week contract).
First years are guaranteed accommodation. Residential and age restrictions apply.
International students: guaranteed housing.
accommodation@qmu.ac.uk
www.qmu.ac.uk/accommodation/

Queen Mary, University of London

Queen Mary (QMUL) enjoyed record applications and enrolments in 2013, as it reaped the benefits of joining the Russell Group of leading research universities. With a big medical school contributing to a high volume of research, it fitted the profile of the group better than some of the other new entrants. It has since launched a life sciences initiative, bringing together the Faculties of Science and Engineering, Humanities and Social Sciences, and Barts and the London School of Medicine and Dentistry to work together to realise the social and economic promise of personalised healthcare and to address major public health issues both locally and worldwide. The school's Institute of Dentistry moved into the first new dental school to be built in the UK for 40 years, when it occupied new facilities costing £78 million in the Royal London Hospital in 2014. The medical school, which has introduced a new BSc in Global Health, is rated in the top 100 in the world, but QMUL is still best known for its strength in the humanities, where it boasts a clutch of high-profile academics.

Queen Mary has the highest proportion of undergraduates from working-class homes in the Russell Group – more than a third. Many come from London's ethnic minority groups, although QMUL also attracts students from 150 countries outside the UK. It is aiming to be among the top ten universities in the UK by 2015, although has set its own criteria, which give more weight to research than is the case in *The Times and Sunday Times* league table, where it remains outside the top 30. There has been particular success in attracting overseas students, who make full use of a unit specialising in English as a foreign language and now account for more than a fifth of undergraduates. There is a flourishing exchange programme, which includes universities in the USA and Japan, as well as Europe, while more than 2,000 students are in Beijing taking joint degrees from QMUL and the Beijing University of Posts and Telecommunications.

QMUL outperforms most London institutions in the National Student Survey. Most lectures are filmed and made available through the Virtual Learning Environment to allow students to go back over parts that they may not have understood. The majority of undergraduates take at least one course in departments other than their own. Interdisciplinary study has always been encouraged: for example, medics can choose selected modules in English and drama.

The arts-based Westfield College and scientific Queen Mary came together in 1989. Now the self-contained campus in

---

Mile End Road
London E1 4NS

020 7882 5511 (admissions)
admissions@qmul.ac.uk
www.qmul.ac.uk
www.qmsu.org
Affiliation: Russell Group

Edinburgh
Belfast
Cardiff
LONDON

The Times and Sunday Times **Rankings**
Overall Ranking: **37** (last year: 37)

Student satisfaction:	=89	80.0%
Research quality:	=25	23.0%
Entry standards:	=27	424
Student–staff ratio:	10	12.0
Services & facilities/student:	15	£2,233
Expected completion rate:	35	90.8%
Good honours:	49	70.3%
Graduate prospects:	=47	70.3%

the newly fashionable East End of London is the most extensive in the capital. Some £250 million has been spent over the last 15 years on new facilities and strengthening the academic staff. The main campus includes a state-of-the-art learning resource centre with 24-hour access and an award-winning student village with 2,000 en-suite rooms. An arts quarter contains research and teaching facilities, as well as a conference centre. The £20-million Arts2 building, featuring a drama studio and lecture theatre opened in 2012. There is even room for the second-oldest cemetery in England, the Grade II-listed Nuevo Jewish burial ground dating from the 18th century. The historic People's Palace building, which brought education to the Victorian masses, is still Queen Mary's most recognisable feature, and has been restored to host cultural events for the institution and the local community.

The Barts and the London School of Medicine and Dentistry is based in nearby Whitechapel, in the £44-million Blizard Building. Next door is the new BioEnterprise Innovation Centre for science companies. The Centre of the Cell is also located on the Whitechapel campus, the first such interactive facility to be based within a working medical school research laboratory to give young people a glimpse of how scientists operate. Grades improved spectacularly in the last Research Assessment Exercise, when almost two-thirds of the work submitted was rated world-leading or internationally excellent, propelling Queen Mary into the top 25 UK universities for research.

Social life centres on the campus, which features a refurbished students' union with a new bar and a subsidised health and fitness centre, which has helped improve the sports facilities. Students welcome the relatively low prices (for the capital) in east London, and their proximity to the lively youth culture of Spitalfields, Shoreditch and Brick Lane. Queen Mary students can use the sports facilities at the Queen Elizabeth Olympic Park, including the Copper Box indoor arena and the Aquatic Centre's swimming pool.

Undergraduate Fees and Bursaries

» Fees for UK/EU students 2015–16   £9,000
» Placement year   £1,800
» Year abroad   £1,350
» Fees for international students 2014–15   £13,250–£15,950
   Medicine and dentistry   £19,900–£30,400
» Household income below £25K; a bursary of £1,571 a year; £25K–£42.6K, £1,256 a year.
» Other academic and targeted scholarships available.
» Check the university's website for the latest information.

Students

Undergraduates:	**10,950**	(35)
Postgraduates:	**3,120**	(935)
Mature students:	**13.2%**	
International students:	**21.6%**	
Applications per place:	**7.1**	
From state-sector schools:	**85.8%**	
From working-class homes:	**34.6%**	
Satisfaction with students' union	**71%**	

For detailed information about sports facilities:
www.qmsu.org/sportandfitness/

Accommodation

Number of places and costs refer to 2014–15
University-provided places: 2,337
Percentage catered: 4%
Catered costs: £175 upwards a week.
Self-catered costs: £120–£180 a week.
First years giving Queen Mary as firm choice get priority, if terms and conditions are met. Residential restrictions apply.
International students: All new incoming students meeting criteria are judged equally.
www.qmul.ac.uk/studentlife/accommodation/

Queen's University, Belfast

Queen's had been climbing our league table, breaking into the top 30 for the first time in more than a decade in last year's *Guide*. But it has slipped back this year, mainly because it could not repeat its best-ever performance in the National Student Survey. The undergraduate intake grew by more than 15 per cent, as Queen's achieved one of the biggest increases in applications at any university. A member of the Russell Group of leading research institutions, it is in the top 200 in the QS World University Rankings and is in the process of recruiting scores of high-calibre academics, partly in order to move towards the top 100 over the next few years. More than half of the university's submission to the last Research Assessment Exercise was rated as world-leading or internationally excellent, placing Queen's in the top ten in 11 subject areas. Its international profile is such that it is a favourite destination for American Fulbright Scholars, while it is also among the top ten universities in Europe for the number of students who go on work placements abroad as part of the Erasmus scheme.

Queen's is recognised as Northern Ireland's premier university, with graduates in senior leadership positions in 80 of the province's top 100 companies. It has launched a £140-million fundraising campaign, "Beyond", with a focus on the student experience, including the City Scholars programme, which provides financial support and internships sponsored by alumni worldwide. Strictly non-denominational teaching is enshrined in a charter which has guaranteed student representation and equal rights for women since 1908. The university is one of two in the UK to hold gold Athena Swan Awards for tackling the unequal representation of women in science, engineering and technology. Queen's was one of four university colleges for the whole of Ireland in the nineteenth century, and still draws students from all over the island. However, the majority of students come from Northern Ireland, and Queen's suffers in the comparison of entry grades because relatively few sixth-formers in the Province take four A levels.

Over the past ten years, Queen's has invested £350 million in its campus, and plans to spend as much again over the next decade. The plans include a new home for the School of Law, a postgraduate and international student centre, a new building for biological sciences and a computer centre. The biggest current developments are a £175-million Institute of Health Sciences and the £32-million Centre for Experimental Medicine, which will open in 2015. Completed projects include the £50-million McClay Library, which added

---

University Road
Belfast BT7 1NN

028 9097 3838 (admissions)
admissions@qub.ac.uk
www.qub.ac.uk
www.qubsu.org
Affiliation: Russell Group

The Times and Sunday Times **Rankings**
Overall Ranking: **38** (last year: =29)

Student satisfaction:	=36	83.3%
Research quality:	40	18.7%
Entry standards:	39	391
Student–staff ratio:	=37	15.5
Services & facilities/student:	46	£1,739
Expected completion rate:	=27	92.2%
Good honours:	38	72.6%
Graduate prospects:	32	75.1%

200 PCs, the award-winning Elms Student Village, and a student guidance centre. The students' union has had a £9-million refurbishment and includes an area for students to improve their enterprise and employability skills. Skills development is embedded in all the university's courses and the Degree Plus programme provides official recognition of extra-curricular activities and achievements to help graduates in the job market. A tangible example of the accent on employability was the opening of the First Derivatives Trading Room in the Management School. Queen's also opened the UK's first Graduate and Executive Education Centre this year, which has quickly become a hub for business in Northern Ireland. Undergraduates are encouraged to take language programmes from a "virtual" language laboratory, which provides online tuition from any computer in the university. IT facilities are good: Queen's was the first institution to meet the national target of providing at least one computer workstation for every five undergraduate students. Support for students has been enhanced by the establishment of new mentoring schemes involving students and alumni.

The university district is among the most attractive in Belfast. The university's highly successful international arts festival has been running for 50 years, and Queen's boasts the only full-time university cinema in the UK, as well as an art gallery and theatre, all of which are open to students and the wider community alike. The much-improved city centre is not short of nightlife, but the social scene is still concentrated on the students' union and the surrounding area. Sports facilities, which include a university cottage in the Mourne mountains, have seen a £20-million programme of investment. The new facility at Upper Malone features an arena pitch which can host football, rugby or Gaelic sport, another 14 pitches, a 3-km recreational trail and conference facilities. The Physical Education Centre provides physiotherapy, sports massage and podiatry, while a new Elite Athlete programme offers up to £8,000 of support for leading performers.

Undergraduate Fees and Bursaries

» Fees for NI/EU students 2014–15 £3,685
» Fees for English, Scottish, Welsh (RUK) students £9,000
» Placement year £720
» Fees for international students 2014–15 £12,650–£16,225
   Medicine and dentistry £16,750–£31,590
» The top 50 NI students on STEM course, year 1 scholarship of £1,000.
» RUK students (excluding medicine & dentistry) with at least AAB at A-Level or equivalent, annual fee waiver of £2,500 or £1,750 plus benefits package; with ABB or equivalent, annual fee waiver of £1,750 or £1,000 plus benefits package; with offer grades, annual fee waiver of £1,250 or £500 plus benefits package.

Students

Undergraduates:	14,145	(3,925)
Postgraduates:	2,510	(2,115)
Mature students:	17.2%	
International students:	5.8%	
Applications per place:	6.1	
From state-sector schools:	98.2%	
From working-class homes:	31.0%	
Satisfaction with students' union	78%	

For detailed information about sports facilities: www.queenssport.com

Accommodation

Number of places and costs refer to 2014–15
University-provided places: around 2,000
Percentage catered: 0%
Self-catered costs: £66–£110 a week.
First-year students are guaranteed accommodation if conditions are met.
International students: as above.
accommodation@qub.ac.uk
www.stayatqueens.com

University of Reading

In recent years, Reading has invested more than £400 million on its main campus and in 2015 will add another campus in Malaysia. Undergraduates have already begun courses in business and English on a temporary site close to the stylish new premises that the university will open at the Iksandar Education City, on the southern tip of Malaysia. Degrees in law, the built environment, psychology and pharmacy will be added when the University of Reading Malaysia is fully operational. The project will add to the growing complement of international students taking Reading degrees: new enrolments were up by more than a quarter in 2013. The university's courses and research in agriculture and development have long attracted students from around the world. Around a fifth of undergraduates now come from outside the UK, taking the full range of subjects.

Originally Oxford University's extension college, Reading was one of only two universities established between the two world wars. The attractive main campus, set in 320 acres of parkland, now has a modern feel and has won the Green Flag environmental award for four years in a row. Recent building projects include a new student services centre and business school, £100 million on new and redeveloped halls

of residence, a refurbished sports centre, and new catering facilities. The £17-million Hopkins Building added laboratories and teaching space for pharmacy and cardiovascular research, and there is a new world-class Chemical Analysis Facility. The £11-million Minghella Building for film, theatre and TV opened in the spring of 2011, while a separate Enterprise Centre brings together academic expertise with local and international technology-based businesses.

Reading did well in the last Research Assessment Exercise, despite entering a much higher proportion of its academics than many of its peers. There are international centres of research excellence in areas such as food security, agriculture, biological and physical sciences, meteorology, and European histories and cultures. Another research centre opened in January 2014, in the School of Psychology, which will focus on dementia.

As well as its sites in Reading, the university also owns 2,000 acres of farmland at nearby Sonning and Shinfield, where the renowned Centre for Dairy Research (CEDAR) is located. To these has been added the former Henley Management College, which became the university's business school in 2008. The college's attractive site, on the banks of the river at Henley-on-Thames, houses postgraduate and executive programmes, while undergraduates are taught on the main

---

Whiteknights
PO Box 217
Reading RG6 6AH

0118 378 8618/9
student.recruitment@
  reading.ac.uk
www.reading.ac.uk
www.rusu.co.uk
Affiliation: none

The Times and Sunday Times Rankings
Overall Ranking: **33** (last year: 35)

Student satisfaction:	30	83.7%
Research quality:	=27	22.7%
Entry standards:	44	376
Student–staff ratio:	=24	14.7
Services & facilities/student:	55	£1,594
Expected completion rate:	=31	91.4%
Good honours:	39	72.5%
Graduate prospects:	42	71.8%

Whiteknights campus. All undergraduates take career management skills modules that contribute five credits towards their degree classification. The online system, which has 200 web pages of advice, exercises and information, has been bought by 30 other universities and colleges. Sessions are delivered jointly by academics and careers advisors, with input from alumni and leading employers. Recent graduate employment figures have been good and the university is hoping to improve them further by providing placement opportunities for all students.

Reading is one of the medium-sized campus universities that have demonstrated their appeal through the National Student Survey: often appearing in or near the top 20 on this measure. About one undergraduate in six is from an independent school and just under a quarter come from working-class homes – below average for the university's subjects and entry qualifications. The university is devoting more than a quarter of the extra income from £9,000 fees to attempts to broaden the intake. It expects to provide cash bursaries for about 2,500 students in 2015–16.

Sports facilities have been extended. Water sports are a strong focus, with off-campus boathouses on the Thames and a sailing and canoeing club nearby. Representative teams have a good record in inter-university competitions and the campus was chosen as a pre-Olympics training camp for basketball and fencing. The town may not be the most fashionable, but Reading has plenty of nightlife and an award-winning shopping centre. It also offers temporary and part-time employment opportunities for students. London is easily accessible by train, but the cost of living is on a par with the capital. The halls of residence are either on or within easy walking distance of campus. The latest will provide an extra 650 rooms in time for the start of the 2014–15 academic year. The large students' union has been voted among the best in Britain, and has won numerous awards, including Best Bar None status for encouraging safe drinking. Students who live off campus can make use of the free night bus service to take them back into the town centre.

Undergraduate Fees and Bursaries

» Fees for UK/EU students 2015–16 £9,000
» Placement year / year abroad £1,350
» Fees for international students 2014–15 £13,230–£16,500
» Household income below £25K, a bursary of £1,000 a year; placement bursaries of £200–£1,000.
» 50 per cent fee waiver for Foundation degree in Early Years Learning.
» Other academic and targeted scholarships available.
» Check the university's website for the latest information.

Students

Undergraduates:	8,795	(115)
Postgraduates:	2,720	(1,805)
Mature students:	7.9%	
International students:	15.2%	
Applications per place:	6.9	
From state-sector schools:	84.9%	
From working-class homes:	23.3%	
Satisfaction with students' union	85%	

For detailed information about sports facilities:
www.sport.reading.ac.uk

Accommodation

Number of places and costs refer to 2014–15
University-provided places: about 5,000
Percentage catered: 18%
Catered costs: £131.36–£174.34 (40 weeks, catering during terms).
Self-catered costs: £99.89–£154.98 (40–51 weeks).
First-year undergraduate students are guaranteed a place if conditions are met.
International students: guaranteed if conditions are met.
accommodationonline@reading.ac.uk
www.reading.ac.uk/life/life-accommodation.aspx

Robert Gordon University

Robert Gordon (RGU) has come together on one site for the first time since long before it became a university in 1992. A £120-million development programme has enabled all teaching to take place on the Garthdee campus, on the south side of Aberdeen, overlooking the River Dee. The Schools of Engineering, Computing Science and Digital Media, Pharmacy and Life Sciences moved from the historic Schoolhill site in the city centre in 2013. Development is continuing, however, with a new building for the Scott Sutherland School of Architecture due to open in September 2015. A striking new green glass library tower with spectacular views over the river and city has become a landmark at the heart of the campus, which is full of graceful curves. Previous developments at Garthdee included additional specialist facilities for the Faculty of Health and Social Care. The Aberdeen Business School, designed by Norman Foster, is being upgraded with new teaching and student learning spaces and an open plan area with IT access, group study areas, exhibition and seminar space.

The university has generally been among the leading post-1992 institutions in our league table, but it has slipped 12 places this year and has been overtaken by several others in that peer group.

Graduate employment remains the university's strongest suit. RGU regularly features among the top ten universities on this measure. Close links with the North Sea oil and gas industries help in this respect – among the new facilities is a DART (Drilling and Advanced Rig Training) simulator that provides a full-scale reproduction of an offshore platform or land rig within the Energy Centre. Work placements lasting up to a year have become the norm on all the university's courses. With nursing and health sciences now accounting for a large share of the places, RGU gives itself the soubriquet of the Professional University. The creative industries are a growth area and there is a full portfolio of courses in business, design and engineering. Flexible programmes, with credit accumulation and transfer, make for easy movement in and out of the university for an often mobile local workforce.

Named after an eighteenth-century philanthropist, RGU has a pedigree in education that goes back 250 years. The university now offers about 150 degrees. Students from the city's two universities mix easily, and there is healthy academic rivalry in some areas. There is also a partnership with North East Scotland College, which allows students to progress from a college-based Higher National Diploma to the third year of an RGU degree course. Almost a third of RGU's

---

Garthdee House
Garthdee Road
Aberdeen AB10 7QB

01224 262728 (enquiries)
ugoffice@rgu.ac.uk
www.rgu.ac.uk
www.rguunion.co.uk
Affiliation: none

The Times and Sunday Times Rankings
Overall Ranking: **64** (last year: =52)

Student satisfaction:	=75	81.3%
Research quality:	=61	5.3%
Entry standards:	=40	384
Student–staff ratio:	=84	19.3
Services & facilities/student:	99	£1,246
Expected completion rate:	97	81.3%
Good honours:	=82	63.2%
Graduate prospects:	10	80.5%

submission in the last Research Assessment Exercise was considered world-leading or internationally excellent. Three research institutes have since been launched to focus on the university's strengths in business and information; innovation, design and sustainability; and health and welfare.

Like many modern universities, Robert Gordon recruits most of its students locally, nearly 60 per cent of them female. However, overseas student numbers have been growing sharply and the overall demand for places has been more consistent than at most universities north of the border. Efforts to extend access beyond the normal higher education catchment have produced a diverse student population, with three in ten undergraduates coming from working-class homes and 92 per cent from state schools or colleges.

The university has a strong focus on new technology. An award-winning virtual campus was launched with an online course in e-business for postgraduates. It also enables management undergraduates to receive course materials via an intranet, and other degree and short courses are available. The Moodle system is used across Robert Gordon courses for both on-campus and distance learning students, providing teaching, notes, online forums for discussion and electronic submission options.

Aberdeen is a long way to go for students from other parts of the UK, but train and air links are excellent, and the city regularly features in the top ten for quality of life. There is a £12-million sports and leisure centre, which includes a centre of excellence for the region in hockey, as well as a 25-metre swimming pool, three gyms, a climbing wall and bouldering room, a café bar, three exercise studios and a large sports hall. Sports scholarships are available to budding athletes, with Commonwealth Games gold medal-winning swimmer Hannah Miley among the recipients. Although accommodation can be expensive in the private sector, low prices in the students' union partially compensate, and there are enough residential places to guarantee housing to first years from outside the local area.

Undergraduate Fees and Bursaries

» Fees for Scottish and EU students 2014–15   No fee
» Fees for Non-Scottish UK (RUK) students 2014–15

£5,000–£6,750

Pharmacy   £8,500
» Fees for international students 2014–15   £10,500–£13,500
» Academic and targeted scholarships available.
» Check the university's website for the latest information.

Students

Undergraduates:	**7,170**	**(1,885)**
Postgraduates:	**1,825**	**(2,125)**
Mature students:	**23.5%**	
International students:	**11.4%**	
Applications per place:	**5.3**	
From state-sector schools:	**92.1%**	
From working-class homes:	**29.4%**	
Satisfaction with students' union	**63%**	

For detailed information about sports facilities:
www.rgu.ac.uk/rgusport

Accommodation

Number of places and costs refer to 2014–15
University-provided places: 1,753
Percentage catered: 0%
Self-catered costs: £96 (single) – £187.00 (flat) a week.
All first-year students are eligible to apply for student accommodation. Residential restrictions apply.
International students: given priority for accommodation.
accommodation@rgu.ac.uk
www.rgu.ac.uk/student-life/accommodation

Roehampton University

Roehampton will become the last university in London to increase its fees for degree courses to £9,000 in 2015. The rise only amounts to £250 a year, but the university does not offer bursaries to students from poor backgrounds, so only those winning scholarships will receive financial support on entry. Roehampton is investing £75 million on its attractive 54-acre main campus in south-west London. Much of the money is going on student accommodation and a new library will open in 2016. The Grade II-listed Downshire House will house a centre for Therapies Education and accommodate 200 students. The university has already provided an additional 400 rooms in a new complex that includes a swimming pool and other facilities, 20 minutes from the main campus by public transport, at Vauxhall. It is also opening a new School of Law in September 2015, which will also operate a legal advice clinic for the local community. Recent projects include a £4-million facility for the School of Arts and a new national centre of excellence for teaching citizenship education, human rights and social justice, as well as a newsroom for journalism and media students.

Although an independent university only since 2004, Roehampton has a distinguished history dating back to the 1840s, its colleges having been among the first in the country to open higher education to women. Today the university has diversified into business, the arts and humanities, social sciences and the human and life sciences, while maintaining its historic strength in education, which still accounts for a quarter of the students. The university has embraced the new School Direct system of teacher training, operating in partnership with schools as well as running its own postgraduate and undergraduate training programmes. An additional attraction on the main campus is the Glion Institute of Higher Education, a Swiss hospitality management college offering undergraduate and postgraduate programmes in its first overseas venture. The university is in partnership with Laureate, Glion's owners, to offer courses online. Numbers are expanding rapidly in business, information systems, education and public health, and the university is aiming to have 4,000 online students by 2019.

Roehampton is a collegiate university with four distinctive colleges, which still maintain some of the traditional ethos of their religious foundations: the Anglican Whitelands, the Roman Catholic Digby Stuart, the Methodist Southlands, and the Froebel, which follows the humanist teachings of Frederick Froebel. Students need not follow any of these denominations to enrol in the colleges. The colleges' leisure

---

Erasmus House
Roehampton Lane
London SW15 5PU

020 8392 3232 (enquiries)
enquiries@roehampton.ac.uk
www.roehampton.ac.uk
www.roehampton
  student.com
Affiliations: Cathedrals
  Group

The Times and Sunday Times **Rankings**
Overall Ranking: **73** (last year: 80)

Student satisfaction:	=54	82.6%
Research quality:	57	7.7%
Entry standards:	=107	287
Student–staff ratio:	96	20.2
Services & facilities/student:	19	£2,153
Expected completion rate:	94	81.8%
Good honours:	87	62.1%
Graduate prospects:	101	56.9%

facilities and bars are open to all members of the university. The university also has a Jewish resource centre and Muslim prayer rooms. All four colleges are based on a single campus, with stunning parkland and lakes, on or adjacent to Roehampton Lane. It is the first Living Landscape University in London, having joined the Beverley Brook Living Landscape, which neighbours and extends onto the campus. The scheme will provide opportunities for students to learn practical conservation, as well as teamwork and leadership skills.

The Quality Assurance Agency complimented Roehampton on the accessibility of academic staff to students and the positive ways in which they responded to student needs. New schemes to support students into future employment include graduate mentoring from alumni in professional roles and internships in a number of departments, as well as a Santander Internship Scheme providing paid placements for students in local businesses and the chance to study abroad with no additional tuition fees. Successes in the last Research Assessment Exercise, when Roehampton entered a much higher proportion of its academics than most of its peer group, added to the university's reputation. A third of the submission was judged to be world-leading or internationally excellent. Dame Jacqueline Wilson, former Children's Laureate, who taught on both the children's literature and creative writing Master's degrees, has become the university's new chancellor, taking over from the journalist John Simpson.

Over 95 per cent of undergraduates were state educated, 42 per cent coming from working-class homes. Most first years who want a hall place are offered one, with priority going to those living furthest away. While rents are not cheap for those who prefer the private sector, students like the proximity of central London and the lively and attractive suburbs around Roehampton. The sports facilities on campus have been enhanced, with a new gym, two football pitches, running track and a multi-use games area. The sport performance and rehabilitation centre provides state-of-the-art laboratory facilities and performance coaching. The university is a high-performance centre for British fencing and sitting volleyball.

Undergraduate Fees and Bursaries

» Fees for UK/EU students 2015–16   £9,000
» Foundation degree   £7,900
» Fees for international students 2014–15   £11,500
» Selection of targeted scholarships, including 4 Roehampton scholarships of £27,000 fee waiver for residents of Wandsworth, music and sports scholarships, and £1,000 a year for male primary education students with household income below £25K.
» Check the university's website for the latest information.

Students

Undergraduates:	**6,140**	**(235)**
Postgraduates:	**1,215**	**(1,470)**
Mature students:	**20.7%**	
International students:	**9%**	
Applications per place:	**3.8**	
From state-sector schools:	**95.7%**	
From working-class homes:	**41.7%**	
Satisfaction with students' union	**75%**	

For detailed information about sports facilities:
www.roehampton.ac.uk/Sport-Roehampton

Accommodation

Number of places and costs refer to 2014–15
University-provided places: 1,500
Percentage catered: 0%
Self-catered costs:£105.35–£119.70 (standard) – £135.80 (en suite) a week.
First years are given priority if conditions met. Local restrictions apply.
International students: guaranteed for first year
accommodation@roehampton.ac.uk
www.roehampton.ac.uk/Accommodation/

Royal Agricultural University

The Royal Agricultural University (RAU) has grown by almost 50 per cent in five years, but still has fewer than 1,200 students, making it the smallest publicly funded university in the UK. Its size prevented it from attaining university status until 2013, when the rules changed, and it still does not appear in our main table because, with only six degree subjects, it does not offer the broad spread of courses necessary for a meaningful comparison with less specialist universities. It does appear in the relevant subject tables and has a global reputation in its field. Every monarch since Queen Victoria has visited the attractive campus near Cirencester, in the Cotswolds. A new School of Equine Management and Science was established in 2014, joining those focused on agriculture, food and management; business and entrepreneurship; and real estate and land management.

The RAU was the first agricultural college in the English-speaking world when it was established in 1845 on the initiative of the Fairford and Cirencester Farmers' Club, which was concerned at the lack of government support for education, particularly in relation to agriculture. As the Royal Agricultural College, it launched its first degree in 1984 and was fully independent until 2001, when it began to receive state funding. It now has students up to PhD level and also delivers degree courses in Hong Kong and China. The number of female students has been rising but, perhaps not surprisingly in view of the range of subjects on offer, the university is one of the few in the UK that has a majority of men. Almost nine out of ten undergraduates are school or college leavers, rather than mature students, and there is a small contingent of international students, who pay fees of £10,000 a year.

The institution embarked on its biggest-ever campus development programme in the run-up to university status. A new teaching block opened with seven well-equipped teaching rooms; a biomass heating system has been installed as part of the university's green agenda, but also as a teaching resource; a postgraduate study centre has been added; and a new accommodation block has opened with 50 en-suite rooms. The two university farms, both close to the campus, cover a total of 1,200 acres. Coates Manor Farm focuses on arable farming, while Harnhill Farm is an example of an integrated livestock and cropping system. In addition, there is an equestrian centre providing stabling and livery facility, and students also have access to a large dairy complex. All are run as commercial enterprises. In 2014, the RAU added a Rural Innovation Centre, which

Stroud Road
Cirencester
Gloucestershire
GL7 6JS

01285 889912 (admissions enquiry)
admissions@rau.ac.uk
www.rau.ac.uk
http://rau.ac.uk/student-life/
  leisure/student-union
Affiliation: none

The Times Rankings
The Royal Agricultural University does not appear in our main league table this year because its courses do not cover the broad range of subjects needed for meaningful comparisons to be made with less specialist institutions.

will allow the university to develop its work within the areas of research translation, innovation and agri-technologies.

Relatively low grades in the last Research Assessment Exercise hold the university back in our agriculture table. Fewer than ten academics were entered and only 15 per cent of the work submitted was considered internationally excellent.

The institution has always had a reputation for attracting well-heeled students: around half of the undergraduates come from independent schools – a higher proportion than at Oxford or Cambridge. But 36 per cent come from the four poorest socio-economic groups – also one of the largest proportions in the UK – contributing to a unique student population, in which perhaps only one in seven does not fall into either category.

All business, equine and agriculture courses include a 20-week work placement. There is an extensive network of student placement sponsors in the UK and overseas, and part-time work is available both in the university and in nearby Cirencester. The university has been rated within the top 10 UK universities and colleges for its Enterprise activities. On campus, there is a well-stocked library and computer suites, as well as specialist laboratories. The virtual learning environment ensures that all teaching materials are available online 24 hours a day.

The small campus in the countryside provides a collegiate atmosphere and is the centre of social activities, including four balls each year. There are eight halls of residence on campus for undergraduates with enough rooms for most first-years to be offered a place. Private rentals are available in Cirencester and the surrounding area. Sport plays an important part in student life and, in addition to the normal range, there are clubs for polo, clay pigeon shooting, beagling and team chasing (a cross-country equestrian sport). There are ample opportunities to explore the Cotswold countryside and London is only 90 minutes away by train.

Undergraduate Fees and Bursaries

- » Fees for UK/EU students 2015–16   £9,000
- » Fees for international students 2014–15   £10,000
- » Disadvantaged students with household income below £25K, fee waiver or accommodation discount of £1,000–£3,000 a year.
- » Household income £25K–£42.6K and in financial need, fee waiver or accommodation discount of £1,500 in year 1.
- » Skills bursary of £250 in years 1 and 2 to enhance development of personal and professional skills.
- » Academic scholarships, internships, and bursaries up to £1,000 for student-led projects.
- » Check the university's website for the latest information..

Students		
Undergraduates:	**905**	**(50)**
Postgraduates:	**180**	**(25)**
Mature students:	**14.3%**	
International students:	**10%**	
Applications per place:	**3.2**	
From state-sector schools:	**50.3%**	
From working-class homes:	**35.8%**	
Satisfaction with students' union	**59%**	

For detailed information about sports facilities:
www.rau.ac.uk/student-life/leisure/sports-clubs

Accommodation

Number of places and costs refer to 2014–15

University-provided places: 320

Percentage catered: 20%

Catered costs: £4,780–£7,768 a year; £3,780–£6,768 a year for dinner, bed & breakfast.

Self-catered costs: £4,826 a year.

First years cannot be guaranteed accommodation.

International students: as above.

www.rau.ac.uk/student-life/living/accommodationion

Royal Holloway, University of London

The University of London's "Campus in the Country", as Royal Holloway likes to be known, has had a £100-million makeover in the last five years, producing an impressive range of academic and social facilities. The programme included a £5-million refurbishment of the 450 student rooms in perhaps the most distinctive university building in Britain. The Founder's Building, which also houses teaching and exhibition space, is modelled on a French chateau and was opened by Queen Victoria. It is the centrepiece of 135 acres of woodland between Windsor Castle and Heathrow, which was the Olympic village for the rowing teams in the 2012 Games. Other projects included extensions to the School of Management and the main library, as well as new student residences, which have been praised for their comfort and eco-friendly features. A new student services centre opened in 2013, following the £1.2-million refurbishment of the students' union in the previous year. The construction of a new studio theatre within the listed building that houses the Drama and Theatre Department was also completed in 2013. There is performance space on two levels, with seating for 175 people, rehearsal space, a

workshop and foyer. The university has also redeveloped an old Victorian boilerhouse, turning it into a multifunctional space for lectures with retractable seating for performances and events.

Both Bedford College and Royal Holloway, which amalgamated to form the existing college in 1985, were founded for women only, their legacy commemorated in the Bedford Centre for the History of Women. However, the gender balance in the student population is now roughly equal. Although still best known for the arts, Royal Holloway has a broad portfolio of subjects, including a science Foundation year for those wishing to change academic direction. There are now a record number of full-time students, and both applications and enrolments increased in 2013. The programme of student support includes £1 million for postgraduates so that students who graduate with large debts are not deterred from continuing their studies.

Two of the three faculties have been reorganised, leaving Science unchanged, to encourage an interdisciplinary approach to teaching and research. A separate Faculty of Management and Economics has been created, while humanities subjects have been brought together with the arts in a new Arts and Social Science Faculty. New degrees for 2015 will see law taught for the first time and also include BAs in digital communication and liberal arts. Of

---

University of London
Egham
Surrey TW20 0EX

01784 414944 (admissions)
admissions@rhul.ac.uk
www.royalholloway.ac.uk
www.su.rhul.ac.uk
Affiliation: none

The Times and Sunday Times Rankings
Overall Ranking: **=34** (last year: 28)

Student satisfaction:	=57	82.4%
Research quality:	15	27.7%
Entry standards:	36	405
Student–staff ratio:	=35	15.4
Services & facilities/student:	68	£1,462
Expected completion rate:	26	92.3%
Good honours:	35	74.0%
Graduate prospects:	76	62.8%

the work entered for the 2008 Research Assessment Exercise, 60 per cent was rated world-leading or internationally excellent, cementing Royal Holloway's place among the top 25 research universities. Royal Holloway has been named an Academic Centre of Excellence in Cyber Security Research by the UK Government – one of only eight such awards nationwide.

Royal Holloway draws a fifth of its undergraduates from independent schools, but the proportion coming from working-class homes has been rising. The ethnic mix is above average and the projected dropout rate of 6 per cent is below the official benchmark. The new Royal Holloway Passport is intended to enhance graduates' employability. The scheme recognises the additional skills that students gain from many extracurricular activities and which future graduate employers greatly value. An Advanced Skills Programme, covering information technology, communication skills and foreign languages, further encourages breadth of study. The university offers a number of e-degrees and promotes numerous opportunities to study abroad, building on the international flavour of the campus and its links with institutions such as New York, Sydney and Yale universities. Royal Holloway is only just outside the top 100 universities in the world in the *Times Higher Education* rankings, scoring highly for its international outlook.

Nearly 3,000 students live in halls of residence and there are plans for 600 additional places. The college's green belt location at Egham, Surrey, ensures that social life is concentrated on the active students' union. However, the centre of London is only 35 minutes away by rail for those determined to seek the high life. Sports facilities are good and a new 3G football and rugby pitch is to be installed. Royal Holloway claims to be "the University of London's best sporting college". It has had considerable success with its "student talented athlete award scheme" (STARS). Students enjoy an active cultural scene, and a thriving Community Action programme involves over 1,000 students volunteering with various local organisations and charities. Many students come from London and the Home Counties, and go home at the weekend, but the lively students' union puts on entertainment and activities seven days a week.

Undergraduate Fees and Bursaries

» Fees for UK/EU students 2015–16 £9,000
» Fees for international students 2014–15 £12,900–£14,600
» For all English students with household income below £25K, a bursary of £1,750 a year; £25K–£30K, £1,000 a year; £30K–£42.6K, £500 a year.
» For mature students with household income below £25K with conditions, bursary of £1,000 a year.
» Care leavers provided with £5,000 bursary and free year-round university accommodation for duration of study.

Students

Undergraduates:	6,690	(560)
Postgraduates:	1,710	(600)
Mature students:	8.8%	
International students:	25.7%	
Applications per place:	6.3	
From state-sector schools:	82.1%	
From working-class homes:	26.7%	
Satisfaction with students' union	64%	

For detailed information about sports facilities:
www.royalholloway.ac.uk/sports

Accommodation

Number of places and costs refer to 2014–15
University-provided places: 2,978
Percentage catered: 37%
Catered costs: £86–£163 a week (30–38 weeks).
Self-catered costs: £122–£153 a week (30–38 weeks).
First years are guaranteed accommodation provided conditions are met.
International students: as above.
studentaccommodation@rhul.ac.uk
www.royalholloway.ac.uk/studyhere/accommodation/home.aspx

University of St Andrews

St Andrews has once again won our award for the best Scottish university, registering by far the best scores north of the border in the National Student Survey and remaining Scotland's only representative in the top 20 of *The Times and Sunday Times* league table. It has not been out of the top five in the last eight years. St Andrews, which celebrated its 600th anniversary in 2013, is Scotland's oldest university and the third oldest in the English-speaking world. International students account for more than four of every ten of the intake and give the university a cosmopolitan feel. The university is particularly popular in the United States, which alone provides nearly a fifth of the first-year students, many on Study Abroad programmes. There are eight applicants for every place, with 41 per cent of the UK undergraduates coming from independent schools.

Along with Edinburgh, St Andrews has the highest fees in the UK for undergraduates from England, Wales or Northern Ireland. It charges them £9,000 a year for the full four years of a degree, although there are bursaries for students from low-income families. Scots and other EU students continue to pay nothing. With almost 30 per cent of St Andrews students coming from south of the border,

the new fees might have been expected to hit recruitment, but both applications and enrolments rose in 2013 and all available places were filled before Clearing began. The projected drop-out rate is extremely low, at less than 3 per cent.

Although the university has fewer than 10,000 students, it offers a wide range of courses. Its reputation has always rested mainly on the humanities, which have a £1.3-million research centre. An £8-million headquarters for the School of International Relations opened in 2006, with Europe's first Centre for Syrian Studies, an Institute of Iranian Studies and a Centre for Peace and Conflict Studies. St Andrews has the largest mediaeval history department in Britain and has now added film studies and sustainable development. It has also taken over the running of the town's Byre Theatre. During the day, its main auditorium will be used for lectures and the studio theatre for teaching drama, leaving both free for public performances in the evenings and at weekends.

The town of St Andrews is steeped in history, as well as being the centre of the golfing world. The university at its heart accounts for half of the 18,000 inhabitants. There are close cultural and social relations between town and gown, although some cracks are beginning to show. The university was originally organised along collegiate lines, and the United College (arts and

---

College Gate
St Andrews
Fife KY16 9AJ

01334 462150 (admissions)
student.recruitment@
st-andrews.
  ac.uk (pre-recruitment)
www.st-andrews.ac.uk
www.yourunion.net
Affiliation: none

ST ANDREWS
Edinburgh
Belfast
London
Cardiff

The Times and Sunday Times Rankings

Overall Ranking: **3** (last year: 4)

Student satisfaction:	7	86.3%
Research quality:	=13	28.0%
Entry standards:	6	523
Student–staff ratio:	=8	11.8
Services & facilities/student:	13	£2,346
Expected completion rate:	4	96.9%
Good honours:	3	88.3%
Graduate prospects:	18	79.1%

sciences) and St Mary's (theology) remain a part of student life. Postgraduates join St Leonard's College. New students ("bejants" and "bejantines") acquire third- or fourth-year "parents" to ease them into university life, and on Raisin Monday traditionally give their academic mentors a bottle of wine in return for a receipt in Latin, which can be written on anything. Many of the main buildings date from the 15th and 16th centuries, but sciences are taught at the modern North Haugh site a few streets away. Everything is within walking distance, but bicycles are common.

The university has been expanding both teaching and research in the sciences. A £45-million Medical and Biological Sciences Building opened in 2010, one of the first UK medical schools whose research facilities are fully integrated with the other sciences, offering an important new dimension to medical training and research. A £5-million Bio-medical Sciences Research complex, to lead the fight against superbugs and serious viral, bacterial and parasitic diseases, followed in 2011. The university has the largest optical telescope in Britain and is planning a Green Energy Centre and a Knowledge Exchange Centre for spin-out companies, new business and prototype testing. Nearly 60 per cent of the work submitted for the 2008 Research Assessment Exercise was rated as world-leading or internationally excellent.

More than half of all students live in halls and new apartments will be available for 2015 entrants following the demolition and replacement of houses on the Fife Park site. Self-catering accommodation for 920 students during term and three-star accommodation for golfers and other tourists in vacations won the Green Tourism Business Scheme's Gold Award. Students do not come to St Andrews for the nightclubs, but there is no shortage of parties in a tight-knit community. A £12-million extension and redevelopment of the Students' Association building has begun, but it will not be complete until the end of 2015. The university is also planning a £14-million transformation of its sports facilities, with a new sports hall, a larger and better-equipped fitness suite, tennis centre, expanded changing facilities and other improvements.

Undergraduate Fees and Bursaries

» Fees for Scottish and EU students 2014–15   No fee
» Fees for Non-Scottish UK (RUK) students 2014–15   £9,000
» Fees for international students 2014–15   £16,230
   Medical science   £24,500
» For Scottish students with household income below £42.6K, 50 academic bursaries of up to £2,000 a year.
» For RUK students with household income below £42.6K, bursary to top up student's official grant and loan to £7,500 a year.
» For all students on the basis of need, over 200 accommodation bursaries of £1,000.
» Other scholarships and bursaries are available.

Students

Undergraduates:	**6,465**	**(950)**
Postgraduates:	**1,680**	**(370)**
Mature students:	**3.3%**	
International students:	**41.7%**	
Applications per place:	**7.9**	
From state-sector schools:	**58.9%**	
From working-class homes:	**13.1%**	
Satisfaction with students' union	**72%**	

For detailed information about sports facilities:
www.st-andrews.ac.uk/sport

Accommodation

Number of places and costs refer to 2014–15
University-provided places: 3,578
Percentage catered: 53%
Catered costs: £137–£219 (33 weeks).
Self-catered costs: £81–£194 a week (38 weeks).
Single first-year undergraduates are guaranteed accommodation if they apply by 30 June in year of entry.
Policy for international students: as above.
accommodation@st-andrews.ac.uk
www.st-andrews.ac.uk/accommodation/ug/

University of St Mark and St John

The Plymouth-based University of St Mark and St John plans to double in size over the next decade, but will still have only 5,000 students when the programme is complete. The aim is to develop a "credible and critical mass" in each of its specialist subject areas, to make economies of scale and invest in development. The cost will be relatively modest because the spacious greenfield campus has spare capacity following investment in buildings and sports facilities totalling £20 million in recent years. But the university has promised to increase staffing levels in line with student numbers to maintain the small class sizes that are one of its selling points. There will be more students from overseas, but most will still come from Devon and Cornwall.

Marjon, as the institution was known in its days as a university college, was already increasing in popularity before full university status arrived in 2013, and there has since been further modest growth in undergraduate enrolments. Expansion will involve increases in postgraduate teaching and research, but the removal of courses below degree level. Tourism will be one of the few additions at undergraduate level, but the university has already been reorganised into three faculties: education and social services; sport and health sciences, and language and creative industries. Professor Cara Aitchison, the Vice-Chancellor, plans to build on existing strengths, which took the university into the top five for student satisfaction in 2013. It has since been named as the best in the UK for promoting social mobility by securing graduate level jobs for students recruited from poorer backgrounds. However, satisfaction levels declined in the 2014 survey and Marjon has dropped more than 30 places in our table.

Established in 1840 as a Church of England teacher training college in London, with the son of poet Samuel Taylor Coleridge as its first principal, the university describes itself as "arguably the third oldest Higher Education Institution in England". The College of St Mark and St John only moved to Plymouth in 1973. Still officially a Church of England Voluntary Institution, it was one of several religious foundations among the latest crop of universities. The attractive modern Chaplaincy Centre is at the heart of the campus, but there is less emphasis on religion in the new university's promotional material than at some of its counterparts.

The new university lists sport at the top of its list of specialisms, followed by education, languages, journalism and the creative arts. The Elite Sport Scholarship programme produced a gold medallist at

Derriford Road
Plymouth, Devon PL6 8BH

01752 636890 (admissions)
admissions@ucpmarjon.ac.uk
www.marjon.ac.uk
www.marjonsu.com
Affiliation: GuildHE;
  Cathedrals Group

The Times and Sunday Times Rankings
Overall Ranking: =102 (last year: =71)

Student satisfaction:	=48	82.9%
Research quality:	=117	0.3%
Entry standards:	=115	276
Student–staff ratio:	83	19.2
Services & facilities/student:	119	£803
Expected completion rate:	=83	82.9%
Good honours:	120	51.1%
Graduate prospects:	68	64.0%

the Commonwealth Games in swimmer Ben Proud.

Recent campus developments have included extensive refurbishment of the library to provide a new social learning space. There has also seen a new sports centre, refurbished student housing and a new entrance and student centre. The Journalism and Media Centre opened in 2013, conceived and designed by the lecturers. It includes an iPad teaching room, full iMac classroom, four iMac media editing suites, two of which act as a radio studio, and an editorial meeting room. The three BA programmes – journalism, sports journalism and media production – are strongly vocational, and the new centre is made available to commercial businesses. Teacher training remains strong and new leadership and business management degrees are closely aligned with the university's specialisms in education, media production, outdoor adventure and sport

The university is located on the outskirts of the city, close to the Dartmoor National Park and within easy reach of the sea. The green agenda extends to an on-campus duck pond and nature trail. An orchard planted with local varieties of apple tree celebrates the biodiversity of the campus. Sports facilities are extremely good: there is a 25-metre swimming pool, climbing wall and both grass and artificial pitches. The Ghanaian Olympic team used the campus as its base for pre-Olympic training in 2012, and Plymouth Argyle footballers and Exeter Chiefs rugby players use the university's training facilities such as the gym, sports therapy centre and sports science lab.

There are residential places on campus for 456 students in 7 halls of residence and 38 village houses; rents compare favourably with most universities. Most first-year students from outside the locality are offered places. If none is available, students are offered accommodation with a homestay family until a room on campus becomes available. Those living on campus may only bring a car in exceptional circumstances, but the city centre is a short bus ride from the campus. Plymouth is a lively city that students tend to enjoy.

Undergraduate Fees and Bursaries

» Fees for UK/EU students 2015–16 £9,000
» Foundation degree £5,250–£9,000
» Fees for international students 2014–15 £9,400–10,350
» Fee waivers for high academic achievement and sports scholars will be offered. Details not available in August 2014.
» Academic scholarships and targeted bursaries available.
» Check the university's website for the latest information.

Students		
Undergraduates:	**2,060**	**(85)**
Postgraduates:	**280**	**(240)**
Mature students:	**25.5%**	
International students:	**5.4%**	
Applications per place:	**4.1**	
From state-sector schools:	**96.3%**	
From working-class homes:	**40.7%**	
Satisfaction with students' union	**65%**	
For detailed information about sports facilities: www.marjon.ac.uk/marjon-sport/		

Accommodation

Places and costs refer to 2014-15
University-provided places: 456
Percentage catered: 65%
Catered costs: £115–£130 (inclusive of dining-in-scheme)
Self-catered costs: £85 (small single) – £90 (standard single)
First years are guaranteed accommodation which is allocated on a first-to-go unconditional offer, first served basis.
International students: guaranteed campus or homestay housing.
www.marjon.ac.uk/student-life/university-approved-accommodation/

St Mary's University, Twickenham

St Mary's is the only new university established since the last edition of *The Times and Sunday Times Good University Guide*. It missed out on university status when a dozen other colleges were promoted in 2012, but is making up for lost time with a respectable position on its debut in our league table. St Mary's, which has 5,000 students, including 1,200 postgraduates, is the third Catholic institution to become a university recently. It has four academic schools and a strong tradition in sport, which enabled it to attract the first Mo Farah Academy to develop outstanding young athletes. The academy, established by St Mary's graduate Farah and his wife, Tania, will support training programmes at St Mary's and at Brunel University, as well as providing scholarships for eight top prospects a year.

St Mary's was founded in Hammersmith in 1850 by the Catholic Poor Schools Committee to meet the need for teachers for the growing numbers of poor Catholic children, and moved along the river to Twickenham in 1925. The spectacular Gothic Strawberry Hill House has been its centrepiece ever since, and is undergoing a £9-million restoration. The house was designed and created as a Gothic fantasy between 1747 and 1792 by Horace Walpole, the son of Britain's first Prime Minister. It is set in 35 acres of gardens and parkland close to the Thames, with a variety of modern teaching and residential accommodation. The site constitutes the main campus and there is a hall of residence nearby in Twickenham, while the main sports fields are located in neighbouring Teddington. An £8.5-million sports centre opened there in 2011 with facilities good enough for ten national teams to choose it for pre-Olympic training. A new library, costing £6 million, should be fully open by the start of the academic year in 2015. Other recent improvements include a £350,000 upgrade of the student television studio, which opens in September 2014. There is also a new computer suite with the latest Apple MacPro workstations, offering students 24-hour access to professional-grade creative technologies.

Only a third of today's students are training to be teachers and there are growing numbers taking sport, theatre studies and theology. Sixty per cent of the students are female and about 5 per cent of undergraduates come from outside the UK. There are nearly 500 undergraduate programmes, including a range of Foundation degrees, mainly in the arts and social sciences or sport. The four academic schools cover sport, health and applied

---

Waldegrave Road
Strawberry Hill
Twickenham
London TW1 4SX

020 8240 4029 (admissions)
admit@smuc.ac.uk
www.smuc.ac.uk
www.stmaryssu.co.uk
Affiliation:
  Cathedrals Group; Guild HE

The Times Rankings

Overall Ranking: **100** (n/a)

Student satisfaction:	=82	80.6%
Research quality:	=89	2.7%
Entry standards:	104	294
Student–staff ratio:	115	22.4
Services & facilities/student:	115	£1,005
Expected completion rate:	96	81.5%
Good honours:	93	60.7%
Graduate prospects:	69	63.8%

science; education, theology and leadership; management and social sciences; and the arts and humanities. St Mary's resisted charging the full £9,000 fees for its degrees until 2014, and even in 2015 entrants to Foundation degrees will pay no more than £4,500 a year. Over 35 per cent of the UK undergraduates are from working-class homes and the university has a number of outreach schemes designed to broaden the intake further. The E-Mentoring scheme, launched in 2013, in which current students help selected groups of school pupils throughout the academic year, has received excellent feedback from participants. Other initiatives provide academic support and monitor the progress of under-represented groups once they enter the university.

The university has appointed Francis Campbell, a career diplomat and one-time private secretary to Tony Blair, as its first vice-chancellor. A former ambassador to the Vatican, he helped to secure a Papal visit to St Mary's in 2010. The previous college principal left soon after a critical report by the Quality Assurance Agency led to the postponement of the original bid for university status. Mr Campbell will take over discussions on a "strategic partnership" with Heythrop College, a part of the University of London and the capital's other Catholic higher education institution, which specialises in theology and philosophy. St Mary's has a continued commitment to training teachers for Catholic and other Christian schools, although it admits students of all faiths and none. Its first stated objective is: "To be a distinctive institution within UK higher education, providing a unique experience for our students and staff by virtue of our values and identity as a Catholic university."

Students like the combination of an attractive setting in south-west London that is only half an hour from the West End by train. Sports facilities are excellent and attract elite performers. As well as European Games gold medals for alumni Mo Farah and Jo Pavey, 2014 has seen two current undergraduates win gold medals as part of the victorious Great Britain rugby sevens team at the World University Championships.

Undergraduate Fees and Bursaries

- » Fees for UK/EU students 2015–16 £9,000
- » Foundation degree £4,500
- » Fees for international students 2014–15 £9,900
- » Household income below £25K and meeting specific criteria, £3,000 cash, fee waiver or accommodation discount, year 1; £2,000 cash, year 2; £1,000 cash, year 3.
- » Household income below £42.6 K and AAB at A level or equivalent, £4,000 cash, fee waiver or accommodation discount, year 1; if grade of at least 60% achieved when progressing from one year to the next, then £2,000 cash, year 2, and £1,000 cash year 3.
- » Awards for students from Catholic schools and for care leavers; sports scholarships.

Students

Undergraduates:	**3,470**	**(315)**
Postgraduates:	**390**	**(790)**
Mature students:	**16.9%**	
International students:	**4.9%**	
Applications per place:	**4.2**	
From state-sector schools:	**96%**	
From working-class homes:	**35.6%**	
Satisfaction with students' union	**63%**	

For detailed information about sports facilities:
www.smuc.ac.uk/sports/

Accommodation

Number of places and costs refer to 2014–15
University-provided places: approx 700
Percentage catered: 100%
Catered costs: £4,056.54 (small twin) – £6,592.80 (single en suite) inclusive of meal plan (37 weeks).
University endeavours to provide accommodation to all new first year students who require it.
International students: some rooms reserved for new students.
accommodation@smuc.ac.uk
www.smuc.ac.uk/student-life/accommodation/

University of Salford

Salford is in the middle of a £500-million, 15-year capital programme which is helping to bring about significant changes in the shape of the university. It has ceased to offer courses in modern languages, linguistics and some areas of politics and contemporary history because of low demand for places, focusing instead on its strengths in media, technology, science, engineering and health. The university's development in MediaCityUK, in Salford Quays, cost £30 million and is designed for 1,500 students on 39 courses to enjoy exceptional opportunities to work with BBC staff and other media professionals using the latest equipment, studios and laboratories. The new facilities have already produced a surge in demand for Salford's media courses. New undergraduate enrolments across the whole university were up by 500 in 2013, partially compensating for a big drop when higher fees were introduced.

There are four campuses, all of them apart from Salford Quays clustered around the River Irwell and within walking distance of Manchester city centre. On the main campus, the £55-million Gateway Project will provide a new entrance from Salford Crescent railway station and more facilities for arts and media students when it opens in 2016. There is also a £38-million Arts and Media Centre on the Adelphi Campus and a £22-million headquarters for the Faculty of Health and Social Care on a third site, with practice clinics, hospital ward facilities and a human performance laboratory. The landscaped main campus is a haven of lawns and shrubberies. University House, where students go for advice and support, has seen a £3-millon upgrade, while a 1960s teaching building has been remodelled and extended to accommodate six lecture theatres equipped with large screen displays, a series of learning and breakout spaces, plus a café.

Salford, which has around 20,000 students, has been overtaken by a number of post-1992 universities in *The Times and Sunday Times* league table. It suffers particularly from low scores in National Student Survey, which left it among the bottom ten universities for student satisfaction. However, Salford does well on the Government's access measures: 43 per cent of the undergraduates come from working-class homes and there is a high proportion from areas sending few students to higher education. The projected dropout rate has fluctuated. The latest figures were up to almost 18 per cent, higher than the national average for the subjects and students' qualifications.

The university's growing involvement in health has seen the establishment of a national centre for prosthetics and orthotics, and Salford has a high reputation for the

---

The Crescent
Salford
Greater Manchester
M5 4WT

0161 295 4545 (enquiries)
contact via website
www.salford.ac.uk
www.salfordstudents.com
Affiliation: University
   Alliance

The Times and Sunday Times **Rankings**
Overall Ranking: **105** (last year: 98)

Student satisfaction:	=119	76.4%
Research quality:	56	9.3%
Entry standards:	=57	341
Student–staff ratio:	57	17.0
Services & facilities/student:	66	£1,481
Expected completion rate:	=111	77.6%
Good honours:	=72	64.3%
Graduate prospects:	=102	56.8%

treatment of sports injuries. The School of Nursing and Midwifery, which received outstanding ratings from its regulatory body, runs Europe's first nursing course for deaf students. There is also a BA in journalism and war studies – the only undergraduate degree in the UK to combine the two disciplines.

Engineering is the university's traditional strength, attracting many of the 3,000 overseas students. The university opened the world's first Energy House in 2011 – a full-size traditional terraced house built in a laboratory for students, researchers and industry to study domestic energy consumption.

Two-thirds of all courses offer work placements, half of them abroad and almost all counting towards degree classifications. The university has partnerships which provide research and work experience with the BBC, Adobe and Carnegie Mellon University, in Pittsburgh, and the Salford China partnership programme among others. There is a particular focus on the Middle East, where the University of Salford Abu Dhabi works with a number of universities in the region.

The Enterprise Academy scheme was commended by the EU after it helped 32 student businesses become established. Students are offered training in entrepreneurship and business skills, as well as a business mentor, while an innovative scheme also provides professional training and work experience for unemployed and under-employed graduates. Salford led the way in formally recognising interaction with business and industry as of equal importance to teaching and research. The university entered a relatively low proportion of its academics for the 2008 Research Assessment Exercise, but still had among the lowest grades of the pre-1992 universities. The university has since established nine interdisciplinary research centres and a graduate school.

Salford's location is one of its main selling points. There are 2,400 residential places within ten minutes' walk of the main campus, owned either by the university or a partner organisation. New student apartments will be ready in time for the 2015 entry, adding 1,367 bedrooms in a new complex costing £81 million. It will include a cinema, gym, TV and games room, group study lounges and a launderette.

Undergraduate Fees and Bursaries

» Fees for UK/EU students 2015–16 £9,000
» Foundation year £5,500–£8,000
» Placement year no fee
» Fees for international students 2014–15 £11,090–£12,800
» For students with at least ABB at A Level or equivalent, £2,000 cash scholarship in year 1.
» Sports and asylum seekers' scholarships.
» Check the university's website for the latest information.

Students

Undergraduates:	**13,760**	**(1,750)**
Postgraduates:	**1,765**	**(1,885)**
Mature students:	**31.1%**	
International students:	**11.2%**	
Applications per place:	**4.7**	
From state-sector schools:	**97.6%**	
From working-class homes:	**42.8%**	
Satisfaction with students' union	**64%**	

For detailed information about sports facilities:
www.sport.salford.ac.uk

Accommodation

Number of places and costs refer to 2014–15
University-provided places: 1,314 plus 1,121 managed by specialist providers.
Percentage catered: 0%
Self-catered costs: £67.48 (standard) – £92.96 (en suite).
First years are guaranteed accommodation (terms and conditions apply).
International students: as above.
accommodation@salford.ac.uk
www.accommodation.salford.ac.uk

University of Sheffield

The accolades keep rolling in for Sheffield from its students. They voted it into top place in *Times Higher Education* magazine's 2014 student experience survey, giving it the highest scores in the UK for the students' union, social life, facilities and accommodation. The students' union was already the most popular in the National Student Survey (NSS) and the overseas students placed Sheffield top for facilities, student services, accommodation and social activities in the International Student Barometer. But the university did not maintain last year's high levels of satisfaction in other parts of the NSS and has slipped out of the top 20 despite substantial growth in both applications and enrolments. An additional 900 undergraduates more than compensated for a dip in 2012. But there is more to Sheffield than social life: it is in the top 75 universities in the world, according to the QS rankings, and attracts more than 5,000 international students. Its UK students are more diverse than those in most other Russell Group universities: more than 85 per cent of the undergraduates come from state schools or colleges and almost one in five comes from a working-class home.

The main university precinct now stretches into an almost unbroken mile-long "campus" that ends not far from the city centre. Most university flats and halls of residence are within walking distance, in the suburbs on the affluent west side of Sheffield. There has been sustained investment in new buildings and facilities over recent years – notably the conversion of the former Jessop Hospital into a new centre for the arts and humanities. Recent developments have seen the renovation of the original University Library and the refurbishment of the Arts Tower, still the tallest university building in the country after more than 40 years. The university is expanding the highly rated Faculty of Engineering, which has 4,000 students, with the opening of the £21-million Pam Liversidge Building, named after one of UK's leading female engineers. It includes an eye-catching atrium and a Graduate School, but will be overshadowed by the £81-million Diamond, the first phase of which is due to open in 2015 with a range of specialist engineering features. Sheffield is the lead institution for systems engineering, smart materials and stem-cell technology in a research network of European, American and Chinese universities. There is a separate technology park centred on an advanced manufacturing research centre, in which Boeing is the senior partner.

The students' union was extended for the second time in three years in 2013, creating more facilities for students and staff. A

Western Bank
Sheffield S10 2TN

0114 222 8030 (enquiries)
http://ask.sheffield.ac.uk
www.sheffield.ac.uk
www.shef.ac.uk/union
Affiliation: Russell Group

Edinburgh
Belfast
SHEFFIELD
London
Cardiff

***The Times and Sunday Times* Rankings**

Overall Ranking: **21** (last year: =18)

Student satisfaction:	=42	83.0%
Research quality:	16	27.3%
Entry standards:	=21	439
Student–staff ratio:	=26	14.9
Services & facilities/student:	39	£1,801
Expected completion rate:	=16	93.9%
Good honours:	20	78.5%
Graduate prospects:	27	76.9%

new employability strategy includes two internship schemes offering 75 placements within the university. A high-tech library and learning centre adds to the student experience. The £23-million Information Commons operates 24 hours a day throughout the year, providing 1,300 study spaces and 500 computers linked to the campus network, as well as 110,000 books and periodicals.

Sheffield academics performed well in the last Research Assessment Exercise, when more than 60 per cent of their work was judged to be world-leading or internationally excellent. Former Home Secretary David Blunkett is a visiting professor in the Politics Department, where he was an undergraduate, helping to establish the world's first Centre for the Public Understanding of Politics. The growing School of Management, which is one of 57 in the world to receive accreditation from all three leading agencies, moved into new premises in 2013, following an £11-million refurbishment of the former School of Law.

Residential accommodation is plentiful and first-years from outside Sheffield are guaranteed a room. Private housing is reasonably priced in student areas close to the university. The Endcliffe student village caters for 3,500 students in a mix of refurbished Victorian houses and new flats, while the Ranmoor Village houses over 1,000 students in self-catering apartments, which include some family apartments and studios. The excellent sports facilities close to the main university precinct include five floodlit synthetic pitches, a large fitness centre with more than 150 pieces of equipment, swimming pool with sauna and steam rooms, sports hall, fitness studio, multipurpose activity room, four squash courts and a bouldering wall. The 45 acres of grass pitches for rugby, football and cricket are a bus ride away. Sheffield has one of the biggest programmes of internal leagues at any university.

The famously lively social scene is based on the students' union, but also takes full advantage of the city's burgeoning club life. Town–gown relations are much better than in most major university centres, and the latest crime statistics identify Sheffield as the safest big city in England.

Undergraduate Fees and Bursaries

» Fees for UK/EU students 2015–16 £9,000
» Foundation programme (medicine, science, engineering)
  £6,000–£6,650
» Fees for international students 2014–15 £13,390–£17,470
  Medicine £17,470–£31,580
» Cash bursaries on sliding scale of £1,500–£750 for UK students with household income up to £42K.
» In addition, £1,000 a year bursary for those from disadvantaged areas with household income below £25K.
» £500 a year award for local students achieving ABB at A level (or equivalent).

Students

Undergraduates:	**16,885**	**(1,220)**
Postgraduates:	**5,535**	**(1,905)**
Mature students:	**7.3%**	
International students:	**17.8%**	
Applications per place:	**6.6**	
From state-sector schools:	**85.2%**	
From working-class homes:	**20%**	
Satisfaction with students' union	**94%**	

For detailed information about sports facilities:
www.sport-sheffield.com

Accommodation

Number of places and costs refer to 2014–15
University-provided places: 4,961
Percentage catered: 0%
Self-catered costs: £77.35 (single) –£154.56 (flat) a week (43 or 44 weeks).
All first years offered university allocated accommodation or private housing.
International students: as above, providing conditions are met.
accommodationoffice@sheffield.ac.uk
www.sheffield.ac.uk/accommodation

Sheffield Hallam University

Sheffield Hallam has moved up 15 places in this year's league table after a big rise in student satisfaction. Entrants in 2015 will benefit from impressive new buildings on each of the main campuses, as the university nears the end of its £110-million development plan. The focus of current activity is a new teaching and learning centre under construction on the Collegiate campus, in a leafy inner suburb of Sheffield, and a £30-million building on the city centre campus. This will be home to the university's new Sheffield Institute of Education, which brings teacher and workforce education provision together with two research centres. The two projects are the latest in a ten-year programme of investment in buildings and staff. A new social centre has already opened on the Collegiate Campus and a £14-million development allowed the Faculty of Health and Wellbeing to almost double in size, as extra provision was made for nursing, radiotherapy, physiotherapy and social work. The Centre for Sport and Exercise Science, with its £6-million research facility, is one of the largest of its kind in Europe, with more than 2,000 students. The faculty is the biggest provider of health and social care training in the UK and offers the widest range of sports courses.

Previous developments focused mainly on the City Campus, near the railway station and Sheffield's central shopping area. The main learning centre was refurbished and all the departments in the arts, computing, engineering and sciences were brought together for the first time, placing them in the heart of Sheffield's cultural industries quarter. The university had already launched the Sheffield Business School, bringing together business, finance, management and languages, with several of the university's other specialisms. Business and management courses, which account for easily the biggest share of places, have their own city-centre headquarters, as does the students' union, which took over the spectacular but ill-fated National Centre for Popular Music.

Even after a 5 per cent fall in the demand for places in 2013, Hallam was still among the top eight universities in the UK in terms of the volume of applications. The university actually enrolled an additional 250 undergraduates, although this was still 1,000 less than the record total in the year before £9,000 fees were introduced. The university exceeds all of its access benchmarks and the projected dropout rate of less than 10 per cent is lower than average for its courses and entry qualifications. The university has a growing international dimension, with large cohorts taught in partner institutions in Malaysia and other Asian countries. The 2,200 who come to Sheffield from outside

---

City Campus
Howard Street
Sheffield S1 1WB

0114 225 5555 (enquiries)
enquiries@shu.ac.uk
www.shu.ac.uk
wwwhallamstudentsunion
.com
Affiliation: University
  Alliance

The Times and Sunday Times Rankings
Overall Ranking: **62** (last year: =77)

Student satisfaction:	=42	83.0%
Research quality:	=73	4.0%
Entry standards:	76	321
Student–staff ratio:	74	18.4
Services & facilities/student:	51	£1,705
Expected completion rate:	=59	86.1%
Good honours:	68	65.6%
Graduate prospects:	87	59.7%

the EU have given Hallam high marks in the International Student Barometer.

The university traces its origins in art and design back to the 1840s and celebrated the centenary of education and teacher training in 2005. It now has 35,000 students, including high proportions of part-time and mature students, and more than 1,000 taught on franchised courses in further education colleges. Business and industry are closely involved in the development of courses and more than half of the undergraduates take work placements. Hallam claims to have the largest number of students at any university taking courses that include work placements of a year; it offers a full fee waiver for that year out. More than 200 "specialist flexible courses" mix part-time study, distance learning and work-based learning. A "virtual campus" enables all students to access the growing volume of online teaching, assignments and discussion groups even when they are at home or on work placements. Hallam is also the only university to offer the new MEng food engineering degree, having been chosen by the food and drink industry to develop the course.

Unlike many big post-1992 universities, Hallam now guarantees accommodation for first years, although the large local intake means that many live at home. Transport in the city is excellent, with both well-run bus and tram services. Sports facilities

are supplemented by those provided by the city for the World Student Games. The impressive swimming complex, for example, is on the university's doorstep. The university has taken over the management of Sheffield's only athletics stadium. The redeveloped facility will be available to community groups, schools and local clubs, as well as students. The university partnered with the Tour de France to offer volunteering opportunities for students when the 2014 race started in Yorkshire, continuing the tradition of working with major sporting event organisers. Hundreds of students took official roles at the 2012 London Olympics and at the 2014 Winter Olympics in Sochi.

Undergraduate Fees and Bursaries

» Fees for UK/EU students 2015–16 £9,000
» Placement year £1,800
» Fees for international students 2014–15 £11,500–£12,400
» Household income below £25K, a bursary of £200 in year 1; £25K–£42.6K, a bursary of £400–£800 a year on sliding scale; see website for details.
» Fee waivers of £1,800 for those on placement years.
» Enhanced hardship fund.
» Scholarships and bursaries are available.
» Check the university's website for the latest information.

Students

Undergraduates:	21,865	(5,170)
Postgraduates:	2,605	(5,075)
Mature students:	18.7%	
International students:	9.3%	
Applications per place:	5.3	
From state-sector schools:	96.8%	
From working-class homes:	39.8%	
Satisfaction with students' union	57%	

For detailed information about sports facilities:
www.shu.ac.uk/sport/active/

Accommodation

Number of places and costs refer to 2014–15
University-provided places: 4,961
Percentage catered: 0%
Self-catered costs: £77.35–£154.56 a week (43 or 44 weeks).
All first years offered university allocated accommodation or private housing.
International students: as above, providing conditions are met.
accommodation@shu.ac.uk
www.shu.ac.uk/accommodation

SOAS, University of London

The only higher education institution in the UK specialising in the study of Africa, Asia and the Middle East has dropped its full title (School of Oriental and African Studies) and started promoting itself as SOAS, University of London. The school has a global reputation in subjects relating to two-thirds of the world's population and that excellence will be enhanced by a £20-million gift from a graduate with a passion for South-East Asian art. The donation is worth more than a quarter of SOAS's annual income and will fund new posts, building development and scholarships for Asian students to come to London. Professor Paul Webley, the Director, said the money would be "transformational".

There are 5,400 students on campus, plus over 3,000 studying distance learning programmes. They come from more than 130 countries, but two-thirds are from Britain and the rest of the EU – and the proportion is higher still among the undergraduates. Independent school candidates account for almost a quarter of the British entrants to degree courses, while a similar proportion come from working-class homes. The school has almost doubled its investment in student support with the switch to higher fees, as well as increasing its outreach activities, schools. Enrolments have

been rising steadily, bucking the downward trend in the study of non-European languages across the UK. Results in the National Student Survey have been better than for most London-based institutions. Overall satisfaction increased sharply in 2013, contributing to a big rise in *The Times and Sunday Times* league table, but SOAS has dropped back seven places this year.

The school is located at the heart of the University of London in Bloomsbury. There is a second campus less than a mile away and adjacent to two student residences, providing student-orientated facilities such as a Learning Resource Centre and an internet café. The centrepiece of the main campus is an airy, modern building with gallery space as well as teaching accommodation, a gift from the Sultan of Brunei. The library is one of just five National Research Libraries in the country, holding 1.5 million volumes, periodicals and audio-visual materials in 400 languages, and attracts scholars from around the world. More than 40 per cent of degree programmes offer the opportunity to spend a year at one of the school's many partner universities in Africa or Asia.

The school has a much wider portfolio of courses than its name would suggest, offering more than 400 degree combinations and 100 postgraduate programmes. Degrees are available in familiar subjects such as law, music, history and the social sciences,

---

Thornhaugh Street
Russell Square
London WC1H 0XG

020 7898 4034 (student recruitment)
study@soas.ac.uk
www.soas.ac.uk
http://soasunion.org
Affiliation: none

The Times and Sunday Times **Rankings**
Overall Ranking: **31** (last year: 24)

Student satisfaction:	=91	79.8%
Research quality:	=30	21.7%
Entry standards:	=30	422
Student–staff ratio:	=5	11.6
Services & facilities/student:	28	£2,027
Expected completion rate:	63	85.6%
Good honours:	8	84.0%
Graduate prospects:	67	64.2%

but with a different emphasis. There is also a more limited portfolio of Foundation programmes and language courses.

Approximately 45 per cent of undergraduates take a language as part of their degree and the school has now introduced a Language Entitlement programme which offers one term of a non-accredited SOAS Language Centre course free of charge. The school won a Queen's Anniversary Prize for the excellence, breadth and depth of its language teaching in 2010. The £6.5-million Library Transformation Project has added more language laboratories, music studios, discussion and research rooms, gallery space and other facilities.

SOAS is in the top 80 in the QS World Rankings for the arts and humanities, and has been strengthening its academic staff in a variety of disciplines as it approaches its centenary in 2016. The numbers taking distance learning courses, mainly outside the UK, have grown considerably. The transfer of University of London postgraduate programmes previously taught by Imperial College has made SOAS one of the world's largest providers of distance learning at this level. Postgraduates are attracted by a research record which saw more than half of the work submitted for the last Research Assessment Exercise rated world-leading or internationally excellent.

There is no separate students' union building, although the students do have their own recently refurbished bar, social space and catering facilities. The former University of London Union – soon to be a student centre – is close at hand, with swimming pool, gym and bars. The West End is also on the doorstep. Nearly 900 residential places are available within 20 minutes' walk of the school. However, the school has few of its own sports facilities and the outdoor pitches are remote, with no time set aside from lectures. Students tend to be highly committed and often politically active – not surprising since many will return to positions of influence in developing countries – and the variety of cultures makes for lively debate.

Undergraduate Fees and Bursaries

» Fees for UK/EU students 2015–16 £9,000
» Year abroad £1,350
» Fees for international students 2014–15 £15,320
» For students from low participation neighbourhoods, 33 awards: £2,500 fee waiver and £2,000 cash a year; for academic achievers from low-income families, 66 awards of £3,000 cash a year.
» Enhanced study support and hardship funds.
» Check the university's website for the latest information.

Students

Undergraduates:	2,990	(40)
Postgraduates:	1,805	(580)
Mature students:	22.5%	
International students:	39.4%	
Applications per place:	4.2	
From state-sector schools:	76.2%	
From working-class homes:	28.2%	
Satisfaction with students' union	71%	

For detailed information about sports facilities:
http://soasunion.org/activities/sports/

Accommodation

Number of places and costs refer to 2014–15
University-provided places: 774 (Sanctuary Management Services); 107 (intercollegiate)
Percentage catered: 14%
Catered costs: £136.50–£347.55 a week.
Self-catered costs: £147.28–£255.92 a week.
Priority given to first years on first come basis. Residential restrictions apply.
International students: as above, although they are a high priority.
www.soas.ac.uk/admissions/ug/accommodation/

University of South Wales

South Wales (USW), the product of a merger between Glamorgan and Newport universities, makes its debut in *The Times and Sunday Times* league table this year. The two partners came together in 2013 after several years of on/off negotiations and no little political intervention. They formed the largest university in Wales and one of the ten largest in the UK, with around 30,000 students currently across five campuses. A sixth will be added this autumn, when a London Centre for postgraduate and executive education opens in Docklands. However, in September 2014 the university announced its intention to close its Caerleon campus for new entrants in 2015 and transfer the courses to other campuses.

The University of South Wales Group also includes the Royal Welsh College of Music and Drama and Merthyr Tydfil College, and a new strategic alliance with the remaining further education colleges in South East Wales will spread the network even further. The alliance covers 38 campuses, providing 98,000 learners with advice and structured progression routes from further education to university. Even before the merger, Glamorgan and Newport were working together on the Universities Heads of the Valleys Institute, developing adults' skills in the former mining area.

About half of USW's students are full-time undergraduates and one-thirds are at least 21 years old. Three-quarters are from Wales and receive grants to reduce the cost of tuition; undergraduates from other parts of the UK will pay fees of £9,000 for all degrees in 2015–16. The degrees include the full range of science and engineering subjects, from aircraft engineering and mathematics to computing and surveying. The university is also an experienced provider of teacher training. There is a focus on employability and simulated learning to ensure that students learn how their future profession works in real life. There are partnerships with industry leaders and major employers, from British Airways to the National Health Service. Teaching facilities include the university's own aircraft, moot court room, TV studios, stock exchange trading room, hospital wards, and scenes-of-crime house. Sport students train and play on facilities used by Olympic athletes and the All Blacks. The university is also a significant player in the arts, with an internationally acclaimed film school, industry-standard animation facilities, one of the UK's oldest photography schools and a strong reputation for theatre design. The main research strengths are in applied projects, and it is a member of the St David's Day Group, which brings together all of the Principality's universities to focus on research and innovation.

Pontypridd CF37 1DL

08456 76 77 78 (enquiries)
contact via website
www.southwales.ac.uk
www.uswsu.com
Affiliation: University
Alliance

The Times and Sunday Times Rankings

Overall Ranking: **114** (last year: n/a)

Student satisfaction:	117	77.0%
Research quality:	=76	3.7%
Entry standards:	=74	322
Student–staff ratio:	=110	21.6
Services & facilities/student:	92	£1,313
Expected completion rate:	=100	80.8%
Good honours:	96	59.9%
Graduate prospects:	108	55.4%

Two of USW's campuses are 10 miles outside Cardiff, near Pontypridd, while the third is in the city itself. Around £28 million is being spent on improvements, more than half of it on an expansion of the university's campus in the heart of Cardiff. The £35-million ATRiuM building houses the Cardiff School of Creative and Cultural Industries, in the city centre, along with new premises for law and accounting and finance courses. Recent developments include a £15-million expansion of facilities for health, science and sport, as well as new halls of residence. There has also been a new home for the Law School on the Treforest campus and new laboratories at nearby Glyntaff. Amenities on the Treforest campus have been developing, with a modern recreation centre and a new students' union. A £6-milliion Learning Resource Centre opened in February 2014. The high-quality sports facilities have continued to improve: a £4-million sports park opened in 2011. The university also hosts one of six centres of excellence in cricket. USW has been successful in student competitions, especially in rugby, and offers a number of sports bursaries for students with international potential.

The £35-million Newport City Campus opened in 2011 and won an award from the Royal Institute of British Architects for its striking design. It is at the heart of Newport's new Cultural Quarter, designed to attract inward investment and strengthen the local economy. Newport was rated the top university in Wales for enterprise education by the Knowledge Exploitation Fund for three years in a row, helping more than 70 new start-up businesses. The Newport campus is also well-known for photography and film, hosting the International Film School Wales, whose graduates include double-BAFTA winner Asif Kapadia, and Justin Kerrigan, director of the cult movie *Human Traffic*. The Caerleon Campus, a few miles from Newport, which catered for humanities, education, health and social sciences and photography is to close in 2015. The city of Newport is undergoing a £2-billion regeneration programme and has plenty of clubs and entertainment venues, but students in search of serious cultural or clubbing activity gravitate to nearby Cardiff.

Undergraduate Fees and Bursaries

» Fees for UK/EU students 2015–16 £9,000
» Foundation degree £6,750
» Welsh Assembly non-means-tested grant to pay fees above £3,685 (2014–15) for Welsh students.
» Fees for international students 2014–15 £11,300
» £1,500 university accommodation discount (Treforest and Cardiff) for those paying full fees. Not available to those receiving Welsh Government tuition fee grant.
» Flying Start scholarship of £750 and an iPad in year 1 for students with at least 320 UCAS points.
» Check the university's website for the latest information.

Students

Undergraduates:	**15,835**	**(8,665)**
Postgraduates:	**2,475**	**(3,145)**
Mature students:	**28%**	
International students:	**7.8%**	
Applications per place:	**4**	
From state-sector schools:	**98.4%**	
From working-class homes:	**38.5%**	
Satisfaction with students' union	**53%**	

For detailed information about sports facilities:
http://sport.southwales.ac.uk

Accommodation

Number of places and costs refer to 2014–15
University-provided places: 1,867
Percentage catered: 0% but catering package available.
Self-catered accommodation: £79–£160 a week (40–51 weeks).
First-year students are offered accommodation. Local restrictions apply.
International students are guaranteed housing.
accom@southwales.ac.uk (Cardiff, Glyntaff & Treforest)
accommodation@southwales.ac.uk (Newport)
http://accommodation.southwales.ac.uk/

Southampton University

Southampton attracted more than 1,000 additional students in 2013, bearing out the prediction of the Vice-Chancellor, Professor Don Nutbeam, that a substantial shortfall in the previous year would be a one-off. Enrolments were back to the record level seen before higher fees were introduced, aided by substantial investment in new facilities and high levels of student satisfaction. The university has been a fixture in the top 20 in our league table for several years, benefiting from high staffing levels and a good performance in the last Research Assessment Exercise. Southampton is in the top 100 in the QS World University Rankings and the proportion of income derived from research is among the highest in Britain. It has particular strengths in computer science, where Sir Tim Berners-Lee, inventor of the Worldwide Web, is a professor and Nick Jennings was awarded the only Regius Professorship in the subject as part of the Queen's Jubilee. Southampton was a natural choice as one of the Government's eight Academic Centres of Excellence in Cyber Security Research.

The university has introduced a more flexible curriculum at undergraduate level, with some subjects offering a "major/minor" structure that allows students to spend 25 per cent of their time on a subject other than their original degree choice. There are also new inter-disciplinary modules, such as communication in a global world, or sustainability in local and global environments, that are designed to give students a broader perspective. New degrees for 2014 include web science and wildlife conservation. Every undergraduate has an academic adviser to guide their independent learning and progress. Over 85 per cent of the students went to state schools – more than the national average for the courses and entry qualifications and one of the highest proportions in the Russell Group. Students act as ambassadors, associates and mentors in local schools and colleges, as part of the university's efforts to broaden its intake further.

The university is in the final phase of a £250-million programme to upgrade its sites in Southampton and Winchester, having also opened a campus in Malaysia dedicated to engineering in 2012. The new site is on the southern tip of Malaysia, at the Iksandar Education City development, where undergraduates will study for two years before finishing their degree in Southampton. For example, an MEng in aeronautics and astronautics, new in 2014, will be introduced into Southampton's undergraduate study simultaneously. The university has more than 5,000 international students and a network of overseas

---

University Road
Southampton SO17 1BJ

023 80594732 (admissions)
admissns@southampton.ac.uk
www.southampton.ac.uk
www.susu.org
Affiliation: Russell Group

The Times and Sunday Times **Rankings**
Overall Ranking: **18** (last year: 20)

Student satisfaction:	=64	82.2%
Research quality:	=25	23.0%
Entry standards:	=25	431
Student–staff ratio:	13	12.8
Services & facilities/student:	25	£2,058
Expected completion rate:	=23	92.5%
Good honours:	21	78.4%
Graduate prospects:	=24	77.9%

partnerships in 54 countries. Medical students can take part of their course in Europe and other students can spend up to a year abroad, paying only 15 per cent of tuition fees for that year. A specially designed access programme gives students without the necessary qualifications for medicine a year's tuition to enable them to enter the full medical degree course.

The main Highfield campus is in an attractive green location two miles from the city centre. The students' union has been refurbished and a purpose-built student services centre added to bring together learning support and other advisory facilities. The library has been greatly extended and includes social learning space, designed by students. The striking £55-million Mountbatten Building for electronics and computer science and the Optoelectronics Research Centre and the £50-million Life Sciences Building are recent additions. There are three other sites in the city, including the National Oceanography Centre Southampton, based in the revitalised dock area. A £50-million joint project with the Natural Environment Research Council, it is considered Europe's finest. The Avenue campus, near the main site, is home to most of the humanities departments, while clinical medicine is based at Southampton General Hospital, where a new research centre focuses on respiratory diseases. Winchester School of Art, which has been part of the

university since 1996, has also enjoyed significant investment in new facilities. The arts are well represented·in Southampton, too, with three nationally renowned arts centres: the Turner Sims concert hall, the Nuffield Theatre and the John Hansard Gallery, all based at Highfield.

Sports facilities are first class, with an indoor sports complex next to the students' union. The outdoor sports complex has grass and synthetic pitches. The university won a Queen's Anniversary Prize for Higher and Further Education for its research in performance sports engineering in 2011. Over 1,000 elite athletes, including Sir Chris Hoy, were helped in their Olympic preparation by the university's aerodynamics research and wind tunnel complex. Student accommodation is plentiful: two new residential complexes have added 1,460 rooms, making 6,500 in all.

Undergraduate Fees and Bursaries

» Fees for UK/EU students 2015–16	£9,000
» Foundation degree	£9,000
» Placement year	£1,800
» Year abroad	£1,350
» Fees for international students 2014–15	£13,290–£16,320
Medicine	£16,320–£31,500

» Household income below £16K, a bursary of £3,000 a year; household income £16K–£25K, £2,000 a year.
» Around 150 bursaries of £1,000 a year for students from the Access to Southampton programme.
» Other scholarships and bursaries available.

Students

Undergraduates:	**15,520**	**(535)**
Postgraduates:	**5,235**	**(1,825)**
Mature students:	**13%**	
International students:	**17%**	
Applications per place:	**6.7**	
From state-sector schools:	**86.3%**	
From working-class homes:	**22.4%**	
Satisfaction with students' union	**69%**	

For detailed information about sports facilities:
www.southampton.ac.uk/sportandwellbeing/

Accommodation

Number of places and costs refer to 2014–15
University-provided places: more than 6,500
Percentage catered: 8%
Catered costs: £131.32–£169.81 a week.
Self-catered costs: £85.89–£254.80 a week.
All full-time first years are guaranteed an offer of accommodation. Conditions apply.
International students: All non-EU students are guaranteed accommodation. Conditions apply.
www.southampton.ac.uk/accommodation

Southampton Solent University

Southampton Solent is in the middle of a £100-million development programme on its city centre campus. The university has spent more than £40 million expanding and improving its facilities over the last five years and is planning to invest another £59 million over the next two decades. A new £30-million teaching and learning building will open in 2015 on a site that will extend the campus. Other recent developments include a ship handling centre, a media academy, a new site for the Southampton School of Art and Design and FA-accredited football facilities costing £4 million that are used by the city's Premier League team. The campus currently has few architectural pretensions, but is conveniently based in the centre of Southampton.

The largest of the institutions to be awarded university status in the last ten years, Solent also offers the widest range of programmes, stretching from further education courses to doctorates. It has an extensive range of "top-up" and extended degrees; and multiple start dates for its courses. The rebranded Solent Curriculum plays to the university's strengths in "industry-focused" courses. Over 12,000 higher education students embrace a broad-based portfolio that covers business, technology, the creative industries, sport and maritime studies. Students have the opportunity to work on projects for external clients and there is a strong representation of "non-traditional" disciplines, such as yacht and powercraft design, computer and video games, and music journalism and performance. The subject mix may be one reason that the former Southampton Institute is now one of the few universities with a majority of male students.

Solent recruits mainly in London and the south of England, a quarter of the HE students coming from Hampshire, but about 1,500 come from outside the UK. More than a third of the undergraduates come from working-class homes – considerably more than the national average for the university's subjects and entry qualifications – and 97 per cent are state-educated. Its support for students was recently identified as an example of best practice by the Quality Assurance Agency; the dropout rate has improved consistently over recent years. A Graduate Enterprise Centre provides advice and rent-free offices for those hoping to launch their own businesses, helping to bring about 40 start-ups from concept to securing financial backing. A Graduate Associate scheme provides employment places for about 100 recent graduates.

The university is held back in *The*

East Park Terrace
Southampton SO14 0YN

023 8031 9039 (enquiries)
ask@solent.ac.uk
www.solent.ac.uk
www.solentsu.co.uk
Affiliation: GuildHE

The Times and Sunday Times **Rankings**
Overall Ranking: **115** (last year: 114)

Student satisfaction:	**116**	77.2%
Research quality:	**=114**	0.7%
Entry standards:	**=99**	299
Student–staff ratio:	**=80**	18.8
Services & facilities/student:	**89**	£1,335
Expected completion rate:	**115**	76.4%
Good honours:	**=91**	61.1%
Graduate prospects:	**=117**	50.5%

Times and Sunday Times league table by low scores for student satisfaction and for graduate employment prospects. Solent also entered fewer academics for the last Research Assessment Exercise than any university in England – fewer than one in ten of those eligible. But two of the three areas in which it made a submission contained some world-leading research and the university undertakes a wide range of applied research, as well as practice-based research in art and design. Creative Arts and Society courses now attract almost as many students as the consistently popular business school. There are new music studios with an industry-standard recording complex, as well as a performance space and dance studio. The Centre for Professional Development in Broadcasting and Multimedia Production includes an online editing suite, digital television studio and gallery, for use by undergraduates as well as community groups and professionals.

There is particularly strong demand for places in marine and maritime-based courses, which benefit from a world-renowned training and research facility for the superyacht, shipping and offshore oil industries. The university is higher education's premier yachting institution, with a world champion student team that has won the national championships four times in six years and alumni that have gone on to win Olympic and Paralympic gold medals. Three new boats support courses at the purpose-built Watersports Centre, where some activities are targeted towards disadvantaged young people. The Lawrie McMenemy Centre for Football Research is helping to cement the university's reputation for academic study of the sport and, having assumed responsibility for sport development in the city, Solent has also become the country's largest provider of coaching education. A new School of Health, Exercise and Social Science was launched in 2013 to encourage collaboration in health and exercise science, social work and psychology.

Students like the university's location, close to the city centre's shopping area and growing complement of bars and nightclubs. There are more than 2,300 hall places, most of which are allocated to first years. Sports facilities include a sports hall and fitness suite on campus and outdoor pitches, tennis and netball courts four miles away.

Undergraduate Fees and Bursaries

- » Fees for UK/EU students 2015–16 £9,000
- » Placement year / year abroad £1,350
- » Fees for international students 2014–15 £10,080–£11,140
- » New bursary scheme to help with additional course costs in development for 2015–16.
- » Combined fee waiver and cash award for Foundation year students and for local students from low participation areas.
- » Check the university's website for the latest information.

Students

Undergraduates:	**10,155**	**(1,360)**
Postgraduates:	**165**	**(410)**
Mature students:	**21.4%**	
International students:	**13.1%**	
Applications per place:	**3.9**	
From state-sector schools:	**97.1%**	
From working-class homes:	**36.5%**	
Satisfaction with students' union	**54%**	

For detailed information about sports facilities:
www.solent.ac.uk/sport/sport-solent.aspx

Accommodation

Number of places and costs refer to 2014–15
University-provided places: 2,340.
Percentage catered: 0%
Self-catered costs: £89.95–£124.88 a week (41 weeks).
First years are allocated 90% of rooms.
International students: some accommodation is set aside.
accommodation@solent.ac.uk
www.solent.ac.uk/studying/accommodation/accommodation.aspx

Staffordshire University

Staffordshire has decided to concentrate most of its activities on Stoke-on-Trent and by September 2016, only the highly rated nursing and midwifery degrees and other courses in paramedic and public health will remain on the Stafford campus. Timescales are still to be finalised, but students beginning degrees in computing and entertainment technology in 2015 may start their courses in Stafford and move after the first year. Professor Michael Gunn, the Vice-Chancellor, said concentration made economic sense and would offer the best possible student experience: "Students generally show a preference for an edge-of-city campus with brilliant learning and teaching facilities, good public transport links and social activities – all of which we have in Stoke-on-Trent." Staffordshire's engineering provision had already moved to Stoke in 2013 and the university is planning further development there. The aim is to create an award-winning, teaching-led university by 2017, with a focus on employability, enterprise and entrepreneurialism.

The reorganisation follows a review of the university's academic portfolio. A £30-million science block opened on the Stoke campus in 2012 in order to create a focal point to help drive up the numbers of young people in the region opting to study science, maths and engineering subjects, where career prospects are good. Staffordshire is at the heart of Stoke's University Quarter project, which is designed to transform the South Sheldon area as well as encouraging greater participation in higher education. The university has made a commitment to students and employers through the Staffordshire Graduate programme to ensure that, alongside their academic learning, all students are equipped with employability skills. From 2015–16 for the first time, fees for all undergraduate courses will be £9,000.

The university's two main sites both have modern halls of residence, sports centres and lively students' union venues. Some £12 million has already been invested in the Stoke campus to create a more attractive study environment with dedicated student spaces, exhibition areas, cafes and landscaping. Much larger sums will follow to ensure that the campus can comfortably accommodate the extra students. There is a 25-acre nature reserve – part of the university's sustained green commitment – as well as a business village offering affordable business space for start-up companies. The teacher training programmes, which rank in the top 30 in the *Good Teacher Training* guide, are based on a third site in Lichfield. The site houses

---

College Road
Stoke-on-Trent ST4 2DE

01782 294400 (admissions)
enquiries@staffs.ac.uk
www.staffs.ac.uk
www.staffsunion.com
Affiliation: million+

The Times and Sunday Times **Rankings**
Overall Ranking: **101** (last year: 108)

Student satisfaction:	77	81.2%
Research quality:	=110	1.0%
Entry standards:	117	273
Student–staff ratio:	=61	17.7
Services & facilities/student:	=77	£1,416
Expected completion rate:	=100	80.8%
Good honours:	=102	58.5%
Graduate prospects:	105	55.9%

an integrated further and higher education centre, developed in partnership with South Staffordshire College, as well as business start-up units. There are also 15,000 students taking Staffordshire courses outside the UK, almost half of them located around the Pacific Rim. They now make up more than a third of the university's intake, adding to a growing cohort of international students on the university's UK campuses.

Staffordshire is a pioneer of two-year fast-track degrees, which are now offered in accounting and finance, computing science, business, English and law. There already was an extensive portfolio of two-year Foundation degrees, largely taught by the university's UK partners, which include the National Design Academy. With almost all of its undergraduates state-educated and 44 per cent coming from working-class homes Staffordshire exceeds all the benchmarks for the breadth of its intake. There is good provision for students with disabilities and more than one undergraduate in five comes from areas with little participation in higher education, one of the biggest proportions in the country. The downside is the dropout rate, which, although improving, was projected at more than 18 per cent in the latest survey – well above the national average for the university's courses and entry qualifications. Staffordshire entered only a small proportion of its academics for the last research assessments, but has made a larger submission to the Research Excellence Framework, whose results are due at the end of 2014. Applied research has led to the development of new products in markets as diverse as medical technology and recycling.

Stoke is not the liveliest city of its size, but the University Quarter is attracting more social and leisure facilities. The campus is within easy reach of the city centre and has a buzzing students' union. Stafford is the more attractive setting and offers a better chance of a residential place, but the town is quiet and the campus is a mile and a half outside it. Sports facilities are good and will see more investment as numbers on the Stoke campus rise. Good coaching has helped attract some outstanding athletes, who have access to a sports performance centre to help with training schedules, psychological support and dietary assessments.

Undergraduate Fees and Bursaries

- » Fees for UK/EU students 2015–16   £9,000
- » Foundation degree   £9,000
- » Placement year   £1,200
- » Courses at partner colleges   £5,400–£6,990
- » Fees for international students 2014–15   £10,000
- » Students from deprived areas and with lowest household incomes, 500 bursaries of £200 cash and £800 accommodation discount or for travel costs or institutional services in year 1; £100 and £400 each in years 2 and 3.
- » Check the university's website for the latest information.

Students

Undergraduates:	**10,470**	**(7,010)**
Postgraduates:	**1,100**	**(2,440)**
Mature students:	**32.5%**	
International students:	**3.8%**	
Applications per place:	**4.3**	
From state-sector schools:	**98.3%**	
From working-class homes:	**43.7%**	
Satisfaction with students' union	**72%**	

For detailed information about sports facilities:
www.staffs.ac.uk/teamstaffs

Accommodation

Number of places and costs refer to 2014–15
University-provided places: 1,041 (Stoke); 605 (Stafford)
Percentage catered: 0%
Self-catered accommodation: £80–£108 a week (38 weeks).
First years have priority, if conditions are met.
International students: have priority, if conditions are met.
accommodation_stoke@staffs.ac.uk
accommodation_stafford@staffs.ac.uk
www.staffs.ac.uk/support_depts/accommodation/

University of Stirling

Stirling's strategic plan makes no mention of expanding – indeed, it describes the university's relatively small size as an asset – but it is certainly doing so. It has almost doubled its intake of new undergraduates in two years, far outstripping the record enrolment of 2010. There is plenty of room for more: the spacious main campus would be capable of considerable expansion and the student experience seems not to have suffered. Stirling won *Times Higher Education* magazine's 2013 award for the most improved student experience. Applicants are attracted by the spectacular setting and community feel of a university that still has only about 12,000 students.

The main campus nestles at the foot of the Ochil hills around a loch in a 330-acre estate, although still within easy reach of Edinburgh and Glasgow. It is particularly well provided with sports facilities, having been designated Scotland's University for Sporting Excellence in 2008. The campus is home to national swimming and tennis centres, as well as a golf course and a football academy. The sports centre was recently refurbished and now comprises of a central gym, two strength and conditioning areas with weightlifting platforms and a cycle studio. A new High Performance Sports Science and Sports Medicine Facility opened in 2012. The university runs an international sports scholarship programme and manages Winning Students, the national sport scholarship programme for students in colleges and universities across Scotland.

Academic facilities include a modernised library, a dedicated study zone and more than 700 computers for student use, many available 24 hours a day. The university also has a purpose built faith centre/chaplaincy which is open to students and staff of all faiths. A joint venture with INTO University Partnerships will establish teaching centres on the campus and in London to provide preparatory courses for international students beginning in September 2014. There are two other campuses: one for nurses and midwives in the modern Centre for Health Science, in Inverness, and a Western Isles campus, located in Stornoway, where the teaching accommodation is an integral part of the Western Isles Hospital.

Stirling was the British pioneer of the semester system, which has now become so popular throughout higher education. The academic year is divided into two blocks of 15 weeks with short mid-semester breaks. Students have the option of starting courses in February, rather than September, and can choose subjects from across all seven Schools. Degrees are built up of credits accumulated through modules taken and awarded each semester, rather than at the end of the academic year. Undergraduates

---

Stirling Campus

Stirling FK9 4LA

01786 467044 (admissions)
admissions@stir.ac.uk
www.stir.ac.uk
www.stirlingstudentsunion.
com
Affiliation: none

The Times and Sunday Times Rankings

Overall Ranking: **53** (last year: 51)

Student satisfaction:	86	80.3%
Research quality:	49	13.7%
Entry standards:	43	380
Student–staff ratio:	42	15.7
Services & facilities/student:	62	£1,517
Expected completion rate:	=79	83.3%
Good honours:	85	62.8%
Graduate prospects:	46	70.5%

can switch the whole direction of their studies, in consultation with their academic adviser, as their interests develop. They can also speed up their progress on a Summer Academic Programme, which squeezes a full semester's teaching into July and August. Full-time students are not allowed to use the programme to reduce the length of their course, but part-timers can use it to make rapid progress.

The intake is surprisingly diverse, with nearly 95 per cent of undergraduates state-educated and almost 30 per cent coming from working-class homes. Two-thirds are from Scotland, but the remainder come from more than 100 different countries. International exchanges are common, with many of Stirling's students going to American, Asian and European universities each year, while 175 Study Abroad or exchange students come in the opposite direction.

The university has nominated five "core areas" for teaching and research: health and well-being, culture and society, environment, enterprise and economy, and sport. In the last Research Assessment Exercise, Stirling produced the best results in Scotland in film and media, nursing and midwifery, education and sport.

The first two phases of a £38-million expansion of student accommodation were completed by 2014, with the third phase due to be ready in 2015. Students appreciate the individual attention that a small campus university can offer, although some find the atmosphere claustrophobic. Stirling is not the top choice of night-clubbers, but the students' union won "Best Bar None" status for three years in a row and there is a lively social scene. The MacRobert Arts Centre offers a full programme of cultural activities, while the surrounding countryside offers its own attractions for walkers and climbers. The campus has been described by police as one of the safest in Britain and last year launched the Safe Taxi Scheme. A Counselling and Wellbeing service offers support for mental and emotional health, while the Disability Service supports a full range of student needs.

Undergraduate Fees and Bursaries

» Fees for Scottish and EU students 2014–15   No fee
» Fees for Non-Scottish UK (RUK) students 2014–15   £6,750
» Fees for international students 2014–15   £11,000–£13,100
» For RUK students with at least ABB in one sitting at A Level or equivalent, "Merit" bursary of £1,000–£2,000 a year.
» A range of sports scholarships for all students. .
» Check the university's website for the latest information.

Students

Undergraduates:	6,355	(930)
Postgraduates:	2,400	(1,045)
Mature students:	20.5%	
International students:	8.2%	
Applications per place:	6.7	
From state-sector schools:	94.4%	
From working-class homes:	27.3%	
Satisfaction with students' union	60%	

For detailed information about sports facilities:
www.stir.ac.uk/sport-at-stirling/

Accommodation

Number of places and costs refer to 2014–15
University-provided places: 3,000
Percentage catered: 0%
Self-catered costs: £72–£199 a week (37–50 weeks).
All first years are guaranteed suitable housing arranged by the university.
International students: as above.
accommodation@stir.ac.uk;
www.stir.ac.uk/campus-life/accommodation/newundergraduates/

University of Strathclyde

Strathclyde was established in 1796 as a "place of useful learning", so it was an apt choice as *Times Higher Education* magazine's 2013/14 Entrepreneurial University of the Year, the first Scottish institution to take the title. The award recognised the culture of entrepreneurship fostered at the university through education, research, mentoring and partnership programmes. Strathclyde Enterprise Pathway allows students to develop, enhance and test their transferable skills, while alumni and businesses in the Strathclyde 100 network support the university's emerging entrepreneurs. Students and alumni have established 84 companies employing 200 people, while the university itself has more than 50 spin-out companies, making annual sales of £80 million.

The university promises courses that are both innovative and relevant to employers' needs – hence product design and innovation, energy systems or international business with modern languages. It has set itself the target of becoming one of the world's leading technological universities, and the Vice-Chancellor, Professor Sir Jim McDonald, has been seeking improvements in research to achieve this goal. The university has invested £89 million in a new Technology and Innovation Centre that opened in 2014, bringing academic and industrial researchers together, with financial support from government, industry and Europe. Strathclyde has also been chosen as the European partner for South Korea's global research and commercialisation programme and as the UK headquarters of Fraunhofer Gesellschaft, Europe's largest contract research organisation. Almost 60 per cent of the university's submission was rated as world-leading or internationally excellent in the last Research Assessment Exercise. The business school, which is rated among the top 30 in Europe by *The Financial Times*, is normally considered Strathclyde's greatest strength. It is among the largest in Europe and one of only 55 in the world to be "triple accredited" by the main international bodies. The school has opened its own Indian branch campus near Delhi. The engineering faculty is the largest in Scotland and home to the biggest university electrical power engineering and energy research grouping in Europe.

With more than 20,000 students, including part-timers, Strathclyde is the third-largest university in Scotland, but its numbers swell to more than 60,000 when short courses and distance learning programmes are included. For the second year in a row, degree applications dropped but there was still a small increase in enrolments. Mature students account for one third of the undergraduate population. The university has endorsed

---

16 Richmond Street
Glasgow G1 1XQ

0141 548 2762 (prospectus)
contact via website
www.strath.ac.uk
www.strathstudents.com
Affiliation: none

GLASGOW
Edinburgh
Belfast
London
Cardiff

The Times and Sunday Times **Rankings**

Overall Ranking: **39** (last year: 42)

Student satisfaction:	=59	82.3%
Research quality:	44	16.7%
Entry standards:	=13	470
Student–staff ratio:	=84	19.3
Services & facilities/student:	42	£1,753
Expected completion rate:	62	85.7%
Good honours:	33	74.4%
Graduate prospects:	=24	77.9%

an international movement to establish "Age-Friendly" universities. Strathclyde's Learning in Later Life programme has established itself as one of Scotland's most successful routes to education for older people, while the Centre for Lifelong Learning has been one of the foremost providers of education to people in later life for some four decades. Strathclyde actively promotes wider access, comfortably exceeding the UK average for state-educated students. The projected dropout rate has fallen to 6 per cent and is now lower than average for the university's subjects and entry qualifications.

Strathclyde, which has taken to adding Glasgow to its name, has been carrying out an ambitious £350-million development programme. All courses are taught on the city-centre John Anderson campus, with the Faculty of Humanities and Social Sciences at its heart, enabling staff to work more closely with colleagues in research, teaching and partners in collaborative ventures. The developments feature new and improved teaching areas, study space and facilities for students tailored to their specific subjects. A Confucius Institute supports the teaching of Chinese Language and the Strathclyde Institute of Pharmacy and Biomedical Sciences, a centre for excellence in drug discovery and development research, opened in 2011. Away from the campus, the Advanced Forming Research Centre,

a research partnership with international engineering firms, has opened near Glasgow Airport.

There is a student village on the main campus with 1,400 places and another 500 residential places nearby in the Merchant City. The ten-floor union building attracts students from all over Glasgow. There are numerous cultural and political clubs and societies, plus over 40 sporting clubs and university teams. Proximity to Glasgow's vibrant and celebrated music scene is a plus, and for those with more sophisticated tastes, there are numerous theatres and arts organisations, as well as standout museums such as the Kelvingrove Gallery, one of Scotland's top attractions. On the sporting side, Strathclyde was the only training venue in Scotland for the London 2012 Olympics, and the university's students and alumni made up 5 per cent of Team Scotland in the Commonwealth Games, when the campus formed part of the cycling road race route.

Undergraduate Fees and Bursaries

» Fees for Scottish and EU students 2014–15   No fee
» Fees for Non-Scottish UK (RUK) students 2014–15   £9,000
    (capped at £27,000 for any course)
» Fees for international students 2014–15   £12,000–£15,900
» For RUK students , annual bursaries for household income below £20K, £4,250; sliding scale to £42.6K, £2,500–£1,000; year 1 bursary of £1,000 for those in university accommodation; those with at least AAB at A Level or equivalent, bursary of £1,000 a year.

Students

Undergraduates:	**11,525**	**(2,655)**
Postgraduates:	**3,170**	**(2,505)**
Mature students:	**13.5%**	
International students:	**9.1%**	
Applications per place:	**5.8**	
From state-sector schools:	**92.8%**	
From working-class homes:	**25.7%**	
Satisfaction with students' union	**77%**	

For detailed information about sports facilities:
www.strath.ac.uk/sport

Accommodation

Number of places and costs refer to 2014–15
University-provided places: 1,840
Percentage catered: 0%
Self-catered costs: £94–£125 a week (39 weeks).
First years are offered accommodation if they live further than 25 miles from the university.
International students: as above.
student.accommodation@strath.ac.uk
www.strath.ac.uk/accommodation/

University of Sunderland

Sunderland will be one of only two universities in England to charge less than £9,000 for all its degrees in 2015–16. It delivered on a promise to hold undergraduate fees at a maximum of £8,500 for three years, but will now charge £8,750 for laboratory-based science degrees and £8,250 for the remainder, with Foundation degrees priced at £7,000. The savings over 30 years of loan repayments are not large, especially in the sciences, but the university believes that its students are particularly price-sensitive since half of them have a household income of less than £25,000 a year. Students will also continue to receive £550 towards public transport costs or university rents, as well as a Sunderland Scholarship of £1,000 in their first two years if they are among the 98 per cent whose household income is less than £42,600. Sunderland sees transport costs as a key barrier to study, especially in its local communities, which are the lifeblood of the university. Almost 30 per cent of the undergraduates come from areas of low participation – the highest proportion at any university – while 44 per cent are from working-class homes. A pioneering access scheme offers places to mature students without A levels, as long as they reach the required levels of literacy, numeracy and other basic skills.

Sunderland suffered a big fall in the last edition of our league table, partly because it had not managed to keep pace with improvements in completion rates and graduate prospects elsewhere in the university system. But provision for disabled students is excellent, with award-winning information issued to those with disabilities, trained support staff in the libraries and in every academic school, and special modules to help dyslexics. The main campus also houses the North East Regional Assessment Centre, which assesses the requirements of students with disabilities and specific learning difficulties. There is special provision at the five halls of residence.

The university now has three campuses, two in Sunderland and one in London, near Canary Wharf, which offers business, tourism and nursing degrees, as well as postgraduate programmes. Within Sunderland, the university has spent £130 million on its original campus in the city centre and an award-winning 24-acre site on the banks of the River Wear. The Sir Tom Cowie campus, at St Peter's, is built around a 7th-century abbey described as one of Britain's first universities and incorporates a working heritage centre for the glass industry. It houses the business school and the faculties of applied sciences, law, and arts, design and media. A glass and ceramics design degree maintains a Sunderland

---

City Campus
Chester Road
Sunderland SR1 3SD

0191 515 3000 (course helpline)
student.helpline@
   sunderland.ac.uk
www.sunderland.ac.uk
www.sunderlandsu.co.uk
Affiliation: million+

The Times and Sunday Times Rankings

Overall Ranking: **99** (last year: =96)

Student satisfaction:	74	81.4%
Research quality:	=67	4.7%
Entry standards:	=94	302
Student–staff ratio:	66	17.9
Services & facilities/student:	=86	£1,359
Expected completion rate:	103	80.3%
Good honours:	110	54.3%
Graduate prospects:	115	50.9%

tradition, while teaching and research in automotive design and manufacture serve the region's modern industrial base. The large pharmacy department is another strength and the well-equipped Faculty of Applied Sciences is one of the largest in the UK, with over 4,000 students. The £12-million CitySpace has improved the sports and social facilities on the original City Campus and there is a new Sciences Complex and Quad. A £12-million student village is also fully open. The campus includes the Northern Centre for Photography, as well as a one-stop-shop for student services, an outdoor performance area and a design centre.

Sunderland now has more than 15,000 students, including 2,000 from outside the European Union. Many take work placements with the multinational companies that have been attracted to the North East and now have links with the university. The Institute for Automotive and Manufacturing Advanced Practice has a team of 40 researchers and consultants working with local businesses, while nearby Nissan played an important role in designing a course in automotive product development. The media centre provides students with excellent television and video production facilities, including the former Blue Peter studio, which has been transported from the former BBC Television Centre. The popular media courses now include magazine, fashion and sports journalism. The LLB degree includes space law, the first module of its kind in the UK. Sunderland had only moderate success in the 2008 Research Assessment Exercise, although more than half of the 16 subject areas contained some world-leading work.

Sunderland itself is fiercely proud of its identity and has the advantage of a coastal location. The leisure facilities are better than one might imagine: the city has the North East's only Olympic-sized swimming pool and dry ski slope, as well as Europe's biggest climbing wall and a theatre showing West End productions. Those in search of more cultural events or serious nightlife head for Newcastle, which is less than half an hour away by Metro.

Undergraduate Fees and Bursaries

» Fees for UK/EU students 2015–16   £8,250–£8,750
» Foundation degree   £7,000
» Fees for international students 2014–15   £9,500
» Household income below £42.6K, a bursary of £1,000 in years 1 and 2.
» For all first-year students, £550 towards local transport costs or campus accommodation; discounted travel pass in years 2 and 3.
» For those with ABB at A level or equivalent, £1,000 fee waiver in years 1 and 2.
» Up to 100 scholarships of £1,000 in years 1 and 2 in science and technology subjects.
» Fee waiver of £1,200 a year for students on Foundation degrees at partner colleges.

Students

Undergraduates:	**9,800**	**(1,940)**
Postgraduates:	**2,375**	**(840)**
Mature students:	**22.3%**	
International students:	**24%**	
Applications per place:	**4.5**	
From state-sector schools:	**97%**	
From working-class homes:	**43.9%**	
Satisfaction with students' union	**57%**	

For detailed information about sports facilities:
www.unisportsunderland.com

Accommodation

Number of places and costs refer to 2014–15
University provided places: 1,490 beds in halls, 548 (The Forge).
Percentage catered: 0%
Self-catered costs: £76 (standard room;) for 40 weeks – £92 (en suite) for 50 weeks. Option to purchase catering vouchers.
New first years are guaranteed accommodation in accordance with the university's allocation policy.
International students: as above.
residentialservices@sunderland.ac.uk
http://services.sunderland.ac.uk/facilities/residentialservices/

University of Surrey

Surrey's new £40-million veterinary school – only the second to be established in half a century – will be fully open for the start of the academic year in 2015, with world-class clinical skills centres, pathology facility and teaching, research and diagnostic laboratories. It will add to the attractions of a university that has been making rapid progress up *The Times and Sunday Times* league table and growing considerably in popularity with applicants. The demand for places doubled in six years, despite sharply increasing entry standards, with applications growing again by an extraordinary 42 per cent in 2013. New undergraduate enrolments grew by a third as a result. The university has been among the most innovative in the UK in recent years, reducing its dependence on state funding even before the introduction of £9,000 fees, developing and extending the campus in Guildford, and launching a joint venture in China. Student satisfaction rates have improved by leaps and bounds, placing Surrey among the top five universities in the 2013 National Student Survey.

The university has remained true to its technological history with large numbers taking engineering and science subjects, but it has other strengths in business and the sector-leading School of Hospitality and Tourism Management. Surrey has also incorporated the Guildford School of Acting and opened the £4.5-million Ivy Arts Centre in 2011, with a 200-seat theatre and workshops. Undergraduates in most subjects undertake work placements of one year, or several shorter periods, often abroad. As a result, most degrees last four years. The format and the subject balance combine to keep Surrey at or near the top of the graduate employment league, and the dropout rate is low. All students are encouraged to take a free course in a European language alongside their degree, in a programme known as the Global Graduate Award. Over 91 per cent of Surrey undergraduates are state educated and nearly 28 per cent are from working class backgrounds.

International activities have been increasing. Surrey has one of the largest proportions of overseas students at any university – more than a fifth – and is a member of the University Global Partnership Network (UGPN) involving North Carolina State University and the Universidad de Sao Paulo in Brazil. The biggest development has seen the opening of a campus in Dalian, China with the Dongbei University of Finance and Economics.

More than half of the work submitted for the last Research Assessment Exercise was considered world-leading or

---

Guildford
Surrey GU2 7XH

0800 980 3200 (enquiries)
ug-enquiries@surrey.ac.uk
www.surrey.ac.uk
www.ussu.co.uk
Affiliation: none

The Times and Sunday Times Rankings

Overall Ranking: **11** (last year: =12)

Student satisfaction:	4	86.9%
Research quality:	=35	20.3%
Entry standards:	=30	422
Student–staff ratio:	=35	15.4
Services & facilities/student:	18	£2,167
Expected completion rate:	34	91.0%
Good honours:	=18	79.0%
Graduate prospects:	=7	81.8%

internationally excellent. More recently, Surrey's chemical engineering received two awards for innovation and excellence from the Institution of Chemical Engineers and the university has secured £35-million funding from business and government for a 5G communication research centre, which will be the first in the world dedicated to mobile technologies. Electronic engineering was one of 12 university departments in any subject to be awarded a Regius professorship as part of the Queen's Jubilee. The proportion of its research income coming from private business and industry has grown to about 70 per cent in little over a decade. BP sponsored the new Centre for Petroleum and Surface Chemistry, for example. The Surrey Research Park is one of the largest in the UK still to be owned, funded and managed by its host university.

The compact campus is a ten-minute walk from the centre of Guildford. Many of the buildings date from the late 1960s, but the refurbished and extended library and learning centre, and the gleaming Duke of Kent Building, which houses the growing health and medical provision, offer a striking contrast. The campus includes two lakes, playing fields and enough residential accommodation to enable all first years to live in. The virtual learning environment, SurreyLearn allows students to work with others on their courses online and to take part in discussions and blogs, as well as allowing lecturers to set coursework and interact with students. The Manor Park campus, which is effectively an extension of the university's Stag Hill headquarters, provides over 1,500 residential places for students and staff, as well as a reception building with café, bar and lounge areas. The impressive Surrey Sports Park, with extensive indoor and outdoor facilities, opened in 2010. The main campus is the centre of social life, and has seen recent improvements to leisure facilities including new dining and social areas. Guildford has plenty of retail, cultural and recreational facilities and the proximity of London (35 minutes by train) is an attraction to many students, although it also helps account for the high cost of living.

Undergraduate Fees and Bursaries

» Fees for UK/EU students 2015–16 £9,000
» Placement year £1,800
» Fees for international students 2014–15 £13,665–£14,550
» Household income below £25K and from disadvantaged area, £1,800 as campus accommodation discount (or cash if living off campus) in year 1; £1,800 cash in other years.
» Scholarship of £2,000 cash in year 1 for those with A*A*A* at A level or equivalent.
» Sports and other scholarships available.
» Check the university's website for the latest information.

Students

Undergraduates:	**8,905**	**(895)**
Postgraduates:	**2,565**	**(1,530)**
Mature students:	**15%**	
International students:	**22.2%**	
Applications per place:	**7.9**	
From state-sector schools:	**91.1%**	
From working-class homes:	**28%**	
Satisfaction with students' union	**81%**	

For detailed information about sports facilities:
www.surreysportspark.co.uk

Accommodation

Number of places and costs refer to 2014–15
University-provided places: 5,063
Percentage catered: 0%
Self-catered costs: £67.00–£155.50 a week.
All first years are guaranteed a place if conditions are met. International non-EU students are guaranteed accommodation for the standard duration of their course. Remaining places are allocated to final year students.
www.surrey.ac.uk/accommodation

University of Sussex

Sussex is planning to grow by 50 per cent by 2018 in order to provide opportunities for a broader range of students and achieve the "critical mass" that the university considers necessary to be successful in research. It is still some way off its target of 18,000 students, but has taken more in each of the last two years, despite a drop in applications in 2013. Undergraduates are offered a 21st-century version of the interdisciplinary approach that has been Sussex's foundation in the 1960s, with encouragement to study outside their core area. Sussex has reviewed all its courses since the switch to higher fees and has become a late covert to the semester system. The university believes that two 12-week teaching periods with a mid-year assessment period improves the way students learn and are assessed. Student support includes a work-study programme to help students earn money, funded work placements and three years' aftercare for graduates to help them into a career. The Sussex Plus programme documents and credits students' extra-curricular skills, while a new initiative, Startup Sussex, supports students' creative business ideas and social projects.

The campus, four miles from the centre of Brighton in the suburb of Falmer, is already serving a record number of students: 13,000 students, of whom 9,500 are undergraduates.

The university has completed a £100-million campus development plan, refurbishing Sir Basil Spence's original buildings and adding new ones. A striking new £29-million academic building offers a mix of lecture theatres, study and teaching space, and a social centre. The Gardner Centre will be brought back to life during the 2013–14 academic year as an interdisciplinary arts hub for the university and the wider community, named after the university's former Chancellor, Lord Attenborough. The library, which has undergone a £6-million redevelopment and introduced 24-hour opening during term-time, has seen a 50 per cent increase in use. An investment of £1.5 million in IT developments has doubled the number of computers available to students and installed Wi-Fi in all the student residences.

Arts and social science students take the biggest share of places, but the life sciences are not far behind. Dedicated student social space is being created in each of the university's 12 schools to encourage staff and students to engage both academically and socially. Relations with neighbouring Brighton University are good. The two institutions opened a joint medical school in 2003, which is split between the Royal Sussex County Hospital and the two universities' Falmer campuses.

Sussex generates more than a third of its income from private sources, largely

---

Sussex House
Brighton BN1 9RH

01273 876787 (enquiries)
ug.enquiries@sussex.ac.uk
www.sussex.ac.uk
www.bsms.ac.uk
www.sussexstudent.com
Affiliation: none

The Times and Sunday Times **Rankings**
Overall Ranking: **25** (last year: 32)

Student satisfaction:	=66	82.1%
Research quality:	17	25.7%
Entry standards:	33	411
Student–staff ratio:	47	16.5
Services & facilities/student:	22	£2,114
Expected completion rate:	36	90.5%
Good honours:	29	76.3%
Graduate prospects:	28	76.1%

in research contracts. Its reputation was enhanced by good results in the last Research Assessment Exercise, when almost 60 per cent of an unusually large submission was rated as world-leading or internationally excellent. The first fruits of a £50-million fundraising campaign have seen the opening of major research centres on adoption, corruption, Middle East studies and consciousness science. Although little more than 50 years old, the university can count three Nobel prize winners amongst its alumni.

Sussex is committed to taking candidates with no family tradition of higher education and has a dedicated scheme to support them. There are also a much larger numbers of mature students than most of its peer group of institutions. The proportion of working-class students is lower than the national average for the university's subjects and entry grades, but this is attributed to the university's south coast location. The projected dropout rate has improved to 5 per cent and is lower than the university's benchmark. Sussex has always attracted overseas students in large numbers and has seen big increases recently. The university has performed consistently well in the International Student Barometer, which gauges overseas students' satisfaction. Together with first years, they are guaranteed a place in university-managed accommodation that has been expanded and upgraded in recent years. There are

now more than 5,000 residential places, and Sussex's plans for the future include a major housing development to replace old accommodation, as well as the construction of a new biomedical sciences building to complement the highly rated Genome Research Centre.

The campus is located within the newly created South Downs National Park, with excellent transport links into town. There is no shortage of social events on campus and Brighton has plenty to offer. Sports facilities were good enough to house pre-Olympic training. Sports scholarships are available to outstanding athletes, including four reserved for basketball and hockey players. Sussex has also opened a purpose-built childcare facility for 100 pre-school children of students and staff.

Undergraduate Fees and Bursaries

» Fees for UK/EU students 2015–16	£9,000
» Placement year	£1,800
» Year abroad	£1,350
» Fees for international students 2014–15	£13,750–£17,000
Medicine	£26,100
» Students with household income below £42.6K, a £2,000 university accommodation discount (or £2,000 fee waiver) and £1,000 cash in year 1 and Foundation year; £1,000 a year in subsequent years.	
» Check the university's website for the latest information.	

Students

Undergraduates:	**9,565**	**(25)**
Postgraduates:	**2,685**	**(870)**
Mature students:	**13.7%**	
International students:	**22.6%**	
Applications per place:	**4.9**	
From state-sector schools:	**86%**	
From working-class homes:	**23%**	
Satisfaction with students' union	**72%**	

For detailed information about sports facilities:
www.sussex.ac.uk/sport/

Accommodation

Number of places and costs refer to 2014–15
University-provided places: 5,041
Percentage catered: 0%
Self-catered costs: £82.20–£144.00 (single) a week. Some shared rooms available.
First-year students are guaranteed accommodation if conditions are met.
International students: given priority providing conditions are met.
housing@sussex.ac.uk
www.sussex.ac.uk/residentialservices/

Swansea University

Swansea's new Bay Campus will ready for the start of the academic year in 2015, relieving the pressure on what had become the smallest main site at any pre-1992 university. Designed for 5,000 students and home to the College of Engineering and School of Management, it is said to be the only UK university campus with direct access to a beach. The first phase of the development on the eastern approach to Swansea will include residences with 900 rooms and a library with spaces for 650 students. The focus will be on applied research with industry, but the project will also free up space on the original Singleton campus – itself not far from the sea – where the university has already invested £73 million. Applications have risen by more than 20 per cent this year and last, and the intake of new undergraduates was 770 up in 2013, reaching record levels, so extra capacity cannot come too soon. Swansea was the UK's first campus university when it opened in 1920, enjoying a prime position at the gateway to the Gower peninsula, which was subsequently declared the UK's first Area of Outstanding Natural Beauty. Recent developments have seen the opening of a £1.2-million facility in the university library to house the Richard Burton archives. Other additions have included the £4.3-million Digital Technium Building, now part of the College of Engineering, and a second Institute of Life Sciences building with a Centre for NanoHealth based within it. Applications for engineering more than doubled in recent years, while the Institute of Life Sciences is home to Blue C, one of the few supercomputers in the world dedicated to life science research. The College of Medicine is celebrating its tenth anniversary in 2014 and is one of the fastest-growing in the UK. Its focus is a four-year graduate entry course, and it adopts a distinctive multi-disciplinary approach to research, with an unusually high level of collaboration with industry.

The university, which became independent of the University of Wales in 2007, regained its place in the top 50 of *The Times and Sunday Times* league table last year, scoring particularly highly on graduate prospects. It made further advances this year. It now has more than 14,000 students and about 350 degree courses in a modular scheme. Undergraduates are encouraged to stray outside their specialist area in their first year. There is good provision for disabled students, whose needs are addressed through a £250,000 assessment and training centre. The student services team was judged the best in the UK in 2013, with those in admissions winning a similar accolade in 2014. Nine out of ten undergraduates come from state schools and

Singleton Park
Swansea SA2 8PP

01792 295111 (enquiries)
admissions@swansea.ac.uk
www.swansea.ac.uk
www.swansea-union.co.uk
Affiliation: none

The Times and Sunday Times Rankings

Overall Ranking: **43** (last year: 47)

Student satisfaction:	**73**	81.5%
Research quality:	**=45**	16.0%
Entry standards:	**=57**	341
Student–staff ratio:	**=37**	15.5
Services & facilities/student:	**52**	£1,680
Expected completion rate:	**39**	90.1%
Good honours:	**44**	70.7%
Graduate prospects:	**20**	78.6%

colleges, but the 28 per cent share of places going to students working-class homes is less that the UK average for the university's subjects and entry grades. The projected dropout rate of 5 per cent, by contrast, is significantly better than Swansea's benchmark figure.

Swansea has links to more than 100 partner institutions worldwide and offers many degrees that include opportunities to study abroad. Popular study abroad summer programmes allow students to experience living and studying in India, China, Africa, Japan and the USA. The university has won more than £100 million in European funding for projects such as Graduate Opportunities Wales, which steers students towards small firms through industrial placements and vacation jobs. Its medium-term target is to be recognised among the top 200 universities in the world, although it is still some way off that objective. Closer to home, the department of adult and continuing education teaches mature students in locations throughout the Valleys and elsewhere in South Wales. The South West Wales Reaching Wider Partnership, based in the Centre for Academic Success, encourages students who would not usually aspire to attend university, including those from areas of economic disadvantage, to consider higher education.

Even before the opening of the new campus, the 1,900 computers available for student use represented one of the best ratios at any university. The opening of two new halls of residence has taken the total number of residential places to about 3,500. The sports facilities in the £20-million Sports Village include an athletics track, grass and all-weather pitches, squash and tennis courts plus the indoor athletics training centre and gym. The 50-metre pool is the Wales National Pool and one of only five facilities in the UK to be awarded Intensive Training Centre status. The campus is the focal point of most students' leisure activities, but the city has a good range of leisure facilities.

Undergraduate Fees and Bursaries

» Fees for UK/EU students 2015–16 £9,000
» Foundation degree £7,500
» Welsh Assembly non-means-tested grant to pay fees above £3,685 (2014–15) for Welsh students.
» Fees for international students 2014–15 £11,750–£14,000
» For those with household income below £15K, a bursary of £500 year 1, £1,250 years 2 and 3;
£15K–£25K, £500 year 1, £750 years 2 and 3;
£25K–£30K, £500 years 1 and 2 only.
» Priority subject bursary of £500 a year when household income below £30K.
» Award of £1,500 in years 1 and 2 for those with AAA at A level or equivalent; £1,000 in years 1 and 2 for AAB or equivalent. Sports scholarships and care leaver's bursaries available.
» Sports scholarships and care leaver's bursaries available.
» Check the university's website for the latest information.

Students

Undergraduates:	**10,075**	**(1,830)**
Postgraduates:	**1,735**	**(715)**
Mature students:	**17.3%**	
International students:	**10.9%**	
Applications per place:	**4**	
From state-sector schools:	**91.6%**	
From working-class homes:	**28.2%**	
Satisfaction with students' union	**71%**	

For detailed information about sports facilities:
www.swansea.ac.uk/sport/

Accommodation

Number of places and costs refer to 2014–15
University-provided places: about 3,500
Percentage catered: 5%
Catered costs: £90.50 a week (40 weeks).
Self-catered costs: £82–£177 a week (40–51 weeks).
First-year students holding a firm offer are guaranteed accommodation if conditions are met.
International students: offered up to 3 years.
accommodation@swansea.ac.uk
www.swansea.ac.uk/accommodation/

Teesside University

Teesside will charge £9,000 for all its degree courses for the first time in 2015, but the average fee of just over £8,000 after all forms of student support have been taken into consideration, will still be among the lowest in England. Foundation degree students will pay £6,000 and there will be no fees for students on work placement or years abroad. The university's aim is to achieve regional, national and international recognition as the UK's leading university for working with business – the university won a Queen's Anniversary Prize for its services to business and enterprise in 2013 – but it has also pledged to demonstrate a "real and continuing commitment" to social inclusion. The university is in the top ten for the proportion of UK undergraduates coming from working-class homes – over 47 per cent – and the 27 per cent share of places going to students from areas of low participation in higher education is twice the national average for Teesside's courses and entry qualifications. The projected dropout rate continues to improve and is now well ahead of the university's benchmark, at less than 10 per cent.

More than £200 million has been invested in the university in recent years, and work has now started on a new £20-million teaching building at the centre of the campus and extensive landscaping and remodelling at the "campus heart". It will provide a mix of flexible modern teaching space and offices, freeing up space to further develop the library, which last year underwent a £2-million refurbishment. Computer provision is generous, with 2,700 workstations for student use. Other recent developments include a centre for creative technologies for computing, media and design, where specialist facilities include a new digital sound and TV studio. But the flagship project has been DigitalCity Innovation, the university's centre for digital excellence and entrepreneurship. Some 430 new businesses and 600 jobs have been created by the new centre and by graduate enterprise.

There are 20,000 students, including 2,000 postgraduates. Almost two-thirds of the students are from the North East and around a third of the full-time undergraduates are 21 or over on entry. Applications for 2013 were up about 2 per cent and enrolments by over 100 places. Scores in the National Student Survey had been improving, but that came to at least a temporary halt in 2013, against the national trend. However, the students' union is rated among the top ten in the country. Refurbishment in 2014 produced a new-look bar, social learning space, a shop and postgraduate lounge.

Five further education colleges in the Tees Valley each have a centre offering the

---

7 Borough Road
Middlesbrough TS1 3BA

01642 218121 (switchboard)
enquiries@tees.ac.uk
www.tees.ac.uk
www.tees-su.org.uk
Affiliation: University
  Alliance

The Times and Sunday Times **Rankings**
Overall Ranking: **94** (last year: 93)

Student satisfaction:	=51	82.8%
Research quality:	=102	1.7%
Entry standards:	=72	324
Student–staff ratio:	=80	18.8
Services & facilities/student:	90	£1,329
Expected completion rate:	98	81.0%
Good honours:	101	58.6%
Graduate prospects:	=96	58.0%

university's Foundation degrees and other courses, and the university has a £13-million campus in Darlington with a focus on business services, professional education and training support.

The 11,000 health students are by far the largest group in the university. Computer animation and gaming, nursing and allied health, and design continue to be key strengths for Teesside. The university supports the career development of its graduates for a minimum of two years after graduation and is expanding paid work placements as part of a student's course. The Get Ahead scheme provides three-month paid internships and training for graduates, as well as helping to provide summer placements for second-year students.

Teesside has quite modest numbers of international students but features regularly among the leaders in the International Student Barometer, which measures satisfaction among overseas students.

Only a small proportion of Teesside's academics were entered for the last Research Assessment Exercise, but 30 per cent of their research was considered world-leading or internationally excellent. Five research-led institutes focus on digital innovation, health, culture, social science and technology.

Teesside's main campus is at the heart of Middlesbrough town centre with a wealth of high street and independent retail shops, bars, cafés and restaurants on the doorstep.

The area offers exceptional connectivity, a beautiful coastal fringe and the nearby North York Moors. The cost of living is another attraction: both university rents and those in the private sector are reasonable. The university has a new partnership with mima (Middlesbrough Institute of Modern Art), a part of the Plus Tate network, which has displayed works by some of the biggest names in the art world. Sports facilities include a newly refurbished gym on campus and a water sports centre on the River Tees. The university supports elite athletes with scholarships, coaching and access to the latest sport science techniques. A £17-million sport and health sciences building has a hydrotherapy pool among its facilities.

Undergraduate Fees and Bursaries

» Fees for UK/EU students 2015–16	£9,000
» Year 4 of MEng degree	£4,450
» Foundation degree	£6,000
» Placement year / Study abroad	no fee
» Fees for international students 2014–15	£10,450
» Range of scholarships available.	
» Check the university's website for the latest information.	

Students

Undergraduates:	9,355	(8,475)
Postgraduates:	680	(1,455)
Mature students:	36.6%	
International students:	4.1%	
Applications per place:	3.8	
From state-sector schools:	98.8%	
From working-class homes:	46.9%	
Satisfaction with students' union	82%	

For detailed information about sports facilities:
www.tees.ac.uk/sport

Accommodation

Number of places and costs refer to 2014–15
University-provided places: 1,149
Percentage catered: 0%
Self-catered costs: £57.45–£94.40 a week (40 weeks).
First years are guaranteed a place if conditions are met.
International students: guaranteed accommodation if conditions met.
accommodation@tees.ac.uk
www.tees.ac.uk/accommodation

Trinity Saint David, University of Wales

Two mergers in three years created the University of Wales Trinity Saint David (UWTSD), the second adding the former Swansea Metropolitan University. The university does not appear in any of our league tables, having chosen not to release data, but it expects to return next year. Swansea Met boycotted league tables throughout its brief existence as an independent university, and the new institution felt that a partial assessment might mislead prospective students. The old Trinity Saint David finished just outside the bottom ten on its last appearance in the table and was in the bottom four for overall satisfaction in the 2013 National Student Survey, but this year it achieved one of the two biggest increases in the UK, improving by 5 percentage points. Both applications and enrolments have dropped since the announcement of the second merger. Swansea Met continues to list its courses separately through UCAS and saw a decline in applications of almost 14 per cent in 2013.

The university also has a London campus, near the Oval cricket ground, for international students taking business, management and IT degrees. And a group structure connects UWTSD with two large further education colleges in south-west Wales, Coleg Ceredigion and Coleg Sir Gâr, in Carmarthenshire. The university offers students the choice of a rural or urban experience – from the green campuses of Lampeter and Carmarthen to the urban surroundings of Swansea. The university markets itself as both old and new since in the whole of England and Wales, only Oxford and Cambridge were awarding degrees before St David's College, Lampeter. The college went on to become the smallest publicly funded university in Europe before merging with Trinity University College, 23 miles away in Carmarthen, in 2010.

The UWTSD Lampeter Campus (formerly University of Wales, Lampeter) has continued to make a virtue of its size by stressing its friendly atmosphere and intimate teaching style. It remains a small, rural community that suits students who seek a close-knit campus experience. Based on an ancient castle and modelled on an Oxbridge college, St David's College was established to provide a liberal arts education. The original quadrangle remains, but there have been significant changes in recent few years, notably the introduction of such subjects as anthropology, archaeology, Chinese, classics and philosophy. There is a strong research culture on the campus as well as unique resources, including an archaeological dig site at nearby Strata

---

UWTSD

Carmarthen Campus
Carmarthen SA31 3EP
01267 676767

Lampeter Campus
Ceredigion SA48 7ED
01570 422351

Swansea Campus
Mount Pleasant
Swansea SA1 6ED
01792 481000

Florida and a collection of medieval manuscripts housed within the Roderic Bowen Library and Archives.

The Carmarthen Campus was established in 1848. It has a long history of teacher training and has developed a reputation for education-related programmes including early childhood, social inclusion, and youth and community work. In addition, the university offers a range of programmes in the creative and performing arts, as well a growing portfolio within the School of Sport, Health and Outdoor Education, which makes use of the natural resources of west Wales, supplemented with expeditions around the UK and to extreme climates in various parts of the world.

The Swansea Campus began life as a college of art in 1853, subsequently joined by education and technical colleges. Based in the centre of Wales's second city, Swansea Met became a university only in 2008 and had expanded to about 6,000 students before becoming part of UWTSD in 2013. Its automotive engineering courses – especially those focused on motorsport – are its best-known feature, but there has been strong demand for places on a variety of vocationally oriented courses. The campus surpasses all its benchmarks for widening participation in higher education.

There has been recent investment across all of the university's campuses, including a £30-million programme in Swansea, where there is a new building for the Business School and the city's former library has been refurbished for the School of Design and Applied Art. This and the university's Dynevor campus will form a cultural quarter in the city centre.

In Lampeter, a new hub has opened for student services and the sports facilities were extended in 2013, while Carmarthen has seen refurbishment of student accommodation and the opening of a new Centre for Learning and Teaching. The university has strong links with industry and a focus on the future employment of its graduates. It provides employability support that runs alongside academic programmes, with work placement schemes and internships to provide opportunities for students to build core skills to improve their future career.

Undergraduate Fees and Bursaries

» Fees for UK/EU students 2015–16 £9,000
» Placement year £1,800
» Welsh Assembly non-means-tested grant to pay fees above £3,685 (2014–15) for Welsh students.
» Fees for international students 2014–15 £9,000
» Household income below £18K and not receiving Welsh Tuition Fee Grant, bursary up to £1,000.
» Scholarships and bursaries available, including residential bursaries of up to £400 and Welsh-medium scholarships up to £600.

Students

Undergraduates:	**6,690**	**(3,035)**
Postgraduates:	**1,140**	**(960)**
Satisfaction with students' union	**67%**	

Student numbers obtained by combining Trinity St David and Swansea Metropolitan figures for 2012–13. It is not possible to give combined figures for the other measures usually shown here.

Accommodation

Number of places and cost refer to 2014–15
L refers to Lampeter, CM to Carmarthen, S to Swansea
University-provided places: 623 (L), 631 (CM), 300 (S)
Percentage catered: 0% (L), 75% (CM); 0% (S).
Catered costs: £88–£111 for (38 weeks) (CM) a week.
Self-catered costs: £63–£87.50 (38 or 42 weeks) (S & L) a week.
First years can normally be placed in university accommodation.
International students: guaranteed housing for first year.
Contact: www.uwtsd.ac.uk/accommodation/

University of Ulster

The first phase of Ulster's £250-million campus in Belfast's Cathedral Quarter is due to be completed by the start of the academic year in 2015, although the main part of the development will not be ready for occupation until 2018. That will allow the 12,450 students on the Jordanstown site – historically the main teaching centre – to transfer into the city. Only the High Performance Sports Centre, which houses the Sports Institute for Northern Ireland, will remain in Jordanstown.

The university, which is among the top 20 universities for the volume of applications it attracts, is planning to expand, but will do so initially through the Magee campus in Derry-Londonderry. It has taken 300 additional undergraduates in each of the last two years. Most students are from Northern Ireland and paid less than £3,700 in 2014–15, when fees for students from other parts of the UK were £6,000. Ulster has over 26,000 students, including 3,500 part-timers. All undergraduates complete their studies on a single campus, each of which has well-equipped library and computer facilities.

The existing Belfast campus concentrates on art and design, architecture and hospitality.

The main Jordanstown building, seven miles out of Belfast, will remain the location for courses starting in 2015 in business and management, the built environment, computing and engineering, health and sport sciences, and social sciences. Some £20 million has been invested in the sports facilities at Jordanstown, including outdoor and indoor sprint tracks, sports science and sports medicine facilities, which will remain available to students. The university's specialist engineering facilities will also stay on the campus, much of which will be given over to housing, shared between students and the local community.

Magee has a focus on the creative and performing arts, nursing and social work, computing, business and management, and social sciences. Magee was a central hub for events associated with Derry-Londonderry as the UK's first City of Culture in 2013, hosting an international conference on music, a festival of creative and performing arts, and a history symposium. The university has signed an agreement with the City Council, which will see it almost double its footprint in the city. There will be growth in computer science, engineering and creative technologies. A £12-million Centre for Stratified Medicine has opened near the campus, at Altnagelvin Hospital.

The fourth campus, at Coleraine on Northern Ireland's north coast, focuses on environmental and life sciences, humanities, modern languages and tourism management. A Confucius Institute opened there in 2012

Cromore Road
Coleraine
Co. Londonderry
BT52 1SA

028 7012 3456
 (switchboard)
enquiry via website
www.ulster.ac.uk
www.uusu.org
Affiliation: none

The Times and Sunday Times Rankings
Overall Ranking: **69** (last year: =73)

Student satisfaction:	=36	83.3%
Research quality:	=52	11.0%
Entry standards:	88	310
Student–staff ratio:	=61	17.7
Services & facilities/student:	61	£1,524
Expected completion rate:	102	80.6%
Good honours:	69	65.3%
Graduate prospects:	94	58.2%

to foster academic, cultural, economic and social ties between the university and China. Coleraine is home to the £11-million Centre for Biosciences, whose academics produced the most highly rated work in the last Research Assessment Exercise, achieving grades that were among the top three in the UK. Almost half of the university's whole submission was considered world-leading or internationally excellent. The university is spending £15 million at Coleraine on new students' union and catering facilities, and a new teaching block, which will open in 2015.

Ulster also offers courses in business, computing and engineering in partnership with the QA Business School at their branch campuses in London and Birmingham.

The university has a growing number of international students – about 1,600 from 80 different countries. The eLearning at Ulster programme provides an alternative mode of study, offering courses online to students all over the world. The university has committed itself to becoming the leading provider of "professional education for professional life". One aim is for an increasing number of degrees to provide placement opportunities and professional accreditation. The majority of courses now include the option of a year-long work placement. The National Student Survey has been showed increased levels of satisfaction.

Nearly 100 per cent of undergraduates are from state schools and 45 per cent come from working class backgrounds – among the highest levels at any UK university. Ulster is adding to its portfolio of programmes to widen participation in higher education with a £360,000 project to engage some of Coleraine's most disadvantaged communities. The university runs workshops in primary schools, as well as organising a range of activities to encourage secondary pupils to try a degree. Its award-winning sports outreach programme has been particularly successful. The projected dropout rate had been improving but, at 17 per cent, remains higher than the UK average for Ulster's subjects and entry qualifications.

Accommodation is guaranteed for all first-years students on all four campuses and the students' union is also active at every location. The social life inevitably varies depending on location.

Undergraduate Fees and Bursaries

» Fees for NI/EU students 2014–15 £3,685
» Fees for English, Scottish and Welsh students £6,000
» Placement year / year abroad £1,836
» Fees for international students 2014–15 £10,110
» For NI students with household income below £19.2K, bursary of £358.
» Range of scholarships available.
» Check the university's website for the latest information.

Students

Undergraduates:	**16,085**	**(4,575)**
Postgraduates:	**2,325**	**(3,480)**
Mature students:	**23.7%**	
International students:	**12.2%**	
Applications per place:	**5.2**	
From state-sector schools:	**99.9%**	
From working-class homes:	**45%**	
Satisfaction with students' union	**52%**	

For detailed information about sports facilities:
www.sportsulster.com

Accommodation

Number of places and costs refer to 2014–15
University-provided places: 2,425 over three campuses.
Percentage catered: 0%
Self-catered costs: average £68 (standard) – £98 (en suite) a week (37 weeks).
First-year students are guaranteed accommodation if conditions are met.
International students: same as above.
accommodation@ulster.ac.uk
www.accommodation.ulster.ac.uk/

University College London

UCL has been the biggest beneficiary of the Government's decision to extend student choice by allowing universities to recruit as many candidates with top grades as they like (and can attract). It has increased the size of the undergraduate intake by more than a third in two years. Having taken an additional 800 students when £9,000 fees were introduced, UCL added another 500 in 2013 without having to reduce its entry requirements. It was already comfortably the largest of the University of London's colleges, with 26,000 students and more than 700 professors – the largest number in Britain. UCL includes several specialist schools and institutes, and will add the university's Institute of Education when a merger is finalised at the end of 2014, following a two-year "strategic partnership". The expansion has demonstrated the pulling power of a university that is in the top five in the world in the QS rankings, which place more emphasis on research. In *The Times and Sunday Times* league table, it remains in the top 10 with the best staffing levels in the country and good scores on all measures.

UCL's excellence is built on a history of pioneering subjects that have become commonplace in higher education: modern languages, geography and fine arts among them. Since 2012, there has been a new requirement for a foreign language GCSE at grade C or above, although students are allowed to reach this standard during their degree if they have not taken a language at school. UCL has done better than most London institutions in the National Student Survey. All first-year students are helped to make the academic and social adjustment to university life through the Transition Programme, which includes a variety of activities such as peer mentoring and workshops. There is a commitment to teaching in small groups, especially in the second and subsequent years of degree courses. Although not high, the projected dropout rate of 6.4 per cent has risen above the benchmark set for entrance requirements and grades. UCL is conscious of its traditions as a college founded to expand access to higher education, but the 34 per cent share of places going to independent school students is one of the highest in Britain. About one undergraduate in five has a working-class background. Concerted attempts are being made to broaden the intake with summer schools for state-school students, outreach activities and campus-based programmes. The focus is mainly but not exclusively on schools in London and the South East. UCL sponsors an academy as part of its contribution to the local community.

UCL won the largest amount of funding

Gower Street
London WC1E 6BT

020 7679 2000 (main switchboard)
undergraduate-admissions
  @ucl.ac.uk
www.ucl.ac.uk
http://uclu.org
Affiliation: Russell Group

Edinburgh
Belfast
Cardiff
LONDON

The Times and Sunday Times **Rankings**
Overall Ranking: **9** (last year: 9)

Student satisfaction:	**101**	79.0%
Research quality:	**=4**	33.0%
Entry standards:	**7**	521
Student–staff ratio:	**1**	10.2
Services & facilities/student:	**6**	£2,453
Expected completion rate:	**18**	93.6%
Good honours:	**4**	86.7%
Graduate prospects:	**=7**	81.8%

from the UK research councils of any university in 2013: some £135 million. In the last Research Assessment Exercise, two-thirds of its submission was judged to be world-leading or internationally excellent. The medical school, with 11 associated teaching hospitals, is a large and formidable unit. Its credentials were strengthened still further with the announcement that UCL will be a founding partner in the new Francis Crick Institute (formerly UK Centre for Medical Research and Innovation) that will open in 2015, next to St Pancras Station. The centre will undertake cutting-edge research to advance understanding of health and disease. The various acquisitions mean that there are now outposts in several parts of central and north London, including the School of Pharmacy, which joined in 2012. There is also an archaeology and conservation campus in Qatar, but the main activity remains centred on the original impressive Bloomsbury site. UCL is pioneering the idea of education for global citizenship, ensuring students are given opportunity and encouragement to explore academic ideas from different cultural perspectives and to work on problems of international importance, as well as contributing to their local community and the university's social and cultural life. A quarter of all undergraduates spend part of their course at one of UC's 300 partner universities overseas.

The academic pace can be frantic but, close to the West End and with its own theatre and recreational facilities, there is no shortage of leisure options. Students will also have access to the facilities (including rooftop swimming pool) of the student centre in the former University of London Union building in Bloomsbury. Residential accommodation is plentiful and of a good standard. Indoor sports and fitness facilities are close at hand, but the main outdoor pitches, though good enough to attract professional football clubs, are a (free) coach ride away in Hertfordshire. Hockey players have access to Astroturf pitches at the Old Cranleighans ground, in Thames Ditton.

Undergraduate Fees and Bursaries

» Fees for UK/EU students 2015–16 £9,000
» Year abroad £1,350
» Fees for international students 2013–14 £15,200–£20,100
  Medicine £29,900
» For all UK/EU students with household income below £12K, a bursary of £3,000 a year; household income £12K–£25K, £2,000 a year; £25K–42.6K, £1,000 a year.
» High-achieving students at London state schools, 20 awards of £4,000 a year.
» Range of departmental and academic scholarships.
» Check the university's website for the latest information.

Students

Undergraduates:	**13,700**	**(885)**
Postgraduates:	**8,645**	**(3,045)**
Mature students:	**6.5%**	
International students:	**37.7%**	
Applications per place:	**7.3**	
From state-sector schools:	**65.7%**	
From working-class homes:	**20.2%**	
Satisfaction with students' union	**68%**	

For detailed information about sports facilities:
http://uclu.org/services/active-uclu

Accommodation

Number of places and costs refer to 2014–15
University-provided places: 5,201 (including 542 intercollegiate places)
Percentage catered: 30%
Catered costs: £167.30 – £203.10 a week (40 weeks).
Self-catered costs: £132.50 (single) – £211.40 (en-suite single) a week (39 weeks).
First years are guaranteed accommodation if conditions are met.
International students: as above.
www.ucl.ac.uk/prospective-students/accommodation

University of Warwick

Warwick is our University of the Year after moving up two places in *The Times and Sunday Times* league table and topping five subject tables – only two less than Oxford and more than any non-Oxbridge university has ever managed. The campus seems to have been permanently under development since the university opened in the 1960s. No sooner had the latest £150-million capital programme entered its final year than another £250 million of investment over the next five years was announced. The focus will be on teaching and research infrastructure, beginning with a £15-million learning centre. The new plans also include new interdisciplinary research labs, a new humanities building and improved facilities for a number of other subjects. The first phase of a £30-million extension to Warwick Business School will open in April 2015, making it one of the largest business schools in the UK. Warwick is also about to start building the £100-million National Automotive Innovation Centre (NAIC) on its campus, in which research engineers from car manufacturers will work closely with Warwick Manufacturing Group. NAIC is part-funded by Government as well as by Jaguar Land Rover and Tata Motors.

The most successful of the "plate glass" universities of the 1960s, Warwick has never been out of the top ten in our league table and is near the top 50 in the QS World University Rankings. The university has global ambitions and has expanded a portfolio of international activities that includes a base in Venice and a close partnership with Australia's Monash University. Warwick is also the only European institution to be involved in the Center for Urban Science and Progress, a consortium of leading universities established in New York.

The university has reconfigured its research around its "Global Research Priorities" programme, which focuses on key areas of international significance. Current themes include energy, connecting cultures, food security, global governance, individual behaviour and innovative manufacturing.

The university does not neglect its locality, however. Its mission statement stresses community links and the extension of access to higher and continuing education. There is a smaller proportion of independent school students than at most Russell Group universities – around a quarter – although this does not translate into large numbers of working-class undergraduates. The university took nearly 500 additional undergraduates in 2013, following a small decline in the previous year. The dropout rate is among the lowest in Britain, at little more than 4 per cent. The university plans to spend £1.65

Coventry CV4 7AL

024 7652 3723 (admissions)
ugadmissions@warwick.ac.uk
www.warwick.ac.uk
www.warwicksu.com
Affiliation: Russell Group

The Times and Sunday Times **Rankings**
Overall Ranking: **8** (last year: 10)

Student satisfaction:	=24	84.0%
Research quality:	=9	29.0%
Entry standards:	8	510
Student–staff ratio:	=19	13.9
Services & facilities/student:	14	£2,314
Expected completion rate:	8	95.7%
Good honours:	=13	81.0%
Graduate prospects:	=21	78.1%

million in 2015–16 on a "student lifecycle" approach to widening participation, helping non-traditional students from before the application stage through to employment or postgraduate study. The scheme will include bursaries of up to £3,000 a year for those from families with a combined income of less than £35,000.

Almost two-thirds of the work submitted for the 2008 Research Assessment Exercise was considered world-leading or internationally excellent, placing Warwick among the top ten UK universities. The university has invested shrewdly in business, science and engineering and there is now a thriving graduate entry medical school, with over 2,000 students. An analytical science research facility for physics and chemistry has been completed recently. A £12.5-million building houses a digital laboratory for manufacturing and engineering research, and a clinical trials unit.

Warwick is also one of the few leading universities to embrace 2+2 Foundation degrees, running courses in social studies and health and social policy, along with three-year foundation degrees in early years and person-centred counselling and psychotherapy.

Warwick added further study spaces in its Rootes Grid in 2013 and created a dedicated off-campus study facility for students living in nearby Leamington Spa. In 2014, it created an additional Dining Grid area where students can eat and study.

The 750-acre campus is three miles south of Coventry and three times as far from Warwick. The university has a wide range of on-campus accommodation (6,300 rooms currently and with plans to build even more residences on campus). The sports facilities are both extensive and conveniently placed and include a high quality running track, an indoor climbing centre and an indoor tennis centre. The main sports centre and gym completed an extensive refit in 2013 and further investment is planned in its sports facilities and the already extensive Warwick Arts Centre. Coventry has a growing range of student-oriented facilities and good travel links to London and other parts of the country.

Undergraduate Fees and Bursaries

» Fees for UK/EU students 2015–16 £9,000
» 2+2 degree £6,750
» Foundation degree £6,000
» Fees for international students 2014–15 £15,070–£19,220
   Medicine; graduate entry £17,595–£30,650
» English students from state schools, household income up to £16K, a bursary of £2,000 a year; £16K–£25K, £1,500 a year; £25K–£35K, £1,000 a year. Additional awards of £1,000 a year subject to criteria.
» Benefactors Scholarships of £2,000 a year, with priority to those with low incomes and from areas of low participation in higher education.

Students

Undergraduates:	12,395	(3,975)
Postgraduates:	5,390	(4,390)
Mature students:	6.8%	
International students:	24.3%	
Applications per place:	6.5	
From state-sector schools:	75.5%	
From working-class homes:	19.5%	
Satisfaction with students' union	79%	

For detailed information about sports facilities:
www2.warwick.ac.uk/services/sport

Accommodation

Number of places and costs refer to 2014–15
University-provided places: 6,382 (on campus); 2,000 (head leasing)
Percentage catered: 0%
Self-catered costs: £81–£160 a week (30, 39, 40 and 51 week contracts).
Warwick Accommodation plans to accommodate all first years in campus accommodation (terms and conditions apply).
International students: as above.
www2.warwick.ac.uk/services/accommodation

University of West London

West London (UWL) is nearing the end of its £50-million Future Campus project, which is bringing major improvements to the university's main site in Ealing. A refurbished students' union with a modern bar area, café and gym opened in 2013, alongside a new performance centre. During 2014–15, the university will open a new library, refectory, bookshop and a social space at the heart of the Ealing campus. Existing teaching and social space will also be upgraded as part of the project. The campus had already seen significant investment, as the university opted for the narrower geographical focus implied when it dropped the tarnished title of Thames Valley University. The Slough campus closed and most activities were concentrated on the institution's original base, as UWL set about becoming the country's leading university for employer engagement, with an accent on the creative industries and entrepreneurship.

Like other universities to have changed their names in recent years, UWL enjoyed immediate growth in applications. By 2013, this had developed into rising enrolments, but then came a Home Office ban on recruiting foreign students as the university was accused of failing to carry out adequate checks on English language competence. Although the university generally enrolled relatively small numbers of undergraduates from outside the European Union, the action put a damper on UWL's progress. Professor Peter John, the Vice-Chancellor, had spoken of a "new dawn" with students attracted by a guaranteed work placement, in-study financial support and good employment prospects. Although degrees will cost £9,000 a year in 2015–16, the average, allowing for all forms of student support, will still be among the lowest in England, at £7,832.

The pre-registration nursing courses that dominated the Slough campus have moved to Reading, leaving just part-time business courses and some post-registration nursing at a different site in Slough. The Reading campus, known as the Berkshire hub, is within walking distance of the mainline station and focuses entirely on nursing and midwifery. The landmark Paragon Building in Brentford, not far from the Ealing campus, will remain the headquarters of one of the largest healthcare faculties in Britain with top quality ratings for nursing and midwifery. The site contains residential places, as well as teaching facilities.

Amid the reconstruction, new Honours degrees have been launched in areas such as video production, 3-D design, entrepreneurship, computing and information systems. The portfolio of two-year Foundation degrees is growing, with employers such as Compaq, Ealing

---

St Mary's Road
Ealing
London W5 5RF

0800 036 8888 (admissions)
courses@uwl.ac.uk
www.uwl.ac.uk
www.uwlsu.com
Affiliation: million+

The Times and Sunday Times Rankings
Overall Ranking: **109** (last year: 112)

Student satisfaction:	**107**	78.5%
Research quality:	**=94**	2.0%
Entry standards:	**118**	256
Student–staff ratio:	**=70**	18.3
Services & facilities/student:	**53**	£1,637
Expected completion rate:	**=111**	77.6%
Good honours:	**117**	52.0%
Graduate prospects:	**=55**	67.6%

Studios and the Savoy Hotel Group helping to provide courses. Some are run in conjunction with Stratford-upon-Avon College – one of several partner institutions. New degrees to be launched in 2015 will include policing, building surveying, psychology with substance use and misuse studies, film music composition and operating department practice. Undergraduates have access to an award-winning Student Portal, which combines academic study with social networking.

Including part-timers, who account for nearly a third of the places, three-quarters of the students are over 21, and about 60 per cent are female. More than 40 per cent of the undergraduates come from working-class homes. The university is also very ethnically diverse with only 45 per cent of the undergraduates of white, UK origin. Student satisfaction ratings have been improving, but UWL finds itself towards the bottom of the National Student Survey. However, the School of Hospitality and Tourism is recognised by the Académie Culinaire de France for its culinary arts programmes, while the London College of Music, which is part of the university, has some of the longest-established music technology courses in the country. The university improved its ratings considerably in the 2008 Research Assessment Exercise, but entered only a small proportion of its academics. Only nursing and midwifery was judged to have world-leading research.

The town-centre sites in Ealing and Brentford are linked by a free bus service. The busy Ealing base is within easy reach of central London without the metropolitan hassle that students encounter at some institutions in the capital. Almost half of UWL's students are from London or Berkshire. Residential accommodation is growing and the Paragon building, in Brentford, won *Building* magazine's Major Housing Project of the Year award. The Student Village in Ealing can accommodate up to 440 students and the Paragon up to 839. However, students who rely on private housing find the cost of living high. The new gym is reserved for student use, and the students' union has also established links with local sports teams, ensuring that all the university's sports clubs have access to good facilities in the vicinity.

Undergraduate Fees and Bursaries

» Fees for UK/EU students 2015–16   £9,000
» Placement year   £1,000
» Fees for international students 2014–15   £9,950
» Household income below £25K, 500 awards of £1,000 a year university accommodation discount or for transport costs.
» £100 credit for learning materials for all new students.
» Fee waiver of £1,500 a year for part-time students with household income below £42.6K.
» 75 Vice-Chancellor's Scholarships for Schools: £9,000 fee waiver in year 1.
» Check the university's website for the latest information.

Students

Undergraduates:	**7,400**	**(2,780)**
Postgraduates:	**690**	**(715)**
Mature students:	**40.7%**	
International students:	**18.1%**	
Applications per place:	**5.7**	
From state-sector schools:	**96.2%**	
From working-class homes:	**42.2%**	
Satisfaction with students' union	**69%**	

For detailed information about sports facilities:
www.uwlsu.com

Accommodation

Number of places and costs refer to 2014–15
University-provided places: 1,279
Percentage catered: 0%
Self-catered costs: from £90.00– £190.42 a week (44 or 52 weeks).
First years are allocated housing on a first come, first served basis.
International students: same as above.
onestopshop@uwl.ac.uk
www.uwl.ac.uk/students/undergraduate/accommodation

University of the West of England, Bristol (UWE)

The University of the West of England, Bristol (UWE) is the biggest higher education institution in the South West of England, and is implementing a £250-million campus masterplan to ensure that it is competitive in teaching, research and student facilities. Applications rose both in 2014 and 2013, following a big drop when higher fees were introduced. A new students' union will be open on the main Frenchay Campus for the start of the academic year in 2015 and there are new specialist drama facilities on the Bower Ashton Campus. Eventually, there will even be a 20,000-seat stadium shared with Bristol Rovers on land bought by the university to extend the main campus. UWE currently has three sites in Bristol, mainly in the north of the city, and regional centres near hospitals in Gloucester and Bath that concentrate on nursing and allied health professions. The attractive Glenside Campus, which houses health subjects, has been refurbished and a new computer learning zone added. The main campus, four miles out of the city centre, has already doubled in size and seen a number of improvements, including the opening of the UK's largest robotic laboratory and the biggest exhibition and conference centre in the region. The main library is open around the clock during term time.

More than half of the students come from the West Country and there are close links with business and industry. These provide guest lecturers and professors involved in practice, as well as a wide range of work placements, including one of the largest internship schemes at any university. Recent links include Aardman, CERN in Geneva, Hewlett Packard and the BBC, joining about 6,700 smaller organisations. UWE's careers and employment service was rated the best in the country at the 2014 National Undergraduate Employability awards, partly for an innovative web-based jobs and placement service it runs with the local chamber of commerce. The university also runs the UWE Bristol Futures Award to certificate extra-curricular activities and encourage students to acquire leadership qualities and other skills that will help in the employment market. A tradition of vocational education regularly helps the university to a healthy graduate employment record.

Law received a commendation from the Legal Practice Board and UWE is one of just four universities recognised by the Forensic Science Society for the quality of courses in the subject. There are some 85 undergraduate and postgraduate courses with professional accreditation and the team

---

Frenchay Campus
Coldharbour Lane
Bristol BS16 1QY

0117 328 3333 (admissions)
contact via website
www.uwe.ac.uk
www.uwesu.org
Affiliation: University
  Alliance

The Times and Sunday Times Rankings
Overall Ranking: **68** (last year: 60)

Student satisfaction:	93	79.7%
Research quality:	=67	4.7%
Entry standards:	=59	339
Student–staff ratio:	=92	20.0
Services & facilities/student:	44	£1,750
Expected completion rate:	=71	84.7%
Good honours:	=50	70.0%
Graduate prospects:	52	68.3%

entrepreneurship degree has a ground-breaking course structure where students learn through the day-to-day management of their own business. UWE radiography students have won Radiographer of the Year in five of the last six years, while there have also been successes at the British Book Awards. Only two new universities entered more academics than UWE in the 2008 Research Assessment Exercise. More than a third of the work was judged to be world-leading or internationally excellent. Physiotherapy and other health subjects, media studies and general engineering produced the best results.

UWE has broadened its intake considerably in recent years. The proportion of independent school entrants has dropped to less than 8 per cent, while the share of places going to students from working-class homes is more than 30 per cent. The dropout rate had been coming down significantly, but the latest projection is further above the national average for the university's subjects and entry qualifications. A network of 15 colleges stretches into Somerset and Wiltshire, offering UWE programmes. Hartpury College, near Gloucester, is an associate faculty of the university, specialising in agriculture, equine studies and other land-based courses. There is also an expanding international network, with institutions in a number of countries offering UWE degrees. The university's own international college, run in partnership with the Kaplan group, provides preparatory courses for a growing number of students from outside the UK coming to Bristol. International students also have their own online careers information resource.

Bristol is a hugely popular student centre: an attractive and lively city, but not cheap. University accommodation has become more plentiful in recent years, with about 4,000 places available, including nearly 2,000 in a new £80-million student village on the Frenchay campus, which has more places opening in September 2014. There is also accommodation for nearly 300 students on the Glenside campus. A £5.5-million sports complex at Frenchay has a 70-station fitness suite, while the separate Wallscourt Farm gym is designed for elite athletes. The university was chosen as a pre-Olympics training site for badminton, fencing, table tennis, indoor volleyball and wrestling.

Undergraduate Fees and Bursaries

» Fees for UK/EU students 2015–16 £9,000
» Fees for international students 2014–15 £10,750–£11,750
» Household income below £25K and with selection criteria and (a) liable for accommodation costs, a bursary of £2,000, year 1, £1,000, years 2 and 3; or (b) living at home, £500, year 1, £250, years 2 and 3.
» Range of departmental and academic scholarships.
» Check the university's website for the latest information.

Students

Undergraduates:	19,230	(2,955)
Postgraduates:	1,485	(3,760)
Mature students:	22.1%	
International students:	7.9%	
Applications per place:	4.5	
From state-sector schools:	92.4%	
From working-class homes:	31.1%	
Satisfaction with students' union	64%	

Information about sports facilities: www1.uwe.ac.uk/aboutus/departmentsandservices/professionalservices/centreforsport

Accommodation

Number of places and costs refer to 2014–15
University-provided places: about 4,000
Percentage catered: 0%
Self-catered costs: £3,598–£6,672 (40 to 45 weeks).
First-year students are guaranteed housing in university-approved accommodation provided requirements are met.
International students are offered accommodation where possible.
accommodation@uwe.ac.uk
www1.uwe.ac.uk/students/accommodation

University of the West of Scotland (UWS)

Undergraduate enrolments at the University of the West of Scotland (UWS) have declined for three years in a row, but they started from an unusually high base with the merger of Paisley University and Bell College, in Hamilton, prompting the biggest increases in applications at any UK university for two successive years. UWS is now among the largest modern universities in Scotland, and has been adapting to its increased size with a new £81-million campus in Ayr for 3,500 students. This will be followed by £53 million of transformation of the Hamilton campus, which has already seen the construction of a £2-million engineering centre. The developments are part of a £200-million plan for the university's four bases in Dumfries, Paisley, Ayr and Hamilton. A £5.5-million library and student services centre was added in Dumfries soon after the merger, and the hub of a £1-million employment centre serving all four campuses was a new feature in Paisley.

The university is based in an area of low participation in higher education, but is within reach of nearly 40 per cent of the population of Scotland. UWS has continued its parent institutions' strong records in attracting under-represented groups onto courses. Hundreds of youngsters aged 14 and 15 attend the "University Experience" to sample a week of student life. Almost all UWS's students are state educated and 40 per cent are from working-class homes, but the projected dropout rate of more than 30 per cent is the highest in the UK. That is more than twice the benchmark set according to the subject mix and entry qualifications. Growth since the merger has been fuelled mainly by the move to an all-graduate nursing profession – the School of Health, Nursing and Midwifery is the largest north of the border – but degrees in subjects such as computer animation, commercial music, computer games technology, sports studies and music technology have all been popular.

Over £9 million was invested in student facilities in Paisley in the early years of UWS. The main campus, 20 acres in the town centre, has also benefited from a new library and learning resource centre, a £5-million students' union building, and recently upgraded indoor and outdoor sports facilities. UWS is bringing more students into Paisley town centre with the completion of a £17.6-million student accommodation development. The investment includes the refurbishment of some 160 university-owned flats, as well as the construction of a new £13.2-million student residence with 336 bed spaces, divided into flats for six students, each with

---

Paisley Campus
Paisley
Renfrewshire PA1 2BE

0800 027 1000 (enquiries)
uni-direct@uws.ac.uk
contact via website
www.uws.ac.uk
www.sauws.org.uk
Affiliation: million+

The Times and Sunday Times Rankings
Overall Ranking: **118** (last year: 117)

Student satisfaction:	=102	78.9%
Research quality:	=67	4.7%
Entry standards:	=99	299
Student–staff ratio:	113	22.0
Services & facilities/student:	=96	£1,279
Expected completion rate:	121	67.8%
Good honours:	=102	58.5%
Graduate prospects:	92	58.4%

large en-suite bedrooms and with a shared kitchen and lounge. The Dumfries campus, which is operated in partnership with Glasgow University, has over 500 students. The Hamilton campus contains a students' union, an upgraded leisure centre and some accommodation, as well as teaching space. The Ayr campus is shared with SRUC (Scotland's Rural College) and has a prize-winning library with flexible space for individual or group study, presentation and seminar areas.

Paisley pioneered credit transfer in Scotland, including credit for non-academic achievement, and the modular course system covers day, evening and weekend classes. Most students either take sandwich degrees or have work placements built into their courses, earning an average of £10,000 in the process, but the impact on graduate employment has not been as great as elsewhere. Courses are strongly vocational, with business, multimedia and health subjects by far the most popular choices. There are close links with business and industry and all students are offered hands-on computer training. Paisley was the first UK university to be approved by Microsoft, Macromedia and Cisco, and has the status of Microsoft Academic Professional Development Centre. A games development laboratory, supported by Sony, is part of a £300,000 package of investment in multimedia and games facilities. Research grades improved in the last assessments, although UWS made only a small submission. A quarter of the work was rated as world-leading or internationally excellent, with biomedical sciences and social policy and social work producing the best results. The university returned to *The Times and Sunday Times* league table three years ago after blocking the release of data until all the statistics related to the new institution.

Paisley is Scotland's largest town, while Hamilton ranks fifth. In both places, the university draws a high proportion of the students from the local area, many on part-time courses. Numbers at Paisley have grown particularly rapidly in recent years and there are almost 1,000 international students, thanks to a growing number of Chinese and Indian nationals and long-established links with over 50 EU institutions.

Undergraduate Fees and Bursaries

» Fees for Scottish and EU students 2014–15   No fee
» Fees for Non-Scottish UK (RUK) students 2014–15   £7,250
» Placement year   £1,820
» Fees for international students 2014–15   £10,300–£10,815
» Scholarships and bursaries available.
» Check the university's website for the latest information.

Students

Undergraduates:	**9,760**	**(4,035)**
Postgraduates:	**630**	**(940)**
Mature students:	**45.4%**	
International students:	**6%**	
Applications per place:	**4**	
From state-sector schools:	**98.5%**	
From working-class homes:	**39.8%**	
Satisfaction with students' union	**66%**	

For detailed information about sports facilities:
www.uws.ac.uk/study-at-uws/life-at-uws/sports-and-social/

Accommodation

Number of places and costs refer to 2014–15
University-provided places: 852 (496 at Paisley; 200 at Ayr; 156 at Hamilton)
Percentage catered: 0%
Self-catered costs: £82 (Hamilton) – £106–£137 (other campuses) a week.
First-year students have priority (conditions apply).
International students: single students guaranteed accommodation if conditions are met and applications received by 27 July.
placetostay@uws.ac.uk; www.uws.ac.uk/accommodation

University of Westminster

Westminster's Broad Vision initiative goes further than many of the programmes at other universities designed to encourage students to range beyond their specialist subject. Undergraduates are given opportunities for interdisciplinary learning and collaborative research that straddle the arts and sciences as an optional module on many courses. The programme has produced exhibitions, published books and articles, and presented at conferences, festivals and symposia. The university changed its undergraduate structure to promote deeper learning through year-long modules and weaves work-related skills into degree programmes.

These initiatives are among a number of features that distinguish the university from similar institutions. Almost a third of the students are part-timers, for example, at a time when part-time numbers have been dropping sharply elsewhere. There are more than 5,000 students from outside the UK – among the most at any post-1992 institution – and the largest numbers at any UK university from ethnic minorities. Westminster's courses are taught in nine overseas countries, from Sri Lanka to Uzbekistan, a characteristic which won the university a Queen's Award for Enterprise.

The university was one of many to be left with empty places in the first year of higher fees, but it more than made up for the shortfall in 2013, recruiting an additional 700 undergraduates as applications increased by almost 12 per cent. The university has continued to invest heavily in its buildings and facilities, with major refurbishment taking place at three of its campuses. The £20-million project at the Marylebone Campus was completed in the autumn of 2012, providing a new social and learning hub for the Faculty of Architecture and the Built Environment and Westminster Business School. Significant progress has also been made on the £38-million redevelopment of the Harrow site, home to the highly rated Faculty of Media, Arts and Design. Students there are already benefiting from new library and resource centres, and bigger open spaces and better natural light for the fashion and fine art learning areas. The project, to be completed by 2014, will eventually include spaces for a gallery and catwalk, flexible performance areas, a café, reception and multimedia newsroom. Major refurbishment work at the Regent Campus and Little Titchfield site was completed in 2013, while the School of Life Sciences has recently invested £2 million in modernising its laboratories.

Restoration of the Regent Street Cinema, which is considered to be the birthplace of British cinema and is now housed within the Regent Campus, will

---

309 Regent Street
London W1B 2HW

020 7915 5511 (enquiries)
course-enquiries@
westminster.ac.uk
www.westminster.ac.uk
www.uwsu.com
Affiliation: none

The Times and Sunday Times **Rankings**
Overall Ranking: **112** (last year: =106)

Student satisfaction:	=112	77.7%
Research quality:	=63	5.0%
Entry standards:	=80	317
Student–staff ratio:	=97	20.3
Services & facilities/student:	=86	£1,359
Expected completion rate:	109	79.1%
Good honours:	75	64.1%
Graduate prospects:	116	50.6%

be completed in 2015. The headquarters building, near the BBC's Broadcasting House, houses social sciences, humanities and languages. Westminster offers one of the widest ranges of language teaching of any British university and partners the School of Oriental and African Studies in leading the Routes into Languages programme to encourage more people to learn a language. The Architecture Department is rated joint second in the UK by architects in practice in the *Architects Journal*: students and staff have collected more than 20 RIBA and professional prizes in a year. The Business School has been selected as a Centre of Excellence by the Chartered Institute for Securities & Investment – one of only 12 centres worldwide.

Westminster hit the headlines in the 2008 Research Assessment Exercise, when it was rated top in the UK for media studies with one of the highest proportions (60 per cent) of world-leading research in any subject. More than a third of all the work submitted by the university was rated in the top two categories.

Almost half of the UK undergraduates are from working-class homes – a much higher proportion than the national average for the subjects offered – and the university also exceeds its benchmark for the admission of students from state schools and colleges. The projected dropout rate has been improving and is now lower than at many similar institutions. Westminster has added considerably to its stock of residential accommodation in recent years. The latest development saw the opening of a student village for first-years close to Wembley Stadium and Wembley Park tube station, with speedy links to all the university's campuses. The university had already added a £6-million block of halls in Harrow and refurbished its Marylebone halls, but there is no way round the capital's inflated housing market at some stage. The Harrow campus is lively socially, but those based on the other campuses tend to be spread around the capital. Sports facilities are also dispersed, with playing fields and a boathouse in Chiswick, west London. Smoke Radio, Westminster's student radio station, has won several awards and has now spawned Smoke Television.

Undergraduate Fees and Bursaries

» Fees for UK/EU students 2015–16   £9,000
» Fees for international students 2014–15   £11,750
» Fee waivers given on a course-by-course basis to local students.
» Details of scholarships and bursaries for 2015–16 not announced in August 2014. Check university website for details.

Students		
Undergraduates:	**12,290**	**(3,470)**
Postgraduates:	**2,215**	**(2,195)**
Mature students:	**19.8%**	
International students:	**22%**	
Applications per place:	**5.3**	
From state-sector schools:	**95.7%**	
From working-class homes:	**49.3%**	
Satisfaction with students' union	**51%**	

Information about sports facilities: www.westminster.ac.uk/study/current-students/support-and-facilities/sport-and-leisure

Accommodation

Number of places and costs refer to 2014–15
University-provided places: 1,960
Percentage catered: 0%
Self-catered costs: £105.00–£199.01 a week (38–51 week contracts).
First-year students have priority for 1,000 rooms. Residential restrictions apply.
International students: as above.
studentaccommodation@westminster.ac.uk
www.westminster.ac.uk/study/prospective-students/student-accommodation

University of Winchester

Winchester has increased the size of its undergraduate intake for three years in a row and has seen further growth in applications in 2014. The numbers recruited from outside the UK have trebled since 2010 and the university is now among the leading group of post-1992 universities in *The Times and Sunday Times* league table, with consistently good student satisfaction scores. The university is one the few to have appointed its own ombudsman to handle complaints. It is involved in a national initiative to promote social entrepreneurship and offers support to graduates who wish to start their own businesses. Winchester students can also take advantage of exchange schemes with American universities in New York, Maine, Oregon and Wisconsin, as well as with universities in Japan.

The university traces its history as an Church of England foundation back to 1840 and has occupied its King Alfred campus since 1862. The compact site is on a wooded hillside overlooking the cathedral city, a ten-minute walk away, with views of the surrounding countryside. Known as King Alfred's College until 2004, the university is still best-known for teacher training, although it now accounts for only 12 per cent of the places. Ofsted rates the teacher training courses as outstanding. It is one of the largest providers of primary school training in England, but courses on the main campus also span business, arts, humanities, health and social care, and social sciences. Degrees range from choreography and dance, through social work, business, accounting, law, media and teacher training to modern liberal arts. Winchester improved on already respectable grades in the 2008 Research Assessment Exercise, when more than a third of the university's work reached the top two categories, and there was some world-leading research in four of the six subject areas.

Almost a third of the British students are from working-class homes and 97 per cent are state educated. Winchester is particularly proud of its low dropout rate, which improved again in the latest projections, remaining below 10 per cent and lower than the national average for Winchester's courses and entry qualifications.

The main campus is well equipped, with its theatrical performance spaces, sports hall and fitness suite now supplemented by the £3.5-million Winchester Sports Stadium. Open to local people as well as students, the stadium has an Olympic standard 400-metre eight-lane athletics track with supporting facilities for field events and also a floodlit all-weather pitch. There are six performing arts studios in a new building that opened in 2010 on the King Alfred campus, offering the latest technology for student productions.

Winchester
Hampshire SO22 4NR

01962 827234 (enquiries)
course.enquiries@winchester.ac.uk
www.winchester.ac.uk
www.winchester
  students.co.uk
Affiliations: Cathedrals Group,
  GuildHE

The Times and Sunday Times **Rankings**
Overall Ranking: **61** (last year: =57)

Student satisfaction:	=31	83.5%
Research quality:	=73	4.0%
Entry standards:	=74	322
Student–staff ratio:	59	17.3
Services & facilities/student:	108	£1,139
Expected completion rate:	=41	89.2%
Good honours:	=50	70.0%
Graduate prospects:	114	51.7%

A new Learning and Teaching Building on the King Alfred campus has significantly improved the facilities for lectures and independent study. The low-energy building has a number of eco-friendly features which helped win an award from the Royal Institute of British Architects in 2013. Winchester is among the top 40 universities for environmental performance, as measured in the People and Planet green league.

The award-winning University Centre transformed the students' union, adding a nightclub, cinema, catering facilities, a bookshop and a supermarket at a cost of £9 million. A "learning café" creates an informal working space with networked PCs and wireless internet access. An award-winning extension to the library made room for 200,000 books, 450 study spaces and 150 computers. Building on the success of the Learning Café, the university has developed a second social learning space, with PC access, a café, informal seating areas and outside terracing. The students' union achieved one of the best ratings in the 2013 National Student Survey.

A £12-million student village, a short walk from the main campus, provides more than 700 residential places. The business school is also located on the West Downs campus. A second village, with en-suite rooms arranged in cluster flats, opened in 2010, and a third village has added another 350 en suite study bedrooms. The latest development includes a large gym, available to members of the community as well as students and staff. The new gym is part of a major investment by the university to enhance its sports facilities. Winchester guarantees campus accommodation to first year full-time undergraduates, international students and students with medical needs as long they apply by the deadline.

Students value the close-knit atmosphere and find the city is livelier than its staid image might suggest, with a number of bars catering to their tastes. Southampton is not far for those who hanker after the attractions of a bigger city, and London is only an hour away by train.

Undergraduate Fees and Bursaries

» Fees for UK/EU students 2015–16	£9,000
» Foundation degree in childhood studies	£4,200
» Placement year	£1,350
» Fees for international students 2014–15	£10,800
» Household income below £25K, a bursary of £1,000 a year; £25K–£42.6K, £600 a year.	
» Academic, sport and music scholarships available.	
» Check the university's website for the latest information.	

Students

Undergraduates:	**4,815**	**(560)**
Postgraduates:	**215**	**(805)**
Mature students:	**13.6%**	
International students:	**6%**	
Applications per place:	**5**	
From state-sector schools:	**97%**	
From working-class homes:	**31.6%**	
Satisfaction with students' union	**80%**	

For detailed information about sports facilities:
www.winchester.ac.uk/campuscitylife/Sportsfacilities

Accommodation

Number of places and costs refer to 2014–15
University-provided places: 1,687 on campus; 225 off campus
Percentage catered: 5%
Catered costs: £114 a week (term-time only).
Self-catered costs: £81–£130 a week (37–40 weeks).
First years are guaranteed accommodation if conditions are met.
International students: non EU, as above.
housing@winchester.ac.uk
www.winchester.ac.uk/startinghere/Student%20accommodation/Pages/Studentaccommodation.aspx

University of Wolverhampton

Wolverhampton has declined to release any data for use in league tables since 2009, when it finished just outside the top 100. Its intake of undergraduates has dropped by more than 1,000 since then. A statement on the university's website says that tables such as ours disadvantage universities like Wolverhampton and do not represent a fair picture of their strengths. As a result, it is missing from both the main ranking and all the subject tables. The statement advises applicants to use publicly available data, including results from the Research Assessment Exercise, which it claims recognised the university's research as world-leading. In fact, 6 per cent of the Wolverhampton submission was awarded the 4* rating that signified world-leading research. Overall student satisfaction – described as high by the university – dropped sharply in 2013, leaving Wolverhampton in the bottom dozen universities on this measure, and it fell further in 2014.

The university's success in widening participation in higher education is such that only one institution in the UK has a higher proportion of undergraduates coming from working-class homes. Almost all the students are from state schools and nearly one in five comes from an area of low participation. The university draws two-thirds of its 20,000 students from the West Midlands. A third of the places are filled by mature students and about the same proportion come from the region's ethnic minorities. Big outreach programmes take courses into the workplace. Wolverhampton has abandoned its £100 fee discount and will be charging the full £9,000 for degree courses in 2015–16.

The university is in the throes of a £45-million redevelopment of its City Campus. A new £21-million Science Centre, with well-equipped laboratories, teaching and meeting rooms, will be fully open by the end of 2014. A new £18-million building for the Business School near the Molineux football ground on the City Campus North, is scheduled to open in time for the start of the academic year in 2015. Student facilities have been improved with the redevelopment of the students' union on the City Campus and the opening of a new union bar on the Walsall Campus. The three West Midland campuses each have their own learning centres and are linked by a free bus service. The original site is in Wolverhampton city centre, while sport and performance, education and part of the School of Health and Wellbeing are based in Walsall. A purpose-built campus at Telford in Shropshire focuses on business

**Wulfruna Street
Wolverhampton WV1 1LY**

01902 321000 (enquiries)
enquiries@wlv.ac.uk
www.wlv.ac.uk
www.wolvesunion.org
Affiliation: million+

The Times and Sunday Times **Rankings**
Wolverhampton blocked the release of data from the Higher Education Statistics Agency and so we cannot give any ranking information.

and engineering in a county with only one specialised higher education institution of its own, Harper Adams University. The university also offers part-time courses at Stafford. A branch campus in Mauritius opened in 2012, offering law degrees and an MA in education.

Wolverhampton has been investing heavily in its "New Horizons" infrastructure programme. At Telford the £7-million e-Innovation Centre has won awards for the support it offers to e-businesses. A 350-bed student village and sports facilities, including a Sports Science and Medicine Centre which was used to train Olympic contenders, opened on the Walsall Campus. In 2011, the Performance Hub, the university's centre for performing arts, opened on the same campus. The £15-million facility has exceptional facilities for music, dance and drama. Wolverhampton was the third university in the UK to be awarded All-Steinway School Status.

The university pioneered interactive multimedia communication degrees, as well as offering one of the first degrees in British sign language and one of the first in virtual reality design and manufacturing. It was the first university to be registered under the British Standards for the quality of its all-round provision. Wolverhampton stresses innovation and enterprise in its work with students and businesses, encouraging student start-up companies and leading a project to develop student placements for those who wish to become entrepreneurs. The Flying Start Programme for Sports Business was the first of its kind in the UK, providing specialist workshops. Teacher training courses are rated highly by Ofsted, and Wolverhampton academics have been awarded six National Teaching Fellowships. Research mainly serves the needs of business and industry, as well as underpinning teaching. A relatively low proportion of academics were entered for the last Research Assessment Exercise, but 30 per cent of their research was considered world-leading or internationally excellent. The university has set aside £6 million to finance new research projects.

The city of Wolverhampton has a growing nightlife, and the university has been voted the friendliest in the West Midlands. The cost of living is reasonable, and Birmingham is only a metro tram ride away.

Undergraduate Fees and Bursaries

- » Fees for UK/EU students 2015–16 — £9,000
- » Foundation degree — up to £7,570
- » Foundation degree at partner colleges — up to £6,000
- » Placement year / year abroad — No fee
- » Fees for international students 2014–15 — £10,700
- » For students with at least ABB at A level or equivalent, a bursary of £2,000 in year 1.
- » Fixed number of scholarships for sport and for students from partnership schools, £2,000 in year 1.
- » Access bursaries of £2,000 in year 1 for disabled students with hearing loss and care leavers.

Students

Undergraduates:	**12,360**	**(4,065)**
Postgraduates:	**1,620**	**(1,910)**
From state-sector schools:	**98.6%**	
From working-class homes:	**53.2%**	
Satisfaction with students' union	**64%**	

For detailed information about sports facilities:
www.wlv.ac.uk/sport

Accommodation

Number of places and costs refer to 2014–15
University-provided places: 1,603
Percentage catered: 0%
Self-catered costs: £72–£98 a week (37 weeks).
First-year students are offered accommodation provided requirements are met. Residential restrictions apply.
International students: same as above.
Contact: accommodationservices@wlv.ac.uk
www.wlv.ac.uk/default.aspx?page=20639

University of Worcester

The demand for places at Worcester has doubled in seven years, as a series of impressive developments have taken place. A second campus in the heart of the city opened in 2010 and a spectacular library and history centre – the first joint public and university library in Britain – was opened by the Queen in July 2012. The facility has won 47 national and international awards, including Best Civic Building, Best University Contribution to the Community and Best University Library Team. In 2013 the university opened a 2,000-seat indoor sporting arena, which was one of only two specialist sports venues in the UK designed specifically for wheelchair athletes as well as the able-bodied. It has already hosted the first ever British Universities and Colleges Wheelchair Basketball championship as well as a host of top-flight and student netball, basketball and international wheelchair sports events. Sport, education and business courses have been particularly popular as applications have risen, and there have been increases, too, in biochemistry, journalism, illustration, nursing and several other health subjects.

The university has three campuses less than a mile from each other and all close to the city centre. A fourth campus – a science, health and enterprise park – is currently under development, and will provide new business links and work placement opportunities for students. The main St John's Campus occupies a parkland site 15 minutes' walk from the city centre. It includes science facilities, the National Pollen and Aerobiology Research Unit, the digital arts centre and drama studio, and a modern AstroTurf pitch. The City Campus occupies the historic buildings of the former Worcester Royal Infirmary. It includes teaching, residential and conference facilities and is the site of Worcester Business School. The Hive, neighbouring the City Campus, houses the new library and history centre, which brings together many services from Worcestershire County Council, including archaeology and history, with those of the university. The Riverside Campus, mostly for performance sport, includes the University of Worcester Arena. A mobile 3-D motion analysis laboratory has been used by the England and Wales Cricket Board. Sports scholarships are offered in partnership with Worcestershire County Cricket Club, Worcester Wolves Basketball Club and Worcester Hockey Club. The university's commitment to disability sports extends to the UK's first disability sport degree.

First as a post-war emergency teacher training college and later as a university college, the institution has always been the only provider of higher education in

---

Henwick Grove
Worcester WR2 6AJ

01905 855111 (admissions)
admissions@worc.ac.uk
www.worcester.ac.uk
www.worcsu.com
Affiliation: GuildHE

The Times and Sunday Times **Rankings**
Overall Ranking: **107** (last year: 102)

Student satisfaction:	=95	79.3%
Research quality:	=117	0.3%
Entry standards:	98	300
Student–staff ratio:	=104	21.1
Services & facilities/student:	116	£984
Expected completion rate:	=64	85.4%
Good honours:	=102	58.5%
Graduate prospects:	82	60.7%

Herefordshire and Worcestershire. The university remains strong in education and also in nursing and midwifery. Ofsted rated the primary and secondary teacher training "outstanding" for the second time in succession in 2014, and Worcester received the best possible inspection report from the Nursing and Midwifery Council. Worcester is the partner university for the National Childbirth Trust, delivering all of the trust's antenatal training. The six academic departments also cover applied sciences, geography and archaeology, a business school and arts, humanities and social sciences. An emphasis on employability in the curriculum was commended in an audit by the Quality Assurance Agency.

The 23 academics entered for the 2008 Research Assessment Exercise (RAE) represented the smallest contingent from any university in England, but Worcester has entered four times as many academics for the successor to the RAE, the Research Excellence Framework, which will be published at the end of 2014. Only English had any world-leading research in 2008, although there are pockets of excellence such as the Association for Dementia Studies and the National Pollen and Aerobiology Research Unit, which produces all of Britain's pollen forecasts.

More than a third of the undergraduates come from working-class homes. The projected dropout rate is better than average for Worcester's subjects and entry standards. The share of degree places going to students from working class backgrounds is a little lower than average for Worcester's courses and entry qualifications, but the university has long-established projects working with primary schools to try to broaden the intake further. There are excellent links with local businesses and students have access to an extensive learn-while-you-earn programme. A number of local partner colleges offer Worcester courses, as well as less conventional study centres such as hospices and specialist national organisations.

The cathedral city is not large, but is safer than many university locations, and has its share of pubs and clubs that cater for a growing student clientele. Student satisfaction dipped slightly in 2014 but a recent survey placed the city among the top ten locations in the UK for happiness. An active students' union acts as a social hub.

Undergraduate Fees and Bursaries

» Fees for UK/EU students 2015–16 £9,000
» Foundation degree £6,500–£9,000
» Fees for international students 2014–15 £10,920
» Award of £1,000 in year 1 for those with Distinction, Distinction, Merit at BTEC or equivalent.
» Award of £1,000 for academic achievement after year 1 and year 2.
» Enhanced student hardship fund.
» Check the university's website for the latest information.

Students

Undergraduates:	7,255	(1,480)
Postgraduates:	615	(960)
Mature students:	22.3%	
International students:	6.2%	
Applications per place:	4.6	
From state-sector schools:	96.4%	
From working-class homes:	36.1%	
Satisfaction with students' union	69%	

For information about sports facilities: www.worcester.ac.uk/your-home/sport-at-worcester.html

Accommodation

Number of places and costs refer to 2014–15
University-provided places: 974 university-owned; 360 university-managed.
Percentage catered: 0%
Self-catered costs: £86–£141 a week.
First-year students are guaranteed accommodation, on a first come, first served basis, if conditions are met.
International students are accommodated if conditions are met.
accommodation@worc.ac.uk
www.worcester.ac.uk/your-home/accommodation.html

University of York

York has launched a series of initiatives to boost its students' transferable skills and networking opportunities to enhance their employability prospects. Every student has an online tutorial to identify key strengths and career development needs. York is the first UK university to host its own crowd-funding website, and over 2,000 students attend workshops, seminars and networking events with York alumni working in senior positions in a range of industries, who advise on securing internships, volunteering experience and graduate employment. The university has established a Winter Interns programme to provide employment opportunities to recent graduates and provide them with graduate level training.

The university celebrated its 50th anniversary in 2013, a year after joining the Russell Group of leading research institutions. It remains well inside the top 20 in *The Times and Sunday Times* league table and has been growing in popularity with prospective students: applications and enrolments both rose significantly in 2013. However, scores in the National Student Survey – a traditional strength of the university – slipped in 2014, although the medical school, which is assessed separately, still finished in the top ten. York was among the top ten institutions in the last Research Assessment Exercise, when more than 60 per cent of the work submitted was judged to be world-leading or internationally excellent. Nearly 30 per cent of the full time students are postgraduates.

York decided more than a decade ago that it was too small to maximise its research capability, play a leading role in the economy of the region and satisfy the growing demand for its places. In an audacious move for a highly selective university, it opened a second campus to accommodate up to 50 per cent more students and strengthen its research. Seven new buildings have opened on the £750-million Heslington East site, including two residential colleges, each accommodating more than 600 students. The second phase is now under way and refurbishment is taking place on the original campus. A £21-million "hub" for the campus expansion opened in 2010 and a £20-million refurbishment of the university library was completed in 2012. The latest development has seen new undergraduate laboratories and a Green Chemistry Centre of Excellence added at a cost of £10 million.

The original campus occupies 200 acres of landscaped parkland, a mile outside the historic city centre. Students join one of the nine colleges, which mix academic and social roles. Most departments have their headquarters in one of the colleges, but the student community is a deliberate mixture

---

Heslington
York YO10 5DD

01904 324000 (admissions)
ug-admissions@york.ac.uk
www.york.ac.uk
www.hyms.ac.uk
www.yusu.org
Affiliation: Russell Group

The Times and Sunday Times Rankings
Overall Ranking: **16** (last year: 11)

Student satisfaction:	=54	82.6%
Research quality:	=9	29.0%
Entry standards:	17	446
Student–staff ratio:	30	15.0
Services & facilities/student:	30	£1,995
Expected completion rate:	=20	93.2%
Good honours:	16	80.0%
Graduate prospects:	37	73.8%

of disciplines, years and sexes. Nursing apart, only archaeology and medieval studies are located off campus, sharing a medieval building in the centre of the city. Expansion has allowed York to introduce new subjects. The first undergraduates in law and in writing, directing and performance in theatre, film and television graduated in 2011. Medicine had already been introduced in 2003, in partnership with Hull University. York also runs its own nursing and midwifery programmes and launched a biomedical sciences degree in 2013.

Entrance requirements are high, but the university is getting closer to meeting its targets for broadening its undergraduate intake. The share of places going to students from areas of low participation in higher education now exceeds the national average for York's courses and entrance qualifications, although the same is not true of entrants from working class backgrounds. Every student has a supervisor responsible for their academic and personal welfare, and undergraduates are entitled to free language tuition and have access to a Mathematics Study Skills Centre. Students can also take the York Award, comprising a range of courses, work placements and voluntary activities which aim to prepare students for employment. Over 600 students work as volunteer teaching assistants in local schools.

Social life on campus is lively. There are television and radio stations, as well as several student newspapers and magazines. Sports facilities are good, and include four sports halls and a dance studio. The £12-million York Sports Village opened on campus in 2012, featuring a 25-metre pool, learner pool, 100-station gym, full-size 3G pitch and three further five-a-side pitches. The university has the only velodrome in Yorkshire, which opened this summer, a 1-km cycling track and a new athletics track. Tennis and squash facilities have been refurbished and £30,000 invested in bespoke team coaching. Cultural events abound on campus and in the city, which is also famous for a high concentration of pubs and its music scene. The free Festival of Ideas brings world-class speakers to the campus and includes a lively student fringe festival.

Undergraduate Fees and Bursaries

- » Fees for UK/EU students 2015–16 £9,000
- » Placement year / year abroad £1,350
- » Fees for international students 2014–15 £14,340–£18,660
  Medicine £25,420
- » Foundation year fee waiver: household income below £25K, £5,600; above £25K, £3,000.
- » Household income below £25K, accommodation bursary of £2,400, year 1, £1,800 subsequent years; £25K–£35K, £1,000 a year.
- » Awards for care leavers, Foyer students and those who have completed Realising Opportunities or Next Step York schemes.
- » Separate scheme for Hull York Medical School.

Students

Undergraduates:	**11,245**	**(935)**
Postgraduates:	**3,180**	**(790)**
Mature students:	**9.2%**	
International students:	**14.7%**	
Applications per place:	**6.2**	
From state-sector schools:	**78.1%**	
From working-class homes:	**20.7%**	
Satisfaction with students' union	**56%**	

For detailed information about sports facilities:
www.york.ac.uk/study/student-life/sport/

Accommodation

Number of places and costs refer to 2014–15
University-provided places: 5,702
Percentage catered: 14%
Catered costs: £124.67–£155.19 a week.
Self-catered costs: £101.92–£135.03 a week.
First-year undergraduates are guaranteed accommodation if terms and conditions are met.
International students: as above.
accommodation@york.ac.uk
www.york.ac.uk/study/undergraduate/accommodation/

York St John University

York St John is the only university in the UK to have increased its enrolment of undergraduates for the last four years in a row, but it has dropped more than 20 places after a big drop in student satisfaction. The university attracted one of the biggest increases in the country when higher fees were introduced and added another 14 per cent in 2013. Its popularity continued a well-established trend: undergraduate applications have risen by 60 per cent since university status arrived in 2006. Professor David Fleming, the Vice-Chancellor, said the university had invested in the quality of its teaching and the campus environment, as well as offering a strong package of fee waivers and student support. The university will charge perhaps the lowest fees in England on its Foundation degrees in education and theology, which will cost £3,500 in 2015–16, but the fees for all Honours degrees will be £9,000.

York St John is a Church of England foundation that dates back to 1841, when the Diocesan Training School opened with just one pupil on the register, in whose honour the students' union is named. The 11-acre site faces York Minster across the city walls and is a five-minute walk from the city centre. Now serving 6,000 students, the campus has seen £91 million of development in recent years and more is planned. The Fountains Learning Centre, which provides a striking entrance to the university, has been refurbished. It now has 530 computer workstations, multimedia group-work facilities, 24-hour access to enhanced self-service facilities and an enlarged book stock, as well an internet café and lecture theatre. Nearby, the prize-winning De Grey Court, which cost £15.5 million and serves the health and life sciences, links the university quarter with the city centre.

Divided between York and Ripon for most of its existence, the institution diversified beyond teacher training in the 1980s and decided in 1999 to concentrate all its teaching on York. The university's mission statement says its provision is "shaped" by the York St John's church foundation, although it welcomes students of all beliefs and none.

The Business School, launched in 2008, is now the biggest faculty, having overtaken Education and Theology, as well as Health and Life Sciences. The university has launched a number of successful enterprise initiatives. Its latest venture, the Phoenix Centre, a business incubation facility, supports both the university's graduates and new local businesses. Almost two-thirds of the students are female and there is a growing cohort of international students. More than 95 per cent of the UK undergraduates attended state schools or

---

New Mayor's Walk
York YO31 7EX

01904 876598 (information hotline)
admissions@yorksj.ac.uk
www.yorksj.ac.uk
www.ysjsu.com
Affiliations: Cathedrals
Group, GuildHE

The Times and Sunday Times Rankings
Overall Ranking: **87** (last year: =64)

Student satisfaction:	=87	80.2%
Research quality:	=110	1.0%
Entry standards:	=94	302
Student–staff ratio:	=104	21.1
Services & facilities/student:	101	£1,207
Expected completion rate:	33	91.3%
Good honours:	78	63.5%
Graduate prospects:	66	64.5%

colleges, over a third of them coming from working-class homes. The projected dropout rate of less than 4 per cent maintains the impressive improvement of recent years and is now among the ten lowest in the UK.

The Faculty of Arts, which was formed in 2001, has been one of the main points of expansion, especially in degree programmes such as film and television, media and American studies. The university was awarded a national centre for excellence in creativity, based on its work in English and theatre studies, although funding for such programmes has now ceased. Another music technology suite has been added and performance spaces include two dedicated TV studios, digital non-linear edit suites, digital imaging equipment and equipment for sound manipulation. Drama, dance and performing arts was the most successful field in the 2008 Research Assessment Exercise and the only one to contain world-leading research.

Relatively high numbers of local mature students ease the pressure on residential accommodation. As a result, first years who want to live in university-owned accommodation are now guaranteed places. A new hall of residence for 250 students opened in 2013, ten minutes' walk from the campus, increasing the number of bedspaces to over 1,800, and the university offers a choice of catered, semi-catered and private accommodation.

The Foss Building houses a sports hall, climbing wall, basketball, netball, indoor football and cricket nets. The university has also acquired a 57-acre site 15 minutes' walk from campus, where it has made huge improvements to the sports facilities, with cricket, rugby and football pitches, tennis and netball courts, and a six-lane athletics track. The site includes the Rowntree Theatre, which is used mainly by local performance groups.

The students' union was recognised in the latest NUS awards as Small and Specialist Union of the Year, having doubled its number of societies and society members. York is popular as a student city with a growing range of clubs as well as, supposedly, a pub for every day of the year.

Undergraduate Fees and Bursaries

» Fees for UK/EU students 2015–16	£9,000
» Foundation degree in Education & Theology	£3,500
» Fees for international students 2014–15	£9,500–£11,500
» Household income: below £25K, a bursary of £1,000 a year.	
» Check the university's website for the latest information.	

Students

Undergraduates:	**4,360**	(875)
Postgraduates:	**310**	(505)
Mature students:	**9.7%**	
International students:	**5.3%**	
Applications per place:	**5.2**	
From state-sector schools:	**95.3%**	
From working-class homes:	**34.6%**	
Satisfaction with students' union	**76%**	

For detailed information about sports facilities:
www.yorksj.ac.uk/ysjactive

Accommodation

Number of places and costs refer to 2014–15
University-provided places: 1,850
Percentage catered: 8.5%
Catered costs: £124.08–£148.87 a week (33 weeks).
Self-catered costs: £82.72–£150.77 a week (44–48 weeks).
First years choosing university as first choice are guaranteed accommodation. Residential and age restrictions apply.
International students: guaranteed housing.
www.yorksj.ac.uk/campus-residential-services/
campus-residential-services/accommodation.aspx

Additional Institutions of Higher Education

This listing gives contact details for other degree-awarding higher education institutions not mentioned elsewhere within the book. All the institutions listed below offer degree courses, some providing a wide range of courses while others are specialist colleges with a small intake. Those marked * are members of GuildHE (**www.guildhe. ac.uk**). The list includes private institutions. Fees are given for UK/EU undergraduates for a single year of study.

BPP University
6th floor, Boulton House
Chorlton Street, Manchester M1 3HY
Campuses in Abingdon, Birmingham, Bristol, Leeds, London, Manchester.
0330 060 3100   www.bpp.com
Fees 2014–15: £7,000 (two-year course);
              £6,000 (three-year course).

Conservatoire for Dance and Drama
(Comprised of Bristol Old Vic Theatre School, Central School of Ballet, London Academy of Music and Dramatic Art, London Contemporary Dance School, National Centre for Circus Art, Northern School of Contemporary Dance, Rambert School of Ballet and Contemporary Dance, Royal Academy of Dramatic Art.)
Tavistock House, Tavistock Square
London WC1H 9JJ
020 7387 5101   www.cdd.ac.uk
Fees 2015–16: £9,000

Glasgow School of Art
167 Renfrew Street, Glasgow G3 6RQ
0141 353 4500   www.gsa.ac.uk
Fees 2014–15: Scotland/EU, no fee
RUK £9,000

Guildhall School of Music and Drama
Silk Street, Barbican, London EC2Y 8DT
020 7628 2571   www.gsmd.ac.uk
Fees 2015–16: £9,000

ifs University College
ifs House, 4–9 Burgate Lane
Canterbury, Kent CT1 2XJ
Student campus:
25 Lovat Lane, London EC3R 8EB
020 7337 7111   www.ifslearning.ac.uk
Fees 2015–16: £6,000

The University of Law
Birmingham, Bristol, Chester, Guildford, Leeds, London (Bloomsbury and Moorgate), Manchester, York.
0800 289997   www.law.ac.uk
Fees 2015–16: £9,000 (two-year course)
              £6,000 (three-year course)

Leeds College of Art*
Blenheim Walk, Leeds LS2 9AQ
0113 202 8000   www.leeds-art.ac.uk
Fees 2015–16: £9,000

Liverpool Institute for Performing Arts*
Mount Street, Liverpool L1 9HF
0151 330 3000   www.lipa.ac.uk
Fees 2015–16: £9,000

New College of the Humanities
19 Bedford Square, London WC1B 3HH
020 7367 4550   www.nchum.org
Fees 2014–15: £17,814

Pearson College
80 Strand, London WC2R 0RL
0203 7335 573   www.pearsoncollege.com
Fees 2014–15: £8,250

Plymouth College of Art*
Tavistock Place, Plymouth PL4 8AT
01752 203434   www.plymouthart.ac.uk
Fees 2015–16: £9,000

Ravensbourne*
6 Penrose Way, Greenwich Peninsula,
London SE10 0EW
020 3040 3500   www.ravensbourne.ac.uk
Fees 2015–16: £9,000

Regent's University London*
Inner Circle, Regent's Park,
London NW1 4NS
020 7487 7700   www.regents.ac.uk
Fees Spring 2015: £15,054

Rose Bruford College of Theatre and Performance*
Lamorbey Park, Burnt Oak Lane,
Sidcup, Kent DA15 9DF
020 8308 2600   www.bruford.ac.uk
Fees 2015–16: £9,000

Royal College of Music
Prince Consort Road, London SW7 2BS
020 7591 4300   www.rcm.ac.uk
Fees 2015–16: £9,000

Royal Conservatoire of Scotland
100 Renfrew Street, Glasgow G2 3DB
0141 332 4101   www.rcs.ac.uk
Fees 2014–15: Scotland/EU, no fee;
RUK £9,000

Royal Northern College of Music
124 Oxford Road, Manchester M13 9RD
0161 907 5200   www.rncm.ac.uk
Fees 2015–16: £9,000

Royal Welsh College of Music and Drama
Castle Grounds, Cathays Park,
Cardiff CF10 3ER
029 2034 2854   www.rwcmd.ac.uk
Fees 2015–16: £9,000

St Mary's University College*
191 Falls Road, Belfast BT12 6FE
028 9032 7678   www.stmarys-belfast.ac.uk
Fees 2014–15: £3,685; RUK £9,000

Scotland's Rural College
Campuses at Aberdeen, Ayr, Broxburn,
Cupar, Dumfries, Edinburgh
0800 269453   www.sruc.ac.uk
Fees 2014–15: Scotland/EU, no fee;
RUK £5,600

Stranmillis University College
Stranmillis Road, Belfast BT9 5DY
028 9038 1271   www.stran.ac.uk
Fees 2014–15: £3,685; RUK £9,000

Trinity Laban Conservatoire of Music and Dance
Music Faculty: King Charles Court
Old Royal Naval College,
Greenwich, London SE10 9JF
020 8305 4444
Dance Faculty: Laban Building, Creekside
London SE8 3DZ
020 8305 9400   www.trinitylaban.ac.uk
Fees 2015–16: £9,000

University Campus Suffolk
Waterfront Building, Neptune Quay
Ipswich IP4 1QJ
Other campuses at Bury St Edmunds,
Lowestoft, Otley, Great Yarmouth
01473 338000   www.ucs.ac.uk
Fees 2015–16: £9,000

Writtle College*
Chelmsford, Essex CM1 3RR
01245 424200   www.writtle.ac.uk
Fees 2015–16: £9,000

Index

A levels
   choosing 20–21
   results different from offer 207–8
   and UCAS tariff 18
Aberdeen, University of 61, 250, 300–1
Abertay University 64, 250, 302–3
Aberystwyth University 63, 196, 250, 304–5
academic courses 22–4
Academic World Ranking of Universities
   49–50, 52–4
access agreement 211, 227, 229
access courses 26
access initiatives, university admissions 212
accommodation 233–42
   after first year 238
   choices 235–6
   cost of 233
   parental purchase 238
   private halls 236–7
   university 33, 236–8
accommodation agreements, university 238
accounting 37, 39, 40, 69–71
Adjustment Period, UCAS 204, 207–8
admissions tests 20–22
Adult Dependants' Grant 224, 228
Advanced Highers, and UCAS tariff 18
aeronautical and manufacturing engineering
   38, 40, 72–3
African studies 39, 41, 159–60
agriculture and forestry 39, 40, 73–5
American studies 39, 41, 75–6
anatomy and physiology 38, 40, 76–7
Anglia Ruskin University 64, 250, 306–7
animal science 39, 41, 78–9
anthropology 39, 41, 79–80
application process 199–210
   decisions 204, 205
   international students 266
   parental involvement 258
   see also UCAS
application timetable 204, 205
Apply, UCAS 200–3
archaeology 39, 41, 80–82
architecture 23, 38, 41, 82–4
architecture, history of 39, 41, 139–40

art, history of 39, 41, 139–40
art and design 39, 41, 84–7
   end of UCAS Route B 199
Arts University Bournemouth 62, 250,
   308–9
Arts, University of, London 63, 254, 310–11
ARWU World Ranking 49–50, 52–4
assured shorthold tenancy 240
Aston University 61, 196, 198, 250, 312–13
astronomy 38, 40, 171–3
Athletic Union 247
audiology 165

Balliol College, Oxford 275
Bangor University 61, 196, 250, 314–15
Bath, University of 60, 196–8, 316–17
   and sport 245, 250
Bath Spa University 62, 250, 318–19
Bedfordshire, University of 64, 250, 320–21
biological sciences 39, 40, 87–90
BioMedical Admissions Test (BMAT) 20
Birkbeck, University of London 25, 322–3
Birmingham, University of 60, 196–8, 250,
   324–5
Birmingham, University College 211, 250,
   238–9
Birmingham City University 63, 250, 326–7
Birmingham Conservatoire 326
Bishop Grosseteste University 64, 250,
   330–31
Bologna process 47
Bolton, University of 64, 250, 332–3
Bournemouth University 63, 250, 334–5
BPP University 26, 30, 212, 564
Bradford, University of 63, 250, 336–7
Brasenose College, Oxford 275
Brighton, University of 63, 338–9
   and sport 244, 250
Bristol, University of 60, 196–8, 250, 340–41
British Council 263, 265
British University and College Sport
   (BUCS) 243, 244, 247
Brunel University 61, 342–3
   and sport 245, 250
Buckingham, University of 26, 30, 61, 212,
   250, 344–5

Buckinghamshire New University 64, 250, 346–7

BUCS *see* British University and College Sport

budget, personal 231

building 38, 40, 90–91

bursaries 214, 227–8

business studies 37, 39, 40, 91–5

buzzword, UCAS 200

Cambridge University 60, 67, 196–8, 348–9
  admissions tests 21
  application and acceptance by course 274
  application process 201, 269–75
  choosing a college 270–73
  college profiles 287–97
  and sport 245, 250
  state school applicants 270
  Tompkins Table 270, 272

Cambridge Online Preliminary Application 273

campus universities 27, 31

Canterbury Christ Church University 63, 250, 350–51

Cardiff University 61, 196–8, 250, 352–3

Cardiff Metropolitan University 63, 354–5
  and sport 245, 250

career planning 44

casual work 37

catered accommodation, university 237

Cathedrals Group 32

Celtic studies 37, 39, 41, 95–6

Central Lancashire, University of 63, 197, 250, 356–7

CF 206

chemical engineering 38, 40, 96–7

chemistry 37, 38, 40, 97–9

Chester, University of 62, 250, 358–9

Chichester, University of 62, 250, 360–61

Child Tax Credit 224

Childcare Grant 224, 228

China, studying in 45, 49

Christ Church College, Oxford 276

Christ's College, Cambridge 287

Churchill College, Cambridge 287

CI 206

cinematics 39, 41, 111–14

cities, world, most popular for students 47, 48–9

Citizen's Advice Bureau 240

city universities 27, 31

City University London 61, 250, 362–3

civil engineering 38, 40, 99–101

Clare College, Cambridge 287–8

classics and ancient history 39, 40, 101–2

Clearing 31, 32, 199, 206, 208–9

colleges
  further education 29, 212
  higher education 29, 564-5
  private 30

Combined Honours 24

Commonwealth Games 243

communication and media studies 39, 41, 102–5

Community Service Volunteers 209

complementary therapies 165

completion measure, and league table 59

computer science 37, 38, 40, 105–8

Confirmation of Acceptance for Study 266

Conservatoire for Drama and Dance 564

Conservatoires UK Admissions Service 199

contracts, accommodation 240–41

Corpus Christi College, Cambridge 288

Corpus Christi College, Oxford 276

cost of accommodation 235

Council Tax 242

counselling 165

countries, best to study in 46, 48–9

course, choosing 15–27, 31–2, 201
  and graduate employment 24

Coursera 25

Courtauld Institute of Art 196, 198, 447

Coventry University 61, 250, 364–5

Cranfield University 298

Creative Arts, University for the 63, 250, 366–7

creative writing 39, 41, 108–10

credit card 230

cross-border studying, finance of 226

Cumbria, University of 63, 250, 368–9

dance 39, 41, 111–14

De Montfort University 62, 250, 370–71